D0992039

THE LAST ROYAL REBEL

THE LAST ROYAL REBEL

The Life and Death of James, Duke of Monmouth

Anna Keay

B L O O M S B U R Y

LONDON · OXFORD · NEW YORK · NEW DELHI · SYDNEY

Bloomsbury Publishing
An imprint of Bloomsbury Publishing Plc

50 Bedford Square   1385 Broadway
London   New York
WC1B 3DP   NY 10018
UK   USA

www.bloomsbury.com

BLOOMSBURY and the Diana logo are trademarks of Bloomsbury Publishing Plc

First published in Great Britain 2016

© Anna Keay, 2016
Maps by John Gilkes

British Library Cataloguing-in-Publication Data
A catalogue record for this book is available from the British Library.

ISBN: HB: 978-1-4088-2782-6
ePub: 978-1-4088-4608-7

2 4 6 8 10 9 7 5 3 1

Typeset by Newgen Knowledge Works (P) Ltd., Chennai, India
Printed and bound in Great Britain by CPI Group (UK) Ltd, Croydon CR0 4YY

MIX
Paper from
responsible sources
FSC® C020471

To find out more about our authors and books visit www.bloomsbury.com. Here you will find extracts, author interviews, details of forthcoming events and the option to sign up for our newsletters.

For my father and mother

Contents

Map		ix
A Bird's Eye View of Whitehall Palace		x
The Lineage of the Duke of Monmouth		xii
Author's Note		xv
1	Abduction	1
2	An Infamous Mother	13
3	A New Life	35
4	Homecoming	45
5	Vicious and Idle	64
6	Coming of Age	84
7	The Soldier and the Sun King	106
8	A Rising Sun	130
9	Care But Not Command	151
10	The Ties Begin to Break	165
11	Finding New Friends	185
12	Icarus	204
13	Exclusion	226
14	Opposition Leader	246
15	Town and Country	265
16	Desperate Measures	286
17	Love and Loss	309
18	The Reluctant Rebel	329
19	The Last Battle	349
20	The End	364
Epilogue		377
Notes		389
Bibliography		435
Acknowledgements		447
Index		449

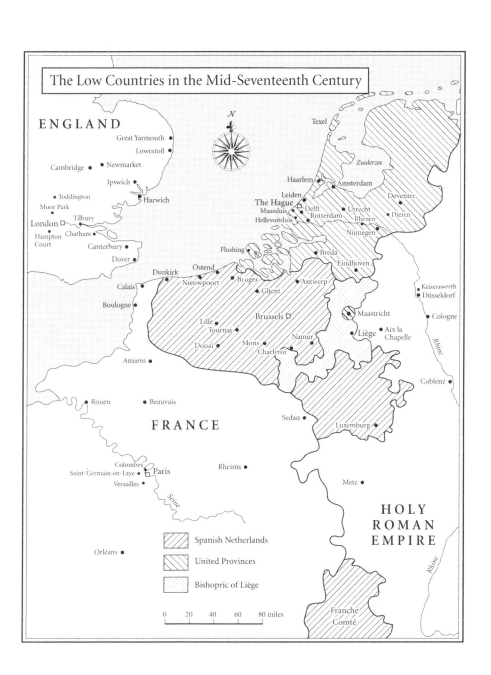

The Low Countries in the Mid-Seventeenth Century

ENGLAND

Great Yarmouth
Lowestoft
Cambridge Newmarket
Ipswich
Toddington
Moor Park
London Tilbury
Hampton Chatham
Court
Canterbury
Dover

Dunkirk Ostend
Nieuwpoort Bruges
Calais
Ghent
Boulogne

Lille
Tournai
Douai Mons
Amiens
Charleroi

Rouen Beauvais

FRANCE

Colombes
Saint-Germain-en-Laye Paris
Versailles

Orléans

N

Texel

Zuiderzee

Haarlem Amsterdam
Leiden Deventer
The Hague Delft Utrecht
Maassluis Rotterdam Rhenen Dieren
Hellevoitsluis Nijmegen

Flushing Breda
Eindhoven

Antwerp
Keiserswerth
Düsseldorf

Brussels Maastricht
Cologne
Namur Liège Aix la
Chapelle

Coblenz

Sedan

Luxemburg

Rheims
Metz

HOLY
ROMAN
EMPIRE

Spanish Netherlands

United Provinces

Bishopric of Liège

0   20   40   60   80 miles

Franche
Comté

A Bird's Eye View of Whitehall Palace, c. 1695 by Leonard Knyff. The Duke and Duchess of Monmouth's lodgings centred on the five-bay, three-storey building towards the left of the engraving, facing the river across the Privy Garden. St James's Park, with its avenues and canal, stretches into the distance behind. Also overlooking the Privy Garden, viewed obliquely, is the Privy Gallery, rebuilt by James II. To the right of that,

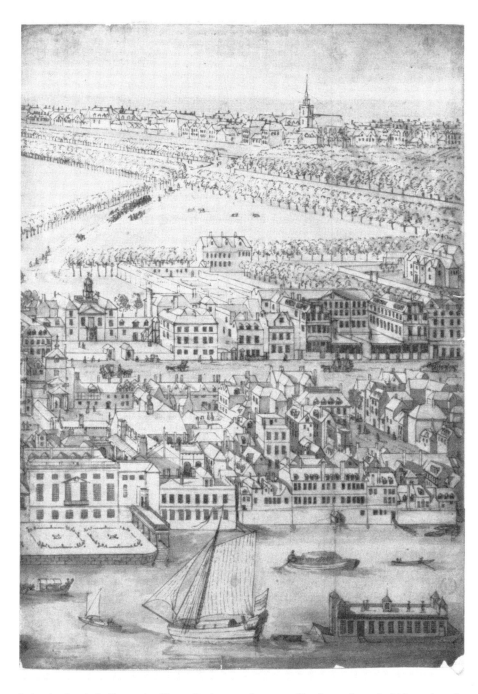

facing the river, is the Banqueting House. Carriages can be seen on King Street, the road which ran through the middle of Whitehall, passing on the right the gated forecourt of Horse Guards with its distinctive cupola. The Privy Stairs, the pillared royal landing stage, can be seen jutting out into the river against the later terrace.

THE LINEAGE OF
THE DUKE OF MONMOUTH

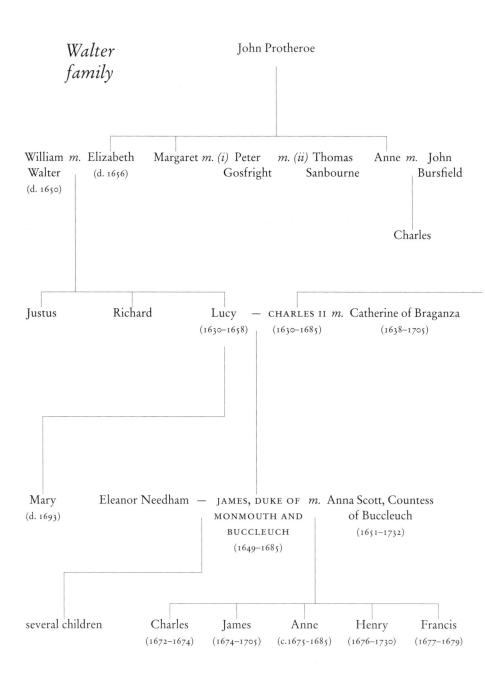

*Walter
family*

John Protheroe

William *m.* Elizabeth
Walter (d. 1656)
(d. 1650)

Margaret *m. (i)* Peter *m. (ii)* Thomas
Gosfright Sanbourne

Anne *m.* John
Bursfield

Charles

Justus

Richard

Lucy — CHARLES II *m.* Catherine of Braganza
(1630–1658) (1630–1685) (1638–1705)

Mary
(d. 1693)

Eleanor Needham — JAMES, DUKE OF *m.* Anna Scott, Countess
MONMOUTH AND of Buccleuch
BUCCLEUCH (1651–1732)
(1649–1685)

several children

Charles
(1672–1674)

James
(1674–1705)

Anne
(c.1675–1685)

Henry
(1676–1730)

Francis
(1677–1679)

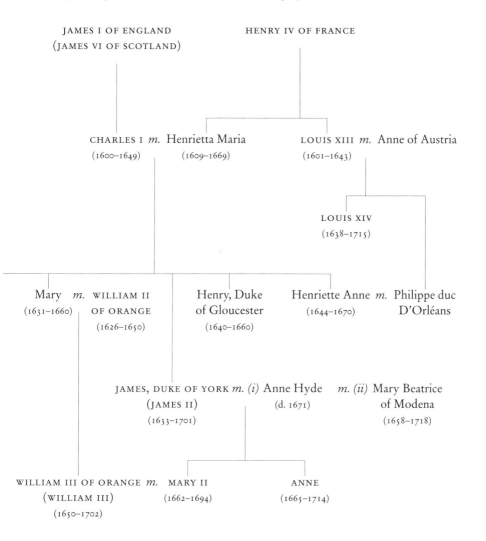

House of Stuart
Kings of England & Scotland

House of Bourbon
Kings of France

JAMES I OF ENGLAND
(JAMES VI OF SCOTLAND)

HENRY IV OF FRANCE

CHARLES I *m.* Henrietta Maria
(1600–1649)   (1609–1669)

LOUIS XIII *m.* Anne of Austria
(1601–1643)

LOUIS XIV
(1638–1715)

Mary *m.* WILLIAM II
(1631–1660)   OF ORANGE
(1626–1650)

Henry, Duke
of Gloucester
(1640–1660)

Henriette Anne *m.* Philippe duc
(1644–1670)   D'Orléans

JAMES, DUKE OF YORK *m. (i)* Anne Hyde   *m. (ii)* Mary Beatrice
(JAMES II)   (d. 1671)   of Modena
(1633–1701)   (1658–1718)

WILLIAM III OF ORANGE *m.*   MARY II   ANNE
(WILLIAM III)   (1662–1694)   (1665–1714)
(1650–1702)

Author's Note

The dates here are shown in the Old Style, Gregorian Calendar, for events in Britain (though with the new year taken to begin on 1 January) and in New Style, Julian Calendar, when the story takes place on the continent – with both shown for clarity where relevant.

The original spelling has been retained in quotations throughout. These are broadly phonetic, so readers may find it useful to read words aloud if the meaning is unclear.

Chapter 1

Abduction

On a cold December evening in 1657 an English army officer loitered in the backstreets of Brussels, intent on abduction. His target, walking close by the side of an expensively dressed young woman, was an eight-year-old boy with dark eyes, a bright, animated face and brown hair that lay in soft curls on his shoulders.

The magnificent city of Brussels, which had once been home to the dukes of Burgundy, was now the capital of a satellite state of Spain, the Spanish Netherlands. From within the Coudenberg Palace, looming high in the darkness on its rising ground, a Spanish governor-general administered the region, brushing past the catafalque of the city's last Habsburg princess, Archduchess Isabella, as he went about his business. From its tapestried halls, his despatches were carried daily to his royal masters in Madrid.

Below the palace, in dimly lit alleyways, lurked the kidnapper, Sir Arthur Slingsby. Here, among inns, brothels and merchants' mansions, lived his client – a man who called himself King Charles II. He was the eldest son of the recently executed King Charles I, and grandson of both James I / VI of England and Scotland and Henry IV of France. But with his kingdoms now commanded by Oliver Cromwell, he had no government to instruct, no army to command, no palaces to occupy; his title was, in truth, more aspiration than actuality.

Slingsby's quarry was Charles II's own son. His instructions were to take the child from Charles's former lover, the notorious

Lucy Walter. But as the kidnapper made his move, rather than a stealthy abduction, a violent public fracas unfolded. Wild screams of maternal horror drew crowds as Slingsby attempted to wrench the boy from his mother's arms. Lucy's desperate cries – whether of love, or of cold determination, it was impossible to tell – echoed between the tall houses in the still, night air, receding only after the appalled onlookers intervened and carried mother and son to safety.

News of the incident spread swiftly across Europe, and a fortnight later King Philip IV of Spain received a detailed account of the event, which his agent described as 'most barbarous, abominable and unnatural'.[1] But Charles himself felt no such qualms. He now considered the woman to whom he had clung in ecstatic abandon eight years before a dangerous liability, bent, as he put it, on 'ruining her innocent child by making a property of him to support herself in those wild and disgraceful courses she hath taken'. This was Charles's second attempt to snatch the child, and it would not be the last. The boy, whose name was James, would one day become the Duke of Monmouth. Now, as so often, he represented something extraordinary to those around him. His short but spectacular life would be as magnificent and as mesmerising as fireworks. For thirty-six years he would light up the firmament, inspiring by turn delight and disgust, adulation and abhorrence and, in time, love and loyalty almost beyond fathoming.[2]

To understand how this royal child had come into the world at all, and what a world it was, involves retreating ten years to the mid-1640s. Charles II was then still Prince of Wales, the seventeen-year-old heir to the thrones of England, Scotland and Ireland. Brought up in the rarefied world of the Stuart court, he had seen his universe turned on its head when civil war had broken out between his father, Charles I, and his subjects. The causes, though complex, stemmed largely from the king's determination to impose his florid and ceremonious form of religious worship on his three kingdoms. This was anathema to many of his subjects who preferred the simpler worship ushered in by the Protestant reformation. For four years Charles I fought the parliamentary army in a series of battles across the middle shires of England, before he was finally defeated.

During these years his son and heir Charles had turned from twelve-year-old bystander to active participant. In 1645, aged fifteen, the prince had been given nominal command of the royalist forces in the west of England. But the men he oversaw were no match for the increasingly professional and well-trained parliamentary army. Pushed further and further west, until he was pinned down in the south-western tip of Cornwall, he was finally forced to leave England in March 1646. As the prince sailed, Charles I had tried to bargain with his opponents, until, undone by his own intransigence, he was taken prisoner.

The young prince reached Paris in July 1646. Though this was the France of Louis XIV, the French golden age was yet to come: the Sun King was a boy of eight and Versailles still a hunting lodge. During this French minority political power had been vested in the hands of a regent, Louis's mother Anne of Austria, who was guided in everything by the powerful Italian prelate Cardinal Mazarin. Prince Charles's mother, Queen Henrietta Maria, was the sister of the recently deceased Louis XIII and, being a 'daughter of France', had been warmly welcomed by her sister-in-law. Given apartments in the main royal palace of the Louvre, a summer residence at St Germain-en-Laye, and a substantial allowance, Henrietta Maria had established a new centre of gravity for the exiled royalists. It was to her court that Prince Charles reluctantly travelled in the summer of 1646.

Having already seen more than someone of his position might expect in a lifetime, Charles was at sixteen tall and dark and developing a fledgling moustache. He had the height of a man but had yet to throw off the self-consciousness of the adolescent. At eighteen he was described by a contemporary as 'one of the most gentle, innocent, well-inclyned Princes, so far as yet appears, that lives in the world [with] a trimme person, and a manlie carriage'.[3] On his arrival in France in the summer of 1646 he joined his mother in the suburban splendour of St Germain-en-Laye, which from its long ridge commanded the plain on which Paris stood. At the court entertainments and balls that their royal mothers arranged for Prince Charles and King Louis, the young first cousins shuffled awkwardly, straitjacketed by protocol, and remained silent rather than risk dishonouring their families.

As Paris smouldered with France's own political protests, the Fronde, in England Charles I was imprisoned in Carisbrooke Castle on the Isle of Wight, while his younger son, James Duke of York, made a daring escape from the parliamentary army disguised as a woman. All the while the Prince of Wales was consigned to playing pet to the great ladies of the French court, ever in the eye of his mother. Confined to his chamber by illness in the winter of 1647, Charles's frustration must have been acute.[4]

Then suddenly, in June 1648, everything in England seemed set to change. With the king captive and incapable of compromise, the possibility that there might be no reconciliation between Parliament and monarchy had started to become horribly real to both sides. As the moderates were being squeezed out of the parliamentary regime, the country began to enter uncharted territory. It was far from clear what would happen should Charles I continue to refuse the rebels' demands. Many of the possible answers were unthinkable.

A royalist backlash ensued. Parts of Kent broke into open rebellion against Parliament, and one of the most senior naval officers in the land, Sir William Batten, declared for the king and led a dozen warships, the bulk of the parliamentary navy, into mutiny. But a navy alone could not retake the kingdom: land forces were needed. Clear that 'it is Scotland, and Scotland only [that] can save the King', Charles I's Scottish supporters galvanised. A week later, on 9 July, the king's principal Scottish adviser – his 'polar or northern starr', the Duke of Hamilton – led an army of 10,000 men over the border to mount a challenge to Cromwell. With both an army and a navy suddenly unexpectedly in play, the king's prospects were transformed. Unable to act himself, he sent from his prison on the

Isle of Wight the orders for which his son had been waiting: at last Prince Charles was to enter the fray.[5]

All the ports along the south coast of England were firmly in parliamentarian hands, so the naval mutineers made instead for Holland, where they were allowed to moor at the Dutch docks at Hellevoetsluis. The Prince of Wales was to travel to Holland and take command of the ships. Then, somehow, he was to join forces with the Scots. Much remained unclear. Acutely conscious of the need to ensure his teenage son had experienced advisers about him, the king dispatched a flurry of letters to his various councillors – most in retirement while the prince lived with his mother in France – with orders to go to him in Paris. But the slow movements of these middle-aged administrators were no match for the speed of a young man with great deeds in his sights. As Sir Edward Hyde, the privy councillor appointed to guide the prince, forced gouty feet into his boots on Jersey, Charles was already hurrying through the ceremonies of departure from the French court.[6] A week later he rode out of Paris with his first cousin, Prince Rupert, at his side: brilliant, brave and ten years Charles's senior, no companion could have added more to the sense of eager anticipation than this swashbuckling soldier.[7]

By 19 July, Charles was in Calais, where he learnt that his brother, the fifteen-year-old Duke of York, had already reached Hellevoetsluis and was taking command of the fleet himself.[8] Any intention of waiting for the councillors to gather was abandoned and Charles and Rupert sailed at once for the Dutch Republic. They reached Hellevoetsluis shortly afterwards, and as the Prince of Wales boarded the English flagship, the thousand men of the fleet cheered with delight.[9] But despite the drama and exhilaration, the immediate departure for which he longed was not possible. Practical concerns intervened to force a delay: food, drink and supplies were needed to sustain an invasion fleet, while positions of command had to be filled and a plan agreed. Such matters would require the financial assistance of Charles's brother-in-law, the Prince of Orange, and a few days' organisation. A week at most: but what a week it would prove to be.

Hellevoetsluis, the Dutch equivalent of the English naval head-quarters at Chatham dockyard, stands on the north side of one of the great ragged inlets that perforate the Dutch coast. Here channels had been cut and berths hollowed out of the sludge at the water's edge to allow the ships of the formidable Dutch navy to berth safely – protected by the inland position and the town's substantial defences. Exactly forty years after these events, Charles's nephew, William of Orange, would set sail from these very docks to invade England. Though it was ideal for preparing invasions, the port had little else to recommend it, and so with provisioning under way, Charles abandoned its briny streets and an hour or so later was riding along the elegant boulevards of The Hague to visit his younger sister, Mary.[10]

Only eighteen months apart in age, Charles and Mary had grown up together. As was normal for royal offspring, they and their siblings had lived in their own royal palaces away from their parents. Here they were waited on by their own staff – at first nurses and 'rockers', later governesses and tutors – and shared with one another the sort of warmth and companionship which children of their position seldom received from their parents. Charles and Mary had played and prayed together in the state rooms of St James's and Richmond palaces, and hand in hand learned the complex manoeuvres of court dance from their French dancing master.[11] When Mary had been just nine she was married to William of Nassau, the teenage son of Frederick Henry, Prince of Orange. She arrived in Holland in 1642 to find herself a child alone in a foreign land, loathed and lied about by her manipulative mother-in-law, Amalia van Solms, and able only to look on as her beloved family's troubles unfolded across the Channel.

The happiness felt by brother and sister at their reunion in The Hague in July 1648 must have been intense. A week of delay was turned into a week of delight, as an impromptu family reunion took place, drawing together in the palace of the Binnenhof, a moated complex in the middle of the city, a whole generation of young Stuarts. Charles, Mary and her husband William, and their brother

James, Duke of York, were joined by their slightly older cousins, Prince Rupert and two of his brothers Maurice and Philip, whose mother, Charles I's sister, Elizabeth of Bohemia, had been living in exile at The Hague for thirty years. An official dinner was held at the palace, at which the cousins dined in state and every courtly nicety was observed. A rail divided the dining table from the rest of the room, against which the citizens of The Hague pressed to gaze at this impossibly glamorous gathering. The festivities flowed on long after the formalities had ceased, hosted by Mary's husband William II of Orange – who, at twenty-two, had already established a reputation for gambling, drinking and womanising.[12]

Finally delivered from the controlling eye of his mother, and still without the services of Sir Edward Hyde thanks to the intervention of a band of pirates off the Dutch coast, Charles was, for perhaps the first time in his life, completely free from supervision. This sense of liberation, cut with the anxious anticipation of what lay before him, proved a powerful aphrodisiac. The young prince spent one of those warm summer nights entwined with a beautiful, knowing young woman of his own age. The relationship was brief and would have been entirely inconsequential, but for the fact that when he sailed out with his navy on 26 July, she was pregnant.[13]

The woman was Lucy Walter. The circumstances of her affair with the prince and her subsequent reputation might conjure up an image of a bawdy backstreet girl, but this was not how her story had begun. Eighteen years earlier, when the cannons of the Tower of London had sounded to celebrate the birth of the Prince of Wales, Lucy had been born in Pembrokeshire, in the south-western corner of Wales. There her father was a landowner of some means, possessing some hundred acres including Roch Castle, a small but handsome medieval tower house that still stands pertly on a rocky outcrop a mile from the sandy western shore. The Walters were a respectable gentry family with good connections – her mother's uncle was the Earl of Carbery – and despite the remoteness of their Welsh estate they retained ties to London and its fashions.[14]

Though Prince Charles underwent the stiff and formalised upbringing of an heir to the throne, he witnessed in his parents a marriage of genuine love and fidelity. Charles I and Henrietta Maria's engagement had been as much a matter of politics as any of its age, and the two had been married by proxy long before they actually met, but their initial frostiness melted and affection blossomed into love. The harmony and happiness this brought the royal couple – despite the horrors contemporaries ascribed to the influence of the Catholic queen – was palpable. Even in the bleakest moments of the civil war the king would sit down to write warm and loving letters to his wife. In adulthood Charles II would become a byword for infidelity, but it was not for want of example.

Lucy's experience could not have been more different. Her childhood was dominated by the violent and destructive relationship between her mother and father. According to Lucy's mother, Elizabeth, William Walter was a serial adulterer who began an affair with their maid when Lucy was six. The maid gave birth to two illegitimate children while still living with them, for whom Elizabeth then had to provide. When she protested, William responded with brutality – verbal and physical – and then abandoned her. Encouraged by her friends and family, Elizabeth eventually fled Wales with her three children, and made for London. There she pursued a case for financial support and a legal separation from her husband.[15]

In 1641, when Lucy was eleven, her parents' lawsuit reached the House of Lords. It was decided in Elizabeth's favour. William Walter's property was sequestered and he was ordered to pay his wife £60 a year for the care of their children. But her victory would be short-lived. After four more troubled years, during which the civil war raged, the Lords again considered the case and were sufficiently convinced by William Walter's counter-claims against his wife – including reciprocal allegations of adultery and abandonment – that in 1647 they reversed their original decision. It is hard to know now where the truth lay in these embittered mutual accusations. William Walter was clearly a violent brute, but Elizabeth Walter seems also to have been a poor role model, and even her own family would accuse her of failing her daughter. Whatever the truth of it, few children could have had a bleaker experience of relations between men and women than poor Lucy Walter.[16]

The sting in the tail of the Lords' final decision in the Walters' case was that the couple's children were ordered to return to their father 'for their Keeping and Education'. This dreadful prospect provoked immediate action and at some point in 1647 Elizabeth Walter and her daughter Lucy made their escape and sailed for Holland.[17]

The small, sorry farce of the Walter family was played out against the epic backdrop of the civil war. As the royal palaces had been looted, and Rubens's magnificent altarpiece was ripped from Henrietta Maria's chapel at Somerset House, so Roch Castle was burned by royalists. For Lucy and Charles, as for many others in this extraordinary age, certainty and stability evaporated and they were thrust into premature adulthood. By the time the House of Lords ordered that she and her brothers should return to their father, Lucy was seventeen and already ravishing.

Even those who despised her – and in time there would be many – conceded that Lucy was bewitchingly beautiful. With long glossy black hair, pale skin and full red lips, she caught the eye immediately. She was not particularly accomplished – the domestic events of the previous years had interrupted her education – but she had both a coquettish charm and a quick, knowing manner that proved irresistible to men.[18] She was also ambitious, despite – or perhaps because of – the poverty and disarray brought about by her parents' separation: a provincial gentry girl who aspired to the elegance and opulence of the London elite. She longed for jewellery, fine clothes and beautiful, expensive things. Her enemies would later accuse her of becoming a prostitute and while such a stark description seems harsh, she soon began to acquire wealthy suitors who were prepared to spend money to enjoy her company. Among them was the second son of the Earl of Leicester, a brilliant twenty-four-year-old parliamentary colonel called Algernon Sidney who, it was claimed, was willing to part with fifty pieces of gold in her pursuit.

When Sidney's regiment was suddenly mobilised the two parted, never to meet again. But he must have been reminded of his time with her when, thirty-five years later, the earl was introduced to her son, James, and the two started to talk of treason.[19]

Elizabeth Walter had a series of brothers and sisters to whom she had turned when her marriage collapsed, and it was her sister Margaret, and Margaret's Dutch husband, Peter Gosfright, who facilitated her flight to Holland with Lucy in 1647, where they travelled under the alias 'Barlow'. Not long after their escape Margaret was arrested. Behaviour that might have been overlooked in wartime London met with stern disapproval in the Protestant trading towns of the Netherlands. Peter Gosfright's family took a dim view of the pair and were scandalised when Mrs Walter returned to London leaving her teenage daughter alone in Holland, already 'in an ill way of living'. With connections and charm, and with the Dutch towns home to hordes of downhearted English royalists, Lucy made friends fast. Within months she was installed as the mistress of one of the most eligible, the Earl of Leicester's third son, and Algernon's younger brother, the handsome royalist exile Colonel Robert Sidney.[20]

Whether it was Lucy who pursued Prince Charles, when he came to The Hague in July 1648, or Charles who sought out Lucy, is not clear. According to one source Charles was the predator, who 'hearing of her, found means to get her from her Collonel, she not being averse to so advantageous a change'. On the other hand Lucy was much the worldlier of the two and the young Prince of Wales was a spectacular conquest. Either way, the pair seems to have been equally willing. Robert Sidney was quickly cast off – muttering bitterly that as Lucy was 'already sped' (no longer a virgin) anyone was welcome to her – and the affair was consummated.[21]

Consumed by the prospect of reclaiming England and rescuing his father, the Prince of Wales probably thought little of Lucy Walter as he sailed out of Hellevoetsluis less than a week later.[22] The reality of what he found in England would be a sorry substitute. Entering the Channel, the fleet had been unable to land at any of the south-eastern coastal forts. After weeks of indecision and infighting of the sort the teenage prince lacked the experience or authority to resolve, and a spell blockading the Thames, Charles's forces ran out of supplies and by September they were back in Hellevoetsluis. There the awful news greeted them that the Duke of Hamilton's army had been defeated by Parliament's best general, Oliver Cromwell, on a rough moor north-east of Preston. Two thousand of Hamilton's 10,000 men lay dead and three times as many captured. The heroic royalist recovery they had all believed in was all but over.

The five months that followed were no better. Though it had failed, the royalist uprising had been a reminder of the loyalty most people still felt to the king. As the Prince of Wales docked in the Netherlands that September a parliamentary deputation set off from Westminster to visit Charles I at Carisbrooke Castle. They came with a mandate to agree terms within forty days that would reinstate the king but with checks on his power. The conditions included the militia being put under parliamentary control for a limited period and the establishment of Presbyterianism. The commissioners, and the majority of the political class, were desperate for Charles to accept so that peace and order could be restored and the real radicals kept from power. They had reason to worry, as the soldiers of the army were enraged by tales of the commissioners trading their hard-won victories for lucrative posts in a new royal regime. But the forty days expired with no agreement. The commissioners wept with frustration at the king's refusal to concede. The army demanded the treaty be abandoned and Charles I tried for treason.

Knowing that the House of Commons, even now, would not vote to try their king, a small group of radicals took matters into their own hands. On the morning of 6 December, when the MPs began arriving at the Palace of Westminster, the London brewer turned parliamentary officer, Thomas Pride, stood defiantly on the steps. Behind him, with their swords drawn and muskets at the ready, was a contingent of the 7,000 soldiers who occupied London. In Pride's hand was a list of all the moderate MPs; as each one arrived, each was either turned away or arrested, so only the radicals remained. This act of political cleansing, known as 'Pride's Purge', saw the House of Commons reduced by half; only when it was done was the seal set on the king's fate.

The remaining MPs, the 'Rump', could now push through their measures and moved to put the king on trial. The House of Lords, implacably opposed, was simply ignored. A High Court of Justice was established and the king was summoned to Westminster Hall to answer the charge of making war on his own people. Like many vanquished leaders tried for their alleged crimes, Charles I refused to recognise the authority of the court and would not register a plea. No plea was taken as confirmation of guilt.

The Prince of Wales spent the nail-biting months between September and January at The Hague. Though he lodged in princely splendour with his sister and brother-in-law in the Binnenhof, he was powerless. In November, as the forty-day period ended, he lay incapable in isolation, his body covered in the rampant pustules of smallpox.[23] When he recovered, now reunited with Sir Edward Hyde and the rest of his council, he had experienced men about him, but lessons learned in the past had little application in this radical new world. As events in London unfolded, and the implications of a trial became clear, the prince despatched increasingly desperate letters to the crowned heads of Europe, begging them to intervene, emphasising the terrible precedent the execution of a king would set for all monarchs. A blank page, ready to receive any terms, bearing the signature 'Charles P' at the bottom, survives with the eighteenth-century inscription: 'Prince Charles his Carte Blanche to the Par[liamen]t to save his Father's Head'. But it was all to no effect. The radicals were now unstoppable.[24]

On the morning of 30 January, Charles I was marched across the park from his son's former rooms at St James's Palace, where he had lodged during his trial. From the principal audience chamber of Whitehall Palace, the Banqueting House, he walked out onto a timber stand where the executioner waited. Charles had already assumed the glassy calm of the martyr, and was serene as he laid his pale neck on the block. As the executioner raised his axe the crowd froze, and as it fell monarchy was no more.[25]

Chapter 2

An Infamous Mother

In April 1649, nine months after his parents' fleeting first meeting at The Hague, and three months after the execution of his grandfather, the future Duke of Monmouth was born in Rotterdam.

The prosperous port had grown up around the point where the Rotte river fanned out to discharge itself into the wide Meuse delta, which in turn met the sea some twenty miles north-west. By the seventeenth century the town was a distinctive triangle of waterways: the base the long waterfront of the Meuse, defined at each corner by the two principal forks of the Rotte which diverged upstream at the apex. An almost Venetian complex of canals lay within the densely settled triangle, providing ample harbour for the fleet of trading vessels that docked there. Prominent among them were the ships of the Dutch East India Company, which returned from their 10,000-mile trading odysseys laden with peppercorns, cloves and nutmeg. Expanding trade over the previous century had made Rotterdam a cosmopolitan place. To hear English spoken there in the 1640s was commonplace: scores of English merchants operated from the city, and from the 1630s St Peter's church in the Hoogstraat was available for English Protestant worship.

The nine months of Lucy's pregnancy had been the most eventful in English history. The child had been conceived when it seemed, briefly, that all might be saved. As he formed a heart-beat Cromwell's army had cut down Hamilton and the resurgent royalists on Preston Moor; as he started to move the parliamentary commissioners had delivered their terms to the king, and as his eyes opened in the murky world of the womb his grandfather had been beheaded. Just three weeks before he took his first breaths of salty Dutch air, Parliament formally abolished monarchy in England.

As Lucy's abdomen swelled and her shapely figure filled out, she was not often to be found at the late-night court revels. Charles returned to The Hague in September 1648, and was at the Binnenhof five months later when he received the news of Charles I's execution. Tears coursed down his cheeks at the horror of it all: the loss of his father, the murder of his sovereign, and the weight of responsibility that he now bore. He was just fifteen miles away that spring when Lucy gave birth. Six weeks later, having outstayed his welcome in The Hague, and determined to do something even if it was not at all clear exactly what, he left for Paris. Whether he visited his baby son before he left is not certain, but likely: he loved small children and the baby was consoling evidence of the strength of the royal genes.

By July, Charles had reached Paris and was staying with his widowed mother at the palace of St Germain-en-Laye. It was six months since the execution of the husband that she loved so intensely, during which time she had not seen her eldest son, making for an emotional reunion. Henrietta Maria ensured that Louis XIV and the Bourbon royal family welcomed Charles, personally, with warmth and sympathy. But to her disbelief there was still no official French condemnation of the execution of Charles I. Cardinal Mazarin was too shrewd to make an enemy of the new English regime before it was clear what power it might wield. This put Charles in a deeply uncomfortable position: uncertain whether, if he appeared in Paris, he would be treated as a king. To prevent the question even arising he stayed out of the capital, and those who wished to see him journeyed out to St Germain. When it became clear his ten-day stay was to be extended, Lucy herself travelled to France and on 18 August 1649 she shared a coach from Paris to St Germain with the young gentleman scholar John Evelyn. He did not warm to her, considering this brittle beauty both 'bold' and 'insipid', but even he could not deny she was lovely to behold.[1]

While it was a century since any English sovereign had fathered a bastard child, the phenomenon was reasonably common in Europe. Henrietta Maria had grown up alongside her father's nine illegitimate children. Her half-sisters' rooms had adjoined her own, and the girls had always been lavished with attention and honours. She must have been aware of her grandson's birth and may even have met him at St Germain. It seems unlikely that Lucy would have left the baby behind: at three months old he was already her greatest asset.

The execution of Charles I horrified most of his subjects: as well as widespread disapproval of the rigged House of Commons, the Scots and Irish, whose king he had also been, had had absolutely no say in the decision. When the news reached Edinburgh there was outrage. Men of influence wore mourning to register their fierce disapproval, and the royal throne in the chamber of the Scottish Parliament was draped in black. On 5 February 1649, rejecting the English Parliament's proceedings, they declared Charles II King of Scotland. The difficulty for Charles was that the Scots were committed to Presbyterianism, as expressed in their 'Solemn League and Covenant', a creed which his father had detested and had died rather than allow. Any agreement that would allow him to take the throne in Scotland, and from there to launch an invasion of England, would require a compromise on this issue.

If a deal with the Scots necessitated negotiating with Presbyterians, a deal with the Irish – also appalled at the execution of their king – involved an agreement with Catholics. Thanks to the careful skill of the Marquis of Ormond, Charles's lord lieutenant in Ireland, a deal had indeed been struck, but the new republic despatched Oliver Cromwell to Ireland with an army ensuring nothing could come of it. In late September 1649, frustrated with loitering at St Germain, Charles moved to Jersey, poised to attack England – be it with the Scots or the Irish. Six months later a Scots delegation ready to talk terms finally sailed south. The venue for the parley was to be the Dutch town of Breda and so Charles returned once again to the land of his son's birth.

Part of the United Provinces (as the Dutch Republic was properly called) but only a few miles from the border with the Spanish Netherlands, Breda was a frontier town. Regularly besieged over centuries past and those yet to come, it had been grabbed by the Spanish as recently as 1625 – an event which Philip IV had commissioned Velasquez to commemorate – only to be snatched back by the Dutch the following decade. The town and its medieval castle, surrounded by a complex of defensive angular moats, knew conflict and conference equally well, and it would be here ten years hence that Charles would sign the treaty for his restoration to the throne.

In 1650 this was still a world away, and the Scottish commissioners were in no doubt that they held all the cards. Given the disparity in their negotiating positions, Charles knew he had to play perfectly his only trump: being king. The full ritual rigmarole of a diplomatic reception at Whitehall Palace was laid on for the meeting. A coach was despatched to bring the commissioners to the king's lodgings at the castle, and as they disembarked they were greeted and solemnly accompanied towards him in ceremonial stages. At the door of the outer rooms, Thomas Wentworth, son of the Earl of Cleveland and as devoted a royalist as ever fought, met the delegation and led them gravely to the royal bedchamber where the audience was to take place.

Charles maintained this stately style throughout the two-month negotiations, creating eight Knights of the Garter in as many weeks. He did everything he could think of to inspire confidence in the negotiators: Lucy Walter was persuaded to bring baby James to Breda, she and Charles still being on amicable terms. The child was proudly paraded before the Scots delegation over those weeks: a healthy one-year-old boy offering encouraging evidence of their young king's virility.[2]

Charles II was a very different creature to his father and the Scottish delegates were charmed by him. But when they wrote back to their masters in Edinburgh, the concessions he had coaxed out of them were flatly refused. Desperate to revive his cause, and feeling his opportunity ebb, the new king conceded. All the Scots' terms, including that he would name sign his name on the Solemn League and Covenant, were agreed to and at the end of the first week in June, Charles sailed for his kingdoms.

When John Evelyn had ridden with Lucy Walter to St Germain-en-Laye in August 1649 he had described her as Charles II's 'mistress'. If this was still true then, relations were certainly cooling by the following summer. Fidelity would never be Charles's strong suit and, as he strolled with his cousin Sophia (future grandmother of George I) one warm evening in southern Holland, he told her she was much more beautiful than 'Mrs Barlow' (the assumed surname that Lucy retained for life). But Lucy herself was another matter. While Charles's presence may have kept her behaviour in check, when he sailed for Scotland – hoping never to return – she quickly resumed her 'loose' ways. However the clearest evidence of the breakdown of relations between Charles and his former lover by June 1650 was that he had already ordered what would be his first attempt to abduct their son.

When Charles sailed for Scotland, Lucy travelled to the port of Schiedam, just three miles west of Rotterdam. Here her baby was being looked after by an English wet nurse in the household of the merchant Claes Ghysen, while Lucy herself lived in relative splendour at the house of a Mrs Harvey in Rotterdam. There can have been few people Charles trusted as he did the man who organised this first attempted kidnap. Thomas Eliot had served him from before his father's execution and would continue to do so for almost thirty years, until he died in service in 1677. As a groom of the bedchamber he was one of a small cadre of servants who attended the king in his bedchamber and acted as his informal agents. Eliot was loathed by Edward Hyde and his fellow councillors for precisely the reason that Charles trusted him: he was unscrupulous, irreverent and loyal to no one but the king. When Charles travelled to Scotland that June, three of these grooms travelled with him, while Eliot remained behind, his task already determined. He in turn gave instructions to John Griffith and James Eliot, two young men attached to the exiled court. Their job, as they later recalled, was: 'to take the duke [of Monmouth] aforsaid from his mother by any means they could'.[3]

The plan they settled on was simple. Lucy Walter's taste for invitations from affluent men was well known. She was therefore invited, perhaps by the wealthy Earl of Craven, to go to the Rotterdam fair. While she was away their agent, Paul Watts, who had apparently infiltrated Lucy's household, managed to carry James and his nurse away. Returning that evening to find her baby gone, Lucy was horror-struck. Hysterical, 'she Rent her Apparrel, Tore the Hair from off her Head, and whole shours of Tears bewailed the greatness of her Loss', but she soon regained her composure and sped into action. Ordering horses, she rode through the night to Maassluis, a town eight miles down the Meuse, where she suspected her son was being put aboard a ship for England. She assumed the abduction had been ordered by the English republic and had no inkling of the truth.

Reaching Maassluis she was informed that the mayor of the town was the only person likely to be able to help her. She tracked him down, just about to board a boat for The Hague from the town's enclosed harbour. When her entreaties and promises of money failed to move the mayor, she tried another tactic. Throwing gold coins at the mayor's feet, and crying at the top of her voice that a royal child had been abducted, Lucy caused a commotion which drew scores of townspeople to the waterfront. Embarrassed into action, the mayor promised to intervene on condition that she went 'into some house and made no noise about it'; true to his word he closed the port and ordered a thorough search of every vessel.

Precisely what happened next is not certain. But ten or twelve days later, in the village of Loosduinen, two miles south of The Hague, James was discovered. The boy had been here all along. Years later John Griffith recalled cradling the child in his arms,

showing that Watts had managed to hand him over to his paymas-
ters. Whether, in the end, James was found because Lucy tracked
him down, or whether Eliot and Griffith gave up their captive
because the abduction had simply become too public to continue,
is unclear. According to one account, Lucy regained possession of
her child only after a lawsuit. Mother and son were reunited, and in
the process 'Mrs Barlow' revealed herself as a force to be reckoned
with.[4]

While this desperate drama was unfolding in August 1650, Charles
was hundreds of miles north, with troubles of his own. Arriving in
Scotland, his elation at finally setting foot on the soil of which he
claimed to be king was soon punctured. He found himself virtually a prisoner of the Scottish Presbyterian leadership and even
his coronation at Scone palace was a form of persecution, as the
Scots minister enumerated agonisingly the faults of his father and
grandfather before the enthroned king. His Scottish sojourn would
be cut short by war. In 1650 the English parliamentary army had
invaded and when Charles and the Scottish army retaliated they
finally met their defeat at the battle of Worcester in 1651. Fleeing
from the battlefield, as was the loser's only real option, Charles
spent the following six weeks on the run, adopting a series of
disguises and darting from one hiding place to another, including,
famously, clinging to the branches of an oak tree in Boscobel Wood.
Finally, on 15 October 1651, he reached the south coast and sailed
for France and freedom.

Charles arrived back in Paris exhausted, defeated and looking
more like a tramp than a king. But, despite the disaster that was
the Scottish expedition, his status had been transformed: he was
now a crowned king and an international celebrity. The silk-clad
aristocrats of Paris's finest drawing rooms trilled with excitement
at his stories of his adventures after Worcester. He spared them
no dashing detail: the moonlit manhunts, the daring disguises,
the rustic helpers, the brushes with disaster. The story spread fast
and by November the Doge of Venice was hearing it from his

ambassador to Paris, and the Grand Duke of Tuscany recounted it to the Florentine courtiers.[5]

Whatever the scale of Lucy's fury when she discovered that Charles was behind the attempt to kidnap her son, the attraction of reasserting her status as the consort of the most glamorous man in Europe was irresistible. Sometime that winter Lucy reappeared in Paris, in the hope of re-establishing herself in Charles's affections. But she was to be disappointed. He would have nothing to do with her, and her credit with the Parisian beau monde quickly expired. Lucy was still in Paris the following spring as English newspapers reported with delight that the English ladies at the Louvre had attempted to poison her during a court banquet. This was probably just scurrilous gossip, but her stock had clearly fallen dramatically and, with scandal in the air and Paris itself simmering with civic unrest, she packed her bags and returned to the Netherlands.[6]

Charles remained in Paris for two more years. During this time Lucy continued her harlot's progress and James grew from baby to boy. Circumstances at The Hague had changed dramatically since the halcyon days when the exiled Stuarts had revelled at the court of William II. In November 1650, at the age of just twenty-four, William died of smallpox. A week later, on her nineteenth birthday, his widow Mary gave birth to the child who would one day become King William III of England. But at the time, with her mother-in-law and the leaders of the Dutch Republic hovering around him, the child's future was uncertain and her position an uncomfortable one. As a teenage widow and mother of an infant boy little more than a year younger than Lucy's own child, Mary perhaps felt some sympathy for her brother's former mistress. Lucy now lived prominently in a house on the Denneweg, just a few minutes' walk from the Binnenhof, and the two women periodically crossed paths. Mary's letters to Charles written in 1654 refer coyly to Lucy as his 'wife' in The Hague, someone who pressed her for help, though she was busy enough already with a number of new 'husbands'.[7]

Among those who passed through The Hague and caught Lucy's eye was the Irish soldier Theobald, Viscount Taaffe. An exuberant figure, Taaffe was a lover of gossip and good times, a drinker and a dancer, and a fixer of parties and fun. Already in his fifties, he had, like many noblemen of his generation, lived a peaceful rural life before the civil war exploded his world. When he had sailed from Ireland to fight for the king in 1643, he left behind his wife and seven young children. A decade later, when the war was finally lost, his wife was dead, the children had grown into adults and the existence they had known had been extinguished. In truth Taaffe had been an awful military commander, and the life of aristocratic exile that followed suited him far better than that of the soldier. When the new King Charles returned to Paris from Scotland in 1651 the two men had become fast friends, despite their age difference, and kept in close touch through the years that followed – sharing the entertainments and intrigues of exile. It is no surprise that when Taaffe and Lucy met they were instantly attracted to one another. By 1654 their affair was public knowledge and the following year, if not before, Lucy gave birth to a second child, James's younger sister Mary. Lucy and Lord Taaffe were clearly more than just occasional lovers, and at one stage there was even talk of marriage. Taaffe treated her kindly – he was one of the few people who ever really did. Crucially he represented Lucy favourably to his friend the king, gently encouraging him to provide her with what she needed most: money.[8]

Charles's main concern when it came to Lucy was not her welfare, or even that of their son, but preventing her from embarrassing him and blighting his cause at home and abroad. For the English republican regime nothing was more welcome than lurid evidence of the exiled king's decadent lifestyle, and Charles squirmed with discomfort as reports of Lucy's promiscuity seeped out of The Hague. These were particularly unwelcome at this time as his position had just become even more precarious. In 1654, as relations between the French and Lord Protector Cromwell became increasingly close, Charles felt he had to leave Paris. With no major European country now willing to give him sanctuary, and no princely sponsor to pay his bills, he was forced to drift amid the mini-states of northern Germany looking for support. Perhaps persuaded by the argument that if Lucy were more financially secure she would be less reckless in her behaviour, in January 1655 Charles granted her an annual allowance of 5,000 livres. In reality, however, he did not have 50 livres, let alone 5,000 to give, and little if any money was ever actually paid. So, despite Charles's pleas to Lucy to 'go to some place more private than The Hague, for her stay there is very prejuitiall to us both', she remained firmly installed in the Dutch capital, her two illegitimate children living proof of her dissolute character.[9]

In the summer of 1655 Oliver Cromwell gave the brilliant young naval officer William Penn (father of the future founder of Pennsylvania) command of a fleet of thirty-seven ships, and instructions to sail for the Caribbean to attack Spain's lucrative West Indian empire. Despite some serious mishaps, Penn returned in October with Jamaica his trophy.

An enraged Philip IV of Spain, casting about for the means of revenge, fixed upon the English republic's most conspicuous enemy, the exiled Charles II. Discussions were slow and tentative at first, but in them Charles and his councillors thought they spied an oasis in the desert of their exile. With this enticing prospect in sight, and with the stiff and decorous agents of the King of Spain now calling, the problem of Lucy Walter became more acute. A new approach was clearly needed. One was suggested by Charles's suave Irish Protestant agent, Daniel O'Neill. Lucy, O'Neill purred, had been mistreated and mishandled and would respond better to a gentler approach. Agents were despatched to The Hague to reassure her that Charles would not attempt to kidnap James again and to try to persuade her to leave the city. Though she gave encouraging answers, again she did not move. O'Neill went to speak to Lucy himself but was so appalled by what he found that he wrote at once to the king, utterly disowning his former advice: 'I am much troubled to see the prejudice hir being here does your Matie for every idle action of hirs brings your Matie upon the Stage and I am noe less ashamed to have so much importuned your Matie to have beleeved hir worthier of your care.'

His report was damning. The agent had arrived in The Hague just as a scandal far worse than anything Charles could have feared was about to erupt: he received intelligence that Lucy had been poised to murder her maid by stabbing a large upholstery needle into her ear as she slept. The crime was designed to prevent the woman publicly accusing her of living an immoral life and of having had two abortions. O'Neill quickly paid the maid off. Whether the accusations of abortions were true is uncertain – there had certainly been miscarriages – Lucy's reputation was already so terrible that it barely mattered. She had avoided being marched out of The Hague 'for an infamous person' only because of her connection to Charles II. O'Neill was now adamant that the only solution was to get the boy away from his mother as soon as possible.[10]

While O'Neill fumed, a slyer approach to neutralising Lucy was being suggested, or at any rate facilitated, by the king's widowed sister. Mary of Orange had living in her household one Thomas Howard, the younger brother of the Earl of Suffolk. In the autumn of 1655, Howard visited Charles II in Cologne with a proposition. Mary wrote to Charles in January to confirm that Tom was ready to put this scheme into action after she had left The Hague, so that he might proceed 'without suspicion'. The moment the princess's carriage trundled out of the city Howard would get to work.[11]

Tom Howard must have presented an appealing prospect to Lucy who, with little if any of the promised 5,000 livres having material-ised and two children to support, had limited resources. Compared with the raucous, ruddy Taaffe, Howard was a picture of youthful elegance. The thirty-five-year-old son of one of the great English noble families, he had grown up at Audley End in Essex. In the late 1640s he had abandoned England for Holland, where Prince Fred-erick Henry of Orange had given him the command of a troop of horse in the Dutch army. By 1656 Tom Howard was a prominent figure at the Binnenhof: he was Master of the Horse to the Princess

of Orange, and was married to Walburga, the daughter of Frederick Henry's great favourite Johann van den Kerckhoven, and now
governess of the two-year-old William of Orange. Visiting Lucy
almost daily, Howard's courtship was swift and effective: a few
weeks of his false charm succeeded where years of hectoring had
failed and by the spring, Lucy left The Hague without a murmur,
on the arm of Tom Howard. In April, dripping with the diamonds
with which he had showered her, she went with her lover to view
De Ruit, a country house just north of Delft (the town where the
young Johannes Vermeer was starting to paint). A month later,
on 13 May 1656, she bought it from Elizabeth Pentland for the
substantial sum of 10,000 guilders – the idea and the funds both
having been provided by Howard.[12]

But just as Charles II was drawing a sigh of relief that Lucy was
out of the way, a chance gust blew Howard's plan off course. In early
February, Elizabeth Walter died in London and, as her parting shot,
she disinherited her three children and left her considerable estate to
the family of the elder of her two sisters, Margaret Gosfright. One
of the witnesses to the will had been Lucy's brother Justus, who, a
matter of weeks after their mother's death, sailed from England for
Holland in search of his sister. Justus had found Lucy preparing
for her move from The Hague. The news he bought caused her to
interrupt her plans, and the moment the house sale was completed
coaches were readied to take Lucy and Justus to England to try and
recover their mother's estate.

Howard must have cursed. All his work had been designed to
prevent Lucy from feeding republican propaganda, and now she
was bound for the dragon's den itself. What she might do there
could only be imagined. Furthermore, to take the king's son into
republican England, where his grandfather had been executed and
his family condemned, was to expose him to real danger. Howard
had only one option if he was not to abandon completely his enterprise: he would have to go with her.[13]

The strange party comprising Lucy, her two children, maid,
brother and lover set off for England. Their route involved travelling

by road to the south-western Dutch port of Flushing, from where they were to sail. On their way in mid-May they skirted a few miles north of Antwerp, the richest city in Europe, and only about an hour's ride away from Charles himself, who was just taking up residence in the Spanish Netherlands. A few weeks earlier he had signed the treaty with Philip IV which included, crucially, a commitment from Spain that it would support a royalist invasion of England. Even the sober old chancellor, Sir Edward Hyde, had leapt with delight when he had heard the news.

As Lucy and Charles's trajectories of travel ran close, their paths suddenly crossed. On or around 22 May, in a house near Antwerp, the two met. The visit was brief, a day and a night at most, and we know very little of what passed between them. What is certain, however, is that James, now seven, was present and that for the first time since he was a baby, he saw his father. The child that Charles was introduced to had clearly inherited his mother's dramatic looks. He had large brown eyes, full lips, dark curly hair and smooth pale skin. Despite seven years of chaotic living, his manner was bright, engaging and unaffected. The meeting, while short, would prove significant; but if he had hoped to persuade Lucy not to make the journey to England, then Charles was unsuccessful. The following day she and her son rejoined the main group, and travelled on to Flushing.[14]

The party reached London in the second week of June 1656. A decade on from the end of the civil war proper, the capital had seen six years of republican government. To Lucy, returning for the first time since the mid-1640s, it must have seemed familiar yet foreign. The streets bustled, trade thundered on and the royal palaces still stood. But at the Tower of London the Crown Jewels had been melted down; the pinnacles of the White Tower now glittered with the gilded arms of the republic, while the stakes on London Bridge bristled with the decomposing heads of royalists. The atmosphere was changed too under Puritan rule: the theatres had been shut, horses were stabled in St Paul's Cathedral and soldiers loitered on every street corner. The dizzy idealism of 1649 had quickly dissolved into a hybrid of republic and monarchy. Those who had assumed power after the regicide had given way, in 1653, to a single charismatic head of state. Lord Protector Cromwell knew only too well how fragile his regime was, and with royalist uprisings permanently rumoured and periodically materialising, national security had become an obsession. A regime bordering on a police state had resulted, in which the country was divided into twelve regions, each managed by a major general responsible for ensuring security, preventing royalist rebellions and enforcing moral and religious conformity. This was reinforced by a sophisticated spy network in which news of any royalist activity, at home or abroad, was reported to the intelligence chief and master propagandist John Thurloe.

On entering this politically charged environment, Lucy, Justus and Howard, blithely unaware of just how conspicuous they were, took lodgings above a barber's shop in London's most fashionable thoroughfare, the Strand. Their rooms overlooked the great classical facade of Somerset House. Once Henrietta Maria's London palace, it had been the site in 1649 of the extraordinary sale of almost every tapestry, painting, bronze and sculpture in the royal collection. Now denuded of its royal insignia, Somerset House had become a vast barracks and headquarters of the army: every Thursday afternoon Cromwell himself rode in through its gatehouse to take dinner with his captains. If Thurloe's spies had not known of Lucy's movements all along, they soon caught wind of them and were instantly on her trail. They pursued the pair down Thames-side streets, and mother and son only escaped thanks to a waterman who whisked them across the river before they could be pinned down. But with their identity exposed, capture was inevitable, and less than a fortnight after their arrival in London, the whole party – Lucy, the children, the maid, Howard and Justus – was seized.[15] Seven-year-old James was marched through the ominous triple gates of the Tower of London at his mother's side. Three decades later, he would be a prisoner within its blackened stone walls once more.

Over the course of six centuries the Tower had become home to a bewildering mix of royal and governmental institutions. The mangy lions of the royal menagerie stalked their sorry cages at the western entrance; in the narrow lane between the two vast curtain walls the noisy hammers and presses of the Mint struck discs of metal – some of them the recast gold of the Crown Jewels – into the new money of the republic; in the inner ward the vast Tudor storehouse stood jammed with arms and armour of England's first standing army. Resplendent in the centre was the great square keep built by the Conqueror himself, its dazzling white now dirtied, packed with gunpowder in thousands of volatile barrels.

The commander of the castle in 1656 was John Barkstead, a man as little likely to pity Lucy and her terrified children as anyone alive. A hard-line radical, he had attended every day of Charles I's trial, and had not shared some of his comrades' qualms when it came to the king's execution: Barkstead's spidery signature is still visible on Charles I's death warrant. As one of Cromwell's major generals, he enthusiastically carried out the Protector's orders in London, closing down the boisterous bear gardens on the South Bank, arresting prostitutes, and striving to prevent the celebration of Christmas. Barkstead was notorious for his brutal treatment of prisoners, and it was he who personally interrogated Lucy. Tough as ever, Lucy carefully repeated the story that she and her companions had rehearsed. She was, she maintained, the respectable widow of a Dutch ship's captain, and had come home to England to collect a legacy left by her mother. But Barkstead already knew too much, including that she had borne Charles Stuart a child. Lucy quickly improvised, conceding that this might have been true, but that the baby had died and it had been more than two years since she had seen the exiled king. When Howard was interviewed he told the truth about his position at the court in The Hague, but claimed to have met Lucy and her children for the first time during the crossing to England.

Despite their rapid readjustments their stories might still have stuck, had it not been for the fact that the maid, Anne Hill, had already confessed everything. An illiterate woman only seven months in Lucy's service, Anne's loyalty did not run deep. She had little reason to protect a mistress famous for her cruelty to servants and who even appears to have kept Anne prisoner at one stage. From the maid Barkstead learned of Lucy's relationship with Tom Howard, her precarious financial position, the meeting with Charles Stuart near Antwerp and, crucially, that the boy who travelled with her was indeed the son of the exiled king.

With the facts now before them, Cromwell and his councillors made an unexpected decision: they let them go. The reason was all too apparent. Given her reputation, the damage Lucy Walter could do free and left to her own devices far exceeded any advantage to the republic of keeping mother and son locked up. And so on 12 July, a fortnight after their capture, the Lord Protector signed the warrant for the party's release. The news was announced in that week's edition of the government rag *Mercurius Politicus*. Alongside appeared a report on the 5,000 livres annual allowance which Charles had promised Lucy, the details of which had been found among Lucy's papers on her arrest. With it a gleeful editorial comment was addressed to Charles's supporters: 'those that hanker after him may see they are furnished already with an Heir apparent'.[16]

While young James had been incarcerated with his mother and sister in the Tower, his father's prospects had improved considerably. The new treaty with Spain brought with it the opportunity, finally, for Charles II to re-establish himself amongst the fraternity of kings, to live and be treated as a sovereign. This sort of affirmation had been painfully absent over the past three years. Though the civic magistrates of the free city of Cologne had received Charles warmly, hardly any of the princely rulers of the region had endorsed him. The elector-archbishop of Cologne tolerated his presence but avoided any public statement of support for Charles's claim to the English throne. No royal palace was put at his disposal – he lived instead in a rented house – and no ceremonious exchanges of pleasantries had broadcast his regal status. But with his fortunes now tied to the Spanish there was an opportunity for redress.

The treaty Charles had signed with the Spanish in April 1656 said nothing about where he was to live and how he would be treated. These questions had, instead, to be pursued after the event. While negotiations were under way the royalists moved from Cologne to the ancient Flemish town of Bruges. This brought them into Spanish territory, but this was not their goal. Bruges, though once the seat of the powerful counts of Flanders, was now a genteel backwater; political authority was firmly established in Brussels, and agreement for the exiled court to settle there was what Charles sought.

The new governor-general of the Spanish Netherlands, who was en route to Brussels as the treaty was being signed, was Philip IV's illegitimate son Juan José. Exactly Charles's age, and with a string of military victories to his name, it was this formidable figure that Charles hoped to ensnare. A meeting was duly arranged between the two, both sons of kings and yet each denied his royal patrimony – Juan José by birth and Charles by circumstance. At their encounter, in the stiff surroundings of the Coudenberg Palace, Juan José denied the English request for sanctuary in Brussels. But amid the formalities the two men recognised something familiar in the other and a flame of fraternity was kindled. Instructing his entourage to remain in Bruges for the time being, Charles fanned his new friend-ship with princely presents, including a fine pack of hunting dogs, and found his care rewarded. By the end of the summer Juan José, while standing firm on the question of the exiled king's court, wrote warmly that he hoped Charles would come to Brussels to assist him with various matters. Thereafter Charles shuttled regularly between Bruges, where his household was based in a large house on the main square, and Brussels, where he also took lodgings.[17]

Despite his lack of money, Charles was able to beg enough credit – thanks not least to his visible friendship with the governor-general – to fund the sort of lifestyle he needed to keep up with Juan José and convince the sophisticated Bruxellois of his status. He gave generous alms to the poor, threw splendid birthday dinners attended by liveried attendants, played tennis at the Coudenberg, and kept packs of spaniels and exotic monkeys on golden chains. While the serious-minded Spanish counsellors who advised Juan José and wrote to Philip IV looked on stony-faced, Charles found his stock slowly rising. But then in 1657, after a year of carefully accumulated credibility, fate threw a grenade into the heat of a July afternoon – when through the Brussels city gates trundled a coach carrying Lucy Walter and her children.[18]

Following their release from the Tower of London a year earlier, the entire party had returned to the Netherlands. Lucy installed herself and her children at the new house, De Ruit. Justus, reluctant to relinquish such a comfortable arrangement, remained with them and settled into lavishly furnished rooms on the ground floor. Lucy's brother shared her expensive tastes and together they pored gleefully over the jewel-encrusted rings and necklaces, miniatures and cameos which Tom Howard's money had bought, and talked excitedly of the new coach lined in gold-fringed red velvet that was on order. Meanwhile Howard's court position gave him the perfect excuse to escape and return to The Hague, though he left his possessions as reassurance of his return. Lucy clearly expected the arrangements at De Ruit to last: she and Justus set about planting the gardens, work began on renovations to the house itself, and two portraits of Howard were among the works of art that adorned the walls. But it was not to be. Within a few months Lucy began a personal descent from which she would never recover. It started with a violent dispute with a wine merchant named Gerrit Veldt, which resulted in her imprisonment in Veldt's house. In the legal adjudication that followed, she was arrested, and the damaging statements of a host of servants were publicly aired. When she was finally released she was ordered to leave Delft.[19]

It is unclear from the surviving evidence precisely what had happened, but whatever the sorry details, Lucy was in serious trouble. She must have called for Howard's help from her prison cell, probably via John Harvey, her agent and a relation of her former landlady, but her desperate pleas went unanswered. In the end it was Robert Sidney, the lover of almost a decade before whom she had suddenly dropped when Charles arrived in The Hague, who came to her aid. And it was Sidney, together with Justus, who ensured that all the documents in the house, including letters from King Charles II, Tom and some of Howard's own papers, were secured in a travelling case and taken away to the Harveys' house.[20]

Lucy's calls for assistance may have elicited no response from Howard, but her removal of the sumptuous contents of De Ruit certainly did. She arranged for the swift sale of the house for two-thirds of the purchase price of only a year earlier, throwing various fixtures and fittings in with the sale. Howard's lawyers were instantly at hand, halting the transaction with the claim that most of the goods were not Lucy's to sell. As the lawyers fought it out through June and July 1657, Lucy's anger mounted. That Tom's affections had evaporated was clear, but she now started to doubt his motives in their affair altogether. It was in this thunderous mood that she left Delft for the Spanish Netherlands, not to see Charles II – though he was there – but to wreak her revenge on Tom Howard.[21]

News of Lucy's arrival in Brussels in late July 1657 made Charles II's heart sink. At her side was a new player: Charles Bursfield – son of her mother's younger sister, Anne – who had materialised from England, probably in answer to Lucy's pleas for help. Determined to defend his comely cousin's honour, and bristling with all the self-righteousness of the teenager, he challenged Tom Howard to a duel. Howard laughed Bursfield away, little suspecting how deep the youngster's indignation ran. The cousins, now equally aggrieved, next plotted his murder. The day chosen was Friday 24 August: Bursfield waited in an alleyway near Charles II's lodgings, as Tom walked deep in conversation with a lawyer named Fleming. In his hand Bursfield clutched a spike-like 'stiletto' dagger, designed to despatch a victim even through armour. As Howard passed, Bursfield leapt out and thrust the dagger towards his chest. Howard shot his right hand up to intercept the blow and the dagger sank deep into his arm, just below the elbow. Such was the violence of his assailant's thrust that the spike plunged through eight inches of flesh, re-emerging at Howard's wrist. The lawyer fled in terror, Howard collapsed, and Bursfield, feeling sure he had inflicted a mortal blow, disappeared.[22]

But the blow was not fatal. Tom Howard was found and ministered to, as word of the horrific attack, and Lucy's role in it, spread like fire. Charles II's friend and great swordsman, the Earl of Bristol, exploded with laughter when he heard of Howard's teenage assassin, but Edward Hyde could not see any cause for mirth: 'You may bee merry concerning Mrs Barlo,' he wrote, 'but I cannot bee.'[23] Neither could Charles. His response to this alarming incident was the recruitment of Arthur Slingsby to abduct James from his mother in Brussels. But six years after the first kidnap attempt in Rotterdam, they were again thwarted by Lucy.

On 6 December 1657, the evening after the public fracas in sight of the Coudenberg Palace, mother and son were given refuge by a royalist soldier, the Earl of Castlehaven. The following day Don Alonso de Cardenas, Philip IV's ambassador to the exiled English court, assured them of his protection. Initially no one knew for sure on whose orders Slingsby had been acting, but as soon as the Spanish king learned the truth letters were despatched to Charles, who had taken the precaution of spending that week in Bruges, away from the action.

Charles chose his words carefully in response; to apologise or express rage was to jeopardise all his hard work. Instead his carefully penned reply oozed charm. Thanking the ambassador for his kind intervention, he confirmed that he had indeed commissioned Slingsby to 'get the child', and explained that, despite the regrettable 'noise and scandal', the abduction of the boy remained his goal. Indeed, he went on, he would be grateful for any assistance the Spanish could give in the matter, which would, he contested, 'be a great charity to the child, and to the mother herself, if she shall now at length retire to such a way of life [that] may redeem in some measure the reproach of her past ways'. He ended with vague statements about his intention to disown both mother and child if he could not have his way.

The letter, followed by a communiqué along similar lines to Juan José, worked and the Spaniards now became accomplices in Charles's efforts to extract James from his mother. Cardenas's secretary attempted to talk Lucy into giving up her son, and she offered to allow him to be brought up according to his father's instructions – so long as he continued to live with her in Brussels and she was paid a pension. But Charles was not in the mood for accommodations, and with the Spaniards having swiftly got the measure of their guest, Lucy's protectors now became her gaolers. Christmas 1657 saw Lucy under house arrest in Brussels, threatening to publish Charles II's letters to her unless she was paid her promised pension. Then, three months later, the deed was done.[24]

Responsibility for the third, and final, kidnap attempt was given to Thomas Ross, the thirty-seven-year-old son of one of Charles I's footmen and a go-between in the endless furtive communications of exile. It was an unlikely choice, as Ross himself admitted. Bookish and warm-hearted, he was no natural abductor. The snatch itself was, it seems, effected on Ross's instructions by Edward Progers, another of Charles's grooms of the bedchamber, who had taken up the role when his master was just sixteen and would hold it until the king's death. In the end, the simplest of diversions was all that was needed to seize the boy. One day in April 1658, Progers simply 'took him away from his Mother whilst she was seeking for a paper' elsewhere in the house. Ross's instructions were 'to bestow him for awhile in a place out of the knowledge of his mother or anyone else but such as I took to help me'.[25]

On discovering James was missing, Lucy 'immediatly went in Quest after him'. But this time, finally, she could not manage it. Her courage, her determination, her fury, were not enough: with Ross periodically moving the boy to keep the trail cool, she could not find him. For six months she remained in Brussels, and continued to be a thorn in the side of the exiled royalists. Howard's lawsuits against her rumbled on, and October saw her fighting with one of

Charles II's chaplains, Dr Ffloyd. Gradually her strength began to deteriorate as she succumbed to a mysterious illness. Though sickness slowed her, she continued the search. In autumn she left Brussels for Paris, presumably on hearing that James might be there.[26]

In the French capital she became reacquainted with John Cosin, the distinguished Master of Peterhouse who had acted as chaplain to the English Protestants at Henrietta Maria's court. With her health failing fast, Lucy confessed to Cosin her desire to live a different life and be reconciled with God. Now without her son, with no income, and with disease gripping her lovely body, she may well have contemplated the afterlife. But she had precious little time to bargain for salvation and in the chilly first week of December, nine months after James's abduction, she died.

Lucy Walter was buried somewhere in Paris, her possessions bundled up and passed to her aunt. She was not alone during those final weeks. Watching her in Paris and present at her burial had been William Erskine, an official at the exiled court. He had probably been sent by Charles II to spy on Lucy. What he saw confirmed his view that she was 'a very ill woman' and as he witnessed her coffin being interred he shed no tears. What had killed this vigorous and vivacious twenty-eight-year-old woman is uncertain. Her critics, principal among them Charles's brother the Duke of York, would later claim it was venereal disease. In life Lucy tended to vindicate those who believed the worst of her, and so it may have been in death.[27]

Chapter 3

A New Life

James had just turned nine when he was abducted. He was snatched from his mother with nothing but the clothes he wore and found himself surrounded by total strangers. Utterly disorientated, this child, with no education, no family and no identity to speak of, lacked even a surname. From week to week Lucy's situation had swung from luxury to poverty, as she was buffeted between honey-tongued suitors and heavy-handed creditors. He had seen palaces and prison cells and been treated as both prince and pauper. Addressed by his mother's servants as 'the master', he was draped in jewels and rich fabrics and paraded before important visitors. Yet theirs had been a hand-to-mouth existence, with spells of real poverty, dogged by the threat of arrest for Lucy's various crimes. All the while mother and son had lived in fear of the abduction that would eventually separate them.[1]

Few children could have had a more chaotic upbringing. At nine James lacked the education of a four-year-old, his mother had not taught him to count to twenty, let alone write his name, and he never knew for sure the date of his birthday. But however negligent she was, Lucy knew the value of a royal child. While she did not provide conventional maternal love and stability, she probably spared him the outright brutality she showed others. One of James's most enduring images of his mother was of her fighting off Slingsby in Brussels the previous winter. Her determined struggle to keep her son told him all he needed to know. For James her memory

would be sacred and his desire to defend her posthumous reputation would, in time, have far-reaching consequences.

The wall hangings in James's first apartment at Whitehall Palace
five years later would depict Venus, the goddess of maternal
beauty, and her boy child Cupid. Twenty years after that he would
commission the court artist Godfrey Kneller to paint his mother.
The poised, graceful beauty he portrayed, proudly displaying an
image of her young son, was the person James chose to remember
and carry with him to his new life.[2]

For Charles II, separating his son from Lucy had been a matter of
self-interest. The decisions about James's future to which he now
turned were, similarly, governed by a sense of his own position.
Charles had never quibbled with Lucy's assertion that James was
his son, and as such the boy required a respectable upbringing.
Two or three months after the abduction, when it was felt that any
immediate danger of Lucy reclaiming him had passed, James was
put into the care of Charles's friend William Crofts.

In his thirties and a career courtier with a big character, Crofts was
precisely the sort of man whose company Charles most enjoyed.
Crofts had been attached to the Stuart court since before the civil war
and had spent the three years immediately after the regicide travelling
between the princely cities of the Baltic trying to raise money and
troops for an invasion; when that had come to nothing he had returned
to Paris to rejoin Charles.[3] A scandal over a duel two years later had
caused him to fall out of favour at the Louvre, and the following
year he had taken a comfortable house six or seven miles north-west
of Paris at Colombes, a fertile plain around which the Seine snaked
towards the sea.[4] It was a house with happy associations for Charles.
Just before he had left France in 1654 – pre-empting his eviction by the
unsentimental Cardinal Mazarin – he had visited Crofts at Colombes.
Coming for three days, he stayed for three weeks, reluctant to leave
his friend's house and the plays, music and laughter with which it was
filled. After Charles's departure, Crofts remained in France acting as
an agent with his powerful French cousins.[5]

The month after James was finally taken from Lucy, William Crofts was made Lord Crofts of Saxham. The service he was about to undertake was one for which the penniless king could offer only titular reward. His establishment at Colombes was comfortably removed from scandal-mongers of Brussels or Paris, making it possible for a child to appear as an unspecified young kinsman without provoking comment. But as important as the character of Crofts himself, or the gentle obscurity of his house, was his neighbour: James's grandmother, the dowager queen Henrietta Maria.

For over twenty years Crofts's career had been tied up with that of Henrietta Maria. As a youth he had found his first court position as her page, before being promoted to captain of her guards, stationed within her apartments and responsible for her security. His sister Cecily had been one of her maids of honour, dancing in the theatrical performances in her apartments in the heady days before the civil war. His brother too had frequented them until the queen's dwarf, Jeffrey Hudson, shot him in the head in a 'duel' which everyone but the persecuted Hudson had treated as a joke.[6] Come the mid-1650s Crofts and the redoubtable queen had known one another well for decades and a web of honour and loyalty lay between them. When Henrietta Maria was lent the money to buy a country house she joined Crofts at Colombes, taking a riverside house from one of the Fouquet family. Whenever Charles II needed to rein in his mother he turned for this delicate service to William Crofts.[7]

By 1658 Henrietta Maria was in her fifties and, sapped by sorrow, had turned increasingly to her Catholic faith for solace. In 1651 she had stopped the Anglican services that had always been held for her Protestant servants, and in 1654, encouraged by her confessor Walter Montagu – a Catholic convert and amateur dramatist who Charles II called the 'queen's evil genius' – had tried to convert her youngest son, Prince Henry, to Catholicism. When Charles II heard that his mother was enrolling his brother in a Jesuit seminary, he was horrified; if news reached England that the Stuart heirs had become Catholics any hope of a restoration would be extinguished.

He dispatched a volley of letters ordering his brother to resist (something Henry needed little encouragement to do), his mother to desist and his representatives to extract the boy. Crofts was instrumental in the unenviable task of removing Prince Henry from his mother's clutches. Though she could hardly blame her youngest son for obeying his brother and sovereign, she was furious and stubbornly refused his requests for her blessing on his departure.[8]

Since those events of 1654 relations between Charles II and Henrietta Maria had remained cool, and for four years no meeting had taken place between them. In July 1658, just three months after James's abduction, Henrietta Maria set out from her lodgings at the Louvre to attend the admission of the Duke of Sully's granddaughter as a Carmelite nun at the convent north-west of the city in Pontoise. She passed through Colombes as she did so. Unusually – perhaps having learned the identity of Lord Crofts's new ward – she did not stay at her own house but lodged instead with Crofts and so began her relationship with her first grandson.[9] With the arrival in her melancholy world of James – bright-eyed, winning and under the wing of her liegeman – the queen's cold heart warmed. Those who saw them together three years later were left in no doubt about the strength of feeling she had developed for the boy; as the Venetian ambassador put it: he was 'dearly loved by the widowed queen'.[10]

While Henrietta Maria had been prevented from educating Prince Henry as a Catholic, no such sensitivities governed the upbringing of her bastard grandson. She was able, therefore, to arrange for her Catholic chaplain, Stephen Gough, to take over James's spiritual education without complaint. Gough, like a number in the Queen's circle, was a high-Church Anglican turned Catholic by the experiences of the civil war, but unlike some he supported the royalist cause with little anti-Protestant bias. The sort of Catholicism he began to teach his charge was learned and tolerant, and James would remain in touch with Father Gough for the rest of his life.[11]

James's education was only in part religious. Overall responsibility for his upbringing lay with his guardian Lord Crofts. When Charles II had been a boy in the 1630s, before war tore all order apart, the brilliant horseman William Cavendish, Earl of Newcastle, had been his governor. Newcastle had acted as his mentor and taken responsibility for ensuring Charles had all the sporting, military and artistic accomplishments of a prince. The business of Charles's academic education had been managed separately by a series of distinguished scholars. A similar arrangement was instituted for James. Crofts, in Edward Hyde's words, 'took care for the breeding him suitable to the quality of a very good gentleman', ensuring he learned how to dance, fence and hunt. James's academic schooling – which started with teaching him to read and write – was the responsibility of his tutor, Thomas Ross, the man who had successfully masterminded the boy's abduction. When James became his pupil, Ross was thirty-eight and without children of his own, and he quickly developed an indulgent affection for James that went well beyond his task as schoolmaster.[12]

An ignorant and uneducated pupil, the bastard son of a disreputable mother, might have made an unenticing prospect for the men put in charge of James. But just a few weeks after the kidnap, Thomas Ross was already enchanted. He wrote warmly to the king's principal secretary of state of the boy's qualities: he was 'so pretty a child', full of 'wit', and – despite his ignorance – showed 'a great desire to learn'.[13] Perhaps the most remarkable thing was how little his mother's calculating ways had affected him. Instead of being sly or cynical, he was sunny and sincere. His good looks combined with this unaffected and willing character made him almost irresistible.

If James presented a captivating figure to his tutors, Crofts must also have been an appealing guardian. Handsome, boisterous and impulsive, prone to swordfights and seductions, he was the sort of man who would have beaten a path to Lucy's door – indeed he had seen Lucy in her prime in Paris in 1649, when John Evelyn had travelled to court with her. While he was loathed by the more serious-minded administrators of the king's council – Edward Hyde spat with irritation when Charles II made him a gentleman of the bedchamber – Crofts proved magnetic to a spirited nine-year-old.

For a boy who had known men only through their stormy affairs with his mother, to form an enduring relationship with an adult man must have been rewarding.[14]

Sixteen fifty-eight was a turning point in the life of James 'Crofts', as it was in the history of Britain. On a stormy night in early September 1658 Oliver Cromwell lay fevered and incoherent in his rooms at Whitehall Palace. When dawn started to break his confused murmuring ceased and he fell into a coma. Twelve hours later he was dead. Fifty-nine years old, he had changed England more than any single person before or since. A republican revolutionary whose career had been won in the mud of the battlefield, he died in regal luxury in the state bedchamber of Charles I's principal palace. He had been troubled as he felt death's approach, and asked his chaplains whether grace, once reached, could be lost. Reassured by their replies, he had mumbled 'I am safe for I know I was once in grace'. The celebrations of the royalists were soon dampened as power passed without hitch to Cromwell's thirty-two-year-old son Richard, in fulfilment of his father's instructions. But obscure and without obvious talents, this new Cromwell's regime was fragile. Though the counter-revolution was not upon them yet, the royalists felt sure the regime could not last long.[15]

While England's fate looked uncertain, things were changing on the continent too. Two months earlier the armies of Louis XIV of France and Philip IV of Spain had clashed near Dunkirk in an encounter known as the battle of the Dunes. English republican soldiers fought with the French, while English royalists fought with the Spanish. The Spanish had been trounced, and the wheels were set in motion for an end to the conflict between these two powerful nations. A year later, in October 1659, the French and Spanish chief ministers, Cardinal Mazarin and Don Luis de Haro, met to agree the terms of peace in the border town of Fuenterrabia, where the south-western tip of France meets the northern corner of Spain. Charles decided to attend the negotiations in person; he was both worried the Spanish might use the treaty as an opportunity to withdraw their support, and hopeful that the French might back him now the war was over. Atrocious weather delayed his ship off the western coast of France, so when he finally reached Spain he was weeks late. Assuming the meeting was long over, he trundled a hundred miles inland towards Madrid only to discover the delegates were still in Fuenterrabia and was forced to retrace his tracks.

Charles caught the tail end of the negotiations and was just in time to see the signature of the treaty, as part of which the young Louis XIV was betrothed to the Spanish infanta, Maria Theresa. The expedition was a mixed success. Charles made little progress with the icy Cardinal Mazarin, but he had kept the Spanish confidence, even extracting some of his allowance, and was thrilled when Luis de Haro treated him with the same deference as the King of Spain himself. In this positive mood he left Spain for Brussels, having promised to visit his mother on the return journey.

With relations with Cardinal Mazarin still shaky, there was no question of Charles II appearing publically in Paris, and so the meeting was to be at Colombes. Charles travelled from Bordeaux to Chartres in less than a fortnight, and was met there by Crofts and Lord Gerrard, who accompanied him the final sixty miles.[16] Whether young James travelled with his guardian on this important journey to meet his father is uncertain, but likely. On 24 November, Henrietta Maria came to Colombes from Paris with her youngest daughter and ladies. The following day at around noon a clattering cavalcade of horses and coaches announced the arrival of her son.

Much had changed in the five years since the row over Prince Henry's religion, so much so that Charles did not recognise his teenage sister and warmly greeted one of the queen's attendants before having his mistake pointed out. The plan had been for Charles to stay at his mother's house, in the suite of rooms usually occupied by her companion and advisor Henry Jermyn. But after the introductions and embraces Charles changed his mind, and lodged instead with Lord Crofts. No explanation for this change of plan was given, but perhaps the cause, and certainly the effect, of this domestic rearrangement was the strength of the relationship he was developing with the dark-eyed boy who was always now to be found at Crofts's side.[17]

Charles spent just a fortnight at Colombes before unfolding affairs in England drew him back to Brussels. But those short November days would be forever bright in his memory as they saw him forge the two most profound and enduring personal relationships of his life: with his sister and with his son.

Henriette Anne was the last of Charles I and Henrietta Maria's eight children and had been born in 1644 amid the discomfort and distress of the civil war. Smuggled out of England by her governess, she had arrived in Paris in 1646 and would live there for the rest of her life, going on to marry Louis XIV's brother the Duc d'Orléans in 1661. She was ten when her brother left France, and while they corresponded periodically it was on being reunited at Colombes in 1659 that an intimacy and affection blossomed between the two that would never falter. Within weeks of the visit, Charles and Henriette Anne began a frequent exchange of letters which would continue for the rest of her life, and in which he characterised himself as a 'brother that loves you more than he can expresse'.[18]

The froideur between Henrietta Maria and her son swiftly dissolved in the convivial atmosphere of the gathering in Colombes that autumn. The king, everyone agreed, was wonderfully cheerful, and acts of forgiveness on both sides were salve to old sores. In generous spirit Charles brushed off his mother's past intransigence, and delighted her by making Henry Jermyn Earl of St Albans. When Charles left he had begun to form a bond with his son every bit as strong as that with his sister. Events over the next three years, until they met again, would show that after that fortnight the king's interest in James had become personal rather than political. No longer simply an inconvenient piece on the political board, James was now 'a person I have so great a kindnesse for'.[19] A miniature of him by the brilliant portraitist Samuel Cooper probably dates from this time, perhaps a commission from the king as a keepsake.[20] Being the king's illegitimate son was in itself no guarantee of importance – the position carried no income, office or expectation.

But being a bastard son who enjoyed the affection of his royal father would change James's life absolutely, and set him on a path to both triumph and tragedy.

While Charles, Henriette Anne and James were rediscovering one another at Colombes, England was falling apart. Richard Cromwell, utterly unable to reconcile the enmities his father's death had only multiplied, lasted little more than six months. The army, deeply dismissive of their young civilian leader, soon rose up and forced Cromwell's resignation and the abolition of the office of Protector and of the Protectorate regime altogether. A return to the early radicalism which had brought about the revolution a decade earlier seemed certain. But political stability once lost was to prove impossible to regain. The army and Parliament were at logger-heads, with the army first recalling and then expelling the 'purged' Parliament. Even as Charles left Crofts's house and returned to Brussels in December 1659, the rank and file of the army rebelled, overwhelming its generals and reinstating the dismissed Parliament. George Monck, Oliver Cromwell's stalwart Scottish general, supported the uprising and on Parliament's request rode to London to try and hold the peace.

When General Monck arrived in the capital he was shocked by the reality of Parliament's approach to governing. Alarmed by their heavy-handedness and troubled by the aggression they directed to ordinary Londoners, he soon became convinced that only a moderate regime enjoying popular support could restore stability. On 21 February 1660 Monck declared that the less radical MPs who had been 'purged' by Thomas Pride back in 1649 were to be readmitted. In a single stroke history changed course. The execution of Charles I, the abolition of the monarchy and all that followed had not been the will of the people nor even the elect-orate – but of a domineering political minority who had used force to remove moderates from the House of Commons. With the most powerful man in the kingdom now insisting on their reinstatement the outcome was inevitable: the revolution was over.[21]

Three months later Monck as head of the army and Edward Montagu, who led the navy, prepared to welcome the return of the king. After so long, a swift exchange of letters between Charles II and a new parliament (the purged MPs had swiftly dissolved themselves to allow for an election) was all that had been needed to effect a restoration of the monarchy. Agreement was made easy by Charles's determination that it should be: a general pardon was to be issued to all but those who had actually signed his father's death warrant, while the thorny issue that had lain at the heart of the civil war – the religious complexion of country – he proposed referring to Parliament. Montagu's young kinsman, Samuel Pepys, arranged for a team of painters to cover the republican insignia on the naval fleet with the royal arms.

On 23 May 1660, Charles boarded the navy's greatest vessel – once the *Naseby*, now the *Royal Charles* – off the Dutch coast and, after fourteen years' absence, sailed home.

Chapter 4

Homecoming

Charles II rode into Westminster and reclaimed his kingdom on 29 May 1660, his thirtieth birthday. As he did so his horse's hooves clattered past the very spot where his father's head had fallen a decade earlier. The pealing church bells, the cheering cries of thousands of spectators and the girls in white strewing rose petals in the procession's path all contributed to an ecstatic pageant amid which the past must have seemed remote indeed. In the months that followed monarchy was reassembled, the army paid off, the Church of England re-established and the Crown Jewels remade. George Monck, Cromwell's trusted general, was made a duke and Edward Hyde, councillor to the exiled king, an earl. Old enemies were bound together in the new regime.

As London rang with celebrations, James, now eleven, remained in peaceful obscurity at Colombes. His existence was not unknown at the new court, however, and the Venetian ambassadors dispatched to London to congratulate Charles II on his restoration confirmed that the king had a son who was being raised a Catholic. Incorrect on various details, they had clearly heard of him only at second or third hand.[1] News of this boy, and of the king's affection for him, also reached the ears of the Scottish noblewoman Margaret Leslie, Countess of Wemyss, and in his distant and indistinct figure she saw the answer to her troubles.

Margaret Leslie was the forty-year-old daughter of the Earl of Rothes. In her mid-twenties, and already a widow, she had married the pale nineteen-year-old Francis, Earl of Buccleuch. After five happy years of wedlock the earl died in 1651, leaving Margaret with two infant daughters into the eldest of whose hands, according to the conditions of his will, the wealth of the richest family in Scotland now passed. As Margaret grappled with her second widowhood the late Earl of Buccleuch's sister and her powerful husband, the Earl of Tweeddale, circled menacingly, for should the girls die, or marry into their own branch of the family, the wealth would be theirs. Desperate to avoid such an outcome, Margaret waited as long as she dared and then married her frail older daughter, Mary, to the teenage Walter Scott, Earl of Tarras. All seemed secure, but it was not. The legality of this marriage between children was contested, and then Mary became ill, developing a tumour in her arm which even the healing touch of the restored king could not cure. On 12 March 1661 she died, and her fortune, and vulnerability, passed to her ten-year-old sister Anna. Suddenly exposed, and desperate to save her second daughter from the fate of the first, the countess cast around for the powerful supporters she needed. And thus two months after Mary's death she wrote to King Charles II and offered the hand of her daughter, now Countess of Buccleuch in her own right, to James, the bastard son he was believed to have fathered in exile.[2]

It was a massive gamble. The Buccleuch fortune was substantial and Margaret was depending on the king caring enough for his son to protect this inheritance for his sake. Furthermore she had never met the boy and to put her family's wealth and name in the hands of this unknown illegitimate child was a risk indeed. Charles, however, was delighted. He wrote warmly to Margaret (now Countess of Wemyss following her third marriage) accepting her offer 'most willingly' and, to her relief, describing her troubles over the Buccleuch inheritance as something 'I look upon now as my own interest.'[3] The arrangement was made in the summer of 1661 and within a year its implementation would begin in earnest.

The prospect, and then the reality, of the restoration of the Stuart monarchy had instantly transformed Cardinal Mazarin's attitude to Charles II. Lord Crofts now found himself in urgent demand by the French premier keen to make amends, and his formerly thankless role of Anglo-French go-between became suddenly much more rewarding. Mazarin asked Crofts to present Charles II with France's warm congratulations. He bent the rules of protocol in order to ladle him with honour and even sought his advice on what lavish gift could best express this sentiment.[4] Just as Crofts came and went between Paris and London, so James's other patron, the queen mother, Henrietta Maria, travelled to England in October 1660 to celebrate her son's restoration. She returned just three months later to see Henriette Anne marry Louis XIV's brother Philippe, Duc d'Orléans and it may be that young James 'Crofts' accompanied his guardian or grandmother on one of these trips. But he perhaps more likely watched the comings and goings from Thomas Ross's supervision in Colombes. Once Henriette Anne's marriage had taken place, and his own with the young Countess of Buccleuch had been arranged, it was only a matter of time before James would be called to England.

In the spring of 1662 the newlywed Duc and Duchesse d'Orléans came to Colombes. Henriette Anne, who was only five years James's senior, had developed a real affection for her favourite brother's young son at the Colombes congress three years earlier.[5] But this visit was to be a farewell, for Henrietta Maria was now set to return permanently to England and James was to accompany her. The young Countess of Buccleuch was brought to London by her mother to await James's arrival, and in preparation for his entry into London society, the Catholic tutors approved of by Henrietta Maria were banished and Protestants substituted in their place.[6]

That James should arrive in England a practising Protestant of the right sort was essential, for his journey was to take place at precisely the moment when England's new religious regime was being instituted. Charles had declared himself happy to acquiesce in the will of Parliament in relation to the religious complexion of the country. This looked likely to mean that the re-established

Church of England would encompass many of the new breeds of Protestantism that had sprung up in the decade before – Quakers and Presbyterians of various varieties – perhaps even Catholicism would be allowed. But in the end it was not to be. The 'Cavalier' Parliament that had swept to power in the general election of 1661 agreed a narrow definition of acceptable religious practice. A set of rules for worship was set down in a new Book of Common Prayer the following year, the use of which was to be mandatory in all churches. As a consequence some 2,000 clergymen were ejected from the re-established Church. To be a non-conforming Protestant or a Catholic was now not actually illegal, but it was legislated against so as to make life very uncomfortable for any but Anglicans. Though Charles II had not wished it, the religious 'settlement' of 1662 enshrined a deep and fundamental division in English society that would haunt him and, in time, play a defining role in James's own life.

In early July 1662 James prepared to leave France for England. The Duc and Duchesse d'Orléans accompanied the party as far north as Beauvais before returning to Paris. Charles II's brother, the Duke of York, was to ferry the queen mother and her considerable entourage over from Boulogne in a series of ships while the king himself was to wait to greet them in another vessel just off the English coast. When the king left London for Dover in the royal barge on 19 July it was already raining hard and temperatures were dropping.[7] As James, his grandmother and their companions arrived at Boulogne, the wind picked up. The Duke of York, who was also Admiral of the Fleet, sailed the next day accompanied by a bevy of distinguished companions, including the vice-admiral, Lord Sandwich, and Lord Crofts himself. Mid-crossing a tremendous storm hit. Battered by gales, heavy seas and relentless rain, the ships floundered. Ropes and sails were shredded and dozens of men thrown overboard and drowned. The king's own vessel was swept aground on the sand-banks in the Thames estuary and was in danger of being wrecked. The Duke of York, caught in the water between Dover and Calais, watched as the wind snapped the mast of his warship, while the first boat in the flotilla, a yacht captained by Sandwich and carrying Crofts, disappeared completely in the eye of the storm. They were feared dead until they materialised, dazed and shaken, days later. The ordeal had driven Crofts to weeping hysteria, and even Sandwich, the greatest sailor of the age, conceded it had been horrible.[8]

The storm passed as quickly as it had broken. On Friday 25 July the queen mother, James and the rest of her entourage – including the king's cousin, Prince Edward of the Palatinate – boarded fresh ships and crossed the Channel in just a few hours. They landed at Dover to be welcomed by Charles II, Prince Rupert, the Duke of Buckingham and a host of other grandees, then sailed up the Thames to Woolwich. Here the company parted. Henrietta Maria travelled to Greenwich to her miniature park-side palace, built by Inigo Jones in the 1620s. The king and much of the rest of the party were rowed on through London to Hampton Court. It was not just James who was contemplating wedlock in 1662. Two months before his arrival in England his father had finally married, taking as his bride the shy and formal Portuguese infanta, Catherine of Braganza. After a ceremony in the governor's house at Portsmouth the couple travelled north and took up quarters in the capacious Tudor palace for the summer, its acres of shady gardens providing respite from the summer heat.[9]

Here at Hampton Court, James made his public debut at the English court. His very existence was a surprise to some, while the tenderness with which the king treated him astonished everyone. Suddenly courtiers and diplomats could talk of nothing but the 'great affection' of the king for this thirteen-year-old new arrival. Though James went under the surname 'Crofts', Charles made no effort whatsoever to deny the rumours that he was his son. The stir only increased when it was confirmed that James was already engaged to Scotland's richest heiress. The warmth and familiarity that Charles showed his son was visible to even the most fleeting visitor. For those who had known anything of Lucy, his affection for her child was a cause for alarm. But the king was oblivious. A fortnight later he and Queen Catherine left Hampton Court for London in a magnificent river pageant. With this the king returned to London, and there was never any doubt that James was going with him.[10]

In August 1662 James arrived in the great city which would be his home for the next twenty years. Considerably larger than the Dutch towns of his childhood, London was still much smaller than the scene of his adolescence, Paris. With a population of over 300,000 it had been growing rapidly until the civil war brought so much to a standstill. To a visitor then, as now, the city was an eclectic mix of old and new. The great structures which punctuated the skyline – the Tower of London, St Paul's Cathedral, the Royal Exchange, Westminster Abbey – spoke of a prosperous royal past, while the medieval streets of narrow timber buildings between them recalled the busy bargaining of merchants and traders over as many centuries. But while the buildings were old, the spirit was new. Peace and a popular new regime brought with them a wave of relief that was intoxicating. The return of a royal court to Whitehall Palace two years earlier had seen an explosion in demand for luxury products which the drapers and goldsmiths, masons and painters clamoured to meet. Since Charles II had returned to London on his birthday in 1660 the public ceremonies and celebrations had come thick and fast. The processional arches erected for the coronation still stood astride the principal road through the city, though their painted canvas was now torn and faded.[11]

With the ferocious civil and moral grip of the major generals gone, an orgy of exuberance and amusement had taken hold. The playhouses of London, comprehensively shut down in the 1640s, now reopened their doors and theatres sprang up across the capital in a matter of months, the industry flourishing with the king's own patronage. In Moorfields, diners at the music hall were served supper while musicians with jesters and performing animals provided a cabaret of entertainment. In Vauxhall visitors paid handsomely to promenade along the immaculate avenues of the New Spring Gardens. On the Thames a thousand vessels teemed across the water affording glimpses into the riches of the riverside mansions as they passed. At Whitehall a floating bowling green, complete with artificial grass and potted trees, bobbed in the tidal waters beside the palace. The spectacles were legion: cockerels, bears and bulls fought to the baying cries of gambling spectators; at St Bartholomew's fair camels, lions and flamingos with collars and chains were marvelled at; wrestlers, tightrope walkers, dancers and acrobats performed at taverns and on greens. The latest craze was coffee houses: eighty had opened over the capital in just a few years, and here Londoners sipped and gossiped, their chatter fuelled by the pamphlets and newspapers which had become a staple of life in the capital during the wars.

But all the drinking and dancing was a carefree veneer on a still fragile world. In London and England as a whole, the destruction of civil war was still apparent and the danger of further disorder was real. Everywhere the steady thud of rebuilding could be heard. As James and the royal party had been rowed up the Thames from Woolwich in July 1662, the Tudor palace of Greenwich was being rebuilt while the hunting park on the rising land behind – its deer killed and oaks felled in the wars – was crisscrossed by avenues of sapling trees. Rapid re-badging was evident everywhere, promoted equally by government officials and ordinary citizens keen to cash in. The lions at the royal menagerie, the republican warships, and the countless weather vanes were given new royal identities, while statues were re-erected and churches repaired.

All the while the grisly justice of the age was never far away as sentences were meted out to the signatories of Charles I's death warrant. Only three months earlier James's former gaoler, the erstwhile Lieutenant of the Tower, John Barkstead, had been dragged through London on a wooden sledge to Tyburn for execution. Unrepentant till the end, and though he was too ill to stand, Barkstead chewed nonchalantly and swigged from a hip flask as the executioner tore off his wig and fitted the noose. The severed heads of regicides and republican sympathisers crowned the city's gatehouses, while the executions, burnings and brandings continued through James's first autumn. Oliver Cromwell's own head, hacked off his two-year-old corpse, was exhibited outside the Palace of Westminster, a cautionary tale to would-be radicals. While the gaiety was real, it could dissolve at a moment's notice, as it did when a plot against the king was rumoured to have been uncovered just three months after James's arrival. The capital suddenly filled with thousands of armed soldiers, doors were broken down and over 300 people were arrested.[12]

James would have many more arrivals in London in the years that were to come, and they were seldom without drama, but the contrast between his first and second was as night and day. In 1656, illiterate and obscure, he had slipped in with his mother and her lover on the scent of money. They had put up in rented rooms above a barber's shop before being captured, imprisoned and interrogated. Six years later, draped in French finery and with the mannerisms of the first salons in Paris, James was becoming the darling of the royal family and was known by all to be King Charles II's son. What a changed world it was: Barkstead's severed head was on a spike and when James glimpsed his former lodgings on the Strand it was from the sovereign's coach where he luxuriated on velvet seats with the king's mistress, the queen and the king himself.[13]

The delight with which the king received James may at first have been more than personal feeling. It had, after all, been three years since he had seen his son, and their relationship was based on little more than a fortnight's real acquaintance. There was also, perhaps, an element of policy: Charles II had to ensure the Buccleuch family did not have second thoughts about the marriage which was set to bring such wealth. But even with all these qualifiers, James blazed into his father's world like a comet. That he so mesmerised Charles was thanks not just to his own appeal, but to the particular emotional state in which he found his father in 1662.

When the monarchy was restored Charles II had ended four-teen years of exile. He had agreed to the restoration on terms that were remarkably clement given what his family had experienced –

perhaps because of his desperation for the throne, or because he had a political sophistication alien to his own father. The religious regime was being determined by Parliament, but at the king's insistence an Act of Indemnity and Oblivion had pardoned almost all but those who had actually tried Charles I in 1649, and no attempt was made to turn back the clock on the sale of royalists' lands over the past eighteen years.

For Charles the restoration had brought an end to the long shame of exile – poverty, obscurity and enforced idleness – and like his subjects he threw himself into his new life with gusto. He responded to the clamouring crowds and endless congratulatory addresses with charm, humour and patience. Perhaps only a sovereign who had felt the grinding absence of such things for so long could truly appreciate their value. Energetic in mind and body, the new king was an enthusiast with wide-ranging interests, among them science, theatre, sailing and sex. Before the restoration, in the period when he travelled between Brussels and Bruges, he had fathered a second son, this time with Catherine Pegge, the daughter of a Yorkshire royalist. Come the restoration he was embarking on a new affair with the promiscuous beauty Barbara Villiers, the wife of the royalist lawyer Roger Palmer. This passionate relationship would last seven years and produce four further children. But while clearly enjoying his liaisons – he was infatuated, for a period at least, with the formidable Barbara – and having a genuine affection for the queen, the strongest of Charles's emotional attachments were to his siblings. His brother James was his heir and lieutenant, his sister Mary a stalwart friend in friendless times, his brother Henry constantly at his side and his youngest sister Henriette Anne his darling.

Then in September 1660 tragedy had hit. Henry, praised by even the irritable Hyde for his 'comeliness and gracefulness of his person and the vivacity and vigour of his wit and understanding', had caught smallpox. Within days the prince, who had only just turned twenty, was dead. Charles was devastated. One contemporary described his 'grief unspeakable', as the king wept with open despair at his brother's death. He withdrew from all court events, giving instructions that no one was even to attempt to see him.[14]

Mary, widow of the Prince of Orange and mother of the now ten-year-old William of Orange, had been travelling to England to join her siblings at the time of Henry's death, and her arrival gave her grieving brother some solace. But tragedy was to come of tragedy when she too contracted the disease. By December she lay dying at Whitehall, racked with despair that she was abandoning her son: 'my greatest pain is to depart from him,' she wept, 'Oh my child.' Charles II's companion since infancy, and supporter and friend in exile, Mary had been back for only a matter of weeks before her death. The love between the siblings had been reciprocal until the end: she left the care of her son to Charles (though the Dutch government would prevent him from fulfilling her wish) and asked to be laid to rest beside Henry in Westminster Abbey.[15]

The effect on Charles of watching two siblings die within weeks of one another, and in particular of losing his young brother, had been profound and left him bereft of something which only the arrival of his son would supply. But if in his grief Charles felt predisposed toward a younger kinsman, the strength of emotion that his son would release in him was still extraordinary. To the magnetic good looks which James had inherited from his mother, and which were commented on by all who saw him, had been applied the rich polish that came from Lord Crofts's tutelage. He had acquired the accomplishments and affectations not just of an English gentleman, but of a Parisian aristocrat.[16] This was a powerful combination; for the English court in 1662, France was synonymous with style and sophistication. In their taste in clothes, dancing, furniture and music the English beau monde looked to Paris alone for example. This hallowed place that most had never seen, James knew intimately.[17] In listing his merits his father cited proudly the 'suavity of manners' that his son's French education had cultivated.[18]

Thanks to the efforts of Thomas Ross and Lord Crofts, James's accelerated education at Colombes had been a success. To dancing, riding and hunting he brought a natural aptitude and grace of

movement that made him a pleasure to watch.[19] Spurred on by
an eagerness to learn which Ross had seen in him from the first,
he could not now just read and write but was capable, when he
applied himself, of penning letters in as even a script as any young
nobleman of the age.[20] But if his person was lovely to the eye, if
his manners were elegant enough for the drawing rooms of Paris,
and his deportment a delight, the transforming agent was his
energy. A lifetime's apprenticeship in the languid affectations of
the French court could not subdue the sheer vitality that flowed
in the boy's veins. In France he already had a reputation for being
'high-spirited', and the same characteristic was commented upon
the moment he arrived at Hampton Court.[21] Never still, his natural
mode was motion; he never sat when he could stand, never stood
when he could dance or run. When Samuel Pepys accompanied the
king and his companions on an inspection of various naval yards in
1665 he saw James close to, and described him as 'the most skittish,
leaping gallant that ever I saw, always in action, vaulting or leaping
or clambering'.[22]

When the court returned to London the king decided that James
should no longer live with Crofts, or even with Henrietta Maria,
but with him. The principal royal residence was Whitehall Palace,
an aggrandised bishop's residence which Henry VIII had taken from
Cardinal Wolsey after his fall. Built on a long narrow site between
the Thames and the open ground of St James's Park to the west, it
was the epicentre of royal and government life until a catastrophic
fire would decimate it in 1698. It was so hemmed in by buildings on
all sides it looked more like an affluent quarter of the city than like
a stand-alone palace. The public road which now bears its name,
known then as King Street, ran through the middle of the palace,
with two covered bridges sailing over it that connected the buildings near the river with those facing the park.

Here at Whitehall, James was assigned a suite of rooms overlooking the Thames. They were located next to the privy stairs, a
two-storey jetty which allowed the sovereign to disembark from

the royal barge and walk directly into the heart of his private apartments. Courtiers and politicians visiting the palace bound for the council chamber or chapel royal were not allowed to land on the privy stairs, using instead the hall stairs, three hundred feet to the north. James's rooms were at the bottom of the back stairs that led up to Charles II's private bedchamber, and so at the inner hub of the king's existence. With the Thames lapping at the brickwork, he spent those warm September nights just yards from the father who could not now bear to be without him.[23]

The weeks that followed must have been a blur, but glimpses of them remain in the memoirs and diaries of the curious courtiers who craned their necks for a view of this new celebrity. Little more than a week after the court had come to London from Hampton Court, Samuel Pepys went to an assembly in Henrietta Maria's presence chamber at Somerset House. The new queen consort, Catherine of Braganza, sitting formally beside her mother-in-law, of whom Pepys was getting his first glimpse, was ostensibly the chief attraction. But, as he noted in his diary, it was 'Mr Crofts the King's bastard' who was the real highlight.[24]

Just as Henrietta Maria had taken to James a year or two before, so the women around the king clamoured to be close to this motherless son. Beautiful, fiery and strong-willed, Barbara Castlemaine, Charles II's mistress, was cut from the same cloth as James's own mother. The two immediately took to one another and in the calendar of court social occasions, when the king was paired with his new queen, James and Barbara often formed a couple in a hand of cards or a dance.[25] But she was not alone. Queen Catherine, who had only been in England a few months, was also drawn to the boy. Naive and hopelessly ill-prepared for the knowing world of the English court, she seemed younger by far than her twenty-four years. The queen's immaturity, and the youth of the ladies who attended her, gave James companions of his own generation, and during his first months he was frequently to be found in his young stepmother's apartments at Whitehall, playing cards with the maids of honour and sharing a joke with this new-found family.[26]

As soon as the court returned to London and the sensational news of his relationship to the king had broken, it was obvious to all that the boy would soon receive a title to rescue him from the unsatisfactory moniker of 'Mr Crofts'. Lady Wemyss was understandably keen that an English title of the highest order should be given to the boy to whom her daughter was betrothed. But when the king consulted Lord Clarendon on the matter, the lord chancellor was implacably opposed. A child born to a king out of wedlock might sometimes be given a peerage on the continent, but not in England, where such 'unlawful acts ought to be concealed, and not published and justified'. Even in France, he lectured, where royal bastards were sometimes ennobled, these were the children of aristocratic mothers and not of disreputable harlots. Henrietta Maria, whose affection for James was beyond doubt, and who had at first supported the proposal, was soon persuaded it was a bad idea. His marriage to Anne, she argued, would bring his wife's Scottish title, Earl of Buccleuch, which was quite enough for someone who was too young yet to have proved himself worthy of higher rank. After her discussion with the king, the dowager queen summoned Lord Clarendon and barked at him that it must not be allowed to happen. Unmoved by the Buccleuch family's arguments that their heiress deserved an additional title, Charles himself – as would be the case so often – decided, quite simply, to do what he thought was best for James. He had, as he put it, 'an anxious concern, on account of the singular affection wherewith we have cherished him, that nothing may be wanting to him'. Waving aside the barrage of advice, on 10 November 1662 he signed the papers making his son Duke of Monmouth and Earl of Doncaster.[27]

A dukedom was a magnificent prize. In 1662 there were only seven English dukes. Two, the Duke of York and Duke of Cumberland (Prince Rupert), were members of royal family. The remaining five were august figures: George Monck, now Duke of Albemarle, to whom Charles owed the restoration of the monarchy; his distant cousins the Dukes of Somerset and Richmond; the son of his father's adored friend the Duke of Buckingham, and the Duke of Norfolk, already the sixth to hold a title given in the fifteenth century. Many of the leading politicians of the day held Scottish or Irish peerages, and only sat in the House of Lords thanks to lesser English titles. Why Charles chose 'Monmouth' for his son's dukedom is not obvious. It was not a royal title, though it had royal associations through Henry V's alias Henry of Monmouth. It had been given only once before as a title, to the courtier Robert Carey who had brought King James of Scotland the news of his accession to the English throne. The death without sons of Carey's heir, the 2nd Earl of Monmouth, in 1661 may simply have left a handsome-sounding title available. But as significant as the magnificence of the title itself, was that the open secret now became officially sanctioned fact, since the instruction the king signed for the paperwork to be drawn up described James, in black and white, as 'Our Naturall Sonne'. For the first time in his life James could give his name and that of his father without hesitation. [28]

As soon as the date for her fiancé's departure from Colombes had been agreed, Anna, Countess of Buccleuch, and her mother had set out for London. Taking lodgings on the Strand, Lady Wemyss engaged a series of tutors to try to transform this slight eleven-year-old girl into a lady. French gowns and ribbons and lavish jewellery were ordered for the young heiress, and silk liveries with ostrich plumes for her pages. A French teacher was taken on, a dancing master engaged, and Anna was taken to a host of plays to furnish her with fashionable subjects of conversation. On the day when the king and queen entered London in their magnificent flotilla, Anna and her mother watched from raised seats, which had been specially erected on the riverside, straining their eyes for sight of the boy to whom their fortunes would shortly be bound.[29]

Before the marriage could take place the financial arrangements for the young couple had to be resolved. Anna's late father had tied up the vast Buccleuch estates in a tight entail, which meant that they would be inherited by his eldest daughter, along with his title, which could pass through the female line, on condition that her husband take on both the name and coat of arms of the Buccleuch family. To ensure the terms of the entail were met and that the new Duke of Monmouth and his future children could enjoy this inheritance fully, the king summoned the most senior lawyer in Scotland, the president of the court of sessions, Sir John Gilmour.[30]

As well as receiving the income from his wife's Buccleuch estates, Monmouth was to have his own income: the proceeds from the tax on the export of undyed woollen cloth which was taken abroad to be finished. Wool being one of England's principal industries, this was expected to provide him with a colossal income of £8,000 a year – something approaching £1 million in modern money.[31] But while the king could provide his son with a spectacular income, and an heiress for a bride, he was still vexed by a question at once obvious and obscure. As an illegitimate child, would Monmouth and his heirs be prevented from enjoying the full range of property rights enjoyed by a child born in wedlock? Might his illegitimacy mean that at some future date he could be denied this magnificent settlement or titles? With Lady Wemyss certain that her relatives would exploit any tiny loophole, Charles was convinced that something more had to be done.[32] By the time Gilmour arrived in London in November 1662 he had decided what this should be: he would set in train a legal 'legitimation' of the boy. This would involve lifting any formal bars on inheritance and office-holding that might hamper his progress in life – something which James V of Scotland had done for his illegitimate sons to enable them to hold church offices.[33] However simple the king's intentions, this apparently innocuous request would unleash a demon that neither Gilmour, nor Monmouth nor the king himself would ever be able to contain. For while the king had in mind nothing more than a legal formula that would allow his son to pass on his property, and was not for a moment contemplating a change in Monmouth's status in relation to the royal succession, as soon as the word 'legitimise' was even whispered, it passed like a plague from Gilmour's paper-strewn office in Whitehall to the coffee houses of London and the popular and political world beyond. All nuances were lost, and the possibility that the king would lift Monmouth's illegitimacy entered the collective imagination. It would remain there until two decades later it seemed set to become reality.

In January 1663, after much poring over precedents, Gilmour gave his advice to the king. Despite the clarity of his instructions, he risked royal displeasure by advising the king not to proceed. First, Gilmour explained, he could find no precedent for this sort of legitimation in Scottish law (James V's sons had been legitimised in relation to the Catholic Church). Second, because it was unnecessary: he could see no basis on which the boy or his heirs could be denied their inheritance. Finally – and crucially – because of the danger of what it might imply. Gilmour put it delicately: 'a misconstruction might be putt upon it'. Or, in the plainer words of Lady Wemyss's relation Sir Gideon Scott, it might 'provocke his highness the Duke of Yorke'.[34]

This, of course, was the rub. The arrival of the king's son at court, and rumours of some sort of legitimation, started tongues wagging about the succession to the throne. Charles II was, so far, without a legitimate child. His heir was his brother, the Duke of York. All this talk of legitimating the king's bastard son clearly made uncomfortable listening for York. Lady Wemyss's advisors knew this, and urged her to be sensitive to it.[35] But the gossip was already rife that the king's affection for the boy would alone be enough for him to change the succession in his favour. When the king received Gilmour's advice he was briefly reassured. But Lady Wemyss was not, and four days later the king dictated a new letter of instructions to Gilmour, asking that he and a group of others look at the matter of the young Duke of Monmouth's rights once more.[36] After a month's further discussion and deliberation, the advice was the same, and the king finally decided to leave the matter there.[37]

The story was well and truly out when, in February 1663, far too late to make much difference, an effort was made to hush the whole matter up. Shortly after Gilmour's advice was accepted, the Earl of Lauderdale, who managed the king's Scottish affairs, wrote asking him to: 'Use all fair means you can to get those parchments into your hand that concern that old Legitimation, And if you can do it send them safe to me.'[38] The paperwork was, it was realised, dynamite. If in gathering it in Lauderdale hoped to keep under wraps the fact that the king had wanted to legitimise his bastard son, he was naive at best. As Gilmour and his assistants had begun their research in the autumn the word in the street was that the king would somehow 'acknowledge' the duke, but come the following spring it was more precise: Pepys's crony Robert Black-burne remarked that it was common knowledge 'that the King entends to legitimate the Duke of Monmouth'.[39]

As the lawyers and the parents ruminated about such matters, the two children around whom it all revolved began to grow accustomed to their new world. That Monmouth – as he now was – was thor-oughly enjoying his fame and fortune was clear to all who saw him. Sitting in the royal box at the court theatre or watching his father receive the Russian ambassador, while magnificent hawks being given as gifts swooped above periwigs of the crowd, the boy's joyous exuberance was plain to see.[40] In March he was at Newmarket with the king and all the bucks of the court, hunting daily, betting extrava-gantly on the flat races and joining in with such enthusiasm that when he was thrown from his horse and knocked unconscious, he jumped shakily up determined to see if his bet had come good.[41] Though she still lived with her mother on the Strand, Anna came to court almost daily with Lady Wemyss when Monmouth was there, tipping the royal doormen and her fiancé's coachman for taking them home in the evenings.[42] Her slight frame and youth were the things about her upon which, at first, everyone commented. Despite the glamour of her new life, this twelve-year-old girl did not find being thrust into this court maelstrom easy after the comfortable Scottish childhood from which she had been plucked. When she wrote to her stepfather, the Earl of Wemyss, that autumn, she apologised for not sending him a drawing as her mother had suggested, 'but there is not so much merriness at my heart'. The happiness of her early youth was some-thing which she would hereafter remember with a wistful air.[43]

Everyone could now see plainly that generosity to Monmouth won the king's approval, and absence of it won his displeasure, and so the prizes came thick and fast.[44] En route to Newmarket, Monmouth had stopped in Cambridge, where he was made an honorary MA and a banquet and performance were staged in his honour at Trinity College. Back in London he was elected a Knight of the Garter, so entering the most prestigious club in the kingdom, joining his father, his uncle the Duke of York and his cousin Prince Rupert.[45]

Amid all of this, with the paperwork still being done till the last moment, the marriage finally took place.[46] The date was Monday 20 April 1663, the day after Easter. The ceremony was held within the king's apartments at Whitehall, and was followed by a supper party hosted by the Earl and Countess of Wemyss at their London house.[47] The bride wore a white and silver gown cascading with ribbons and lace. Lady Wemyss spared no expense; the embroidery of the petticoat alone cost £19 and the bride's garters and shoelaces almost £10. It was a thrilling day for all involved, and in the interlude between the ceremony and the party the king dashed off a note to his sister in Paris, reporting breathlessly that: 'You must not by this post expect a long letter for me, this being James's marriage day. And I am going to sup with them, where we intend to dance and see them abed together.' The public 'seeing to bed' of a royal couple on their wedding night, to which Monmouth's cousin William of Orange would be subjected when he married Princess Mary some years later, was thought inappropriate for such a young couple. It was done as a ritual only, and rather than spending the night together the couple returned home with their respective parents.[48]

Three days later was St George's Day and the third anniversary of the coronation. The whole court moved to the rather dilapidated castle at Windsor and in an age-old ceremony Monmouth was formally installed as a Knight of the Garter in the splendid gloom of St George's Chapel. His fellow initiate was the future King of Denmark; over the stall was his new coat of arms and buckled around his leg the dazzling diamond-encrusted Garter ordered by his father 'for our deare Sonn James duke of Monmouth'. Amid all of this, on the date his mother had failed to impart to him, Monmouth turned fourteen. An astonishing nine months it had been. At the ball after the Garter Feast he danced with his stepmother, the queen, holding his hat respectfully in his hand as he did so. The king came over to kiss him, and then indicated that he should put his hat back on. This single gesture confirmed that, whatever Monmouth's birth, he was a member of the royal family. As Samuel Pepys wrote prophetically in his diary on the night of the Monmouths' marriage, which had been nothing short of a royal wedding, 'what it is that speaks of his being a bastard I know not'. Little wonder the political world raised an eyebrow. Their fears about what it all meant for the future would not be misplaced.[49]

Chapter 5

Vicious and Idle

The king and Lady Wemyss had agreed that after the marriage of their children, aged fourteen and twelve, the couple would separate until they were old enough to live together. Monmouth was to go on an educational tour of the continent, and Anna to return with her mother to Scotland.[1] But when the time came Charles could not bear to be parted from the son with whom he had been so recently united. He insisted on a change of plan that would keep the pair in London indefinitely. Anna's mother felt she could not object and prepared to return to her own husband in Scotland despite her daughter's pleas for her to remain.[2]

Four months after the wedding, the king and much of the court left London on a progress to the west, taking in Bristol, Bath and Oxford. In reality, ten weeks' travelling between country houses and county towns was far more of an education for the young Monmouth than a continental tour would have been. While he had ample experience of the cities of the Low Countries and northern France, he had yet to stray beyond London in his unfamiliar father-land. Monmouth had known only extremes, and the lives of the respectable people of these English towns were almost as foreign to him as the court of the young Louis XIV would have been to them. Over the weeks that followed he was at his father's side, staying with Lord Seymour at Marlborough House, with Sir James Thynne at Longleat and with Lord Herbert at Badminton. He saw Maiden-head and Newbury, Bristol and Bath, Cirencester and Woodstock.

The royal party reached Oxford on 23 September and was met by Lord Clarendon, who proudly entertained them at his new house Cornbury Park. They then proceeded into Oxford itself, where the king and queen lodged at Christ Church college. Not to be outdone by their academic competitors, the university gave Monmouth an honorary MA in a magnificent ceremony. They neatly explained that '"though he was a Mr. of Arts at Cambridge first, yet that made him but the fitter for Oxon" – as if Cambridg[e] had bin a nursery to Oxon'.[3]

Travelling with Monmouth was his erstwhile tutor Thomas Ross, who had the difficult task of keeping his young charge under control and maintaining some order in their arrangements. Knowing of Lady Wemyss's plans, he worried that Anna was about to be abandoned to the morally murky world of the Restoration court.[4] And well he might. Accompanying the royal party to Oxford was the king's mistress Barbara, Countess of Castlemaine, whose own lodgings were just a stone's throw from the royal apartments at Christ Church. Only weeks before she had given birth to Monmouth's half-brother, Henry, later Duke of Grafton, who would grow to be first his understudy and then his adversary.[5] Being on the move suited the restless Monmouth perfectly. Thomas Ross, who felt sure the terms of his marriage were not as watertight as the king believed, struggled to get the boy to write the necessary letters, and indulgently bemoaned 'my Lord Duke's perpetual hurrying up and downe'. To the Earl of Wemyss, Ross could only pass on Monmouth's flimsy apologies, 'desiring your excuse that he writes not at this time, the gentlemen of this country soe continually employing him with visits and hunting that hee has noe leisure'.[6] It was not that Monmouth could not write: the few surviving letters which Ross did torture out of him are laboured but immaculate; but few fourteen-year-old boys would have sat patiently with pen and ink while the thrilling life of the court went on around them.

When the king returned to London, Monmouth was to continue to lodge with him at Whitehall, but a separate establishment was needed for Anna.[7] No doubt because of the concerns being voiced about the suitability of court for so young a girl, somewhere at one remove from London was settled upon. To the west of the city, away from its crowded streets, the route of the Thames curved west through lush parks and pastures towards Oxford. For centuries the court had travelled up and down the river between the palaces and castles that stood on its banks, among them Richmond, Hampton Court and Windsor, and beside them a string of courtier houses had grown up. In January 1664 the king bought for the Monmouths a large brick manor house that stood a few fields north of the Thames at Chiswick, some ten miles by river from Whitehall. Built by a prosperous courtier in the reign of James I, Chiswick House had by the Restoration become the property of one of the king's grooms of the bedchamber, John Ashburnham. Described as 'a large great house & faire large Garden', it was considerable without being enormous. The H-shaped building, with Dutch gables to the main south front and projecting wings to the rear, had some forty rooms and stood in trim formal gardens (which would be transformed the following century when the property was acquired by the 3rd Lord Burlington). For the house, its lands and contents, the king paid £7,000 in March 1664, and before the summer Anna and her ladies were installed.[8]

While the purchase of Chiswick was being organised, plans were in train for improving Monmouth's own lodgings at Whitehall. He temporarily reoccupied his rooms by the privy stairs when the court had returned to London in October 1663, but it was clear that these were inadequate for someone who, after the king, the Duke of York and Prince Rupert, was now the first man in the kingdom.[9] That very month the Office of Works was instructed to create new apartments for the duke.[10] Though space at Whitehall was short the king was determined his son should have rooms of status and splendour, giving the royal surveyor, John Denham, a difficult task. The solution he and his architects hit upon was an imaginative if unlikely one: to convert the largest and best of the royal tennis courts, which stood right at the heart of the palace, into the grandest apartment outside the royal suites themselves.

Henry VIII had built no fewer than four tennis courts at White-hall and, like his predecessor, Charles II was a keen player, but he considered the merits of Denham's scheme worth the sacrifice.

The recreational buildings of Whitehall Palace lay clustered on the west side of the road which bisected the site. Here, near the Tudor cock-pit which gave this part of the palace its name, stood Whitehall's best tennis court – an imposing rectangular structure with its east side along the road. It looked from the outside like the great hall of a Cambridge college, with brick walls and large stone windows. The court itself was on the ground floor, and its four large windows were set high in the walls clear of the balls. Externally, slender turrets stood at its corners, each topped with an onion dome punctuating the palace's skyline. In November 1663 the royal masons started work. The high interior of the tennis court was divided by the insertion of a floor in the process of which a series of brick chimney flues were built, the largest in the short end wall, replacing a great window. The large stone windows were taken down and a run of five tall timber casements inserted instead. White Portland stone chimney pieces were erected in the rooms, while all three floors were connected by fine timber staircases. At the end of the works the Tudor tennis court had been transformed into a tall Restoration townhouse, looking something like a slice of the facades William III would create three decades later at Hampton Court.[11]

Only the king and his immediate family were catered for by the royal furnishing department, the Great Wardrobe; the scores of courtiers with rooms in the palaces were expected to provide their own furniture. But the king bent the rules of royalty when it came to Monmouth. The Wardrobe was instructed to provide him with his pick of furniture on loan – though in reality the arrange-ment would extend without payment for the rest of his life. The sequence of large rooms on the first floor, comprising a dining room, a withdrawing room, a bedchamber and a closet and stool room, were ready for furnishing by March 1664. For the dining room Monmouth had a set of six tapestries of Cupid and Venus –

a striking subject for the young son of a famous beauty. A dozen high-backed chairs with upholstered seats stood against the walls, and Turkish carpets covered the stone floors. In the drawing room four large landscape paintings, each measuring eleven feet across, hung on the walls while the bedchamber beyond was provided with a lavish state bed upholstered in red velvet, fringed in gold, and surmounted by foaming plumes of ostrich feathers. On the floors above and below were a series of chambers for the footmen and pages, cooks and grooms and a richly decorated privy, or 'stool' room.[12]

By the spring of 1664, therefore, Monmouth and Anna were set up in the new homes the king had provided for them, but despite this separation they saw one another almost daily in the kaleido-scope of court events. The life of the king and those close to him was lived almost entirely in public. Every morning after being dressed and shaved by his staff, he would engage in a series of ritualised spectator events. Three times a week he dined before a crowd in the presence chamber, every Friday in the 'touching' season he healed the sick in the Banqueting House, on Sundays he processed to the chapel royal, and most evenings he attended the court assemblies or 'circle' held in the queen's apartments. No event – the presentation of diplomatic credentials, the death of a foreign ruler, the knighting of subjects, the launching of a royal ship, or one of the many saints' days – was without its protocol.[13]

As the months passed Anna's shyness subsided and she became more used to the people and practices of the court. She was taken under the wing of various senior courtiers. The Duchess of Albe-marle, a farrier's daughter who had been General Monck's seamstress before their marriage, became a friend, entertaining Anna in her lodgings and taking her to the theatre. Monmouth's old guardian, William Lord Crofts, who, as a gentleman of the king's bedchamber, regularly waited on the king in his private apartments, had finally married in 1661, and he and his wife also took a close interest in the Monmouths. The night before the couple's wedding Lady Crofts had sent a page to Anna's rooms with a necklace as a wedding gift.[14]

Unable to have her mother with her indefinitely, Anna was provided with two respectable lady companions, her gentlewomen, to guide her. Mrs Howard and later Diana Vernatty were paid £30 a year to manage the household and personal affairs of the young duchess, assisted by their junior Mary Minterne.[15] Thanks to a combination of personal ability and the efforts of the teacher her mother had had the foresight to engage, Anna had become a wonderful dancer, the best of any lady at court.[16] With her grace of movement this pale girl, slowly growing into a tall young woman, could hold her own alongside her cosmopolitan husband at court masques and balls.[17] Quickly too, she had seen that what had done for Wemyss Castle would not do at Whitehall. French earrings and gloves, wigs and dresses were ordered. Her Scottish page, Gordon, was quietly pensioned off and polished metropolitan boys were engaged instead, clad in silk with dress swords at their side. She kept black and pink bullfinches in delicate cages in her rooms, took up the fashionable instrument of the guitar, and was soon betting enthusiastically on the card games that they all played in the royal apartments.[18]

Though little more than children, Monmouth and Anna now inhabited a thoroughly adult world. The king, while delighting in his son's company, clearly considered the four years of tuition he had received in France as quite enough. No more formal education took place. As Charles's own schooling had been abruptly interrupted by civil war when he was twelve, he probably saw no reason for his son to be at his schoolbooks at fourteen. Monmouth could now read and write and spoke excellent French. After his arrival at court he refined various other accomplishments, among them dancing – tutored by his French dancing master – but he studied little, if anything, that required him to sit still.[19] The truth was that there was now no one to instil discipline in his life. Lord Crofts had been relieved of his role as governor and no successor was appointed. While happily recognising Monmouth as his son, the king clearly did not see himself as taking on the task. Instead it was left to Thomas Ross to try to supply the sort of guidance and steady counsel of which his young master had had so little.

No longer his tutor, now his secretary, Ross loved him too much simply to abandon his former responsibilities – despite being given the lucrative post of keeper of the king's library. As well as handling the duke's paperwork, he stood over the boy making him reply to his father's affectionate letters when they were occasionally apart. This was no easy task, and Ross found that just two letters 'made a poore yonge Duke sigh and sweat this morning exceedingly being not used to write'.[20] Privately he tried, too, to give the boy some sort of moral instruction. He bought a large and beautiful bible from Francis Bowman, Oxford's best bookseller, in the hope that his master might consult it. But his task was an almost impossible one. Monmouth was sharp and quick to learn but, like the king, had neither the patience nor the appetite to make much of a scholar. [21]

In the relative seclusion of Colombes, and with Lord Crofts to second him, Ross had been able to hold his pupil to his lessons. But with the infinite attractions of the Restoration court now at his feet, there was little chance of keeping his attention. Having given up hope that Monmouth would read whole books, Ross drew up short summaries 'least long discourses and recepticons of the same things should seeme tedious to yo[u]r Gr[ace]'. The works he précised were carefully chosen: letters of advice written by great men to their heirs, in which the central message was that young princes and noblemen must not simply wallow in their inheritances, but should aspire to become models of honour and heroism by their own deeds. 'Hee is miserable, who hath no other Tytle to true Heroick Nobility but what was left him by his Ancestors,' counselled Ross. His message for Monmouth was twofold: he needed to live up to the honours his father had heaped on him, and to do all the more because his own ancestry on his mother's side was rather short on 'heroic nobility'. It seemed to Ross that his efforts fell on barren ground. This was in part his own fault. He tried to explain to Monmouth that 'to bee affable courteous and Civill bee in themselves vertues very desire-able in all men, yet they comonly degenerate into the vices of sloth and Luxury'. But he chose to do so when they were both aboard the warship the *Royal Charles*, while it was being prepared for battle against the Dutch. Unsurprisingly Monmouth looked not the least interested and Ross gave up. But though they would lie dormant for a while yet, the seeds he had been sowing would, in time, begin to germinate.[22]

Monmouth certainly preferred action to intellect, but more importantly he came of age in a post-war court that encouraged every one of the vices Ross enumerated. Self-indulgence in all its forms was the leitmotif of the Restoration court, and against the exuberant example of Monmouth's father, uncle and almost every glamorous figure that strode or swept along the silk-hung corridors of Whitehall, Ross's sermons were useless. The king, himself not yet thirty-five, was a sexual glutton. Not content with his wife and rapacious mistress Lady Castlemaine, he spent the first year of Monmouth's life at court in pursuit of the fifteen-year-old Frances Stuart, who had also just arrived from France. 'La Belle Stuart' delighted in the childish games which courtiers could be found playing of an evening at Restoration Whitehall – cards, blind man's buff or hunt the slipper. Unusually, this famous beauty – who would be the model for the figure of Britannia on English coinage until 2008 – did not succumb to the king's advances, but many others did.[23]

For Monmouth, it was at first simply a matter of trying to keep up with court hedonism. Activities such as hunting or horse-racing, which required physical strength or grace, he soon mastered; at the gaming tables, however, he always had more enthusiasm than ability. Visiting Portsmouth in the autumn of 1664 the gold flowed from Monmouth's purse, in the words of one contemporary, as freely as if there were treasure ships in dock. While Ross might transcribe grave words of advice, he was not unsympathetic. 'The Truth is,' he wrote to a friend 'I cannot desire my poor little L[or]d to be singular, and sit by with a stoicall countenance w[he]n every one ventured his 5th and looses it with a chearfull satisfaction.'[24]

The Monmouths had, by any standard, an enormous income. While the white draperies licence which the king had given James in 1662 never produced the promised £8,000 a year, it brought in several thousands, while Anna's estates in Scotland yielded some

£7,000, giving them approaching £13,000 to spend annually.[25] By comparison, Monmouth's butler William Robinson, earned £15 a year, his steward, William Ford, who ran his household, £100, and Thomas Ross £200. Even the annual salary of the lord treasurer, one of the highest-paid men in the entire kingdom, at £8,000 came nowhere close to Monmouth's income.[26] And yet as quickly as it came in, it went out.

The Monmouths were in effect part of the royal family, expected to live like princes but without the staff of the royal household to support them. The teenage couple employed their own servants, forming a troupe of fifty, among them nineteen livery servants dressed in the yellow silks that identified their employers.[27] The extravagance of their lifestyle was in part a necessity. Moving about with the king involved considerable costs: the rent of appropriate lodgings in the various towns where the court stayed; the caravan of vehicles necessary to carry their clothes and furniture, plate and saddlery from place to place; and all the associated costs of keeping fifty people on the move. Even at Whitehall life was expensive. In a vivid sign of Monmouth's place in his father's affections, the king often came to their apartments for supper. Father and son would eat side by side in Monmouth's new dining room, with Venus and Cupid as their backdrop. But while the royal wardrobe had provided the furnishings, the food and service was from the Monmouths' own income. The expense to the couple of having the king to supper was often as much as £120 for a single month – indeed Monmouth was eventually given an additional allowance of £4,000 a year to cover it. On top of this the queen came to eat with Anna on other evenings, bringing further costs. The frequency of royal guests meant the six footmen and other household servants had always to be at the ready, and their chief cook, Thomas Busse, on perpetual standby. When the queen dined with the Duchess of Monmouth on a hot evening in July 1666, just weeks before the Fire of London broke out, she was served cheesecake, savoury tarts and pigeon pie. To these were added the exotic delicacies that sent the costs soaring: among them olives, capers, imported tropical fruit – they spent £170 with the fruiterers in only nine months – wine, beer, exquisite confectionery and even 'champaign wine' brought specially from France for the young duchess to serve at her table.[28]

Lucy Walter had revelled in beautiful clothing and jewellery – her loveliness had, after all, been her livelihood – and from his mother Monmouth had acquired a lifelong taste for elegant and expensive dress. At fourteen his expenditure on his own clothes was already astronomical.[29] Among the fifty staff was his French valet St Gill Vanier, whose taste for Parisian style chimed with Monmouth's to costly effect. From 1666 to 1667, Monmouth spent £544 with his tailor Mr Watts, £139 on hats, £89 on shirts and other linen, and a further £396 on items bought by St Gill directly. The bill he ran up with the king's own French tailor, Claude Sourceau, was £833 in little more than a year. The duke's annual expenditure on wigs alone was almost double St Gill's £20 salary.[30] Against an allocation of £1,200 for all personal expenses the duke was soon spending over £1,600 simply on clothing.[31]

That a teenager who had never had any money of his own might have some trouble in managing a fortune was not unpredictable, and the king had appointed the distinguished lawyer Edward Thurland to advise him.[32] But Monmouth was deaf to whatever guidance Thurland gave, and from the first spent well beyond even his magnificent means. He ran through his entire income for 1664 long before the year had ended. Ashen-faced after a particularly disastrous night's gambling, he was suddenly reminded of the real pennilessness of his childhood and started to panic – seeing 'poverty (like an armed Hollander) ready to assail him'. Ross borrowed £2,000 and Monmouth sat down to write to his father, this time without complaint.[33] The king agreed to help, and instead of the unpredictable income from textile exports, granted him a fixed annual allowance, or 'pension', of £6,000. Alerted to his son's troubles, he also appointed a commission to manage his affairs and 'see that his household is well ordered and settle his debts'.[34] Composed of busy men with matters of state to manage, among them Thurland and Lord Crofts, the commissioners made some efforts to chase additional sources of income for the couple, but were too distracted to be of much use. Monmouth, meanwhile, considered his problems solved – to predictable effect.[35]

Matters came to a head again just a year after he had first raised his problems with the king. In the summer of 1665 the bubonic plague seeped from London's docks and, in the heat and press of the city, was soon claiming scores of victims a day. Anyone who could get out, did so. The theatres closed and the court packed up and headed west. In Oxford the king and queen and Duke and Duchess of York lodged at Christ Church as usual. Monmouth and Anna, now sixteen and fourteen, and finally living together, set up in comparable state at adjoining Corpus Christi college. Much of their household accompanied them, though at least one – their footman Bryte – stayed behind, already infected with the plague's pustulating sores.[36] As thousands a week died agonising deaths in London, their corpses piled up on street corners before being tipped into mass graves, the court revelled blithely on. In November, Monmouth hosted a ball. With crowds of would-be spectators clamouring outside, a select group of his guests, among them Queen Catherine and all the beauties of her court, danced and sang until two in the morning.[37] When the winter weather finally stalled the plague, and the king decided the court was to return to London, the Monmouths found that their credit had expired. Over £1,000 in debt, they realised, to their acute embarrassment, that they could not leave Oxford. Anna, who was her husband's equal when it came to spending, protested bitterly that 'she had not the money to buy herself stockings'.[38]

On learning how bad things had become, the king decided more direct management of their affairs was needed. He summoned Stephen Fox, brilliant financial fixer and Paymaster of the King's Guards, to take charge. Fox had made his name, and won the king's perpetual gratitude, as the manager of the meagre royal finances through the bitter years of exile, somehow keeping them all from destitution. He was hugely overqualified to sort out the Monmouths' sorry finances, but had good reason to agree. First it was a personal request from the king. Second, he had recently bought the neighbouring property to theirs in Chiswick and was looking to expand.[39]

Fox, whose financial acumen had already made him rich, lent the couple £500 on the spot to enable them to leave Oxford. On inspecting the mountain of bills that had defeated their Steward, William Ford, he established that they were actually almost £1,800 in debt. He took personal control of matters and from then on all of the couple's income came directly to Fox and was distributed by him to various officials of their household. Knowing the king's feelings for his son, Fox took the view that the solution was not for Monmouth and Anna to curb their extravagance, but for the king to give them more money.[40]

Having offloaded his financial troubles onto Fox's broad shoulders, Monmouth threw himself back into the amusements of court life with abandon. He had forgotten his financial woes even before he left Oxford, and thought nothing of presenting the president of Corpus Christi with a magnificent silver tankard in thanks.[41] Luckily for him, however, Monmouth's profligacy and Fox's ability were well matched. Fox negotiated a three-year advance of the couple's pension – a colossal £18,000 – to refill their coffers. He then set about making the most of other sources of income. The trustees of the Buccleuch estate were put under pressure to ensure the proceeds were playing their part in relieving the Monmouths' financial difficulties. But the real answer was in the stream of applications he put to Charles II on Monmouth's behalf. Every few months in the years that followed, the king agreed a further sum of money for his son, for 'expenses' of various sorts, some specified – the buying of coach horses or particular journeys – but many not. In this way as much as (and sometimes more than) £10,000 a year was added to the couple's income. Fox met no resistance; in his own words, 'the King was pleased to consent to whatever Sir Stephen Fox proposed, not only for their necessary support but even Splendour'.[42]

In time Monmouth's means grew to almost limitless proportions. He no longer lagged behind the Restoration bucks, but was becoming their ringleader. His infectious energy and unslakeable thirst for life's pleasures soon made him the favourite of the gossips and scandalmongers. He became friends with the fastest men at court, regardless of their age. One was the wild Earl of Oxford, who lived openly with the actress Roxalana in Covent Garden, and whose riotous parties were periodically closed down. Like Monmouth, Oxford was a Knight of the Garter. The evening of the annual ceremony of the order in 1667 the pair were found careering around Hyde Park in a Hackney cab still in their hallowed robes of office, oblivious to the scandalised onlookers, their shouts of exhilaration rising into the darkness.[43]

Amidst all this, Monmouth and Anna were not destined for a happy marriage. Given the circumstances of their union and the examples that surrounded them it would have been extraordinary if their relationship had been one of emotional intimacy or sexual fidelity. The king's affairs were legion, and while he was fond of Queen Catherine, and refused ever to countenance divorce, he thought little of ignoring and humiliating her. The nature of the court calendar was such that Monmouth tended to be with the king and Anna with the queen. This both kept them apart and encouraged the duke to ape his father's casual neglect in his dealings with his own wife. Anna would not conceive their first child until 1672, at the age of twenty-one; as she gave birth to five more over the remainder of the decade, it seems unlikely the couple had slept together often, if at all, before then.

Monmouth had turned sixteen in the spring of 1665. With good looks, immense wealth and worshipped by the king, he found he already had the pick of the court beauties. His father's marital infidelity offered nothing but encouragement to adolescent urges and he soon embarked upon his own. According to one contemporary, 'those who before were looked upon as handsome were now entirely forgotten at court: and all the gay and beautiful of the fair sex were at his devotion. He was particularly beloved by the King, but the universal terror of husbands and lovers.' When the Duke of Ormond's son, John, set his heart on one Miss Malet, he knew the moment she caught the eye of the Duke of Monmouth his cause was lost; defeated, he bitterly dismissed her as 'fitter to be a mistris then a wife'. Sir George Carteret, treasurer of the navy, complained of the 'baseness and the looseness of the court' in 1667 and told 'several stories of the Duke of Monmouth' to prove his point. 'Whoreing and rogeuing' were soon considered Monmouth's principal pastimes. Even Samuel Pepys, who gained much vicarious pleasure from dissolute celebrities, declared himself disgusted with one 'who spends his time the most viciously and idly of any man, nor will be fit for anything'. Carousing and gambling all night and sleeping all day took its toll and, Monmouth's angelic features started to turn wan and plump. It was clear that he needed something other than drinking and dancing to occupy him and, for better or worse, the opportunity was about to present itself.[44]

In dynastic terms alone the queen, Catherine of Braganza, had not been much of a catch for the restored Charles II. The Braganza family had been sovereigns of Portugal only since the country had declared independence from Spain two decades earlier. Catherine's brother, King Alfonso VI, was mentally unstable and partly paralysed, and so ruled in name only. But the shortcomings of the House of Braganza had been outweighed by the material benefits of the match. Catherine's magnificent dowry included £300,000, free trade with Brazil and the East Indies and the important strategic and trading posts of Tangier in north Africa and Bombay in India. These territorial acquisitions gave a massive boost to English international trade, which in the following century would take over the world. In 1660 the Royal African Company had been established, whose investors – among them the king, Duke of York and Prince Rupert – hoped to earn fortunes from exporting gold and slaves from the West African gold coast. In the Americas a series of trading colonies in the Caribbean and along the eastern seaboard had been gradually expanded over the 1650s.

Charles II's desire to capitalise on this growing maritime trade quickly brought England into competition and then conflict with

Europe's greatest trading nation, the Dutch Republic. There was a political as well as economic reason for the restored king to want to harry the Dutch. After the death of Charles II's brother-in-law, William II, in 1650, the stadtholder's infant son, William III, was the head of the Orange dynasty. But exploiting the hiatus of William II's demise, the republican leader Johan de Witt and his supporters had seized power and Charles II's sister Mary, her son and the House of Orange as a whole were excluded from government. All of which left the Stuart family spoiling for a fight with the Dutch government that had ousted the Oranges. In 1664 one of Prince Rupert's former captains, Robert Holmes, now working for the Royal African Company, attacked a series of Dutch trading posts in West Africa. Meanwhile the king 'gave' James, Duke of York, the small Dutch enclave of New Amsterdam in North America, its situation being an irritation in the midst of England's other lands. The colony was quickly seized from the Dutch and renamed New York in James's honour. Several months later, in a culmination of all these acts of aggression, war was finally declared between England and the Dutch Republic.

The civil war had turned the English nobility into warriors for the first time since the Wars of the Roses. The king, the Duke of York and their cousins had all witnessed the bloody battles of the 1640s and after the war had ended, both Prince Rupert and the Duke of York carried on martial careers, though Charles himself had no further appetite for fighting. York served under the King of France and then the King of Spain in the 1650s, and Prince Rupert ran what remained of the mutinied fleet of 1648. At the restoration the Duke of York was given the post of Lord High Admiral with Prince Rupert and a series of experienced Cromwellian naval commanders beneath him. To one who, in the words of his secretary, 'had been bred to arms', the outbreak of war with the Dutch brought the Duke of York the exhilarating prospect of action once again.

As soon as war was declared York began assembling a fleet in the seas between England and Holland that would number some hundred vessels. On 23 March 1665, the Duke of Monmouth visited his uncle on the flagship the *Royal Charles* and was instantly intoxicated by the atmosphere; over the two months that passed before the first battle he returned repeatedly.[45] On 3 June, when the English and Dutch fleets finally met in the waters off Lowestoft, Monmouth was on board. The cannons of 200 ships roaring in a deafening engagement could be faintly heard in both London and The Hague, and the result was a resounding victory for the English. They lost only one vessel to the Dutch twenty-six, and killed the Dutch commander-in-chief, Jacob Opdam. Monmouth stood by his father aboard the *Royal Charles* again when the king knighted the officers who had fought, and later that month he and the king together undertook a detailed inspection of a royal shipyard with the young navy official Samuel Pepys as their guide.[46] The Duke of York commissioned the best artist in England to paint the principal officers of the battle – 'the flaggmen of Lowestoft' – and the finished portraits (now in the National Maritime Museum) hung prominently in his apartments at Whitehall. For Monmouth the experience of life aboard the royal gunships, his uncle in personal command, the public celebrations of the victory and the honours bestowed on the officers had a profound effect and left him hankering after glory.

Lowestoft would, however, be the high point in a war that soon started to go wrong. As the battle was being fought, plague was already gripping London. It would kill around 100,000 people over the coming months, and its human and economic effects sapped the swaggering spirit that had sparked the war and seen Londoners cheer it on. Though Lowestoft was a victory, the loss of life had been great. Among the scores of English sailors who died was the king's close friend Charles Berkeley, Earl of Falmouth, who had been standing next to the Duke of York when his brains were blown out by enemy fire. The king was devastated, and would not allow his brother to command the fleet in battle again. If Lowestoft had sparked in Monmouth a hankering for the hero's life, it also convinced his father that the risks of combat to those that mattered to him were simply too high.[47]

The Dutch war would last two more years. As the ships of the navy were slowly repaired over the winter of 1665/66, attention was turned to the country's land forces. Before the civil war there had been no permanent army in England. A series of royal bodyguards, the Yeomen of the Guard and the Gentlemen Pensioners, protected the sovereign in the royal palaces and beyond.[48] A handful of forts and castles on the frontiers, among them Dover Castle, had standing garrisons, while in an emergency the lord lieutenant in each county could raise a militia, an assemblage of amateurs drawn from all able-bodied adults. A more reliable subset of the militia, the 'Trained Bands', which regularly assembled and drilled, had been created in the reign of Queen Elizabeth. All this might enable the government of the day to defend the kingdom if attacked. On the rare occasions when there was active engagement abroad, Parliament had to agree special funds to raise a temporary army. This would then be made up of members of the Trained Bands who could be persuaded or coerced into fighting, the personal retainers of the nobility and hired foreign mercenaries.

The civil war had, of course, brought about a quite different set of circumstances. After two years of fighting and military stalemate, Parliament had decided to reform their forces from top to bottom. The 'new model' army thus created was centrally controlled, highly trained and commanded by impassioned experienced soldiers appointed on ability rather than rank. It soon annihilated its royalist opponent and after the war was won had stayed on, albeit reduced in size, ensuring the security of the republic until the restoration. In 1660 the republican army had been paid off, the cost and concept of a permanent professional army being anathema to almost all English people. But while the old army was disbanded, a far smaller permanent force under royal command did, in reality, come into effect. In the first two years of the reign two regiments of infantry and two of cavalry were created, with the job of protecting the king, and by extension the government, in the capital.

In June 1666, the Dutch navy trounced the English in the Four Days' Battle, killing over 4,000 English mariners, and it was feared that the now resurgent Dutch forces might actually land on English shores. Lord lieutenants of the coastal counties were instructed to mobilise their militias immediately and orders were issued for nine cavalry troops, each numbering about eighty men, to be raised, with one of the commanding commissions being granted, doubtless to his utter delight, to the seventeen-year-old Duke of Monmouth.[49] But the appointment of these new land forces was, it was accepted, largely presentational, a gesture designed to deter the Dutch from landing; there was next to no expectation that they would see any real action.

The armchair military command Monmouth now acquired made little difference to his reputation for laziness, vanity and debauchery. Though his troop would not be formally mustered for a year, at which time it was incorporated into Prince Rupert's regiment, Monmouth started – between court balls and ceremonies – to make appointments.[50] His recruits were not a promising lot, drawn from the dissolute young noblemen with whom he drank and gambled in London. Robert, Lord Mandeville, the idle son of the lord chamberlain, and Philip Stanhope, Lord Chesterfield, whose principal accolade was that of having been the first to seduce Barbara Castlemaine, were among the 'young Hectors' Monmouth gathered about him. Monmouth clearly enjoyed playing the part of soldier, but there was little evidence he took it seriously or had any appetite for the sort of application or arduous work that real valour was made of.

As Monmouth made his appointments, a second tragedy, as destructive as the plague of the previous summer, befell London. A fire that started at the house of the baker Thomas Farrier on the night of 1 September, spread by wind and feeding on buildings left dry by a hot summer, became a ravenous inferno that would rage for four full days. At the end, London was devastated: over 13,000 buildings were incinerated, among them the Guildhall, the Royal Exchange, fifty-two livery and company halls, and eighty-four churches, including the city's greatest, St Paul's Cathedral. The king visited the stricken wards of the city twice daily during the fire, personally directing the efforts to quell it, 'sometimes on horseback sometimes on foot, giving orders for pursuing the work, by commands, threatenings, desires, example, and good store of money which he distributes to workers'.

Monmouth, on the other hand, was mentioned in no despatches for acts of personal heroism or self-sacrifice. His first concern was to secure his moveable possessions, which he did by paying an exorbitant sum to hire scores of carts to carry them to safety. Then on the afternoon of Monday 3 September he rode into the city with the King's Guards to view the blaze at the junction of Cornhill and Lombard Street (now the site of the Bank of England). Here he saw the chaos and panic, the crush of people, carts and coaches as thousands of desperate householders tried to salvage something of their property and livelihoods, and the violent and terrifying reality of the fire itself. He surveyed the scene from his saddle and, without even dismounting, turned and rode away.[51]

The Great Fire devastated the English economy and made an end to the expensive Dutch war essential. In May 1667, eight months later, with Anglo-Dutch peace talks now under way, Monmouth and his cronies rode up to Harwich, supposedly to support the militia, though in Pepys's view, really intent on 'debauch[ing] the country-women thereabouts'. The duke's arrival, in absurdly extravagant dress, having already spent over £740 on his own cavalry attire, brought the whole county flocking to the town to see him, providing a dangerous distraction from the serious matters at hand.[52] Thomas Ross, as ever, tried to make up for his master's shortcomings, and badgered him into sending a report on military matters to his father. Then suddenly, on the evening of 12 June, the posing and partying was interrupted with the sickening news that booming cannon fire had been heard. It came not from the open seas to the east, but from the south, the direction of the royal dockyard at Chatham where the principal ships of the English fleet lay at anchor. The news hit Monmouth like a physical blow and he rose from his revels, mounted his horse and rode south like the wind. As one who was with him remarked, the words on everyone's lips were 'God preserve Chatham'.[53]

Despite the treaty negotiations the Dutch, furious at endless English acts of provocation, had been set on landing a devastating final blow. On 10 June, Cornelius de Witt, brother of the Dutch premier and an officer of the Dutch fleet, had sailed quietly up the River Medway, cutting the chain across the entrance and capturing the poorly defended Upnor Castle, which supposedly protected it. Arriving at the docks they opened their cannons on the unmanned fleet: a number of the best ships in the English navy, among them the *Royal Oak* and *Loyal London*, were burned at anchor and several others were sunk. The most important vessel in the country, the *Royal Charles*, which had brought the king home in 1660, was captured and towed off as a trophy (its prow is still one of the treasures of the Rijksmuseum in Amsterdam). The raid was both a body blow to the English navy – only one of the country's five best warships now remained – and a national humiliation. The whole incident was a personal public relations disaster for Charles II. The ill-preparedness for the raid chimed with public distaste at the immorality of court life to elicit outright disgust at king and court. As a royal bastard famed for his louche lifestyle, Monmouth epitomised the court's failings. This was reinforced when it was reported that the king had spent the evening of the Chatham raid supping with his mistress and the Duchess of Monmouth, after which the three had careered around Lady Castlemaine's apartments trying to catch a moth.

But while Monmouth and his cronies' Harwich revels were further grist to the mill of public outrage, the events of that evening were in fact a portent. Though it was in vain, in the urgency with which Monmouth rode through the night towards the burning fleet he showed a flash of something brave and brilliant that was yet to come.[54]

Chapter 6

Coming of Age

The recriminations that followed the disaster of the Dutch war were bitter and the general mood in England in the autumn of 1667 was downhearted. Freezing weather offered little cheer, and in early November, Monmouth's uncle and the heir to the throne, the Duke of York, contracted smallpox. It was only seven years since both Prince Henry and Princess Mary had been killed by the disease, and there was nothing to say it would not now claim York. The long Matted Gallery that led to his apartments at Whitehall was closed off, and the duke placed in quarantine with only a skeleton team of attendants.[1] York would recover, but a few weeks later Monmouth himself fell ill. He developed a raging fever, and it was feared that he too had the pox. After a frightening week of containment, however, he was declared safe.[2] As he recuperated he talked enthusiastically of joining the army as soon as he was well again. Determined to try and distract him from this ambition, Charles decided on a diversionary tactic: now, he declared, was the perfect time for Monmouth to pay his respects to his cousin, King Louis XIV.

No European figure in the Duke of Monmouth's lifetime was more prominent or powerful than his father's iridescent cousin Louis XIV of France. Twenty years earlier, at the age of only four, Louis had inherited the throne of France. His very birth – to a so-far childless thirty-seven-year-old mother – was considered a miracle, and his name 'le Dieu Donné', Gift of God, set the tone for a life to be lived in superlatives. The French king and Monmouth probably met seven years earlier at the wedding of Louis's brother, the Duc d'Orléans, to Henriette Anne. But it was in the early weeks of 1668 that Monmouth was really to feel the rays of this dazzling sovereign on his own skin.

On 13 January 1668 Monmouth set out for France, on a trip that was part recuperation, part recreation. Lord William Russell, son of the Earl of Bedford, was his chaperone. In his late twenties, cosmopolitan, amusing and with Monmouth's own appetite for both adventure and expenditure, Russell was an ideal companion; it was the beginning of a friendship that would blossom once again in the most serious circumstances.[3] Paris was a beacon of delight for any English aristocrat of the age, and Monmouth and Russell plunged into the city at its most alluring, for between Twelfth Night and Ash Wednesday the Paris carnival took place. During this orgy of indulgence before the fasting season of Lent the capital blazed with parties, balls, entertainments and public spectacles. The butchers of Paris led fattened oxen through the streets, acrobats performed amazing feats in the open air and everyone, from paupers to princes of the blood, participated.[4]

Acutely aware of the potential for Monmouth to reel out of control, Charles II put him in the charge of his beloved younger sister, Henriette Anne, now Duchesse d'Orléans following her marriage. As Monmouth travelled south, the king's letter to Henriette Anne kept pace with him in the post. Knowing she would understand his concerns, Charles explained: 'I put him into your hands to be derected by you in all things.' As well as ensuring he behaved properly, the king asked Henriette Anne to 'put the thought of goeing into the army out of his head'.[5] The truth of the matter, however, was that the court of Louis XIV in the winter of 1667/68 was more likely than perhaps any place or time of the century to give a young aristocrat a hunger for war.

Louis XIV had grown up under the influence of Cardinal Mazarin, who had instilled in him a deep and insatiable yearning for the glorification both of France and of his office as sovereign, and an understanding that he would achieve this only through sheer hard work. The moment Mazarin died in March 1661, Louis took hold of the reins of government himself and set about putting this into practice. His attention was irresistibly drawn to France's north-eastern border. The Spanish Netherlands (broadly modern Belgium), he felt, had to be annexed, both because the territory had repeatedly been seen as the way to mount a foreign invasion of France, and because it was in itself a glittering prize, with the great city of Antwerp its principal jewel.

When war had broken out between England and the United Provinces in 1665, an existing alliance between the French and the Dutch had brought Louis XIV in on the Dutch side. Though Louis had no real desire for war with England, it presented him with the ideal excuse to build up an army that he could use, the moment the time was right, to pounce on the Spanish Netherlands. Even in the late seventeenth century, territorial invasion was seldom done without a pretext, however flimsy. In this case Louis XIV argued that his wife, Queen Marie-Thérèse, was, as the child of the first marriage of Philip IV of Spain, entitled to this portion of her father's inheritance.

The army that Louis began to amass in 1666–67 soon numbered some 70,000 men, extraordinary in an age when a few thousand was more the norm. The king revelled in the business of building his forces, taking the luminaries of the court – including the queen and his mistresses – to review the troops and sleeping in a six-chambered military tent of Chinese silk. In May 1667 Louis XIV had invaded and with his immense army, well managed and supplied thanks to the sort of attention to administrative detail Mazarin had instilled in him, the cities fell like dominoes. Charleroi, Tournai and Douai among others were taken over the months that followed, culminating in the capture of Lille at the end of August. A temporary truce was declared, and it was in this calm that the Duke of Monmouth's trip to Paris was planned. But as Monmouth and Russell sailed for France, unbeknownst to all but a few, Louis XIV was preparing to launch a surprise winter invasion of the southern part of Spain's territory, the Franche-Comté. Monmouth rode into Paris shortly before Louis rode out to join his army, which in a blistering wave of attacks, took the province. A fortnight later the king returned in triumph. Any notion that the trip to France would cure Monmouth of his desire to join the army was now laughable.

The speed and effectiveness of Louis XIV's assault on the Spanish Netherlands had startled his neighbours and the rulers of Sweden, the Dutch Republic and England had swiftly clubbed together to declare their opposition – with Charles II signing their pact, the 'triple alliance', the day Monmouth sailed for France. This left Monmouth in an uncomfortable position, as would often be the case for members of the Stuart family in their dealings with France. On the one hand he arrived in Paris as a member of the extended French royal family, visiting his aunt (Louis XIV's sister-in-law) and his grandmother (Louis XIV's aunt), and was received with familial warmth and affection. On the other hand, England was officially allied against France. As Louis launched his attack on the Franche-Comté, it became increasingly awkward that Monmouth was in Paris at all. As Charles II wrote to Henriette, if her husband, the Duc d'Orléans, left for the front then 'it will not be decent for him [Monmouth] to stay in Paris, with everybody in the field and on the other side'.[6] But the Duc d'Orléans was a different creature from his warmongering brother and was not eager to forgo Paris for the mud of the battlefield. When Monmouth arrived in France he had been plunged not only into the gorgeous world of the Parisian court, but into the fragile and fractious sphere of the Orléans's marriage.

Henriette Anne was as widely loved as it was possible to be at the faction-ridden French court. She had grown up at Henrietta Maria's side, speaking French and educated as a Catholic, and had known Monmouth since their time at Colombes in the late 1650s. As soon as Charles II had been restored to the throne, she became a highly desirable bride, and in 1660, declaring himself hopelessly in love with her, Louis XIV's brother, the Duc d'Orléans, had asked for her hand in marriage. The happiness the pair experienced together lasted about a fortnight. Tall and slight, with a long face, even white teeth and pale skin, Henriette was not considered a beauty, but her character and manner radiated loveliness. By contrast Orléans's dashing good looks disguised an ugly personality; vindictive, suspicious and neurotic, he quickly tired of his bride, and turned his attention instead to a series of attractive young men. But in so doing he remained fiercely jealous of those close to Henriette, accusing her of liaisons and infidelities and forcing her to abandon her friends. When the nineteen-year-old Duke of Monmouth arrived at the Palais Royal, one of the triumvirate of royal palaces on the north bank of the Seine, he found an uneasy threesome, with Orléans's lover, the twenty-five-year-old Chevalier de Lorraine, having taken up residence with the duke and duchess.[7]

Perhaps all the more because of these strained domestic arrangements, Henriette fell upon her nephew, child of her adored older brother, with unbridled joy. Five years older than Monmouth, she threw herself into the role of guardian with gusto: after formally introducing him to King Louis and Queen Marie-Thérèse in the royal palace at St Germain-en-Laye, she set about launching him into Paris society. Dressing him in the finest clothing the city had to offer, she threw balls and staged plays in his honour – including a special performance of Thomas Corneille's *Laodice* in her own rooms – and introduced him to everyone who was anyone. In the Palais Royal, which Louis had assigned to his brother and sister-in-law, Monmouth was given his own apartments. Having been received '*très favorablement*' by the French king, Monmouth was lodged and lauded as royalty and, in a city in which royal bastards were members of the most respectable ranks of society, he was in clover. Paris delighted him and the feeling was mutual. Louis XIV's cousin, Mademoiselle de Montpensier, one of the most formidable ladies of the age, arrived in Paris to find 'the King of England had sent his son, the Duke of Monmouth, to the French Court and he was received very handsomely by his Majesty. Indeed he was so extremely amiable and good-looking that everyone spoke very highly of him.' The Duc d'Orléans's chaplain, Daniel Cosnac, similarly, admired the fine figure and beautiful face of this young visitor. The combination of good looks and gallantry that had set hearts aflutter in London was a hit in Paris, too, and the ladies of the Louvre, young and old, flocked to this glamorous Englishman who spoke such perfect French.[8]

As Monmouth and Henriette Anne danced and dined their way through the Paris carnival, laughing and chattering, sometimes in the English that her husband did not understand, he grew thunderous and – whipped up by the dangerously destructive chevalier – finally exploded with rage. The falling out that resulted between the Duc and Duchesse d'Orléans was bitter and Louis XIV himself had to intervene. He forced a reconciliation at the royal hunting palace at Villers-Cotterêt, fifty miles from Paris, and Monmouth returned home to England. Fortunately for all concerned, the embarrassing fracas was buried under bigger news, for Louis XIV had just agreed to a peace treaty with the triple alliance.[9]

Monmouth returned to London in March 1668, and in April, Louis signed the Treaty of Aix-la-Chapelle, relinquishing the Franche-Comté, but being confirmed in his conquest of the towns in the north, including Charleroi and Tournai. As soon as the deal was done, covert negotiations were opened for a new alliance between England and France, which Louis saw as the route to breaking the triple alliance against him, and so reviving his expansionist ambitions. Charles II, the slipperiest of fish when it came to foreign relations, was encouraging, attracted by the advantages that might come to him should he switch sides. So it was that two months after the Treaty of Aix-la-Chapelle had been signed, Monmouth returned to Paris, officially to attend the festivities celebrating the treaty but also, confidentially, as a go-between. His task was to talk to Henriette about the putative Anglo-French treaty and, in particular, the notion of a face-to-face meeting to ratify it, which Charles II described to his sister as 'the greatest hapyness to me imaginable'.[10]

Back in Paris, Monmouth lodged again at the Palais Royal – the Duc d'Orléans's 'rediculous fancy' about his wife's relationship with him having temporarily moved on to another of her friends. With him this time was one of Charles II's trusted creatures, James Hamilton, groom of the king's bedchamber. As a personal servant, and son of an English gentry family long established in France,

Hamilton was the perfect person to help facilitate the secret diplomatic discussions. Despite Hamilton's assistance, Monmouth's first
foray into public affairs was not a success. While he had all the
charm and manners of a diplomat, he was wildly careless about the
papers and protocols that went with it. Not only had he failed to
write and thank the duchess for her hospitality on his first visit –
Charles II had to personally apologise to his sister for the missing
letter – but on this second visit he managed to lose his official documents somewhere between London and Paris. Little wonder one
contemporary said of him at the time, that he lived 'in a mad ramble
after pleasure, and minded no business'. Charles II made more
indulgent excuses, but it was not a good start.[11]

If Monmouth was reluctant when it came to the paperwork of
diplomacy, he was consoled by its perquisites. Thanks to the wily
Stephen Fox he had been provided with colossal sums of additional
money to fund these two French trips: £4,000 in February simply as
'royal bounty', £2,500 more in April for travelling expenses, and a
further £500 for 'the King's special service' – presumably in connection with the putative Anglo-French treaty.[12] When he returned,
the spoils of shopping included a spectacular new coach which his
yeoman of the stables, John Heron, was paid almost double his
annual salary to bring home. His personal success during his winter
visit had given him real confidence and he cut his long hair short
just before he sailed for France in June, causing a sensation when
he arrived in Paris. His new hairstyle was the talk of the town,
commented on in both royal and diplomatic correspondence. The
look was made all the more a personal signature when his troupe
of cherubic young pages all appeared with similar shorn locks. Like
his mother, Monmouth knew how to make an entrance.[13]

The finale of Monmouth's trip, and perhaps the apogee of the
many eye-watering spectacles of the Sun King's reign, was the
'Grand Divertissement royal' staged by Louis XIV on 18 July 1668.
This outdoor extravaganza at the palace of Versailles was a public
celebration of the territorial expansion of France confirmed by the
Treaty of Aix-la-Chapelle. Over the past five years Louis XIV had

been aggrandising his father's hunting lodge at Versailles, and the building that Monmouth's mother had visited with John Evelyn in 1649 had already been substantially rebuilt, though it would be twenty years yet before it would reach its full gargantuan glory. As well as extending the house, the king had commissioned André le Nôtre to create hundreds of acres of formal gardens fanning out from a central east–west axis and it was here that the 1668 *divertissement* took place. Over the course of twelve hours on a summer's late afternoon and evening, the king, his guests and hoards of spectators moved through a series of vast temporary buildings erected within the avenues and groves of the gardens. The event began in the late afternoon with a 'collation', an al fresco buffet, held in one of the wooded '*bosquets*' with a fountain shooting thirty feet into the air behind the tables encrusted with exotic food. It then moved on to a spectacular tapestry-hung theatre for the first performance of Moliére's new comedy *Georges Dandin*, and after that to an octagonal hall for a seated banquet. As each opulent venue was vacated by the royal party, the spectators swarmed in to pillage what remained of the food and wine. The final location, to which the company moved, now in darkness, was another building raised for the evening, a ballroom where the king and his party danced past midnight. Finally as the revellers entered their coaches, the gardens and the palace were illuminated with lanterns and torches, and the skies set ablaze with fireworks.

Monmouth was not simply among the thousands of spectators to whom the king opened the gates, or one of the hundreds of courtiers given privileged access, but was in the royal party itself as the guest of the king's brother. Little wonder that Charles II wrote to his sister that 'we are here in great expectation of the relation of the entertainment at Versailles. I hope James will be the first messenger to bring it.'[14]

When Monmouth landed at Deal in Kent on 31 July, his ears still ringing with the fireworks of Versailles, he was burning with a new ardour. In his father Monmouth had long known a model of mellow royalty, a king who, though not yet forty, had imbibed as much danger and drama, heroism and horror as any man could want. Experience and adversity, civil war and exile had engendered in him humour, languor and heavy-lidded cynicism; he was now intent on leisure. But in the young Louis XIV, Monmouth saw something quite different, a man who was just beginning and whose whole person thrilled with a desire for conquest and accomplishment. Those few months in Paris in 1668 would prove a turning point for Monmouth. A man of leisure he no longer wished to be: action now called him.

The urgency of Monmouth's desire to participate, to command, to direct, was immediately obvious, and Charles II saw he had to respond. Within just two weeks of his return from Paris, not only was there no more talk of dissuading Monmouth from joining the army, but a deal had been struck which saw him take on his first real post of command. The position, one he specifically sought, was that of Captain of the King's Life Guards. The beginnings of the British army proper had come in the first year or so of Charles II's reign, when four regiments had come into being. The public distaste for a permanent brigade of armed men, made no less strong by bitter experience of the New Model Army, was such that the regiments were billed as being for the personal protection of the king – hence the word 'guards'. Though technically new, they incorporated men and officers from both the former royalist and parliamentarian forces. Two infantry regiments, the 1st and 2nd Foot Guards, soon known as the 'Grenadiers' and the 'Coldstreams' respectively, and two cavalry regiments, the Life Guards and the Royal Horseguards, or 'Blues', were therefore created. The position of Colonel of the Life Guards, both in charge of the premier cavalry regiment and captain of its most distinguished troop, the King's Own Life Guard, had been given to the loyal royalist commander Charles, Lord Gerard of Brandon, in 1660, confirming a command he had nominally held since the 1640s. By 15 August it was public knowledge that Brandon had agreed to relinquish the post to Monmouth in return for Chiswick House and £800 in cash; and within a month the paperwork was done.[15]

The day after the duke received his commission from the king he was formally installed at a muster of the Life Guards in Hyde Park. The nearly 500 men who made up the three troops assembled in battle formation in the park, with Monmouth proudly at their apex, while the king rode among them making his inspection. The event concluded with a thunderous sounding of the guns, and Monmouth – as ever – looked sensational. Mounted at the front of his regiment, whose clothes were 'uniform in everything', he was clad in the best cloth and cut: a red jacket lined in blue, gold lace dressing and with drooping white feathers in his hat, he was indeed a 'mighty fine' sight.[16] Now in charge of a regiment proper, Monmouth's thirst for command was briefly satisfied. With no enemy to fight, he contented himself with parades and processions and the king with the knowledge that his beloved boy faced no actual combat. Neither them yet had any inkling of what would happen when he eventually felt the bloodied mud of the battlefield beneath his immaculate boots.

While Monmouth had been whirling his way around the salons of Paris in the spring of 1668, his wife had remained in England, soon to undergo her own life-changing experience. Close to the queen and taken particular care of by the king, she had more money to spend than any woman at court.[17] She was not yet out of her teens and with as yet no pregnancies to restrain her, she danced and acted on every available occasion to widespread admiration. Just before Monmouth sailed for France in January 1668 they had both played roles in a court performance of John Dryden's *The Indian Emperor* in the great hall at Whitehall, which Charles II had converted into a theatre. While almost all the amateur actors performed their parts 'like fools and sticks', Anna was singled out for praise. On Shrove Tuesday, when Monmouth was at St Germain for his audience with Louis XIV, Anna and her ladies performed their own masque at Whitehall, the duke's absence no obstacle to their pleasure.[18] But on 9 May, when Monmouth was back, disaster struck. During a gathering which Anna was hosting in their Cockpit lodgings, she stumbled as she danced, falling with such force that she dislocated her hip. In agony she was attended by the royal doctors who attempted to reset the joint. Three days passed and it became clear the operation had been unsuccessful. The procedure was repeated with, in the king's own words, 'all the torture imaginable'.[19] A week after the accident, with little apparent concern for his injured wife, Monmouth set sail again for France, while Anna was taken to Bath where it was hoped the hot springs would help her heal. Accompanied by both her own and the king's doctors, and with an elaborate chair made to carry her, she took the waters.[20]

When Monmouth returned to England, nearly three months later, Anna was still in Bath. It became clear that, as was so often the case with seventeenth-century medicine, the problem was less the original injury than the measures taken to heal it, and the 'ill setting' of her hip was as much to blame as the fall.[21] The sums laid out in relation to her 'lameness' were enormous. In the six months after the accident over £700 was spent on her recuperation, and the best physicians and surgeons in France consulted by correspondence for their views on the case. As well as the payments to a host of doctors and apothecaries, smaller sums hint at the agony she endured, among them £20 to 'a Dutch operator' and £13 to 'several bonesetters'.[22]

Anna returned to London with Monmouth in the autumn of 1668 and re-entered society, at first receiving visitors from her rooms and later appearing once again at court occasions. She would walk with a limp for ever more and though she would start dancing again a year or so later, her awkward movements now provoked more pity than praise.[23] With the accident something of Anna's youthful optimism was crushed. In its place grew up a brittle self-indulgence, tinged with the careless selfishness of the spoiled child, which was given almost limitless scope by the couple's money and the duke's frequent absences. She spent with abandon, never considering the cost or the consequences. At twenty she spent a cool £1,200 – some £140,000 in modern terms – on a single pair of diamond earrings.[24]

Though Monmouth brought his wife back to Whitehall in the autumn of 1668, he was not much in evidence as she recuperated.

His new role as Captain of the Life Guards, though prestigious, was not terribly time-consuming and left plenty of room for pleasure. He continued to keep company with his fast friends, frequenting London's most fashionable nightspots, among them Chateline's in Covent Garden, where Pepys saw Monmouth and 'a great many blades' late one evening that year. As often, however, he was with his father and uncle, the Duke of York, who both still in their thirties, were as vigorous as he. For all his famed appetite for women, Charles II also enjoyed a range of largely male activities, among them horse-racing, yachting and hunting. The three men were often to be found messing about on boats, official inspections of the royal dockyards and capering on their racing yachts blending easily together. In August 1668 the king, Monmouth and York took their barges to Vauxhall before travelling upriver together for a day's fowling. A fortnight later the three were together again, for a week's hunting deer at Bagshot, a royal hunting ground south of Windsor Great Park in Surrey.[25] Gatherings of the same group at Newmarket were also common. Professional jockeys being a thing of the future, it was the king and Monmouth, among others, who would ride the horses in Newmarket's famous flat races. In October 1671 the king was the victor, with Monmouth riding at his side; on other occasions Monmouth rode and his father and uncle looked on.[26]

So it was that Monmouth's character was formed in a mixture of company his own age and of his father's generation. In some matters he seemed absolutely the equal of his older companions. He could ride as well or conquer a beauty as quickly and effectively as his father or uncle. But on occasion his youth, inexperience and a persistent streak of naivety suddenly told. He alone believed the Marquis de Montburn's claims that his daughter's looks were a product of nature and not cosmetics, until 'he was quickly laffed out of it'. While, having begged the French society astrologer, Abbé Pregnani, to come to England, he placed all his bets at Newmarket on the Abbé's astrologically inspired tips; peals of laughter followed as every horse lost.[27]

The new command of the Life Guards and the duke's success in Paris had only increased his attractiveness to and appetite for women. A French contemporary described his appearance at this time in rapturous terms: 'His figure and the exterior graces of his person were such, that nature perhaps never formed anything more complete. His face was extremely handsome; and yet it was a manly face, neither inanimate nor effeminate; each feature having its beauty and peculiar delicacy: he had a wonderful genius for every sort of exercise, an engaging aspect, and an air of grandeur.'

The effects were predictable: 'the astonishing beauty of his outward form caused universal admiration: those who before were looked upon as handsome were now entirely forgotten at court: and all the gay and beautiful of the fair sex were at his devotion'.[28] Just as the three men, father, brother and son enjoyed the same outdoor pursuits, so they were all relentlessly unfaithful to their wives. Charles II is famous for his numerous mistresses, but he was not the exception. The Duke of York was just as prolific, indeed the king remarked to the French ambassador: 'I do not believe there are two men who love women more than you or I do, but my brother, devout as he is, loves them still more,' adding on another occasion, in a timeless fraternal dig, that York must have been given his mistresses by his priest as a penance.[29]

These royal liaisons occasionally brought the three men into uncomfortable tangles. When, having failed with Frances Stuart, the king directed his attentions towards the beautiful young comic actress Nell Gwyn, it was one of a rich seam of relationships between actresses and aristocrats which Monmouth would soon mine himself. When one particular young actress caught his eye, the king plied her with gifts and jewels, but was furious to discover that another courtier had already seduced her. He 'wanted to know who had deflowered her' but 'on learning that it had been the Duke of Monmouth, went away disturbed and never sought her again'.[30] Another common hunting ground for predatory courtiers was the maids of honour, 'unmarried gentlewomen' who attended the queen and the Duchess of York, and the ladies of the bedchamber, their senior, married, equivalents. The king had forced Queen Catherine to accept the indomitable Countess of Castlemaine as one of her ladies, while the Duke of York had affairs with several of his wife's maids of honour, among them Goditha Price and Arabella Churchill, whose brother John would serve as a soldier under Monmouth's command. Monmouth also had an affair with one of the Duchess of York's maids of honour, Mary Kirke, whose sister Diana would go on to marry the reckless Earl of Oxford, in the early 1670s (and is famous as one of Peter Lely's bare-breasted beauties). Such relationships were, on the whole, fluid and fleeting, and Monmouth was soon fending off other suitors from Mary's door.

While Monmouth seems to have been no better or worse than his father or uncle, he was unquestionably promiscuous. The gossips might hesitate before defaming their sovereign or his heir, but they had few qualms about repeating scurrilous stories of the Duke of Monmouth – indeed his own illegitimacy made him an especially satisfying target. Stories of his sexual exploits – visits to the city's brothels, seductions of respectable women, orgies, venereal disease and blackmail – were commonplace, lapped up enthusiastically by prurient observers from foreign courts or county towns. One visitor to the English court in 1668 said of Monmouth: 'His inclination leads him to the pleasures of the senses and of wine; he has lately recovered somewhat from the latter, but in the former he is easily pleased, and very often has paid, in the hands of the doctors, the penalty of his too ignoble and imprudent sensuality.' Where actuality ended and exaggeration began in many of these tales is unclear, but there is no doubt that Monmouth was a serial womaniser.[31]

By 1670 Charles II had fathered eight illegitimate children – seven since Monmouth himself – and the Duke of York had fathered seven children with his wife and a further three with Arabella Churchill. But the great irony was that alongside all this visible virility the one person whose defining task it was to provide children, the queen, remained conspicuously childless. Poor Queen Catherine, presented daily with the living evidence of her husband's fecundity, suffered visibly as her own infertility became increasingly apparent. Prone to prolonged menstrual bleeding, she found conception, which came so easily to Barbara Castlemaine and Arabella Churchill, almost impossible. Long summer visits to the springs at Tunbridge Wells and Bath were undertaken to try and improve matters, but to no avail. The effect this had on the shy Portuguese princess was crushing. In the autumn of 1663 the king had looked in on her on his way to Lady Castlemaine's apartment only to find the queen ashen and dangerously unwell. Through her snatched breaths she told him that death would not be unwelcome, as it would free him to marry another who would be able to provide as she could not. The king, startled and shaken, pleaded with her not to despair. Slipping into unconsciousness she hovered between life and death for a matter of days. When she awoke, she was still delirious and, convinced she was pregnant, raved to the king about an imagined baby; marvelling that she had had no morning sickness, and saying she hoped their son would be handsome. With poignant tenderness the king indulged her delusion and murmured gently that their phantom child was 'a very fine boy'.[32]

Catherine did recover, and would in the end outlive her vigorous husband, but any real expectation that she would produce an heir soon faded. In the eight years following their marriage she conceived perhaps twice, in 1666 and 1669, but in neither case did the pregnancy reach twelve weeks. Apart from the personal tragedy this represented for Catherine, the queen's inability to bear children had profound political consequences: for the king, for his brother and heir, the Duke of York, and for the royal son so often at their side.[33]

While Monmouth's place in the king's heart was beyond doubt, he also had a close and affectionate relationship with his uncle. Only three years younger than Charles II, James, Duke of York was in many ways a slightly duller version of his technicolour sibling. The king, while no Adonis, made a striking impression with his height, his dark hair and eyes, his strong features and the deep furrows scored across his cheeks. York was in all senses slighter. Shorter than his brother, his colouring was fair, his eyes blue, his hair and stubble sandy. While the king strode about with a straight back dispensing good humour and wry lines, York slouched, dressed carelessly and scuttled rather than strode. He was a military and naval man by experience and inclination, lacked his brother's quick wit, and his conversation seldom went much beyond soldiery, ships and shooting. Without his brother's charm, his idea of romantic small talk was stories of 'broken legs and arms, dislocated shoulders and other entertaining adventures'.

Temperamentally York was also quite different from his brother. Whereas Charles was morally dexterous and mercurial in his allegiances, York saw the world in clearer and more distinct terms. He was physically brave and personally loyal. He had – above all – inherited their father's complete belief in the sanctity of royal authority. According to a contemporary who knew him well, York 'was bred with high notions of the kingly authority, and laid it down for a maxim that all who opposed the king were rebels in their hearts'. That a military man should have an authoritarian streak was not surprising, and this trait was not, as yet, a cause for public concern. Despite all their differences, however, the bond between these brothers was strong, partly from genuine affection and partly of necessity. In the words of one observer, York lived on good terms with his brother 'not entirely because he has to and not entirely because he wants to'.[34]

As boys the brothers had shared much of the experience of childhood and civil war; York had stood at their father's side at Nottingham Castle when the royal battle standard was first raised, and after the regicide had, with his brother's agreement, spent much of the interregnum as a hired soldier, fighting first for the French and then the Spanish. When Charles II was living in Brussels under Spanish protection in the late 1650s, and trying to grab his son from Lucy Walter, York began an affair with one of their sister Mary's ladies-in-waiting. This was Edward Hyde's daughter, Anne. When Anne became pregnant in the spring of 1660, just as the restoration was taking place, York had declared his intention to marry her. Henrietta Maria, who loathed Anne's father Hyde, was apoplectic with rage and Charles II was also infuriated, as the marriage of his brother could have been a powerful diplomatic bargaining chip. At first refusing them permission, he gradually softened as Anne became more visibly pregnant and, finally, relented. In October the pair were secretly married. A furore resulted, but after Anne gave birth to a son, who was third in line to the throne, passions calmed. The boy and the three other sons she bore would die in infancy, but two of her daughters, Princess Mary (born 1662) and Princess Anne (born 1665), would survive the precarious early years of any seventeenth-century childhood and, in time, would each rule England.

While the scandal of York's relationship with Anne Hyde would pass, his marriage to the chief minister's daughter involved him much more closely in the vicious world of Restoration politics than he ever could have wished – and clearly had not anticipated. Now Earl of Clarendon and lord chancellor, Hyde was in effect 'prime minister', and with the authority came relentless jealousy and jostling for position. The new regime gradually declined in popularity, discredited by a series of disasters and disappointments – the infertility of the queen, the Medway raid, the decision to sell the English-controlled town of Dunkirk to the French. The country's accumulating woes were all to a greater or lesser extent blamed on Clarendon. The chancellor's adversaries, among them the Earl of Bristol and the Duke of Buckingham, and with Henrietta Maria always in the background, fanned the flames of discontent in the hope that he could be toppled. As Anne Hyde, now Duchess of York, gave birth to ever more children and the queen did not, the chancellor was even accused of deliberately choosing a barren wife for the king so that his own grandchildren would inherit the throne.[35]

In this charged atmosphere Charles II's unstinting love for the Duke of Monmouth – the sort of handsome son for whom the queen was not alone in longing – started to take on a new significance. Clarendon's enemies, keen to remove the Hyde family – including his son-in-law the Duke of York – from power, were pleased by rumours that the king intended to somehow promote Monmouth within the royal family. The king had, of course, explored a technical 'legitimation' for his son in advance of his marriage in 1663, simply as a mechanism to ensure he and his heirs could have full possession of the Buccleuch estates, and not in order to give him a right to the throne. This subtlety was, however, lost in transmission. In the rumours and gossip that circulated, encouraged now by Clarendon's foes, something far more radical was on people's minds. Might the king give Monmouth the full status of a son – a Prince of Wales – and so instantly supplant Clarendon's son-in-law and grandchildren in the line of succession?

On the face of it this was an astonishing suggestion. And yet it was not without precedent. While there had been no English royal bastards for a century, anyone with a decent grasp of history would know what the tangled complexities of the Tudor succession had amounted to. Henry VIII's three legitimate children had each been born after his marriage to their respective mothers. Irrespective of this he would go on to issue a series of Acts of Succession between 1533 and 1543 that declared them legitimate or not in various combinations, so confirming the principle that with parliamentary assent the monarch could determine the legitimacy of his children more or less at will.[36] What was to prevent Charles II from doing the same now?

For Samuel Pepys and his cronies the gossip in the winter of 1662/63 had been of little else, as he wrote his diary on New Year's eve: 'the Duke of Monmouth is in so great splendour at Court and so dandled by the King, that some doubt, if the King should have no child by the Queen (which there is yet no appearance of) whether he would not be acknowledged for a lawful son'. The rivalry which such suggestions had the potential to introduce into the relations between Monmouth and York was plain to see: the Scottish lawyers had warned of it in 1662/63; Pepys feared it and the Earl of Sandwich gave him the strong impression shortly after the Monmouths' marriage that 'all is not kind between the King and the Duke, and that the King's fondness to the little Duke doth occasion it'. Accusations were hurled in Parliament that Clarendon (of all people) had been 'venting scandal against the King, as though the Duke of Monmouth were to be legitimated'. As the king's affection for his son endured, so did the rumours.[37]

Part of the tenacity of the gossip about the Duke of Monmouth being made his father's heir came from the fact that a second rumour with the same implication had also long drifted about. This was the story that there was no need for any legitimation, Acts of Parliament or troublesome paperwork because Charles II and Lucy Walter had in fact been married. As she had died in 1658, this had no bearing on the validity of his marriage to Catherine of Braganza. Within three months of Monmouth's arrival in England, Pepys's friend Mr Creede had told him that it 'is whispered that young Crofts is lawful son to the King, the King being married to his mother'.[38] Monmouth in his youth encouraged the story, threatening when he was fourteen to kill anyone who said otherwise. This says more about Monmouth than the question of their marriage however; for him to have taken any other line would have been tantamount to confirming the common view that his mother was a whore.[39]

Indeed, rumours of his parents' marriage gave Monmouth a welcome opportunity to recast his personal history. The affection in which he held the memory of his mother had not been diminished by time and when his elevation to great status brought various Walter relatives out of the woodwork, he welcomed them warmly. In February 1663 Lucy Walter's dissolute brother Justus appeared at Whitehall and thanks to Monmouth secured a minor court position. He seems only to have been a fleeting presence, but his spell at court is very likely connected to the arrival in the Monmouths' household of one Cornelia Walter. With no named office or duties she was clearly not a servant, but she received a modest annual pension and would remain part of the Monmouths' establishment for at least a decade.[40] Also on the pay roll was a cousin through Lucy's aunt, Margaret Sanbourne, while Monmouth would later employ another cousin from her first marriage to the Dutchman Peter Gosfright.[41]

Whether a legal legitimation were to happen, or an overlooked marriage acknowledged, if the rumours were to amount to anything it would only be because the king wished it so. And this was the rub: what exactly were his intentions? On the one hand the king had described Monmouth plainly as his 'natural', that is illegitimate, son in the paperwork relating to his dukedom and marriage. When directly confronted on the question of whether Monmouth might be made his heir Charles was straightforward: 'he loved James well, but for his brother the crown was his right and he knew none more worthy of it'. And yet for all this clarity, the king clouded the issue in countless ways in his treatment of Monmouth. Many of the usual indicators of royal bastardy were avoided. After his first year in England the qualifier 'natural' was dropped from all official documents, and thereafter he was simply 'Our Deare Sonne' or 'our entirely beloved Sonne'. When the duke was introduced into the House of Lords in 1670, the words of his original creation were repeated, but the reference made in them to his being the king's 'natural' son was deliberately omitted – to describe Monmouth as illegitimate by 1670 was considered to be in bad taste.[42]

On numerous other occasions Monmouth was treated as a member of the royal family proper. The coat of arms he was given in April 1663 was simply a rearrangement of the royal arms, with no 'baton sinister', the heraldic device that denoted bastardy. They were changed in 1667 to a more conventional form, but only because Thomas Ross had initiated an investigation of whether the first set were indeed correct. Monmouth wore the same purple mourning clothes as the king, duke and Prince Rupert when members of foreign royal families died, while when the royal family adopted special insignia for feast days, such as the embroidered leeks worn on St David's Day, they were provided by the royal wardrobe for the king and queen, the Duke and Duchess of York, Prince Rupert and Monmouth. The king's mistresses and other children were outside the royal circle, but the Duke of Monmouth was within it.[43]

Given the ambiguity about who, precisely, Monmouth was, it is not surprising that when in 1667 the Duke of Buckingham urged the king to declare that he had married Lucy Walter, offering to rustle up some plausible witnesses to corroborate it, he was not convinced by the king's refusal. 'The King would not consent to this, yet he put [it] by in such a manner as made them all conclude he wished it might be done, but did not know how to bring it about.'⁴⁴ The discomfort all this speculation had the potential to introduce into the relationship between Monmouth and his uncle, York, was considerable. But the two men remained on warm terms regardless.⁴⁵ Monmouth and Anna were godparents to the Yorks' children – Anna to her namesake the future Queen Anne in 1665 – and York always called Monmouth 'nephew' (later claiming he did so because it pleased the king). In part, doubtless, the older man knew that to take these rumours seriously would only diminish his own status and that to fall out with Monmouth would harm his relationship with the king. But more than this, the bonds of family and friendship were genuinely strong. York had experienced just the sort of active military service under the great French generals that Monmouth's trips to France had left him hankering after, and being allowed to stand on his uncle's flagship in the great sea battle of Lowestoft must have been deeply thrilling for the teenager. When York was asked in the early 1670s whether there really was a risk of Monmouth challenging his place in the succession, he answered confidently that loyalty and lack of ambition on the part of both the duke and duchess was such that he had no fear.⁴⁶ But the 'universal whisper' did not abate. Knowing looks were exchanged in Paris in 1668, as the duke's dashing charm and princely bearing seemed to add credibility to the rumours that had already reached France.⁴⁷

In the autumn of 1667 the Earl of Clarendon had fled England, following the king's heavy hints that his future was looking bleak, and in the spring of 1668 he was officially banned from ever returning. Unshackled now from his unpopular father-in-law, York might have breathed a sigh of relief, and many felt that the danger of a change to the succession had been successfully averted. Little did anyone know that in the winter of 1668, as Clarendon settled down to write his memoirs from a comfortable exile in Marseille, the Duke of York was about to make a second personal decision with seismic political consequences. At some point in the winter of 1668/69 this son of a Protestant martyr knelt down before the elderly Jesuit priest Father Simons and asked to be received into the Catholic Church. It was now only a matter of time before the 'universal whisper' that Monmouth could take his place would become a roar.[48]

Chapter 7

The Soldier and the Sun King

Louis XIV was left hamstrung by the Treaty of Aix-la-Chapelle. He was full of expansionist energy and spoiling for a fight but could not resume his assault on the Spanish Netherlands without bringing a massive counterattack from the Spanish assisted by England, Sweden and the Dutch Republic – which he knew not even his army could withstand. He had, therefore, to look elsewhere and his sights quickly settled on the prosperous Dutch Republic itself. Careful diplomacy would be necessary to isolate the republic and so enable the French to cross its borders unopposed, and Louis began to pick off the republic's allies one by one. In the summer of 1668 Monmouth had been an early go-between in the discussions about a possible Anglo-French alliance and these progressed over the following year. Louis XIV was, in time, adamant that England should commit to joining him in attacking the republic. Charles II, who harboured a massive grudge against the Dutch as a nation for the Medway raid and against the republican regime for ousting his sister and her son, needed little persuasion to turn on his supposed ally. He nonetheless attempted to keep in with the Dutch and the Swedes while the negotiations slowly progressed. For Louis the prestige a successful assault on the republic might bring was an end in itself. An added attraction was that because of the proximity of the Dutch Republic to the Spanish Netherlands the Spanish might be provoked into attacking him – which would allow him to resume his aggression without breaking the terms of the Treaty of Aix.[1]

Added to the headings under which international treaties have always been made – mutual military support, trade deals, non-proliferation pacts – the discussions between the English and French would include an explosive additional element: in return for a cash payment of several hundred thousand pounds Charles II was to declare himself a Catholic. There is no real evidence that he actually intended to do so – he knew perfectly well it would be personal political suicide and there is little indication that he was genuinely a Catholic – but it says something about his character that for money he was prepared to play such a dangerous game. The bait of Charles II's conversion would be enough to tempt Louis, who proudly styled himself the 'most Christian' king, to hand over a considerable sum and, so long as it remained a secret element of the treaty, it would be next to impossible for anyone actually to hold him to it. The terms of the treaty were finally thrashed out in the spring of 1670. The deal would bind the signatories to a joint attack on the Dutch Republic, with Charles providing 4,000 infantry and sixty ships, in return for an annual payment of £230,000. The United Provinces, still in the hands of the republican De Witt, was to be carved up, with the rump to be ruled by Charles's nephew William. In addition, Charles would declare his conversion to Catholicism at an unspecified moment for a cash payment of £160,000. In an age when the total annual income of the Crown was around £900,000 these sums were large and after the various catastrophes of the last few years, Charles needed money. In the 1590s Henri of Navarre had converted to Catholicism to secure the French throne, famously taking the view that Paris was 'worth a mass'. Now, almost a century later, his grandson Charles II seems to have taken a similarly pragmatic view.[2]

The treaty between England and France was genuinely secret, and the clauses concerned with Charles's religious conversion utterly so. The king had revealed that aspect to only a handful of people, having gathered a tiny group, among them the Duke of York and Clarendon's successor as chief minister, Lord Arlington, on 25 January 1669 and brought them into his confidence. The signing of an international pact was not easy to effect inconspicuously, but the original notion that Charles, Henriette Anne and Monmouth had discussed of a Stuart family gathering provided the ideal cover. In the early summer of 1670 the French court was due to travel to Flanders to view the territories which Louis had conquered two years before. This would bring them within only a short sailing from the English coast and so enable Henriette Anne to visit her brothers and nephew in London without alerting the suspicions of De Witt and the Dutch Republic. This was all well and good, but for the ever complicated personal politics of the Orléans marriage.

It clearly had to be Henriette Anne who made the journey to England: she both had the pretext and enjoyed the confidence of the two kings. But as a seventeenth-century wife she could travel only with the consent of her husband. Things were not easy in the Orléans household. A few weeks earlier, finally losing his temper with his brother's favourite, Louis had ordered the arrest of Orléans's lover the Chevalier de Lorraine. A daily stream of pathetic and poisonous letters now flowed from the imprisoned Lorraine to the distraught Duc d'Orléans. Smarting with resentment towards both his brother and wife, and casting about for revenge, Orléans refused to allow Henriette Anne to travel.

For weeks Louis, his ministers and Charles's agents tried to talk the Duc of Orléans round. In the end it was only a direct command from Louis as sovereign that elicited the duke's consent, and then on terms designed to disappoint. Henriette was not to be allowed to travel to London but must remain in the port of Dover – which Charles II protested was a miserable place – and was to return after just three days. The leisurely family reunion that Charles and his sister had longed for was not to be. Furthermore, Orléans, still jealous of his wife's friendships and frightened of '*la beauté et l'adresse du duc de Monmouth*', stipulated that Monmouth was to be banned from the meeting altogether.[3]

In mid-April the French royal party finally set out for Flanders, with Henriette Anne tired and fragile. The visible contempt with which the Duc d'Orléans treated his wife shocked those who witnessed it. Still looking for the means to prevent the trip, he was insisting, it was rumoured, on having sex with her every night in the hope that pregnancy would force a cancellation. At Lille the party divided, and on 14 May, Henriette and her retinue of over two hundred sailed from Dunkirk. Between four and five in the morning of 16 May her ship dropped anchor beneath Dover's chalky cliffs and the royal barge bearing the king, the Duke of York, Prince Rupert and the Duke of Monmouth was rowed out. There in the dawn light this pale and persecuted princess stepped into the arms of the tall men of her family who loved her so much.[4]

The visit would in the end last two weeks, business necessitating an extension and, once the meeting was under way, making attempts to curtail it futile. Monmouth was present throughout, despite Orléans's objections. While the diplomats dealt with the paperwork, the royal party made the most of their fortnight together. The sprawling castle on the Dover cliffs was pressed into service as lodgings for Henriette Anne, while every respectable house in the town was taken by either French or British courtiers. The Duke and Duchess of Monmouth brought their whole household with them, spending almost £700 on accommodation in the town during the visit.[5] Entertainments were laid on: a trip to Canterbury with dinner at St Augustine's Abbey; a visit to view the fleet at anchor; and a party on 29 May, the anniversary of the restoration and the king's birthday.[6] While the French party could not go to court, the pleasures of court could be brought to Dover. The players of London's best theatre company, the Duke's Men, established by the celebrated playwright William Davenant, performed comedies on twelve consecutive nights. English plays with a French flavour were chosen: Thomas Shadwell's *The Sullen Lovers* – a recent hit and one of Charles II's favourites – and John Caryll's new work *Sir Salomon Single*. The atmosphere was high-spirited and Monmouth, who was already on familiar terms with many of the visiting delegation and could slip effortlessly between conversation in English and French, was in his element. David Nokes, the most brilliant comic actor of the century, came on stage as the ludicrous Sir Arthur Addle in *Sir Salomon Single*, dressed in a costume that was a deliberate parody of the French courtiers' distinctive short coats. When the Duke of Monmouth then leapt up onto the stage to complete the caricature by buckling his own belt and sword round Nokes's waist, the English spectators' titters escalated into roars of laughter. Ever careless of his possessions, Monmouth did not bother to reclaim the sword, and Nokes kept it until his death nearly thirty years later.[7]

On 2 June, with tears on all sides, Henriette Anne said farewell to her brothers and nephew and sailed for France. There was good reason for melancholy: the family reunion was over, Henriette Anne was returning to her miserable marriage and England was now committed to war. But no one knew how soon tragedy would unfold. Less than a month later, after drinking a glass of chicory water, Henriette Anne suffered an agonising seizure and cried out that she had been poisoned. In barely twelve hours she was dead. Between the spasms of pain, she took the ring from her finger and pressed it into the hand of the English ambassador, asking him to take it to her brother and to tell him that her love for him had been above all things.[8]

When Charles II was brought the news he was devastated. He withdrew completely for several days, remaining in his bedchamber, closeted with his grief.[9] Instant suspicion surrounded her death, as the Duc d'Orléans's terrible treatment of his wife was well known, and an autopsy was demanded. Over a hundred officials looked on as Henriette Anne's slight body was slit open and her intestines dissected by a legion of doctors. But no sign of poisoning could be detected. Though cleared of any culpability, the Duc d'Orléans's bad behaviour did not end with his wife's death. When Charles II asked for his letters to his sister to be returned, the duke was forced to admit he had been through them all himself in a frenzy to see those from Monmouth that he was sure would confirm his jealous suspicions. He did not find the evidence he sought, but that Orléans should have so resented their relationship is testimony to the closeness between Monmouth and Henriette Anne – and to the grief he too felt on hearing of her death.[10]

Shortly before the Dover meeting, in the spring of 1670, Monmouth had turned twenty-one. While he had been at the heart of court life for eight years, his youth had prevented him from actually participating in the governance of the country. With majority came the opportunity for him to hold office. Within weeks of his birthday the king made him a member of the Privy Council, the seventeenth-century equivalent of the cabinet, and that autumn Monmouth took up his seat in the House of Lords, with the king looking proudly on.[11] From the first he responded with enthusiasm to this new access to the institutions of government. In the few weeks of the year that remained after his introduction into the Lords at the end of October 1670 he attended six times, and would attend a further fifteen times before Parliament was prorogued at Easter. This was not simply a matter of accompanying his father, who was present only occasionally, but of relishing admission to the adult world of business that had so far been closed to him.[12] But as soon as he had entered the political world he was embroiled in a major scandal.

Behind the secret treaty of Dover was Charles II's need for money. In the autumn of 1670, as various new areas of taxation were being discussed in Parliament, a provocative counter-proposal was made that there should be a tax on theatres. Sir John Berkenhead replied that the theatres had done the king loyal service and acted for his pleasure, prompting Sir John Coventry to ask boldly whether it was the actors or the actresses who most pleasured the king. While the king's *affaires* might be the subject of coffee house tittle-tattle, for reference to be made to them in the House of Commons was quite another matter. The comment was reported to the king, whose anger overwhelmed his usual languor and who declared himself determined to take 'severe notice of this, that nobody should dare to talk at that rate for the future'. He decided that some of his Guards should ambush Coventry and 'leave a mark upon him' that would teach him a lesson. That night as Coventry walked home in the small hours a gang of Guards appeared out of the shadows and surrounded him. His servant's torch was thrown down and in the darkness, though he put up an impressive defence, he was pinned down, his own cloak used to restrain him, and his nose slashed with a blade, so that the tip was almost severed. The assailants then melted away into the darkness, regrouping to report events and have their wounds dressed at the house of their captain, the Duke of Monmouth.[13]

When news broke the next morning there was a terrific scandal. Coventry showed his mutilated face to his colleagues and an assault on a Member of Parliament was looked on as a blatant attack on Parliament's privileges. Furthermore Coventry recognised some of his attackers as members of the Life Guard and the Duke of Monmouth was accused of having ordered the attack. The word about town was that, following Coventry's speech, Monmouth had sent some of his officers to murder him.[14] As Captain of the Guards, Monmouth presumably had ordered the attack, but the initiative was clearly the king's and he had taken no personal part in the lynching. Indeed he must have felt some unease given that Sir John Coventry was one of his friends. As ever, to lay the blame at Monmouth's door was easy: it implicated the court at the highest level while avoiding accusing the king directly. A few months later a beadle died in a late-night brawl between a group including Monmouth and his friend Christopher, Duke of Albemarle, and the watch.[15] If Monmouth's popular reputation was already as a seducer and a spendthrift, it was now becoming tinged with something much nastier.

In August 1670 the king's childhood friend, the Duke of Buck-ingham, had arrived in Paris to negotiate the treaty which, unbeknownst to him, had in fact already been signed. The French and English kings, and others in the know about the Dover deal, happily strung Buckingham along and in December a public treaty was concluded covering the same ground as its secret forebear but without reference to Charles II's conversion. War with the Dutch

James, later Duke of Monmouth, by Samuel Cooper, painted soon after his abduction from his mother in 1658. His enchanting appearance and irrepressible energy were crucial to winning his father's love.

Charles II by the studio of Adriaen Hanneman, painted around the time he met Lucy Walter, both then aged eighteen.

Lucy Walter attributed to Nicholas Dixon. Though painted after her death this miniature captures something of Lucy's allure.

LUCY WALTER

The Binnenhof Palace in The Hague (*above*) where the princes of Orange lived and the Estates General met. Charles II is shown dancing at a ball there in 1660 (*below*), watched by members of his family, including his young nephew William of Orange who can be seen standing behind the dancers. It was after just such a party ten years earlier that Monmouth was conceived.

James, Duke of Monmouth aged fourteen. In the nine months since his arrival in England he had been made a Duke, married to an heiress and created a Knight of the Garter.

Anne Dutchefs of Monmouth and Buccleugh.

Monmouth's bride, Anna Scott, was just eleven when they married, but quickly acquired expensive and exotic tastes, not least for imported food and wine.

Charles II by
Antonio Verrio,
in the late 1670s.

James, Duke of York
with his first wife,
Anne Hyde, by Peter
Lely. Monmouth was
genuinely close to his
uncle until personal
and political differences
made enemies of them.

The arms granted to Monmouth in 1663, without a 'baton sinister' denoting illegitimacy.

The Duke of Monmouth on horseback, *c.* 1668. This enormous painting shows Monmouth at nineteen and his most dissolute, dressed in theatrical military style before the realities of command changed him.

Lucy Walter holding a miniature of Monmouth, by Godfrey Kneller, *c.* 1680. Painted as an official enquiry was revealing the sorry truth of her life, it portrays Lucy as the respectable and devoted mother Monmouth chose to remember – for both personal and political reasons.

was now agreed, but there was to be a delay before any actual action. As Louis continued to barter terms with other European powers to isolate the Dutch, he was also engaged in a major campaign of refortification – prompted by the crumbling defences he had seen on the French court's tour round Flanders the previous summer. The following spring Louis XIV set out to inspect progress on one of the major undertakings, the rebuilding of the fortifications of Dunkirk.[16] While Louis was at Dunkirk personally overseeing the works and inspecting tens of thousands of soldiers camped there, Monmouth and an extensive entourage travelled to the city to formally bring him the news of the death of the Duke of York's wife, Anne.

Both the son of a king, and as a favourite of the French court, Monmouth was welcomed warmly by Louis and lodged in the house of his greatest general the Vicomte de Turenne – who gave him a personal tour of the works to the city and the army under his command.[17] Louis's own delight in his military endeavours knew no end. He commissioned a vast model of the city and its defences, the first of a series which would soon fill the Grande Galerie in the Louvre and which can still be seen at the Musée de l'Armée in Paris. A spectacular 'military feast' was staged in Monmouth's honour: enormous tents were erected on top of the newly built bastions in which the banquet was served and a play performed. All the while the musicians of the army – trumpeters, drummers and all – played rousing tunes punctuated with cannon fire at appropriate moments.[18] When Monmouth left he carried with him a host of presents from the French king, among them a diamond-encrusted portrait of Louis and a jewelled ring worth £2,000. The honour that Louis XIV had heaped on Monmouth was so conspicuous that it caused the Dutch at last to wonder whether something was afoot.[19]

It was no coincidence that both Monmouth and the Duke of Buckingham, the two men being considered for command of the English regiments Charles II was now committed to providing to fight the Dutch, visited Louis XIV at Dunkirk in 1671. The clear priority was to find someone to take the position who would please both Charles II and Louis XIV. Buckingham, unaware the secret treaty of Dover had been signed months before, was delighted with what he felt had been his masterful diplomacy and convinced the role was his. In reality neither the French nor the English wanted Buckingham while Charles, doubtless pressed by Monmouth himself, favoured his son. Whatever misgivings he had had about the risk to Monmouth's life seem to have been assuaged, perhaps by his sheer enthusiasm, perhaps by the assumption that, like Louis, he would command from the safety of the camp and would not lead any attacks in person. In Monmouth's favour were his personal closeness to Charles and his familiarity with Louis and the luminaries of the French court, which he paraded by throwing a lavish dinner for the visiting Duc de Guise and a host of French dignitaries shortly after his return from Dunkirk. But weighing heavily against him were his youth and complete lack of any military experience – which hardly recommended him to the imperious generals who led the French army. In September 1671 Louis was explicitly sounded out. Whatever his misgivings, Monmouth was Charles's preference and, it was argued, would be a huge asset to the undertaking as he 'would be followed by all the young nobility in England'. The arguments worked and in January 1672 it was common knowledge that the regiment of English soldiers to be sent to France would fight under the personal command of the young Duke of Monmouth.[20]

The pace of events quickened in the early months of 1672 and the recruitment of the men to form Monmouth's regiment became a matter of urgency. Despite Charles II's confidence, it was not an easy task: the prospect of fighting overseas for the King of France and being commanded by one of the court's most famous reprobates did not appeal to everyone.[21] Nonetheless the recruiting parties beat their drums in London and other cities calling for volunteers, for whom the joining fee of five shillings held considerable appeal, and by Easter some 2,000 men had been recruited.[22] Meanwhile Monmouth himself participated in the usual round of court parties and progresses, travelling with the king to Norfolk and Suffolk and designing the clothes for his new regiment.[23] With the whole notion of standing armies very much in its infancy, the concept of a consistent uniform for forces on any given side was not widely established. Monmouth envisaged 2,500 soldiers dressed in his own yellow livery and plans for these suits were well advanced when news of his intentions reached Paris. A complete French military uniform was immediately posted to London with warnings that 'it will be taken ill' if the English troops were dressed otherwise.[24] Monmouth's original notion was not just vainglory; colonels had historically determined the dress of their men, often in personal colours, but this was not to be Louis XIV's way.

On 17 March 1672 Charles II declared war on the United Provinces, Louis XIV did likewise, and a fortnight later Monmouth and his officers, among them Sidney Godolphin and Sir Thomas Armstrong, sailed for France. Sixteen companies of just over a hundred men made up the core of the regiment which would be known as the 'Royal English'. They gathered at Dieppe where they waited for instructions, as Monmouth travelled to Paris to present himself to the French king. He was received by Louis and Queen Marie-Thérèse with great warmth and appeared at several Parisian parties looking, according to Madame de Sévigné, every bit as dashing as he had at the Palais Royal four years earlier. But the visit was to be brief as Louis was now ready to attack and so with his equipage 'the most *magnifique* I ever saw in France', Monmouth rode out.[25]

Given the terms of the Treaty of Aix, Louis could not attack the Dutch on the nearest south-western border, as it would have involved entering the Spanish Netherlands, while the great Dutch stronghold of Maastricht, an island of territory outside their principal border, was so well fortified as to be too risky a task for the first attack. So he settled, instead, on a simultaneous assault on a string of Dutch towns along the Rhine on its south-eastern edge. After a council of war in Louis's magnificent tent, which Monmouth was allowed to attend alongside the now remarried Philippe d'Orléans, the forces split. The main French army marched north-east from Paris across the lands controlled by the Archbishop of Cologne, which formed a convenient corridor through the Spanish Netherlands. Meanwhile Monmouth and the Royal English were with the section of the army taking a longer way round, marching east from Paris, through Rheims and Metz. They reached the Rhine over a hundred miles south of the Dutch border at Coblenz, then travelled north through Cologne and the strategic stronghold of Kaiserswerth to rendezvous with their colleagues.[26]

Their longer route meant that Monmouth and the Royal English were still on the move as Louis swiftly took a series of Dutch fortified towns. On 12 June 1672 the French army crossed the Rhine, the cavalry riding through the wide waters while the engineers erected a bridge to carry the infantry. A day or two later Monmouth and the Royal English arrived and joined the invasion force as it entered the heart of the republic. Major towns fell fast, Arnhem, Deventer, Nijmegen and a successful assault on Utrecht bringing them within only twenty miles of Amsterdam. Mass panic took hold, as one correspondent from Rotterdam, the city of Monmouth's birth, wrote, Louis XIV 'gains every day so much upon us that we are become like people deprived of all reason'. With the scale of the emergency evident, and total subjugation to the French looking a near-certainty, the Dutch took the one remaining course of action that could save them. On 22 June they smashed down the sluices at Muiden just outside Amsterdam, and allowed the salty waters of the North Sea to pour in torrents over the precious farming lands between the Zuiderzee and the Rhine. Amsterdam became an island and the French army cut off from its quarry. Only by consigning itself to the sea could the Dutch Republic escape the French.[27]

One of England's reasons for declaring war on the Dutch was, on paper at least, to unseat the brilliant and brutal Johann De Witt, who had ousted Charles II's nephew William and the House of Orange two decades earlier. The anxiety and then outright terror provoked by the French invasion began to destabilise De Witt's regime, and compound the growing unpopularity of one who had been in power for so long. Meanwhile William was beginning to assert himself. Now twenty-one, educated by scholars, among them De Witt himself, Mary Stuart's infant son had grown into a tough and serious young man, determined to recover his family's positions and defend the independence of the United Provinces. In 1671 he gained a seat on the Council of State and by the summer of 1672 had convinced his fellow councillors to make him the leader of the Dutch army, as admiral and captain general. This put Charles II in an uncomfortable position, as one of his arguments for war had evaporated and his son might now face his nephew across the battlefield. The king's first minister, Arlington, and the Duke of Buckingham were despatched to Holland to try and broker a peace.

Arlington and Buckingham arrived at the French army encampment at Zeist just outside Utrecht in the high summer of 1672 to try and devise a deal that everyone knew Louis XIV would make impossible. The Duke of Monmouth was to act as their third ambassador, both because of his closeness to Louis XIV and after proving himself a useful participant in dealings with the Danish ambassador the previous year.[28] When they found Monmouth they found a changed man. The three months since the duke had left London had seen him take on real responsibilities for the first time. He had marched several thousand men over 500 miles of foreign ground and now camped and held command alongside the seasoned generals of Louis's army, among them the king's cousin the Prince de Condé, and his host from Dunkirk, the incomparable strategist and soldier, the Vicomte de Turenne. At last Monmouth's restless energy had found its release.

His own troops, he soon realised, were a pitiful bunch compared with the drilled and disciplined soldiers of the French army – a sorry collection of largely untrained and unskilled men who knew nothing of modern warfare. While it was generally agreed that 'never was there a more miserable regiment' than the Royal English, and Monmouth himself could only apologise for them, their commanding officer was getting an altogether different press. The despatches sent from Utrecht reported not without a tone of surprise that 'the Duke of Monmouth is in infinite reputation here'.

For once, it was not simply for his charm or the cut of his coat, but for 'his great application to his businesses, which has already in this short time made him in the opinion of all the old experienced officers of this army a very able Commander and is like in a little time to equall theirs of the first rank'.[29]

Having been given the responsibility he had begun to crave, and now part of Europe's most spectacular and sophisticated military machine, a force that numbered some 150,000, Monmouth had started finally to concentrate on something other than his own amusement. Thomas Ross accompanied him, making regular journeys back to London to give the king detailed reports of the duke's health, but it was now Monmouth himself who sat down to write letters that kept his affairs in order. Sincere and solicitous, they no longer rang with the careless tone of the indulged child but expressed instead the new attentiveness of a man who recognised he needed the aid of the administrators. To the Earl of Lauderdale, looking after his property in Scotland, he pledged: 'I shall never forgit your kindnes to mee,' and to Joseph Williamson, the new secretary of state – no grandee – he also picked up the pen himself, thanking him in heartfelt language for sending the money for his regiment and pledging to manage it well: 'I will a sur you the effects of your kindnes will make me live within compas.'[30]

Monmouth, Arlington and Buckingham trooped dutifully back and forwards between the French and Dutch camps. Buoyed by the speed and success of his invasion Louis would offer peace only on deliberately humiliating terms, while William of Orange, incredulous that his royal uncle should still be assisting the French, declared that he 'would rather dye a thousand deaths than submitt'.[31] Encouraging William to accept a deal that might allow him to proclaim himself king rather than just stadtholder, the English ambassadors found they patronised this diminutive Dutchman to little effect. He remarked coolly that he preferred the title of stadtholder, which the Dutch people had just granted him, and would not capitulate. Holding off Louis XIV and defending the United Provinces would go on to be William's life's work. For Monmouth and William, first cousins, this al fresco diplomacy was not their first encounter. They may have met as children of lone mothers in The Hague in the 1650s, but if so they cannot have remembered it. Much more recently, however, William had paid a visit to his uncle Charles II in London, and had lodged in rooms adjoining Monmouth's at White-hall.[32] Though there was barely a year between them in age, these now motherless young men – Monmouth, tall and fair of face and figure; William, small, stiff and unsociable – were utterly different in appearance, ambition and allegiances. But in time they would become close friends and collaborators and it would be to them that England would look for salvation.

In August, with the flooded landscape preventing the French army from advancing, the campaigning season nearing its end and no deal struck, Louis XIV returned to Paris. As he withdrew The Hague erupted. Ire against the De Witt brothers drove a baying and bloodthirsty mob to drag them into the streets where the two men were murdered and mutilated, their fingers, eyes and toes hacked off as mementos. To this day Johann de Witt's shrivelled tongue can be seen at The Hague's Historisch Museum, testimony to the wave of violence which ended his regime and brought William of Orange to power.

The hiatus in the campaign was fortuitous for Monmouth person-ally, as it enabled him to return to London in August 1672 for a significant event. After almost a decade of marriage his wife was about to give birth to their first child. Despite his desire to be with his troops, and the fact that he and Anna had quarrelled seriously before he left, Monmouth was determined to be in England for the event.[33] After years of ignoring his wife, Monmouth had been undergoing, not so much a change of heart – for his heart was little touched by Anna – but of mind. Louis XIV's wife, Marie-Thérèse, had been pregnant with their second son throughout Monmouth's 1668 visits to France and this seems to have planted in him a desire to have children himself. A new interest in his relationship with Anna had probably contributed to Monmouth's decision to acquire

Moor Park in Hertfordshire in 1670. This handsome and substantial house only fourteen miles north of London had belonged to the Duke and Duchess of Ormond and had been coveted by Anna since she had stayed there in 1665.[34] Monmouth had shown no interest: his life was at court with the king, or in France, and he had little appetite for the countryside. When the king travelled to Newmarket or Audley End, he was assigned extensive rooms within the palaces themselves, and had no need of his own satellite residences.[35] At Whitehall the house created for the couple near the cockpit had been expanded over the following years, and within days of the death of the Duke of Albemarle in January 1670 the 'great roome' of his lodgings was annexed to it with over £1,000 spent on improvements.[36]

It was probably therefore to please Anna that Monmouth asked Sir Stephen Fox, and Fox brokered the deal with the king that saw Charles II buy Moor Park and its contents for the Monmouths in April 1670.[37] Acquired fully furnished for £13,200, the house could be occupied immediately and was given a standing staff of six who remained there when the Monmouths were not in residence.[38] For Monmouth, either at court or on the continent, the main use of Moor Park was as a source of supply: fruit for his table and hay for his horses – about to be magnificently stabled in new buildings north of Whitehall.[39] For Anna it provided a retreat from the claustrophobic court. As her pregnancy progressed no expense was spared to ensure she was well looked after and provided for. Childbirth was a serious business in an age when even among the aristocracy a third of all children died before they were five, but also provided an opportunity for conspicuous consumption, with lying-in clothes rivalling wedding gowns in their magnificence.

The expenditure on Anna's first birth was huge. The bill for her linen and clothing, the basket and swaddling clothes for the baby and the attendance of a doctor and two midwives was just under £2,000, of which almost half was spent on lace.[40] But this was only the beginning: there were the silver vessels for the baby's nursery, the

cost of extra staff for three months, among them the wet nurse, Mrs
Southhouse – whose importance was reflected in the generous £60
she was paid for eighteen weeks' work – a dry nurse, Mrs Maugridge,
a rocker, Mrs Gettings, two nursery maids and a 'Chamber Keeper'
for the infant. Luckily the money was forthcoming as the king,
who did not baulk at helping with arrangements for his first grand-
child, made a one-off payment of £5,000 to cover the Duchess of
Monmouth's lying-in expenses. The healthy baby Anna produced
was baptised Charles on 6 September; the Archbishop of Canterbury officiated and the king himself was a godfather. The king's
usual christening present of plate to children of the aristocracy
increased almost threefold in scale for Monmouth's baby.[41]

It may have been the comforts of his new home at Moor Park
and the domestic concord following the birth of baby Charles
that made Monmouth feel reluctant about returning to the Royal
English. Perhaps more important, however, was his sobering sense
of his own inexperience and the shortcomings of his ramshackle
regiment.[42] In the thick of winter he sailed for France for a two-
month visit. The crossing was atrocious, with awful weather
battering the vessel which only narrowly avoided being wrecked.
His reception in Paris was warm and honour-laden now that he was
a soldier of France.[43] The poor reports of the Royal English had had
some impact and eight companies of Guards were to accompany
Monmouth to augment the regiment.[44] Monmouth found Louis
emboldened by the successes of the previous summer and set on a
second major assault as soon as the season permitted.

As part of his preparations Louis had decided to integrate the
foreign troops more fully into his army, which would involve
giving Monmouth a position within its hierarchy. Proposing an
elevation from his existing rank of colonel, the secretary of state for
war, Louvois, suggested the position of brigadier or even the more
senior role of *maréchal de camp*. But the previous year's experience
of the French army in action had checked Monmouth's cockiness,
and he declined the role of *maréchal de camp*, protesting that he
was not experienced enough and would be happy with brigadier.

The Marquis de Saint-Maurice was impressed by the duke's humility and, struck by his intelligence and his application, wondered whether Charles II had deliberately sent him to fight abroad to enhance his reputation among the English people.[45] Keen to flatter his ally and to smooth their troubled family history, Louis XIV was at pains to bestow honour on Monmouth during his winter visit. A ball was thrown for him in Paris and hosted by the Duc d'Orléans himself. Afterwards Monmouth was presented with a diamond-studded sword worth £5,000 which Louis gave 'with his compl[i]m[en]t – that he would not have him receive it from any other hand but his owne'.[46] That was January; come April, Louis XIV had decided on his plan of attack and had elevated Monmouth not to brigadier or even *maréchal de camp* but to the still more senior rank of lieutenant general, second in status only to the handful of marshals of France.[47]

The Third Dutch War, as the Anglo-French campaign against the Dutch would be called, was not fought on soil alone. Part of the terms of the treaty of Dover had committed the English to providing sixty ships to fight the Dutch at sea, commanded by James, Duke of York. But pitched against the great Dutch naval commander De Ruyter the English had again been having mixed success. At the battle of Solebay on 28 May 1672 the flagship *The Royal James*, commanded by Edward Montagu, Earl of Sandwich, was bombarded by the Dutch and sank to the sea bed, taking Sandwich with her. The following summer there would be even less to celebrate, not least when in July the Dutch recaptured New York.

Though Monmouth described Louis looking 'the most pleased that ever I saw any man in all my life' when he gave him news of the Anglo-French naval victory that spring, Louis's own focus was on the land war, and his target in the spring of 1673 was the Dutch stronghold of Maastricht.[48] Standing forty miles beyond the United Provinces' main border it was a Dutch enclave in a sea of foreign territory, surrounded by the Spanish Netherlands and the lands of the bishopric of Liège. The fortress of Maastricht was arguably the strongest in Europe. It straddled the Maas, or Meuse, river, enveloping a crossing of such strategic importance that it had been fortified by the Romans and remained so ever since, each century bringing new waves of defensive features.

Two hundred years earlier gunpowder had transformed the business of war, and guns big and small had replaced the crossbows and colossal catapults of the Middle Ages. The high walls of castles, which easily threw off arrows, shattered like thin ice under the massive momentum of a cannonball, and so many were left ruined or abandoned. Fortresses had to be redesigned as sprawling squat structures of brick, set out in the ever more complex geometrical shapes which allowed for a maximum field of fire. Maastricht was one such, with multiple layers of stocky walls with jutting defensive bastions that had been augmented only thirty years earlier when William of Orange's brilliant grandfather, Prince Frederick Henry, had captured the city from the Spanish.

The main body of the city stood on the west bank of the Maas river, its smaller sister settlement of Wyck on the east bank, reached by a single bridge. Both were encircled by high medieval stone walls punctuated by gates with double-drum gatehouses. Outside this a further circle of deep wide ditches had been created by the Dutch to strengthen the city, themselves protected by further embanked walls. At various strategic points, on corners and protecting important entrances, were a series of huge detached bastions with high brick walls: those with a triangular footprint known as demilunes, and those with two pointed projections toward any attacker, appropriately, hornworks. The river provided a barrier to the east, forcing any approaching army to cross the open ground to the west and so face an impassable hail of fire from the cannons mounted along the walls and on the bastions.

To break through Maastricht's mighty defences needed not so much a brave soldier as a brilliant engineer, and in Sébastien Le Prestre de Vauban, Louis had found the greatest of the age. From a minor gentry family in Burgundy, Vauban's sheer skill in managing and manipulating the terrain in the business of siege warfare, both in defence or attack, had elevated him to the position of Engineer in Ordinary to the King at just twenty-two. By 1673 he was a highly experienced engineer and in the first fortnight of June he unrolled his plan for taking Maastricht. Twenty thousand peasants were to excavate a web of covered trenches traversing the open ground from the French headquarters at the village of Wolder, almost two miles west, right up to the ditches of the fortified city. Through this subterranean labyrinth the French army would swarm towards its prize. Vauban's technique allowed large numbers of attackers to approach the fortress without ever exposing themselves to the wide fields of fire which the banks and ditches of the outworks provided. This was by now common practice, but at Maastricht he tried a new arrangement of trenches. Rather than creating more or less direct lines from the attacker's headquarters to a point on the city's defences, the approach was to be through a series of ditches dug parallel to the city walls, so leaving the defenders uncertain about the point of final attack until the last hours. But to take the city the attackers would still need to emerge from their trenches into the city's ditches, and dodge both the gunners above and their minefields below to mount the walls of the raised bastions. Vauban knew this was the hardest part: 'I know nothing more difficult to surmount than the outer edge of the ditch, the counterscarp,' he wrote.[49]

Monmouth arrived in France in April 1673 to his new rank and the daunting realisation that he was no longer tagging along, but was to carry the full weight of military responsibility on his shoulders. Louis divided his 40,000 men into a series of sections, or '*quartiers*', who made their camps in a menacing circle a mile's radius from the city. Each *quartier* was led by a senior officer: the king himself taking responsibility for the headquarters at Wolder to the west, his brother the Duc d'Orléans for the forces on the east bank of the Meuse facing Wyck – but with Vauban and the Duc du Lorges actually in command – and the Comte de Montal for the forces to the north. The original plan had been for Monmouth to fight as part of Orléans's *quartier*, which he may not have welcomed given their history. Instead, however, in recognition of the French king's 'greatt respect' for Monmouth and the positions French commanders had been given in the Anglo-French naval fleet, he changed the plan and gave Monmouth his own *quartier* on the north-west, 'a greatter comand then any hath Monsieur [i.e. Orléans] being excepted'. Louis gave Monmouth an extra *maréchal de camp*, the experienced Chevalier de Fourille, to lodge with him and provide additional counsel but otherwise Monmouth was on his own. At twenty-two, with next to no experience of siege warfare, he was now a lieutenant general in the French army with nine battalions (some 8,000 men) under his command.[50]

The excavation of the trenches was the first undertaking, which the French carried out under cover of darkness. The effort was disrupted by cannon fire from the city, but the strange reticence of the Dutch to fire more forcefully meant the digging covered ground fast. As the hordes of men plied their spades and the carpenters sawed the timber for the gun emplacements, Monmouth watched Louis XIV admiringly, drinking in the powerful combination of energy and application with which he approached the almost surgical task of capturing a city. The experienced soldier and diplomat Sir William Lockhart, who was with the army over those days, wrote that the French king 'continews still indefatigable doing all the functions of a greatt captaine and good soldier, the D[uke] of Monmouth taketh pleasure to follow so greatt and good example and dayly gaineth more not only the kings esteeme but everybodys'.[51]

The senior officers each led the action in twenty-four-hour shifts. On Tuesday 10 June it was Monmouth's turn. Three days earlier in darkness and driving rain the engineers had erected three large gun platforms which now stood proud of the warren of trenches and bore massive cannon. With heavy artillery in place the attack on the town's defences, starting with the counterscarp, could begin. Six in the evening was the moment when the commanders changed shift, and as this hour drew near Monmouth wrote his father a letter fizzing with anticipation, determined that tonight 'I shall make a lodgement apon the conterscarpe'.[52] Trenches dug in the Low

Countries tended to flood – as the soldiers of the First World War would also find – but the downpours of June 1673 exacerbated the problem. As Monmouth had explained in one of his despatches, ''Tis sutch rainy weather that in the trench wee ar up to the knees in water wch is not very comfortabell espetualy when wee ar to stay 24 houers in the trench beefor wee ar relived.'

Monmouth and his men entered the trenches on 10 June. But as they waded towards the city in the muggy evening air they found the water in the furthest tunnels was now waist-high. Soldiers were exposing themselves to enemy fire by trying to bypass the drowned ditches, and Monmouth realised the attack he had hoped to make was impossible under such conditions. Rather than move forward he directed his energies instead to clearing the water and excavating new trenches. The work was hazardous, as the Dutch guns were finally bearing down on them, and he narrowly avoided serious injury when a bullet flew between his legs. Everyone was nervous about how such an inexperienced commander would fair; William Lockhart hoped only that Monmouth would not embarrass himself. Louis sent volleys of emissaries down to him in the trenches 'to enquire after his health and to charge him not to expose himself'. By daybreak the tunnels were just twenty yards from the outer ditch, sixty yards nearer than when Monmouth had taken over, and 'his Grace tooke such care that the Trenches should be drie before the Duke of Rohanez relieved us, that his men yesterday in the evening past safe and drie to their several Posts'. As he returned to his tent, Monmouth broke the seal on his letter to his father to add a hasty postscript of 'my night's Trench'. Making no mention of the bullet that nearly felled him, which he knew would appal his father, he reported breathlessly 'they have fierd exstremly but I have gott wth in thourty peasess of the counterscarp and could have mead a lodgement apone it but the king would not for fear of the minds [mines]'. He then added some brief words of reassurance – 'I am very well' – before sealing it and giving it to the courier.[53]

The reason for the Dutch reticence to fire sooner was now becoming clear. They had been saving their powder until the French army reached the foot of the walls; their bullets and shot now rained down, slowing French progress. It would be four more days before they could make a major assault and when the hour came it was once again Monmouth's shift. At 6 p.m. on 14 June he took command and the order to attack was given. In the fading light the duke and his men filed through the last stretch of tunnels before ascending the bank of the fort's outer ditch and from here surging up the high-sided 'half-moon' bastion that defended one of the city's main gates. With Monmouth were many of the Royal English. Waiting for his word in the tunnels behind were the French musketeers, commanded by none other than their sixty-two-year-old lieutenant, Charles de Batz-Castelmore, Comte D'Artagnan.[54]

Now Monmouth and the French were in control of the bastion and its approach, communication channels back to the tunnel complex could be opened. The work of consolidating this advance continued through the night, with Monmouth passing back and forward between the trenches and the half-moon bastion to see work progress. At noon the following day, as relays of his men went down into the tunnels for refreshment, Monmouth suffered a catastrophic setback. The true reason the Dutch had been content to let the French come so close before firing was revealed: their outworks were absolutely laced with mines. An enormous mine exploded below Monmouth's men, its blast throwing fifty soldiers into the air, ripping limbs from bodies with its force. The Dutch swiftly exploited the disarray and counterattacked – doing so with 'great order and bravery, the Hand Grenados flying very thike amongst our men', and forcing Monmouth and his men back into the tunnels.

Furious at having lost the advantage, Monmouth was determined to retaliate. Not waiting for reinforcements, and with only a dozen or so men with him, he 'leape[d] over the banke of the Trench in the face of our enemy', his sword held before him. His shocked men, not knowing what else to do, followed him and together they charged forward, utterly exposed, towards the barricade the Dutch had hastily erected in front of the half-moon bastion. To have any hope of regaining their position they would have to pass single-file through a narrow gap, laying themselves open to a barrage of enemy fire as they did so. D'Artagnan advised against it, but the duke, burning with the ardour of the amateur, would not be dissuaded. He led the charge himself, and as they were twice repelled, he twice pushed back until, with the light fading, he finally fell exhausted onto the regained bastion. At his side were those who had escaped the bullets, among them Captain Churchill, the future Duke of Marlborough. Sprawled in the ditch below were those who had not. First among them was the crumpled figure of D'Artagnan himself, a single bullet to the head bringing down the most celebrated soldier in French history. Casualties notwithstanding, possession of the half-moon meant that the fall of the city was now inevitable. Assuming this was the spearhead of a massive advance, and not the impulsive attack of a tiny detachment of men, the Dutch took fright and the garrison started to mutiny. The defeated Dutch commander, General de Fariaux, led his 5,000 men out of the fortifications in surrender just a few days later. As he did so he paused before the Duke of Monmouth and saluted him in respectful acknowledgement 'that the honour of taking the Towne' had been his.[55]

The accounts written by participants in the hours afterwards make it clear that the attack had been a thing of real danger.[56] Hundreds died, were dismembered or wounded, and the exploding mines very nearly brought defeat. Unquestionably the sheer strength of the French army funnelled safely through Vauban's parallel tunnels was going to bring Maastricht to its knees sooner or later – the speed with which the Dutch surrendered after the events of 25 June speaks for itself. But Monmouth's own part was one of real bravery. When he had told an anxious Marquis de Saint-Maurice, whose eldest son fought under him, that he would not ask the boy to go anywhere he would not go himself, it was not simply a figure of speech. Louis XIV and the Duc d'Orléans remained in their palatial tents a safe distance from the front throughout the siege, delegating their command to the lieutenant-generals who served beneath them. Monmouth, by contrast, led the attack in his *quartier* himself, wading through miles of trenches in mud up to his thighs. More than this, it was his personal bravery that began the crucial attack to retake the bastion. He put his men in danger, it is true, but himself most of all, and the whole occasion involved a physical hardship of the sort he had never before experienced. The following day he apologised to Lord Arlington for not writing to him straight after the attack: 'I swer I was so wery then that I could not write,' explaining his brevity with the words: 'I hope you will pardon mee if I troubell you no longer for I am so wery that I am not eabell to say one word more.'[57]

After the siege, having watched his men die before his eyes, Monmouth showed little of his former swagger: rather a palpable sense of how lucky they had been. In his letter to Arlington he referred to the victory simply as 'the good loke [luck] I have had the last time I was apone dity [duty]'.[58] When Louis greeted him as he finally emerged, shattered, from the trenches (in a scene recorded on the walls of one of the refectories at Les Invalides) he declared that Charles II would be overjoyed when he heard what had happened. Monmouth replied only that the cannon fire could have been worse. Louis said that, while he approved of such modesty, 'we know what it is that you have done'.[59] Those who were there agreed with William Alington, Monmouth's *maréchal de camp*, when he concluded at the end of his detailed account of events written the following day that 'some old commanders say, this was the bravest and briskest action they had seen in their lives, and our Duke did the part of a much older, and more experienced general'.[60] Finally, Monmouth had proved himself.

Chapter 8

A Rising Sun

'The joyfull news of the Duke of Monmouth's successe' at Maastricht was brought to Charles II in a series of despatches that left him elated. His faith in his wayward son had at last been proved, and 'his Majesty sheweth as much satisfaction as you might easily imagine he would'. When he received Louis XIV's detailed account of Monmouth's exploits, Charles initially protested politely that the French king must be exaggerating. Louis responded vehemently that *'Je ne vous dis rien que les éloges de toute l'armée ne confirment'* (I tell you nothing that the praise of the whole army does not confirm), and gave yet another account of how the young man's bravery had won the day. Fireworks and public services of thanksgiving were staged in Paris as Monmouth took his leave from an ecstatic French king in early July. Travelling north to Calais he found five English frigates waiting to bring him home, and as he sailed for England the cannon of the Calais ramparts thundered a farewell salute.[1]

It was long after dark on the evening of Saturday 12 July 1673 when Monmouth reached London. He strode into his father's apartments to a thunderous welcome. The following morning he rode out with the king and the Duke of York to view the troops who were assembled on Blackheath, pending a further wave of action on the continent, and on Monday he rode north to Moor Park. Anna and their year-old son, Charles, were now installed here, and Monmouth spent two nights in their company.[2] But they did not detain him long, and on Wednesday he was back in London where he remained, mustering the Royal Life Guards, and throwing a party for the king and 'all the gallants' at the Chelsea house of John, Lord Robartes, where he had had the gardens and bowling green illuminated with hundreds of lanterns 'in an extraordinary manner'.[3]

With Monmouth's spectacular success the talk of the town, there was intense speculation about which great office he would now be given. Four days after his arrival he asked his uncle James, Duke of York, to dine and the pair spent the whole afternoon together in Monmouth's Cockpit rooms. They must have had much to discuss: during the 1650s York too had fought with Turenne for the French, while among those who died at Monmouth's side was Sir Henry Jones, one of his uncle's servants. York was almost as proud as the King was of his nephew's success, 'it being observed by those that are nere his Royal Highnesse that he has a particular kindnesse and affection for his Grace'.[4] But while his avuncular affection was sincere, it now contended with a bitter new reality. For just as Monmouth's prospects were soaring, York's career had suddenly collapsed.

The government had known from the first that a war against the Dutch would be unpopular with English Protestants, particularly those who sympathised with the Calvinism which predominated in the republic. So in March 1672, just two days before war had been declared, the king issued a 'Declaration of Indulgence' which suspended the penal laws against nonconformists. Low Church Protestants were to have freedom of worship if they received a licence and Catholics were to be allowed to worship in private. The measure was intended to placate nonconformists and prevent them siding with the Dutch in the war. Unfortunately for the king, and nonconformists of all complexions, the move would spectacularly backfire.

The king's chief advisors, who effectively made up the government at this time, were a disparate set of men whose names, it was realised, could be arranged to spell the word 'cabal'. 'C' was the loyal and cultured Thomas Clifford, now Lord Treasurer; 'A' his former patron, Sir Henry Bennet, Lord Arlington and the 'smoothest man at court', who, as secretary of state was well suited to a post responsible for relations with foreign powers; the king's childhood friend, the maverick and unpredictable Duke of Buckingham, was 'B', who had influence without holding a major office of state; the serious and experienced Anthony Ashley Cooper, the second 'A', had long been chancellor of the exchequer; while 'L' was the uncompromising Earl of Lauderdale, who managed Scotland as the king's commissioner. All received honours as the war was launched and the regime came under pressure: Ashley became Earl of Shaftesbury and was made lord chancellor, Lauderdale was made a duke and Bennet an Earl. But the Cabal's supremacy would be undone by the very measures which defined it. Parliament had not been consulted about the Declaration of Indulgence, as it was within the king's powers to issue without their consent. When the MPs and Lords assembled in early 1673 and were asked to grant extra funds to continue the fighting, the Cabal faced a barrage of opposition.

The fact was that although the Declaration had been intended to placate Low Church nonconformists, the freedom it had also allowed Catholics was deeply controversial. Taken together with the alliance with Catholic France and widespread rumours of the Duke of York's conversion, it created suspicion that Catholicism was infiltrating the state at the highest level. In the end it became clear that Parliament would grant money for the war only if the Declaration of Indulgence was abandoned. The effects split the Cabal, some feeling war was more important than Indulgence, others that defending the king's ruling on religious toleration was now more significant than the war.

Charles II, who had only reluctantly agreed to it, took the view that the Declaration of Indulgence had to be sacrificed to continue the war. Parliament, now with the wind in its sails, pushed not simply to stop the religious toleration of the Declaration, but to enact stricter measures against Catholics by means of a Test Act, or in the words of its full title: 'An act for preventing dangers which may happen from popish recusants'. This piece of legislation, which received royal assent on 29 March, required anyone holding civil or military office to take Anglican communion within three months of appointment and to swear an oath explicitly denying transubstantiation – the real presence of Christ in the bread and wine taken at communion. By April 1673 Charles II had secured the money to keep on fighting, but only at the cost of excluding Catholics completely from any role in government.

It was against this charged backdrop that the Duke of Monmouth's successes on the French campaign were achieved. While he was fighting for the French king there had never been any suspicion that he was anything other than Protestant. His childhood tuition at Colombes by the Catholic Father Gough was not widely known, and on his arrival in England the Archbishop of Canterbury had appointed a chaplain to guide him. That position, paid a handsome £50 a year, was held from 1665, if not earlier, by James Gardiner, a churchman with impeccable Anglican credentials who would go on to be Bishop of Lincoln.[5] Despite Monmouth's disreputable lifestyle, he attended the chapel royal regularly, and on Sunday 27 July, a fortnight after returning to England, he went to the parish church of St Clement Danes on the Strand and took communion according to the requirements of the Act. Also receiving the bread and wine that day, and with his secretary John Locke acting as witness to both, was the brilliant, diminutive lord chancellor, Anthony Ashley Cooper, now Earl of Shaftesbury.[6] The lives of these two men were to be intertwined in the years that lay ahead of them. Now they were both insiders; six years hence they would be the titans of the opposition.

With no qualms about taking the 'Test' and as a man 'upon whom, indeed, all the world now looks as a riseing sun', Monmouth's name was linked by court gossips to a host of glittering positions, among them command of the navy, the army, and the Duke of Lauderdale's position as the king's lieutenant in Scotland.[7] In reality Monmouth had started accumulating offices since he had first shown his promise in the 1672 campaign. In the winter of 1672/73 he had been made lord chief justice of the royal forests south of the Trent. The royal forests were not so much areas of woodland, but huge tracts of land that, since the early Middle Ages, had formed a distinct legal entity and which were administered for the king by two officials, one for the north and one for the south. Though the chief justices were less important than they had been, and deputies were appointed to do the real work, the post still brought considerable responsibilities and patronage.[8] The spring of 1673 had brought a bigger catch, as the Catholic Lord Bellasis was forced to resign the related positions of governor of Kingston upon Hull and lord lieutenant of the East Riding of Yorkshire. The city of Hull standing on the north bank of the wide Humber estuary was one of the foremost trading towns of the east coast and a place of real strategic significance for command of both land and sea. It had been hotly contested during the civil war and after the Restoration retained a standing garrison under the command of a governor, to ensure peace and prevent rebellion in the north and to protect the country from attack from the Low Countries.[9] It was a perfect fit: a substantial garrison command provided an additional string to Monmouth's military bow, while a serving soldier close to the king was the sort of influential army man that pleased a garrison town. The mayor and burgesses of Hull were so delighted with the king's choice of new governor that in July they elected him their high steward as well.[10]

While anything now seemed possible for Monmouth, for the Duke of York the scene was starkly different. The strict terms of the Test Act had been passed just days before Easter, one of the three occasions in the year when everyone at court took communion in the chapel royal. York attended the service but at the crucial moment when the royal family came forward he slipped away. John Evelyn, who watched from within the chapel, expressed the horror of his contemporaries. York's failure to take communion, he wrote, 'within a day of the Parliament sitting, who had lately made so severe an Act against the increase of Popery, gave exceeding grief and scandal to the whole nation, that the heir of it, and the son of a martyr for the Protestant religion should apostatize. What the consequences of this will be, God only knows and wise men dread.'[11]

The king himself was infuriated by his brother's behaviour and tried repeatedly to make him understand just how dangerous it was for them both. But York was determined to make his conversion public, seeing it as a matter of conscience from which reasoned arguments could not dissuade him.[12] In the face of his brother's refusal to compromise, there was little the king could do. The following Sunday almost all the other main officers and men of the court had attended chapel and taken communion, among them Prince Rupert and the Duke of Monmouth, who was then just about to sail for the Maastricht campaign. But no amount of general conformity could relieve the shock and disbelief at the Duke of York's conversion.

York initially thought he might be able to hold his offices through an exemption from the conditions of the Test Act. But he soon realised there was no way out and in June 1673, on almost the very day that Maastricht fell, he had resigned the position of lord high admiral.[13] In so doing he offered further confirmation of his change of faith. The same month the lord treasurer, Clifford (the C of the Cabal), also resigned. To many it seemed as if rumours that Catholicism was becoming rampant were indeed justified.

The Duke of York's commitment to Catholicism did not diminish in the face of the public reaction it provoked; if anything it became greater. That he was not content with the sort of covert, crypto-Catholicism which might have escaped scrutiny only added to the alarm which those around him felt. As next in the line of succession, he was, after all, poised to become the head of the Anglican Church. Towards the end of her life, his wife Anne had written a detailed account of her own conversion, which revealed something of the couple's experience. She admitted to being influenced by witnessing Catholicism on the continent during the 1650s. Conceding that she had little real understanding of scripture, she described being thrilled by the clarity of Catholic doctrine, which 'I found so easy'. Similarly her husband was drawn by the absolutes of Catholicism. His dogmatic attitude to power and authority gave

him an instinctive preference for the uncompromising attitudes of
the Catholic Church over the many debates and divisions within
Protestantism. Just as he resented parliamentary interference in
royal affairs, he, like his wife, was attracted by the doctrine of papal
infallibility. The implications of the duke's conversion would be
profound. The anxiety of a Protestant country facing the prospect
of a Catholic king would be the overriding issue of English politics
for the rest of the century.[14]

In the spring of 1673 the Duke of York was a widower with two
daughters, Princesses Mary and Anne, who had been brought up
as Protestants, and so the likelihood was that if there was to be a
Catholic monarchy, it would at least be for quite a short time. But
this all changed when in September 1673 York, now forty, married
the fifteen-year-old daughter of the Duke of Milan, Mary Beatrice
d'Este of Modena. A decade earlier the choice would have raised
few eyebrows, but for York to marry a Catholic from a family
with close ties to Louis XIV so soon after resigning his offices was
highly contentious. The marriage was concluded by proxy before
the couple met and, once done, the young bride and her mother set
off for England. As they travelled across the continent, Parliament
assembled for the first time since passing the Test Act in March. The
House of Commons complained bitterly and sent an urgent demand
to the king for it to be called off and for the duke to marry a Protestant instead. The king protested that it was too late. Unbowed, the
Commons retorted they would grant no more money while their
concerns about popery lay unaddressed. Realising he was going to
get nowhere Charles prorogued Parliament until the new year.[15]

As the Duke of York welcomed his timid and reluctant teenage
bride in the face of widespread opposition, the royal family made
a clear show of unity. York travelled to Dover to receive the Italian
party, including Mary Beatrice's mother and uncle, while the king,
Monmouth, Prince Rupert, and a bevy of government ministers,
intercepted them at Woolwich on their way to London. On introducing his bride to the court at her first 'circle' at Whitehall, York

told her to kiss the hands of the king's children by Lady Castlemaine. When Catherine of Braganza made her formal visit to the newly-weds York asked Monmouth to act as his lieutenant. Monmouth stood with the duke and duchess at the entrance to their lodgings as the queen alighted from her sedan chair. As York led Queen Catherine into their rooms, Monmouth followed with Mary Beatrice on his arm.[16]

Despite such demonstrations of family unity there was no escaping the fact that Monmouth was being celebrated just when his uncle was being castigated, was being cast the hero as York was the villain. When York resigned as lord high admiral, Monmouth was named to the commission set up to exercise its responsibilities, and it was widely rumoured he would soon be given the post itself. That the relationship between uncle and nephew remained close despite all this is a measure of the genuine affection and loyalty between the two Jameses. The younger, acutely aware of the sensitivities, was anxious not to make his uncle's position worse, and was also not at all convinced of his own readiness for high office. When it was speculated he might be given charge of the navy, he surprised onlookers by seeking nothing more senior than the captaincy of a single vessel.[17] In November 1673 the king offered to make him Commissioner of Scotland, in place of the Duke of Lauderdale, whose bullying ways were causing the king trouble, thus proposing an appointment which government officials had for some months considered a certainty. But again it was Monmouth himself, as his new secretary James Vernon recorded, who turned down the role. He explained to his father that while the war continued he wished to 'appear in action', be it on land or sea. But even if there were peace, he could not have accepted such a position as he 'feared that his employment would draw upon him the envy of the Duke [of York]'. The king, impressed by his son's maturity, could only agree.[18] So it was that a fork in the road had been reached, and Monmouth had passed up high office rather than displease his uncle. In placing family harmony above personal position he had set the course for his own career over the next few years – one which, had it not been for extraordinary circumstances that had already begun to unfold, might have continued for many decades to come.

The fallout of the Duke of York's conversion took its toll on the government and the 'Cabal' shattered under the pressure. Clifford, having resigned his office after the Test Act passed, was gripped by a profound melancholy and was found dead some months later, probably by his own hand. To his position of lord treasurer was appointed Thomas Osborne, a blunt but effective Yorkshireman soon to be made Earl of Danby. Arlington, who had been the king's chief minister since the fall of Clarendon, was losing power and stepped back from front-line politics, taking up the post of lord chamberlain in 1674. Buckingham, whose dissolute personal behaviour made him deeply unpopular, was dismissed from his offices in the spring of 1674 while Lauderdale's heavy-handed management of affairs in Scotland was losing the king's confidence. But most significant of all were the changing allegiances of Anthony Ashley Cooper, Earl of Shaftesbury, who had taken communion alongside Monmouth in July 1673.

Shaftesbury, now in his early fifties, was one of the few people who had been major players in national politics during both the Commonwealth and Restoration periods. From an old Dorset family and orphaned young, he had been given a Puritan education by his grandfather, which contributed to his decision to switch sides from the king to Parliament in 1644. An acute intellect and political flair saw him rise fast within the Commonwealth regime and in 1653 he had been a member of Oliver Cromwell's Council of State, and taken an active role in the business of forging new models of government in a world without kings. As the regime began to crumble he, as a former royalist, was among those approached by Charles II's agents and in 1660 he became convinced that the great republican experiment had failed and joined those who brought about the return of the king.

In the years since the restoration, Shaftesbury had been a government official of senior standing, reaching the pinnacle of his career in government as lord chancellor from 1672. He held office despite falling dangerously ill in 1668, when his liver ruptured. His friend, the Oxford academic John Locke, had recommended and supervised a highly perilous operation, which, while successful, left a small copper tube protruding from his side from which fluid could be drained. His small stature, colourful medical history and awkward gait made his person easy to mock, but Shaftesbury's mind was sharper than steel.

For Shaftesbury, with his Puritan upbringing and republican experience, the events of 1673 were to prove a real turning point. The heir to the throne's conversion to Catholicism, taken together with his absolutist instincts, represented, in Shaftesbury's view, a threat to the liberty of the English people so serious that it would turn him from a pillar of government to its most relentless and effective critic. When he could see that Charles II was neither going to persuade York to abandon Catholicism nor banish him from court, Shaftesbury began quietly to encourage parliamentary opposition. It was he who ensured it was able to voice its anger at the Duke of York's marriage. The king, soon realising his minister's disloyalty, expelled Shaftesbury from the Privy Council in November 1673. When asked to return the insignia of the position of lord chancellor, Shaftesbury reportedly remarked: 'It is only laying down my gown, and putting on my sword.'[19]

After the stand-off with Parliament in October 1673, it was clear Charles II had to do something or he would have real trouble on his hands. War with Catholic France against the Protestant Dutch had always been a bitter pill for his subjects to swallow and people increasingly wondered why they were at war at all. When the Earl of Sandwich had been drowned in the naval battle of Solebay in 1672, John Evelyn had remarked that it showed 'the folly of hazarding so brave a fleet, & loosing so many good men, for no provocation in the World but because the Hollander exceeded us in Industrie, & in all things else but envy'.[20] But if the war had seemed acceptable enough when the Dutch were led by the De Witt brothers, it seemed downright perverse in 1673 with the king's nephew William III their leader. Furthermore, smouldering unease at fighting with a Catholic king against a Protestant nation turned to outrage when English Protestantism itself seemed to be threatened by the Duke of York's conversion. An end to the war was inevitable, and in the last months of 1673 English and Dutch diplomats talked terms. William of Orange was naturally keen to pick off one of Louis XIV's key allies, but also felt that in time he might be able to persuade his uncle to join him against the French, and so did not push his luck in demanding concessions. Early in 1674 the terms of the second Treaty of Westminster were thrashed out. The English had made no territorial gains, but at least the Dutch were to return New York, and so there were also no losses. In a nod to the promises made to Louis XIV in 1670, the Royal English were not to be withdrawn but were to be allowed to continue to fight for Louis until he and William made terms themselves.

While the Duke of Monmouth was a member of the Privy Council, and attended the House of Lords every day during Parliament's short sitting in October 1673, he was observing policy rather than making it. The members of the now fracturing Cabal were figures of his father's generation who were well known to him, each having played a personal role in his career. Clifford had been one of the rather inattentive commissioners for Monmouth's estates in the 1660s, as had Lauderdale, who ten years earlier had helped broker his marriage to Anna.[21] The unreliable Buckingham had been Monmouth's boon companion in many a court revel of the 1660s and had, with the elegant Lord Arlington, been his co-negotiator in the attempts to make peace between Louis XIV and William III in 1672.[22] Even the cerebral Shaftesbury was more than an acquaintance. When Monmouth received his first civil office, as chief justice of the southern royal forests in 1672, he had appointed as his deputy 'my very noble Lord and worthy friend, Anthony Earl of Shaftesbury'.[23]

With the sands of international relations and domestic politics shifting fast, it was unclear from one week to the next what the future held for Monmouth. When he had left his regiment in July 1673 it was with the express purpose of raising more troops and returning. Come early September he was poised, instead, to take up a captaincy in the navy, with Vernon sent to inspect the condition of the ship he was to command. But only a fortnight later that plan too had been abandoned and Vernon was packing his bags to return to his regiment in Flanders.[24] Vernon set off, but the days passed and Monmouth did not travel. He was still 'preparing' at the end of the month, and in mid-October the Venetian ambassador complained: 'Monmouth is always talking of his journey but never makes it.'[25] He was unquestionably anxious to return to 'action' and the delays were not of his making but stemmed from uncertainty about Louis XIV's plans, and a wider question about the longevity of the war itself. As autumn turned to winter it was too late in the year for any more fighting, and anyhow, peace was now being talked in earnest.

Whatever else had passed between Monmouth and his wife when he visited her for three days at Moor Park on his return from Maastricht, they had re-consummated their marriage. By Christmas, Anna was visibly pregnant, and the couple prepared for a second child to join Charles, Earl of Doncaster. Then, as so often in seventeenth-century families, death intervened.

In the late afternoon of Sunday 8 February the secretary of state's ground-floor rooms at Whitehall, directly under the king's great bedchamber, were a hive of activity. Here Arlington's industrious clerks plied parchment and ink preparing the papers of the peace treaty with the Dutch, which was almost ready for the king to sign. Immediately overhead, courtiers and diplomats clattered into the royal apartments to attend the king after his dinner, as was usual on Sunday afternoons. But Charles was not to be found there. Instead he was a stone's throw and a world away in the Monmouths' apartments, sitting with his son and daughter-in-law as they kept a vigil for their eighteen-month-old son, from whose small body the life was draining. At four the following morning the child died. Monmouth was inconsolable. Despite his lack of warmth for Anna, the strength of feeling he had for this little boy expressed his true capacity for love. In the bleak melancholy of the next morning the king put his name to the Treaty of Westminster. Monmouth, shat-tered and sorrow-stricken, was still 'in great affliction for his only son' three days later.[26] But amid the misery he too, with the new lord treasurer, Lord Danby, and the secretaries of state, signed the articles of peace. So it was that on a single day, it seemed, his career had ended and his heart had been broken.

Monmouth's illegitimacy was an irrelevance as the Earl of Doncaster was laid to rest in the Stuart royal vault at Westminster Abbey. His tiny coffin lay with those of Charles II's own brother and sister, whose deaths the king had felt so keenly over a decade before.[27] Sad and worried for his son, Charles felt the need to do something to take Monmouth's mind off his grief. So he sacked the wayward Duke of Buckingham as Master of the Horse and gave the position to Monmouth instead. By the end of April 1674 the new master was exercising his responsibilities.[28]

One of the three most senior court offices, alongside the lord chamberlain and lord steward, and answerable directly to the king, the Master of the Horse had complete responsibility for the royal stables. The role brought with it considerable prestige, including the right to ride beside the king in all processions, and had been held by a string of luminaries – the Earl of Leicester had been Master of the Horse to Queen Elizabeth, the Duke of Buckingham to James I and General Monck to Charles II.[29] But it was also a major court department with serious practical responsibilities and a large budget. Charged with almost all aspects of royal transport, including coaches and carriages, and responsible too for the royal race and hunting horses, it had a standing staff of some 160, among them the royal footmen, grooms, pages and equerries as well as an army of tradesmen and suppliers. The master oversaw the various royal stables, of which the most substantial by far was the Royal Mews at Charing Cross, a vast complex of stalls and hay barns, granaries and riding houses ranged over four red-brick Tudor court-yards that covered almost all of what is now Trafalgar Square. Built largely for Mary Tudor in the 1550s, its enormous outer courtyard was 800 feet wide and 400 feet long, with a horse pond at its centre. North of this were the courtyards known as the 'Green' or 'Upper' mews and to the west the back or 'Dunghill' mews. Almost 300 horses and thirty coaches could be accommodated here, while the buildings also housed a large number of the staff of the office. The Master of the Horse's own house was a new structure of eleven main rooms, standing at the western side of Dunghill Mews with a street front onto Hedge Lane.[30]

Monmouth was an obvious choice for the position and his appointment had been anticipated for almost a year.[31] His own stables had long been a subject of general admiration. Before his first visit to Paris in 1668, they had been formed of some thirty horses and nineteen staff. But on his return he put things on to an altogether different footing, almost doubling the staff and appointing a Gentleman of the Horse, Charles Godfrey, on a salary of £50 to oversee them – displacing his Porter, John Clerke, who had until then been paid just £8 a year for much the same task. The following spring the king agreed Monmouth should have an additional grant of £500 to buy a string of coach horses. Coachmen, postilions and grooms, all dressed in Monmouth's eye-catching yellow livery, made him unmistakable wherever he went. When he travelled by coach the vehicle was accompanied by his liveried footmen running alongside to ensure its smooth passage (footmen would not be indoor servants until a century later).[32]

Monmouth's four young pages were a particularly prominent part of his stables and, like their royal equivalents, they were supposed to 'attend' their master on all public occasions; gentry boys barely in their teens, they were paid a handsome salary for their services. Dressed in yellow riding breeches, silk embroidered stockings bearing Monmouth's cypher and a coronet, with swords at their sides and their hair curled and powdered, they were a picture of elegance and Monmouth delighted in their immaculate appearance.[33] Twelve pairs of shoes and two of boots were allowed each every year, while one Monsieur Pinson was employed to teach them to read and speak French so that they, like their master, would impress their Parisian hosts. Their hair was cut short like Monmouth's own when he visited France for the fete at Versailles that summer, and come the 1670s they too wore the wigs that had become his preference.[34] While Anna was spending months on end in Bath, and their household was partly disbanded, the pages were tutored intensively to improve their writing. They later received dancing and even wrestling lessons.[35] Where Monmouth went his pages followed, travelling with him to Newmarket and Southampton, accompanying him during the Duchesse d'Orléans's visit to Dover, and even wading after him through the waterlogged tunnels at Maastricht.[36]

The duke was a brilliant horseman: his fervour and fearlessness caused falls at first but he soon became an accomplished equestrian.[37] The quality of the grazing at Chiswick and then Moor Park was important to him, and his horses enjoyed the pastures at each and benefited from the cut hay sent to London. Monmouth sought the finest animals from around Europe, using all his contacts to acquire them. In December 1671 the Swedish diplomat Lindenov wrote home anxiously that: 'The duke of Monmouth is asking me often for news regarding his horses. He is in great need of them; for two horses for his bay team have died, and he has been unable to find any of the proper colour to replace them.'[38] Meanwhile, Secretary of State Williamson spent many hours organising the transport of a single horse, given by the Bishop of Strasbourg to Monmouth as a gift.[39]

The Monmouths' Cockpit lodgings at Whitehall, even after their expansion following Albemarle's death, could not begin to accommodate this large equestrian establishment for which rented stables had long been necessary. In the spring of 1673 Monmouth took a hundred-year lease on a piece of ground immediately to the north of the Royal Mews, backing on to the Green Mews, in order to build his own stables and coach houses there, on which work was soon under way.[40] He probably already knew the office of Master of the Horse would come his way, and when it did the fact that his own stables adjoined the Royal Mews only made the office seem all the more made for him.

Monmouth began his tenure as Master of the Horse grieving for his son, but what he found on becoming acquainted with his staff and the workings of the department soon both interested and irritated him enough to propel him into action. Well over 200 horses belonging to the king and queen formed the core of his responsibilities, ninety sporting animals, among them 'Hunting Race[ing] or Running Horses', eighty-two coach horses of various sorts, and around thirty others mostly used in the wagons of the baggage train. The staff responsible for managing them were another matter, however. Monmouth swiftly realised that 'many inferior Tradesmen and Artificers that have noe skill or Experience in keeping, dressing or feeding horses have acquired and procured themselves to be admitted and sworne into Groomes, Littermen, Sumptermen and other places in Our [i.e. the King's] Stables in which they neither have nor can doe service', while a host of people unconnected with the department had taken up residence in the expansive accommodation of the mews.[41]

Two seasons in the French army, Europe's most sophisticated and well-managed military establishment, had taught Monmouth the value of well-run institutions, while Louis XIV's personal interest in administration had shown him that such concerns were not below the dignity of the greatest prince. This was experience Monmouth would bring to bear on the Royal Stables. In his first three months in office he had a detailed post-by-post proposal drawn up for reducing and reordering the staff and management of the department. By the end of June his plan was ready to present to the king. Charles II was delighted with reforms which would both save him money and put his stables in better order. Permission was given for Monmouth to dismiss the unqualified staff, evict the extraneous people living in the mews, reform the allowances for feeding the various categories of horse, and set the royal equestrian establishment on a new footing. A year later the financial arrangements of the department were also restructured.[42]

Assuming the post of Master of the Horse added considerably to the geography of Monmouth's influence. The Royal Mews stood at the top of King Street (today's Whitehall), commanding the road from Westminster to the City as it turned a corner into the Strand, and was made, in effect, larger still by the stables he had built himself on the leased ground to its north. This was now his fiefdom, and the lines between what was his personally and what was 'his' as Master of the Horse were blurred by the unusual entitlement of the master to use the staff and equipment of the departments as his own. To the south of the mews, King Street led to Whitehall Palace and Monmouth's own apartments on the St James's Park side of the palace. Between the palace and the Royal Mews stood another part of his bailiwick, the 'Horse Guards'. One of the most prominent public buildings of the Restoration, it opened onto St James's Park, where an area of open ground was used for drilling and military inspections. This structure was the headquarters of the royal cavalry regiment, of which Monmouth was captain, and had been erected in the mid-1660s, presumably at the instigation of his predecessor Lord Gerard (it would be replaced with the existing building of the same name by William Kent in the 1750s). Though he had turned down major political office, the duke's influence was highly visible and growing fast.[43]

Monmouth may have pored over the paperwork of the Master of the Horse's department with the clerk of the stables, but his new-found industry had not displaced his former self-indulgence; the two simply coexisted.[44] There was no tension for Monmouth between his military reputation – both the daring exploits of the battlefield and the sober management of men and money – and the dress and deportment of a dandy. Amid the discomfort and danger of the French campaigns, he had fitted in an impressive amount of shopping. On his return to England for the birth of his first son in August 1672, he had brought with him over £2,000 of Parisian furniture and plate. Among this assemblage were fourteen cases containing bedding alone and a magnificent silver looking-glass with accompanying silver pier stands. Customs officials opened just one box of another consignment from Paris in October 1672 to find that it contained 'an embroidered suit with silver and gold, and another of silke, a peruque [a wig], a hat, a gold sword, four pair of shoes and another hat'. As for Anna, the bill for customs and carriage alone for the clothes she bought in Paris that autumn was almost £150.[45]

Though they shared a love of luxury goods, Monmouth and Anna's relationship remained at best uneasy. Anna was no doormat; now in her mid-twenties she had lost her shyness and had become both sharp and politically aware. Not content simply to bow to her husband's will, and with Moor Park to herself, she became increasingly independent. After dining with Monmouth and Anna at Lord Arlington's in 1673, John Evelyn noted that 'she is one of wisest & craftiest of her sex'. Her awareness of 'her oune affaires' was probably behind the arrangements laid by Sir Stephen Fox when Monmouth went to fight the Maastricht campaign. As Monmouth was dodging the bullets, Fox was procuring the king's agreement to a generous financial settlement for Anna and her issue in the event of the duke's death. It was a provision for which she would one day have reason to be grateful.[46]

Anna and Monmouth had fallen out in 1672, but he had become 'friend[s] now again with his wife' just before Charles had been born that summer.[47] The boy's death was a tragedy they shared, as they shared the birth in May 1674 of the child they had conceived immediately after his return from Maastricht. Another son, he was christened James, after both his father and great-uncle, and assumed the titles of his dead sibling.[48] A gossipy account of life at the English court in the mid-1670s, though unreliable in detail, captures the essence of the Monmouths' relationship: 'Marriages thus arranged are not always happy; in fact it was the duke's idea only to observe conventional decencies with his Wife & as she was very proud it was easy for her to discover her husband's sentiments. Thus her own affections chilled; & she contended herself on her side in performing her duty without making any display of tenderness.'[49]

Monmouth showed Anna little warmth or tenderness, and she – with an imperious sense of both the ancient title she held in her own right and her status as daughter-in-law to a king – was certainly not going to stoop to seek them. The truth was that Monmouth's appetite for affection was already satisfied, not by his wife, nor even by his mistresses, but by his father. The family he felt part of was not that born of his marriage, but that which his relationship with the king placed him among. If there was one thing every observer of the age agreed upon it was the strength of the king's love for Monmouth. He was, of course, not the king's only illegitimate child. Since the restoration Monmouth had acquired numerous half-siblings: four from his father's affair with Barbara Castlemaine (three sons and a daughter), two from Nell Gwyn, and in 1672 Louise de Keroualle, a French lady-in-waiting who had come to Dover with the Duchess of Orléans, had given Charles II a further son. Added to this host, a fifteen-year-old boy had arrived in England in 1672 and was acknowledged by the king as another son born during the exile, the result of an affair with Catherine Pegge. Known as Don Carlos, he was created Earl of Plymouth in 1674. To all these children the king felt and showed fondness, especially when they were very young and his interest in their mothers still alive. But Monmouth was different, both in his position and in the strength of the king's attachment to him.

When a few years later John Dryden wrote his epic poem *Absalom and Achitophel*, in which Charles II appeared as King David and Monmouth as his son Absalom, he gave his own account of their relationship. Monmouth's good looks and irrepressible energy made him shine more brightly than any of the king's other children: 'Of all his numerous progeny were none / So beautiful, so brave as Absalom.' The king's love for Monmouth was, in Dryden's interpretation, a hankering for his own youth: 'With secret joy, indulgent David view'd / His youthful image in his son renew'd.'[50] There was certainly something in this: Monmouth was a younger and better-looking version of the king himself. The eighteen years between them were no longer such a gulf. By the 1670s Monmouth was in his twenties and the king had only just turned forty. The two could and did enjoy one another's company as friends. They shared energy and appetites: for company and carousing, for riding and dancing, hunting and sailing. That said, Charles was always at heart a father to Monmouth before he was a friend. While the king's own infidelity was famous, he pressed his son to be more attentive to his wife, and on the one occasion when their seductions actually crossed he was visibly shaken.

Monmouth's angelic appearance and spirited personality as a child had first lodged him in the king's affections. The wording used by the king in granting his son's dukedom six months after his arrival in England had given a sense of it, describing him as 'a young man of the highest promise, whose uncommon abilities. . . and whose very early maturity of understanding and suavity of manners are sufficiently well known to us'. But already the king's sense of responsibility towards the boy was palpable; in his own words Charles felt 'an anxious concern' that Monmouth should receive everything 'that may act as a spur and incitement to him'.[51]

Monmouth, for his part, reciprocated. His father was his north star: protector, supporter, friend and sponsor. He both loved and respected Charles, addressing him always with deferential formality and never disobeying an instruction. Charles's affection was apparently limitless, but Monmouth had not become careless of it. Instead he began, in his twenties, to realise how fortunate he was, writing to Charles that 'all that I will troubell you w[i]th now is to desier the continuans of yr Matys kindnes wch I shall ever try to deserve'. He was anxious to please and amuse one who had a quick mind and wit. From Maastricht he had sent his father a curious historic medal that had been discovered when the trenches were being dug, which he knew would interest him. He ended his letter with an impish sign-off: 'I hope your Maty will pardon mee for troubling of you w[i]th so long a letter but tis a faught [fault] that I am not often g[u]ilty of therfore may bee easeur pardon.'[52]

While all Charles II's other children had living mothers who protected and educated them and fought for their status and financial security, Monmouth had lost his when he had been kidnapped fifteen years earlier. It may be that a sense of accountability for the boy's loss was part of the subtle cocktail of Charles's love. But whatever its genesis, from the moment the boy had taken up lodgings by the Privy Stairs at Whitehall the king had been both mother and father to him. Charles felt himself responsible for Monmouth in a way he never did for his other children. When he had sent him to Henriette Anne in Paris in 1668 he trilled indulgently to her of the child's appearance and behaviour, always calling him 'James' and remarking with wry understatement that 'you may easily guess that I am some thing concerned for this bearer James'. As Monmouth reached adulthood the king's affection deepened rather than diminished; in the words of the Duke of York: 'as he [Monmouth] grew up the King's kindness increased'. Motherlessness was proving a positive advantage. With no cast-off mistress to complicate or cool their relationship, Monmouth and Charles could revel unfettered in their intimacy.[53]

Charles II's idea of fatherhood was unconventional and Monmouth had known next to nothing of paternal discipline and rules, but he nonetheless showed all the characteristics of a doting parent. He was protective and demonstrative, he spoiled Monmouth and took disproportionate pride in any achievement, and whatever his son's shortcomings they could not lessen his love. Unlike the passion that might be felt for a mistress or a court 'favourite', what Charles felt for Monmouth was not the finite and mutable passion of a lover, or even the enduring fondness and affection of a sibling, but the boundless and unbreakable love of a parent for a child.

Chapter 9

Care But Not Command

At Windsor the Thames briefly diverges from its east–west course to loop suddenly north and then south again, leaving a tongue of low-lying meadow reaching away from the great rocky ledge on which the castle stands. Part of the 'little' hunting park of medieval Windsor, it is now known as the Home Park and is peppered with the pavilions and parking spaces of the Windsor Cricket Club. Here over five days in the summer of 1674 the Duke of Monmouth would lead an extraordinary theatrical extravaganza which caused this patch of pastoral Berkshire to be known for centuries after as Maastricht.

The political struggle which followed the Duke of York's resignation as lord high admiral was a real one and the king felt its pressure. In the stand-off between king and Parliament in the autumn of 1673 boundaries which would become political battle lines had been drawn between an anti-Catholic Parliament and a king determined to uphold the principle of hereditary succession even though it would bring a Catholic to the English throne for the first time since Mary Tudor. The degree to which the situation worried the king was revealed by a marked change in how the court operated in the spring of 1674. The confirmation of the Duke of York's daughters as Anglicans took place in January 1674, and then in April, just before Easter, the king announced that the entire court would go to Windsor Castle for St George's Day and remain there for the rest of the summer. This was highly significant. As yet the crumbling medieval castle had been very little used by Charles II. Only three Garter Feasts had been held here – among them that in 1663 when Monmouth had been installed as a Knight of the Garter. Additionally the king had made a small number of overnight stays whilst hunting in the surrounding landscape. But the court as a whole had never 'removed' to Windsor. The royal family had spent previous summers at Whitehall with odd weeks at Hampton Court and September progresses in southern England. Now, however, Charles decided to move the court out of London, and in so doing away from the crowds who showed their anti-Catholic feelings so loudly through bell ringing and bonfires, and away from his increasingly troubled relationship with Parliament. Windsor was beset by no such bothersome neighbours and was big and splendid enough to accommodate everyone.

Here, during the court's hundred-day stay at Windsor in the summer of 1674, an epic re-enactment of the siege of Maastricht was staged. Designed 'to celebrate the memory of that Glorious Action and gratifie the active Gallantry of divers brave Spirits', it must have been the king's initiative, since Monmouth's own attitude to the siege remained ambivalent. If ever the pride of a father was expressed in actions it was in this great theatrical event. A 'fort' was specially built at the foot of the terrace of the castle 'representing the aforesaid Garrison of Mastrick'. Measuring about eighty yards square it had walls twelve feet thick, topped by cannon, and was encircled by a moat and counterscarp and garrisoned by 500 men. The exercise, which took place over five days, was for the 'city' to be captured by a force commanded by Monmouth and the Duke of York. As had been the case in reality, the attack was oblique, from the east, and the two dukes started excavating their trenches some 300 yards from their target. Seven hundred men, all serving soldiers, formed the besieging force and on Friday 14 August they started attacking under 'fire' of the defending garrison. On Saturday, York erected a bastion, only to be beaten out of it by the defending force, while the culmination came on Tuesday when in a long day's full-frontal assault the attackers took the 'city'.

The whole re-enactment was watched not just by the king and court, but by waves of spectators who came from London to view the 'mock siege' and who told their friends of developments – ''tis reported that the Duke of Monmouth is taken prisoner' wrote one gripped contemporary to a country friend on day four. The finale was spectacular. John Evelyn recorded how: 'Great gunns fir'd on both sides, Granados shot, mines Sprung, parties sent out, attempts of raising the siege, prisoners taken, Parlies & in short all the Circumstances of a formal siege.' The fortress fell as the stars came out, after which the thousand or so spectators drifted home. Evelyn shared a coach to London with his friend Samuel Pepys, who agreed 'it made a formidable shew'.[1]

That the Duke of York participated wholeheartedly in this theatrical celebration of Monmouth's campaign is striking. He must have known that his nephew had declined the Scottish commissionership, and in his enthusiastic participation in the Maastricht re-enactment he was perhaps showing his gratitude. Or put less generously, York could live with Monmouth the military hero; it was Monmouth the figure of political weight that he feared. The decision that Monmouth made in the autumn of 1673 to decline political high office led him to take on a collection of significant but less politically charged positions that would define his professional existence for the next four years.

As his approach to the Mastership of the Horse had suggested, Monmouth was showing genuine aptitude for managing people and activities, which came as something of a surprise to those who had known him in the 1660s. He would go on to bring to almost all his significant roles an appetite for reform. He would also show genuine concern for the people with whom he worked. A bright streak of compassion and humanity was being revealed in the duke, which stood in stark contrast to his youthful reputation for casual violence. This was born of a new respect for his fellow men learned away from the ribaldry and cynicism of the court, and of the maturity which his growing years and responsibilities had brought.

While he would accumulate many offices, the mainstay of Monmouth's career would be the army. The peculiar terms of the Treaty of Westminster meant that the regiment of the Royal English, of which Monmouth was colonel, was to continue to fight for Louis XIV in a war from which England had now extracted itself. This eccentric arrangement made it impossible for Monmouth to rejoin his men and left him the difficult task of commanding a regiment at arm's length. The troops he had left behind in July 1673 had been sorry to see their commanding officer leave, partly because it meant they were without a protector, but also because his conduct, both personal and military, had won their affection. As Sir William Lockhart put it, on the day he left, 'their are many vowes made for his happy and speedy returne'.[2] Lockhart himself, an English diplomat, and James Vernon, the talented private secretary to Sunderland, Charles II's ambassador to France, had each observed Monmouth with growing admiration during that campaign, and both would afterwards enter his service. A warm and appreciative ally when it came to those he respected, Monmouth had sent a special despatch to the king from Maastricht to sing Lockhart's praises: 'I forgott to tell your Maty that Sr William lokard was wth me in the trenches and I find him a pone all occassions the readist in the world to serve mee and I do assur you sr hee dos his businss heer very well.' Lockhart for his part was so swept along with the charismatic young duke that the fifty-two-year-old retired soldier had followed him into the trenches without even a breastplate.[3]

When Monmouth realised he could not rejoin the French army, he asked Lockhart to take 'care of my concerns of my regiments in France'. But although Lockhart himself was a seasoned soldier, Monmouth had a much keener concern for his men than the older man. One of the issues that worried him was their winter pay, which the French had failed to remit. He instructed Lockhart to go in person to see Louvois, Louis XIV's war minister, whilst also sending his own plea: 'I beg you to have the kindness to cause the arrears of half-pay to be paid us. . . that the officers may employ it for supplying each company with what is necessary for the winter.'

It would not be until March that the money finally materialised and then, concerned it would not be fairly apportioned, Monmouth asked to examine the regiment's account books.[4]

In dealing with his senior military officers the duke showed compassion and empathy even at one remove. When Louis XIV dismissed Henry Staniers, one of the English officers, Monmouth wrote asking him to reconsider as it was damaging not only to Staniers's 'honour but his fortune, since he had never learned any employment but that of a soldier'. Instances of personal kindness towards even those who had not behaved well would recur. On discharging an officer Monmouth added gently: 'I would not have you discouraged or surprised, for I am very well satisfied you have behaved on all occasions as became you.' After his regiment was involved in the battle of Strasbourg, he dispatched a series of personal letters to his officers, among them John Churchill, now a colonel himself. He concluded them simply: 'I own myself a debtor to every individual person that performed his duty on that occasion.'[5]

Alongside this deep sense of responsibility for his regiment was a determination to improve its effectiveness. Though Monmouth had won personal accolades when the Royal English first joined the French army in 1672, Louis XIV had made no secret of his 'dissatisfaction over the slight service rendered by the English, who are undisciplined and their commanders lack experience'. The sting of rebuke remained and Monmouth resolved to remedy it. In 1675 he drew up a code of conduct for his men covering military discipline, sobriety and personal behaviour. In addition he changed the financial arrangements to prevent the embezzlement of funds issued for recruitment.[6] Despite his own immense personal extravagance, he became hawk-eyed about financial management in his regiments, in particular in ensuring his men were promptly paid. When one of his captains, Robert Ramsay, presented incomplete accounts, Monmouth rebuked him sternly: 'I expected that the Major at his coming over should have brought with him the whole account of the regiment, that I might have known its condition. . . I can't but look on it as a great neglect that it should not be done in all this time and I expect it to be sent over by the first opportunity.'[7]

Keen to feed his son's appetite for work, and aware of his frustration at the mismanagement of military matters, in January 1674 the king gave Monmouth a new role with the aim of 'initiating him into business'. The job, which 'has as yet no name', gave him shadow oversight of the whole army, not just his own regiments. He was to make 'an inspection into all things relating to the forces now on foot' and to approve all army paperwork before it was passed to the king for signature. The arrangement was to be in the nature of an apprenticeship, and implicit in it was the promise of some more formal role in the future.[8]

With the concept of a permanent army still novel, there was little established practice in the business of who actually ran it. George Monck, Duke of Albemarle, had unquestionably been head of Charles II's army in the 1660s, and was styled 'captain general' or just 'general'. Arguably, however, the title had been personal to Monck, and on his death, in January 1670, it was not reissued. Instead the king declared he would sign all important military documents himself while the administration of the army became, in effect, an additional responsibility of the secretary of state. In the spring of 1673, before his resignation, the Duke of York had been given the exotic title *generalissimo*, but had stepped down from his offices before it was clear exactly what this was to have meant.[9]

Monmouth was therefore 'intrusted with the care tho' not the command' of the army at time when there was no more senior English army officer on the scene. As Monmouth's interest and ability became obvious successive secretaries of state were only too happy to let him take on the real work.[10] Though he was still only in his mid-twenties, two seasons spent on campaign had given him as much recent experience as any senior officer in England, and this he brought to the role. Administration was a dry enough business on its own, but having witnessed first-hand the consequences of administrative negligence, he knew its value. When letters arrived from his regiments complaining there was 'not one bit of bread

left, we having so many hungry souls to feed', there was no question of this being a simple matter of bureaucracy.[11] Already by the
end of the year, the duke's role was passing from apprenticeship to
actuality.[12]

As with his efforts with his own regiments, Monmouth brought
to the army as a whole a determination to improve order and effectiveness. In December 1675 he published 'An Abridgement of the
English Military Discipline'. A practical guide for senior army
officers, it covered a miscellany of topics including the proper form
of drills, marching, salutes, presenting arms, setting up camps and
aspects of siege warfare. In his new capacity Monmouth also began
to explore better formal arrangements for injured soldiers. Having
struggled to find positions for disabled servicemen, he knew just
how unsatisfactory existing arrangements were. It must have seemed
yet another example of how poorly the English army measured up
to its French equivalent. After all he had watched the masons toiling
on the massive walls of Louis XIV's palatial hospital for injured
soldiers, Les Invalides, on the walls of which Monmouth was personally depicted. In 1677, if not well before, Monmouth raised with
his father the notion of a comparable British foundation, a royal
hospital for wounded soldiers. Charles showed some interest, and
Monmouth wrote to Louvois asking him to send over 'the plan of
the Hotel des Invalides drawn with all the fronts, for the King will
be very glad to see it'. It was soon public knowledge that Monmouth
wanted his father to build a hospital and that Charles was enthusiastic. But the funds were not easily available and the project stalled.
One enterprising consortium who sought a licence to build an insur-
ance office offered the incentive of a fifth of their projected profits
for 'the Duke of Monmouth towards the maintenance of a hospital
to be shortly erected by the King'. While this particular ruse did
not work, Monmouth's financial adviser Sir Stephen Fox eventually
came up with a plan which did, and on 17 February 1682 Charles II
laid the foundation stone of the Royal Hospital at Chelsea.[13]

By the summer of 1676 all the regular army regiments were taking
their orders from the Duke of Monmouth and the king added

to his responsibilities a wider operational brief, which included army billeting.[14] But to make clear that, despite appearances to the contrary, this was still not the Duke of Albemarle's old role as captain general the king added weakly that he would continue to issue personally 'some kinds of warrants and military orders which belonged to the office of the late General'.[15]

Given Monmouth's obvious ability as the head of the army, it was, on the face of it, strange that he had not been made its captain general. But once again the stumbling block was the Duke of York. When Monmouth had asked York whether he would support his request to the king to be made general, York turned him down. Monmouth explained the difficulty he faced in having responsibility for the army without actually being the senior commanding officer: there was always a risk the troops would refuse to follow his orders. It was not an unreasonable point, and instances of officers ignoring Monmouth's instructions would occur.[16] But York was unshakable, arguing first that Monmouth was already the most senior officer, as Captain of the Life Guards, and so could give orders anyway. He then changed tack to argue, instead, that there was no need for a general in peacetime. After a further discussion with Monmouth on the question, York ended with a tight-lipped summation: 'He would never speak to the King about it, nor consent there should be any general, as it was a post not fit for any body in the time of peace.' York's objections were not without substance, but they were not ones in which he really believed. The truth was that he did not want Monmouth doing a job he felt should be nobody's if not his own. It was at this moment, as York would freely admit a few years later, that his jealousy was truly unleashed.[17]

While the army was the centre of Monmouth's professional life during the mid-1670s, this was not to the exclusion of his other interests, personal or professional. On 11 July 1674, Charles II had written to Cambridge University declaring the Duke of Buckingham's tenure as chancellor over, and suggesting in an insistent tone that they choose in his place 'our dearly beloved son James Duke of Monmouth'.[18] Two weeks later, Monmouth was unanimously elected.

The appointment as chancellor of Cambridge University of a royal bastard, who had, at best, a patchy education, was bound to provoke comment. Acutely aware of this, Monmouth's first letter to the vice-chancellor was laced with apology. He expressed gratitude for 'y[ou]r famous university's ready complyance and expedition in my election', and pledged to do everything in his power to serve them, ending, with gentle self-deprecation, that 'I shall always appear more a friend to that Renowned body then an orator.'[19] If some at the university dismissed such language as courtly convention, they were soon surprised. When its senior officers waited on Monmouth at Hampton Court they came away delighted. The duke, one wrote, had received them with real warmth and sincerity and when they mentioned that they had a letter for the king, Monmouth 'imediately replied that he would bring the king into the next room, which his Grace immediately did where I had the honor to kisse the king's hand on my knees'.[20]

It was in connection with his inauguration as Chancellor of Cambridge that Monmouth sat for a painting which would come to play a powerful part in his celebrity.[21] The work was a full-length portrait in Garter robes that was to hang in the Regent House, the home of the university's governing body. The artist chosen was the anglicised Dutchman Peter Lely, a favourite of the Duke of York. The work was a dazzling image of Monmouth not as a soldier, but tall and graceful as the premier courtier and aristocrat who would enhance the university's own splendour. Just before the king's visit on 4 October 1674, the painting was completed and taken to Cambridge, where it was duly hung.[22]

Only a decade after the king viewed this masterful depiction of his son, Lely's gorgeous canvas would be torn from the wall and burned in the street before a crowd of spectators. Yet despite its early destruction, the painting remains well known, because the moment it was finished Lely found he had a lucrative trade in supplying copies. Just how many the artist himself produced and how many more versions were done by other artists is unknown. However, even though others must also have been destroyed, at least nineteen versions in oil, either full or half length, survive in Britain today.

Among those commissioning copies of Lely's portrait was Monmouth himself. Eighteen months later, in the early months of 1676, Lely was paid a hefty £75 for a version for Monmouth to present to Nell Gwyn. By 1676 the former actress, now retired from the stage, was living comfortably in the house the king had bought her on Pall Mall, which looked towards Whitehall across St James's Park. She had had two sons by the king and he had granted her £4,000 a year to support them. In August 1674, as Monmouth and York attacked the mock 'Maastricht', the king had distributed a host of titles among his children: his eldest son with Barbara, now Duchess of Cleveland, was made Earl of Northumberland; his son with Louise de Keroualle, now Duchess of Portsmouth, was made Duke of Richmond; and Don Carlos was made Earl of Plymouth. The simultaneous marriage that month of the king and Barbara's two daughters to newly enno-bled bridegrooms may have been the spur. Smarting with indignation at all this largesse was Nell Gwyn, whose own son remained without a surname or title. She lobbied the king hard for remedy, and looked to Monmouth for support. He overshadowed all his siblings from his unassailable place in the king's affections. But as he was not the child of a rival mistress he did not represent a direct threat to his siblings' mothers. Indeed the fact that he had received the highest honours from the king set a precedent which they argued should be followed. With Monmouth her ally, Nell won the king over and her son was created Earl of Burford in December 1676. The friendship she devel-oped with Monmouth would be important and she would ever after count herself his supporter and champion.[23]

If Monmouth's growing influence was expressed in the number of portraits Peter Lely found himself churning out, so his contin-uing closeness to both the king and the Duke of York – despite the pressures – was given visual expression. In 1676 the Dutch engraver Abraham Blooteling, who worked in London and Amsterdam, produced a trio of large mezzotints of Monmouth, Charles II and the Duke of York, regarded still as among the greatest works in the medium of the age. The three images were the same size, double the usual size of contemporary prints, and each was based on a portrait by Lely. They must have been created with royal approval – thus may even have been a royal commission – and depict Monmouth and York as equals without any emblems or insignia to distinguish between the heir to the throne and the bastard. When a new warship *The Royal James* was launched in July 1675 Monmouth and York travelled to Portsmouth together to attend its inauguration. As the two dukes looked on, it would have been hard to say for sure which one was the real 'royal James'.[24]

York certainly now felt threatened by his nephew, he had blocked his promotion in the army, and in 1676–77 he also saw off suggestions that Monmouth should be made lord lieutenant of Ireland.[25] But, remarkably, Monmouth's loyalty to his uncle still held. He showed no signs of resentment, indeed the two were, on the face of it, as close as ever. Often forming a threesome with the king, they spent long days inspecting docks, hunting together in the home counties and taking river excursions in the royal barge.[26] In August 1675, with the court at Windsor, the Duchess of Monmouth invited the Yorks and the two princesses for a picnic at Cranbourne Lodge in the Windsor hunting park: 'They din'd in fresco abroad in ye fields under trees, & spent ye afternoone in gentle recreations, as cards, walking & ye like, but after supper her R[oyal] H[ighness] and ye young company diverted ymselves with dancing & made it pretty late before they came home.'[27]

In the winter of 1676 when a thick fall of snow turned Whitehall white, the royal family spilled out into St James's Park to play together as affectionately as any in the kingdom. Mary Beatrice, Duchess of York, still in her teens, was 'much delighted' and pelted her husband with snowballs. He gave chase and she tore into the palace and down the galleries until he finally caught up with her in the furthest room of their apartment. Monmouth meanwhile rigged up a special horse-drawn sledge, which he alone could master, and thundered across the icy park at great speed drawing behind him first Mary Beatrice, and then the king himself. Ever the daredevil, he rode his horse the length of the frozen canal though no one believed the ice could hold.[28] Despite their great difference in age, Mary Beatrice and the Duke of York had quickly become fond of one another, and at seventeen she gave birth to her first child, Catherine Laura. York chose Monmouth alongside his daughters, Princesses Mary and Anne, as her godparents. When their second daughter Isabella was born the following year, Anna, Duchess of Monmouth, was godmother.[29]

As Monmouth's intimacy with his father's family held, there appeared from the shadows a vivid reminder of his mother. Monmouth had last seen his sister, Mary, when he was barely eight years old and she no more than four. When Lucy Walter had died in 1658 her daughter was adopted by the man who was almost certainly the girl's father, the boisterous Irish soldier Theobald Taaffe, soon to become Earl of Carlingford. Mary would re-emerge in the early 1670s as a member of his household in Ireland, her expenses supplemented by an allowance from Charles II.[30] Shortly before 1672 she married one of Carlingford's Fermanagh neighbours, William Sarsfield of Tully Castle. Keen to exploit his new wife's famous family, Sarsfield took Mary to London and through Thomas Ross and the king's groom of the bedchamber Edward Progers (who as agents in Monmouth's kidnap had known Mary as an infant) inveigled his way into the duke's presence. We cannot know what precisely he felt on being reintroduced to someone who been part of the bittersweet and now infinitely remote life they led before their mother's death, but his actions were expressive.

Having been lobbied by his new brother-in-law, Monmouth spoke to the king, who agreed to grant the young couple his old family estate of Lucan on the outskirts of Dublin. This was done on the explicit understanding it would be settled on Mary and the two children she had quickly borne her husband – whose names, Charles and Charlotte, were a blatant expression of the royal connections Sarsfield sought to exploit. Monmouth further arranged for William's younger brother, Patrick, to be given a commission in the Royal

English regiment in France and took another relative into his own service. But the Sarsfields were a bad lot and as soon as William had his hands on the property he plundered it for its value, reneging on the agreement. Monmouth, appalled, tried to stop the transfer, but before he could post the letter he received the unexpected news that his disreputable brother-in-law had died of smallpox. Mary, rescued from her husband, was now at the mercy of her in-laws and Monmouth was genuinely worried about her welfare. He passed his concern on to the king, and when the king ordered that she be given an allowance of 600 guineas a year, it was to be done quickly as 'it will set his Ma[jes]ty much at ease to have her settled'. The following year Mary married William Fanshawe, son of a respectable English gentry family, and the couple took up residence in St James's, a stone's throw from Whitehall where William Fanshawe would hold the position of Master of Requests. It would prove a much happier match, though the wrangling over the Sarsfield lands would never abate.[31]

Monmouth's growing stature and influence did not stem his sexual appetite, and if anything it made him an all the more appealing target for gossips and satirists. In March 1676 George Etherege's seminal Restoration comedy *The Man of Mode* was first performed at the Duke's Theatre in its magnificent new Thames front premises at Dorset Gardens. The plot saw the lead character, the fashionable rake Dorimant, attempt the seduction of a young gentlewoman recently arrived in London, whilst trying to shed a long-standing mistress and incidentally taking another – all amid a tangle of affairs and amours between a variety of thinly veiled court caricatures. It was instantly the talk of the town, with everyone attempting to identify the characters. Peter Killigrew, who attended the first night, gave his sister a detailed account and declared that 'Dorimant means the Duke of Monmouth', citing his 'intrigues' with three women as evidence: Moll Kirke, Eleanor Needham and Lady Henrietta Wentworth.[32]

Mary, or Moll, Kirke had been Monmouth's 'newest mistress' in October 1674 but, to his irritation, she had soon moved on to the Earl of Mulgrave. The daughter of Mary Townsend, a famous courtesan of the 1640s, and the Keeper of Whitehall Palace, George Kirke, Mary was a born courtier. When she was abandoned, pregnant, by Mulgrave the following year, her brother Percy, who had a commission in Monmouth's regiment, challenged the earl to a duel for having so 'debauch'd & abus'd his sister'. Monmouth's trusted lieutenant and master of the horse Captain Charles Godfrey was Kirke's second, and her return to respectability, through her marriage in 1677 to Sir Thomas Vernon of Hodnet, may well have been orchestrated by Monmouth's secretary James Vernon. So while Mary Kirke may have jilted Monmouth, he helped her when she needed it most.[33]

Less fleeting was Eleanor Needham, whose sister Jane was also a famous beauty. As she was unmarried and held a position as a maid of honour to the Duchess of York, the pregnancies in which the affair resulted had to be handled discreetly. In August 1675, 'having managed an intrigue of love with his Grace ye D. of Monmouth a little too grossly', she disappeared from court. A few weeks later she was 'catched abroad' with the duke, but was thought likely to return shortly – presumably after the child had been born.[34] Though there is little to indicate the relationship was a grand passion, Monmouth ensured Eleanor was comfortably set up in a house on Russell Street in Bloomsbury and the children bore the name 'Crofts', as he had once done. One daughter, Henrietta, would grow up to marry the future Duke of Bolton.[35]

The third name mentioned in the context of Monmouth's amours in March 1676 was a new one: Lady Henrietta Wentworth. Not quite sixteen, she was the daughter of the royalist Lord Wentworth who had been with Charles II in exile, and had first met Monmouth at court the previous year. Her resemblance to 'Harriet Woodvill', the dignified heroine of Etherege's play, was striking. Quite unlike the comely courtesans Monmouth had so far been drawn to, Henrietta was a poised and independent-minded young noblewoman. Now she caught his eye. In time she would be the love of his life.

Chapter 10

The Ties Begin to Break

The elegant figure of the twenty-six-year-old James, Duke of Monmouth, strode purposefully across the boarded floor of the House of Lords on Tuesday 13 April 1675, his long frame made taller still by the high red heels on his immaculate white shoes. It was the start of the new parliamentary session and the chamber was crammed. Sitting on the long red benches were almost ninety peers, all draped, like Monmouth, in voluminous crimson parliamentary robes lined with white taffeta. The oblong chamber itself was smaller and plainer than its modern-day successor and with its high walls lit only by dormers in the vaulted ceiling it had a gloomy, almost cavernous, atmosphere. The walls themselves were cloaked to the ground in tapestries depicting the defeat of the Spanish Armada, over which candle sconces dangled, glimmering with dim additional light. Hidden behind the white coffering of the plastered barrel vault erected fifty years before was a medieval roof, as the chamber was, like all the buildings at Westminster, a remnant of the medieval palace that had been abandoned by Henry VIII after a fire in 1512.

Tightly packed on the benches against the long right-hand wall were the senior noblemen in ascending order of precedence. Chief among them, and so closest to the throne, were the Duke of York and Prince Rupert. Monmouth took his place here, with Rupert on his right hand and the two non-royal dukes on his left, each bearing four stripes of ermine on his sleeve. Below the dukes were the earls. Here sat the king's chief minister, Danby, his long thigh almost touching the short limb of his adversary, the diminutive and determined Lord Shaftesbury, both with three ermine stripes. The barons with their two stripes sat in the benches across the centre of the room. Opposite, either side of the flat marbled fireplace, were the dozen clergymen, bishops and archbishops dressed in sober black and white without the luscious curling wigs of the peers. First among them was the half-blind seventy-seven-year-old Archbishop of Canterbury, Gilbert Sheldon. In the middle of the room the judges perched on the large upholstered seat known as the woolsack, while the clerks who carefully noted all proceedings faced the throne. At the far, high end of the room was the dais on which the royal throne stood, shaded by a canopy of state embroidered with the royal arms and suspended by thick ropes from either side of the room.

When all the peers had assembled the door opened and in trooped the heralds in their playing-card tabards signalling the arrival of the king. Also dressed in red and white robes, he wore the solid gold crown of state encrusted with large coloured gems, which glinted in the gloom. After prayers and the admission of new peers the members of the House of Commons were summoned from their larger chamber in the former St Stephen's Chapel. The MPs, dressed in civilian clothing rather than robes of state, crammed into the room at the low end, held back by a wooden rail, and here they stood to hear their sovereign's speech. There had been no general election since 1661, so these were members of the same group of 538 men who had been elected over fourteen years earlier in the heady early days of the Restoration. Charles II cleared his throat and began reading: 'My Lords and Gentlemen,' he opened. 'The principal end of my calling you now is to know what you think may be yet wanting to the securing of religion and property, and to give myself the satisfaction of having used the uttermost of my endeavours to procure and settle a right and lasting understanding between us.'[1]

These conciliatory words, which seemed to promise the defensive religious policies which the bishops and many of the rank-and-file

MPs sought, were carefully chosen. The stand-off between an anti-Catholic Parliament and a king determined to uphold the principle of hereditary monarchy had put Charles and his ministers in a tricky position. They could not afford simply to ignore Parliament, as they needed the taxes it alone could agree. Furthermore the bad feeling between the government and Parliament risked spilling out of the chambers of the Palace of Westminster into the streets, and this both represented a threat to public order and carried worrying echoes of the events of his own father's reign just thirty years before. The new prime minister, the Earl of Danby, saw he needed to keep Parliament happy if the government was to function, which involved promoting anti-Catholic measures and drawing back from France – and the wording of the speech was chosen to allude to this. Having completed his address the king left the chamber and the session began.[2]

The appeasing tone taken by the king was spectacularly short-lived. At the head of the legislation the government sought to promote was 'A bill to prevent dangers from disaffected persons', or 'Danby's Test' as it would come to be known. This would require all office-holders, including member of the Commons and Lords, to swear an oath not to 'endeavour to make any alteration in church or state'.[3] Danby saw it as a way of promoting Anglican conformity, and so pleasing the Anglican high command and the parliamentary rank and file, but it was also designed to strengthen the authority of the government. But while any measures that might further prosecute or exclude Catholics had widespread appeal, the proposed bill was regarded by many as a fundamental assault on parliamentary liberties. The conventional formality of thanking the king for his speech gave way to furious exchanges as a group of peers, among them the Earl of Shaftesbury, demanded that the clerks record their objections to a 'Manner of Proceeding not so suitable with the Liberty of Debate necessary to this House'.[4] Over the following weeks in a series of long sittings the bill was debated and widely condemned as 'most destructive of the Freedom which they ought to enjoy as Members of Parliament'. In the end, sensing defeat, the government quietly let it drop.

This was not the only cause for conflict in the short session. The Commons almost immediately asked the king to dismiss the Duke of Lauderdale, his chief minister in Scotland, whose heavy-handed ways were causing resentment, as 'a Person obnoxious and dangerous to the Government', before going on to propose that the prime minister himself be impeached for various trumped-up crimes.[5] By early June the king had had enough and adjourned Parliament until October. When it reassembled things had become worse still, not least because the Duke of York had now stopped attending Anglican services. At his opening speech the king set out his bargain explicitly: he would support measures for 'the security' of Protestantism, and in return they were to grant funds for building ships. But again the meeting was not successful, Shaftesbury got into a number of heated rows in the Lords, in which 'angry words' were exchanged. Finally the king lost his temper and prorogued Parliament, declaring that it need not meet again for more than a year.[6]

Throughout the long and bad-tempered sessions in the spring and autumn of 1675 the faultless figure of James, Duke of Monmouth, was regularly to be seen on the peers' benches. He attended twenty-seven of the forty-four days that the house sat in the spring session, and was in his seat for all the major discussions of 'Danby's Test', hearing at close quarters the speeches and expostulations of the emerging opposition.[7] The proposed legislation seemed to confirm growing suspicions about the government's intentions. These Shaftesbury would articulate in an anonymous pamphlet published that autumn in which he argued that the government was intent on emasculating Parliament and introducing an autocracy into England, which would see the people enslaved and monarchy and episcopacy become unassailable.[8] But if Monmouth felt any sympathy for Lord Shaftesbury and his colleagues he certainly did not show it. His presence was a statement of loyalty, to his father, who attended almost every debate, and to his regime. Moreover he had a professional interest in the session, as the future of his regiment, the Royal English, still fighting for the despised king of France, was being hotly debated in the Commons.

While the Treaty of Westminster of January 1674 had seen Charles II agree a peace with the Dutch, they and the French remained very much at war. Louis XIV had been forced to abandon all his territorial gains from the campaign in which Monmouth had fought, retaining only Maastricht itself. Yet, despite this, he was as determined as ever to devour his north-eastern neighbours, especially the Spanish Netherlands. For Charles II the years between 1674 and 1677 would see a tug of war in which the English Parliament urged the king to join forces with the Protestant Dutch to help them defeat Louis XIV, while the French, on the other side, anxious to prevent this, offered Charles II substantial financial incentives if he agreed not to call Parliament. Charles II's natural sympathies remained with the French, and though in the parliamentary session of 1675 the government agreed that those men who had joined up since January 1674 should be brought home, Monmouth's regiment remained in French service. The king positioned himself as peacemaker, which enabled him to take the French backhanders without actively being in alliance with them and so stave off his subjects' anger. Once again, he had no qualms whatsoever about outright double-dealing in foreign affairs.

Monmouth, meanwhile, had his hands full with the labour-intensive business of running the army while attending to the affairs of his other offices. He was also beginning to take a modest, but active, role in national business. When Shaftesbury's pamphlet accusing the government of seeking to become absolute appeared (entitled 'Letter from a Person of Quality to his Friend in the Country'), Monmouth sat on the committee charged with investigating. Shaftesbury, Buckingham and others went on to argue in a further publication that because the king had prorogued Parliament for over a year it should be automatically dissolved and new elections held. Monmouth again sat on the committee which investigated, and which ordered the pamphlet's public burning as 'seditious and scandalous'. Shaftesbury, Buckingham and their allies were sent to the Tower of London when they refused to ask the king's pardon on their knees. When, a few months later, the king relented and released Buckingham, Monmouth joined Danby and the Duke of York in arguing vigorously that he should not 'suffer his authority to be trampled on'. Shaftesbury, meanwhile, whiled away the days before his eventual release annotating lists of the members of the two houses, labelling his friends with a 'w' for 'worthy', and his enemies with a 'v' for 'vile'. Next to Monmouth's name he inked out three 'v's.[9]

In the spring of 1677 Louis XIV attacked the Spanish Netherlands with tremendous force. William of Orange joined forces with his bruised neighbour, the Spanish governor general the Duke of Villa Hermosa, to mount a counterattack. The order that the most recent recruits to the Royal English were to be brought home worried Monmouth, as he knew the officers of the skeleton regiment it would leave behind would struggle to maintain discipline. But despite his protests, and his contributions to the discussions in the king's inner council, the Committee for Foreign Affairs, the decision stood.[10] Thus a few months later the beleaguered remnants of the Royal English were mobilised and by the high summer were helping to defend Louis XIV's recent conquests against the Dutch. In July, Monmouth journeyed to Flanders to support them while his half-brother, Don Carlos, now Earl of Plymouth, and Lord Ossory pointedly volunteered on the other side, with the Dutch army.[11] Monmouth's journey was billed as one of research rather than combat, and he and his companion the Earl of Feversham took only two men with them, but no one was deceived. The continued presence of the Royal English in the French army was a provocation and the situation was palpably absurd. In the first week of August 1677, as William of Orange and Villa Hermosa tried to retake the city of Charleroi, there were sons of Charles II fighting on both sides. When Lord Ossory mistakenly left his coat with its Garter star at an inn near Charleroi, Monmouth, passing through, picked it up thinking it was his own.[12] The Spanish had been little troubled by the Royal English, but when a royal military hero joined the French army they were furious, writing angrily to Charles II that Monmouth, 'a prince of so great reputation and most approved valour, has betaken himself to the military service of France'.[13]

William of Orange's lack of success in the summer of 1677 convinced him that a proper alliance with the English was essential if he was to hold Louis XIV at bay. Accordingly in the early autumn a proposal was revived for his marriage to the Duke of York's daughter, Mary. The notion had been discussed before, but the Duke of York had always been against it – as had Monmouth – hoping that she might marry the French dauphin instead. However in the face of his own monumental unpopularity, even York could see the benefits of uniting his oldest child to the most prominent Protestant in Europe.

The marriage went ahead on Sunday 4 November 1677, William of Orange's twenty-seventh birthday. Performed in Princess Mary's bedchamber at St James's Palace it was a match deeply reminiscent of his own parents' wedding thirty years earlier. Neither bride nor groom regarded the event with much pleasure. William's own memories of Whitehall were excruciating. On his last visit six years earlier the king had got him horribly drunk at a supper hosted by the Duke of Buckingham. Trying to refuse at first – protesting that he 'did not naturally love' such occasions – he was soon paralytic and had to be dragged away after breaking and entering the maids of honours' apartment.[14] Mary, for her part, was a romantic and emotional teenager, given to penning long passionate letters to friends, and at fifteen was already unusually tall. She could hardly have been more cast down by the sight of her suitor. Almost six inches shorter than she, with a large Roman nose and black teeth, William of Orange was ugly, asthmatic and short on charm. When her father called Mary into his closet to tell her that the marriage had been agreed, she burst into tears. Desperate at the thought of leaving England to live abroad with this joyless man who made no attempt to court her, Mary knew she had no say in the matter. While she nursed her self-pity the public mood was one of delight. The lord mayor's feast on 29 October was particularly spectacular, with four elaborate pageants being performed in the streets of London, and Monmouth joining William, the king and Queen, Duke and Duchess of York and Prince Rupert for the magnificent banquet in the Guildhall.[15] Despite all the bonhomie, Monmouth and William were on chilly terms, having faced one another on opposing sides at Charleroi only three months before. When Monmouth was given the task of showing William the royal docks, he managed to lose the stadtholder somewhere between Chatham and Sheerness, and was forced to chase after him round the coast to Margate.[16]

On the morning of the wedding day Mary, her eyes swollen from weeping, asked her friend Anna, Duchess of Monmouth, to look after her sister Princess Anne after she had gone and 'to think often on her'. The sight of Anna's husband, Monmouth, so self-possessed and attractive, can only have exacerbated the princess's dismay. Later that evening, when the king drew the curtains on the hapless newlyweds' bed with the helpful cry: 'Now, nephew, to your worke! Hey! St. George for England!' Mary's misery was complete. But outside the city streets blazed brighter with celebratory bonfires than they had at any time since the Restoration, as England had now finally tied itself to the Dutch.[17]

While Monmouth had no love for William III, and must have pitied his miserable cousin as she left Whitehall, by the winter of 1677 he had had enough of the French himself. He had clearly savoured both his first taste of command and the celebrity he enjoyed in the drawing rooms of Paris, but that had been five years ago and the relentless business of trying to ensure his men were paid and properly provided for had been a thankless task ever since. In December when he wrote to Louvois he did not cloak his irritation in his usual gracious prose: 'I cannot refrain from expressing the regret I feel at the bad treatment the king's subjects have received for some little time.'[18] Come the first week in January, Danby told William of Orange that Charles II had just given instructions for the withdrawal of the Royal English from the French army. Only a matter of weeks later, in a classic bit of seventeenth-century side-switching, Monmouth found himself gathering men to fight with William against the French.[19]

Though the Anglo-Dutch alliance was now public, Charles II and Danby quietly continued trying to broker peace between the

French and Dutch. Apart from anything else it meant they could still claim the subsidy which Charles II received from the French in return, in effect, for not going to war against them. Meanwhile Monmouth leaped into action.[20] Not waiting for his formal commission to be signed, he applied himself to the task of planning the defence of the coastal ports of Ostend, Bruges and Niewport against Louis XIV. He appointed the naturalised Frenchman Louis Duras, now Earl of Feversham, as second-in-command for the mission, and the pair accompanied the first 500 men to Ostend in early March.[21] Monmouth's instructions were to stop the French from capturing Bruges. When he arrived in Ostend, however, he realised things were going to be difficult. Just maintaining discipline among English recruits in a Catholic country was a challenge and he immediately issued strict orders for behaviour: outlawing drunkenness, the mistreatment of landlords, offensive behaviour to Catholic priests and violent brawls.[22] The carefully preserved rights of the burgers of Ostend meant Monmouth could not billet his men in local inns and houses as usual and so had to set up a series of large encampments instead. Presenting himself to the Spanish governor of Ostend, he discovered what a sorry and dispirited lot the Spanish forces were. The port's whole garrison was little more than 400 men, and as Monmouth wrote to the king 'they ar the miserablest creaturs that euer I saw'. He realised at once that his orders for marching to Bruges were probably misconceived, as the city looked about to fall, and it would be better to concentrate on preventing the capture of Niewport. The trouble was the Spanish had more or less given up trying to save the seaports, and were Niewport to fall too, then the Flemish townspeople would very likely simply open their gates to the French rather than trying to fight them. Monmouth wrote urgently to the king, asking for permission to march to Niewport, but ending: 'Whatsoever you doe, bee pleased to doe it quike, for one day lost is a great matter hier,' and signing himself, as ever, 'your dutifull Monmouth'.[23]

As he raced about Ostend and galloped between Flemish towns, establishing how things lay, Monmouth received orders from his father to return – as his visit was technically only to accompany the first body of soldiers to Ostend. His frustration at leaving less than a week after arriving and at such a critical stage was enormous, but he quickly put his affairs in order before complying. Writing gracious letters to Villa Hermosa and his deputy the Marquis d'Ossera he agreed, after consulting with them, that his troops should go to Bruges after all (there were as yet not enough to defend Niewport), and appointing one Mr Gosfright, probably a relation of his uncle Peter Gosfright, as paymaster to ensure the funds were properly managed.[24]

Back in London on 11 March, Monmouth immediately signed orders for ammunition and warm bedding for his encamped men. As he had taken leave, he had reassured the Spanish officials that he would impress on the king the need for reinforcements. But back in London he admitted it was a strange situation. With the towns-people ambivalent about whether it was better to be subjects of the king of Spain or of the king of France, he was doubtful whether they wanted English protection at all, 'the French use the conquered so wel' that they would arguably 'rather have them masters then we releevers'.[25]

The subtlety of the situation in Flanders was of little interest to the MPs of the Parliament that had finally reassembled, who simply wanted England to go to war against the French Catholics with the Protestant Dutch. When they first gathered in mid-January the king's opening words had been: 'When we parted last, I told you, that before we met again, I would do that which should be to your Satisfaction: I have accordingly made such Alliances with Holland, as are for the Preservation of Flanders'. But trouble would come, he had continued, not without menace, if the funds to support the English troops were not speedily granted.[26] The preparation of this army, which was to include eleven new regiments on top of those already standing, was the task that lay before Monmouth. Given the responsibility involved and the high profile the expedition had already acquired, it was clearly essential he be given a proper commission. Accordingly on 13 April 1678 orders were finally given for a warrant to be drawn up for Monmouth to be appointed captain general of all the land forces in England and Wales.[27]

While so much of the political tension that Monmouth saw all around him was about religion, he himself remained quiet on matters of faith. He attended the chapel royal and his parish church, St Martin's in the Fields, he employed a chaplain and swore the oaths of Protestant conformity required by the recent legislation. But while he was a conforming Anglican in behaviour, he did not share the automatic anti-Catholicism of most of his contemporaries. His grandmother, Henrietta Maria, and aunt Henriette Anne, to whom he had been close, had both been Catholics, as were the queen, the king's mistress and the Duke and Duchess of York. When he issued orders for his troops in Ostend he added an additional stipulation 'That whatever souldier shall att any time meet the secrement in the Street hee shall either avoid by going some other way or be bareheaded whilst it passes by on paine of severe punishmt.'[28] He did not seek out the world of the Church or involve himself in religious controversy. While he exercised influence over some appointments, he freely admitted that 'the preferments of the church are out of my way'.[29] When he was petitioned by Irish clergy regarding their tithes, he passed on their paper to the Earl of Ormond but was careful to emphasise 'I do not find in myself any desires to invade the rights of the church, which I wish reather should be preserved.' Protestant non-conformists played no part in his world.[30]

The experience that would change Monmouth's outlook came from an unexpected direction: not from Flanders, Paris or the United Provinces – cosmopolitan worlds he knew first-hand – but from somewhere he had never been and from whence came his wife, his name and one dukedom and half his vast income: Scotland. Monmouth was, in name at least, lord high chamberlain of Scotland and a member of the Scottish Privy Council, but neither of these actually involved him doing anything much. When suddenly in 1677 his attention was drawn north to this place he knew only by report it was not because of any office he held, as a peer, army officer or administrator, but as a landowner.[31]

Monmouth's marriage in 1663 had brought with it the accumulated wealth of the Buccleuch family, whose estates were focused in the borderlands south of Edinburgh, with the family's seat at Bowhill near Selkirk. To this patrimony more estates had been periodically added, among them the castle and lands of Dalkeith just outside Edinburgh, where General Monck had set up his headquarters in the 1650s and which Anna would one day rebuild. Monmouth and Anna happily consumed the thousands of pounds of income that poured south from these estates every year, leaving their management in the hands of their agent Sir James Stansfield. Then on 17 March 1677 Monmouth received a letter from the lords of the Scottish Privy Council in Edinburgh reprimanding him for the 'unlawful assemblies' – illicit non-conformist prayer meetings – taking place among his tenantry on the Dalkeith lands. He immediately instructed Stansfield to do everything necessary to 'prevent and suppress' these illegal gatherings, declaring that 'I shall be unsatisfied till I hear that his Majesty's peace is preserved and the laws of the kingdom complied with.'[32]

Stansfield looked into the matter and provided a detailed account of what he had discovered. Reading this caused Monmouth to reconsider, and when he wrote to the council it was not to confirm the punitive measures he had taken, but to argue instead that his tenants should be acquitted.[33] Exactly what had happened in Dalkeith we do not know, but it prompted Monmouth to take an interest in the experience of landlords and tenants in Scotland, and thereby in politics altogether, which would soon grow.

Scotland's religious complexion was different to England's. The reformation in Scotland had come later and was more radical than in England and the reformed Church which emerged in the 1560s was broadly Calvinist. Charles I's efforts to impose High Church Anglican worship on Scotland in the 1630s had been disastrous and the Covenanting movement reaffirmed the Scots' desire for a simpler liturgy and a Church structure without bishops. This was realised during the interregnum. But after the turmoil of the

1650s, the desire for order and stable government was as strong in Scotland as in England. In 1661, Charles II wrote to the Scottish Privy Council stating that the sort of Presbyterianism the Scots had had for the past twenty years was inconsistent with monarchical authority and declared that the Church in Scotland would hence-forth be Episcopal. This established a profound tension in Scotland, as something like a third of all ministers, who could not accept bishops, were now excluded from the official Church. It hit hardest in south-west Scotland, where Presbyterianism was most deep-rooted and, in some cases, ninety per cent of ministers resigned their livings. These ministers and their congregations did not disap-pear, but simply relocated out of the churches to assemble instead in houses, barns and even in the open air, in gatherings known as conventicles. But in so doing they broke the law, raising the ques-tion of what, exactly, the government would do about it.[34]

The scale of Scottish non-conformity remained large and growing despite various policies to address it. Come the mid-1670s, with Danby and the English bishops thirsty for evidence that dissenters were being prosecuted, the pressure to act was greater still. John Maitland, Duke of Lauderdale, who remained the king's represent-ative in Scotland, though once a Covenanter himself, saw the issue as being about the assertion of royal authority and was determined to demonstrate the firmness of his grasp. Lauderdale pledged 'this game is not to be played by halfes, we must. . . crush them, so as they may not trouble us any more'. His solution was to assemble an army of some 8,000 men (a separate body to any controlled by Monmouth, the Scottish and English armies being distinct), many recruited from the Highland clans, and send them to south-west Scotland to 'keep the peace'. In reality the imposition of this force was far more likely to provoke rebellion than to prevent it, and it may be that this was part of Lauderdale's plan, giving him a cast-iron excuse for the sort of absolute crackdown he sought. In a bit of clumsy vindictiveness, Lauderdale deliberately quartered many of these troops on lands belonging to his enemies, first among them being the Scottish opposition leader, the Duke of Hamilton.

The 'Highland Host' as the army became known, was empow-
ered to root out and destroy non-conformist meeting places and was
virtually unaccountable. Unleashed in January 1678, they ran riot,
terrorising the countryside, destroying buildings, stealing property and violently molesting householders. In the twenty-one days
the Earl of Strathmore's regiment were quartered in Lanark they
were reckoned to have done £3,544 of damage, their crimes encom-
passing widespread robbery, the destruction of several houses and
the demolition of the town tollbooth.[35] As Monmouth knew better
than most, any quartered troops were a menace to their hosts and
in this respect the bad behaviour of the Highland Host was not
an exception. But in Scotland, as in England, landowners were not
used to billeting men and – more to the point – the Host's mandate,
to find rebels in the very towns where they were staying, made for
certain confrontation between soldiers and civilians.

The leading landowners of south-west Scotland were therefore
facing the wholesale destruction of their property for something
which, after all, they could not themselves easily control – the religious preferences of their tenants. Their powerlessness was further
compounded by a particularly controlling measure Lauderdale
had taken the trouble to institute just before the Highland Host
marched in – an order through the Scottish Privy Council forbid-
ding Scottish noblemen from leaving the country without a formal
licence. Soon orders were issued for all weapons to be seized,
including those of the nobility themselves. By forcing senior Scottish noblemen to relinquish their own arms Lauderdale imposed an
intolerable indignity on a martial class. As one friend wrote to the
Duke of Hamilton: 'There ar[e] few honest men but say that if the
Duke of Hammiltone be putt to walk without his sword they will
even lay aside theirs and beare him company.'[36]

As the Host was on the rampage in Ayrshire, and as ever more
demeaning acts of submission were required of the landowners
there, some noblemen attempted to make the king aware, in the
belief that he would countermand Lauderdale. Among them
was Hamilton's brother-in-law the young John Kennedy, Earl

of Cassilis, who wrote to James, Duke of Monmouth describing Lauderdale's punitive measures and the highlanders' barbarities, which he characterised as 'the greatest complaint of violence, rapine and all manner of oppression that ever was heard in the world'. Cassilis had already been ordered by the Scottish Privy Council to impound arms, to destroy several meeting houses in his lands in south Ayrshire, publicly burning their timbers, and to produce a list of those who had erected them. Despite complying with all of this, 1,500 men were quartered on his estate and went on to cause 'plunder and other exactions with many insolencies and cruelties'. Cassilis enclosed in his letter to Monmouth an account of events which was intended for the king, with the plea that 'many of these proceedings were illegal and not warranted by the statues and customs of Scotland'. Why Cassilis targeted Monmouth is not clear, but the fact that Monmouth had resisted prosecution for meetings on his own estates the previous year gave grounds for thinking he might be sympathetic. Appalled by what he read, Monmouth took the letter straight to the king. When Charles asked Lauderdale for an explanation he was swiftly reassured by the duke's silver-tongued agents that they were just 'idle ridiculous stories'.[37]

Monmouth dutifully handed to Lauderdale the paper Cassilis had sent him.[38] But unlike the king he was not reassured. In the first days of April, Charles II saw a clutch of Lauderdale's colleagues in his bedchamber and quizzed them again on reports of murders, rapes and robberies. After the king had declared himself satisfied, Monmouth came into the room and reopened the subject, asking whether it was lawful or right to expect a landowner to be responsible for the conformity of his tenants, and pointing out that it was hard to expect a landlord to turn his tenants off the land in large numbers. The delegation responded curtly that it was better for the fields to lie waste than be a 'nurserie for rebells'. Monmouth then took another tack and asked a series of detailed, probing questions about the legality of the quartering arrangements, a subject he understood intimately, given he had been responsible for billeting English soldiers for several years. The meeting lasted two hours before the king's patience expired. 'I will maintain my authority,' he announced, and would not challenge Lauderdale's actions.[39]

A day or two later the Duke of Hamilton and the other opponents of Lauderdale's policy arrived in London, without the licence they were supposed to have secured to leave Scotland. They went straight to see the Duke of Monmouth, who was further alarmed by their vivid first-hand account of affairs. The king would not see Hamilton face to face but appointed intermediaries to hear his grievances. At another conference in the king's bedchamber at Whitehall on 15 April 1678 Lauderdale's right-hand man, the Earl of Moray, gathered with Danby, the Duke of York, Prince Rupert and Monmouth to discuss 'the affairs of Scotland'. The king declared, again, that he was satisfied with Lauderdale's judgement and Danby and York agreed, approving of his authoritarian approach. Monmouth, however, was vociferous in his support of Hamilton and of the persecuted people of south-west Scotland, taking the part of 'defending the uest [west] country'. The king's own hard-heartedness owed much to the bitter memory of his humiliation at the hands of Presbyterian Scots during his visit in 1650–51, when he had been forced at his own coronation to sit through an hour-long sermon enumerating the sins of his father. He declared that he, unlike many there, knew Scotland, and told Monmouth that he might 'close his eyes and shit' in Scotland 'for ther uas not on of them better than another'. While the company guffawed with laughter Monmouth smarted at their levity and lack of concern for the outright injustice he now felt so keenly.[40]

In the days that followed, unbowed, Monmouth acted as an agent ferrying letters and petitions from Hamilton and the other Scots opposition figures directly to the king – not because the king wished it, but because he was now determined to pursue the matter. On 19 April Monmouth passed Moray in the privy gallery at White-hall, and waved in front of him four or five papers which he was going to show to the king that night.[41] Moray relayed to Lauderdale how Monmouth was pressing Hamilton's case with the king, railing about the destruction and waste, and the fact it would make 'hundreds of poor people com up & petition the King'.[42] But still the king backed Lauderdale completely, with the Duke of York not far behind; all was well 'bot for the D. of Monomout', Moray wrote, 'I apprehend th[at] Lord hes not bene what he ought iff he mynded graetitud or obligation.'[43] While the king was growing irritated and on several occasions declared the matter closed, Monmouth's familiarity with his father and the king's affection for his son prevented it being so. On the evening of 24 April, Monmouth talked privately to the king of the ruination of Hamilton's lands and of all his horses being taken, so his wife could not even ride out, and he went on to expand on his belief that householders were not being paid for housing the belligerent highlanders. The king looked on, apparently bored, but afterwards asked Danby to investigate whether the soldiers' quarters were being paid for, and instructed Lauderdale to leave Hamilton's horses alone.[44]

After several more attempts, which were parried each time, Monmouth finally managed, in spite of his father's antipathy to Hamilton, to arrange for the two to meet. The summit took place in the late afternoon at Secretary Coventry's office under the Whitehall privy gallery and lasted some two hours. Present were just the king, Hamilton and his colleagues, Danby and Monmouth. Ultimately the king asked Hamilton to put his grievances in writing. Fearful for the consequences if he did so, Hamilton declined and there the meeting ended. While no change had been secured for Hamilton the encounter lodged doubt in the king's mind, and orders for the disbanding of the Highland Host soon followed.[45] According to the well-informed Scottish cleric Gilbert Burnet, 'the madness of this proceeding' eroded the king's confidence in Lauderdale to such an extent that he decided he would appoint Monmouth to his position as soon as a respectable interval had passed.[46]

For Monmouth the whole business was a watershed. The duke, just turning twenty-nine, had taken an active part in domestic political affairs of the first consequence. His participation was not simply to support the government line but saw him take on his father's ministers, and indeed the king himself, to argue a counter case almost alone. The reason for the change, and for his sudden entry into the political arena, was not self-aggrandisement, party-politicking or a personal grudge (of all of which he would one day be accused) but stemmed from his own keen sense of injustice. As such it was in character: the instincts which saw him back the western Scots in 1678 were the same as those which he had demon-strated over the past six years, and which flowed from the personal sympathy he felt for the wronged.

The affair of the Highland Host saw Monmouth drawn for the first time to an opposition group by a positive force, fellow-feeling with persecuted people. His interest was more than fleeting, and three months later he would again press the concerns of the Scot-tish opposition, feeling, he explained to the king, a responsibility as he 'had sayd so mutch in that bussines'.[47] At precisely the moment this was unfolding, and perhaps partly provoked by it, the Duke of York did something at once both innocuous and inflammatory which finally severed Monmouth's loyalty to him and brought him into a much more fundamental conflict with his father's regime.

Monmouth was feverishly busy in the spring of 1678, sending contingents of soldiers out to join the defence of Flanders and lobbying almost daily for the Scots opposition. With the country now on the brink of war the Duke of York's arguments against appointing a captain general on the basis that it was unnecessary in peacetime had been overtaken by events, and Monmouth was at last to be given the position. Over the previous fifteen years he had been appointed to a series of offices by the king, each conferred by an official document. In the very first months after his arrival in England the king had described him in such papers as his 'natural', or illegitimate, son but within a year the qualifier had been dropped and thereafter he was addressed simply as 'our dearly beloved son'.[48] In accordance with this long practice, when the attorney general was ordered to draw up the commission as captain general in April 1678, he was instructed to address it to 'our most entirely beloved son James Duke of Monmouth'.[49]

As Monmouth was taking the reins of the army, the Duke of York looked on, boiling with bitterness. He could see that war would make it impossible for him to continue to block his nephew's progress, and would provide new scope for Monmouth to burnish his reputation as soldier – now fighting for a Protestant cause. That the commission of captain general might under other circumstances have been his own can only have aggravated him further. Added to all of which the debates about affairs in Scotland going on at court were demonstrating how much Monmouth's political awareness and independence had grown. The certainty York once felt that Monmouth was too loyal ever to present a real threat to him had all but evaporated. Monmouth seemed to be swiftly slipping his uncle's grip and York cast round for any means, however slight, to hold him back.

Saying nothing to the king, York had a quiet word with the attorney general, William Jones, towards the end of April 1678. Asking him as a lawyer to ensure proper drafting, York made casual mention of the importance of the word 'natural' being included in Monmouth's commission. Though this broke with fifteen years' practice, it was unquestionably the proper form of address. Jones acquiesced and included the qualifier. Knowing this small but significant change was unlikely to escape notice, York followed up with a brief note to the secretary of state asking him 'if my Nephews Commission for Generall be not yett signed' to 'speake with me before you present it to his Ma[jesty]'. When they met, York was reassured to see the commission was as he had specified.[50] Uncomfortable at what he could see was happening, Williamson seems to have tipped Monmouth off, and shortly afterwards Monmouth himself strolled into the secretary's office also asking to see the document. Having inspected it he simply instructed his own secretary James Vernon to scratch out the word 'natural', which he did, apparently without any objection from Williamson.

The commission that Williamson laid before the king on the green baize council table at the end of their meeting on Sunday 27 April 1678 had an unusually messy section in its first line, where the word 'natural' written by Jones had been erased by Vernon. The king, not given to reading the detail of such papers, inked his name at the top, before sauntering down into the privy garden to enjoy the spring sunshine. York immediately pounced on Williamson and demanded to see the final document. On reading it, he exploded with fury and demanded an explanation. Williamson mumbled incoherently and looked at his shoes. York shot down into the garden, paper in hand, in a fever of indignation and accosted the king among the white marble statues. The king, ever keen to avoid an argument, simply took a pair of scissors from his pocket, cut a square out of his own signature and ordered another to be drawn up. York insisted that Williamson be punished for changing the wording of a document drafted by the attorney general, until it became clear that the alteration had been on Monmouth's instruction. The truth of the matter was, of course, that the one who had first altered a royal instruction without approval had been York.[51]

This apparently minor incident was a vivid statement of hostility. By insisting that Monmouth's bastardy be formally referenced, York was challenging the king's special treatment of his son and, in effect, attempting to eject him from the royal family. Such an unequivocal act of personal antagonism, from one to whom Monmouth had in the face of provocation shown only loyalty, wounded and angered him deeply. On the surface nothing seemed to have changed. The king doubtless told Monmouth to ignore the matter, and continued to call him 'our most entirely beloved sone' in correspondence.[52] Monmouth went on with his duties. But beneath this the events of April 1678 had altered everything. On the one hand the affair of the Highland Host showed that the opposition's claim that the government was trampling the liberties of its subjects had real substance. On the other, the loyalty to his uncle, that had until now prevented Monmouth listening to those who claimed York threatened the very foundations of the nation, stood in the way no more.

Chapter 11

Finding New Friends

Monmouth rode out of Brussels before sunrise on Sunday 4 August 1678, passing through the very streets where, twenty years earlier, he had last walked with his mother. Here Arthur Slingsby's bungled kidnap had taken place, and he must have remembered it well: her beautiful face, her screams, his terror. The city had changed little since those days. The king of Spain still commanded this distant place from his sun-bleached palaces, and a Spanish governor-general still occupied the lofty rooms of the Coudenberg Palace.

Now, however, Louis XIV's fearful army was drawing near. The last few days had been a blur of activity. Monmouth had landed at Ostend the previous Tuesday, and had sent word to William of Orange that he would bring eight English battalions to join him in the southern Spanish Netherlands. Speed was vital if he was to reach the combined Spanish and Dutch forces before they engaged the French. Mobilising 17,000 men was no small task and Monmouth moved swiftly. Despatching orders and making arrangements, he sped ahead of his army preparing the ground for them as they marched east to Antwerp and then south to Brussels, ensuring at each stage that the city gates were open and enough bread and beer awaited them. Leaving Ostend on Wednesday afternoon, he covered 150 miles in just over forty-eight hours. When he arrived in Brussels at eight on Saturday morning he had not slept for two nights. He remained only long enough to pay his respects to the wife of the Spanish governor-general and to snatch a few hours' sleep, before setting out again. It was high summer and the air grew quickly warm as he and the advance party of 200 English cavalry, all dressed in blue and red uniforms, thundered towards Mons.

François Montmorency, Duc de Luxembourg, the French commander in Flanders, had, for the last two months, held Mons, forty miles south of Brussels, in a stranglehold. Without actively mounting a siege, he and an army of 50,000 had been slowly suffocating the city by preventing any traffic or supplies passing in or out. While peace talks between Dutch and French diplomats were taking place in Nijmegen they had been rumbling on for nearly two years without conclusion, and William was determined to prevent the fall of another city. By mid-morning Monmouth and his cavalry caught up with the rear of William's army as it marched determinedly towards its target, just in time to join the audacious attack which he was about to unleash on the unsuspecting French.

The Duc de Luxembourg's army headquarters was a few miles outside Mons itself, in the scenic grounds of the Benedictine abbey of St Denis. Here over six centuries the monks had tamed areas of dense forest on the undulating terrain, channelling the fast-flowing rivers to feed mills and fish ponds, and creating pastures on the gentle slopes. It was in this verdant, sun-dappled landscape, both productive and picturesque, that the French army was based. Luxembourg was housed comfortably in the monastery itself, while his men camped in open pasture between two dense woods. The protection the forest afforded made any attack difficult, but William, undaunted, decided on near-simultaneous assaults from both north and south. So little did Luxembourg expect it that when he heard the first booming report of the Dutch cannon he was sitting down to dinner at the abbot's table.

Over the following hours a ferocious and unusually bloody battle was fought. Monmouth, as ever, was in the thick of things, 'in person wherever any action or danger was'. At a crucial moment when he led a direct charge on the French, the Spanish troops who were to take his command turned back, claiming not to know who he was (which given that he had only arrived a few hours before may have been quite true). Only the English followed him as he surged into the eye of the battle, and narrowly avoided capture. By dusk, after seven hours relentless fighting, the French smelled defeat and Luxembourg issued the order to withdraw. It was a victory certainly, but one for which the price had been shockingly high. Some 6,000 corpses lay amid the trees and the fields, a far greater death toll than for almost any battle of the war, with casualties in comparable numbers on each side. Among the wounded was Monmouth's friend Thomas Armstrong, who had taken three bullets in the leg; Lord Ossory, who arrived with five English regiments, lost twenty-two of his officers. While Monmouth may have comforted himself that the prize justified the cost, they then received devastating news: the diplomats at Nijmegen had signed a treaty and the war had been over before the battle had even begun.

The experience of fighting alongside William of Orange would change Monmouth's view of his dour Dutch cousin for ever. Louis XIV, for all his energy and eye for detail, was an armchair soldier with no appetite for putting himself in danger's way. William, next to whom Monmouth fought for most of the day, was, he now realised, altogether different. James Vernon, Monmouth's secretary, wrote a detailed account of the expedition, and noted that not only were the Dutch soldiers disciplined and reliable, but the stadtholder was chief among them, commenting admiringly that he had 'charged himself at the head of a battalion'. William, like Monmouth, was not one to leave before the battle was ended, as was common for princely commanders, but stayed throughout. When night came the soldiers slept on the battlefield as they had been arrayed, ready for any surprise counterattack. The stadtholder did not withdraw to a silk tent, but spent the night among them in his coach. By its side in the trampled grass that had that day seen so much death, lay the Duke of Monmouth, his heavy cloak keeping out the rising dew.[1]

With the battle and now the war over, there remained the anticlimax of the aftermath. The Duc of Villa Hermosa claimed he could not provide the food he had promised to feed the English soldiers, and Monmouth had to start buying provisions for his 15,000 men from his own pocket. Arrangements for the wounded, as ever, troubled him. He wrote sharply to the surgeon-general asking detailed questions about medical supplies and arrangements, and insisted that the army surgeons should take their orders directly from him. He visited the various hospitals, and stopped off in Antwerp specially to see the young colonel, Henry Sidney, lying sick with disease like many who had survived the fighting. Sidney himself would recover to become an important English agent in Holland, and a decade later the key intermediary in William's invasion of England.[2] The truce now agreed, Monmouth and a clutch of senior Dutch officers dined convivially with their erstwhile opponent the Duc de Luxembourg – who Monmouth knew well from his days fighting with the French. The fifty-year-old Frenchman was gracious in defeat, remarking to Monmouth's valet St Gill that 'it was his own misfortune to be the enemy to so brave a man'.

William himself was anxious to return to government in The Hague, but agreed to inspect the English battalions still camped outside Brussels as he passed. That Monmouth should have been so keen for this to happen was a measure of his new respect for the stadtholder. Racing ahead to snap his troops into shape, Monmouth drew them up in formation. Straight-backed at their head, pike in hand, he offered the salute as William passed three times up and down the line. The inspection over, William climbed into his coach and clattered off towards the United Provinces, while Monmouth rode for Brussels and on to England. The whole expedition had lasted barely three weeks and had, militarily, been utterly fruitless. But in personal terms it was significant for both William of Orange and Monmouth. Between these two men the mutual suspicion bordering on antipathy which had clouded their relations until now had suddenly lifted. For seven hellish hours they had been brothers-in-arms, and through the smoke and roar of the battlefield, each had recognised in the other the qualities he respected most.[3] Since the late 1660s the Catholic Louis XIV had enthralled Monmouth with the magnetism of a brilliant older brother. But after the short Flanders campaign William's fortitude and bravery eclipsed Louis's flamboyance and territorial greed, and Monmouth's love affair with France was finally over. In the light of what was already unfolding at Whitehall it did not come a moment too soon.

A month after Monmouth's return from Flanders, Charles II called an extraordinary meeting of the Privy Council at Whitehall. Wednesdays and Fridays were the normal council days, so this was unexpected. The members gathered as the clock outside the council chamber approached ten. Dating from the mid-sixteenth century, this large first-floor room, nestling at the heart of the palace, opened off the privy gallery opposite the royal bedchamber. The king entered this way, a weighted cord quietly closing the gallery door behind him, while the councillors had approached by the staircase that sailed directly into this part of the palace from King Street. The chamber was cool and dim as the company entered. Oak-panelled, its stone-mullioned windows faced north, though their view of the cobbled outer courtyard of the palace was obscured by creamy paper blinds. Overheard the ceiling glimmered with painted and gilded royal arms encircled with the Garter, while underfoot woven rush mats muffled the clatter of shoes on the wide boards. The Tudor character of a room which had been familiar to Thomas Cranmer and Elizabeth I suited the mist of uncertainty that hung in the air that morning. After the king had taken his seat the eighteen other members took theirs, among them the chief minister Lord Danby, the Duke of Lauderdale (still clinging on to power in Scotland), the new Archbishop of Canterbury, the secretary of state, Prince Rupert, and the Duke of Monmouth. The king wasted no time in announcing the news: intelligence had been received of a Catholic terrorist plot for his assassination.[4]

After the shock of the initial revelation it soon became clear that things were more complicated than they initially seemed. The 'conspiracy' had been known about for some time and there was reason to doubt its veracity. The king himself went on to rehearse the strange series of events which had taken place over the past six weeks as Monmouth had made his way back from Flanders. On 12 August one of the assistants from the king's scientific laboratory had handed him a note as he took his morning stroll in St James's Park. The paper was a request that he meet an Anglican minister called Israel Tonge, who claimed to have evidence of a Jesuit conspiracy to kill the king. The meeting had taken place that evening and immediately roused Charles's scepticism: Tonge's manner was both naive and feverish and some of his claims, among them the suggestion that Louis XIV was party to the plot, were highly improbable. Reassured, the king had delegated the matter to Danby to investigate and gone to inspect his buildings works at Windsor. Sure enough various crucial pieces of evidence soon proved to be clumsy forgeries. But in the midst of Danby's covert inquiry the Duke of York became aware of the alleged conspiracy theory and – oblivious to the consequences – demanded a full public investigation. This was precisely what the king had been trying to avoid, aware that any rumour of such a conspiracy would reignite smouldering resentment towards Catholics in England. As Lord Halifax put it: 'considering the suspicions all had of the Duke's religion. . . every discovery of that sort would raise a flame that the court would not be able to manage'. But York was adamant, and anyhow the story was now out.[5]

Once the king had explained the background to the council, Secretary Williamson put a bundle of papers on the table, the evidence as it stood, which was passed round as Tonge was brought in. The council was gentle with this man of visibly limited faculties, who went on to explain that his source was one Titus Oates, who had that day sworn the truth of the accusations on oath before a Westminster magistrate, Sir Edmund Bury Godfrey. The king declared that they could not possibly continue without Oates himself and adjourned the meeting. While the 'plot' was now under official investigation, Charles remained sure it was fiction and he and Monmouth set off for Newmarket straight after the meeting, leaving Prince Rupert to interview Oates. While Charles was sanguine, Monmouth was not. Concerned for his father's safety, he quickly arranged for fifty soldiers of the Life Guards to accompany them. Called at such short notice, they slept in two large tents in the palace grounds.[6] Meanwhile in London, Oates appeared before the council. He was a deeply unappealing figure to behold – squat, red-faced with bulging features and a coarse, swaggering manner – but his testimony was dynamite. Clear, convincing and full of copious details which could be corroborated, he was a far more plausible witness than poor Tonge. Rupert ordered a host of arrests and requested the king's urgent return.[7]

Charles's scepticism remained when he met Oates in person. In his expansive testimony Oates claimed to have seen Philip IV's illegitimate son, Juan José, and Charles casually asked for a description of the man. Oates responded confidentially that he was tall, to which the king – who had known Juan José well in Brussels in the 1650s – replied that he was in fact very short.[8] But if Oates, though more credible than Tonge, was still questionable as an informant, things changed fundamentally a fortnight later. The magistrate to whom Oates had sworn his testimony, Sir Edmund Bury Godfrey, went missing and on 17 October was found dead on Primrose Hill, his own sword plunged into his torso with such force that the tip stuck out several inches at his back. It was no longer possible to dismiss the conspiracy as fantasy; indeed it seemed that it was actively taking effect around them.

Four days after Godfrey's mutilated corpse had been found, Parliament reassembled. While the king's speech was calm and measured, referring to the importance of letting the lawyers untangle the 'plot' in the proper way, Parliament was anything but and demanded that the evidence be handed over to them. There followed exactly what the king had feared, mass anti-Catholic hysteria; in the words of Bishop Burnet 'the whole town was all over inflamed with this discovery'. The fear was not just in London; a week or two earlier the Privy Council had required each of the county lords lieutenant to ensure the houses of all known Catholics were searched for weapons because of 'a dangerous conspiracy', so spreading the story and the suspicion nationwide.[9]

With plausible, if not perfect, sworn evidence and its first corpse, 'the Popish Plot' became a reality in the minds of almost everyone. As head of the army and colonel of the royal Life Guards, Monmouth was instantly plunged into the affair, both as security chief and investigator. The king's cynicism and some obvious holes in Oates's tale might still give reason to doubt the truth of the plot, but as the man with responsibility for the safety of the sovereign and national security more broadly, Monmouth was bound to take it seriously. For every faulty detail Oates provided, scores of others were strikingly accurate. Added to which the affair brought countless tales of villainy to light which were not easily dismissed. On its fourth consecutive day of sitting the council received a report from Monmouth that two of his soldiers had met a man in Romford who had been offered £50 to convert by a Catholic nobleman who, he had claimed, stood poised to arm 300 men in rebellion. The king might be able to take a dismissive attitude, but Monmouth could not.[10]

It was a natural extension of Monmouth's responsibilities and experience that the flood of security reviews and investigations that now followed should have been put into his hands. He was given personal responsibility for protecting Titus Oates, who, after Godfrey's stabbing, was thought a likely next target. He was appointed to the House of Lords committee inquiring into the plot, he led another recommending the measures which the king should adopt to protect his person and he was asked by Charles himself to investigate the circumstances of Godfrey's death.[11] With the House of Commons and the Lords having now taken the investigation of the plot into their own hands, the check of the king's caution was removed and rumours spread like plague. Reports of the sound of digging in Old Palace Yard in the first days of November raised the fear that the 5 November would see a new Catholic attempt to blow up Parliament. Moonlit searches were made; mining experts were brought in to look for signs; Christopher Wren was asked to confirm the warren of cellars had been thoroughly examined, and Monmouth put sentries on duty day and night. Wren's report that there were 'so many secret places' put no one's mind at rest and the question of whether Northumberland House could be used instead was raised.[12]

In this febrile atmosphere, Parliament looked to Monmouth to protect everyone: the king, themselves, Oates and the other informers. All eyes in the House of Lords were on him as he reported on the armed guard he had placed about the king and the further list of measures he thought necessary: including stopping Catholics from coming to court, vetting all the royal guards and kitchen staff and changing all locks and keys at Whitehall.[13] It was to Monmouth that the many tales poured in of mysterious groups of riders seen about the country at night, sightings verified and witnesses' reliability attested by respectable county figures. He was the one taken by informers to dank and disreputable places where treacherous acts were sworn to have taken place. The pressure was immense and perhaps the greatest challenge was identifying who exactly was the enemy.[14]

The plot as Titus Oates described it to the Privy Council was something of a shaggy dog story, long on digressions and incidental details, but short on hard facts.[15] It was clear that the Jesuits were the masterminds, the re-establishment of Catholicism in England was their goal, and the assassination of the king the means by which it was to be achieved; almost every other aspect of the 'plot' was murky. The Duke of York was not directly implicated by Oates. But among the many English Catholics he named as tangentially involved was the Duchess of York's former secretary, one Edward Colman, who he claimed was holding a treasonous correspondence with Louis XIV's confessor. The council included Colman on the list of people who were to be arrested or have their property searched in the rash of orders of late September.[16] He was nowhere to be found, but from his distraught wife a series of letters were extracted and placed in Monmouth's hands.[17] When they were examined and deciphered the sensational discovery was made that he had indeed been in contact with François de la Chaise, one of Louis's confessors, and the letters revealed that he had been seeking money from Louis and the Pope to persuade the king to dissolve

Parliament. Almost no one knew that this sort of arrangement was, in fact, tantamount to official policy and the scandal was instant. Colman's letters both further corroborated the plot and brought the conflagration to the Duke of York's very door. The letters strongly implied that Colman was acting on York's behalf and when this was not denied by Colman the flames engulfed him. In the words of Roger North, the 'discovery of Coleman's papers made as much noise in and about London, and indeed all over the nation, as if the very Cabinet of Hell had been laid open'.[18]

Just as York was being accused of being party to the Popish Plot, so Monmouth was being written in as one of its victims – though this had not been suggested by Tonge or Oates in their early interviews. Soon the story, enriched by a thousand retellings, was that this was a Catholic plot to kill Charles II and Monmouth so that James Duke of York could succeed.[19] Regardless of Oates's claims, Colman's letters were real – not even York denied their authenticity – and were enough on their own to blacken York's reputation for good. In them his own secretary described the future head of the Church of England as committed to Catholicism with 'such a degree of zeal' that nothing mattered to him but the reconversion of the kingdom.[20]

There was now no fighting the flames, and the government did not even try. The Duke of York stood down from the Privy Council and all other bodies of government on 3 November 1678 and the king realised that he needed to take urgent personal action or Parliament would try to remove him permanently. He announced his intention to address Parliament and on Saturday 9 November both York and Monmouth were in the chamber as the two houses gathered to hear him. Exhibiting none of his actual scepticism, he gave a masterful performance. Radiating concerned sincerity, he expressed his gratitude to both houses for their care for his safety, and his sympathy with their desire to protect Protestantism after his death 'and in all future Ages, even to the End of the World'. He then pledged his support for any reasonable measure, so long as it did not interfere with the line of succession or impede the rights of a future Protestant sovereign, to 'make you safe in the reign of any successor'.[21]

That night London went wild. The city blazed with bonfires and hundreds of pealing church bells mixed with the jubilant shouts and cries of celebration. Aldermen overjoyed at the good news opened their cellars and the wine flowed like water; toasts were drunk to the king, to Monmouth and the Earl of Shaftesbury. But what precisely was the news? The wording of the king's speech had not been ambiguous: he was prepared to agree to checks on the powers of a Catholic successor. But between his speech in the Lords' chamber that afternoon and the streets of London that night, all clarity had dissolved. It was widely reported that the king had declared there would be a Protestant successor. In places, amid further ecstatic cheers, a more specific and seismic claim was made: 'that the Duke of Monmouth was to succeed the king'.[22]

The Popish Plot was in truth a fiction. Dreamt up by Titus Oates, as destructive and dangerous a man as the seventeenth century ever saw, it was as Charles II always believed a nonsense of his own concoction. The secretary of state had remarked in October 1678 that, 'if he be a liar he is the greatest and adroitest I ever saw', and so he was. Thanks to his lies many innocent people were executed and imprisoned, and England's political history changed.[23] Oates's skill and the national paranoia about Catholicism were already a combustible combination; put together with the secrets and lies common at Charles II's court the results were an inferno. Then in December, Charles II's former ambassador in Paris, Ralph Montagu, who harboured a personal grudge against Danby, threw in a further grenade. He produced a box of letters in the House of Commons that was opened and read aloud before the transfixed members. These contained the sensational revelation that it was not just York's people who had been in secret correspondence with the French, but the king's. While Charles had been proudly reporting to Parliament his alliance with the Dutch and his intention to declare war on France, behind the scenes his first minister, Danby, was offering to call off the war and dispense with Parliament if Louis XIV paid them 6 million livres a year.[24] A bill to impeach Danby for treason was immediately drawn up. While the Lords resisted, the momentum seemed unstoppable. Finally, on 24 January, Charles II dissolved the Cavalier Parliament, seventeen years after it first assembled, deciding that he had now no choice but to risk a general election.

The events and experience of the autumn and winter of 1678 changed Monmouth. He was about to turn thirty and the investigation of the plot propelled him into the centre of national events in a way he had not known before. While managing the ramped-up security arrangements and various inquiries connected with the plot, and making sure the election took place without violence or coercion, he was also disbanding the army raised the year before to fight the Dutch. This was a highly complex operation which involved getting all 15,000 men home from Flanders, making arrangements for the ill and wounded, organising temporary quarters, and then paying them off in waves. At each stage the soldiers' provisions and discipline had to be managed and as ever Monmouth responded to individuals' troubled circumstances.[25] He stopped paying one of his lieutenants until he had settled his colossal bills with a distressed Dutch tradesman and made special arrangements to allow the infirm Lord Howard of Escrick to retain his rank and salary.[26] Meanwhile the six standing regiments and garrison companies which were to remain required accommodation. Monmouth commissioned a major survey of the country's castles and forts and set about building guard houses and regimental barracks at a number of key strategic locations, among them county towns on the main roads out of London at Hitchin, Newport Pagnell and Sevenoaks.[27]

Over those months Monmouth's stature in the political world visibly grew. He moved from the periphery to the centre of those whose views and actions mattered. As the Duke of Ormond's agent at court wrote with eloquent understatement that December, the Duke of Monmouth 'appears of late to be more a man of business than was expected he would prove'.[28] When Danby's career collapsed, and the departure of the man who had managed the king's affairs for six years became a certainly, a political vacuum was created into which Monmouth, among others, was drawn. This opportunity coincided with Monmouth's own political awakening. His dealings with the Scottish opposition almost a year before had exposed him to the regime's oppressive tendencies while the events of the Popish Plot seemed to confirm the menace of Catholicism. The opposition regarded the army as posing a dangerous threat to national liberties if it were allowed to remain after fighting had finished, and Monmouth himself now rather agreed and both proposed and ensured it was stood down as soon as possible.[29] It had come as a complete surprise to him that while he was marching his men towards Mons, Danby had been discussing cosy financial deals with the French. For one who had watched thousands die about him in a battle which now seemed doubly futile, the revelation was shocking and left him with a disgust for Danby that he did not disguise.[30] As a member of the Privy Council, head of the army and with responsibility for national security, Monmouth was a senior member of the government. But if he had once followed his father's line in an unquestioning manner, he did so no longer. The events of that autumn had demonstrated to him, among others, that Shaftesbury and his colleagues, rather than being a radical fringe, might just have been right all along.

The general election of February 1679 was a catastrophe for Charles II. Though the election of individual MPs was subject to lobbying – Monmouth managed to get Vernon returned as MP for Cambridge University, Thomas Armstrong for Stafford and his paymaster, Lemuel Kingdom for Hull – overall the 538 MPs were not a packed group. The old House of Commons had been fairly evenly divided between those who supported the government and the opposition, but the new one favoured the opposition by two to one.[31] So clear had the distinction become that the two sides started now, for the first time in English history, to be called political 'parties': the king and government on the one hand (known as the court party, or 'Tories') and Shaftesbury and his fellow critics on the others (the country or 'Whigs'). Though the nicknames each gave the other were insults – a 'tory' was an Irish Catholic vagabond, a 'whig' was a Presbyterian radical – they stuck and soon became commonplace.

With the prospect of this hostile group meeting the king had to act fast to try to stave off the political mauling they were bound to inflict on the government, and conciliation and compromise were the mood during the critical weeks between the election and the opening of the parliamentary session. While York's determination to attend the Lords' debates on the Popish Plot during the autumn had in a way been admirable, it had made him doubly conspicuous and he remained a huge political liability. Attempts to persuade him to abandon his faith were futile and shortly after the election the king instructed him to go overseas. York and his family reluctantly set off on an indefinite excursion to Brussels. After asking Danby to resign, and to do so before he was forcibly removed from office, the king went on to make a series of new government appointments. Robert Spencer, Earl of Sunderland – from whom, while he was ambassador in Paris, Monmouth had recruited his devoted secretary James Vernon in 1674 – became a secretary of state. In his thirties, urbane and well travelled, Sunderland shared Monmouth's taste for French fashion and high stakes at the gaming tables. With his arch aristocratic manner and affected court drawl, he was a different creature from his meticulous secretarial predecessors. He was liked by the king – not least because he knew how to handle the Duchess of Portsmouth – but as Shaftesbury's nephew by marriage and with friends in both camps he was a carefully judged appointment. Also back in high office that spring was the Earl of Essex, the able one-time lord lieutenant of Ireland, who in 1678 had started voting with the opposition, and who was now made the head of the new Treasury commission.

It was in this context of shifting relationships and responsibilities that Monmouth and Shaftesbury started talking. What interaction they had had over the five years since the older man had been Monmouth's deputy as chief justice of the southern royal forests is not clear; quite possibly very little. But things were changing. Shaftesbury had been invited to court for the first time since 1675, and dined there with his nephew, Sunderland, with the king's knowledge. That winter Monmouth and Shaftesbury had 'severall private meetings' in which the earl talked of the need to have York removed from court and Danby toppled. As well as a growing sympathy with the Whigs' arguments, Monmouth shared Shaftesbury's antipathy for York and Danby, and this unlikely pair began to find that they had common cause.[32]

While the respect Monmouth commanded in the House of Lords and the council chamber had gradually grown, his reputation in the coffee houses and playhouses of London was sky high. Even before he led the investigation into the Popish Plot, his dashing looks, closeness to the king, and reputation for bravery had begun to bring him popular celebrity. This only increased as York's reputation plummeted and he started fighting alongside the Protestant Dutch. In January 1678 a pamphlet 'describing a vision. . . of an adorable mortal the exact image of the Duke [of Monmouth]' was being sold by Andrew Forrester from his shop outside Whitehall Palace, while a fortune-teller prophesied that the comet that had streaked through the sky in 1677 foretold a change of religion from which the Duke of Monmouth would be the Protestant deliverer.[33] Monmouth's very public role in protecting Protestants and rooting out Catholics in the autumn of 1679 further inflated his credit with the anti-Catholic crowds. Prints of the duke were soon being sold all over the capital and in March 1679 the Earl of Ossory wrote to this father of 'the great credit the Duke of Monmouth is now in, and how vigorously he opposes against the Papists'.[34]

The publication of the exact words of the king's speech in Parliament of November 1678 gave the lie to the reports that Monmouth was to replace York as heir to throne – which had raised such cheers in the wine-warmed revellers – but the story did not go away. Indeed, opportunists of various complexions saw too much personal advantage in them. The unscrupulous Ralph Montagu, not content with bringing down Danby, whispered in the ear of the French ambassador that it would be to Louis XIV's advantage to have Monmouth declared Prince of Wales – claiming it was what both the king and Monmouth really wanted and it needed only the French support to make it happen.[35] Thomas Armstrong was another. A career soldier who had worked his way up through the ranks of the restoration army to the position of lieutenant colonel, Armstrong was brave and hot-headed – valuable qualities in a soldier perhaps, but mixed blessings in a friend.[36] He had taken care to make himself useful to Monmouth between campaigns and, having served under him at Maastricht and taken a bullet by his side at Mons, had won the duke's unshakeable loyalty.[37] In May 1679 he reportedly spoke to his old colonel, and Monmouth's one-time revelling companion, the Earl of Oxford, 'to endeavour to get the succession to be on Monmouth'. Oxford vigorously slapped him down, warning him that if 'he were not quiet, he would send him to a place where he should be nothing'. While some encouraged the chatter, Monmouth himself was not among them. He had lived with rumours of his being made his father's heir since childhood and had never known them to hold any substance. When York wrote to William of Orange in December, grumbling about the 'foolish discourses about towne concerning the Duke of Monmouth', he complained that 'some of his friends talke as indiscretly on the same subject', but even he did not yet accuse Monmouth of encouraging them himself.[38]

Instead Monmouth saw his role differently. His experience told him that he, of everyone, had both the position and persuasive powers to talk his father round, to encourage him to listen to the opposition leaders and so to his subjects. It was a new role, that of broker or negotiator, which he now took upon himself. It involved striking a fine balance. While he unquestionably supported the moves to bring Danby down, he also stood his ground. When Shaftesbury tried to stir up outrage in Parliament about the continued threat posed by imprisoned Catholics, Monmouth took the floor to explain calmly that only one of those held in the Tower now refused to swear the oaths required of them, and he had been given a fortnight to comply.[39]

Behind the scenes it was Monmouth, along with the new centre-ground ministers, who worked on the king to try to persuade him to change his approach. A week or two after Parliament met, Monmouth and a small number of others talked to the king about a radical idea for appeasing the still irate Parliament. Instead of having a Privy Council made up of those who supported government policy – and real government done by a tiny subset of those – the king should create a new smaller Privy Council that would actually include the key opposition leaders. While the precise genesis of the idea is uncertain (the diplomat William Temple claimed it originated with him), Monmouth was crucial to convincing the king, which was no easy task. Of the inclusion of one of the opposition figures, the Earl of Halifax, Monmouth said 'he had as great difficulty in overcoming that, as ever in anything that he studied to bring the king to'. But at a small gathering in Sunderland's lodgings in mid-April, attended by just the king, Monmouth, Sunderland and Shaftesbury, the reluctant monarch was finally persuaded.[40]

On 21 April 1679 a surprised Privy Council was informed that their services were no longer needed. The king intended, they were told in his presence, to 'lay aside the use he may hitherto have made of any single ministry or private advices'. Instead a new council would meet, formed in part of a series of named office holders – among them Monmouth as Master of the Horse – and in part of a number of individuals not in government. The language used that day was rich with contrition: the king was sorry for the way things had been managed in the past, he promised that the new body would be consulted on 'all business' foreign and domestic, and that he would henceforth be guided 'by the constant advice of such a council'. The scale of the shift this involved became clear as the names of the new members were read out: which included such prominent opposition figures as Lord William Russell and the Earl of Halifax, while the revived post of Lord President of the Council was to be given to none other than the Earl of Shaftesbury himself.[41]

It seemed suddenly as if English politics had changed, and a new era of moderation and cooperation was now dawning.

While the king had opened the door to a discussion of the checks on a future Catholic sovereign, all such restrictions had the same problem: what was to stop a new monarch reversing them as soon as he was in power and in command of the nation and its army? The view that a Catholic king posed a threat to the nation was almost universal. A more radical alternative to such checks was hovering on many lips, and was finally given voice when on 11 May 1679 after a debate which wore on into the night, the House of Commons voted that 'a Bill be brought in to disable the Duke of Yorke to inherit the Imperial Crown of this Realm'.[42] This suggestion was warmly received and was just getting its second reading when Charles II made up his mind to step in and prorogue Parliament.

Monmouth heard of the king's intention to prorogue on the morning of 27 May and was appalled. The council had not met for four days and knew nothing of what was as significant a political decision as any. For the king to take it alone would expose his words about the new Privy Council as little more than lies. Monmouth rushed into the royal apartments and begged the king to reconsider, 'earnestly entreat[ing] His Majesty to call his Council before he undertook so weighty a thing; for that he had in his public declaration so promised and declared that nothing should be done without them'.[43]

If the king had ever had any intention of honouring his announcement about the new system of consultation, it had been short-lived. The opposition saw their inclusion in the council as the start of their participation in government, but the king soon decided that the appointments were the end of his concessions and expected them now to come to heel. Before long his loathing for his new councillors became clear. He would remark to the son of one who was disappointed not to be included: 'Doth he imagine I left him out because I did not love him? He was to be left out because I do love him,' adding in a loud aside: 'God's fish! they have put a set of men about me, but they shall know nothing.'[44]

When Charles II announced before an astonished Parliament that it was to be prorogued – having ignored his son's pleas and said nothing to the council – Monmouth's heart was heavy with two bitter realisations. First that there were limits to what even his most passionate pleading could persuade his father to do, and second that his optimism and sincerity were incompatible with his father's cynicism. Taken together they mapped a path to disaster.

Chapter 12

Icarus

In bright noon daylight on 3 May 1679 Scotland's most senior cleric, James Sharp, archbishop of St Andrews, was travelling with his daughter Isabella across the flat open moorland between the Fife village of Kennoway and his seat at St Andrews. The white-haired Sharp had started life as a Presbyterian but had crossed the floor to join the Episcopalians. He was disliked and distrusted by his countrymen on both sides for his fluid loyalties and the corruption of which he was accused. As the coach crossed Magus Moor a gang of horsemen overtook it and fired a series of shots. Bringing the vehicle to a standstill, they revealed themselves as a ramshackle lynch mob, whose hit was largely opportunist (their original target had been a local sheriff). Recognising the passenger, they dragged the archbishop onto the heather, called him a traitor to Christ and clumsily stabbed him to death as the appalled Isabella looked helplessly on.

The brutal murder of Archbishop Sharp, head of the established church in Scotland, instantly accelerated the animosity between Lauderdale's regime and the more politically active Presbyterians. On 29 May, the king's birthday, Robert Hamilton, described by his relation Bishop Burnet as a 'crack-brained enthusiast', led eighty armed supporters to nail a manifesto to the Market Cross at Rutherglen near Glasgow, declaring allegiance to the Solemn League and Covenant and condemning episcopacy and royal supremacy in the Church. Three days later government forces clashed with the rebels at a bloody skirmish at Drumclog; when the former were forced to withdraw defeated, it was clear the situation had already escalated dangerously.

At an extraordinary meeting of the uneasy coalition Privy Council in London the order was issued for the Duke of Monmouth, as captain general of the king's forces, to raise an army and suppress the 'insurrection in Scotland'. With the king, Monmouth, Sunderland, Shaftesbury and Russell all present, Lauderdale must have found the meeting intensely uncomfortable, demonstrating as it did that the kingdom for which he was responsible was now beyond his control.[1]

In a sign of the changing times, the king's commission to Monmouth as captain general of the royal forces in Scotland addressed him with cool professionalism as 'our beloved cousin and councillor'.[2] After making the arrangements for raising the six regiments he judged necessary, Monmouth set out for Scotland. In an age utterly unforgiving of rebellion the instructions he carried with him were unusual. He was authorised to grant pardons to those in rebellion 'without any limitation', and only the clutch of men actually responsible for Sharp's murder were excluded.[3] These remarkably clement terms were drawn up after the king had a series of meetings with Scottish noblemen in London, in which they had argued that if Lauderdale were removed and various grievances addressed, the rebels would back down.[4] Monmouth, as captain general and one of the chief politicians of the day, must have participated in discussions about his mission, and his interest in the plight of the lowland Scots remained. That summer he was once again with Hamilton, Cassilis and other Scottish noblemen presenting the case against Lauderdale to the king and again he succeeded in convincing the king to meet them after he had at first refused. Given Charles's own loveless attitude to the Presbyterians there may well have been some truth in the report of one contemporary that the leeway Monmouth was allowed in the issue of pardons had been his condition for accepting the commission.[5]

Monmouth covered the 400 miles to Edinburgh at speed. He left Whitehall at 3 a.m. on 15 June and spent three days and nights on the road, not stopping to sleep but dozing when he could as his coach jerked and jolted its way north. Something of the pace and energy of his movements even on his return journey are revealed in the experience of the Yorkshire MP John Reresby, who waited to welcome him to Doncaster on his way south. With still no sign of Monmouth well into the night, Reresby gave up and went to bed in the room that had been prepared for the duke. Sometime after midnight Monmouth arrived, ate a quick supper and 'would not have the sheets changed, but went into the same bed', before setting off again at daybreak.

Arriving in Edinburgh at noon on 18 June, Monmouth lost no time – despite the bone-shaking three days he had just spent on the road – and went straight into a meeting of the Scottish Privy Council, informing them of his instructions and of his intention to inspect the army and quell the uprising 'without delay'.[6] The scout he had dispatched had established how things lay: the rebels already numbered around 5,000 and were camped south of Glasgow in the new park of Hamilton Palace, where the River Clyde divided the Hamilton lands from the Bothwell estates to the north. The Duke of Hamilton himself remained in London throughout the uprising, keeping a safe distance from the treasonous activities of the rebels – not entirely easy given their presence on his lands and the coincidence of the ringleader's surname.[7]

Monmouth's antipathy to Lauderdale, plus his reputation as a champion of Protestantism, preceded him and Robert Hamilton and the rebels presented their petition as soon as he arrived. Addressing the duke warmly 'as a reliver of the opprest and a seasonable preventer of all the miseries and ruines That threatine this poor land', they asked leave to come and lay their hearts open to him.[8] If Monmouth was moved by this, he did not show it. Refusing to see the rebels in person, he sent an officer to parley with them on Thursday evening. Having found 10,000 troops already assembled he decided not to wait for the remaining English regiments to arrive. Instead he advanced towards Hamilton, taking up a position six miles north, with the Clyde now the main obstacle between the royal forces and the rebels.[9]

At 7 a.m. on Sunday 22 June Monmouth was ready to attack. His regiments were arrayed along the north bank of the Clyde facing the rebels across the water, with the barricaded Bothwell Bridge the only land access between them. The rebels tried to barter terms again and Monmouth replied that if they would lay down their arms and surrender he would 'interpose for their pardon'. When they refused he declared their demands 'destructive to the king's Authority, and contrary to the fundamental Laws and Constitutions of this Kingdom', and gave the order to attack. The cannon on the rising north bank of the river discharged their devastating loads on the rebels and a direct assault on the bridge began. Outnumbered some two to one, there was little hope for Robert Hamilton's ragtag army and Monmouth soon had control of the bridge. His forces forged over it to attack head-on. The rebel cavalry scattered almost immediately and the foot soldiers that remained were quickly routed. News of Monmouth's 'totall & absolut victory' reached Edinburgh in time for it to be included in a London despatch at midnight. While some 600 rebels had been killed, the casualties on the royal side numbered just four.[10]

In the aftermath of the battle Monmouth discovered that his soldiers were continuing to kill the defeated rebels after he had claimed victory. Disgusted at what he considered to be executions, he insisted the rebels be taken as prisoners, as a consequence of which some 1,200 men were captured. One among them was a John Kid who, like many, surrendered on the promise of his life being spared. He was interviewed in person by the Duke of Monmouth, who confirmed the terms and 'assure[d] me that I should not onely be secure as to the said quarter, but also be civilly used'. While it was explicitly allowed for in Monmouth's instructions, this clemency provoked questions. The Duke of York sneered at it as a cheap bid for personal popularity while the king remarked in a cold aside that if he had been present there would not have been any prisoners to worry about. To these rebukes delivered hundreds of miles from the corpse-strewn banks of the Clyde, Monmouth's reply was brief: whatever others might do, 'he could not kill men in cold blood . . . that was only for butchers'.[11]

Over the first six months of 1679 there had developed, if not exactly a friendship, then certainly an association between the Earl of Shaftesbury, the leader of the Whig opposition, and the Duke of Monmouth. The duke periodically travelled from his base in the West End to gatherings at Thanet House, Shaftesbury's home in Aldersgate Street on the edge of the City of London.[12] When Monmouth had been absent from the House of Lords during a vote on excluding Catholics from Parliament in November 1678, little was read into it.[13] But the winter of 1678/79 had seen Monmouth's behaviour in the House of Lords shift. Appalled by the revelations about the government's secret dealings with France, opposed to the Duke of York on personal and political grounds, and now emboldened and encouraged by his new contacts, Monmouth no longer felt obliged to maintain his unbroken record of support for the government. Danby kept obsessive lists of the voting behaviour of his fellow peers in the various motions against him in the spring of 1679. When he noted those he reckoned to be for or against him in March 1679, Monmouth was still down as a government supporter, though significantly as one of nine who were 'to bee spoke to by the King' to ensure loyalty.[14] When he drew up a second list very shortly afterwards Monmouth had changed columns and was now under 'against' with an added 'x' for 'unreliable'.[15] Sure enough when on 14 April a bill of attainder was presented in the Lords declaring Danby guilty of treason without the need for a trial, Monmouth voted for it, and the bill passed by three votes – though the death sentence would never actually be carried out.[16] The following month there was a vote on whether a committee of both houses should enquire into the trial of the Catholic lords accused of involvement in the Popish Plot, and Monmouth again voted with the opposition.[17]

The Duke of York's explanation for Monmouth's changing political behaviour was that his nephew was a pawn in a sinister political game. He told William of Orange in May that Shaftesbury had made 'a property of him [Monmouth] to ruine our family'.[18] To York it was unthinkable that his nephew could have formed such political views himself. From his Brussels exile York wrote to the king claiming that Monmouth, overwhelmed with personal ambition, was positioning himself as a figurehead for the opposition. Charles II conceded some of Monmouth's recent conduct was 'amiss' but did not accept the argument for his motives. He 'rather blam'd the Duke [of York] for beginning too harshly with him'.[19] The Duke of York's paranoid fear of his nephew's advancement had been visible in the vetoes he had exercised on Monmouth's career over the past six years. He had agreed to go into exile in March 1679 only after the king lodged in the Privy Council Register a signed declaration that 'for the avoyding of any dispute concerning the succession of the Crown. . . that I never gave nor made any contract of marriage, nor was married to any woman whatsoever, but to my present wife Queen Catherine'. The king was perfectly aware of Monmouth's dealings with Shaftesbury and while he did not like it, he did not see it as a serious threat nor did it challenge his 'natural love' for his son. While there might be grumbling about Monmouth's mercy to the Scots rebels, his behaviour had been within the terms of his instructions and his swift quelling of the rebellion spoke of his steadfastness in carrying out royal policy.[20]

In reality Monmouth and Shaftesbury had both shared interests and significant points of difference. They agreed on the need for Danby to be brought to justice for his dealings with the French and, for their own cocktail of reasons, each came to see the exclusion of the Duke of York as essential. By contrast the other new men on the coalition council – Sunderland, Essex and Halifax – had by the summer of 1679 been won over by Charles's offers of limitations on the power of a future Catholic king. Monmouth, like Shaftesbury, believed in the reality of the Popish Plot, but he never developed the feverish anti-Catholicism on which Shaftesbury traded. Monmouth employed a Catholic barber, Thomas Dearlove, until his own departure from England in the autumn of 1679, when he wrote him a generous personal recommendation addressed to his old tutor the Catholic Father Gough in Paris.[21] Both viewed Lauderdale's treatment of the Scottish lowlanders as outrageous, and Shaftesbury's language in Parliament that spring, condemning the indignity to which the 'ancient nobility and gentry' of the kingdom had been subjected, echoed the case Monmouth had made to the king a year earlier. But when news of the Scottish rebellion reached the council, Shaftesbury had argued vehemently against sending an army to suppress it, contending it should be calmed without force. According to Henry Sidney, he was 'ill pleased' with Monmouth, and a number of prominent Whigs, among them Lord Grey of Werk, had refused to serve on the expedition. Monmouth, on the other hand, having secured the wide-ranging rights to pardon, had set about putting down the insurrection with the swift discipline of the professional soldier.[22] While he voted with Shaftesbury on the attainder of Danby, Monmouth did not join the twenty-eight opposition lords in lodging a protest on the voting rights of bishops in the House of Lords on the last day of the parliamentary session. If Shaftesbury ever imagined Monmouth would be his puppet, he was quickly disappointed.[23]

In the weeks before the king's sudden dissolution of Parliament on 27 May 1679 the notion that the Duke of York might be written out of the royal succession went suddenly from outrageous idea to concrete parliamentary proposal, bringing with it the loaded question of who, then, would take his place. There were really only two broad possibilities. First, that the throne would simply skip York and pass to the next in line, his daughter Mary, probably in some sort of partnership with her husband, William of Orange; both as Mary's husband and as a grandson of Charles I – and so fourth in line to the throne himself after Mary's sister Anne – William's participation in his wife's sovereignty was assumed. The second was that Monmouth would be made eligible through his illegitimacy being somehow expunged. As the king's legitimate son he would then leapfrog everyone. A third possibility – that the king would be persuaded to divorce the queen, allowing for a new marriage and legitimate children – was more or less discounted in the summer of 1679.[24]

While Thomas Armstrong might gossip of Monmouth as king, and Shaftesbury let the rumour run to add to the popular clamour against York, Monmouth himself had not talked of it at all. It would have been dramatically out of character for a man who had a few years earlier tried to turn down the position of brigadier in the French army on the basis that he lacked experience suddenly to start promoting himself as the next king, so disinheriting not just his uncle but many other members of his own family. When William of Orange asked him outright about the rumours that he was angling for the throne, Monmouth replied simply that he 'he hadn't the least thought of it and never would have'.[25]

Monmouth was a royal bastard with the ability and appetite for power, but it did not therefore follow that his sights were set on the Crown – indeed precedent suggested something else. It had been over a century since an illegitimate child had been born to an English sovereign, but the last, Henry VIII's son Henry Fitzroy, had been made Duke of Richmond and was clearly being groomed for a career in his father's service. More recently the whole of the southern Netherlands had been governed by Philip IV of Spain's illegitimate son, Juan José, who would go on to be viceroy of Aragon. On the journey from Colombes to Brussels in 1659, Charles II and Lord Crofts – and so presumably the ten-year-old Monmouth himself – had spent two nights with Henri de Bourbon, Comte de Verneuil. An illegitimate son of Henry IV of France (and so Charles II's uncle), Verneuil was made Bishop of Metz, and would go on to receive a dukedom. In 1665 he had visited London as Louis XIV's ambassador charged with trying to mediate between the English and the Dutch. He had lodged in great state at Berkshire House on Pall Mall and remained in and around Whitehall for eight months during which his and Monmouth's paths must often have crossed. On his return to France he was made the governor of Languedoc. In these two contemporary cases in Europe's premier

monarchies royal bastards were given part of their country's territories to manage on the sovereign's behalf. Monmouth quite likely
hoped for something similar – not least as his taking charge of both
Ireland and Scotland had already been seriously considered.

In respect of the Crown itself Monmouth probably saw William
of Orange as the obvious beneficiary should the exclusion of his
uncle ever be effected. For the cosmopolitan Monmouth, William
III was far less alarmingly foreign than he appeared to many
Englishmen – who considered Monmouth's Englishness a heavy
mark in his favour. William and Monmouth were first cousins,
their wives were close friends and after fighting together at St
Denis the previous summer Monmouth regarded the stadtholder
with genuine admiration.[26] Sometime after returning from Scotland
the duke commissioned Jan Wyck to paint a series of large battle
paintings, one showing Bothwell Bridge and another a battle of the
1679 campaign on which Monmouth and William fought together
against the French. An elaborate engraving of the two men by side
at the battle of St Denis dedicated to the Duke of Monmouth had
also been produced. Such pairings are a measure of Monmouth's
respect for his cousin and might even be interpreted as statements
of allegiance.[27]

When Monmouth's dusty coach rumbled back from Edinburgh on
9 July 1679 he passed not through the teeming streets of London
to Whitehall, but up the steep slope to the castellated splendour of
Windsor Castle. Five years before, the king had resolved to bring
the court to the castle every summer and each year the massive
programme of building works he had set in train had to be halted
to accommodate these visits.[28] Under the auspices of the architect
Hugh May the royal apartments built for Edward III had been reno-
vated. The castle then, as now, was formed in a figure of eight, with
the royal apartments in the upper court or ward and the officers of
the Order of the Garter among others, accommodated in the lower.
In May's rebuilding the king's and queen's apartments remained
on the north side of the upper ward, with spectacular views of the

revetments and counterscarps of the 'Maastricht' meadows. May had considered his site carefully and the new buildings retained much of the rhythm of wall and tower characteristic of medieval martial masonry. Inside the interiors were of the first fashion and their exuberant painted allegorical wall and ceiling decoration had just been completed by Antonio Verrio – who had been given a personal dispensation from the ban on Catholics at court. The king's mistress, the Duchess of Portsmouth, and Monmouth, as Master of the Horse, had rooms on the floor below the king's apartments, while the Duke and Duchess of York were lodged on the eastern side of the ward and Princess Anne in the tower on the corner. Separate suites were allocated to Monmouth's children and their governess.[29]

The moment news of Monmouth's success at Bothwell Bridge had reached Whitehall, Charles II, who had been itching to get out of the capital, announced the court's departure for Windsor and by 30 June he was installed there in the new apartments.[30] The suspicion with which the king regarded his new coalition Privy Council was expressed in the geography of their business. Instead of coming to Windsor for their meetings, the members were instructed to gather twelve miles away at Hampton Court, with the king coming over for the day to join them. In anticipation of this arm's-length arrangement the king had ordered the rebuilding of the Hampton Court council chamber a few months earlier.[31]

After the victory at Bothwell Bridge and his humane treatment of the prisoners, Monmouth's popular reputation as a Protestant hero soared. In Edinburgh, where he had remained for a fortnight, he had been feasted by the civic dignitaries and presented with the freedom of the city. At a meeting of the Scottish Privy Council after the battle, it was ordered, with Charles II's agreement, that the lowland Scots should no longer be persecuted and in rural areas south of the Tay indoor conventicles would henceforth be permitted. When Monmouth rode south for London he left 'a mighty reputation behind him in Scotland for clemency and indulgence'. He was welcomed at Windsor as a hero, winning applause from all quarters.

The king received him with 'great tenderness' and was so delighted that he even allowed the troublemaker Armstrong to return. In the opinion of one senior government figure, Monmouth was now 'greater than ever'.[32]

While the Duke of Monmouth's career had taken a dramatic turn for the better, his domestic arrangements had not improved. When Henry Sidney, who Monmouth had visited on his sickbed in Antwerp, saw the duke and his wife at Windsor that month he noted with surprise that the duchess addressed her husband icily as 'sir'.[33] After the death of their first baby, Anna had borne Monmouth a child a year for the following four years, so that they now had three sons and a daughter. But this intimacy ceased with the birth of Francis, named after Anna's father, in November 1677.[34] While Monmouth's experience as an administrator had taught him to be a much more responsible manager of his own money, his continuing infidelity and lack of attention to her only encouraged Anna's extravagance. When he was in France in 1677, Monmouth asked Melville, one of the commissioners for their Scottish estates, to 'lett me know if my wife begins to looke after her bussines at home, and if their bee any hopes of her being a good husiue [housewife]'.[35]

The Monmouths' Whitehall lodgings were now vastly bigger than they had been when they first occupied them in 1665. They had acquired much of what had belonged to the Duke of Albemarle in the early 1670s, whose extensive set of rooms around the Tudor Cockpit, looking out onto St James's Park, backed on to theirs. This more than doubled the size of their apartments. A remodelling to incorporate these rooms had taken place largely at the king's expense during the summer and autumn of 1674, with the birth of their second child, James, providing a subtext. A new dining room was created, and with it a large kitchen, cook's room, larder, cellars and bottle room – filled with the champagne Anna loved to drink – and a confectionary for the preparation of exotic sweet desserts. The expansion allowed for the separate rooms that both fashion and the couple's cool relationship made desirable. So while Monmouth remained in their original street-front rooms

Anna moved into a new apartment that opened off the same principal stairs. These comprised her own dining room, withdrawing room and separate great and little bedchambers, with a closet and privy beyond, all with richly plastered ceilings bearing their entwined initials.[36]

Among the duke and duchess's own rooms was expanded accommodation for their household. This included a new apartment for Francis Watson, who had taken over from Stephen Fox in managing their day-to-day financial affairs and of whom Monmouth had told Charles II in 1674: 'I do a sur you Sr Mr Watson has had great Care of My family and has put it in mutch beater order then ever it was.'[37] Thomas Ross was now largely retired after a distinguished career which had seen him serve outside Monmouth's household, in the royal library and as a diplomatic aide, but always retaining his £200 annual salary and lodgings with the duke. After the death of his wife, Ross had married Anna's lady-in-waiting Mary Mintern, who was also in her fifties and had served alongside Ross for a decade since the marriage of their employers.[38] The gentle old bibliophile must have looked at his former pupil's transformation from selfish wastrel to principled politician with pride, and the mutual affection showed in the allocation to Ross of the loveliest rooms overlooking the Park. Also allocated rooms was William Ford, the long-standing steward, while new wardrobe and linen rooms were created to house the Monmouths' colossal collection of clothes.[39] And all this was on top of the nursery where Lord Doncaster and his three little siblings held sway.[40]

While the froideur between Anna and Monmouth remained, both were still very much a part of the royal family. When the Duke of York complained to William of Orange that the Whigs were cultivating Monmouth it was the ruin of 'our family' that he described as the consequence. Anna remained close to Princess Mary, and in September 1678 when the news of the Popish Plot was breaking, she, the Duchess of York and Princess Anne were on a two-week visit to Mary at The Hague.[41] There the imperious Duchess of Monmouth was temporarily softened by what she described as

Mary's 'extraordinary sueetnes', and witnessed the affection which had unexpectedly unfurled between her friend and the husband about whom only a year before she had wept in such misery. The proud Anna never doubted she deserved the de facto membership of the royal family she and Monmouth enjoyed. The king dined with his daughter-in-law regularly, with or without the duke, and she had no hesitation in creating in her new Whitehall apartments the paired bedchambers, one with a large recess or alcove in which the bed was placed, that were such distinctive features of the king and queen's own rooms. Her hauteur was enough to convince some that the rumours about Monmouth displacing his uncle as heir to the throne were of her invention.[42]

Anna's sense of status and the couple's fast-growing family were probably behind the rebuilding of Moor Park, which was the duchess's principal interest in the summer of 1679. This was not so much a country house – Monmouth had no wish to be many days' journey from court – but more a large suburban villa, as Chiswick had been in the 1660s, and as the Duke of Buckingham, for instance, had built at Cliveden. Hugh May made a model of what he proposed, which involved an extensive rebuilding to create a fashionable 'double pile' house. On 15 September contracts were signed 'for the takeing down one old house and setting up and erecting a new house or pile of Building for his Grace in Moore Parke'. As well as overseeing the king's remodelling of Windsor, May had recently been working on Cassiobury, the home of Monmouth's fellow council member Arthur Capel, Earl of Essex, on lands that adjoined Moor Park, and some of the details were to be modelled on those at Cassiobury. Built of brick, the Monmouths' new Moor Park was substantial without being vast. It was smaller than Ham House in Petersham, which the Duke of Lauderdale had remodelled just a few years earlier. Three storeys over a basement, Moor Park incorporated five suites of rooms over the ground and first floors, one each for Monmouth and Anne and three more which could accommodate their growing family. But, as the couple were about to discover, the orders for rebuilding and the financial outlay they involved could not have been issued at a more inauspicious moment.[43]

The court spent the high summer of 1679 out of the capital. Army affairs kept Monmouth shuttling back and forward between London and Windsor, where the king was, but much other business had ceased. The Privy Council was in recess and Parliament had been dissolved with the year's second general election not due till the autumn. The Duke of York remained in exile in Brussels while Shaftesbury, like many others, had left London for his country estate, not to return until the end of September.[44] It was a quiet time and, with company at Windsor thin, the king spent several days quietly fishing on the Thames. And then something quite unexpected happened. After a short sailing expedition on the Solent, Charles developed a cold.[45] He was forty-nine and in excellent health, so this in itself was no cause for concern. By Saturday 23 August, however, the cold had developed into an alarmingly high fever. The following day, though weak and pale, he seemed better. But in the middle of Sunday night the fever returned, more ferocious than before, and as he soaked his sheets with sweat and began vomiting violently, it became clear he was dangerously ill. Monmouth was at Windsor, standing anxiously by as the doctors came and went. At 5 a.m. scores of glistening leeches were laid all over the king's shivering flesh, in the belief that by feeding on his blood they would relieve the illness. His thirst was immense and he gulped glass after glass of water and wine before enduring the added agony of being unable to urinate.[46]

The whole experience can only have been deeply frightening for Monmouth. But as one of the few Privy Councillors with the king he knew he had to stay calm. After the horror of Sunday night he sat down on Monday morning to write to the lord mayor of London, who given the absence of court and Parliament, was the most senior figure in the capital. The king had been and remained ill, he explained, but had been 'eased' by his treatment and the doctors were giving an encouraging prognosis. He promised to write every day with news.[47] While Monmouth remained level-headed, many about him did not. Three months earlier the dissolution of Parliament had left the question of who would succeed on Charles II's death unresolved. The discussion that in May had seemed almost abstract was now terrifyingly real.

The Privy Council, like the political nation, was split. The earls of Sunderland, Halifax and Essex had become reconciled to the prospect of the Duke of York succeeding Charles II so long as there were strict limitations on his authority. Monmouth and Shaftesbury on the other hand had not, believing, in the words of Algernon Sidney, it was just 'a little golding to cover a poisonous pill'. When Essex and Halifax had failed effectively to oppose the king's dissolution of Parliament in July, Shaftesbury had raged furiously that for this betrayal he would have their heads.[48] If the king were now to die with York out of the country, these three foresaw that Monmouth would 'be at the head of the nation in opposition to the Duke [of York]', which spelled both extreme political instability and the end of their careers.[49] With this prospect looming, action was required. On Monday 25 August, as Monmouth was reassuring the lord mayor, Sunderland sent a covert letter to the Duke of York in Brussels. When York read it three days later he made up his mind in an instant. He had to return.[50]

By Wednesday the king's bedchamber at Windsor was overflowing. Seven doctors attended – each prescribing treatments that were alike only in their ineffectiveness – and with them all the gentlemen of the bedchamber and half the Privy Council. As his fever waxed and waned the king, vomiting, seized by fits and defecating in his bed, endured all the pain and indignity of the dying. Illness was a special sort of torture for a sovereign, every symptom peered at by the scores of spectators who crowded around and all privacy denied to one whose body was not his alone. The Earl of Ranelagh wrote home on Wednesday that for the last four days he had 'hardly been out of his [the king's] bed chamber'. The allegorical figures of Verrio's painted ceiling must have swam before the king's delirious eyes, and the thick summer air been made all the more unbearable by the press of perspiring bodies in the tapestried rooms.[51]

As the king gasped for life, the Duke of York was stealing towards England. With no permission to return, and well aware just how politically incendiary his appearance would be, he travelled in disguise, accompanied by only three others. Crossing the Channel in a French vessel, he arrived in London after dark. There at the house of Allan Apsley his friends told him his movements remained a secret, and he journeyed on to reach Windsor at sunrise. At seven in the morning on Tuesday 2 September, after seven months' absence, and totally unannounced, the Duke of York walked into the royal bedchamber. But the surprise was mutual, for instead of the dying man he expected to see York found his brother, calm and dressed, waiting for his barber to apply the frothed egg whites before he was shaved.[52]

The king had passed out of danger a few days before, but there was no question the whole episode had been a profound shock. For nearly a week it had looked as if Charles II might not live, and as his illness had ebbed and flowed, better one day, far worse the next, the agony and uncertainty was protracted. Algernon Sidney arrived at court to find 'men's minds more disturbed than ever I remember them to have been, so as there is no extremity of disorder to be imagined, that we might not probably have fallen into if the king had died'.[53] The political danger was such that as soon as the king was conscious he was receiving visitors, propped up on a pile of pillows in his bedchamber. Among them was the lord chief justice, William Scroggs, who had – despite massive popular pressure – helped ensure a number of Catholics close to the queen were not condemned to die on Titus Oates's spurious evidence. The feeble and drained king extended his hand for the anxious Scroggs to kiss, 'renewing to him ye assurance yt he wou'd stand by him'.[54]

The reverberations of that week would be felt for the rest of the reign. The panic had polarised allegiances in ways which could not now be undone. In the days after the king's recovery Sunderland tried to convince Monmouth that he had had nothing to do with recalling York, but it was too late.[55] When William Temple arrived at Windsor, he met the Earl of Halifax, who owed his position on the Privy Council to Monmouth's cajoling of the king four months before. Now he was implicated in the enterprise to bring York home, Halifax and Monmouth had parted ways and the earl mumbled to Temple that he was going home 'to think over this new world'.[56]

For Monmouth the behaviour of Sunderland, Halifax and Essex was extraordinary. He had been instrumental in the creation of the coalition council on which they served, and in trying to make it work; together they had spent much of the past nine months advocating measures to limit or bypass York, whose exile was something they had supported as politically essential. Why then, when the king was ill, had they gone behind his back to surreptitiously summon York home? Monmouth was not one for double-dealing and political intrigue; if anything he had a streak of personal and political naivety. His well-attested bravery combined with a clear sense of fairness and justice made him a different creature to the politically and morally adroit operators of the restoration court. A divide began to open up between Monmouth and many of his fellow councillors. In part this was because they regarded him as a political threat as an alternative candidate for the Crown, and in part because he just saw things in more straightforward terms than they.

The king had received his brother with affection. Perhaps after his brush with death he was grateful to see his only living sibling, or perhaps he had been party to York's return. Either way he knew that with the general election only weeks away, York could not stay in England or he risked being excluded or even arrested. York for his part, furious at the prospect of leaving his 'professed enemy' Monmouth with the king while he was banished, argued that if he had to go, then Monmouth should be sent away too.[57] Sunderland, Halifax and Essex also now had reason to want to neutralise Monmouth, who they had angered, and so raised no objection.[58] But as the king had never paid any attention to anyone else's opinion, when it came to his oldest son this in itself was barely material.

The person whom the king's illness had most altered, however, was Charles II himself. Inclined to take each day as it came, and not to trouble himself too much with the future or his own mortality, that week in August had left the normally sanguine sovereign changed.[59] Deeply affected by the experience, he emerged more certain and more serious and seized suddenly with the importance of taking control. His love for Monmouth was unaltered, but as he took slow recuperative walks in Windsor Great Park, passing beneath Edward III's ramparts and among the magnificent trees of the medieval hunting park, he saw his responsibility to the institution for which his own father had died in new terms. The sort of emasculated kingship which he was proposing his brother be given in order to placate the Whigs seemed to him now a betrayal. He had to stop bartering terms and instead assert his authority and that of the ancient office he held. Two days after York's return and a week exactly after his last fit, the convalescing king talked candidly to the French ambassador. The normally languid Charles was '*fort inquiet et fort alarmé*', leaving Barillon certain that great changes were about to occur. The most significant of these was that he had made up his mind that the popular disorder which Monmouth's supporters were whipping up was unacceptably dangerous. He would send York away once again, but he would also banish Monmouth.[60]

On the evening of Wednesday 10 September, in his lodgings at Windsor, Charles finally broke the news to his son. That it had taken him almost a week to do so was a measure of how little he relished the conversation. Monmouth recounted the bones of it to a friend shortly afterwards: 'the K. told him Yorke would not depart if he went not also; thereupon he must go'.[61] Not only was he to leave court and England, but he was to surrender his job as captain general of the army – something else York had demanded in exchange for returning to exile.[62] In the course of the meeting Monmouth's whole firmament cracked. The news was sharper and more shocking than any battlefield blow. For him the love, loyalty and labour he had given the king, as his son, his general and his councillor, were being met with brutal rejection. For one who felt wrongs inflicted on others so keenly, the injustice of his father's actions that September day must have been overwhelming. As he absorbed the news his disbelief turned to bitter fury. If he was not fit to be general, why then was he being kept on as captain of the guards, he demanded, suggesting that the post be given to his half-brother the Earl of Grafton instead. The following morning, his first flush of fury having dulled in dawn's cool light, Monmouth saw the king again and, subdued, took back his resignation of the Life Guards and told his father that he would obey his instructions. Shattered, he instructed St Gill to pack his bags and he left Windsor for London.[63]

The news of Monmouth's banishment, when it got out, was a sensation, and 'like gunpowder set on fire, did in an instant run over ye whole city'.[64] The duke arrived in London to find bonfires already blazing and bells ringing out in loud expressions of popular support for him. Angry crowds gathered round the pyres demanding that any affluent-looking figure drink the Duke of Monmouth's health or be fined and declared a papist.[65] Waves of visitors came to the Cockpit to express their support, among them for instance, the city magistrate Edmund Warcup. The pressure the opposition figures put on Monmouth to disregard his father's orders was enormous – even York admitted that they did everything they could 'to perswade him to disobay his Majesty's comands'. But while the duke agreed despondently that 'he suffred for the Protestant interest', he would not be talked round and began the miserable business of preparing to leave.[66]

Monmouth told the king he needed time to see to his affairs, which was in part a delaying tactic and in part the truth – the range of his offices gave him a great deal to put in order. However resentful he felt, he did not lose his sense of responsibility for his departments and dependents, and he set about paying all his debts.[67] He appointed Viscount Falconbridge to oversee his responsibilities as chief justice of the southern royal forests, gave Stephen Fox power of attorney in relation to the contracts for the rebuilding of Moor Park, and made arrangements for his royal pensions to be received in his absence, which since the birth of his children had risen to £8,000 a year.[68] He submitted the paperwork to reclaim the £3,000 he had spent from his own pocket to feed the army on campaign the previous summer.[69] Though he was being relieved of his command, he was anxious to ensure his men were properly provided for. He left detailed instructions to Fox – as paymaster of the army – for the precise salary to be paid to each rank of soldier for the rest of the year, so that none should fall into arrears. And he dealt with a number of awkward individual disputes: to Drum Major William Young he arranged a payment of £20 for eight months' service the previous year, after his name had been mistakenly left off the army list; to the warring parties in a dispute over who had the right to collect the toll on Sutton Street in Clerkenwell, he decided in favour of the 'tenants and parishioners' on condition that they pay the income to the poor of the parish.[70]

Throughout the fortnight after the king's devastating announcement Monmouth hoped his father might change his mind. Despite the Damoclean sword hanging over him, he attended the Privy Council on 19 and 21 September, sitting in his usual chair, and the king treated him with his accustomed kindness. But the signs were not good. His army commissions, which had always taken so long to materialise, were rescinded with sickening speed. Barely twenty-four hours after his first interview with the king, Sunderland had drawn up the documents formally discharging him of responsibilities he had exercised for five years.[71] On 18 September a rumour suddenly went up that the king had had a change of heart. Within hours Westminster was ablaze with celebratory bonfires, until the story was scotched and the fires doused in bitter disappointment.[72]

When the king decided to send Monmouth away he knew that in the short term it would enflame the popular feeling against the court and the Duke of York. But this, he felt, was a consequence worth enduring to make a public statement of his support for his brother as heir to the throne.[73] What he had not properly considered was what it would do to Monmouth. Those not directly involved were astonished enough: the French ambassador remarked a few days later that there simply could not have been a greater change at court than that which had taken place regarding the Duke of Monmouth.[74] For the duke himself the shock was immeasurable.

The strength of Charles II's feeling for Monmouth owed something to his sense of responsibility for one whom he, Charles, had stolen from his mother. Just as Charles loved Monmouth completely, so too Monmouth's affection was absorbed by his father. The king had smothered him in love without end, and every material or financial expression of it he cared to name. While the king was the centre of his world, Monmouth had been emotionally satisfied. No woman had ever really engaged his heart, and other than those who worked for him, he had formed no very strong personal relationships outside the royal family. Almost everything he had and was physically and personally could be traced in some way to his father. Now suddenly for the second time in his life Monmouth was torn from the one person he loved most, and once again it was his father's doing. All the affection and approval which Charles had lavished on Monmouth since he was twelve years old seemed now, like a candle, to be being snuffed out.

On Wednesday 24 September, Monmouth went to the king's closet at Whitehall to take his leave. The meeting lasted barely half an hour and when he came out his handsome face was swollen and his cheeks stained with tears. Walking down the stairs, he passed the rooms where he had lived during his first year at court sixteen years earlier, before stepping out onto the royal landing stage. Only the handful of people with whom he was to travel were allowed to attend – for neither Monmouth nor the king had any reason to celebrate this parting. They included Charles Godfrey, Monmouth's master of the horse, Robert Langley, one of his long-serving officers, and Charles, Lord Gerrard of Brandon, the twenty-year-old son of his friend the Earl of Macclesfield.[75] At Gravesend he swapped the barge for a yacht and in the early light on Thursday morning he sailed for the continent. As Monmouth watched England recede over the wide grey sea, and with it everything that mattered to him, his heart ached with loss and his mood turned black and bitter.[76]

Chapter 13

Exclusion

When Monmouth sailed from England in September 1679 it was not clear, even to himself, where precisely he was bound. He talked in one breath of Copenhagen in another of Hamburg, while his cousin Prince Rupert had offered him his house on the Rhine in the province of Utrecht.[1] He travelled with just a handful of men, murmuring that Anna and the children could join him once he was settled.[2] From Gravesend his yacht sailed to the Dutch coast, and on the evening of 26 September he reached The Hague, the city of his conception.

Though capital of the wealthy United Provinces, The Hague was not a large city. With only 40,000 inhabitants, it was smaller than Rotterdam and only a fraction of the size of Amsterdam.[3] Compared to Paris and London, with populations approaching half a million, it was tiny. The city owed its status to the fact that for a century it had been the meeting place of the States General, and so the administrative centre of the republic. The Binnenhof, the moated medieval castle of the counts of Holland, stood in the centre of a city framed by a rectangular border of canals, and was both where the States General assembled and where the stadtholder resided – their cohabitation an expression of the hybrid Dutch political system. While The Hague was small and, several miles from the sea, lacked the prosperous docks of Rotterdam and Amsterdam, it was unquestionably affluent. The buildings Monmouth saw from his coach windows were tall brick and stone structures with large windows raised in recent decades, prominent among them the enormous baroque church, the Nieuwe Kerk.

The duke, accompanied by Robert Langley and Charles Godfrey, made for the house of their former fellow officer Henry Sidney, now English envoy-extraordinary to the United Provinces, where they had arranged to lodge. It was not an easy meeting. Sidney had become close to Sunderland and Monmouth did not hesitate to complain to his host of the behaviour of his 'friends'. A day or two later the two men went on an excursion a few miles north to the sandy shores of Scheveningen – from where Charles II had sailed home in 1660 – and there in the salty breeze talked of the events of the past weeks. Monmouth was downhearted and resentful, simmering with bitterness and self-pity as he talked 'a good deal of his own melancholy prospects' and of the anger of 'the people' at his expulsion.[4]

The day after his arrival Monmouth waited on his cousins and friends the Prince and Princess of Orange. But if he had expected a warm reception he was disappointed. William received him with chilling civility, making the merest small talk on trivialities before abruptly terminating the interview. Monmouth perhaps hoped for better from Mary, who from birth had been almost a younger sister to him. But when he walked into her apartments she did not even rise from the gaming table to greet him, coldly extending her hand for him to kiss before turning back to her cards.

The intense frostiness of William and Mary was not born of loyalty to Mary's father the Duke of York for, despite York's attempts to keep William close, the stadtholder regarded his father-in-law with little fondness or admiration. Rather William was fiercely protective of his and his wife's own places within the English succession, and received the rumours that Monmouth was positioning himself as his father's heir with displeasure. Only a few weeks earlier Sidney had talked to William of English politics and reported that the stadtholder 'is convinced that the Duke [of York] will never have the Crown, and I find would be very willing to be put into a way of having it himself'.[5]

Feeling further wounded and wronged, Monmouth announced that he would be leaving The Hague the following day, and William duly invited him to dine before his departure. In the early afternoon he presented himself at the Binnenhof and was taken into William and Mary's apartments on floors one above the other on the western, entrance side of the great courtyard. Thirty-one years earlier William and Monmouth's respective parents – William II and Mary Stuart, Charles Prince of Wales and Lucy Walter – had revelled together after a dinner in those same rooms during the week Monmouth was conceived. But now, as the cousins picked their way through the dishes in near-silence, the atmosphere was funereal rather than festive. They were just rising from the table when Monmouth, desperate at the thought of leaving things this way, asked William in a low and urgent voice if they might have a private conversation. The stadtholder, perhaps moved by their camaraderie the previous summer, or simply mindful of Monmouth's political influence, agreed. They withdrew from the press of the state rooms into the garden of William's closest friend, and fellow veteran of the battle of Mons, Hans Willem Bentinck. Hangers-on, including Henry Sidney, were unable to follow as the two figures – one tall, one short – passed to and fro along the shady walks.[6]

Monmouth began by producing from his pocket the letter that Charles II had given him on his departure and asking William to read it. Rather than reproof, it was full of words of affection and regret at the exile being imposed.[7] In 'very kind' language the king had written that he wished York could have stayed so that Monmouth might have remained too. As such the letter confirmed the case Monmouth put to William: that his expulsion was not a punishment but a measure the king had been persuaded to adopt to ensure the Duke of York returned abroad. William brightened at this, and began to quiz Monmouth closely on the rumours that he sought the throne. The duke conceded 'that he knew some reports had been spread of his having set up pretensions during the Kings illness, but that he was not so mad as to entertain such idle fancies'. William asked him to repeat this, warning that were he to have 'the least thoughts of such pretentions' they could never be friends. Monmouth then promised the prince that he did not, and never would, seek the throne for himself, upon which William remarked – part compliment, part threat – that he knew he would never break his word.[8]

After their meeting in Bentinck's garden relations between Monmouth and William were transformed. William quickly talked his cousin into staying in the Netherlands, offered him a house in The Hague and invited him to hunt at his palace of Honselaarsdijk just outside the city.[9] Monmouth was delighted at this change of heart, and wrote gushingly to his father of the great kindness he had received – cheered by the knowledge that the news would reach and rile his uncle. When this new warmth was questioned by Sidney, William was bullish: 'he said he thought it not fit to make any excuse because he did not think there was any fault' and that 'he used him no better than he thought he ought to do one that the king writ such kind letters to'. After the excursion to Honselaarsdijk, Monmouth passed up the house in The Hague and left suddenly for Prince Rupert's house at Rhenen – news having just been brought that the Duke of York himself was about to arrive in the Dutch capital.[10]

When Monmouth had embarked from the privy stairs at Whitehall a week earlier his misery at leaving was equalled only by his uncle's jubilation. The following day York emerged from his own leave-taking visibly elated, and as he passed the hordes lining the way to his lodgings his proud satisfaction increased. The king's illness had startled many into pledging loyalty to the Duke of York; as Charles himself had publicly endorsed York so others quickly followed suit. York's barge was so thronged with well-wishers when he left that it looked more like the launch of a royal progress than an expulsion.[11]

A week later York, his wife and young family paraded into The Hague, where they were received by his daughter and son-in law. York confided proudly to William that he and Charles II intended to dispense with parliaments altogether. The stadtholder did not hide his disapproval. His mood darkened further when a communiqué arrived from Charles II informing them that he had decided his brother should return to his dominions, albeit to live in Edinburgh. York beamed with delight, for while Edinburgh was not London, it was within the British Isles and so his foreign exile was over. Enclosed in a package from Whitehall was a letter addressed by the king to the Duke of Monmouth, which York ensured was forwarded to his nephew within half an hour of its arrival.

When Monmouth's long fingers broke the seal on his father's letter he was in rented lodgings in Utrecht, waiting for Rupert's house at Rhenen to be ready. Here he had spent the last week unable to rise from his bed, drained by a fever of which he wanted no news to reach home. It was as if his mental anguish had spread to his body. Pale and thin, and with his heart heavy, the arrival of the letters must momentarily have lifted his spirits – it might have been his summons to return. Instead it contained a further inexplicable blow. What precisely the king said to explain why York was to come home but Monmouth was not is not known, but whatever words he used, his promises and professions of love must now have rung hollow. The argument the king had put to him – that he had to go so that York would go – to which Monmouth had responded with obedience despite the agony it caused him, looked now to have been little better than a lie.[12]

York's recall changed everything. Monmouth's fury was shifting from his uncle to his father. To Sidney he said 'many slighting things' of the king, including that he had once heard him admit 'that if he could be well as long as he lived, he cared little what happened afterwards'.[13] In his first wave of rage at his father's betrayal he reeled off into the company of precisely the people who most agitated against the government, exiled English radicals. He went to Amsterdam, the largest city in the United Provinces, where he was wined and dined by such 'fanatics'. There he talked loudly of what a relief it was to be among real Protestants, and made conspicuous appearances at a number of church services with his increasingly large retinue. To the surprise of the grandees of the city he lodged with a Mr May, a barber, who was 'a great enemy of the king's'.[14] Among the English dissidents based in Amsterdam was one Robert Ferguson, a disreputable character who would later play his part in Monmouth's final fate.[15]

From Amsterdam he travelled on to Enkhuizen on the very eastern tip of north Holland, passing over terrain he had last seen in 1672 on Louis XIV's campaign, before journeying south to take up residence at Rhenen. The house here on the banks of the Rhine had been built for Prince Rupert's parents, Elizabeth of Bohemia and Frederick of the Palatinate, in the 1630s. Local dignitaries came to pay their respects and were delighted with 'his noble obliging carriage who neither carries himself lofty nor low, but with such a becoming grace that commands the very affections of all'.[16]

William of Orange, who had also been in the country for a fortnight, invited his cousin to hunt at his large rural estate twenty-five miles to the east of Rhenen at Dieren. Ever fastidious over dress and equipage, Monmouth sent for his own hunting horses and hounds from England on accepting. The two men spent the crisp autumn days thundering through the rides and copses of the vast Veluwe forest, pursuing deer and wild boar with the sunlight gilding the leaves of the beech trees overhead.[17] Here, a hundred miles from The Hague, and away from councillors and diplomats, they talked of people and politics, and what many Whigs hoped for, an alliance between William and Monmouth, started to take shape. The closeness between the cousins had, as predicted, set tongues wagging furiously in London, where 'everybody talks of the Prince's kindness to the Duke of Monmouth'.[18] Monmouth had gained a powerful friend and patron in William, and with a number of shared interests their relationship was politically as well as personally potent. He resolved to use The Hague as his base over the winter, keeping Rhenen as a rural retreat, and planning excursions to various European cities.

But it was not to be. As if to rub salt into his nephew's wounds, York was travelling to Edinburgh by land, going via London, while his daughters were to be taken home in the very yacht which had carried Monmouth into exile. York was warmly received by Charles II at Whitehall, and on 21 October he and the king attended a major feast in the City of London. The event was held by the Honourable Artillery Company, and saw a host of senior city figures pledge their support to York. Radiating self-satisfaction, York turned to his neighbour, Charles Hatton, and remarked that 'this was pritty well for a poor banished man so little a while since'.[19] A leisurely six days later he set out for Scotland on a slow and splendid progress, staying with a string of noblemen on the way. The king had clearly resolved to throw his whole weight behind his brother, and to Monmouth it must have been brutally plain that in doing so the father had decided to sacrifice his son. It needed now only the smallest straw to break the back of Monmouth's resolve.

Sometime in September or October, Thomas Dangerfield, a character every bit as dubious and duplicitous as Titus Oates himself, came before the king claiming to have evidence of a new plot against him, in which, this time, the Whigs were the villains. He reported having intelligence that a coup had been being discussed at various 'mutinous clubs' attended by Monmouth, Shaftesbury and other prominent Whigs. This was at first given some credence, and Dangerfield was paid some money to continue to investigate what – due to 'discovery' of a piece of evidence in an oatmeal jar – became known as the 'Meal Tub Plot'. But Dangerfield produced risibly unconvincing evidence and was soon exposed as a thief and forger, so the game was up almost before it began. Realising this, he quickly recast his story to claim he had been hired by Catholics to invent a plot to defame the Whigs. On 2 November, once Dangerfield's first tale had been discredited the king expressed his relief to the Whig magistrate Edmund Warcup during a private conversation in his bedchamber, remarking that 'he would not believe ill of Monmouth' and 'was glad they found he was not at the Clubbs'.[20]

As ever, news percolated across the Channel and when Monmouth returned to The Hague from his hunting trip on 8 November the story of the Meal Tub Plot awaited him. Over the coming days as news trickled in of its being a fiction, evidence of yet more Catholic wickedness was apparently exposed. Furious, frustrated and with his delicate sense of honour pricked, his resolve shattered.[21] With the utmost secrecy, and without a word to William, he despatched Charles Godfrey to London to make preparations: he was coming home.[22]

During the dramatic events of the past months, Monmouth had seen nothing of his political colleague the Earl of Shaftesbury. From mid-August to the end of September, Shaftesbury had been at home in Dorset, at a distant remove from events, causing several people to wonder what he would make of Monmouth's agreeing to go into exile. Now nearing sixty, and with the metal tube that stuck through his flesh on his side giving him pain, the little earl was becoming physically frail. At St Giles he was content, discussing estate matters with his steward, inspecting the horses in his vast brick stables and tending the ripening fruit in his beloved orchards.

The general election of the early autumn returned a firmly Whig House of Commons and was the magnet that drew Shaftesbury back to London in early October 1679. He found the court a changed place, with compromise utterly evaporated. On 14 October, the day before the king was to start attending again, he was sacked from the Privy Council for the second time in his career. The earl was not surprised, remarking tartly in his written reply that 'he wondered not much to be dismissed, when he so lately saw His Majesty advised to send away even a son with tears in his eyes'. The next day the king announced his intention to postpone Parliament until the new year, convinced that it if it met it would accuse his brother, and perhaps even the Queen, of treason and 'fall upon all that he considered right'. With the king intransigent and any hope of limitations on a future Catholic king fast fading, many were bitterly disappointed. Henry Sidney, then visiting England, wrote to William that 'the scene is quite changed'. Essex, Sir William Temple and Halifax, the members of the coalition council who had closed ranks on Monmouth during the king's illness, were now disillusioned and disappointed. Essex resigned from his position at the head of the Treasury, Halifax was 'out of humour' and talked of retiring, while Temple had withdrawn to his house at Sheen determined to have no further part in public affairs. Their faith in Charles II, like that of many others, had been misplaced.[23]

While William of Orange wanted to keep Monmouth in the United Provinces, there was real advantage for Shaftesbury and the other opposition leaders in their celebrity colleague returning.[24] Popular anti-Catholic feeling remained strong: the Duke of York was regarded with disapproval by most, and a widely admired alternative figurehead had powerful positive appeal. The Whig free-thinker Charles Blount published a luridly provocative pamphlet that autumn entitled 'An Appeal from the Country to the City', which painted a picture of London under a Catholic ruler as a place where ordinary citizens would witness the rape of their wives and daughters, their children's brains being dashed out against walls, their possessions plundered and their throats cut. Smithfield, Blount claimed, would once again ring with the screams of a sovereign burning his subjects – 'imagine you see your father or your mother or some of your nearest and dearest relations tied to a stake in the midst of flames'. The remedy, Blount claimed, was for Monmouth to take over when the king died: 'no person could be fitter. . . as well for quality, courage and conduct'.[25]

Pamphlets lamenting Monmouth's expulsion were followed by reports of his warm reception in the United Provinces, while a campaign was mounted from within the Whig camp to gather evidence to prove that Charles II had married Lucy Walter, which involved tracking down a host of part players in their liaison of thirty years before. But while things could be done to fuel the feeling against the Duke of York, without Monmouth himself they soon began to lack a certain lustre.[26] However, as powerful as any specific stimulus for Monmouth's sudden return was the simple fact that he had no talent for sitting still: patience was not a virtue he possessed, and just as an innate urge to act had called him forth out of the trenches and into the cannon fire at Maastricht, so the clamour and smoke of politics at home inevitably drew him out of exile and into the fray. Action was his métier.

After dark on Thursday 27 November, Monmouth arrived quietly at Charles Godfrey's house in Covent Garden. He stayed just a few hours, and at one in the morning travelled down King Street to his own lodgings at Whitehall. At daybreak he tried, just as York had done at Windsor three months earlier, to see his father in his bedchamber as he rose. If the king's illness had been acceptable grounds for York's unauthorised return, surely the accusations against him made in the Meal Tub Plot would justify his own actions. He was certainly not alone in considering that the revelations would prompt his recall.[27] But unlike York, Monmouth did not move with the collusion of those closest to the king, and he was refused entry. Astonished, he sent a note to the king apologising for returning without his leave and claiming he came only to clear his name of Dangerfield's accusations. The king angrily ordered him to return abroad before his presence in London was discovered. But it was already too late. Silent and nocturnal though Monmouth's arrival had been, the news had spread fast. The nightwatch passed the word around and pealing church bells were even then broadcasting it to the waking city. The streets rung with cheers 'ye Duke of Monmouth return'd!' By nightfall London was once again ablaze. Sixty bonfires were lit either side of the Strand alone. As one astonished observer remarked: 'it is very difficult to express fully ye prodigious acclamations of ye people nor can any one credit them who wase not an eye and eare witness'.[28]

As London celebrated Monmouth's return, his reception at Whitehall became only bleaker. Missives were carried up and down the long corridors between the Cockpit and the royal apartments throughout the day. While he might have expected to feel his father's displeasure, the king's refusal even to see him was shocking. This was a new level of personal rejection – gone were the emotional entreaties and tender words – and as Monmouth bristled with

anger, sadness and bruised pride his line hardened. He had come
to clear his name, and would not leave until he had done so. 'If his
Ma[jes]tie pleased to send him to the Tower or put any other confine-
ment upon him, he was ready to obey him and answer any charge
ag[ain]st him.'[29] His argument in specifics was absurd – Dangerfield
had admitted the accusations against Monmouth were lies almost a
month earlier. But there was a wider point of real substance. Why,
if he had done nothing wrong, was he to remain abroad? 'Banishment,' he insisted 'was the proper badge of a malefactor.' If he was
accused of some wrong-doing he would gladly hear it, and take
the consequences, but 'he could not go beyond the sea without
exposing his life or (what was dearer to him) his honour'.

Monmouth told the king he would not return to exile unless some
substantial charge against him was brought, prompting the king to
respond that he would not enter into a further correspondence but
expected to be obeyed. Monmouth, with the stubborn defiance of
child to parent, again refused. Exasperated, the king ordered him to
leave the palace and, opening the letter in rooms now filled with a
crowd of friends and hangers-on, Monmouth casually agreed, and
moved a few hundred yards north to his house adjoining the Royal
Mews. A last ultimatum was issued: the king, 'out of greate tender-
nesse', gave him till night to leave the country.[30]

It was no ordinary night. Monmouth's return formed the
crescendo of an autumn of popular demonstrations. November was
the season of Protestant celebrations. With Monmouth's banishment, the postponement of the new Parliament and the tales of
further plots, London was feverish. A week before his return a spectacular procession had snaked through the city on the anniversary
of Elizabeth's accession. Countless caricatures of Catholics – Fran-
ciscans, cardinals and Jesuits – were carried through the streets, led
by a hideous devil, towards a colossal bonfire at the city's west gate.
Here a benign figure of the Virgin Queen on Temple Bar, carrying
symbols of Magna Carta and the Protestant religion, had looked
on as each of the Catholic creatures was hurled into the flames as
the crowds roared their approval. All the while the ghoulish figure

of 'Sir Edm. Godfrey on horseback, murdered, in a black wig and pale-faced' looked on.[31]

On the night of Friday 28 November, with Monmouth's return now common knowledge and the stand-off at Whitehall holding, the city again erupted, with chants for 'Protestant Duke James' filling the air.[32] The Whig printing presses had worked fast, tipped off no doubt by Charles Godfrey earlier in the week, and churned out poems celebrating the return of 'Great Monmouth, darling of our British isle'. The bonfires on the Strand threw their sparks high into the darkness as crowds gathered about them, some mild, some menacing. Coaches were stopped in the street and prevented from passing until the inhabitants cried 'God Bless ye Duke of Monmouth'. Many were forced to drink a toast to the duke, either in 'kennel water' or, for a fee, liquor. Even the lord chancellor, Sir Heneage Finch, was made to drink to Monmouth, and reluctantly parted with a shilling for the privilege.[33]

The clamour and disorder of that night only stiffened Monmouth and Charles's respective positions. The adoring hordes reinforced both Monmouth's defiance and the king's sense of the threat he had to crush. Christopher, 2nd Duke of Albemarle, was called to Whitehall the next morning and there a furious king gave him Monmouth's prized first military office, the captaincy of the Life Guard. Over the rest of the afternoon he dispensed all of Monmouth's other royal appointments: chief justice in Eyre, the governorship of Hull, the lord lieutenancies. Even the Mastership of the Horse was taken from him, though the king put this in the hands of a committee, rather than giving it to another individual.[34] Various of those who were to benefit from this sudden shower of honours hesitated, thinking it likely the duke would soon be back in favour and the offices reclaimed. In response the king gave his steely reply: 'No he shall never be restored more.'[35]

November 1679 was a turning point for Monmouth. Unequivocally and publicly he had broken with his father. That break took with it his closest relationship, his royal offices, his home and his income.

In the early weeks it was far from clear whether the schism would hold. A number of close friends tried hard to effect a reconciliation. Nell Gwyn, ever grateful to Monmouth, supped with him every night at Hedge Lane. She went to see the king and 'beggd hard' for a meeting, pleading that Monmouth had grown pale and thin from his exile. But the king was adamant. Anna, too, for whom the king had ever had a soft spot, tried imploring her husband to obey his father's instructions, but she could not move either man.[36]

With the sands of politics clearly shifting, many were keen to keep in with Monmouth, and in December 'all the world' was visiting him at Hedge Lane. However it soon became evident this was no temporary tiff but something far more serious. A few days after his return, the Monmouths' youngest son, Francis, was taken suddenly ill. Just two years old, the boy had remained with his mother in their apartments at the Cockpit when Monmouth was ordered to leave. In the following days Monmouth was discreetly given permission to return to visit his ailing child. On Thursday 4 December, exactly a week after his father's arrival in London, Francis died. Five years earlier when the couple's first son had been taken ill, the king had sat with them at his bedside. This time, however, not even the child's death thawed the king's resolve. When the breath ceased within the child's small frame, the king sent Monmouth's half-brother, the Duke of Grafton, to express his condolences to Anna. Grafton's instructions were coldly clear however: to the Duke of Monmouth he was to say not a word.[37]

Monmouth had begun the year at the height of his power, head of the army, Privy Councillor, security chief, royal adviser and builder of alliances between the fractured elements of the political world. Come its end he had sacrificed everything. Rivalling now his resentment of his uncle was his sense of injustice at his treatment by his father. When he had said that his banishment had wounded his sense of honour, which was dearer to him than anything, it was not simply rhetoric. Over almost a decade of managing men he had developed a deep sense of empathy for those who had suffered injustice. For the underdog, the unsung, the maligned, he felt instant sympathy. This instinct was now, for the first time, directed at himself. Personal suffering and discomfort he saw as part of the brave man's lot, but wrongs had to be righted. A sense of betrayal by his father was mixed with his feeling for human justice and personal liberty, and the cocktail that resulted was stiff indeed.

Not least among the things that Monmouth relinquished in the autumn of 1679 was adulation. For fifteen years he had been adored. As his father's favourite he had enjoyed the attention of scores of others. His sexual affairs had come and gone but thanks to the king he was doted on and indulged, admired and included. The events of the autumn of 1679 took all this from him, and it created a place in the duke's emotional world for love to develop where little had existed before. The winter saw his new associate, the Whig nobleman Ford, Lord Grey of Werke, send his wife, Mary, to Northumberland to separate her from her 'beloved' Monmouth, but the dalliance was fleeting. At the same time, however, a second scandal broke which marked the beginning, in earnest, of the love affair that would outlast everything.[38]

Now nineteen, Henrietta, Countess of Wentworth was the daughter of one of Charles II's most loyal supporters, Lord Wentworth. The old baron had been with him in Breda in 1650 when the deal with the Covenanting Scots had been done, at which the one-year-old Monmouth had also been present. An only child, Henrietta was born in the year of the restoration and was just five when her father died. Thanks to the terms of the barony she succeeded him, holding the Wentworth title in her own right, and her formidable mother, Philadelphia, protected her daughter's inheritance – which included the imposing manor of Toddington in Bedfordshire and land to the east of London at Stepney.[39]

Once in her teens Henrietta had been periodically brought to court by her mother, providing the material which George Etherege had used in *The Man of Mode* in 1676. She probably first met Monmouth in February 1675, when she was fourteen, when they had both participated in John Crowne's masque *Calisto*. This lavish production was staged in the great hall at Whitehall, converted by

Charles II into a permanent court theatre. Crowne had created a performance with music and dance based on a rosy retelling of Jupiter's seduction of the nymph Calisto. It was a ladies' piece, and the lead roles had been played by the Princesses Mary and Anne, then just entering their teens. Henrietta had played Jupiter and closed the entire production delivering the epilogue directly to the audience. Monmouth's role had been fleeting but flamboyant: he and a male troupe danced a minuet dressed in bejewelled Roman military costumes of green, gold and scarlet.[40]

The play had been an enormous undertaking, with some hundred performers and twenty rehearsals. The behind-the-scenes preparations were extravagant, Monmouth's Roman costume was fussed over by his valet, St Gill Vanier, while Henrietta was attended to by a French dresser and another dancer by the king's tailor Claude Sourceau. That Henrietta should have been star-struck by the king's famous son was no surprise, but amid the scores of ladies dripping with gems and silk she too had interested him. A flirtation began, but it was almost certainly no more than that. The following year the characters of the seducer Dorimant and the virtuous heiress Harriet Woodvill in *The Man of Mode* read as caricatures of Monmouth and Henrietta Wentworth. As in the play, though, Henrietta did not succumb to Monmouth's advances. The watershed was not until early 1680, when they had known one another for five years. At the end of January, Monmouth's attentions to her daughter prompted Lady Wentworth suddenly to spirit Henrietta away to Bedfordshire 'in so much haste that it makes a great noise and was sure done in some great passion'.[41] The relationship which had now ignited would burn for the rest of Monmouth's life. When he later copied out an elaborate horoscope in his pocket book a few years later, the date he chose was 1680 and the words that accompanied it: '*il vivra avec plus de plaisir dans le 2 que dans le 1*' ('he shall live more pleasurably as two than as one'). He was alone no more.[42]

The emotional fulfilment that Monmouth was beginning to find with Henrietta Wentworth was an important positive ingredient in the resolution which he would show in his dealings with his father over the coming months. While the falling out of November 1679 was angry and apparently absolute, those who knew Charles II and his strength of feeling for his son doubted even then that it would last. The argument, despite all the terrible things done and said, seemed likely to pass like a lovers' row. At first the king continued to refuse to see Monmouth, and stopped visiting Anna as had been his wont. But there were soon chinks of light.[43] In February, as he walked along the tree-lined avenue in St James's Park known as the Mall, Charles encountered Monmouth's five-year-old second son Henry, taking the air with his governess. Striding forward he swept his grandson off the sandy path, and carried him on his hip down the long walk, lavishing the child with kisses all the way.[44] A few weeks later Monmouth met his father in secret, with the king's visit to a new mistress standing as cover. It looked suddenly as if a reconciliation was about to be announced. Charles offered to readmit Monmouth to his offices if he would divulge the names of those who had been advising him. Monmouth instantly recoiled, refusing to do any such thing, 'upon point of Honour, to w[hic]ch his duty is opposed'.[45]

As father and son took these furtive and faltering steps towards one another the Whigs had other ideas. Before Monmouth had been sent into exile his intemperate former officer, Thomas Armstrong, had been trying to establish that Charles II and Lucy Walter had been married. While Armstrong wished simply to demonstrate that Monmouth was the rightful heir to the throne, the duke himself had more complex motives.[46] He knew no more of the months preceding his birth than anyone else and there were obvious intensely personal reasons why he should wish to know the truth about his parents' relationship – not the least of which was the chance to redeem his mother's honour. There were genuine grounds for doubt about the matter. Rumours of a marriage had circulated from the year he first arrived at court, long before the political crisis gave the question such potency.[47] When Monmouth had been expelled from court in September, whatever restraint he had exercised on Armstrong loosened, the search intensified, and he contributed £30 towards expenses incurred in making enquiries.[48] Members of Lucy's maternal family, the Protheroes, were sought out, and while many were dead, friends and neighbours of Lucy's aunt Margaret and her Dutch husband Peter Gosfright were found. Anyone who had seen or spoken to Lucy during the chaotic cavalcade of her life – herb women and watermen, merchants and inn-keepers – were tracked down and interviewed. The newspapers of the day were dredged up for any clues on her movements, and the date of her death in Paris was finally established.[49]

From all of this a sensational specific 'discovery' emerged at the end of March 1680. It related to John Cosin, the late bishop of Durham, and one-time chaplain to Henrietta Maria in Paris, who had heard Lucy's confession in 1658. The claim was that the dying Lucy had pressed a document into his hand which proved that she and the king had been married. The paper was put by Cosin into a black box and sealed up, not to be opened during Charles II's lifetime. After Cosin's death his son-in-law Sir Gilbert Gerrard had discovered the box and opened it to reveal the dramatic truth.[50] The story was tantalising, and in the first week of April was passing like a wind between London's coffee houses. On 1 May a bookseller in Great Queen Street was selling a pamphlet entitled the 'Popish Massacre' which claimed Monmouth was legitimate; when challenged he shrugged it off saying that the contents of the black box had confirmed it to be true.[51]

The reports gained such credit that the king decided something had to be done. York had by now been allowed to come back to London – Monmouth's own return giving the king little choice. The Catholic duke's presence made it a certainty that any parliamentary meeting would seek once again to introduce an exclusion bill. Charles prorogued Parliament until the autumn, a year after the election, and decided to address the allegations head-on. York wrote to William of Orange in April explaining that the story of the black box 'had been so discoursed on in towne that his Ma[jesty] thinks himself obliged to enquier into it'. It was a dangerous tactic.

For the king to hold an investigation into the stories, even if only to demonstrate their falsehood, risked broadcasting them still wider and lending them a greater ring of validity. Regardless, an extraordinary meeting of the Privy Council was summoned on Tuesday 27 April 1680, to which a dozen judges were invited. The king addressed the meeting directly: a false and dangerous rumour was in circulation about evidence of his having married Monmouth's mother. He was determined to investigate this story to demonstrate that it was utterly untrue. Sir Gilbert Gerrard, who had been lined up in advance, was marched into the chamber to swear publicly under oath that the rumour was without foundation and that there was no such box or paper. The king made an unequivocal declaration that he had never been married to Monmouth's mother, before asking the secretary of state to find out who had started the rumours. The Duke of York was cock-a-hoop and crowed that it would finally reveal Monmouth's villainy and ensure that 'he can never go about any more to pretend to be P[rince] of Wales'.[52]

While the follow-up investigation was being conducted in early May, the king made an unusual late spring visit to Windsor. Another long afternoon fishing on the Thames left him with a cold which quickly developed into something more worrying – wet feet were thought the cause. Though the first fits he suffered passed within a few days the episode was again destabilising in such a delicate political atmosphere. While he was ill, Monmouth wrote to the king 'full of humble duty expressing his infinite grief for being under his displeasure and chiefly now that he may not attend on him'. His anxiety for his father's health was heartfelt but his position was unchanged and he asked the king to 'reflect on the condition he [Monmouth] is in, and on his innocence', signing off, as he always had, 'your dutiful Monmouth'. The king, equally stubborn, scoffed at the wording and replied that if Monmouth would only be a dutiful son, then they might indeed be reconciled.[53]

At the council meeting on Wednesday 12 May, confronted with reams of papers inscribed with the scores of testimonials that had been gathered, and a list of endless further interviews yet to be conducted, the king realised the enquiry into the source of the black box story was going nowhere. He 'cut the matter short and said he would have no more of that Farce'. The Duke of York, dismayed, pushed for the orchestrators to be punished in some way, but the king was impassive, and his order for the enquiry to cease stood. As one onlooker observed, the whole undertaking had in the end done York more harm than good.[54]

As all this was happening the Whig presses churned out a sharp and unusually sophisticated piece of propaganda. Written by Robert Ferguson, it was a twenty-three-page pamphlet entitled 'A Letter to a Person of Honour concerning the Kings Disavowing the having been married to the Duke of Monmouth's mother'. Cleverly turning on its head the king's declarations, it listed a host of reasons why the king might not be telling the truth (not least of which was his poor record of doing so in general), and enumerated the evidence of York's wickedness. Instead of ending with an assertion of Monmouth's legitimacy it left this open and declared it imperative that Parliament be allowed to set matters right.[55] The king was furious and ordered his denial of the marriage written in the council minute book to be publicly printed. The declaration was published on 2 June and a week later it appeared in the *London Gazette*.[56]

The oxygen the council enquiries gave to stories of Monmouth's legitimacy was politically useful to the Whigs, though the real evidence all of this digging actually threw up of Charles and Lucy Walter having been married was flimsy and unconvincing. But while the dossiers and testimonials failed to prove that Lucy had been Charles II's wife, they vividly revealed the sorry truth of her life. What exactly Monmouth knew of his mother beyond his own childish recollections is not clear, but the snatches of her existence which were now exposed were pathetic enough to feed the duke's sense of grievance. They gave bitter glimpses of her acute lack of money, her imprisonment, the sequence of attempts made by Charles to snatch her child from her, and told of her death, alone, in Paris, having been prevented finally from finding her stolen son.[57]

By the end of the month all signs of rapprochement between the king and Monmouth had evaporated. When the king himself contended that not only had there been no marriage but Monmouth's mother had been 'a whore to other people', he delivered a brutal blow to Monmouth's already inflamed sense of honour. As Bishop Burnet, noted this statement was seen, finally, as 'an absolute breaking off'.[58]

Chapter 14

Opposition Leader

The Duke of Monmouth's magnificent plumed horses pulled his coach out of his stables on to Hedge Lane on the morning of 23 July 1680. It was an unmistakable sight. The animals were adorned in gorgeous yellow silk; even their lower legs were bound in satin embroidered with coronets and cyphers. The coach was attended by a phalanx of men – the coachman, postilions and the footmen who ran alongside also dazzling in yellow. Every element, from these golden liveries to the arms emblazoned on the door, exclaimed the identity of the passenger reclining against the padded mohair upholstery within. When this conspicuous cavalcade reached the junction with the road to Oxford (now Oxford Street), instead of driving towards Hampstead bound for Moor Park as usual, the coachman, Thomas Eyres, turned the vehicle sharply westwards. By nightfall they had reached Reading. As Monmouth entered the town he was met with great fanfare by both the town dignitaries and the Berkshire gentry. Alarm bells immediately started ringing at Whitehall. As the French ambassador Barillon wrote to Louis XIV, no one believed for a moment that this was a mere summer hunting expedition. Instead a new front had opened up in the cold war between king and Parliament, father and son.[1]

Come the summer of 1680 the Parliament that had been elected in October 1679, during Monmouth's short Dutch exile, had still not been permitted to meet. The date had now been put back to the end of the year, leaving the opposition without the principal tool with which to pursue the exclusion of the Duke of York. Impatient, and uncertain whether it would sit at all that year, they had started to adopt new measures. Petitions were presented calling for Parliament to meet, while in late June the Earl of Shaftesbury had, sensationally, tried to have York indicted by the grand jury of Middlesex as a common recusant. Though he was foiled, the gesture was a dramatic statement of intent. Monmouth's journey westwards was, it was soon realised, a further tactic to ensure that popular anxiety about the Duke of York did not wilt in the summer warmth. The secretary of state established that Monmouth intended to stay with a series of high-profile Whig landowners in the South West, giving the opportunity for prominent appearances at county towns on his way. Thomas Thynne at Longleat, Sir William Portman near Taunton, and Shaftesbury himself at St Giles in Dorset would be his hosts. On the king's behalf letters were swiftly despatched to all the senior men of the western counties stating baldly the royal displeasure they would provoke should they receive Monmouth.[2]

Monmouth spent the next six weeks on the move. He started at a leisurely pace, going first to Bath, en route to Thomas Thynne at Longleat. In the spa city, notwithstanding the threats from Whitehall, he was given a rapturous welcome. Two hundred men rode out to meet him on the approach road, and as he entered the city the streets rang with church bells and cheering crowds.[3] By mid-August he was staying with Lord Shaftesbury at Wimborne St Giles, where he had been a guest with the king almost twenty years before; the earl had travelled west two days ahead of Monmouth in the company of his friend, the academic John Locke, who had just returned from four years abroad. From St Giles he forged west, accelerating his pace to spend just a night each with a series of Whig supporters, passing through Stroud, Chard, Illminster, Colyton and Otterton in just a matter of days. On 1 September he reached the city of Exeter, the furthest point of his tour of the west country. Here again the king had issued stern warnings against receiving Monmouth, to the bishop of Exeter among others, but again the

welcome was clamorous. Even a government figure conceded that
700 men on horseback and 800 on foot had accompanied Monmouth
into Exeter, where he was entertained in the dean's own house.[4]

It soon became clear that the charm for which Monmouth was
famous at Whitehall and Versailles was no less in evidence in provincial market places and town halls. When he had visited Chichester a
few months earlier, even a hostile witness admitted he had quickly
impressed the crowds. After telling the mayor William Jennings
that 'he look'd like a young man', Monmouth talked seriously to
him about why Parliament must be allowed to meet. He 'graciously
received' a Quaker tobacco-pipe maker, to whom he listened at
length, making courteous enquiries about his congregation. All the
while the old Quaker kept his hat on as his creed dictated, while
Monmouth, dressed in scarlet from head to toe, held his respectfully
in his hand. Charm and celebrity made for a powerful combination. At Ilchester that summer, petals were thrown before his feet;
at other places the crowds jostled just to touch him. The cries of
the people were of loyalty to both the king and the 'the Protestant
Duke' and of 'no Popery'. The Duke of York was condemned by
implication.[5]

Anxious missives passed to and fro between the localities and
London over these weeks, as government officials sought to play
down the whole undertaking. Those who had welcomed Monmouth,
they contested, were 'shabby people' with very few of consequence
among them. The secretary of state reported to William of Orange
that 'among all this company there was not one justice of the peace,
deputy lieutenant or militia officer, neither mayor nor alderman
wayted on him', remarking on the mortification Monmouth must
have felt at this 'cold reception'. Those that had turned out, he went
only, only did so because of 'a great deal of art and pressing invitations'.[6] It was certainly true that there had been both organisation
and orchestration. An itinerary had been worked out and communicated ahead. At George Speke's house at Whitelackington near
Ilminster, Somerset, gallons of beer and cider were laid on which
helped to swell the crowds to many thousands. The claim that the

people who cheered Monmouth were artisans and yeomen rather than gentry had truth in it. Civic office holders and members of the gentry and the nobility did turn out, but they represented the minority of the ruling elite in most localities. Regardless, no amount of Whitehall spin could disguise the enthusiasm with which Monmouth had been heralded by Englishmen and women across the South West.

At no point over those weeks did Monmouth assert a claim to the throne, but his presence alone was enough, on prepared ground, to inflame popular disgust at the prospect of a Catholic king and enthusiasm for an alternative. When he passed through the Somerset town of Crewkerne, among the press of people was one Elizabeth Parcet, a twenty-year-old woman who suffered from scrofula, the disease which it was believed the royal touch could cure. Pushing close to the duke she grabbed his bare wrist, exposed by a drooping glove, pressing her ulcerated hands against his skin. While he may not have altogether enjoyed the experience, Monmouth responded graciously 'God Bless you'. Within a fortnight the young woman's symptoms had gone and a pamphlet had been published in London describing it as a miracle. While Monmouth had made no claim to have the power to cure, his presence in such a charged political climate was enough to make others assume it.[7]

The seriousness with which Monmouth's western tour was taken by the king and his ministers was demonstrated not just by their efforts to undermine it but by the surprise announcement on 26 August that the meeting of Parliament was to be brought forward to 21 October. Monmouth concertinaed his 120-mile journey to Exeter and back into just a week, arriving in London in a cloud of dust on 7 September. Four days later Shaftesbury reached the capital. The earl was more physically disabled than ever, 'a little limping peer – though crazy [in body] yet in action nimble and as busy as a body louse', according to one contemporary. The two men were now in close collusion. Giving an account of the state of affairs in London in July 1680, which recommended who to target with bribes, the French ambassador described Shaftesbury as 'directing all the affairs against the court' and Monmouth as 'currently greater than anyone', two figures of substance with allied but not identical interests. With time now short there was furious campaigning in the weeks before Parliament met. Whatever was to be done when it met might never be undone. Both the Earl of Sunderland and the king's mistress, the Duchess of Portsmouth, fearing that the king would in the end sacrifice York, opened talks with the Whigs.[8]

Replaying his successes of the summer, Monmouth made a visit to Oxfordshire a week after his return, as a guest of Henrietta Wentworth's Whig cousin Lord Lovelace. On 16 September the mayor of Oxford and a phalanx of aldermen greeted him and in a procession formed of the city's bargemen, he rode through the town gate to choreographed cheers of 'God bless the Protestant Duke'. While the MPs for the city and county joined the festivities, the university high command was conspicuous by its absence, as was the bishop. Over the following few days to the chants of 'God bless the Protestant Duke' and 'No York' were added 'no bishops, no university' and 'confusion to the bishop of Oxford', as various local enmities were thrown in for good measure. On Saturday there were races on Port Meadow into which the local nobility entered horses. To the delight of the crowds Monmouth declared he would compete in person. He rode hard, with Lovelace and Thomas Armstrong looking on, and while he was not the victor that day his glamour and gusto won the hearts of the crowds. A poem describing the day spoke of how the 'Boys Monmouth shout and the bells Monmouth ring' and ended that they hoped '. . . in a fortnight to see him K[ing] Jemy ye second'.[9] The news of his reception only further alarmed Sunderland and the royal ministers, with one report stating that 'as he rode along the streets [he] was followed by the rabble with shouts and acclamations that they hoped to see the crown shortly on his head'.[10]

In the fortnight before 21 October the capital filled with peers and Members of Parliament, and the anticipation mounted. While on the face of it clear battle lines had long been drawn, clandestine conversations took place between the two sides. With the king not famed for his loyalty – few had forgotten his abandonment of the Earl of Clarendon – some who knew him well expected that he would in the end agree to his brother's disinheritance. Lord Longford wrote to the Earl of Arran that many 'believe when his Majesty is pressed hard by the Parl[iamen]t yt he will part with the Duke [of York]'.[11] The Earl of Sunderland clearly shared this fear and in those October weeks worked to try and get the government back on the front foot.

The king's mistress, Louise, Duchess of Portsmouth, who had eyed Monmouth with resentment in the 1670s, both as a rival for the king's love and as one whose places she wanted for her own son, had also changed tack. This formidable Frenchwoman, exactly the same age as Monmouth, now saw greater advantage for herself and her son in the Duke of York's exclusion. She had considerable ground to make up with Monmouth, however. When he had been sent into exile the previous autumn, Portsmouth had written him a highly provocative letter claiming she had had a hand in his dismissal. Bragging that 'the K of Engl. is in love w[i]th mee', she blamed Monmouth's fall from grace on his failure to pay court to her: 'Had you not all this while very coldly & very unkindly dealt with me, I had made you ye greatest man in Engl.'[12] A few months later Monmouth had reportedly said that he would only go back into exile if the Duke of Lauderdale and the Duchess of Portsmouth went too; one wag added that should the ship sink and drown them all Monmouth would have felt it worth the sacrifice.[13]

Come October 1680, however, the tables had turned. With Monmouth now independently politically powerful, Portsmouth repositioned herself as a go-between. She did not do this without the king's knowledge and perhaps encouragement. In addition to the widely reported meetings between the duchess and Monmouth, the king himself met his son in his mistress's rooms during those weeks. The French ambassador reported that: 'I don't see a person who is not persuaded that the Duke of Monmouth will soon be replaced in all his employments.' But yet again, both Monmouth and the king stubbornly stood their own ground, each expecting the other to capitulate. In the words of Henry Sidney, when reporting the secret meeting to William of Orange: 'his Majesty was not att all satisfied with him, for he did not make those submissions the king expected from him'.[14]

On the evening before Parliament was finally to assemble the atmosphere in London was electric. The king, under no illusions that a fight for the very monarchy itself lay before him, had packed a reluctant Duke of York off to Edinburgh, returning to Whitehall for a late supper with Lady Portsmouth. Meanwhile in the City Monmouth and Shaftesbury hosted a dinner for over a hundred Whig noblemen and gentry at the Sun Tavern near the Royal Exchange.[15] On Thursday 21 October, what would be known to history as the Second Exclusion Parliament assembled. Parliament had last met almost a year and a half before – when Monmouth was still a senior government figure – and had been abruptly dissolved by the king just as measures to exclude the Duke of York were brought forward. Since then events (including their landslide at the general election and Monmouth's break with his father) had only strengthened the Whigs' resolve. No one was in any doubt that there would be a fresh attempt to remove the Duke of York from the royal succession. When the peers gathered in the Lords' chamber in their flowing Parliament robes the scene was on the face of it little changed from the spring of 1679, not least because the arrangement of seating by rank rather than political allegiance meant everyone remained in the same position. So Monmouth was on the bench with the other dukes: Prince Rupert, now in his sixties, and his former friend, the twenty-seven-year-old Duke of Albemarle, to whom the king had given his captaincy of the Life Guards a year before. All were just three strides from the king.

On 2 November, the House of Commons agreed that 'a Bill be brought in to disable the Duke of Yorke to inherit the Imperial Crown of this Realm'. The man who proposed it, as in 1679, was Lord William Russell, the forty-two-year-old son of the Duke of Bedford – who a decade earlier had been Monmouth's companion on his trip to Paris during the 1668 carnival. A member of the coalition council of the previous year, he was now the Whig leader in the Commons. Russell had become passionately convinced of the threat that the Duke of York posed to a Protestant nation. What he lacked in silken rhetoric he made up for in clarity and conviction: as he had said some years earlier, he 'would rather be thought to mean well and speak ill, than to betray the trust of his country'.[16]

The momentousness of the bill was breathtaking. It contested that because the duke had converted to Catholicism, it was inevitable all England would be forced to do the same if he became king. York was therefore to be 'excluded and made forever incapable to inherit' the English crown. He was to be sent into exile; should he try to assert his authority, or return to England, he would be convicted of high treason. On the death of Charles II the crown was instead to pass as if York 'were naturally dead', so to York's daughter Mary. While the crowds on Christ Church Meadow might lobby for Monmouth, this was not being explicitly proposed in Parliament.

The House of Commons was therefore again attempting to override the hereditary principle of the royal succession. The case against the bill was articulated by Sir Leoline Jenkins in the debate on its second reading in the Commons. The King of England, he argued, held office by divine authority: 'the King has not his Crown by designation; he is not an Elective Monarch'. Consequently 'when God gives us a King in his wrath, it is not in our power to change him; we cannot require any qualifications; we must take him as he is'. The Commons no longer had any sympathy with this time-honoured view. On 11 November, after its two readings, they passed the bill. The support was so great that it was agreed without even a vote and Russell broke into a run as he carried it down the corridors of the Palace of Westminster to the House of Lords. Only they and Charles II stood between the Whigs and their goal.[17]

Everything now depended on whether the Lords could be convinced to support the bill. This chamber of the landed classes was naturally conservative, but as the impeachment of Danby had shown, and indeed that of Charles I's minister, Lord Strafford, forty years before, sheer force of popular demand could cause them to crumble. Some thirty peers were expected to support the bill, while perhaps fifty would be against it, which was close enough to make anything possible. Added to this, many wondered whether the king, while outwardly contesting the motion, might not privately be content to see it pass, in order to put an end to the whole business.[18] Over these nail-biting days Monmouth was highly visible. Friday 29 October was the annual Lord Mayor's Feast. After attending the debate in the House of Lords that morning, Monmouth went on to the Guildhall, where cries of 'long live the Duke of Monmouth' were heard as he passed and prayers were said in his favour.[19] To give him a foot in both the City of London and Westminster, he had taken a house in Bishopsgate Street some weeks before, while continuing to live mostly in Westminster on Hedge Lane. On 31 October he attended the service at St Martin's in the Fields. He remained outside the church for half an hour afterwards where a crowd gathered 'admireing him', removing their hats as was usual in the presence of royalty.[20]

The House of Commons presented the Exclusion Bill to the House of Lords on Monday 15 November 1680, asking the peers for their assent. The Lords' chamber was packed and a debate began which would last the entire day. As the longcase clock by the fireplace chimed through the hours, the winter light died away and the debate continued by candlelight. Charles remained in person throughout, stretching his long legs pacing the room. So determined was he not to miss a moment that he had his meals brought to him just outside the chamber. Shaftesbury led on the case for the exclusion, while passionate and eloquent against was the Earl of Halifax, another of Shaftesbury's nephews by marriage, and the man who two years previously Monmouth had persuaded the king to admit to the Privy Council. On this issue uncles and nephews opposed each other in the nobility and royal family alike.[21]

Monmouth was no parliamentary performer. He had given few speeches in the house, and compared with Shaftesbury and Halifax, the greatest public speakers of their generation, he was utterly amateur. This he knew. He had apologised to the governing body of Cambridge University for his 'defects' and even his father agreed that 'James was no eloquent orator'. But while he was conscious of his failings, he did not lack courage, and during the Exclusion debate he rose to address the chamber and the king in person. His speech in favour of the Exclusion Bill had an energy and effectiveness that both surprised and impressed the audience. Even the cynical French ambassador reported to Louis XIV that it was '*pas mal*'. Monmouth's case was plainly put. Avoiding any specific condemnation of the Duke of York, he spoke simply of the peril he believed lay in the king's submitting to the influence of those around him and ignoring the well-founded concerns of the people. It was an argument made with sincerity: having heard first-hand the testimony of plots to kill the king, he had reason to believe that his father's life really was in danger. But as these impassioned words left Monmouth's lips Charles spat a bitter aside: 'it is a Judas kiss he gives me'. The House of Lords that afternoon saw not only a polity at war with itself, but the raw fury of family betrayal.[22]

With the real strength of the king's opposition to the bill now obvious, and any rapprochement with Monmouth out of the question, the Whig case was nothing like strong enough to convince the wavering peers. The question was put to a vote shortly before midnight, and by sixty-five votes to thirty, and with every bishop voting with the Crown, it was rejected.

Throughout the session from October 1680 to January 1681 Monmouth was utterly focused on Parliament. Of the fifty-seven days when the House of Lords had business, he was absent just twice – giving him a fuller record of attendance than even the Earl of Shaftesbury.[23] He served on the committee enquiring into a new supposed Catholic plot (this time from Ireland) and another considering anti-Catholic legislation. Both before and after the Exclusion Bill was defeated he was a crucial standard-bearer for the opposition, powerfully popular with the House of Commons. When a group of MPs had come to the Lords after electing their

Speaker, they had ostentatiously removed their hats before him, while at the end of the session the Commons petitioned the king to restore Monmouth to all his former offices.[24] On seeing his name in this address the king, his sangfroid now restored, merely raised an eyebrow and remarked that whether he was indeed a 'dutiful son' was rather a matter of opinion.[25] All this enthusiasm notwithstanding, the fundamental aim of the senior Whigs – including Monmouth himself – was not that he should be made heir to the throne, but that the Duke of York be removed from the succession. The latter was the end, the former only one possible means. Ralph Montagu reported during the first weeks of the Parliament that the 'Duke of Monmouth at present shows no other design than that of procuring the good advantage of all the nation by the Duke of York's exclusion'.[26]

Despite the blow of the defeat of the Exclusion Bill, legislation was not the only way of preventing the Duke of York from becoming king, and the Whigs quickly turned to other possibilities. On 15 November 1680 Shaftesbury argued again that the king ought to divorce the queen and remarry, so that he might have legitimate children. Much reference was made to the precedent of Henry VIII on this point. Monmouth himself, the French ambassador felt, was first and foremost hoping he would be readmitted to court, so he could once again use his relationship with the king to pursue the Whigs' aims – much as he had done with the coalition council the previous year.[27]

The king was present during all these enquiries into his personal and political position – which must often have been excruciating – and made clear his adamant opposition to the divorce scheme as well as to Exclusion. But the peculiar intimacy of the House of Lords, in which every man was connected to his peers by class, family and history regardless of party, sometimes told on even the most serious topics. In discussing a royal divorce reference was made to the ability of a healthy man of sixty, let alone the king's age of fifty, to father children – with a knowing nod to a septuagenarian in the room. Laughter erupted across the chamber, consuming even the king himself, and for a few minutes the tension was shattered.[28]

After the defeat of the Exclusion Bill Parliament reached an impasse. The Lords rejected the various means the Whigs proposed to prevent the succession of the Duke of York, while the more determined Whigs refused to discuss the lesser measure of limitations on a future Catholic king. Charles II, enjoying it all not one jot, dissolved Parliament as soon as an excuse presented itself.[29] Having done so in January 1681, it was announced there would be yet another general election, the third in two years. The new Parliament was to meet on 21 March, but instead of gathering in Westminster amid the unruly London crowds, it was to do so in Oxford.

The dissolution of Parliament caused a pause in political proceedings which afforded a new opportunity to rally support for the Whigs. This time Monmouth travelled to Sussex to stay with Lord Grey, the Whig dignitary with whose wife he had had a brief affair two years before. In so doing he presented himself at nearby Chichester, where he was received in the late afternoon by the city's two MPs and 400 men, and conducted towards the cathedral in a celebratory procession lit by flaming torches.[30] But while Monmouth stayed with Grey at his house of Uppark, the government was redoubling its own propaganda efforts. The 'healing' that Monmouth was said to have effected in Crewkerne the previous summer when young Elizabeth Parcet had grabbed his arm was a public relations gift to the Tories. That very month a pamphlet was published ridiculing the episode, by claiming that Monmouth's unlucky half-sister, Mary Fanshawe, also had the healing touch. In the words of the brilliantly barbed satire, she had inherited from her mother 'the curing of the ills of young men by a touch of Her Naked Flesh'. The pamphlet claimed Mary was being called 'Princess Fanshawe' and that it was expected that Monmouth's right to rule would shortly be demonstrated by a lion in the Tower menagerie placing its paw on his head. To round off the satire, the spoof 'authors' of the pamphlet included Monmouth's secretary, James Vernon, and his former mistress Eleanor Needham. A second pamphlet which appeared just as he made his entry into Chichester sent up Monmouth's liaison with Lady Grey by claiming she had been visited late at night by an 'apparition' with a glimmering Garter addressing her as 'sweetheart' and foretelling doom.[31]

The print literature against Monmouth that flowed in earnest from the winter of 1680/81 was relentlessly abusive. It included a pamphlet purporting to contain a speech made during his visit to Oxford the previous year. In only a few short stanzas it dwelt gleefully on his Jesuit education at Colombes, accused him of being unable to read or write, and repeatedly called his mother a whore. Another recounted a further absurd fictional 'healing'. A riposte to the spurious account of his sister's healing was published, railing against its 'venom' and calling it 'a most ridiculous story with little wit', going on to point out the absurdity of the tale of Monmouth's having cured the girl in Crewkerne, not least as only the sovereign (and never his heir) had the healing touch. A rejoinder to the pamphlet on Lady Grey's ghost also followed, condemning it as libellous, and ending with the conclusion that in the case of such 'spirits', 'nothing can curb them or lay them like a good Parliament'.[32]

While Monmouth canvassed in Sussex, practical arrangements were in hand in Oxford. The eight weeks from the end of January 1681 were ones of frantic activity in the ancient university town. This was not the first time the court and Parliament had decamped here – it had been the royalist headquarters during the civil war, and they had sheltered here again during the plague of 1665. The university was expected to put itself entirely at the king's disposal, and by and large it did. While the town was Whig in sympathy, the university was a bulwark of Anglican royalism, with James Butler, Duke of Ormonde, the king's long-standing supporter, its chancellor.

In preparation for the arrival of the court all bachelors of arts and undergraduates were instructed to absent themselves and many fellows and senior university figures chose to move out temporarily. Christ Church, Merton and Corpus Christi colleges were immediately requisitioned as lodgings for the king, queen and diplomatic corps, and the rest of the colleges were made to understand they would be expected to house Privy Councillors.[33] Christopher Wren, as Surveyor General of the Works, was responsible for accommodating Parliament itself and had been in Oxford overseeing arrangements for some time. The two 'houses' of Parliament were to take over the university's own buildings between the High Street and Broad Street. The larger House of Commons was to meet in Convocation House, the ground-floor chamber still used by the university's governing body. Already provided with tiered benches for Convocation, the room was easily adapted for the Commons in everything but size. Wren and the lord chamberlain did little more than create a temporary structure at the high end to bear the Speaker's seat and supply dozens of green baize cushions. The smaller House of Lords was to meet in the Geometry School on the first floor of the schools' quadrangle (now the lower reading room of the Bodleian Library). Here more infrastructure was required. The room had no suitable seating, and so benches had to be imported and a royal throne and canopy of state carried up from London. New woolsacks were made, covered in red canvas and stuffed with wool and hay, and crimson velvet and fine woollen cloth was supplied to cover various seats. The adjacent Greek and Astronomy Schools were used to create withdrawing chambers for the king, the bishops, the lord chancellor, the lord treasurer and others, mirroring those at Westminster. They were fitted out with candelabra, candlesticks, kneeling cushions and chamber pots for their various occupants.[34]

In 1665, when court and Parliament had last been in Oxford, the Duke and Duchess of Monmouth had, on the king's say-so, been assigned Corpus Christi college. Come 1681 Monmouth was on his own, and James Vernon had the task of making the duke's arrangements. Within a fortnight of the announcement of the general election, Vernon was in Oxford trying to secure lodgings for Monmouth, working in concert with John Locke, who was doing the same for Shaftesbury. Monmouth, ever on the front foot with logistics, had already established that Shaftesbury's plan that they should take over a whole college was unrealistic. The king had made it clear that he expected the colleges to make themselves available for government figures, and on 6 February, Vernon confirmed to Locke that 'having a college' was 'past hopes'. Instead Monmouth had instructed Vernon to take for Shaftesbury the house of the mathematician Dr Wallis on New College Lane. Vernon and Locke viewed these lodgings together and concluded that they would suit Shaftesbury well, not least as they had a series of ground-floor rooms which would save the infirm earl from toiling up flights of stairs. Locke plied his tape measure and made detailed notes and sketches of the rooms and furniture. Monmouth himself had arranged to stay with goldsmith William Wright, the city's flamboyant Whig MP. Wright's house stood on Broad Street, only a few moments' walk away, and thanks to the influence of Dr Wallis the Whig grandees were to dine together at Balliol College.[35]

If the king had hoped the defeat of the Exclusion Bill would see a more moderate House of Commons elected he was disappointed. The general election once more returned a substantial Whig majority. It was followed by a series of orchestrated 'addresses' from constituents to their MPs, asking them not to agree any funds for the king unless the Duke of York was excluded. Clearly arranged by the party leaders, these were a statement of intent: the Whigs were going to attempt Exclusion again. On Monday 21 March the session began. Proceedings opened with the king's speech to the House of Lords and Commons gathered in the Geometry School. It was smooth and solicitous in content, laced with promises that while he remained opposed to Exclusion, he would listen to any proposal that might allow for the 'administration of government' to remain in Protestant hands during a Catholic king's reign. What this meant was not at all clear, and anyhow Charles, in reality, had no intention of allowing such a thing, but he knew the value of being able to claim he had been open to discussing it.[36]

Monmouth did not arrive in Oxford in the melée of the days preceding the meeting, but held back and made an eye-catching entry once Parliament was already sitting. His own household had been in the city for three weeks, and were waiting for him at Alderman Wright's as he rode down the High Street, flanked by an entourage of thirty men humming a low vocal drum roll. A plan for the city's mayor and alderman to give him a lavish welcome had been seen off by the royal ministers. Monmouth joined the Lords in the Geometry School that afternoon and was immediately appointed to a committee investigating why the king, disregarding parliamentary process, had not signed the only piece of legislation that both houses had actually agreed in the last sessions – the repeal of an Act of 1593 against Protestant dissenters.[37]

That was Tuesday. On Thursday as the lords milled around in the Geometry School before the house sat, Shaftesbury asked the Marquis of Winchester to pass the king a note which contained, he claimed, a brilliant solution that would make everyone happy. The earl's jovial manner and the indulgent smile of the lord chancellor indicated it was a joke, and Winchester agreed. The king unfolded the letter and suddenly all laughter evaporated. The 'solution' Shaftesbury proposed, which would meet the king's criteria and delight his people, was for Monmouth to be made his successor.

The king slowly smiled and remarked that this would indeed be the solution, if the small matter of trampling all earthly and divine laws was disregarded. Shaftesbury came over in person, and with the light falling through the tall southern windows, the two men talked. After fulminating against religious fanatics, the king went on to say softly that of course he wished he was 'able in honour and conscience to see a child of his own capable of succeeding him rather than his brother and his brother's children', but he would not betray the Duke of York and the principle of hereditary monarchy. There indeed was the heart of the matter. Shaftesbury urged the king to let him and his associates help by changing the law so that what was right might be reflected in statute. But Charles was intransigent. Some men, he mused aloud to Shaftesbury, grew weaker as they aged, but he had surprised himself by finding he had become 'on the contrary, bolder and firmer'. Nothing would change his mind.

During this extraordinary conversation the room had fallen quiet and the groups of bewigged peers turned, transfixed, as their tall sovereign and his small adversary, propped on his stick, spoke of the question which for half a decade had gripped the political world. Monmouth was also in the room and the French ambassador observed how he talked to a companion in a low voice during Shaftesbury's conversation with the king, making plain his 'ridicule of the proposal of the letter presented by Lord Shaftesbury'. Another source reported that when Monmouth was asked by his old friend Lord Arlington what Shaftesbury was up to, he replied 'with some shew of modesty and self-denial' that it concerned himself, adding that in respect of his own position Shaftesbury was 'much more forward than he desir'd he should be'. Some dismissed this as sham reluctance on Monmouth's part, but there is no reason to doubt its truth. Shaftesbury put to the king the notion of Monmouth becoming his heir, while Monmouth was at pains to distance himself from it. And little wonder: it was just over a year since he had promised William of Orange that he would never seek the throne, and for all that he longed to see the Duke of York excluded he did not really believe that he should be made king in his place.[38]

As Charles II reaffirmed his opposition to changing the succession, so the House of Commons began preparing a new Exclusion Bill. And thus a spectacular stand-off was in prospect. By refusing to grant any funds or to assist with any royal bills unless the bill was signed, the Commons could hold the government to ransom. On Saturday, Monmouth reported to the House of Lords on the Elizabethan dissent law, relaying the widely felt outrage that the king had deliberately 'lost' a piece of legislation agreed by both houses in their previous session. As the tension grew the king spoke to

Shaftesbury again, suggesting that he chair a meeting between two men from each side to seek a mutually acceptable solution. Shaftesbury suggested scoffingly that it should happen at Lord Arlington's lodgings, where there would be decent wine – the only good thing that such a meeting could possibly offer. On the face of it Charles was being reasonable, offering further negotiations and willingness to consider other 'expedients'. But it was all fakery. Age had indeed made him bolder, and in just that frame of mind he had already formed a quite different plan.[39]

Charles II's patience with the Whigs had run out with the defeat of the Exclusion Bill in the autumn. The vote had at last given him what he had lacked for two years, certainty that the House of Lords would not support it. Meanwhile the events in Parliament had been being watched by Louis XIV with reptilian vigilance. His determination, as ever, was to prevent the English from forming an alliance against him, particularly with his great enemy William of Orange. For the last few years domestic political turmoil had made any English overseas action unlikely. Now that there was talk of limiting the power of a Catholic sovereign – which might involve appointing a Protestant regent – Louis saw the spectre of Parliament pushing for some sort of formal role for William in English politics. Horrified, he authorised his ambassador to offer Charles II £120,000 a year for the next three years on condition that he did not support Spain against France or call Parliament for that purpose. With nothing to suggest there was any solution to the arguments in Parliament and a useful French bribe now secured for his coffers, Charles made up his mind.

On 27 March, Charles attended chapel in Christ Church Cathedral, and then performed the royal healing ceremony. A short meeting of the inner group of the Privy Council took place that afternoon at Merton College, and the House was scheduled to sit again the following day. After the formal opening of Parliament the sovereign and peers dispensed with their robes of state and attended in ordinary dress. So it was that when the peers gathered on Monday morning, Monmouth strode up the broad, shallow stairs to the chamber in the clothes that his French valet St Gill had laid out for him, with a cravat of Venetian lace tied in a fashionable knot at his throat. The king was brought from his rooms in a sedan chair and took his seat also in familiar court dress. Once proceedings had begun Charles briefly left the room, as he did when he needed to relieve himself or take refreshment. When he returned a few minutes later, he swept into the chamber swathed in thick crimson and silk Parliament robes and wearing the crown of state. Before the dumbfounded Lords knew what was happening the king asked the parliamentary officers to summon the House of Commons. The astonished MPs clattered in, and the shouts of shock and surprise became so loud that the sergeants-at-arms had to cry repeatedly for silence. The king then said curtly: 'we are not like to have a good End when the Divisions at the Beginning are such', and on his nod, the Lord Chancellor Finch announced that Parliament was dissolved. It had sat for one week.[40]

The king marched out of the House of Lords leaving the assembled company stunned. Still pulsing with adrenalin as he disrobed, he declared to a companion that as of the last fifteen minutes England had 'one king [rather] than five hundred'. Colonel Cooke wrote to Ormond that 'though I have seen the distractions and dejections of routed armies (a prospect dismal enough)', they were nothing compared with the scene of disappointment and shock in the House of Lords that day. But their shock would have been ten times greater if they could have foreseen that Charles II would never call Parliament again.[41]

Chapter 15

Town and Country

W hen John Locke and James Vernon had trudged around a
dark and drizzly Oxford looking for lodgings for Shaftesbury and Monmouth in January 1681, Locke had been feeling
terrible. Shivering despite his many layers, he was feverish and
racked by a painful cough. Only sheer determination that it should
be he who made arrangements for Shaftesbury at his university had
raised him from his sickbed. He had reason to feel frustrated: for
weeks his streaming cold had been keeping him from what lay on
his desk, a work of genuine genius.[1]

The debates about the Exclusion Bills over the past two years had
put under a microscope profound questions about the substance
and source of political authority itself. The traditional interpretation – the 'divine right of kings' – was that royal authority was part
of the fundamental order of things and had been given to sovereigns
directly by God, just as he had given parents authority over children,
and people over animals. If hereditary succession had been instituted
by God himself, and royal authority was absolute, then Parliament
could have no right to interfere with it. In 1680 a book by Robert
Filmer entitled *Patriarcha* was published by the Tories which forcefully expressed this view. Now Locke was working on a sensational
rebuttal, almost certainly commissioned by Shaftesbury himself.

The controversial project was a radical work of political
philosophy. Undertaken by Locke in the two or three years after

1679, it would finally be published in 1690 as *Two Treatises of Government*, and even then without a named author. While it remained in manuscript alone during Monmouth's life, it was a coherent expression of the thinking which underpinned the contentions of the Whig leaders during the Exclusion crisis and which must often have been discussed at Thanet House and Hedge Lane. In the *Treatises* Locke argued that human beings were not born into a divinely ordained hierarchy, destined to be ruled by superiors and ultimately a sovereign. Instead, he contended, people were created by God in 'a state of perfect freedom' and equality, regardless of class or race. Government or rulership of any sort, he went on, was simply the authority of each individual transferred voluntarily to a collective body or person for practical reasons. It was therefore susceptible, under certain circumstances, to being taken away or given to another body or person more able to exercise it. This was an argument for government by consent of the governed. By extension it brought with it the ultimate right to resist or reject a tyrannical ruler. It was powerful and, for its time, highly controversial thinking, provoked by the struggle to remove the Duke of York from the succession in which Monmouth was so closely involved. Locke guarded the manuscript closely, shelving it in his library disguised as a book on syphilis. But this secret project would one day be famous the world over as perhaps the most influential work of political philosophy of all time.[2]

After the catastrophe of the Oxford Parliament the king and court went to Windsor, and the Whigs trickled home. For Monmouth it was to an empty home. When he had first been expelled from court in 1679, Anna and the children had remained in their Cockpit lodgings, and the couple had lived apart. While Monmouth had spent the year since the death of their son Francis immersed in politics, Anna had had no such distractions and the boy's death had weighed heavy on her heart. In July 1680, as her husband paraded through the western counties, she had taken to her bed and the king, full of pity, resumed his regular visits to his daughter-in-law. Furious about her husband's relationship with Henrietta Wentworth and troubled by both grief and illness, Anna decided she would make a trip to the continent.[3]

With Monmouth out of town, the duchess had landed at Dieppe on 23 August 1680. She travelled with a battalion of servants and her three surviving children: James and Henry, aged four and six, and Anne, aged five. It is telling that Monmouth had let their children go. Many men of the time would have been highly protective of their young sons as the future of their line. But he did not worry greatly about his dynasty and after the death of his first child, Charles, he seems never to have become close to those who followed. He may also have felt it unreasonable to deny his neglected wife the company of the children of whom she was fiercely protective. In Paris, Anna was seen by doctors who let her blood, while their daughter Anne was also treated. The family then travelled 250 miles south to Vichy in the Auvergne, where they rented a house close to the famous thermal springs. Anna travelled this great distance fearing she might never recover, writing home to a friend, 'if I die be kind to my children'. Come January she was 'better than I was', but still uncertain if she would see England again and, as the Oxford Parliament met, she travelled back to Paris. Her relationship with her husband stayed cold, but he was not forgotten; on the journey north the six-year-old Lord Doncaster bought a pipe and a book of music for his father.[4]

Money was one of the few things which necessitated contact between the couple at this time. By the spring of 1681 it was nearly eighteen months since Monmouth had lost his court offices and the financial pressure was beginning to show. Shortly after his fall from favour, a beggar had accosted him mumbling that she survived on handouts from great ladies; Monmouth had replied wryly that he too 'lived on the charity of a lady'. For now he was without his lucrative court and government offices the revenue from Anna's Scottish lands was crucial. The truth was that no one, least of all Monmouth and Anna, had expected he would be out of favour and office so long, and so no attempt had been made at economies.

To her husband's 'great offence', Anna would run up bills of over £11,000 during her two-year French expedition – against the £6,000 that had been agreed – which did little to improve their relationship. She was colossally extravagant, maintaining scores of servants, dispensing alms liberally and choosing the finest lodgings. The house she took in Paris belonged to Madame Foucault and the rent alone was £3,000 a year, with the cost of hiring furniture as much again. She made countless lavish purchases, among them a mirror set with diamonds for which she paid £340.[5]

The source of Monmouth's money at the time of his disgrace had been fourfold. He had had an annual allowance from the king of £8,000 (increased from £6,000 some years before), something like £3,000 had been brought in by his various jobs (the Mastership of the Horse, for instance, came with a salary of £1,460) and the couple had received £7,000 a year from the Buccleuch estates. All this was inflated by a series of hefty one-off payments from the king, which Stephen Fox estimated to have totalled well over £50,000 during his time managing the Monmouths' money.[6] The salaries, allowance and ex gratia payments had all ceased in December 1679. The impact of this was initially masked by a series of large retrospective payments from his former offices that continued through 1680. Come the autumn of 1680, however, 'our affairs did oblige us to call for some money from Scotland', which in itself was a challenge as the documents relating to the Buccleuch estates had to be ferried for signature to the duchess in France.[7] Monmouth was beginning to feel the financial as well as the personal pinch of his stand against his father and the government.

The events in Oxford during the short week of Parliament's sitting put relations between various of the Whig leaders under real strain. Monmouth was deeply uncomfortable that Shaftesbury had suggested to the king that he be made heir to the throne. When the earl and other Whig leaders went to London to ask the lord mayor to lobby the king for Parliament to be recalled, Monmouth did not join them and went instead to the Northampton races with the Earl of Sunderland, who the king had dismissed as secretary of state a few months earlier. At a meeting at the King's Head tavern on Fleet Street in early April 1681, Shaftesbury once more argued 'for making the Duke of Monmouth King, if occasion should be'. But Monmouth was again not present, and it was reported that he 'is not well pleased with his party'.[8]

A public declaration of the king's reasons for dissolving Parliament, which heavily criticised the opposition, was read aloud in all churches and the government began quiet talks with a number of Whigs, offering them incentives to come back to the royal fold. Old Lord Macclesfield returned to his duties as a gentleman of the king's bedchamber, while the outspoken Baptist Lord Howard of Escrick (brother of Monmouth's one-time army colleague), a mercurial former Leveller, had a secret meeting with the king and a position in Ireland was whispered of.[9] With such approaches being made, it was again rumoured that Monmouth was about to be readmitted to his father's favour. Further fuel was added by the fact that in December 1680 the duke's allowance, which had stopped altogether in December 1679, had started to be paid again. This may in fact have been the result of Anna's influence with Charles, but it nonetheless showed clearly that he had not abandoned the family altogether.[10]

Monmouth was, in truth, readier for a reconciliation with his father in the early summer of 1681 than he had been at any time since his banishment in September 1679. Those closest to him, among them his secretary James Vernon, were urging him to make peace with the king, and he was deliberately distancing himself from his opposition colleagues. He remained convinced that the Whig stance against an increasingly overbearing government – which would only become far more so if York became king – was right. But he was never comfortable with suggestions that he should be king himself and now that Exclusion had failed, the party seemed to have come to a dead end. But such was the sequence of wrongs that Monmouth and Charles felt each had dealt the other, that pride remained the most serious obstacle. The king had to make the first move, Monmouth insisted. When told by an intermediary that, on the contrary, it was he who must request the first meeting, Monmouth complained bitterly that he had already 'applyed' through the Duchess of Portsmouth but had been refused. Deeply uneasy, and torn between loyalty to his new cause and colleagues and a longing to be reunited with everything his life had been before his banishment, he told the go-between that if the king would make some sign that he would accept a visit, he, Monmouth, would ask for one. But if he was at this moment ripe for reconciliation, the king was less so. Together with his ministers, Charles was preparing to follow the sudden dissolution with a further coup de théâtre.[11]

At 6 a.m. on the morning of 2 July 1681 a sergeant-at-arms hammered on the door of Thanet House, the Earl of Shaftesbury's home in the City of London. The earl was woken and presented with a warrant for his arrest for high treason. As he dressed, the sergeant and his men were in his study sweeping armfuls of letters and papers into trunks and boxes which they carried off. By mid-morning he stood before the Privy Council of which just two years earlier he had been lord president. Here, in the presence of the king, he was accused of 'imagining' the king's death, endeavouring to depose him and of planning to raise an armed force to do so. Shaftesbury, incensed, protested angrily that the charges had no substance, and he was involved in no such scheme. He had, he contested, only ever worked for the king's best interest – he just took a different view from the government on what exactly that was. It was to no avail: by noon he was on a vessel making the short but ever fateful journey down-river to the Tower of London.[12]

While some rather unreliable Irish 'informers' claimed to have evidence for Shaftesbury's involvement in a treasonous plot, nothing in Shaftesbury's seized papers corroborated the charges. The shock and injustice of Shaftesbury's sudden arrest appalled Monmouth, and he leapt into action, the recent coolness between them instantly forgotten. He visited Shaftesbury in the Tower that very day and was in court a week later at the hearing of the earl's petition for bail. For four hours Monmouth stood through proceedings, during which he heard himself called a string of insulting names – including a 'blockhead' and a 'tool' – before the petition was dismissed.[13] The government, determined to make Shaftesbury feel the steel of the king's fury, set preparations in train for the earl's trial as soon as the autumn legal term began. The arrest was part of the new policy of crushing the opposition with the sheer pressure of royal authority, but it also had the unintended side-effect of sending a drifting Monmouth reeling back into the arms of his opposition colleagues.

Shaftesbury awaited the trial that would come in November in relative comfort, lodging in the house of the Master of the Ordnance, Sir Jonas Moore, within the Tower of London rather than in a dank cell.[14] Meanwhile the political war of words continued in playhouses and on street corners. Publications and counter-publications were issued by the two sides. In one bearing Monmouth's name, it was complained that he and the opposition peers could not move without being 'pelted with Letters publiquely printed, and spread abroad (what in them lies)' designed to turn people against them. The Tories accused the Whigs of wishing to dispense with monarchy altogether – which was guaranteed to turn almost everyone against them. On 2 November, Monmouth published a furious denial of the claim that 'we, who were for passing the Exclusion Bill, were for the subversion of monarchy', maintaining that, on the contrary, 'we always were and are still readier to expose our lives' for the king and Crown 'than such defamers are or perhaps know how to be'. The paper was pasted up in shops and inns across the capital, fuelling further impassioned public exchanges.[15]

While all this political fencing was going on the playwright, poet laureate and historiographer royal, John Dryden, was crafting a subtler piece of pro-government literature, a thousand-line poem about Monmouth and Shaftesbury entitled *Absalom and Achitophel*. This epic work told the story of the Exclusion crisis through a biblical parallel. Absalom was the third son of King David, famed for his good looks and popularity, who was led astray by the royal councillor Achitophel. Dryden was not the first to see a parallel for Monmouth's recent career in this Old Testament story, but the success of his poem spread the comparison to the whole political world. Monmouth was, in Dryden's hands, Absalom, the king's beautiful and brave favourite child. Physically strong, but personally weak, he was sought out by a smooth-tongued Shaftesbury and lured into seeking the crown for himself. 'Made drunk with honour, and debauched with praise / Half loath, and half consenting to the ill / (For loyal blood within him struggled still)'. The poem cast the Whigs as driven only by personal ambition, Shaftesbury as an outright villain and Monmouth as a puppet. As the new legal term approached, Dryden worked fast and the poem appeared in print just a week before the proceedings against Shaftesbury began. *Absalom and Achitophel* was an instant sensation. Two days before Shaftesbury's trial Sir Charles Lyttelton wrote to a friend raving about 'one of the finest poems. . . that you ever read, wherein there is a great many characters of all ye great men of both sides'.[16]

The indictment of the Earl of Shaftesbury took place in the sessions house where the Middlesex assizes were held, which stood in the west of the City of London on Old Bailey and would later become the central criminal court. Like so much of the City it was a completely new building, its predecessor having been devoured by the Great Fire fifteen years before. The atmosphere in court was highly charged. Dazzlingly conspicuous among the crowd who filled the public benches was Monmouth, together with the Earl of Essex, who had joined the opposition, the Commons leader William, Lord Russell, and his old army friend Thomas Armstrong. The proceedings were raucous, with the 'great rabble' of Whig supporters booing and hissing loudly when the witnesses against Shaftesbury were examined, and a larger crowd of 600 pushing threateningly against the carriages that carried the witnesses to and from the building. The outcome was never seriously in doubt and Shaftesbury was duly acquitted. This was in part because there was no substantial evidence of the treason of which he was accused. But as importantly, he was on home ground. All the senior figures in the City of London were Whigs: the lord mayor, Sir Patience Ward, was a Whig sympathiser, and in May the City's elected assembly, the Court of Common Council, had petitioned the king for Parliament to be urgently recalled. Responsibility for judicial matters was in the hands of the City's two annually elected sheriffs, who were both Whigs and who ensured the jury was full of opposition sympathisers. At the end of the day they gave a unanimous verdict of *ignoramus*, an outright rejection of the indictment.[17] The crowd was ecstatic, 'whooping and hollowing' so loudly that the concluding words of the lord chief justice were drowned out altogether. That night jubilant groups charged about the City: in St Paul's churchyard forty men with drawn swords chanted 'no Popish successor' and 'A Monmouth!'; another gang on horses cried: 'God bless the earl of Shaftesbury'. Four days later the earl petitioned for release and was discharged on a hefty bail. Offering to stand as guarantor was the Duke of Monmouth himself.[18]

The whole episode left the king and his chief minister (and Shaftesbury's nephew) Lord Halifax outraged. Though not unexpected, Shaftesbury's acquittal was an infuriating expression of the limits of the government's power. That Monmouth should offer to stand his bail was downright humiliating. The king's capacity for tolerating, if not condoning, Monmouth's behaviour might be considerable, but not so those who advised him. Under pressure from an incensed Halifax, Charles gave the nine-year-old Duke of Richmond, his son by the Duchess of Portsmouth, Monmouth's most personally prestigious former office, the Mastership of the Horse. This had been held 'in commission' since 1679 on the expectation that Monmouth would at some point be reinstated, and Halifax crowed with pleasure at getting the king to agree to dispose of it.[19] Understanding what this meant, Monmouth put his magnificent coach horses up for sale – he no longer needed nor could afford such a spectacular team. Informed onlookers considered the Duke of Richmond's appointment a clear sign that Monmouth was 'beyond all hopes of ever being restored'.[20] Whether this would prove to be the case remained to be seen. But what was beyond doubt was the heat of the king's anger with the City of London. When the City sheriff Samuel Shute had come out of the Old Bailey to 'calm' the crowd, he had done the opposite, encouraging them to 'Shout, boys'.[21] The king announced privately that he intended to do everything in his power 'to repress these tumultuous riots', and it would soon become clear the government was declaring war on the City of London.[22]

For the next year, with Parliament still in abeyance, the City of London became the principal battleground in the war between the government and the opposition. Shaftesbury had himself elected a member of the Skinners' Company so he could personally participate in city politics. Monmouth had long used his lodgings on Hedge Lane for wining and dining influential city figures, and in February 1682 took a lease on a magnificent new house being built a few streets to the north, on Soho Square, using the remainder of the lease at Hedge Lane as part payment.[23] After Shaftesbury's release it was obvious the government intended to try and wrest control of the city offices from the Whigs, and as the elections of the autumn of 1682 drew closer the two parties jostled aggressively for position.

In April 1682, as the Duke of York returned to London from Scotland, the new lord mayor, though a Tory, dined with Monmouth, Shaftesbury and the other opposition leaders – to the government's dismay. The Honourable Artillery Company then invited York to be a guest of honour at their annual dinner a fortnight later, upon which the Whigs announced they would be holding a rival dinner on the same night with Monmouth as the guest.[24] As the preparations for the Whigs' 'Anti-dinner' in the Haberdashers' Hall gathered momentum, floridly worded tickets were printed for the event. This was the final straw for the king, who banned the dinner as an 'unlawful assembly' designed to stir up unrest. The Whigs gathered to discuss what to do. At a tense meeting Monmouth opened with a long speech arguing that their great and noble cause was not dependent on a single dinner. He did so referencing Christ's conversation with a Samaritan woman, in which He responded to her fretfulness about the place for proper worship by saying that a change was coming which would soon make such questions immaterial. Shaftesbury, infuriated by Monmouth's reluctance to defy the king, gave an irate counter-speech contending that it was vital they demonstrate their power. Monmouth carried the day and the feast at the Haberdashers' was cancelled. Instead a private dinner was held at Viscount Colchester's house, preceded by a noisy procession and pope-burning.[25] The debate about the Haberdashers' feast illuminated the differences between Shaftesbury and Monmouth. The former, now in his sixties, was desperate not to lose momentum, while Monmouth, still only thirty-three, had time on his side and no appetite for contravening direct orders from his father and sovereign. On the ceiling of the dining room, which Antonio Verrio had just been painting at Moor Park, Monmouth had chosen a pertinent allegorical scene: 'Time revealing Truth to the Gods'. He could wait. Shaftesbury could not.[26]

A risk to politicians of both parties was that sooner or later the king and Monmouth would be reconciled, which was likely to bring compromises that neither side wished to make. Even with the chasm between them apparently vast, there remained clear signs that while the king had moments of immense fury with his son, he remained unwilling to cut their ties. From the winter of 1680/81 Monmouth's allowance continued to be paid, and in January 1682 the king had given the Moroccan ambassador permission to visit him as part of his round of formal interviews with the nation's worthies. When the diplomat had expressed the hope that father and son would soon be reconciled, Monmouth gently steered the conversation back to hunting.[27] That it was in the interests of the politicians of both political parties to prevent a reunion was revealed in May 1682. The king was informed that the Duke of Monmouth had offered to come and 'submit' to him but would do so only if he did not have to bow to the Duke of York. Charles responded with 'great indignation', furious that Monmouth was trying to dictate terms to which he would obviously never agree and, as a reprimand, ordered that no person in royal employment should be allowed to speak to or communicate with him. When news of the king's angry declaration reached Monmouth he was baffled. While it was true he was unwilling to capitulate to his uncle, he had not made any such conditional offer through an intermediary, which he knew would only aggravate things further. He protested his innocence, adding that 'he must not only be a foole but ye most impudent man liveing not to understand him selfe & the dutye he owes the King better then if he hoped to reconcile himself to His Maties favour to proceede in such a Method wch were the only way to destroy him with ye Kinge'.[28]

The basis of the story was tracked down to a conversation at Windsor between the minor Whig Sir Robert Holmes and the secretary of state, Viscount Conway, in which the former remarked that while Monmouth might be reconciled with the king, Holmes felt sure he would never surrender to the Duke of York. This innocuous enough remark had then been represented to the king as an official approach from his son – without Monmouth knowing anything about it. Many soon smelled a rat. Some blamed Monmouth's friends, 'officiously. . . tampering & nibbling in the affaire'. Monmouth himself was convinced that the villain was the king's chief minister the Earl of Halifax. He may well have been right. Halifax had certainly talked the king into giving the Mastership of the Horse to the Duke of Richmond a few months earlier.

Later that week Monmouth and Halifax saw one another across the nave of the parish church of St Martin-in-the-Field at the Sunday service. Monmouth, bristling with bitterness, marched up to the earl and announced as archly as his anger would allow: 'my Ld I hear I am mutch obliged to your L[ordshi]p for the advice which you prest last Sunday in Council that the Kg should derect that none of his frends should visit me, but I may assure you the advice was needless as to yr particular [i. e. in your case] for I should never desire any conversation with yr L[ordshi]pp'.

In fact the Privy Council had not yet met since the incident and Monmouth's outburst simply ensured that when it did the ban was made official.[29] Two days later an anonymous source confirmed that rumours were deliberately being spread of Monmouth seeking a reconciliation in order to undermine the Whig cause. The informer ended with a chilling warning: 'Pray desire the Duke of Monmouth to have a care of himself.'[30]

In May 1682 the splendid coach of Anna, Duchess of Monmouth, swept down King Street to Whitehall finally bringing the duchess and her three children home from their prolonged French expedition.[31] Into her Cockpit rooms – from which, significantly, the family had never been expelled – were carried a colossal number of packing cases bearing the fruits of her ever-fertile interest in the lace-makers, goldsmiths and perfumiers of Paris.[32] For the past two years geography as well as politics had divided the principal members of the extended royal family. Anna's arrival at Whitehall coincided with the return to London of the Duchess of York, and came just a few months after York himself had come home – the coast being clearer now that Parliament was not sitting. This convergence brought with it unsettling reminders of the closeness that had existed between this fractured family just a few years before. Anna went to St James's Palace to wait on Mary Beatrice, the Duchess of York, who at only twenty-four was pregnant for the sixth time – though still without a single living child to show for all the agony and anticipation. Monmouth once again saw his children and the king his beloved grandchildren, now two years older. While Anna was based in the Cockpit and Monmouth largely in Hedge Lane, they spent time together at Moor Park, which was finally habitable after the rebuilding. And for the first time in years the couple slept together.

So, like gossamer in dewy grass, the invisible ties among the royal family were suddenly revealed. In August 1682, as Monmouth was being driven through Hyde Park in his coach he saw the Duke of York's vehicle approaching in the distance. It was the first time the two men had encountered one another since the king had sent them both overseas three years before.

As York's coach neared his, Monmouth called to his coachman to stop. His amazed footmen and postilions were instructed to remove their hats, and as York's coach levelled, Monmouth rose and made a deep bow. York, confused and yet transfixed, returned the gesture.[33]

Anna was determined that Monmouth should return to court. It had been inconceivable to her when she had left England in the summer of 1680 that the breach could have lasted this long. But still her family remained divided and her status and income painfully reduced by his political exile – the husband who had once so revelled in splendour, now 'rolls about in an old coach'.[34] On her visits to Mary Beatrice at St James's Palace she used their friendship to try to broker a peace between their husbands. She pressed Monmouth to let her tell the king he would return to the fold, marshalling every argument she could to persuade him it was the right thing to do. At one moment he agreed, but then quickly repented and told her that she could say what she liked to the king on her own behalf, but must make no promises for him.

Monmouth was not alone among the leading Whigs in considering a compromise. Less than a year earlier Shaftesbury himself had written secretly to the king from the Tower offering to leave London and political life altogether if he were released, pardoned and an outstanding debt settled – and it was not the only such approach he would make. Indeed Shaftesbury had gone so far as actually to propose abandoning their cause – and be refused – whereas Monmouth was only contemplating it. The Duke of York ascribed Monmouth's wavering to personal weakness.[35] But resisting the magnetic pull of his family required far more emotional strength than giving in to it, and all the more so now that the Whig movement was gathering a dangerous momentum of its own. In July 1682 – after outright electoral interference by the government – the new Tory lord mayor declared that the Whig candidates had been defeated in the London sheriffs elections. With political control of London slipping from their grasp some among the Whigs started talking in low voices of radical measures that went far beyond elections and representative assemblies.[36]

On Tuesday 5 September 1682 the Duke of Monmouth left his half-finished new house on King's Square, Soho, where now a series of other prominent Whigs had also taken houses, and set out north. He was bound for the famous horse races at Wallasey across the Mersey estuary from Liverpool. Here the 5th Earl of Derby had built a course where races were run for high stakes, an event which when it was revived in Epsom a century later was known as simply 'the Derby'. Monmouth had been expected to attend the September races, and to visit a series of Whig landowners on the way, since the beginning of the summer, which in itself was nothing out of the ordinary. He had been at hunts and races in Sussex and Northamptonshire already that year, each occasion attracting considerable public attention. In August the Earl of Derby, as lord lieutenant of the county as well as patron of the races, had been preparing to receive Monmouth without concern, making a special visit to Wallasey to inspect the track and specify the marquees that would be needed to entertain him.[37]

The journey would not in the end be a leisurely one. While Anna was pleading with Monmouth to return to court, and he was searching his own soul, he had delayed his departure. In the third week of August the Duke of Ormond reported that Monmouth had distanced himself from Shaftesbury and would not be attending the Wallasey races after all. On 1 September the Earl of Derby – who had by now been instructed not to entertain Monmouth – was bright with relief that he might not now be coming.[38] But in the end Monmouth decided that he would go. The loyalty he owed to his opposition colleagues was such that he could not now abandon them. For better or worse, he resolved, he was with them.

Like his 'progress' to Exeter two years earlier, the Wallasey expedition was an opportunity to promote the opposition's cause, and the route was chosen to take in a series of powerful Whig opposition noblemen and towns. Monmouth had to move at speed to make up the time he had lost through indecision. Over the next four days he travelled about fifty miles each day, while also dining and supping with those waiting enthusiastically to receive him. Thursday night he spent in Coventry, Friday at Trentham in Staffordshire. On Saturday he dined in Nantwich and reached Chester in time to attend in a large supper with the mayor at the Feathers Inn, at which all the prominent supporters who had joined him along the way gathered.

Monmouth as ever played his part with zest and charisma. In Chester he agreed to be godfather to the baby daughter of his host, the town's mayor, giving her the name 'Henrietta'. At the Wallasey races he rode the winning horse, going on to present his prize, a silver plate worth £60, to his new goddaughter. The following day he won a barefoot running race and on agreeing to re-run it booted, went on to win again. The crowds who turned out for him were large and enthusiastic, and once again made up mostly of ordinary working people, with a smattering of gentry and nobility. The streets of the country towns he passed through were strewn with sand and flowers, and people crowded in to see him dine. As he rode through Nantwich the women of the town clamoured to touch him. One kissed the tail of his horse while an old woman managed to kiss his knee crying 'you are so like your father that I am sure you are no bastard'. As ever the combination of heroic demeanour, good looks and personal charm won him the hearts of those who flocked to see him; as one sympathetic observer put it, 'the duke's deportment was extremely humble and pleasing'. Influential Whig landowners, Leveson Gower at Trentham, the Earl of Macclesfield at Gawsworth, Lord Delamere at Dunham Massey, entertained him and made sure their retainers swelled the crowds. Monmouth had himself been lord lieutenant of Staffordshire for five years, and so had friends and connections there already. Extensive arrangements had been made to guarantee a good crowd: men rode ahead to announce Monmouth's arrival, strong beer was laid on and blue ribbons provided so people could show their allegiance.[39]

Spirits were certainly high. The Earl of Macclesfield's companions, waiting for Monmouth to arrive in Nantwich, got so drunk
that in their slurred ramblings about Monmouth and York they
started 'mistaking one Duke for the other'.[40] But a keen observer
could see that behind his winning performance Monmouth was
subdued. A big drinker in the past, he had no taste for alcohol
on the Wallasey expedition. Amid all the feasting and revelry he
said little and took hardly a drop. When a tailor in Boughton
drank Monmouth's health, the duke gallantly drank the tailor's
in return then quietly handed the bottle to a gentleman near him.
At the races he 'desired the rabble to leave off their shouting',
and an enthusiast with a trumpet who tried to sound it for him
'was by his command immediately silenced'. Staying in Liverpool on the night of his victory at Wallasey he dined with the
senior Whigs, but when they went out on the town drinking and
gambling, Monmouth left them to it and retired to his lodgings at
ten o'clock.[41]

Though he nodded appreciatively at those who cheered and
shouted 'A Monmouth!', he who had never put himself forward as
a candidate for the throne made no bid for it now – though some
clearly wished he would. In Nantwich, Roger Whitley (who had
first suggested to the mayor of Chester that he invite Monmouth
to the city) was seen to bow so low 'that some affirmed he kissed
his [Monmouth's] hand on the knee [i.e. kneeling]' – a gesture
appropriate only for royalty. While he rode through towns on
horseback – changing from a coach at the outskirts – in a procession of sorts, he was respectfully bareheaded, whereas a royal
prince would have kept his hat on. One account alleged that on
the boat across the Mersey a man had thrust his disfigured child
at Monmouth, who 'laid his hand on. . . and said, God bless you',
which the man took to be the duke touching for the King's Evil. As
had been the case with the young woman in Crewkerne, however,
the incident was not something that Monmouth had invited, but
was prompted by an unexpected act by a member of the crowd. In
fact in this case it probably did not happen at all, or the dozens of

spies watching his every move for evidence of impropriety would surely have seized upon it.[42]

The big question was what was it, precisely, that the Whigs were canvassing for? In 1680, during the western progress, Parliament had been about to meet, and the intention was to ensure the country MPs felt the strength of popular feeling for Exclusion. Now in 1682 there was no sign of Parliament being called and it was obvious that, in the words of one contemporary, 'the Whigs, finding their cause and party daily declining in London', were set on 'raising some considerable tumults in the country'. Some felt sure the ground was being laid for an outright insurrection. The government had observers reporting back daily and the deputy lieutenants of the county had recommended calling the militia out as a precautionary measure.[43] Significantly, however, the king had not prohibited the expedition, something Monmouth was at pains to point out, claiming, probably accurately if rather disingenuously, that he would otherwise not have gone.[44] When an enthusiastic onlooker asked one of Monmouth's servants why the duke would not stay longer in Cheshire, he was told that 'this Majesty had limited him a time, which he would by no means exceed'. This was perhaps just another instance of the Whig habit of implying the king secretly supported Monmouth – though it may also have been true.[45]

As Monmouth made his way back to London, at a less urgent pace than on the outward trip, detailed reports of the events of the previous days were reaching Whitehall. Any evidence of violence or riotousness was watched for closely. The most unruly moment had been when news of Monmouth's victory at the horse race had reached Chester and the town erupted in celebration – led by the mayor's wife whose daughter was to be the beneficiary – with bonfires piled up and church bells rung. The boisterous crowd then broke into St Peter's church, where the bells had conspicuously not sounded on Monmouth's arrival in the city, and pulled the ropes so vigorously that the bells were overturned.[46] Monmouth was not even in the city that night, having already moved on to Liverpool. But similar instances of forced entry to churches to ring bells were cited, as were cases of windows being broken, and it was enough to seriously alarm the government. Five days after the Wallasey races a sergeant-at-arms, John Ramsey, was despatched north from London. In his pocket was a warrant for Monmouth's arrest.[47]

On Wednesday 20 September, now halfway home, Monmouth was in Stafford, a city of which he was technically still high steward, to attend a gathering in one of the town's mansions.[48] A lavish 'treat' had been prepared at which wine, pickled oysters, tongue, anchovies and biscuits were to be served. The mayor, Sampson Birch, claimed to have been pressurised into participating by townspeople threatening to break his windows. As Monmouth walked into the rooms the mayor told him in a low voice what was about to happen, adding sharply that he for one abhorred traitorous activity. Monmouth responded calmly that all 'all good men should abhor it too', before asking the mayor to propose a toast to the king. Once this had been done, and Monmouth had pledged his allegiance, the sergeant-at-arms came forward and presented his arrest warrant, which accused Monmouth of inciting riots. The duke had the paper read aloud to the crowd. It was serious and ominous, not least as the days when the Whigs could depend on London sheriffs to acquit them had now passed. Making no attempt to resist, despite the outrage of the crowd, Monmouth went with Ramsey. By night they travelled thirty miles south to Coleshill, just outside Birmingham, and were expected in London by Saturday. As they travelled the word spread and the crowds only increased: when they passed through Coventry some 700 people assembled to meet him, led in their chorus of 'A Monmouth' by the town's disgusted MP Richard Hopkins. Early the next morning Ramsey realised that Thomas Armstrong, ever with Monmouth and a one-time MP for Stafford, had slipped quietly out of the inn the previous night. On Friday evening, as they reached St Albans, a triumphant Armstrong returned. He had been to London, and secured from Justice Raymond a writ of habeas corpus, which required Monmouth to be immediately brought before a court and the charges against him stated and substantiated. It was thanks to

Shaftesbury that three years earlier the terms of the Habeas Corpus Act had been tightened up.[49]

The following afternoon Monmouth was brought to Leoline Jenkins's office as secretary of state in Whitehall, the very room where four years before he had ensured the word 'natural' was removed from his commission as Lord General of the Army. To begin with he had refused to go to Whitehall at all, but when the sergeant told him, quite falsely, that the king wished to speak to him personally, he instantly complied. On arrival he realised he had been lied to and angrily refused to be examined on the basis that he knew of no sworn evidence against him, and so by the terms of the writ he could not be detained. On being asked to give 'security' for keeping the peace in future he refused and swept out of the room. This refusal created new grounds for arrest, and before Monmouth had even reached the court gate he was detained by Ramsey once again. He spent the next few days under house arrest in Ramsey's lodgings in the Strand, where he received a stream of visits from Shaftesbury, Lord Russell, Lord Herbert and old friends such as Colonel Godfrey. Finally a few days later he was released, but only on the payment of the hefty bail of £10,000 for 'security' against his keeping the peace.[50]

While all this was going on government agents had been following in Monmouth's wake through Staffordshire and Cheshire, searching for what evidence they could find of illegal activity during the Wallasey expedition. Testimonies were taken, questionnaires put about and names named to establish exactly who had done what. Evidence of the smashed windows, of churches broken into so the bells could be rung, and of threats issued and other minor crimes were gathered. Reports were painstakingly taken down of individual acts, such as the reveller at the Chester bonfire who had cried that 'he cared not a fuck for the King or Parliament, God save the Duke of Monmouth', and the rumour that at another bonfire a song had been sung that contained the words: 'Let Monmouth reign'. But nothing could be pinned on Monmouth himself. The job of undertaking any prosecutions was that of the chief justice of Chester, an office not then occupied by some gouty old county barrister, but by the thirty-seven-year-old Judge George Jeffreys.[51]

Just a few years older than Monmouth, this talented and single-minded lawyer had cut his teeth as a barrister in the London of the 1670s. As the City had become increasingly dissatisfied with the government, Jeffreys's political conservatism and thirst for personal success caused him to stick firm to the king. This paid off, and on the king's recommendation he was made the 'Recorder', the principal judge, of the City of London in 1678. A year later he became solicitor general to the Duke of York and was afterwards given a baronetcy by Charles II. But his habit as a judge of telling juries what their verdicts should be enraged many in the City. Such was the strength of feeling against him that during the anti-Catholic processions of 1680 the London crowds had burned a portrait of Judge Jeffreys alongside effigies of the Pope. The following year he resigned his London position, hounded out by his Whig adversaries. The task of trying those who had transgressed the law during Monmouth's visit to Chester would not be a very rewarding one. Monmouth himself could not be snared and in court the townsmen refused to submit to Jeffreys's overbearing instructions. At one point they started to hum in low harmony in a defiant statement of their allegiance to their political cause and the town's ancient liberties. Jeffreys muttered darkly that 'full justice will be done'. Though he had failed to catch him this time, he had now fixed Monmouth's scent and would pursue him and his supporters to the death.[52]

Chapter 16

Desperate Measures

As Monmouth set out for Cheshire in September 1682 the Earl of Shaftesbury knew his own time was running out. When he had been incarcerated in the Tower of London the previous year, the king's own physician had been called to examine him and had reported that his health was dangerously fragile. Living as a semi-invalid in Thanet House, his frail body was finally beginning to fail, and as it did so his mind became ever more animated. They had to act, he felt; they had do something to prevent everything he had passionately laboured for from turning to dust. With the Tory sheriffs now finally being sworn in, he knew he was highly vulnerable to rearrest, and had become convinced that 'patience would be our destruction'.[1]

For some time, both while the Exclusion was still a possibility and since, there had been discussions among the Whigs about what they would do in the event of Charles II's sudden death. On at least two occasions the king had been taken ill, making a plan for this eventuality an urgent necessity. The critical thing was that Parliament should meet before a successor was declared, and they were in broad agreement that they would take up arms to ensure this happened. This resort to arms for a very specific defensive purpose was one thing, but in the summer of 1682 Shaftesbury himself became convinced that an armed uprising against the government was the best, indeed now the only, course of action. He had badgered Monmouth on this point before the duke left for Cheshire, pressing him to look for an opportunity to start an uprising during that very trip, which had doubtless contributed to Monmouth's own hesitation about going at all. When Monmouth arrived back in London from Cheshire he found Shaftesbury's conviction on this point stronger than ever.[2]

After his release on bail in late September, Monmouth visited Shaftesbury at Thanet House. With him was William, Lord Russell, the erstwhile leader of the Whigs in the lower house, and he who, two years before when they had the wind in their sails, had run from the Commons to the Lords with the Exclusion Bill in his hand. Russell and Monmouth had rekindled their friendship over the preceding year or so. Ten years older than Monmouth, Russell was a different creature to the fast-living friends, such as Lord Grey and Thomas Armstrong, that Monmouth was often drawn to: men of swagger and superficial charm. In the decade since he had accompanied Monmouth to Paris in 1668, Russell had grown into a man of principle, beneath whose sometime abrasive exterior lay a wry sense of humour, real loyalty and deep personal strength. By 1682 he had won both Monmouth's respect and affection. It was in front of both men that Shaftesbury, fidgeting with nervous energy even in his sickbed, announced his plan: they should immediately seize the king's guards and take the city by force. Monmouth and Russell were incredulous. What would happen then, Russell asked, would they go on to 'massacring the guards and killing them in cold blood'? Monmouth, aghast, asked where exactly the earl had quartered the 10,000 men necessary to do such a thing. They received no satisfactory answers, and as they left the house Russell recalled how Monmouth 'took me by the hand and told me kindly: my lord I see you and I are of a temper; did you ever hear so horrid a thing?'[3]

Shaftesbury on the other hand was enraged. After they left he fulminated against their lack of commitment. Monmouth, he spat, was a coward whose reluctance showed he was no more than a spy sent by his father to hold them back – after all, everyone knew he still lived on his royal allowance. Reluctantly, Monmouth and

Russell came to the conclusion that their friend was losing his reason. Shaftesbury, knowing he had already talked to too many of his plan, felt sure he would hear the thump of the sergeant-at-arms' mace on his door once again. Sometime in the first few days of October 1682, in utter secrecy, he had his most trusted servants help him out of Thanet House and was spirited away into the narrow alleys of Wapping.[4]

Concerned rather than relieved, Monmouth and Russell tried to make contact with him. A few weeks later they heard that Shaftesbury and his shadowy friends were planning an immediate uprising of some sort. The earl's fury with Monmouth had subsided to the point that he stopped accusing him of being a spy, and conceded that he had been 'true enough to the cause'. But he was now intent on a rebellion without him and had a common-wealth rather than a monarchy in his sights. Monmouth and Russell persuaded the earl at least to delay his rebellion a week or two, arguing that it would allow important intelligence from the country to be received. In mid-November a meeting was arranged at Shep-herd's, a wine merchant's on Abchurch Lane near the Monument. Russell and Monmouth arrived together, and were joined by Lord Grey and Thomas Armstrong, but they found that Shaftesbury was not coming in person. He had sent two 'retainers' to represent him instead: the former Cromwellian soldier John Rumsey and the stooping pamphleteer, radical Presbyterian minister and serial intriguer Robert Ferguson. These two hardly lent plausibility to Shaftesbury's scheme and when they too talked of overwhelming the city guards, Monmouth and Russell remained unconvinced.[5]

Shortly afterwards, the expected intelligence arrived which showed that, as with the 'invisible' London army, there were no rebel regiments in the shires ready to march on the capital. Shaftes-bury, crushed and expecting arrest at any moment, had himself carried to Gravesend, where he was taken aboard a vessel bound for Amsterdam. Here a few weeks later he was glimpsed, limping along a city street supported by Ferguson and another man. The liquid had now ceased to seep from the tiny pipe in his side and, on the morning of 21 January 1683, with Ferguson at his bedside, this most remarkable of English politicians lost the power of speech and died.[6]

Monmouth's Cheshire expedition, the battle for control of London (which the Whigs had lost) and the whispers of risings and rebellions had all helped to whip up popular feeling against the government. This had now gathered a momentum which none of the remaining senior Whig figures had the power to control. As ever the fifth of November 1682 was a lawless night. The city was blazing with bonfires, when, at about ten o'clock, five or six hundred 'ordinary sort of people' marched through the streets shouting 'A Monmouth, No York!' Gone was the good humour of previous years; members of the crowd tried to burn down the Mitre Tavern on Poultry, the windows of prominent Tories were smashed and series of lynchings attempted. Arrests followed, and thirteen men would be condemned to death. Five days later, when six apprentices were put in pillories for riot, 'not a pin's head was flung at them'. Instead the miscreants were fed oranges and chocolate, while others on the Gracechurch Street pillory were bought wine from neighbouring inns with which they gleefully drank the health of Lord Shaftesbury and the Duke of Monmouth.[7]

It was in this atmosphere, and after Monmouth had confirmed Shaftesbury's death by making a visit to Ferguson's lodgings, that the remaining Whig lords gathered. The architect of bringing together an otherwise quite disparate group was the sly and unreliable Lord Howard of Escrick, of whom Charles II would later have reason to say he 'was so ill a man that he [Charles] would not hang the worst dog he had upon his evidence'. Howard saw an opportunity to harness the ardour that was visible on the streets by uniting the relatively conservative Monmouth and Russell with the Earl of Essex, himself and the radical republican Algernon Sidney.

Sidney and Monmouth were on the face of it unlikely bedfellows. Though now sixty, Sidney remained as angry, able and ferociously independent-minded as he had been in his youth when he had eyed

up the young Lucy Walter and celebrated the execution of Charles I
as the 'justest and bravest act ever committed in England'. His view
of the world was formed in the forge of the English revolution and,
like Shaftesbury, he had held senior office under Oliver Cromwell.
After the restoration he had remained committed to the cause of
rebellion against the restored monarchy and took the view that it
'was all one to him whether James Duke of York or James Duke
of Monmouth was to succeed'. But Howard, himself a creature of
the republican years but with none of Sidney's fierce integrity, used
outright trickery to engineer the coming together of Sidney and
Monmouth, who until that moment had never met.[8]

Thus towards the end of January 1683 it was a decidedly dissonant
group of senior Whigs who assembled, comprising Monmouth,
Russell, Essex, Howard, Sidney and Sidney's republican friend
John Hampden. Howard was clearly keen to yoke the respectability and popularity that Monmouth and Russell represented
to the radicalism and appetite for action he shared with Sidney.
Monmouth and Russell for their part seem to have been driven by
a combination of factors. On the one hand they felt a responsibility
to manage something that they had had such a part in creating, and
to prevent it from veering any further out of control. Furthermore
Monmouth, at least, believed that there really might be an opportunity to compel the king to return to the table with Parliament.
But added to all of this was the simple fact that they were already in
so deep that they could not now easily turn back.[9]

When the talk turned to plans for an uprising, which the more
radical members of the group were determined should remain the
course, Monmouth took a deep breath and spoke seriously of the
challenges of raising a fighting force and 'insisted upon it that it was
impossible to oppose a well-methodized, and governed force with
a rabble hastily got together'. A list of very detailed practical questions were posed which someone with recent experience of military
command was well placed to ask. If there was to be an uprising they
would need to determine where it would start, to understand in
detail how likely each county would be to join, who there might be

the ringleaders, what arms would be required, how they would be acquired, where they would be kept. Secondly Monmouth stated that it was 'absolutely necessary' for them to have at least £30,000 readily to hand. Finally, and crucially, they needed to understand exactly how things stood in Scotland, an obvious source of potential support in an uprising, before there was any point in even beginning work on the first two. Monmouth knew well that money was in short supply all round, as Sidney said himself, neither he nor Howard could raise £5 or five men, let alone £30,000 and an army. All of this threw up a barrage of obstacles to be cleared. The practical challenges Monmouth set out were immense – and if he had only kept this level-headed clarity three years later the course of British history would have been very different. Now, however, he was clear-sighted. An envoy was sent to Scotland, funded by £15 from each participant, and Monmouth left London to go fox-hunting in Sussex.[10]

What precisely happened next among these men is very hard to say, for the evidence comes almost entirely from a single source. The 'history' of the events by Monmouth's Sussex host Lord Grey was written after almost all those involved were dead and while Grey himself was bargaining for his life. Moreover if any reader could have hankered after details confirming Monmouth's weakness and treachery, it was the Duke of York for whom that account would be written. But despite Grey's unreliability it does seem that, as he claimed, there were further meetings between all but Howard (who was already regarded as untrustworthy), that a deputation from Scotland did come to England to participate in discussions, and that a plan was indeed evolving for a Scottish rebellion, led by the renegade Earl of Argyll, to be supported by risings in London, Cheshire and the South West.[11] While neither Monmouth nor Sidney was predisposed to like the other, they shared a sense of the injustices the Scots had suffered at the hands of the government and the importance of this to their cause. When Sidney spoke of the 'the oppressions there' being 'so grievous', Monmouth can only have nodded in agreement. The uneasiness between the leaders remained, however, and discussion of what exactly the rising was trying to achieve was hampered by the difficulty that Russell and Monmouth were for monarchy and the others favoured a republic. Come April, however, the republicans agreed to support a monarchy, and to recognise Monmouth as the general leading the uprising – though there was never any proposal on any side that he would be king.[12]

For Monmouth and Lord Russell the purpose of the proposed uprising was to compel the king to listen to his people; and they remained convinced that 'all would end in an accommodation between the king and a Parliament'. Protecting the king personally and the institution of monarchy as a whole was, for them, of paramount importance. Monmouth, who alone of them had recent experience of fighting, worried the most about the lives that might be lost. As he walked round Soho Square with Lord Grey one May evening, Monmouth talked of his belief that when 'the king saw how strong we were in several places there would be little bloodshed'. It was now almost two decades since he had cast every bet at the Newmarket races on the French astrologer's tips. An optimism bordering on naivety, though attractive in itself, remained a dangerous shortcoming.[13]

As the king's temper cooled, Monmouth's position with his father started slowly improving. When he eventually appeared before the court of the King's Bench in November 1682, the start of the legal term, it was a non-event; the 'Attorney Generall saying hee he had no direction to Prosecute', the duke was released.[14] Though he was kept under close surveillance during his February visit to Sussex, his allowance continued to be paid and in March a royal warrant was approved for a huge quantity of gold and silver plate to be delivered to the duke and duchess. More remarkably still, in April 1683 he was granted permission to visit the Cockpit – overturning a complete ban on his coming into St James's Park or Whitehall that the king had instituted the previous autumn. There was a very particular reason why Monmouth now wanted to visit his wife, and for which his father would have sympathy: six years after the birth of their last child, Anna was pregnant again.[15]

This piece of news coincided with the arrival in London of the Scots delegation. The talk of uprisings suddenly acquired substance, as the Scots were far more enthusiastic than had been expected. These two forces, one drawing him to peace, the other promising only bloodshed, prompted Monmouth actively to pursue a reconciliation with his father for the first time since the months after the Oxford Parliament two years before. In the middle of May the French ambassador noted in his despatch that quiet discussions had indeed begun between father and son; the Duchess of Portsmouth was once again the go-between. What might have become of this can never be known. For as it began a small-time London merchant called Josiah Keeling was preparing to make a sensational revelation to the government which, in only a matter of weeks, would shatter Monmouth's whole existence.[16]

Josiah Keeling was a down-on-his-luck London Baptist. His nominal trade was preserved goods, treated by salt or oil, making him both a 'saltman' and an 'oilman'. He was one of the many religious dissenters who lived and worked in the cosmopolitan metropolis and were shocked and angered at the way the government was trampling on the liberties of his city – something that seemed to be further demonstrated by the unseating of the Whigs from City offices. In the second week of June 1683, consumed by guilt and remorse (or so he claimed), he made an astonishing confession to the Privy Councillor, Lord Dartmouth, who immediately alerted Secretary Jenkins. Four months earlier, he told them, he had been approached by two respectable men in the Sun Tavern behind the Royal Exchange – a famously Whig hostelry. General conversation about recent events, and how Londoners were being treated like slaves, followed. Then Keeling was asked quietly to join a scheme 'to take away the life of the king, and the duke of York'.

Many had already been recruited, he was told, prominent among them a barrister, Robert West, a cheesemonger, a carver and an instrument-maker, all from the East End, and a joiner from South-wark. A member of their gang, the one-eyed malt-maker Richard Rumbold, had a house at Rye near Hoddesdon in Hertfordshire, close to the road from Newmarket to London. The plan was that in a few weeks' time they would lie in wait for the king's coach as it travelled back to Whitehall. Some of their number, disguised as farm labourers, would then pull a cart into the road to stop the vehicle, while others would leap out from behind a wall and, using blunderbusses, would first shoot the coachman and postilions, and then point the barrels through the windows and kill the king and the Duke of York.

Keeling signed up, but the original plan was quickly thwarted by the king's returning from Newmarket earlier than expected in March 1683. Regardless, arrangements for a rebellion remained under discussion, as did talk of assassinating the king, perhaps on his return from Windsor or Hampton Court. This all poured out in the confession Keeling made on 12 June. Jenkins thought it all sounded rather far-fetched and asked him to come back with evidence. He returned with his brother two days later and it quickly became clear it was no hoax.[17]

The assassination conspiracy that was being revealed was a continuation of the radical scheming in which Shaftesbury had been involved just before his flight, which had then extended to talk of killing the king. The conspirators were, in Bishop Burnet's words, 'a company of Lord Shaftesbury's creatures', including both Ferguson and Rumsey, who had represented Shaftesbury at the meeting at Shepherd's wine merchant the previous autumn. This gang, largely made up of artisans with a smattering of City lawyers, were a quite different group, with different ends, to the aristocratic band that Monmouth and Lord Russell had been involved with. But there were individual threads that connected them, not least through Shaftesbury himself, which were about to be revealed with catastrophic consequences.

After Keeling's initial confession began to be corroborated, Jenkins called a Privy Council meeting on 18 June, which took place – highly unusually – at Windsor Castle, where the king was spending the summer. Having been apprised of the situation, Charles asked to see Keeling, who was brought before him later that week at Hampton Court. By now the seriousness of the situation was becoming apparent. For when Keeling's confession led to a number of others being questioned, the trail started to stretch beyond the backstreets of the City of London towards the mansions of the West End. Casual reference was made by a number of those examined to senior Whigs, including Algernon Sidney, Lord William Russell and, to the king's stomach-turning horror, James, Duke of Monmouth.

At the Privy Council meeting on Saturday 23 June a proclamation was ratified for the arrest of a string of minor 'ill affected and desperate persons' on suspicion of plotting the death of the king and the Duke of York. But these obscure men and their ineffectual plans were not what consumed the king's thoughts as he stepped shakily from the council chamber, trying to keep his composure. He went straight to the rooms of his daughter-in-law, Anna, Duchess of Monmouth, and as he explained what had happened, his body began to shudder with sobs. The tears that flowed through the deep furrows of the king's cheeks that afternoon were caused by one overwhelming emotion: fear for his child.

He did not think for a moment that Monmouth had been involved in the plot to kill him. He felt sure he was not capable of such a thing. Monmouth abhorred killing and the king understood as no one else did the strength of the bond between them. Furthermore Robert West had admitted freely that he had never met the Duke of Monmouth, and John Rumsey that while they wanted Monmouth to be their leader, they had 'never said anything of it to his grace'. The reason for the king's terror was not for his own safety, but his certain knowledge that even the slightest brush with treason would, under the Duke of York's vengeful eye, take his son to the scaffold. There was no time to waste, he told Anna, Monmouth had to disappear.[18]

Over the next two days three of the five men who had been involved in discussions about an uprising with Monmouth were taken in for questioning. At the Duke of York's levée on Tuesday morning the

word was that Russell, Grey and Sidney were all already in the
Tower and that the Duke of Monmouth was being looked for but
had not yet been found.[19] The following day Shepherd, the wine
merchant, was interrogated, as were several others, and the tale
grew ever more confused as the two conspiracies became entangled. Despite the garrulousness of the assassination plotters, the
Whig grandees gave away next to nothing. Sidney refused to say
anything at all until there was some definite charge against him;
Lord Russell denied outright there had been any scheming, while,
by a miraculous stroke of luck, Lord Grey escaped from custody
when the hungover sergeant taking him back to the Tower dozed
off in the coach.[20]

Monmouth's absence served only to inflame reports of his guilt
and complicity in the plots, which was the reason Lord Russell had
decided not to flee. Shepherd confirmed the autumn meeting at
his shop, and the talk there of rebellion – though he admitted he
had not heard it all, having been sent to fetch wine, sugar and then
nutmeg from the cellar. Lord Russell unwittingly confirmed this
by conceding he and Monmouth had been at a gathering at Shepherd's, though he claimed it was simply to taste wine. Soon even the
king's deliberately gentle questioning was unable to stem the flood
of accusations and insinuations, and on 28 June the Privy Council
issued a proclamation for apprehending Monmouth, along with
Lord Grey, Monmouth's hot-headed friend Thomas Armstrong,
and the notorious Robert Ferguson (who had absconded immediately Keeling confessed) – all accused of 'treasonable consultations
to levy Men and make an Insurrection in this Kindgome'.

When the proclamation appeared in print the next day, however,
the wording had been altered and all the named men were accused
of planning 'the Death and Destruction of Our Royal Person and of
Our Dearest Brother', with a reward of £500 offered for the capture
of each of them. The accusation against Monmouth had, under
political pressure and against Charles II's own 'natural inclinations',
become one of plotting to kill the king. It was profoundly shocking.
Monmouth would later tell his father that 'there is nothing has

struck me so to the heart as to be put into a proclamation for an intention of murdering you'. His wife would feel it too. Traumatised by the shock and shame of her husband being accused of treason, which threatened every one of her family's titles and estates, the Duchess of Monmouth went into premature labour. On 30 June, her misery complete, she gave birth to a tiny dead baby.[21]

The order for Monmouth's arrest for plotting to murder the king travelled through the country at the speed of a galloping horse. Lords lieutenant, JPs, mayors, and all royal subjects were required to join the search, and within two days a stream of reported sightings of the missing men started pouring in. Monmouth was 'spotted' clambering to safety over the tiles of a house in Westminster, escaping in a boat at Gravesend, lodged at Rocksavage House in Cheshire, sailing north to Scotland and strolling the streets of Dublin.[22] In Cambridge on 16 July the full-length portrait of Monmouth of which the university had been so proud in 1674, was heaved off the wall of the Regent House and condemned as 'being indecent in itselfe', and 'unbecoming' to a loyal university 'to Continue any marke of Honour to a person soe farre obnoxious'.[23]

While Monmouth had followed his father's instruction to leave London, he had drawn the line at actually going on the run while his friends were being taken to the Tower. So instead of sailing to the Dutch Republic – as Thomas Armstrong and Robert Ferguson had quickly done – he went instead to the home of his mistress Henrietta Wentworth at Toddington in Bedfordshire, just thirty miles away.[24] That he was not sought here was thanks to Charles throwing the searchers off the scent – the house of his long-discarded mistress Eleanor Needham was put under surveillance, while Henrietta Wentworth's was not. In the circular letter sent to the lords lieutenant and other senior figures in the northern counties, Secretary Jenkins stated confidently that the king had 'reasons to believe' Monmouth was making for Scotland. But it was all fiction: the king knew exactly where to find him and it was barely an hour's ride from Whitehall.[25]

While the search went on, the Whig grandees in the Tower continued to hold their ground, until, that is, the government caught up with the fatally unreliable Lord Howard of Escrick. Howard had at first swaggered around town showing no sign of concern at the revelations of the assassination plotters. When he heard that he had been named by Robert West, however, he visibly 'changed colour'. Four days later he was found hiding inside a large chimney stack in his house. He burst into tears and started there and then to confess every single name and detail of the Whig uprising on which Russell and Sidney had for a fortnight remained stoically silent. This sealed their fate and implicated the remaining members of the group. The following day John Hampden was arrested and taken to the Tower, as was the Earl of Essex, who had been living quietly at his house at Cassiobury for the last fortnight – determined not to incriminate himself by absconding.[26]

The trial of Lord William Russell began at the Old Bailey on 13 July 1683. As Justice Pemberton opened proceedings at 9 a.m., the king and the Duke of York were half a mile away at the Tower of London inspecting the new ordnance storehouses. A commotion was heard from within the castle as the royal brothers were getting onto their barge at the Tower wharf. The Earl of Essex had just been discovered by his servant lying in a lake of blood, both his jugular veins severed by the French razor still in his hand. The assumed cause, accepted by his own family, was suicide. Ever since his arrest four days before, he had been profoundly melancholy, consumed with self-loathing at having ruined his wife and children and been the one to introduce the fickle Howard to Russell and the others. The news reached the Old Bailey while Howard himself was on the witness stand. He asked for a pause so he could weep false tears for a man who, but for his own confession, would have been at home with his family.[27]

Unlike the distraught Essex, Russell had managed to maintain a remarkable composure over the previous days. He had already understood and accepted his likely fate. Monmouth had sent a message suggesting that he 'come in and run fortunes with him', but Russell had declined, saying it would do him no good to see his friends die beside him.[28] The crowds at the Old Bailey on the day of his trial were so great both outside and in that even his lawyer was unable to find a seat. Lady Russell was in court throughout, given permission by the judge to take notes. As was usual for the time, the defendant faced the prosecution lawyers alone. Ranged against him were a formidable legal team, among them Judge Jeffreys. Jeffreys knew that Russell had been one of those who had worked for his removal from his London office and his concluding remarks were 'full of fury and indecent invectives'. With Howard's detailed confession in their hands, the prosecution made light work of showing that Russell had been involved in discussing a rebellion against the king. At 4 p.m., after an hour's deliberation, the jury returned a guilty verdict.[29]

Eight days later Russell was executed outside his own house in Lincoln's Inn Fields. He had been spared the obscene, prolonged agony of death by hanging, drawing and quartering when the king commuted the sentence to beheading. For this Russell was grateful, telling his friend Gilbert Burnet, who was with him during his last hours, that the pain would last only a few instants, and would probably be no worse than having a tooth extracted. After parting from the wife he adored, Russell was calm, saying that the hardest part was now over. As he stepped out to die he emphasised he had acted only for good, and that 'he was still of the opinion that the king was limited by law, and that when he broke through those limits his subjects might defend themselves and restrain him'.[30]

The anguish for Monmouth of standing by as the two members of the group to whom he was closest, Russell and Essex, each died violently must have been almost unbearable. He would be haunted for the rest of his life by sorrow and a sense of bitter injustice at Russell's execution. That Russell was a good and honourable man who did not deserve to die was his repeated and heartfelt refrain. As well as the misery Russell's death caused one who set such store by loyalty, it also, of course, made it more likely that this would be his own fate. The fact that the king had told him to leave London was a long way short of a guarantee of safety. As the confessions spilled out, more than one revealed that while they were not the instigators, Monmouth and Russell had in fact both been aware that Shaftesbury's former cronies were talking of an assassination. Ferguson himself, according to Rumsey, had been confident of drawing Monmouth in, though after a conversation with the duke he had backtracked with the words there 'was no saying any such thing to the duke'. According to Robert West, when Ferguson had begun gently to raise with Monmouth some sort of detention of the king, 'the duke answered somewhat sternly, *You must look upon me in the capacity of a son*'.[31]

During those weeks in late June and early July the king swung between relief that Monmouth had not been arrested and rage as the details of his involvement in a scheme for an armed rising against the government were revealed.[32] As soon as Monmouth arrived at Toddington on about 26 June he had notified his father of his whereabouts. The vacillating king asked young Lord Bruce, son of the lord lieutenant of Bedfordshire, to take a turn with him around the privy garden. As the two men walked along the sandy paths amid the garden's immaculate grid of rolled grass, Charles bleakly instructed Bruce to go to Toddington to arrest Monmouth. The twenty-six-year-old Bruce admired Monmouth, and could see the despair in the king's eyes. So he replied that he would of course obey any order, but 'represented (what I knew was fallacious) that the house was surrounded with vast ponds, and that there were many vaults underground by which he might escape', the implication being that Monmouth would easily get away. The king instantly brightened at this response and told Bruce that in that case he should: 'Come to me another time for further orders.' Setting his watch by the ornamental sundial in the centre of the garden he strode back to the palace in such good humour that Bruce 'never saw him so full of joy', and the subject was not raised again.[33]

As well as telling the king where he was, Monmouth had found a way of conveying to his father what had actually happened. What puzzled many was why, if Monmouth and Russell had had even the slightest knowledge of an assassination plot, they had not immediately reported such a horrifying design to the government. Lord Russell gave the answer shortly before his execution. They had not taken the assassination plot seriously and he 'could not betray his friends, nor turn informer against them, while he saw there was no danger'. But if things had come to a crisis, continued Russell, he would 'have contrived some notice to have been given to the King of it; and in case of violence would himself have been ready to oppose them with his sword in his hand'. When this was reported to Charles II on the night of Russell's execution on 21 July, 'The King himself confirmed the truth of the greatest part of this account', murmuring within in earshot of his chaplain John Tillotson that 'James (meaning the Duke of Monmouth) has told me the same thing'.[34]

While he was out of the way, Monmouth was not, in his own mind at least, in hiding. He was not secreted in a priest hole, living in disguise or hiding up a chimney like Lord Howard. Instead he was staying as a guest of Henrietta Wentworth and her mother, Philadelphia, the dowager Lady Wentworth. He was attended by three of his servants, took walks in the park and slept every night in one of the great rooms on the first floor. He had very deliberately told the king where he was and when an agent came from the secretary of state two days later to confirm it, Monmouth gave his word that he would remain there. He would later tell Lord Bruce, quite truthfully, that he, Bruce, 'could have taken him out of his bed at that Lady's house without his making any resistance'.[35]

Monmouth's mistress, Henrietta, was now twenty-three and, despite her age and sex, was the owner of Toddington, which she had inherited from her grandfather along with the barony of Wentworth when she was just seven. Five roads converged at the wide sloping green in the middle of the village of Toddington. Half a mile to the north-west was the manor, a grand courtyard house built by Henrietta's forebear Lord Cheyne in the late sixteenth century, which in its time had received both Queen Elizabeth and King James. Formal gardens surrounded the house, while a substantial deer park lay to the south and east, punctuated by dignified oaks of great antiquity.[36]

Like Monmouth's wife, Anna, Henrietta had a strong mother who had determinedly protected her daughter's inheritance during her childhood. When Monmouth's interest in Henrietta had created a scandal at court in January 1680, Philadelphia had immediately whisked her back to Toddington. Now, three years on, Philadelphia had become devoted to him and vowed fiercely that she would go to the king and 'take her oath that she had never set eye on the Duke of Monmouth the whole time he lay concealed'. After the horror of Russell's execution was over, Monmouth began to experience an unexpected peace which left him almost light-headed. Now that the plot had been exposed – and having told his father where to find him – he had finally shed the almost unbearable responsibility which had accumulated over the preceding years. He spent much of those warm weeks alone with Henrietta and snatches of verse that he penned over those weeks reflect his mood:

> Oh how blest and how inocent
> and happy is a country life
> free from tumult and discontent
> heer is no flatteryes nor strife
> for t'was the first and happiest life
> when first man did injoie himself.
> This is a better fate than kings
> hence jentle peace and love doth flow
> ... for a hart that is noble true
> all the worlds arts can n'er subdue.

It was during this time that Monmouth and Henrietta came to believe that their relationship, never simply sexual, was something altogether more serious. Together they knelt and prayed in the Toddington chapel and soon they became certain that, despite his marriage to Anna, there was no sin in their love. Instead, in Monmouth's words, Henrietta was 'his wife before God'. Philadelphia also accepted this and the couple were allowed to occupy adjoining rooms. When a visitor who came to dine at Toddington that summer strayed into Henrietta's chamber, she caught a glimpse of the Duke of Monmouth – stretched out in an armchair talking with easy intimacy to his beloved as she dressed.[37]

Monmouth's determination not to hide and the momentum behind the continuing search for him meant that things could not go on as they were. It was only a matter of time before his whereabouts would become too widely known for the situation to continue. Lord Bruce was horrified when he saw Monmouth walking down a lane near Toddington – completely recognisable despite his 'country habit' – having just been among a crowd inspecting a fallen stag. Hurriedly he had to frantically distract his father, the lord lieutenant of Bedfordshire, to prevent him spotting the country's most famous fugitive in his midst. Towards the end of August an anonymous informant wrote to the Earl of Rochester, a senior member of the Privy Council, reporting that 'the duke lies now concealed in the manor house of Toddington', with detailed suggestions on how best to storm the house. Only absolute resolve on the king's part that Monmouth should not be caught hushed the report up.[38]

Monmouth also knew that things could not go on, and he started making plans to take Henrietta abroad, and to enlist as a professional soldier in the Spanish army. Then, at eleven o'clock one Saturday night in October, a coach crunched unexpectedly over the gravel at Toddington. Out stepped the most senior government politician of the last few years, the Earl of Halifax, who Monmouth had first persuaded the king to admit to the Privy Council in 1679. This was the man who Monmouth had publicly insulted outside St Martin-in-the-Fields the previous summer. Since his heyday leading the government in the parliamentary campaign against the Exclusion Bills, Halifax had been feeling power slipping from him. Lord Sunderland had been readmitted to the Privy Council, the Duke of York was back at court and now being allowed to participate in the council meetings once again. It was clear that if he wished to shore up his position he needed to ingratiate himself with the king in some new way. This, he felt sure, would be most spectacularly achieved by effecting a public and permanent reconciliation between the Duke of Monmouth, his father and uncle.[39]

Monmouth and Halifax talked through the night. The earl's first challenge was to convince someone who regarded him as an enemy of his sincerity; this he finally managed as Monmouth accepted his 'great concern for me' was real and not a trick. To Monmouth's relief Halifax was able to confirm that, despite the wording of the proclamation for his arrest, the king 'could never be brought to believe I knew anything' of the plot to kill him, but had to 'behave himself as if he did believe it, for some reasons that might be for my advantage'. Potential reconciliations between father and son had, in the past, faltered on Monmouth's refusal to acknowledge York as the legitimate heir and to publicly treat him as such. As they talked, Halifax established what he suspected to be the case: that the trauma and tragedy of the past months had sapped Monmouth's defiance. With Shaftesbury, Essex and Russell all dead, and Grey and Armstrong overseas, there was next to no one left for Monmouth to remain loyal to. Exclusion was now impossible; the Whig party had collapsed; his colleagues had gone and his anger had been drowned by the sorrow of the lives lost. Monmouth was finally ready for reconciliation.

Halifax's proposal was that he should write a letter to the king offering to return to court and to ask for his father and uncle's forgiveness. Monmouth at first refused, certain that no letter could heal wounds that were now so deep. But when Halifax said that the king was expecting to hear from him, he promised he would comply. The content of the letter that Monmouth wrote in his steady even script was informed by Halifax who, having witnessed and foiled a number of previous discussions about a rapprochement, knew what Monmouth needed to say to win Charles round. As his coach had pulled away from Toddington in soft dawn light he left behind a draft letter, which the duke read before forming his own.

It was obvious that Monmouth's letter would have to include a statement of his willingness to endorse the Duke of York as heir. Halifax's proposal for proving his sincerity was that Monmouth should suggest that, should he be permitted to return, York himself should be the one to reintroduce him at court. Monmouth did as Halifax instructed, but not without misgivings. He expressed his apology to York as briefly as possible. Halifax's draft had Monmouth say he had been misled into thinking York 'intended to destroy mee'; Monmouth included this but with the pointed rider that he had had 'some justification'. A heartfelt denial of the charge of plotting murder became his opening paragraph: 'I doe call God Almighty to witness and I wish I may dye this moment I am writing if ever it entred in to my head, or ever said the lest thing to anybody that could make them think I could wish such a thing.' He pledged obedience for the future and played to the paternal love he and his father both knew was strong: 'What good can it do youe s[i]r to take your own childs life away, that only erred and venturd his life to save yours.' Like Russell before him, he remained adamant that his actions had been intended only to protect the king and the kingdom from profound harm, however naive that now seemed.[40]

The covering note that accompanied Monmouth's letter to the king was, with Halifax's assistance, provided by Anna, Duchess of Monmouth. She was sceptical of Halifax's sincerity, but was not about to pass up an opportunity, however remote, to bring about a reconciliation. The king had retained his fondness for his resilient daughter-in-law. Though he could not be seen talking to her at this time, he ensured that the Treasury payments to the Duke of Monmouth were not stopped despite the charge of treason against her husband, and in mid-September 1683 instructed the Scottish Privy Council to let Anna receive income from her Buccleuch estates. Monmouth waited anxiously for a response from his father and then, on 20 October, it came. The few lines from the king made him weak with relief and changed absolutely everything. They were, in Monmouth's words, 'very kind, assuring me he believed every word in my Letter to be true; and advis'd me to keep hid, till he had an opportunity to express his Belief of it some other way'.[41]

Five days later Halifax collected Monmouth and took him to meet his father. The location was the court lodgings of one Mrs Crofts, an elderly spinster related to Monmouth's old governor Lord Crofts who could be completely trusted. A visit to court was highly perilous for Monmouth and it was arranged for the end of the day to give him the benefit of fading light. It was, and could only ever have been, an emotional meeting. His first act on seeing his father was to fall to the floor to beg his forgiveness for his involvement in the scheme for an armed uprising. The king received him kindly, but not without chastisement. He vented his anger at those he believed had led Monmouth astray, among them Shaftesbury himself. Having done so he became calm, and when they parted there was peace between father and son for the first time in exactly four years.[42]

It was one thing for Monmouth to win the king round. It was quite another for the king to persuade the Duke of York to receive Monmouth, who for almost five years had done everything in his power to remove York from the royal succession – and whose misdemeanours were those for which Russell had been executed only two months earlier. Charles had told Monmouth to be patient, but events suddenly required them to move fast. As Monmouth left Mrs Crofts's apartment, walking briskly down a dark passage to the waiting coach, he passed Edward Griffin, an army officer, who recognised him. Griffin went straight to the king, who had just returned from the meeting, and told him, breathless, that Monmouth was at Whitehall and could be taken that night if the guards were immediately alerted. The king 'answered him with a disdainful look' and, concealing his intense alarm beneath his haughty demeanour, replied: 'You are a fool; James is at Brussels.'[43]

Certain he was right, Griffin repeated his story to a friend through whom it reached the Duke of York a few days later. York dashed to the king, and asked him to approve a warrant to allow for an arrest within the palace, as he had news of the Duke of Monmouth's being there. The king played for time, asking why he did not detain Monmouth himself if he knew where he was – after all there was a declaration in council for his arrest. When York reiterated that he needed a signed warrant, the king replied vaguely that the council declaration was 'better than all warrants. . . if that be not enough I know not what will serve your turn'.[44]

Any reconciliation between York and Monmouth had to be managed before York tracked him down, which now seemed imminent – there was only so long the king could fend him off with lies and obfuscation. A second clandestine meeting between Monmouth and his father took place on 4 November, to which Halifax and the Secretary of State Jenkins came in order to brief Monmouth on what was to happen next. The reprimands had passed, and Charles was now unequivocally 'very kind' to his son. In Monmouth's words he 'gave me Directions how to manage my Business' and coached him on 'what Words I should say' to York at the meeting the king was hoping to arrange.[45]

That Monmouth should pledge his loyalty to his uncle was clearly essential, but to persuade York to accept such a pledge it was important to pull on all the cords of kinship and former closeness, and to convince York that the mercy was all his. To effect this the king needed not to be seen as the instigator. He went instead, as he seldom did, to see his wife Queen Catherine to ask for her help. She had always been fond of Monmouth, who had arrived in England the same summer as she had, and when the king spoke to her with real feeling of how grateful he would be for her assistance, she quickly agreed. In the second week of November Queen Catherine visited the Duchess of York, and together they spoke to the duke.[46]

Six days later Halifax brought Monmouth a new letter of 'submission' for him to send the king, which the Duke of York was to be told was the first communication that had been received. Unsurprisingly the new letter included a fuller statement of Monmouth's wrongs than he had so far given. It also made much of the fate of Monmouth's children should he be tried for treason, clearly something that had pricked even York's sympathy.

Monmouth must have winced at the wording, not because it admitted he had broken the law – which was undeniable – but because it required him to claim to have done so out of the weak-mindedness of which his uncle loved to accuse him: 'I have been in fault, misled, and insensibly engaged in things of which the consequence was not enough understood by me.' But he was less concerned about making himself look dim and foolish than he was to ensure that nothing he said could be used to incriminate anyone else. Sidney and Hampden were still alive and in prison, while others who had fled might yet be captured. He had pressed Halifax hard on this point a few days earlier, and had been reassured that 'there would be nothing required of me, but what was both safe and honourable'. As a consequence of Monmouth being 'obstinate' on this point, the letter, while it included general statements of regret (of having been 'in fault' and 'offended' the Duke of York), acknowledged no specific crime. Monmouth was still nervous, and before signing asked what precisely was to be done with this letter, saying he 'would have it in no hands but' the king's. Halifax again gave his reassurance, and on 15 November 1683 Monmouth signed his name.[47]

Chapter 17

Love and Loss

At twilight on Saturday 25 November 1683, James, Duke of Monmouth was carried in a sedan chair into the outer court of Whitehall Palace. His three gold-liveried servants stood in attendance as he rose from the chair and walked steadily across the cobbled courtyard, the light from the windows of Inigo Jones's Banqueting House glowing softly above him. The sight there of the most famous nobleman in the kingdom – wanted for high treason – turned every head. Passing under the window of the council chamber where, almost five months before, the proclamation for his arrest had been issued, he pushed open the door of the secretary of state's office. Once inside he stated softly that he had come to prostrate himself at the king's feet.

A message was taken to the king and Duke of York, who came down from the royal apartments above. In the secretary's office, behind a closed door, Monmouth knelt in penitence, professed his sorrow and regret and pledged his loyalty. For an hour they talked, and Monmouth, having been given complete reassurance it would go no further, candidly answered every question they put to him about the Whig conspiracy. After an hour he was given permission by the king to kiss his uncle's hand, he did so and the two men embraced. When the door reopened Monmouth was taken by a sergeant-at-arms not to a prison cell but to his lodgings at the Cockpit.[1]

The next morning Charles had a private conference with a number of his councillors before chapel, and called an extraordinary meeting of the full Privy Council for the afternoon. Here he announced that the Duke of Monmouth had the previous evening confessed his crimes, shown great remorse and apologised sincerely to the Duke of York. Following this, the king went on, the Duke of York had personally asked him to pardon Monmouth. Before twenty amazed faces the king said that he had, after consideration, agreed to his brother's request and was thereby asking the attorney general to stop all proceedings against Monmouth.[2]

Straight after the council meeting a piece of court choreography took place as carefully managed as any performance at Drury Lane, and watched by as many eyes. Monmouth went to the Duke and Duchess of York's lodgings and asked his uncle's forgiveness. York received him, before taking him to the king's apartments where Monmouth repeated the ceremony. York then presented him formally to the queen, the Duchess of York, and others of the extended royal family.[3]

The joy and relief that the king felt at his son's homecoming was immense. At a gathering in the Duchess of Portsmouth's rooms on Saturday night, Charles walked in '*avec beaucoup de joye sur le visage*', such that one fellow guest remarked that there was a 'universal joy in all his actions and in all his words the like of which I had never seen'. Monmouth too was delirious with relief. He wrote in his journal that the king had 'acted his part well and I too' and noted that his father, who 'could not dissemble his Satisfaction, press'd my Hand, which I remember not he did before, except when I return'd from the French Service' ten years before. Over the next few days Charles had Monmouth with him constantly and could not help showing his adoration in his every gesture and glance, treating him 'much more tenderly than he had done formerly'. This was the proof positive of what perceptive people had long believed: that 'the King of England has a fund of tenderness and friendship for the Duke of Monmouth that nothing could destroy'.[4]

The submission that Monmouth made on the weekend of 24/25 November 1683 was painful but sincere. He knew that his meeting

with York in the secretary's office would be extremely uncomfortable. The day before Halifax had 'bad me bear with some words
that might seem harsh' and he had steeled himself for this, and
for the mortification of kneeling publicly before his adversary. It
was true that nothing that could be done over those few weeks could
undo his grievances against York. He felt his uncle had persecuted
him to the extent of trying to 'destroy me' in the late 1670s and
he had become convinced that York, as an authoritarian Catholic,
would imperil the kingdom if he succeeded as king. But these things
notwithstanding, after the terror and tragedy of the past months he
had chosen to make his peace. The written pledge he had made to
his father, looking out on the oaks of Toddington Park, was genuine:
'I will never ask to see your face more if ever I do any thing against
him [York], which is the greatest curse I can lay upon myself.'[5]

York, encouraged by his supporters, had fought against the
proposed reconciliation in the few days after Monmouth's second,
highly orchestrated, letter arrived and the initiative became public.
Various alternatives to his return were proposed, including sending
him to the Tower for a short spell. But the king was adamant, and
in the end simply by 'declareing he would have it soe' prevailed,
writing Jenkins a short note in his own hand stating what Monmouth
was to do. York was furious with Halifax. He knew he had been
the peacemaker and Halifax knew, in turn, that 'the Duke would
never forgive him'. All that said, York was not unmoved by the
sincerity of Monmouth's face-to-face submission in the secretary of
state's office. As the meeting ended Monmouth himself felt warmth
in York's embrace, and even the old cynic the French ambassador
Barillon wrote to Louis XIV that York seemed genuinely satisfied
with his nephew's submission.[6]

For a few precious days it all seemed to be possible. The Duke of
York put some distance between them all by leaving London to go
hunting. Monmouth was to be seen standing behind the king's chair
as he received visitors and carried the sword before his father as he
processed into the chapel wearing the heavy chain of the order of

the Garter. But then, with tragic inevitability, the fragile fabric of reconciliation began to fail.[7]

Only the day after the council meeting Halifax warned Monmouth to be careful, as the Duke of York was starting to suspect that he had been manipulated, adding in code that he 'feared 39 [York] was beginning to smell out 29's [the King's] carriage'.[8] That same day the *London Gazette* published a short account of the events leading up to Monmouth's pardon. The report stated that Monmouth 'shewed himself very sensible of his Crime in the late Conspiracy, making a full declaration of it'. Monmouth had indeed admitted all the details of the conspiracy to his father and York, but he had done so on assurances that it would go no further, and that the sort of careful language used in his letter of submission, avoiding references to a 'conspiracy' or any specific crime, would continue. By contrast the piece in the *Gazette* led many who read it to assume Monmouth would, like others who had confessed, soon be appearing as a witness for the prosecution.[9] Hearing anxious words among those who crowded into his rooms at the Cockpit on Monday morning, Monmouth sent his man, Antony Rowe, out for a copy of the paper. When Rowe read the piece aloud Monmouth exploded with disbelief and declared to the room that he had 'confessed no Plot' and 'did not accuse any man falsely'. The implication that he might behave like Lord Howard, whose testimony had condemned Lord William Russell, shocked Monmouth deeply. 'Not withstanding all reports whatsoever,' he declared 'he would approve himself a man of honour.'[10]

Monmouth rushed across King Street up into his father's apartments with the paper in his hand and his whole body shaking with fear and fury. The king expressed surprise and sympathy and said soothingly that he would simply have the error corrected in the next *Gazette*. Relieved, Monmouth now confidentially repeated his reassurances that there had been no confession to any who asked, adding for good measure that Lord Howard was an infamous liar. But as he did so the king was finding that he had spoken too soon. His ministers told him that he had actually approved the words in the *Gazette*, which were exactly those that had been committed to ink in the Privy Council minute book on Sunday night.[11]

While all this was going on the fearless Algernon Sidney was inching ever closer to the scaffold. The week before Monmouth's return to court he had finally been convicted of plotting the king's death on evidence in his writings. Sidney felt no loyalty to Monmouth and asked pointedly at his sentencing a few days later why the questions at his trial were not now being put to the 'one person I did not know where to find then, but every body knows where to find now, that is the duke of Monmouth'. John Hampden, the sixth of the Whig plotters to have been released on bail, was among the first to crowd into the Cockpit on Monmouth's return. Desperately anxious for his own life, now that the third of their group was facing death, he had asked whether the duke could persuade the king not to execute Sidney. Monmouth had shaken his head. The king had listened sympathetically when Monmouth had spoken 'of how good a man the Lord Russell was and how unjustly put to death' and had even said that he had only agreed to his execution to keep the peace with York. But despite his 'utmost endeavours' there was no saving Sidney. When Hampden had asked him about the rumours of his testifying against them, however, Monmouth had replied passionately that 'he never would'.[12]

Predictably, Monmouth's denial of having confessed to the conspiracy maddened York and those about him, who had been persuaded to accept Monmouth's return on the basis that he had made a full confession. Furthermore it was pointed out to the king that by allowing Monmouth to deny any knowledge of the plot he was undermining the evidence on which the government had already condemned more than one man to die. Monmouth noted in his journal on the morning of Tuesday 27 November that he was beginning to understand 'the storm that was brewing'. A few days later he attended a gathering at the house of Mary, the old Duchess of Richmond, a one-time lady to Henrietta Maria who he knew from his childhood at Colombes. An informant told the king the next day that Monmouth had been heard there talking of the innocence of Lord Russell. The duchess, when asked, protested that 'she heard him say nothing but what became a dutyfull son a Loyall Subject and an honest man'. Though the king had sympathy for his defence of Russell, he was infuriated. He had already warned Monmouth that such talk 'did more hurt than he was aware of', and he now agreed with his Privy Councillors that he must be brought into line.[13]

The remedy that was decided upon that weekend was that Monmouth should sign a public declaration acknowledging both the existence of a plot and his own complicity in it. Halifax, who had managed the original compromise and was in Monmouth's confidence, was given the task of securing the declaration. The draft which Monmouth produced himself was immediately rejected by the council as inadequate. Instead Halifax and Jenkins, who were closer than anyone to the sensitivities, crafted a new letter for which they got the council's approval. This Halifax presented to Monmouth telling him: 'it must be signed and therefore there was no room for further debate'.[14]

The letter that Monmouth was instructed to sign required him to state 'I have owned the late Conspiracy and tho I was not conscious of any design against your Majesties life yet I lament the haveing so great a hand in the other part of the said Conspiracy'. Halifax spent some hours shut away with Monmouth and Anna at the Cockpit on the afternoon of Wednesday 5 December, trying to persuade him to comply. The word 'plot', he coaxed, was unspecific, it was 'a general word, as might signify as much or as little as a man pleased', and anyhow there was no question there had been 'dangerous consultation', which might be all that was meant. Furthermore, stated Halifax, he should think of what greater good he could do his friends by retaining 'the king's heart' through signing such a 'general letter'. If he refused, Monmouth was given to understand, the reconciliation would be over. He remained there agonising, under intense pressure from Anna and Halifax, for some time. Then finally the door swung open and he announced flatly to his those standing by that 'he had done it'.[15]

Halifax was triumphant. It was now in almost everyone at Whitehall's interests to keep Monmouth at court. For the king the motivation was love, for Halifax it was pleasing his master, and for most of the rest it was the value of having the most powerful figure of the opposition with them rather than against them. Halifax celebrated, but as the day wore on Monmouth felt increasingly uncomfortable. He had received a yard of reassurances, it was true, but this might still not be enough to keep Hampden safe. Consumed with worry, he sent a copy of the letter with his footman Bryon to Hampden's house in Covent Garden that night. Hampden was woken and shown the letter. His response when it read it was blunt: 'I am a dead man.'[16]

Monmouth received the news of Hampden's words with a wave of sheer horror. He was 'concerned almost to madness', and striding the room in despair, concluded wildly that perhaps it had all been a trick, that 'they had a mind to ruin him, and he was only brought into court to do a job'. There was nothing for it, 'if he lived till the next day' he said, 'he would have the paper again'.

First thing the following morning he went to the king. His paranoia had subsided but his certainty had not. He implored Charles to return the letter 'in terms full of agony and like despair'. The king tried to calm him, repeating the reassurances that he would not be asked to stand witness against anyone. But Monmouth knew now that this was not enough; his letter alone, he pleaded, 'might have an influence on juries, to make them believe every thing that might be sworn by other witnesses, when from his confession they were possessed with a general belief of the plot'. With Monmouth utterly adamant, the king was confronted with the prospect not just of losing Monmouth again, but of all he had risked to enable his son to return, and 'pressed him vehemently to comply'. But there was no moving him. Charles cried: 'If you do not yield in this you will ruin me,' but still his son knelt before him, tears tumbling from his eyes in despair and desperation, begging him 'as the greatest favour he could beg'.[17]

The personal humiliation and political danger that Charles would bring upon himself if he agreed was almost unthinkable. In what he was asking, Monmouth was placing his honour and loyalty to someone he hardly knew over affection and obedience to his father. But even in these extreme circumstances, when the king's fury and frustration were almost overwhelming, his sense of pity and loyalty to his son were unfathomable. Slowly he put the letter into Monmouth's hand. It was a more profound statement of his love than any other single act of either of their lives. This Monmouth understood. Gulping with emotion and relief, he said 'he owned his life and all to his Majestys grace and favour', and 'never was nor could be more sensible of his favour' than in this act which had secured his honour and his conscience.

The following morning, 7 December, the vice-chamberlain called at the Cockpit to present Monmouth with the inevitable order. He was to leave court and never return. As Monmouth told his family the news, Algernon Sidney mounted the steps of the timber scaffold on Tower Hill where, with a single sure swing of the executioner's axe, his head was severed from his body.[18]

As Monmouth parted from his father the temperature was already dropping. Within a day or two the water in all the city's conduits had turned to ice, and by Christmas the Thames just upriver of London Bridge had frozen right across. Come New Year's Day the bargemen, unable to ply their boats, had set up a series of booths on the ice. Soon a whole street had been created in canvas, with make-shift inns and food stalls, bakers and barbers, a toyshop, a glass shop, and even a printing press where the people jostled for the novelty of buying something marked 'made on the Thames'. Bear-baiting and cockfights were held, sledge rides given and a special Thames lottery offered. Weeks passed and still the world remained frozen. The sooty smoke from the city's coal fires, prevented from escaping by the freezing fog, began to build up in the streets to such an extent that it became impossible to see more than a foot or two ahead. The shrubs and plants in the capital's parks and squares were quickly killed by the depth of the cold, and a few weeks later a sound like gunshot was heard echoing through the streets, as the first of the massive trunks of London's oldest oaks and elms cracked open.[19]

The extreme weather reflected the frigid climate at court that December. Monmouth's long-anticipated return had, in the end, lasted less than a fortnight, and was now definitively over.[20] Straight after the visit from the vice-chamberlain he had left London for Moor Park, where he stayed only to pack for a journey overseas. He knew he had to leave fast. Though his own pardon remained intact, and his life safe, he knew that he could no longer rely on promises made about testifying against others. He made for the coast as England was succumbing to icy paralysis, and sailed at the last possible minute before the seas, full of islands of jagged plates of ice, became impassable.[21]

With the cold still relentless, the government proceeded with John Hampden's trial. The date was set for 6 February, and the proceedings were to be overseen by the new lord chief justice, Sir George Jeffreys. The council was determined to call Monmouth as a witness and, despite Halifax's sharp reminder to the king of the 'regal' promise he had made on this point, Monmouth was subpoenaed to appear. On the last days of January an officer of the court skidded along the hazardous roads to Moor Park to try to present the writ. Failing to find Monmouth he returned to the Cockpit and then to the house of one of Monmouth's servants, but without success. The trial went ahead, but without a crucial second witness to corroborate Lord Howard's testimony, it could not be for high treason. Hampden was found guilty of fomenting disorder, for which he was given a hefty fine but avoided a death sentence. The night before the trial, after six frozen weeks, the thaw began and shortly after the rain started to fall and the ice on the Thames finally cracked.[22]

The news of Hampden's sentence reached Monmouth in Brussels and left him elated. It marked, at last, an end to the revelations and reverberations of the Whig plot. While he had rescinded his written confession, he had sworn to his father to cease all his efforts to unseat his uncle – and he intended to keep his promise. It was, therefore, a new life he was now contemplating. As soon as Hampden's trial was over he returned quietly to England to make arrangements for a permanent move overseas. His appearances at hunts and races were now a thing of the past, and he was careful to be as inconspicuous as possible as he moved around London and the home counties before slipping silently out of England at the end of March.[23]

When Monmouth arrived back on the continent he went equally discreetly to visit William of Orange. The two men had not met since he had stayed in the Dutch Republic during his first banishment five years before. William had watched the unfolding events of the exclusion crisis from across the Channel with intense interest. For his purposes the exclusion of his Catholic father-in-law was much more appealing a prospect than the introduction of limits on the office of king, which diminished the position he expected one day to hold. While he had played a cautious hand, he had made it increasingly clear to Charles II that his sympathies lay with the Whigs, and that he thought the king should call and come to terms with his Parliament. This was not advice Charles enjoyed hearing from his nephew, and if he had ever had any desire to help William fight Louis XIV it had now long since withered.[24]

After Monmouth had briefed William on his affairs he left for Brussels, where he was planning to take up a post in the Spanish army. He had discussed this notion with his old friend Otto del Caretto, Marquis of Grana, in January. This appealing Italian nobleman, with whom Monmouth had fought at St Denis, had been appointed governor-general of the Spanish Netherlands two years earlier. Louis XIV was now attacking the Spanish Netherlands once again and Grana was rallying forces again him. He had come to London in 1682 to try to persuade Charles II to contribute troops to the alliance against the French. The mission had failed but despite the brevity of the trip he had visited Monmouth, who was already talking of coming to join him as a volunteer. Two years on, with nothing now to keep Monmouth in England, Grana agreed that the duke could move to Brussels and join the fight. After a series of prolonged behind-the-scenes meetings, Monmouth was officially received at the Coudenburg Palace in Brussels on Sunday 7 May 1684. The Marquis of Grana sent the captain of his guards in the best state coach to collect his guest, and treating Monmouth as his equal, walked to the door of his antechamber and greeted him 'with great demonstration of joy & respect'. After the formal audience, Monmouth was introduced to Grana's senior officers, before they all sat down together to dine. Word was soon out that Monmouth was to take a senior position in the Spanish army, perhaps commanding the cavalry, and would be remunerated with a pension of £6,000 a year.[25]

A few days later William of Orange arrived in Brussels, having brought a large body of Dutch troops to just outside the city to add to the defence against the French. He and Monmouth traded formal visits and then the two cousins went together to view the Dutch regiments. On 16 May, Grana threw a flamboyant feast for them in the magnificent elevated gardens of the Coudenburg, where they dined in the warmth of the afternoon at three tables set up within the garden's labyrinth. Afterwards the marquis's finest horses were paraded in the park, and he made a gift of a number of them to his guests.[26]

But despite all the bravado, both Grana and William were actually in weak military positions. Louis XIV remained as belligerent as ever and now had Luxemburg under attack, while William was struggling to keep his countrymen behind the war. The members of the powerful States General, those from Amsterdam in particular, had grown unhappy with William's forceful political style and the cost of the war, and when Louis XIV offered a twenty-year truce on highly disadvantageous terms, they were minded to accept. With William struggling to maintain active military opposition to Louis, and Grana, far removed from his Spanish masters, dependent on his neighbour it looked likely both might be forced to capitulate.

The news of Monmouth's second expulsion from court had been greeted with excitement and anticipation by those who had fled England when the two plots had been exposed the previous summer. The experience of exile had brought together a disparate group, some of whom had been involved in the plot to assassinate the king, others connected with the Whig plot. They had expected Monmouth to arrive in their midst at any moment, ready to take up the sword of opposition once again. But they had been disappointed. Lord Grey, after escaping from his gaoler's coach, had been living in the German province of Cleves with Monmouth's outspoken old army friend Thomas Armstrong. Despite feeling aggrieved that he had heard nothing from the duke since his escape, Grey tried to communicate with Monmouth in the spring of 1684 but received a short and distant reply. While they were keen to extract him from Brussels and bring him into their midst, Monmouth was determined to have nothing to do with them. As they rightly concluded, he knew it would 'prejuduce him in England to be where either of us were who were then outlawed'. Robert Ferguson expressed their disappointment: 'all our friends on that side of the water were very sensible of the duke of Monmouth's ingratitude'.[27]

If the rebels were angered by this coolness, Charles II was thrilled. He had survived the humiliation and turmoil of Monmouth's return and expulsion from court relatively undamaged and, as his anger abated, was struck by how fast Monmouth was keeping to his word. The duke had removed himself from England without any publicity or disorder and was refusing to have anything to do with his old associates. Soon a correspondence opened up between father and son once more. The king kept up his public froideur, and forbade the English ambassadors on the continent from seeing him, but it was obvious to many who knew him that this was unlikely to be the full story.[28] While the Duke of York spluttered with indignation when he heard of Monmouth's elaborate reception in Brussels, Charles II did not, having quietly given his consent in a private exchange with Grana some weeks before, and having even helped Monmouth to bring his gold and silver plate over for the ceremonies.[29]

If York was irritated by Grana's treatment of Monmouth, it was nothing compared to his rage when he heard that his son-in-law, William of Orange, had received his disgraced nephew. A stream of letters to the stadtholder was carried from St James's Palace admonishing him for seeing one who had 'been engaged in so horrid a conspiracy for the alteration of the government and ruin of the king and our family'. The only possible explanation for Monmouth's behaviour, sneered York, was 'his vain pretension to the crown'. Receiving no reply from William, he wrote repeatedly to his daughter Mary instead, instructing her to forgo the obedience of a wife and impress upon her husband how scandalous it was that William was behaving so warmly to one of his 'mortal enemies' who was intent on taking the crown for himself.[30] Unflustered, William gave out instructions to his officers that Monmouth should be treated by them with the same honours as the Marquis de Grana.[31]

On 29 June 1684 William of Orange found himself forced to sign Louis XIV's 'Treaty of Truce'. In a bruising personal defeat, he had failed to command the support of the States General and was forced to concede territory and terms to his greatest adversary. The Spanish were expected to sign the truce at any moment, so bringing Monmouth's new job to an end before it had even begun. When a downhearted William decided to withdraw for the summer to his rural palace at Dieren, 150 miles north, he asked Monmouth to accompany him.[32]

At some point in the early months of 1684, perhaps as he arrived in Flanders, Monmouth bought a black leather notebook with a hundred or so blank pages. Small enough to fit easily into a coat pocket, it stayed with him that year, and into its diminutive pages he wrote, making neat transcriptions in the front, and rougher notes of addresses, exchange rates and directions at the back. The book provides a rare glimpse of his state of mind and personal concerns. It shows the intense relief he felt after the horrors of the past year and the contemplation of God that they had provoked. A series of highly personal prayers are written out in his even, elegant hand, one for the morning and one for the evening, each addressing God directly. Starting with a hesitant uncertainty, 'Lord I know not what to pray for as I ought', he went on to express deep repentance for his sins and intense relief at his deliverance. 'Lett me never return to the follys of w[hi]ch I am asheamed w[hi]ch bring sorrow and death,' he wrote, putting a cross in the margin for emphasis, as 'thou in thy manifold mercies hast not forsaken mee, but hath graciously invited mee to repentence.' The prayers speak repeatedly of God as 'Father', mirroring Monmouth's sense of gratitude and deliverance to both the Almighty and to the king.[33] The sense of an intense personal relationship with God, which the notebook reveals, may always have been with him, but part of an inner life almost invisible to the outsider. More likely, perhaps, the traumatic experiences of 1683 had brought out in Monmouth a personal spirituality that had been largely dormant until this time.

Combined with this deep sense of moral and spiritual reprieve, Monmouth was continuing to experience something altogether more temporal that year: love. When he had left Whitehall Anna had not gone with him. After a long meeting, Charles II had agreed that she could be readmitted, alone, into the royal family. On Christmas Day she attended church at St James's Palace, the residence of the Duke and Duchess of York, and, in a deliberate demonstration of reunion, took communion with York's daughter Princess Anne. Monmouth and Anna's paths had parted and their marriage was over. When he left for Flanders in March, Henrietta Wentworth and her mother packed their belongings and made the crossing as well. The respectability of this unmarried young noblewoman concerned him, and she lived alongside him with the greatest discretion over the spring and summer of 1684. Monsieur Fonseca, the Brussels fixer whom Monmouth employed, found him a townhouse and in July an English officer who lodged close by reported that 'it is said here the Lady Harriat W[entwor]th [is] with him' but could not confirm this by any certain sighting.[34]

But while they kept their relationship hidden, Monmouth poured his happiness into his notebook in verse, poor as poetry but intensely genuine in sentiment. While he and Henrietta had known one another for a decade, and been romantically linked for three years, it had become serious and sincere to a completely different degree in 1683. Toddington was synonymous with the contentment and concord he had found the previous year as he laid low at Henrietta's house, and in his poems he blessed the stars that 'did us Tedington give'. Whatever had thwarted their relationship had now passed, 'malice can't w[i]th all her arts / part our two united harts', and peaceful union was his desire, 'lett us now know quietnes / never from each other be'. The happiness that these two felt, now together and away from the unbearable political pressure of the previous year, was mutual. One of Henrietta's friends described them as equally infatuated.[35]

The months of 1684 were, despite all the uncertainties, a time of considerable calm and reflection for Monmouth. He looked back on his life, and took stock. He talked with regret of 'the little care [that] had been taken of his Education'; he bought books and spent time in study. In his notebook he recorded the principal moral tenets of ancient philosophers, made notes on the tactics of the Roman army and listed remarkable natural phenomena from the reigns of William the Conqueror to Queen Elizabeth. Now thirty-five but with a lover a decade his junior, he contemplated his own ageing, noting down recipes for making hair grow thick and dark and for keeping a face fair. Alongside his earnest prayers of repentance he also recorded 'charms', half-religious half-mystical formulae for divining events, including one that would reveal if a person would remain faithful.[36]

In the heat of July, Monmouth and William of Orange hunted together once again in the shady forests at Dieren.[37] Just before William left The Hague he had an excruciating meeting with Thomas Chudleigh, the English ambassador to the United Provinces, in which he was presented with Charles II's official condemnation of his treatment of Monmouth. William was briefly wrong-footed by this galling reprimand and sent Chudleigh reeling from the room, treating him with utter disdain thereafter.[38] William's reasons for entertaining Monmouth so lavishly were complex. On the one hand he felt no necessity to comply with the demands of his uncles, the Duke of York and Charles II, who had completely failed to support his efforts to fend off Louis XIV. He could also see that it might be better to have a potential rival for the English throne in his confidence rather than rattling dangerously about the continent. But there was more to it than this. As soon as Monmouth arrived in the Netherlands in March 1684 he had gone to see William to give him his own account of events – remembering well the promises he had made the stadtholder in 1679. During their meeting, he had explained his actions with intense earnestness and, looking William in the eye, swore that he had never tried to 'make himselfe or be acknowledge[d] as legitimate'.[39]

It was not Monmouth's words alone that convinced William, but Charles II himself. Charles had already established a code by which William would know if a letter represented his true feelings, or those he affected to have for political reasons. The official pardon Monmouth had been granted in December counted for something, but Charles laid out to William in this clandestine correspondence his own continuing faith in his son. Even Chudleigh, whose job it was to hold the official line that Charles II was unhappy with William, expressed frustration because: 'His Maty is not so much offended with ye Prince of Orange as people are made to believe', and that 'there is a private intelligence' between them. William and Mary were left in no doubt that Charles did not consider Monmouth a traitor and that his love was undiminished. Writing to England from Dieren in July, William explained his conduct, arguing that Monmouth 'is his [Charles II's] son, whom he had pardoned for the faults which he may have committed; and though he has removed him from his presence, I know that in the bottom of his heart he has always some friendship for him and that the King cannot be angry with him'.[40]

William and Mary's treatment of the duke was more than a piece of cold political positioning. Mary had grown up with Monmouth and had lived alongside him from her birth to her wedding day. Both Charles II and the Duke of York recognised that since William and Monmouth had fought together in 1678 they had become 'so good friends and agree so well together'. The 'fondness' Mary and William showed for Monmouth in 1684, and the 'caresses' he received that were the 'common discourse of all sorts of people' in The Hague, were the product of personal as well as political dynamics. With Monmouth as guest the atmosphere in the Orange court started to grow noticeably brighter. Onlookers were surprised to see Mary – who never walked out – taking daily constitutionals in the mall with her cousin, while they were frankly amazed when William – who used his asthma as an excuse to avoid dancing – was to be found learning contredanses with Monmouth and Mary most evenings. When the English ambassador in The Hague reported that Monmouth was being treated by William and Mary 'as one of ye family', it was not just a calibration of the formal honours allowed to him, but also an expression of the closeness between them all.[41]

Monmouth was now at a crossroads. On the face of it he had to choose between living in Brussels without the military commission he had expected, seeking a military position elsewhere in Europe or relocating to The Hague. In September he travelled from Dieren to Brussels to discuss the options face to face with Grana. But as well as these obvious avenues there began to emerge another much more extraordinary. In early November it was reported that Monmouth was going to see Grana in Brussels a second time. But the servants he left behind in the Dutch Republic soon found it irresistible to whisper that this was just a cover story: their master's 'true journey is over to England, whither they say he is calld to a private Conference with the King'.[42]

It was a mark of the real warmth of Monmouth's treatment by his cousins that, though his wife was one of the princess's oldest friends, William and Mary received Henrietta Wentworth publicly as his companion. Her own noble status and long acquaintance with Mary were both powerful points in her favour. The couple were inseparable and in the first days of November, Henrietta travelled ahead to Rotterdam accompanied by her mother. Monmouth himself set out conspicuously for Brussels, but along the way he switched vehicles and doubled back, so that while his coach and luggage trundled on he made his way secretly to the coast, travelling the last leg in the back of a wagon. On 9 November he boarded a vessel at Rotterdam with Henrietta and Philadelphia, and the following day they weighed anchor for England. The sense of anticipation and excitement must have been enormous. When he had left the king's closet clutching his retrieved confession a year before he had expected never to see his father again. Now he was on his way home summoned to a meeting of the utmost secrecy. The voyage was a time of intimacy. In his notebook he inscribed simply: 'HW had J', with 9 and 16 November and the location 'poupe', the cabin at the rear of a ship, set out among calligraphical flourishes. He also wrote out a list of boys' and girls' names: Charles, James and Henry; Catherine, Anna and Elizabeth heading each. Whether or not Henrietta was yet pregnant, the thought of children seems to have been on Monmouth's mind.[43]

On their arrival in England, Monmouth had to move with stealth to avoid discovery. He did not stay in London but went to property owned by Henrietta in the village of Stepney five miles east of the city. After a clandestine meeting in London he travelled north through Hampstead to wait for a few days at Toddington, then after a second visit to town, Monmouth and Henrietta made for the busy docks at Tilbury in Essex where they again boarded a vessel.[44] The matter that the king wanted to discuss with Monmouth was extraordinary and unexpected. Unknown to almost everyone about him, Charles was seriously contemplating sending the Duke of York away once more. Precisely why York was to be banished now is unclear, for the scheme was highly secret: only Lord Halifax, Lady Portsmouth and a tiny number of others knew anything of it. But if York were to be sent out of England, the chief barrier to Monmouth being there would be removed. Bishop Burnet was told of the plan by Baptist May, keeper of the privy purse, who had for twenty years been one of the king's closest servants. Whether Monmouth saw Charles in person during his few days in England in late November 1684 is not certain – Burnet thought he did not but several others reported he did – and it would seem strange for the voyage to have been chanced if it were only to exchange letters or messages that could easily have been carried to the continent. Either way, Monmouth left London 'very well pleased with his journey'.[45]

Monmouth landed at Nieuwpoort on the north coast of the Spanish Netherlands at eleven o'clock on a cold December morning and made quickly for Brussels. He slipped into his house, changed clothes and appeared in public. On 19 December he received a letter from Charles II which told him to stay where he was 'till I heard father from him'. A second letter came soon after from Halifax confirming what had been agreed in person: Monmouth would be called home in a matter of weeks. York himself, Halifax said, knew nothing of their meeting. In the margin Charles II scribbled a note reminding him that he should 'trust entirely' in '10' – probably cipher for William of Orange. The letter caught up with Monmouth on the road to The Hague, where on 5 January 1685 the English ambassador reported with surprise that 'the D of Monmouth is suddenly expected'.[46] Monmouth arrived the following day and was immediately visited by the prince's closest advisor, Hans Willem Bentinck, who took him to see the stadtholder. For the next three hours William and Monmouth were shut up together in William's closet. Chudleigh was certain that Monmouth was reporting on his secret discussions with the king and that a 'private under-standing' existed between the three men. Affairs were now afoot that were 'all done by private concert between ye King, ye Prince & Monmouth'. As the two cousins grew closer 'every day', William offered Monmouth his own servants to attend him and ordered one of his palaces in The Hague to be put at his disposal.[47]

The Dutch newspapers now confidently reported that Monmouth would be remaining in The Hague for the rest of the winter. Knowing the call home could come at any moment, the duke avoided moving from the inn where he was lodged. On 3 February a letter arrived from Halifax with thrilling news: 'my Business', noted Monmouth, 'was almost as well as done'. The king was quite decided: York was to be banished; whether he chose to go to Scotland, Flanders or the Netherlands was to be up to him – it 'was all one' to Charles. Halifax advised Monmouth that he must be ready to move at speed when the order to return came, so as not to allow the Duke of York's supporters time to 'counterplot'. Restless and consumed with nervous energy, Monmouth killed time over the coming days attending dinners and receptions but always poised to ride for the coast at a moment's notice. The weather had turned cold and Mary persuaded William to let Monmouth take her skating on the frozen canals. There the duke gave a steadying arm to his normally cosseted cousin as she slipped and slid about in a short skating dress, causing prim onlookers to tut-tut with disapproval. There was general amazement that William, who was 'the most jealous man in the world', was allowing his wife to consort so publicly with this famous gallant – Monmouth was even being allowed to form a couple with Mary in after-dinner dancing. But Monmouth's affection was purely fraternal and William did not flinch, such was the intimacy between the trio. Meanwhile in England, Charles II finally spoke to his brother and announced to the startled duke that 'either the duke [of York] must go, or that he himself would go'. Then on the evening of Friday 16 February, as Monmouth danced at a candlelit ball, one of his servants caught his eye. Gliding from the floor he saw that his man held in his hand a letter from Halifax. His heart pounding, he broke the seal. But as he read the music and light of the ballroom were suddenly drowned by hellish darkness. Halifax's curling script contained not his father's summons, but the news that King Charles II, by grace of God King of England, Scotland and Ireland, was dead.[48]

Chapter 18

The Reluctant Rebel

The speed of Charles II's physical decline had been stunning. On Monday morning he had risen as usual, but when he sat down to be shaved he started shaking, and by Friday morning he was dead. News of his death overtook that of his illness to reach the continent first. He had spent his last days in a delirious haze, tortured by seventeenth-century medicine, and passing in and out of consciousness. Constantly at his side was the Duke of York. Just hours before Charles's death York arranged for Father Huddleston, the Catholic priest who had helped Charles when he had been on the run after the battle of Worcester, to visit the king. There in his bedchamber Charles, who had had known all his life that the survival of the English monarchy depended on his protection of Protestantism, was received into the Roman Catholic Church.

The news when it reached Monmouth left him stunned. To the shock of losing his father would be added mounting disbelief: at the inexplicably swift decline of an apparently healthy fifty-four-year-old, at rumours of his deathbed conversion, and at the wildly suspicious timing of it all, just as York was being asked to leave England. After spending hours locked in conference with William, Monmouth returned to his lodgings, exhausted, as the city bells chimed midnight. Here the vastness of his personal loss broke over him like a tidal wave. Passers-by could hear the muffled noise as he roared with grief, his cries unmistakably those of *'un homme désespéré'*.[1]

The instant word of Charles II's death reached the Whig rebels exiled to the continent they started to mobilise. This was their moment to act. Scattered among various northern European towns and cities were those who had been implicated in the two Whig plots. Thomas Armstrong had been caught and executed six months before, leaving alive only Lord Grey of Monmouth's friends linked to the Whig plot. Dozens of men who had been involved in the radical assassination conspiracy were still at large, among them Shaftesbury's friend and deathbed companion the radical preacher Robert Ferguson. To this varied assortment were also added a series of Scottish exiles, and exceptional among them in every way the powerful chief of the Campbell clan, the Earl of Argyll. To a number of the more active of the dissidents the ideal solution seemed obvious: these two Protestant aristocrats, Monmouth and Argyll, should join forces to lead an uprising to oust the new Catholic king.[2]

Monmouth, however, had other ideas. His thoughts in February and March 1685 were not of England or deposing his uncle, but of his future and Henrietta Wentworth. Six days after he heard of his father's death, he set out for Brussels to collect his belongings and rekindle a plan for joining the Holy Roman Emperor fighting the Turks.[3] During his fortnight in Brussels he began to be approached by the exiled Whigs, anxious to persuade him to lead an invasion. Moses Wagstaffe, one of his servants, recalled the former parliamentarian soldier John Manley visiting them in Brussels twice during those few weeks in February.[4] Pleas and calls to arms came both in person and in letter. But they met the same response. 'Whatever way I turn my Thoughts, I find insuperable Difficulties,' Monmouth wrote to one; 'for God's sake, think. . . of the Improbabilities that lie naturally in our way; and let us not, by struggling with our Chains make then straiter and heavier'. While for the other dissidents, wanted for treason, the future looked bleak unless some sort of drastic action was taken, for Monmouth it was different. His pardon stood and, as he told a correspondent, in the weeks since his father's death, 'I have not only look'd back, but forward', 'I am now so much in love with a retir'd Life, that I am never like to be fond of making a Bustle in the World again.'⁵

While Monmouth rebuffed the rebels' approaches, he was also unable to stay where he was. York had been proclaimed King James II and had made his objection to Monmouth's presence in the Spanish Netherlands threateningly clear. Even the Marquis de Grana felt he had no choice but to ask the duke to leave. Just two weeks after his arrival Monmouth left the city and travelled north back to the United Provinces, agreeing to meet the exiles who were gathering at Rotterdam on the way. He wrote ahead to warn them that he did so only 'that I may not seem obstinate in my own Judgement, or neglect the Advice of my Friends'. Having 'weigh'd all your Reasons, and every thing that you and my other Friends have writ upon the Subject', he was determined to take no part in an uprising.⁶

The new English ambassador in The Hague was Bevil Skelton. During those weeks after Charles II's death Skelton collected every scrap of information he could find on the movements of the English exiles and soon realised that they were flocking together in Rotterdam. Here Monmouth arrived in the first week of April, having waited in Utrecht to be joined by Henrietta, who he then sent onwards to The Hague. A fortnight later Skelton's agents reported that some of the exiles had left 'very ill satisfyd with the Duke of Monmouth's conduct'. But while Monmouth's resolve on his arrival in Rotterdam was holding, the forces that were about to be brought to bear on it would be extreme.⁷

Two Scots were the determining figures in what would unfold over the following three weeks. Robert Ferguson was one. He was a professional schemer of fluid principles who, when the assassination plot had been exposed in 1683, laughed at his fleeing fellow conspirators, declaring fiendishly, 'gentlemen, you are all strangers to this kind of exercise; I have been used to flight and I will never be out of a plot so long as I live'. Ferguson had visited Lord Grey in Amsterdam shortly after Charles II's death and showed his colours. After a prolonged rant about Monmouth's behaviour towards the exiles over the past year, he composed himself and declared with oily magnanimity that 'all these suspicions had now to be laid aside' because 'a perfect unity between us was absolutely necessary to preserve the liberties of the three kingdoms'. When Grey had expressed some uncertainty as to whether Monmouth would be prepared to lead a rebellion, Ferguson's calm cracked and 'in a great passion [he] railed at the Duke of Monmouth, condemning him for great numbness of spirit and slothfulness'. Ferguson was determined to orchestrate a meeting between Monmouth and Argyll, and to push Monmouth into agreeing to lead a rebellion – using whatever means necessary to do so.[8]

The other volatile agent in this political cocktail was the fifty-five-year-old Scottish nobleman Archibald Campbell, 9th Earl of Argyll, who also made his way to Rotterdam that April. His father, the Marquis of Argyll, had been the leader of the radical Presbyterians in Scotland during the interregnum and had been executed in 1660. By contrast his son had rejected his radical politics and became a staunch royalist. Despite his recovery of much of the family's land and titles, the shadow of scores that lay unsettled fell across Argyll's life and he grew up with an arrogance and ability to make enemies that his diminutive stature belied. Argyll was a man who pursued his own advantage relentlessly. In 1681 he had fallen out spectacularly with the Duke of York (then banished to Scotland during the exclusion crisis) when he tried to add a rider to the oath of allegiance that it pertained 'only as far as was consistent with the Protestant religion'. York was incensed and Argyll was found guilty of treason by the Court of Justiciary. Only his escape from Edinburgh Castle disguised as a page in December 1681 had prevented the sentence of death and forfeiture from being carried out. If anyone sought proof that the man who was now King James II posed a threat to his Protestant subjects' liberties, they needed to look no further than his attitude to Argyll's attempt to speak up for the established religion.

After his escape Argyll had briefly appeared in London in 1682. He met Shaftesbury and made contacts among the Whigs that would involve him in discussion about an uprising the following spring. These came to naught and Argyll retreated to the Low Countries, looking for an opportunity to regain his property and throw off the sentence that hung over him.

In truth the idea of a Protestant uprising led by Argyll in Scotland and Monmouth in England appealed to neither man. Monmouth was against an invasion altogether and Argyll recoiled from any enterprise of which he was not the sole commander. Thanks to the devotion of one Ann Smith, a wealthy English widow based in Amsterdam, he had already lined up funds and arms, and his first response to suggestions that he might collaborate with Monmouth were 'tart expressions' that revealed his jealousy of the younger man. When it became clear to Argyll that many of the rank-and-file exiles would only participate if Monmouth was involved, and when he was reassured that he could have total charge of the Scottish leg of the enterprise, he changed his tune. But to Mrs Smith, among others, it was obvious that Monmouth himself remained 'much against' an invasion.[9]

In this situation of mutual distrust and divided ambitions, it took a very particular combination of persuasion and carefully peddled propaganda to bring anything to pass. Ferguson knew well from the experience of the last two years where Monmouth's weak spots lay. The duke had demonstrated an almost unfathomable sense of what honour and justice required of him, together with a strange seam of naivety quite different from the worldly scepticism that was such a feature of his father's court. Both of these were gifts to Ferguson and in April 1685 he and his collaborators set about convincing Monmouth that he was honour-bound to act, and that the circumstances in England were such that if he did so he would meet with certain success.

The arguments advanced were consistent with the rhetoric Ferguson had poured out in lurid pamphlets at the height of the exclusion crisis. In the words of one those involved in these discussions, their 'clear duty in the matter' was to save the Protestants of all three kingdoms from what unquestionably awaited them:

nothing less than the eradication of their freedoms and religion. Those in a position to act had a sacred 'obligation and duty . . . to endeavour the rescue, defence and relief of our Religion, Rights and Liberties and many distressed sufferers on their behalf'. To this general responsibility Monmouth's personal debt to the country's Protestants, the people who had turned out to cheer him in town squares and country lanes up and down the land, was emphasised. Surely 'the Duke would never prove so ungrateful as to see those what have stood up for his interest sink for want of support'? Night after night the case was made to him that, in his words, it would be 'a shame and a sin before God not to doe it'.[10]

Ferguson's second objective was to convince Monmouth that an invasion would not simply be suicide. Monmouth knew that the political climate in England had changed dramatically in the six years since the heyday of the Exclusion crisis. After the final defeat of the Exclusion Bill and the dismissal of the Oxford Parliament, Charles II's crackdown on the City of London had set the tone for a wide-ranging and powerful reassertion of royal authority. Once in the hands of loyal Tories, the City of London had been pushed into surrendering its ancient charter and accepting a new one that removed opposition figures. A similar process followed in towns across the land and, with the central coordination of the Whig movement discredited and dissipated by the exposure of the plots in 1683, the opposition seemed thoroughly spent. All this Monmouth knew, but Ferguson and his cronies now claimed that these setbacks had been superficial and that strong grass-roots support remained for an uprising which needed only his rallying cry to raise it.

A variety of agents and informants were called upon to corroborate the level of support that supposedly existed for an invasion. London was essential and Major Wildman, a former Leveller implicated in the 1683 assassination plot, was a critical potential supporter. Ferguson produced an intermediary, a 'Mr Smith', who brought an encouraging report saying Wildman had told him 'there was never a greater spirit amongst the Common People in England for our purpose' and that 'in the name of all the other Gentlemen of the Duke's [Monmouth's] party in England' he was calling on Monmouth and Argyll to join forces for the 'redemption of three kingdoms'. Wildman, he said, had also pledged to provide 'any reasonable sum' to properly equip an army. It all seemed plausible enough but, unbeknown to Monmouth, 'Smith' was Ferguson's creature, paid by him to peddle lies. He would soon be blackmailing those with whom he had communicated with the threat of exposing them to James II.[11]

To the encouraging messages from England produced by Ferguson was added the Earl of Argyll's own swaggering certainty. When the earl met Monmouth in April 1685 he told him he had decided months ago to invade Scotland, and his bristling sense of competition prompted him to speak in expansive terms of his sure success. He reeled off the resources he already had to hand: 500 barrels of gunpowder, three ships, arms for ten thousand 'and many other things necessary for war'. While he was cagey about the precise details of his plan, as the head of a powerful clan in a disaffected land he spoke convincingly of the thousands who would instantly rally to his cause. He was ready to sail in a fortnight, he maintained, and had come to believe that if 'a rising could be contrived in England to keep time with his in Scotland', so dividing the royal army, he and Monmouth might between them make light work of deposing the Catholic king.[12]

Monmouth was not unaware of how unreliable Ferguson and his cronies were. He had been amazed that Shaftesbury had become so close to them in 1682 and appalled when Ferguson had then slyly hinted to him that Charles II should himself be killed. He also knew enough of what it took to fight a war to know that such reassurances as they received in April 1685, even taken at face value, were still a long way short of the sort of cast-iron arrangements he had been so insistent upon in 1683.

There were two forces that clouded Monmouth's judgement in the spring of 1685. The first was that just two months ago he had lost his father, by far the most influential figure in his life. Still in shock, his sense and clear-sightedness remained shaky. While his resolve not to become entangled in any rebellion was sincere, he was emotionally fragile and more susceptible to pressure than at any other moment in his life.[13]

The second factor was honour. There was a very real possibility that Charles II's death had not been an accident (sensing Monmouth's own suspicions on this point, Ferguson was quick to assert outright that he had been murdered), and Argyll was already poised to attack. For Monmouth to sit on his hands in such circumstances was impossible. After all, he was the man who at twenty-two had leapt alone out of the Maastricht trenches holding only a sword in the face of a barrage of gunfire. In the words of one who participated in the debates over those weeks, 'the Duke of Monmouth was pushed on to it against his own sense and reason, but he could not refuse to hazard his person when others were so forward'. When he first rebuffed the dissidents' approaches he had said he would 'run the hazard of being thought any thing rather than a rash inconsiderate man'. But this was wishful thinking. The truth was he would risk almost anything for honour and justice, however dangerous, and these now loomed so large that any sober judgements about the reliability of his potential colleagues and their plans were fatally eclipsed.[14]

Argyll's 'haiste to be gone' was immense and he 'pressed exceedingly for a categorick answer' from Monmouth and the others involved in the discussions. Under intense emotional pressure from all sides, and alone (Henrietta was still in The Hague), Monmouth finally cracked. A message from the Whig publisher William Disney telling Monmouth 'not to thinke of coming to England' was waylaid by Lord Grey, and after countless meetings in both Rotterdam and Amsterdam, 'Mr Smith's' positive news from London at last 'put the Duke upon entring into a promise to Argyle of invading England in near as short a time as he could land in Scotland'. To do so meant risking his life, breaking his promises to William and forgoing the happiness with Henrietta for which he pined. But he felt that it was what was required of him. He would act, he said, 'as a Protestant and an Englishman, for the Protestant religion and the liberties of the nationes'. While Ferguson offered his unctuous congratulations, Monmouth was unaware that he had been snared

The Duke of Monmouth in Garter Robes by Peter Lely, 1674. One of scores of versions of this portrait of Monmouth painted following his spectacular success at Maastricht. His charm and magnetic good looks caused one contemporary to remark, 'nature perhaps never formed anything more complete'.

Henriette Anne holding a portrait of her husband, the Duc d'Orléans. This image of love is a far cry from the brutal reality of Charles II's sister's marriage.

The mutilated corpses of Johan and Cornelis de Witt, whose fall, as Louis XIV's army threatened to conquer the Dutch republic, brought the young William of Orange to power.

The spectacular temporary ballroom erected at Versailles in 1668. Monmouth was in the royal party sitting with Louis XIV and Marie Thérèse in the foreground.

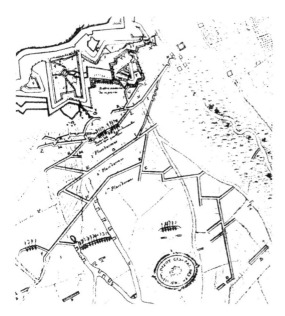

Maastricht, 1673. Louis XIV's army encircled the city (*below*) before Monmouth and his men attacked through Vauban's network of parallel trenches (*above*).

Louis XIV Crowned by Victory by Pierre Mignard, with the fallen city of Maastricht in the background.

Whitehall Palace from the Thames, with the barges of the city livery companies in a water procession. Whitehall was the centre of Monmouth's life for almost twenty years.

After a wildly promiscuous youth Monmouth would, in his thirties, become devoted to Henrietta, Baroness Wentworth, 'whom he called his wife before God to his last'.

Monmouth the professional soldier, wearing the uniform of Captain of the King's Own Troop of Life Guards, by Jan Wyck.

William of Orange (*centre front of the mounted group*) and James, Duke of Monmouth (*right of him*) fighting side by side at the battle of St Denis, August 1678.

Titus Oates giving evidence of the 'Popish Plot' to the King and Privy Council in 1678.

The chamber of the House of Lords. Monmouth was a regular at debates and took his seat near the king, at the far end of the right hand bench.

The River Thames frozen solid and covered with temporary stalls and shops. This was the icy London which Monmouth left behind in December 1683.

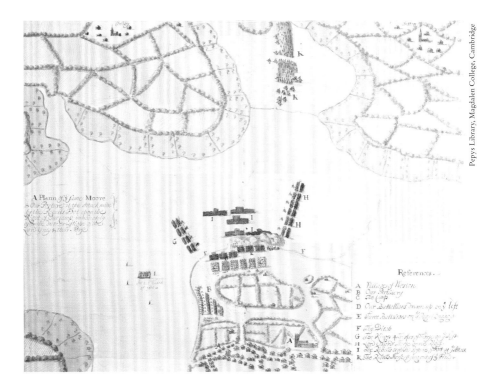

The Battle of Sedgemoor. *Top*: the rebels' cavalry under Lord Grey flee back across the moor (K), having failed to cross the Bussex Rhine (F), leaving Monmouth and the infantry (I) to fight on alone. *Bottom*: the situation as dawn broke, with the rebels surrounded.

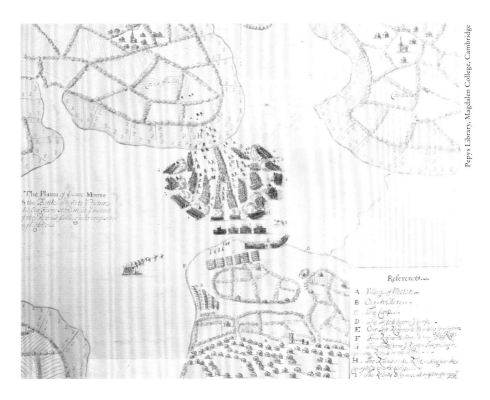

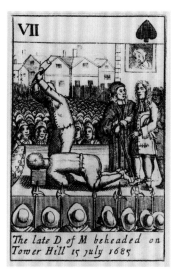

Right: The execution of Monmouth from a set of playing cards of the rebellion.

Far right: The merciless Bloody Assizes of 1685 left the towns and villages of Dorset, Somerset and Devon festooned with mutilated bodies.

The late D of M beheaded on Tower Hill 15 July 1685

Severall of ye Rebells hang'd upon a Tree

JAMES DE MONMOUTH.

Hundreds of paintings and prints of Monmouth were created in the 1680s. After his execution this striking oil painting was inscribed 'Brave, Beautiful, Unfortunate'.

by misinformation laced with outright lies and that the path he had now pledged to take could lead only to tragedy.[15]

During the first week of May, within only a few days of extracting the promise from Monmouth, the Earl of Argyll set sail for Scotland. Thanks to the munificence of the admiring Mrs Smith, he had three ships and was almost as well equipped as he had boasted he would be. With not a moment to lose Monmouth had started making his own arrangements. The scheme that had been agreed was a version of the plan discussed in 1683. Argyll would raise Scotland, the Cheshire Whigs the north-west, Wildman and one or two others, London, and Monmouth himself the south-west. To expand on existing intelligence, Monmouth sent his own agents to England shortly before Argyll's departure: Edward Matthews 'to prepare his friends there for the business' and John Bettiscomb to extract the promised funds from Major Wildman, instruct the Cheshire Whigs – Lord Macclesfield and Lord Delamere – and to make contact with Whigs in the south-west.[16] But the news, when it trickled back, was worryingly ambiguous. In contrast to the confident certainties reported by Ferguson, Matthews had not been able to get a straight answer out of Wildman on either the money or London. Instead he had 'spoke[n] to him only in Hieroglyphics and was something shie of the matter'. But Matthews felt sure the news from the Cheshire Whigs would be more reassuring. From another correspondent, purporting to represent the views of his 'friends', came a message that he should not think of invading England at all, and make instead for Scotland. To further approaches Wildman responded with more enthusiasm, but still no money and an unhelpful postscript that Henry VII had managed an invasion of England with only 140 men. Monmouth started to feel deeply anxious. But it was already too late to think of turning back: he was 'engaged by his promise to my lord Argyle', who by now was already at sea.[17]

The accession of James II, the event dreaded by so many for so long, had in the event gone surprisingly smoothly. Three days after his brother's death the new king announced he was calling Parliament. It had not met for exactly five years. He did so because he needed parliamentary assent to secure the basic royal income, but the news was nevertheless effective in stemming allegations that he was bent on absolutism.[18] On 23 April, as Monmouth was under emotional siege in Rotterdam, James II was crowned King of England in Westminster Abbey. A veil was drawn over the question of whether a Catholic king could be head of a Protestant Church, and the Anglican communion was left out of the coronation service. In time-honoured fashion, many of those who had opposed him as Duke of York changed their tune when he was actually on the throne and in a position to dispense offices and influence. The Earl of Sunderland, who had ricocheted in and out of opposition over the past decade, and had been a one-time supporter of the Exclusion Bill, became his most loyal servant, and devoted himself to making his new master happy.

But while English towns and cities, anxious to please one whom many of them had volubly opposed a few years before, sent loyal addresses to the new king, William of Orange was rather more circumspect. James II's disapproval had caused Monmouth to be ejected from the Spanish Netherlands overnight, but it had no such effect on his son-in-law in The Hague. The stadtholder went through the motions of congratulating his father-in-law on his accession, but when Monmouth returned from Brussels and James II asked that he be expelled, William did almost nothing. He had witnessed first-hand Monmouth's determination not to be drawn into rebellion and was not minded to give his friend up. As the dissidents assembled in Rotterdam in early April the English ambassador confronted William again about Monmouth. William murmured that he would expel him but, in Skelton's words 'gave me little encouragement or hope it would ever be done'.[19] The frustration in London grew with the days that passed. The Earl of Rochester wrote to William claiming that they were not seeking to drive Monmouth from country to country, but surely he could see that they could not have him 'hovering just over against England,

and as it were always in a readiness to transport himself'.[20] Yet still William prevaricated, knowing nothing of Monmouth's change of heart, and even a direct and stern letter from James II a few weeks later did not result in any definite action.[21]

That William of Orange left him alone during these crucial weeks in April and early May 1685 bought Monmouth precious time to make arrangements for equipping the uprising to which he was now committed. Growing concerned about just how much money would appear from England, Monmouth left one of his supporters, Nathaniel Wade, in Amsterdam with a very specific list of things to buy, and returned to Rotterdam.[22] It was clear that to start supplying his arm of the rebellion he would need to provide the initial funds himself. While he had little cash, he had furnished his house in Brussels with considerable splendour, and he set about raising £3,000 by pawning various of his possessions with the merchant Daniel le Blon. Few Englishmen knew better than Monmouth the cost of military equipment, and Wade had instructions to acquire two vessels, armour for 1,500 foot soldiers, four cannons and 200 barrels of gunpowder, all of which came to £3,000.[23] When Monmouth returned to Amsterdam, however, it was to the terrible realisation that there would be no money at all from England: Wildman's infuriating message was that 'the People were well armed and so consequently no need of money'. It was now over a week since Argyll had set sail and Monmouth could wait no longer. He wrote a desperate note to le Blon, offering him all that remained of his belongings. 'I hope this will be wellcome to you,' he scribbled, if it was not 'wee are absolutely ruined.'[24]

Sixty-six boxes and cases of belongings were handed over to le Blon and his associates in Rotterdam on 12 May 1685. They were, in the words of Monmouth's quartermaster, 'all he had in the World'. He had lost none of his taste for beauty and the chairs and stools, tapestries, paintings and gilt-wood chandeliers were all of the first quality. Eighteen sets of cutlery, six candlesticks and six salt cellars featured among £4,000 worth of gold and silver dining plate. Chest after chest of his immaculate clothes were listed by the pawnbrokers, among their contents fifty-six diamond buttons in a velvet case, jewelled mirrors and hats and a pair of diamond-studded shoe buckles. In a remarkable round chest were his heavy silk and velvet Garter robes and with them the massive chain of the order, the first office to which his adoring father had elevated him. What remained of his once legendary stable was taken to the equestrian academy in The Hague and here were disposed of: his horses 'Beaumont', 'Snipe' and the black Spanish stallion 'Forbidden'. Among the acquisitions of more recent times were his five trunks and coffers of books and a collection of mathematical instruments with gold fittings. Henrietta's plate and furniture was mingled indistinguishably with Monmouth's, as were things they had acquired together, including a damask bed bought only months before and a chest containing their linen, in the thick folds of which le Blon's clerk found a seal bearing the Wentworth crest. Here in leather and tortoiseshell was coffered and clasped what was left of a whole life, and in Rotterdam, city of his birth, Monmouth traded it all.[25]

The mass pawning raised £5,770, three-quarters of the total value of the goods. Ann Smith was persuaded to provide a further £1,000 in addition to the £8,000 she had given Argyll. To this a number of supporters added smaller sums, including the one-time lord mayor of London, Sir Patience Ward, who chipped in £500. The lion's share of the new funds went on buying a warship, the thirty-two-gun *Helderenburg*. The three ships were made ready on the island of Texel just north of Amsterdam, where the port officials had been bribed to overlook the military supplies being procured and loaded. Held up by the last-minute need to replace their navigator, on 17 May 1685, a fortnight after Argyll's departure, Monmouth was finally ready to sail for England.[26]

To his intense frustration, however, it would be a further three weeks before the little flotilla was in open water. A series of infuriating delays hemmed them in just off the Dutch coast, first the sighting of English navy ships in the channel and then howling Channel gales.[27] It was June by the time they were on their 400-mile journey from Texel to the south Dorset coast. The delay was highly dangerous, as Argyll had by now landed in Scotland and was beginning to publicise that his was just one element of a national uprising. Monmouth gave the order to sail just as officials of the Dutch States General arrived to arrest them. When they finally disembarked messages were sent to England 'to tell the Lords and Gentlemen of Monmouth's party. . . to get ready to join him when they heard of his landing'. While it was true there had been no money from England, some encouraging reports of the level of support were still coming in. A message arrived from London just as they finally sailed that 'the people were in earnest expectation of us', and that a large detachment of rebel cavalry was setting out from the capital to meet them.[28]

The voyage would take over a fortnight and gave Monmouth ample time to consider and issue orders on how they were going to take the kingdom. The men who accompanied him were a strange fellowship. Ferguson was at his side, sly and obsequious, and claiming the part of army chaplain. With him were a collection of other remnants of Shaftesbury's radical network of lawyers and artisans, among them Nathaniel Wade and Richard Goodenough.[29] The most militarily useful men were a contingent of English soldiers who had absconded from the regiment still serving with William of Orange (who had fought under Monmouth in Flanders in 1678), among them the able officer Samuel Venner.[30] To these were added a series of experienced European mercenaries, including a brilliant gunner. Monmouth's own servants, among them his steward and his long-serving footman William Williams, made another grouping, accompanying him out of loyalty and the scarcity of alternatives. The only nobleman other than Monmouth himself was Lord Grey, whose simmering resentment at Monmouth's coldness over the last two years was temporarily put aside.

The three ships carried just eighty-three men. No more than a single small town could be taken with this size of invasion force, and the plan was utterly dependent on the people of Britain taking up arms. On to the ships at Texel had been loaded weapons and armour for 1,500, the sort of number Monmouth was expecting to spur into rebellion himself in the first few days before the various uprisings coalesced. For the revolution to succeed, Monmouth was counting on ten or twenty times that number being raised and armed by his fellow Whig standard-bearers. As well as the breastplates and gunpowder he carried weapons of different sort: a printing press and a printer to operate it, officers' uniforms – purple doublets and scarlet coats – and a series of large blue flags on which were emblazoned the words under which they would march: 'For God, Freedom and Religion'.[31] Though Monmouth expected to have to engage the county militias, these local volunteer bands did not worry him. Crucial to the scheme's success, however, was that no part of the uprising should face the full force of the professional royal army, if indeed they had to face it at all. The two invasions, in Scotland and England, were designed to divide James II's army; with a bit of luck they might even alarm him into keeping it in London to protect the capital and his family. Additionally, there was reason to think that the army would be diminished by defections. A number of renegades from the regiment serving in Holland had already joined them, and Monmouth's agent, Edward Matthews, had sounded out a series of army officers at home who had indicated they would be willing to rise. As they had wheedled and cajoled him, the dissidents had convinced Monmouth that many soldiers would not fight their former captain general, raising the possibility that there would be no serious fighting at all, and the royal forces would simply 'melt before him'.[32]

There was also the question of what, precisely, they were fighting for. While Monmouth was dashing about trying to arm the expedition Ferguson was preparing their 'declaration'. Full of his fiery rhetoric, it set out the rebels' case for rebellion with little subtlety. James II had overridden the ancient contract between English kings and their people by promoting Catholicism and attempting to turn 'our limited Monarchy into an absolute tyranny'. The slightly uncomfortable fact that Parliament was then assembling was dismissed by the claim that the elections had been interfered with and they would only be 'a company of men... stile[d] a Parliament'. To these charges were added a catalogue of James II's supposed misdemeanours, including his responsibility for Charles II's death. The declaration then set out a progressive manifesto: Catholics were to be excluded from public offices, but both Catholics and dissenting Protestants were to be given freedom of worship. Annual parliaments were to be made mandatory, so no king could again rule without consulting the people, and the ancient charters of England's cities were to be reinstated and measures instituted to ensure only impartial judges were appointed to the judiciary. James II, who was referred to as the Duke of York, would be tried for his crimes. The proclamation was drawn up in the name of 'James Duke of Monmouth', who was described as the 'Head and Captaine Generall of the Protestant forces of the Kingdom'. The question of whether he ought in fact to be the King of England would be a matter for a future parliament.[33]

The weather was fine as the little fleet approached the Dorset coast. With the sea calm and the air warm, Monmouth and his leading men slept on mattresses on the deck of *The Rising Sun*, one of their two smaller vessels.[34] At daybreak on Thursday 11 June, the three ships dropped their sails on a sparkling dawn sea some ten miles south of Lyme Regis. Acutely aware that the delays meant they risked disembarking into the arms of enemy soldiers, Monmouth despatched two scouts in a rowing boat to the tiny fishing village of Seatown four miles along the coast. Landing on the sandy beach, they drew some fishermen into conversation and, sharing their breakfast of wine and cured tongue, asked, casually: 'What news?' The intelligence they received was less bad that they feared. Argyll had invaded Scotland and it was common knowledge that Monmouth would land any day, but the government did not know where to expect him and while the country's militias were being put on standby, there was no welcoming party in Lyme Regis. On receiving this information, Monmouth decided to strike quickly. By noon the three ships were sailing towards Lyme harbour.[35]

A few hours later the unsuspecting worthies of Lyme Regis gathered for their usual Thursday afternoon game of bowls on the town's green overlooking the bay. There was a murmuring comment on how long the harbour agent, sent aboard the unfamiliar vessels in the usual way, was taking to return, but little real concern. Mid-afternoon the town post arrived, and as one of the party read the newsletter, which reported that Monmouth was sailing across the Channel with three ships, they realised with a start what was afoot. Riding to the top of the cliff, the mayor trained his telescope on the ships and saw that a series of small boats, including that of the missing harbour official, were filling up with armed men who were beginning to row towards the shore. With the town completely unprepared, without even a decent stock of gunpowder, and conscious of Monmouth's popularity among the local populace, he mounted his horse and fled.

Monmouth, meanwhile, was optimistic. The fishermen they encountered on entering Lyme bay had welcomed them warmly. They were delighted when the duke spoke to them in person 'very civily', and declared that he would meet no resistance from Lyme.[36] The western sky was starting to turn pink and orange over their heads that evening as all eighty-three men disembarked from their seven landing boats, and crunched across the fossil-rich beach to the west of Lyme harbour. The little army traversed the cliff path to enter the town at the top end, and here Monmouth organised them into orderly formation, so that as they marched down Broad Street they did so 'very well armed and cloathed. . . in a military manner'. The news of the mayor's flight was by now out, and what followed was not combat but coronation. Down the curving arc of Lyme's high street towards the turquoise sea they marched, with Monmouth alone at their head looking every inch the prince. The townspeople flooded into the street and greeted them with ecstatic cheers, crying 'Monmouth and the Protestant Religion!' and straining to kiss the duke's hand. When Ferguson's declaration was read aloud the words were drowned by the noise of the crowd. The imposing figure of Monmouth, dressed in purple with the Garter star shimmering on his breast, and the words 'For God, Freedom and Religion' on the flags that flapped thickly overhead, told them all they needed to know.[37]

While the disembarkation had gone off smoothly, Monmouth knew that it would only be hours before the fleeing mayor reported their arrival and the county militia would be mobilised against them. There was to be no sleeping that night. Instead he divided the army into three parts: two were to guard the town's main approaches and the third to unload the arms from the ships. Lyme town hall was requisitioned as a recruiting station and sixty local men signed up and were issued arms that very evening. The care that Monmouth took in organising this tiny army in a proper military manner was considerable and typical of one who had served in the English army for seven years, run it for four and published the standard work on military training. The eighty-two men with whom he landed were organised to form the skeleton of four regiments, designated by colour: white, red, green and yellow. When he had given out the commissions on board the *Rising Sun*, he had done so in writing rather than verbally, and as new recruits signed up ashore their names and details were carefully recorded as for an army proper. If anyone was expecting this to be a ramshackle rebel band, this was not Monmouth's style. When two of his best soldiers got into a fight, and one shot the other, Monmouth banished the perpetrator. Honourable conduct and military discipline had to be maintained – even if it meant losing his best cavalry officer.[38]

By the following evening matters were still promising. Lyme was secure, their small arms and three cannons had been brought ashore, and recruits were pouring in from the surrounding villages and towns. By nightfall the rebel army, now camped in a field on the town's eastern edge, had grown tenfold to number 800 and 150 horses, making it possible for a cavalry regiment to be formed. The Devon militia, commanded by Monmouth's one-time friend Christopher, Duke of Albemarle, was known to be on the move and

Monmouth, expecting an attack that night, marched the army out to the main approach road, where they slept at the ready, clutching their weapons.[39]

Early on Saturday morning James II was woken in his state bed at Whitehall with the news he knew was coming: Monmouth and his army had landed. An emergency meeting of the Privy Council was followed by an address to the recently assembled Parliament. The elections the previous month had, as Monmouth had anticipated, produced a House of Commons of very different character from the Whig parliaments of five years before. Since then the Tories had acquired a virtual monopoly of local and municipal offices and had a comprehensive majority in the group who gathered at Westminster in May. James II knew enough to emphasise to Parliament his resolution to defend the Church of England, but even this was not without some menace. A month before he had told the Archbishop of Canterbury that he would do so 'unless you first break your word to me', while the fact that he was already encouraging his ministers to attend Catholic mass with him told a different story. Nonetheless news of Monmouth's armed invasion was greeted with widespread horror. That very day Parliament drew up an act of attainder, by which the duke was condemned to death without trial and his lands and titles were forfeit to the Crown. For Monmouth there was now no turning back.[40]

Spirits in Lyme were buoyed by the queues of local men enlisting, to which Monmouth lent his own lustre by standing with the sergeant and offering personal words of congratulations to each new recruit. But beneath his infectiously optimistic exterior he was anxious and longed for sight of the men from other parts of the country bringing their own forces to join him. The large cavalry regiment which Mr Jones had promised was setting out from London as they sailed from Holland and should have reached Lyme – but was nowhere to be seen. For four nights Monmouth waited in Lyme in the hope of one of these groups materialising, but of Jones from London, or Norton from Dorset there was as yet no sign. With the county militia close at hand and their presence at Lyme now well known, the situation was highly dangerous and on Sunday the duke decided he could wait no longer. At 3 a.m. on Monday morning he and his army of around a thousand men set out north for Taunton.[41]

Up and down Dorset's close-hedged lanes the rebels marched north, reaching Axminster on Monday afternoon and Chard on Tuesday. On the one hand they had cause for celebration: the towns put up next to no resistance and the Devon and Somerset militias, which James II had been confident would prevent Monmouth from setting foot outside Lyme, had so far been completely ineffective. They milled about chaotically and sank away as Monmouth approached, while considerable numbers defected to join the rebels.[42] But this disguised the fundamental issue that Monmouth and his principal colleagues could see with painful clarity. While men were joining up, those who were doing so were the working poor, the gentry were nowhere to be seen. There were cheers when forty horses had been brought to join them at Lyme on Saturday, but they were low-grade agricultural animals and the men who brought them were 'few of them armed and all but ordinary fellows'. While such recruits had their uses, the rebel leaders knew that to take the kingdom they needed the support of at least some of the governing classes, the sorts of men who had been Monmouth's hosts in his county tours and who had pushed passionately for reform in the Whig parliaments – people with influence, money, property and patronage. Instead those who rallied to his standard were young weavers and fullers, labourers, artisans and apprentices.[43]

As the rebels camped in a field near Chard on Tuesday night and another gang of 'ragged horses' and 'ordinary fellows' joined them, Ferguson and Lord Grey went to Monmouth. The gentry's reluctance, they told him, stemmed from people's fear that the rebels were republicans. There was only one thing for it: Monmouth had to declare himself king. He resisted; he had never sought the throne and wanted to stick to their plan of letting Parliament determine who was to rule the kingdom – which after all was what he had promised

Argyll before they parted.[44] But though he disliked their remedy, he knew their diagnosis was right. As they rode north, Ferguson and Grey made a second argument. Were Monmouth declared king, then, if they failed, those who had raised arms to join him would avoid execution, for it was widely believed that legislation of the late fifteenth century protected those who fought for one who had been proclaimed king. This new argument was a conclusive one. With his sense of justice, and as 'an utter enemy to all forms of cruelty', the growing ranks of impoverished men who joined him must have filled Monmouth with fear for what would become of them if he did not succeed. This argument finally convinced him and as they rode towards Taunton he at last resolved to do what Thomas Armstrong, the Earl of Shaftesbury, and the clamouring crowds of English townspeople had for so long advocated.[45]

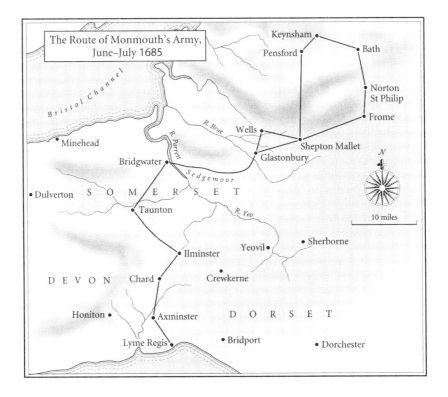

Chapter 19

The Last Battle

On the summer solstice 1685 the Duke of Monmouth was proclaimed King of England. The words were intoned by Joseph Tilley before the medieval market cross in the prosperous cloth town of Taunton. Here, where over a thousand weaving looms operated, the large population of non-conformists regarded the new Catholic king with abhorrence and looked on Monmouth as a liberating hero. When the rebels had entered Taunton two days before, a group of young women had been sent forward to greet them, presenting them with the gorgeous banners they had embroidered.[1] This was a Whig stronghold whose MPs had included William Portman, with whom Monmouth planned to stay during his tour of 1680, and John Trenchard, who was talked of as leading a south-western rebellion during the Whig plot of 1682. But neither was now there to welcome him. Trenchard had fled England and Portman had recanted and was commanding the Dorset militia. The local bigwigs may have been nowhere in evidence, but the townspeople were ecstatic. Once the declaration had been read Monmouth led a procession from the house where he was lodging on East Street, through the town to the field on its edge where the army was camped.[2]

The proclamation made few bones about the situation. Monmouth declared himself king in order to speed up the business of securing the kingdom and to ensure the safety of his troops.[3]

It had been preceded by the first formal council of war, in which the rebels' next steps had been discussed. There they ratified his proclamation as king, and agreed that rather than turning back to engage Albemarle and the Devon militia, they should march on east. While they had not yet combined with any other uprising, they were hopeful that the Whig leaders of Cheshire and Stafford-shire would be on their way south and that they would soon meet support from London.[4]

The decision taken, the army set out first thing the following morning. The length of the train of men that marched along the rough road to Bridgwater was now considerable. The rapturous welcome they had received in Taunton had swelled the ranks with new recruits, and a fourth regiment of 800 men had been created under Colonel Bassett. The whole army now numbered around 4,000 and they had increased their arms with more weapons amassed at Taunton and purloined from the scattering militia. The mood was upbeat. It had been ten days since Monmouth had landed with eighty men, and they remained almost completely unchallenged. Both James II's prediction that they would never get out of Lyme Regis, and Lord Rochester's assertion that they would be defeated in three or four days, had proved spectacularly wrong. What might they now not do, heads held high and marching east towards Bristol and London?[5]

The weather had for all this time remained fine, but on Tuesday black clouds loomed in and rain began to fall as they skirted along the northern edge of the plain known as Sedgemoor, little knowing what notoriety they would soon lend it. Leaving the Somerset Levels behind, they marched on for twelve miles in unrelenting rain until Monmouth called a halt in the lee of Glastonbury Tor. Here amid the ruins of the ancient abbey the sodden army made its camp. The officers organised the lighting of a series of large bonfires in front of which the soldiers steamed their soaking clothes, and when the light faded here they slept, canopied by dripping trees and broken vaults and undercrofts.[6]

The following day, as they continued on to Shepton Mallet, Monmouth discussed his plan. They were going to try to take the great port of Bristol. After consulting his officers, he agreed that they should approach from the far, eastern, side, rather than by the direct western road. On Wednesday night, now at Pensford, only five miles from Bristol, they saw a blazing conflagration on the horizon, actually a ship accidentally set alight in the city's docks, which made them wonder whether fighting might already have broken out. Their warm reception in the towns they passed had been encouraging, cheers had greeted their arrival in most places; in Shepton they had been given free food and in Bridgwater free lodgings. Though there was still no wave of gentry joining their ranks there remained no significant challenge and the militias were still failing to materialise.

And so things stood on the morning of Thursday 25 June. Everything seemed possible, within grasping distance. Bristol was known to have substantial numbers of sympathisers and they were little more than a day from surging into the city. Keeping to the plan of attacking from the east, Monmouth was skirting round the city to the south and despatched one of his officers ahead to Keynsham to prepare for their arrival. The rain was falling once again as the army marched over Keynsham bridge. Then, unexpectedly, they encountered a small detachment of enemy cavalry. A violent skirmish followed, shots were fired with a dozen or so fatalities on each side, and after an hour or so the enemy horse fled leaving behind a few men who were swiftly taken prisoner. When asked for information, the prisoners talked without offering any resistance, but what they revealed was catastrophic.[7]

The news gleaned from the Keynsham prisoners was that just a few miles away was massed not a body of county militia, or even several combined, but the royal army itself, almost 4,000 fully armed and trained professional soldiers. No one alive knew better than Monmouth what this force, which he had spent five years drilling and disciplining, was capable of. The rebel 'army' that he had about him now, enthusiastic but utterly inexperienced, was made up of weavers and farmhands, their few cannon were carried on agricultural carts, and many of their weapons were simply straightened scythes. But it was not just the fact of the royal army's presence that horrified him, it was what it implied, which was soon confirmed. The Earl of Argyll had been caught and his wing of the uprising utterly extinguished.[8]

Monmouth did not know yet just how chaotic Argyll's whole enterprise had been. While he himself had all the tactical ability of a career soldier, genuine grass-roots popularity and no particular personal axe to grind, Argyll was the opposite on every count. Having sailed up the east coast of Britain and round the north of Scotland to reach his western homeland, he had made several brief landings, each spreading news of his approach to government agents, before making a series of indecisive bids to march inland. Arguing incessantly with his officers, who sensibly wanted to make for the Presbyterian heartlands in Ayrshire, he proved a dreadful commander. He burned with desire to reclaim his ancestral lands in Argyll and Bute (he had sworn not to shave again until he did), where he was convinced that his clansmen would rise. But despite such bonds of kinship, and the fact he had begun his expedition with far more men and far better equipped than Monmouth, he raised barely a thousand recruits, and even they soon began to distrust him and peel away. His bid for restitution ended in farce when the fractious earl, now almost alone, got into a fight with an inebriated old man as he tried to retreat across the Clyde. The drunkard finally hit him on the head with his rusty sword, sending Argyll reeling into the water, and then handed him over to the authorities.[9]

Monmouth, meanwhile, knew only that Argyll and his enterprise had failed and was struggling to digest the disaster. He clearly had to get his men away from the royal army. After a discussion about whether to march north to try and find the Cheshire Whigs or south-east, a report that a large body of cavalry was coming to join them from the latter direction decided him. On Friday evening, having narrowly avoided an engagement with their enemy, Monmouth's army marched wearily up lanes musky with elderflowers into the picturesque village of Norton St Philip.

So haphazard and ineffectual was Argyll's invasion that when James II realised that the west country militia were completely failing to challenge, let alone suppress, Monmouth's troops, he was able to swing the whole army into action. On 20 June, with Argyll safely incarcerated in Edinburgh Castle, he despatched three battalions of foot guards and six troops of horse into the west with a commander-in-chief to oversee them and to take charge of the militia. The person chosen was Monmouth's former deputy the French professional soldier Louis Duras, Earl of Feversham. While Feversham was unfailingly loyal to James II, it was a measure of the new king's lack of political sensitivity that he chose a Frenchman to put down a popular Protestant uprising led by a member of the English royal family. Despatched alongside him were a number of others who had once been close to Monmouth. In charge of the cavalry was John Churchill, who had fallen gasping at Monmouth's side when, aged twenty-two and twenty-three, they had taken the half-moon bastion at Maastricht. Much of the infantry was led by Percy Kirke, another of his former officers, and the brother of his one-time mistress, Moll Kirke. Related by blood rather than friendship, and in charge of 2,000 foot, was Monmouth's younger half-brother the Duke of Grafton. In all Feversham had some 3,500 professional soldiers under his command, the lion's share of the army that Monmouth had once called his own.

While the combined government forces – army and county militias – far outnumbered the rebel army, they had not so far covered themselves in glory in their response to the uprising. Despite the protracted delays to Monmouth's departure from Texel, and the numerous details of his preparations which were relayed to London in despatches, the government had failed to establish even which part of the British Isles he was bound for. Almost a week after leaving London, Feversham and the army had struggled to find the rebels, let alone defeat them, and it was little more than luck that had led to the engagement at Keynsham. Monmouth had now managed to withdraw south-east at speed. Feversham was determined to improve his record and despatched Kirk and Grafton with 500 infantry and cavalry to ride after the rebels and hold them while the rest of the army caught up. It was as Monmouth was preparing to move out of Norton St Philip on Saturday 27 June that this large advance force approached.

The Somerset village of Norton St Philip stands on steeply undulating ground at the intersection of five roads, which Monmouth had been careful to secure with manned barricades on their arrival. Tasting glory and the chance to better his glamorous older brother, the twenty-one-year-old Duke of Grafton sped forward with a company of horse only to find himself trapped in a tightly hedged lane, with a rebel barricade ahead and rebel soldiers appearing behind. Heavy fire was exchanged, during which many were killed and Grafton's horse was shot under him. He and his surviving men only escaped by hacking their way through the hedges and bolting desperately across the fields.

As the rest of the royal army started to arrive the rain began to pour down yet again. The two sides, their main forces quite a distance apart, fired their field guns at one another for the rest of the afternoon, but with little effect. After some debate with his officers, Monmouth prepared to mount a full frontal attack, and cut preparatory passages through the hedges. But before they were ready to strike, the royalists, tired, soaking and on the back foot, decided to pull out and withdrew east towards Bradford-upon-Avon. The rebels waited in formation till long after dark, their saturated clothes hanging heavily from their skin. Then, without rest, all 4,000 tramped the seven miles south to Frome in the dripping darkness.[10]

The fight at Norton St Philip had been, on balance, a victory for the rebels. Some eighty royal soldiers were killed, mostly in the shoot-out in the lane, while just eighteen rebels had lost their lives. The rebels were unquestionably inexperienced and ill-equipped,

but with Monmouth at their head they had outclassed their opponents. Monmouth, however, took no pleasure or encouragement
from this. He knew they were doomed. Argyll had been defeated,
the royal army was here; there was no sign of the cavalry promised
by Wildman, Adlam or anyone else and no news of a Whig uprising
in Cheshire. Less seasoned soldiers than he might think victory was
still possible, but Monmouth knew otherwise. He was suddenly
overwhelmed with the horror of it all. For two months since
Ferguson and Grey had talked him round he had been focused on
saving Britain. When he looked out over the three to four thousand
ordinary people camped in the sloping fields, who had put their
trust in him, he felt only despair. For an officer who had always
had an acute sense of the suffering of his men, the plight of these
pitchfork rebels was soul-destroying. In Taunton a distraught wife
had pleaded with him to let her husband leave and Monmouth
had consented – saying simply that he wished no man to fight for
him against his conscience. Such was his melancholy at Norton St
Philip that when Nathaniel Wade and his fellow officers tried to
confer with him, they found him 'so dejected that we could hardly
gett orders from him'. The engagement with the royal army had
propelled him into action, but once his men reached Frome and the
adrenalin subsided he was again filled with sadness.[11]

After thinking it over he set out the situation as he saw it to his
officers. 'Nobody stirred anywhere,' he stated baldly. The promises
of support that had been given before they sailed and since were
hollow, and they had to accept that every single one had failed.
They were alone and with the army now on their tail they faced
near-certain defeat.[12] His sorrow was rich with anger and an acute
sense of what he and the thousands camped in the fields had risked,
and the betrayal that had been their only reward. The news had just
reached Frome that James II had proclaimed that any rebel who
gave himself up within eight days would be pardoned. Monmouth
put it to his council that they should disband there and then. If
they moved quickly the rank and file would be able to avail themselves of the pardon and those who were excluded might yet get to a

port and sail overseas. To this proposal a number of officers readily
agreed: they should cut their losses while they still might. But Lord
Grey, baulking at the thought of a penniless exile, dissented. He put
the argument in terms he knew Monmouth could not resist, and
'opposed it as a thing so base that it could never be forgiven by ye
people to be so deserted and yt [that] ye Duke must never expect
more to be trusted'. At these words Monmouth bowed his head.
He would continue.[13]

The next few days saw the rebels on the move daily, keeping a
step ahead of the royal army. Since Keynsham they had swept south
and now they moved back west again, drawn by news that a thousand men were waiting for them on the Somerset Levels. Here they
camped on Thursday night and the following morning they trudged
into the busy river port of Bridgwater. By this stage they were foot-
sore and weary. They had marched between ten and twenty miles
almost every day for a fortnight since leaving Taunton, tramping
along muddy roads and camping in waterlogged fields. The pressure on Monmouth was immense. Just feeding a few thousand
men on the move was a massive task, and it was to him alone that
everyone looked for direction. When they reached Bridgwater, and
the thousand men turned out to be 160, Monmouth declared that
they would stay there a day or two.[14]

That weekend they rested. On Saturday there was some gentle
drilling and much mending of arms, and Monmouth agreed that
several hundred could travel to Taunton to visit their families. If
he half hoped they might stay away and save their skins he was
to be disappointed. It was testimony to their loyalty to the cause
and their leader that almost every man returned to the rebel camp
on Sunday afternoon. Monmouth for his part was preoccupied.
He ordered their cannon to be set up at the town entrances and
conspicously enlisted a large number of local men to dig trenches
round the town, giving the impression that they were preparing for
a prolonged siege. And then he waited.[15]

In the muggy warmth that Sunday afternoon, as the rebels sharp-
ened their swords and bathed their blistered feet, a Bridgwater

cattleman was tending his beasts on the rich pasture of Sedgemoor a few miles outside the town. As he ambled amid the meadow flowers the thick midsummer stillness became gradually infused with the rumble of men and horses. Wandering south towards the village of Westonzoyland to see what was afoot he realised the vanguard of the royal army had arrived and was beginning to make a camp on the flat pasture at the village edge. Though he had not signed up, he was, like many ordinary folk, instinctively supportive of the Somersetmen who were marching with Monmouth under a slogan he believed in and, looking as aimless as he could, he hurried back to Bridgwater. Once there he went straight to the rebel headquarters and relayed what he had seen. The restless Monmouth was suddenly seized with hope. He pressed a golden guinea, enough to buy a herd of cattle, into the man's hand, and grabbed his 'perspective glass'. The highest vantage point in the town was the tower of St Mary's church, reached by a spiral stair from the nave. Climbing onto the roof, and then up onto the parapet of the stair tower itself, he trained his glass south-eastwards. Sure enough in the shimmering haze he could just make out the royal regiments massing on the level floodplains three miles away.

Flying down the steps, Monmouth called a council of war. Before his assembled field officers he set out the situation. The ditch-digging ruse had worked. Instead of launching an immediate attack Feversham was taking his time. Now was their chance to strike, and looking round the room searchingly, he 'demanded of them if they thought it was advisable to fight'. Even with the odds stacked so spectacularly against them, it might just be that surprise could be their salvation.[16]

At eleven that night Monmouth led his army out of Bridgwater. As they left the dim glow of the cobbled streets and crossed the River Parrett they forged into the darkness where a thick ground fog had already started to gather. He knew that to approach Westonzoyland, three miles south-east, by the direct road that went on to Taunton would be madness, as they would certainly be spotted. Instead he decided they should leave the town by the north-east road towards Bristol and then, after a couple of miles, turn right and forge south, directly across the moor, thereby covering two sides of a triangle to reach the enemy. This meant travelling twice the distance, over five miles, but it kept them as inconspicuous as three and a half thousand armed men could be. By Monmouth's strict orders they marched in absolute silence, the steady stomp of their boots and the urgent beating of their own hearts the only sound.[17]

The plan that Monmouth had hatched in the few hours they had had to organise themselves was daring but simple, and he shared it with his officers just before they turned on to the moor. It hinged on the fact that the infantry of the royal army, almost 2,000 men, were camped in open land at the edge of Westonzoyland, while the cavalry regiments, some 750 men, and almost all the officers, were lodged in the houses of the village half a mile beyond. The rebels would approach the camped infantry undetected from the open moorland to the north. When they were perhaps half a mile away they would spread out silently in a line parallel to their adversaries. The rebel horse would then surge forward to attack the forest of sleeping foot soldiers, catching them completely unprepared and preventing them from even equipping themselves properly, let alone forming a line. As they advanced, their field guns would be rolled into position and their infantry would move forward behind them. In the time it would take the royalist officers and cavalry to arrive on the scene, the rebels would have dispersed the foot, taken control of their opponents' artillery and be masters of the field.[18]

Sedgemoor itself – onto which the rebels now turned south – is what in East Anglia would be called a fen, a vast expanse of absolutely flat ground lying just a few feet above sea level. Annual winter flooding and heavy summer grazing prevented trees from growing and across the open land ran ditches and drains through which the water that had fallen so heavily in recent days was still seeping. The soldiers could see very little and what they could make out was murky and monochrome. But their other senses were fully engaged and as they tramped across the meadows the night air was rich with the sweet, damp scent of the land. The dark sea of reeds that brushed their thighs was flecked with the white heads of cotton grass and peppered with fragrant marsh orchids. Around them water trickled in the sunken streams and from the rushes at the ditches' edge rose the strange squeaky call of the sedge warbler and low trill of the nightjar. It was in this flat, watery darkness that England's last field battle would that night be fought.[19]

For two hours the rebels trooped in the blackness. Progressing south across the moor, they kept on their left the deep drainage channel known as the Black Ditch and on their right rustling fields of corn beyond which, on slightly raised ground in the middle of the moor, was the hamlet of Chedzoy. Ahead, silhouetted against the low southern horizon, was the lone-pinnacled tower of Weston-zoyland church. Jet black against the granite night sky, it was the horned beacon by which they steered their course.

It was now well past midnight and Feversham and his officers had turned in for the night. The main roads were defended with detachments of soldiers, and a series of scouts and patrols had been left scattered around the less obvious routes. But this was standard form, and it never crossed the Frenchman's mind that there was any serious likelihood of a surprise attack. Feeling little urgency, a number of those left on duty left their posts once darkness fell while, such had been the instinctive enthusiasm of the local people for Monmouth's rebels that, as the thousands of men had moved out of Bridgwater, 'not one person' had raised the alarm.[20]

Then, suddenly, chance intervened. Still a mile and a half from the enemy the rebels encountered the Langmoor Rhine, a wide subsidiary drainage channel that ran between Chedzoy and the Black Ditch, cutting right across their path. Straining their eyes in the darkness they found a crossing place and the thousands of men began to file slowly over the deep marshy water. The rebels knew that they might at any moment encounter an enemy patrol and many men carried weapons already primed and loaded. As they crossed the stream, still communicating in only the softest whispers, the silence was broken with a sudden cracking blast. One of the men, Captain Hucker, had fired his pistol into the darkness. Whether he had shot at a phantom adversary or simply pulled the trigger by accident, it was nothing short of a catastrophe. The crucial element of surprise on which absolutely everything depended had, in a single second, been sacrificed. Stunned, Monmouth knew they had to act with immense speed if they were to reach the royal army in time to effect anything of their plan. He ordered the cavalry to begin their charge immediately. Lord Grey had this distinguished command, while Monmouth reserved to himself the less glorious task of leading their foot soldiers. Grey streaked ahead into the darkness with 600 mounted men thundering behind him, while Monmouth marshalled the foot and led all 3,000 in a breathless run towards the royal camp.[21]

Sure enough the gunshot had been heard by a royal guardsman on the moor. He galloped at full speed to Westonzoyland, where Feversham and the royal command were raised with blasting trumpets and the desperate cry 'the Enemy is Engadged'. As Grey and the rebel cavalry reached the royal camp, the royal drums had already started booming their alarm. Furthermore, while Feversham had given no orders to expect a nocturnal attack, a wily Scottish infantry officer named Mackintosh had muttered that he would be willing to bet that 'the Duke would come' that night. Taking matters into his own hands he had briefed his men about the positions they should take if a surprise attack were launched, and ordered them to sleep fully dressed and with their weapons at their sides.[22]

While he was an able horseman, Lord Grey was no battlefield regular. In fact he was no soldier at all. Unlike many others he had never fought with the royal army on a continental campaign or in the civil war. Though he had flamboyantly signed up to lead a regiment during the 1679 Scottish rebellion, he had pulled out at the last minute claiming that his conscience prevented him from fighting.[23] His position as second-in-command and head of the rebel cavalry in 1685 owed much to his status as the only other nobleman involved in the uprising. When Monmouth had sent him to Bridport a few days after they had landed at Lyme,

Grey had, according to another officer, quite simply 'run away' from the skirmish, abandoning a detachment of foot soldiers as he did so. Monmouth had received the report with disbelief and gave instructions that Grey must follow the advice of the professional soldier Samuel Venner. But Venner had left the rebels after Norton St Philip and Grey was now on his own. His lack of experience and bravery, taken together with the critical situation they found themselves in, would further foul the rebels' chances. As Grey neared the royal tents at the eastern end of their camp he realised that while they were now only a stone's throw away, another deep channel, the Bussex Rhine, cut across the ground between them. Even a leaping horse could not clear it. Before he could decide what to do, from the darkness on their left a troop of royalist cavalry emerged and attacked. One of Grey's officers, the old Cromwellian soldier John Jones, fought bravely, desperately trying to push them back, and so capture the bridge over the Bussex Rhine. But it was in vain. Grey meanwhile rode along the ditch looking frantically for another crossing point, but without success. The royal foot, who had now identified the rebel horses in the gloom, started firing heavily over the ditch. Frightened, disorientated and now separated from his junior officers, Grey panicked and led the bulk of the cavalry in a disorderly flight back onto the black expanse of the moor.[24]

Monmouth, unaware of Grey's failure, and utterly focused, led the rebel foot across the moor. But he arrived only to discover, to his disbelief, that the cavalry had already fled. The plan all along had been that the bulk of the fighting was to have happened before the infantry was engaged. Consequently the best of the weapons and men had been concentrated in the first cavalry wave. Now he realised it would be foot soldiers, weavers and labourers with makeshift weapons and just three field guns, who would fight this fateful battle. There seems to have been no question of his abandoning the cause, and instead in darkness still unbroken, Monmouth and his infantry commanders pulled almost 3,000 panting men into a shallow arc just thirty or forty yards from the ditch. On the other side John

Churchill had just arrived to take command of the royal infantry. It was now between one and two in the morning and Monmouth galloped back to bring the cannon forward and set the three pieces up along the line. As he did so his infantry started discharging their weapons, raining fire into the darkness ahead. For almost two hours the two sides fired at one another. While the gunner in charge of the rebel cannons did an expert job, Monmouth's infantry lacked the weaponry, the ammunition and above all the skill to wreak real damage on the enemy. With the royalists in charge of the two crossings over the ditch they were unable to advance.[25]

Then, as the absolute darkness began to turn almost imperceptibly indigo, Feversham finally started to counterattack. A troop of royal cavalry ventured tenatively over the eastern ditch crossing and engaged the far end of the rebel infantry. The rebels, under the old Cromwellian colonel Abraham Holmes, fought fiercely and pushed them back. The royalists' second-in-command, Captain Sarsfield, whose brother had married Monmouth's sister, Mary, was among those brought tumbling down from their horses. But despite this shaky start, it was increasingly clear to even the most die-hard rebels that there was no hope. The royalists still held 600 cavalry in reserve and just a few miles south several thousand men of the militia also waited in the wings. The rebels, on the other hand, had already thrown forward all that they had and it was nowhere near enough.[26]

The air was thick with smoke and periodically lit up by exploding charges, as Monmouth dashed back and forward between the infantry and artillery. He was to be found both shoulder to shoulder with his foot soldiers and directing the fire of the chief gunner. Then shortly before 3 a.m. his longest-standing and most loyal servant, William Williams, came to him. The royal cavalry were now pushing forward on both flanks and would very shortly encircle the whole rebel army. If he wished to do anything other than surrender he had to go, and he had to go immediately. Nodding in numb agreement, Monmouth let Williams unstrap his armour and took 100 guineas from the funds in Williams's charge. Then he and a few others mounted already exhausted horses and rode east towards the low Polden Hills, which were framed against the brightening sky.[27] The nocturnal greys were becoming infused with colour as Monmouth rode up the hill. When he turned towards the flat arena of the moor behind him, he saw a sight that would have broken a heart far harder than his.

As daybreak exposed the rebels' miserable condition the royal cavalry had accelerated. The rebels fled north across the moor with the cavalry in thunderous pursuit. But there would be no escape. Hundreds were trapped by a further deep drain across their path. Here as they scrambled for footholds in the muddy water the mounted soldiers fired mercilessly. Soon the ditch was bridged by bloodied corpses. Those who made it scrambled, mud-soaked, through the swaying cornfields, only to be picked off by the royal guns trained on their backs. Fewer than 200 rebels had been killed in the course of the battle itself, but in the retreat a thousand were slaughtered. When Monmouth had led the royal army against the Scottish rebels at Bothwell Bridge he had forbidden battlefield executions as butchery. Now he stood on the Polden Hills, with the south-west wind blowing his greying hair from his brow, as Churchill, Kirke, Grafton and Feversham wreaked just such bloody butchery on those who had risen to his call. As the wind brought gunshot mixed with the muffled cries of his dying men, Monmouth could do nothing but watch.[28]

Chapter 20

The End

Sedgemoor was an absolute defeat for the rebels, and within hours reports of the battle circulated throughout the kingdom. But against the tide of jubilant official notices there ran a powerful counter-current. The bravery of the rebel army and its commander won the respect of even the most ardent royalists. An officer in the royalist camp confirmed the courage of the rebels, 'who fought very valiantly, the duke being at the head of them with a pike'. Colonel Oglethorpe, who commanded the royal Horse Guards, was also fulsome in his praise of Monmouth: 'all agree that hee acted the part of a great Generall and charged a foot in the head of his army'. In London the rebels' courage and Monmouth's skill was the talk of the town, such that even James II 'himself had said he [Monmouth] had not made one false step'.[1]

For Monmouth, however, all this counted for naught compared with the death he had seen and which now lay in prospect. As he was removing his armour on the battlefield the figure of Lord Grey had materialised from the gloom and followed him as he rode east. Monmouth felt certain that had Grey not led the cavalry away from the front they might still have prevailed. But now they were fugitives, and Grey convinced Monmouth that they should stick together. If they could reach Grey's Sussex lands they would find loyal supporters who would see them safely to the continent.

The battle had been lost at dawn on Monday morning. Before the day was out their horses were collapsing and the fugitives abandoned them to continue on foot. Over two days and nights Monmouth, with Grey, Antony Buyse, a German gunner, and a handful of others would cover some sixty miles, travelling by the most obscure and circuitous paths to avoid discovery. By Tuesday morning they had reached the ancient woodlands of Cranborne Chase. Monmouth's state of mind as they stumbled down the deep lanes and drank thirstily from streams edged by wild garlic must have veered between hope and despair. His head surely throbbed with the slaughter he had seen on the battlefield, and the knowledge that his prospects were now bleak confirmed his sense of God's displeasure. But ringing in his ears were the tales his father had told of his own escape from a similarly bloody battlefield at Worcester in 1651. Charles II had been on the run for six weeks before he sailed safely from the south coast. He had made hiding in haystacks and oak trees badges of heroism rather than humiliation. It could be that Monmouth too could pull off such a feat. He might yet escape and be reunited with his beloved Henrietta.[2]

On Tuesday, after thirty-six gruelling hours, the group which was now a dozen strong, split. They were less than ten miles from the coast and Grey had gone ahead with three men. Early that afternoon, as he skirted the Dorset village of Horton, he was recognised and seized by a government patrol answering to the thirty-five-year-old Lord Lumley. Making no attempt to conceal his companions' movements, Grey immediately volunteered that they should be able to capture Monmouth there the following morning.

That night Monmouth and the few men with him crossed the fields towards Horton by moonlight. As they did so they passed barely a mile from Wimborne St Giles, home of the late Earl of Shaftesbury, which Monmouth had first visited with his father in the plague summer of 1665. It must have been a bittersweet recollection. When the rebels' legs simply could carry them no further, they stopped and crumpled in a state of complete exhaustion into a series of dry ditches and hollows. Little did they know that, thanks to Grey, the fields and woods were being combed by the militia, their appetites whetted by the £500 reward they had already secured.[3]

At 4 a.m. the sniffer dogs finally found a trail and Antony Buyse was discovered beneath the branches of a field hedge. Knowing they were close now, the search party spread out over the surrounding fields and lanes and were soon rewarded. Monmouth lay interred in a dry ditch, over which he had drawn a thick roof of bracken. Sheer exhaustion and the stealth of the search party meant that the first he knew of their arrival was the jubilant cries as they tore away the bracken and dragged his now thin frame roughly from the hollow. The face that their lanterns revealed was not, however, familiar. After four weeks on the road and the rigours of battle Monmouth was almost unrecognisable. He had barely slept and had not eaten a meal for two days and three nights, surviving only on water and peas foraged from fields. Dressed in the torn and stained coat of a cart-maker, he had no sword or pistol, and carried just his watch and notebooks. Only the badge of the order of the Garter in his pocket confirmed his identity. His smooth skin, once the toast of Paris, was now sunburned and drawn and his chin covered by a tangled beard, which had turned almost white. Trauma and tragedy had now overtaken him. He was finally broken. As he fell to the floor his whole body shook violently and when he opened his mouth he could make no sound.[4]

The following day Monmouth found himself eight miles away in the town of Ringwood at the edge of the New Forest, about to be taken to London. Given food, clean clothes, and allowed to bathe and shave, he had recovered some physical composure, but his mind was another matter. The betrayals seemed to tower over him, bearing down on one whose adult life had been defined by trying to do what he believed was right. The falsehoods of Ferguson and Grey were now obvious to him. They had undermined his resolution not to act and tricked him into believing it was his sacred duty to be their leader. After preaching to the rebels before they marched out of Bridgwater, Ferguson had fled north from the battlefield and since gone to ground. Grey had not only aided Ferguson in the initial deception, but had compounded this by talking him out of abandoning the enterprise at Norton St Philip, deserting the battlefield at Sedgemoor and betraying him at Horton.[5]

The sentence that awaited Monmouth would be death. This he knew. He was thirty-six and, in his own words, 'as fearful as other men are'. The prospect of a violent, public death can only have horrified him. But he was also a man of real physical bravery; he had put himself in the way of mortal danger on numerous occasions without showing the least flicker of fear. He had also repeatedly chosen honour over personal ease. What haunted him now was not the image of the executioner, but of Henrietta, of the prospect of leaving her, the fear of what her life and condition would be without him. She had sacrificed her chastity, her country, her possessions and her honour to live with him, and now he was abandoning her. So it was that amid the fog of melancholy and self-pity a single positive thought started to form in Monmouth's mind. He had been betrayed and deserted by everyone. He would now cast them all off and stop at nothing to try to find his way back to her.[6]

Asking for pen and paper, he sat down and, steeling himself, wrote to his uncle the king. The tone he took was one of total submission. He set out his remorse and related with stark candour how the uprising had begun. Citing William of Orange as a witness to his original resolution not to take arms against James II, he spoke of the 'horrid people' who had led him to believe that it would be a sin not to invade, and pleaded to be allowed an audience, pledging his loyalty in lavish and fulsome terms. He then penned a second letter in a steady hand to his stepmother, Catherine of Braganza, remembering how she had talked York round once before over his readmission to court. He told her that he was 'from the bottom of my hart convinced now I have bine disceaved in to it, and how angry God Almighty is with me'. He asked that, in memory of

Charles II, she represent to the king his supplication and pledge of loyalty should his life be spared.[7]

On Sunday 12 July, Monmouth was brought to Whitehall by barge to see the king. By chance, an old friend of his who had just come upriver from the city landed on the pier at the same time and was transfixed by the sight of Monmouth disembarking. He was flanked by soldiers carrying pistols in their hands and looked 'lean and pale and with a disconsolate physiognomy'.[8] At the bottom of the back stairs, by the rooms he had himself once inhabited, were the lodgings of William Chiffinch, the keeper of the king's closet. Here Monmouth was admitted to his uncle's presence. He would try everything, he resolved, burning now with the thought that this new course could be his salvation. Here, with Catherine of Braganza also present, he knelt at James II's feet and begged forgiveness. All and every argument he could think of he now mustered to try to convince his uncle not to execute him; he pledged loyalty, relayed Ferguson's claim that those closest to the king had known of the uprising and argued that he could be useful in helping prevent future rebellion.[9]

There was, however, never any real question of James II letting Monmouth live. It would have been unthinkable for a reigning king to have pardoned one who had launched an armed invasion. But despite all that had passed, James could not look down on his penitent nephew, thin and pale before him, without pity or a memory of how close they had once been. While several who were not there would elaborate on what they thought had passed at the meeting, James II himself would always be reticent. He reported to William of Orange a few days later that Monmouth had not deported himself regally, but he did not elaborate. He simply observed that, rather than dwelling on politics, Monmouth 'seemed more concerned and desirous to love'. The meeting ended and Monmouth was taken to the Tower. But he had seen the glimmer of sympathy in his uncle's eye and hoped that somehow all might not be lost.[10]

On the day of Monmouth's capture, his children – two sons and a daughter – had been sent to the Tower to prevent their becoming figureheads for any further uprising. Their mother had gone with them, and that evening she and Monmouth were allowed to meet. Anna's anger with her husband was understandable and the meeting was not a success. The Lord Privy Seal, the young Earl of Clarendon, was present on Anna's request, and it was to him that Monmouth addressed himself almost exclusively, emphasising the various points he had made to the king, including his hope that the king might show him mercy. Even a delay in the sentence could be his salvation (an astrologer had told him he might yet live if he could only see out St Swithin's Day a few days hence) and he pressed for this as well. After a while Anna could bear it no more and interrupted her husband mid-sentence. Dismissing his words as 'digressions and imaginary expectations of life', she insisted that he confirm that she and their children had had nothing to do with his uprisings or his association with the Whig opposition. This he did and there they parted.[11]

The pity Monmouth had detected in his uncle's eyes was not enough to secure him the reprieve he craved. The following day, as the duke paced his room at the Tower, James II issued a series of orders. The original sentence of hanging, drawing and quartering – a fate of unspeakable agony, in which death was prolonged with the most extreme torture – was commuted to beheading. This was normal in the case of the execution of a member of the aristocracy, as was the stipulation that, instead of any ghoulish displaying of the severed head on London Bridge, Monmouth's body was to be given to his family to bury. But the sentence was to be carried out publicly on Tower Hill, and not within the relative privacy of the Tower of London itself – as, for instance, Elizabeth I had allowed for the Earl of Essex and Mary I for Lady Jane Grey. But James II did agree that the wooden platform on which the execution was to take place could be draped respectfully in black, and gave permission for Monmouth to be allowed servants to attend him, and to see his wife and children before his death. A delegation of bishops was then despatched to confirm that the execution would take place the following morning and to prepare his soul for the afterlife.[12]

When Monmouth received the official confirmation of his sentence, the feverish hope had already fallen from him. It was all over, he now saw, and with this certainty came a stillness that he had not known before. He felt God close, and an increasing confidence that He would be his guide. It was in this serene mood that the bishops of Ely and Bath and Wells addressed him at the Tower of London on Wednesday afternoon. Their task was to secure from him a comprehensive admission of his sins, which might ease his passage in the afterlife – and help James II discredit his cause. Monmouth regarded all three with suspicion, and asked that his parish priest, Thomas Tenison of St Martin-in-the-Fields, be allowed to join them.

The clergymen set about stressing to Monmouth the importance of acknowledging and repenting his sins. Calm and considered, and responding particularly to Tenison's candid manner, Monmouth acknowledged that he was not the true king, nor had ever been, and that he regretted the invasion. He also willingly acknowledged and denounced the debauchery of his youth. 'It was too true,' he said, 'that he had for a long time lived a very dissolute & irregular life & being guilty of frequent breaches of the conjugall vow.' When it came to his affair with Henrietta Wentworth, however, he refused point-blank to offer any sort of apology or remorse. Though 'the world had much aspersed her' for their relationship, he said, she was 'a virtuous Godly lady & far from deserving the unkind censures she lys under on his accompt'. When the bishops responded that, as Henrietta was not his legal wife, she was therefore his whore and their relationship a sin, he was unyielding. Yes, Anna was technically his wife, but they had been married when they were children and were too young to understand what it meant. As a consequence he had never developed 'that perfect love & affectione for her that either she deserved or he wished himself to have had towards her'.

This was the reason for his 'goeing so frequently astray from her & the running after other women'. But 'the ladie Henrietta Wentworth was the persone in the world that cured him of that wandring appetite', and in her love he had found complete fulfilment. For two years, since their time together at Toddington, he had lived a different life and had been devoted to her completely. They had sought God's guidance on their relationship through fasting and prayer, and he 'doubted not that it was pleasing to God and that this was a marriage, their choice of one another being guided not by lust but by judgement'.

As dusk gathered the clergymen kept up their campaign: Tenison coaxing, the bishops hectoring. When Monmouth spoke of receiving communion the following morning, they threatened to withhold it if he still refused to acknowledge all his sins. The prospect of meeting his death without the cleansing force of communion troubled Monmouth, and he spent much of the night in prayer, asking God to send him a sign if he was mistaken in his stand. The clerics were with him throughout, and watched him when he slept. As morning broke, he was surer still. If they would not give him communion, so be it. He felt certain now that God was with him and as dawn turned to sunrise he prayed alone.

The Lieutenant of the Tower was to collect Monmouth at 10 a.m., before which he was to be allowed to see his wife and children. Anna arrived with the children and was surprised to see Monmouth calm and steady. The composed dignity of his resolve was far harder for her to take than the frenzied optimism of two days before. Their meeting was 'the mourningest scene in the world'. To all those present Monmouth stated his wife's complete innocence in respect of his actions and shortcomings. Her attempts to reconcile him to his father were acknowledged and he gave her 'the kindest character that could be'. When finally he asked her forgiveness for his failings and expressed his hope that she would continue to be kind to their 'poor children', she could bear it no more. Her imperious expression cracked and tears streamed down her crumpled features. Sinking to the floor, she clung to her husband's knees and, rocking with sobs, asked for his forgiveness in return.[13]

When Monmouth stepped out of the Lieutenant of the Tower's coach that had carried him the short distance out on to Tower Hill he was a picture of composure. Dressed in sombre grey, lined with black, and wearing an immaculate wig, he greeted the city sheriff. When he had arrived at the Tower by river a few days before, the thousands of spectators had 'seem'd very much troubled'; the mood now was similarly sorrowful. The huge crowd that had gathered did not jeer and jostle, but let him pass, the bishops following. He walked with all the upright bearing and dignity of a prince, 'no man observed more couradge, resolutione & unconcernedness'. Sir Stephen Fox, his old friend and financial fixer, was there, and when he spoke of how sorry he was at what had come to pass Monmouth said simply: 'And so am I too, but since it is God Almighty's pleasure I am going to perform his will.'[14]

Stepping up onto the scaffold, Monmouth addressed the crowds. Things seemed very clear to him now. Gone was the smarting fury at those who had misled and betrayed him. 'I shall say but very little,' he announced. 'I come to die', adding with emphasis, 'I die as a Protestant of the Church of England.' The clerics tried to talk him into condemning all acts of resistance to royal authority, but Monmouth would not be drawn; instead he was intent on protecting the honour of the woman he loved, and so he spoke the words he had rehearsed: 'I have had a scandal raised about me about a woman, a lady of vertue and honour. I will name her the Lady Henrietta Wentworth. I declare, that she is a very virtuous and Godly woman. I have committed no sin with her; and that which had passed betwixt us was very Honest and Innocent in the sight of God.'

When asked to denounce his invasion as a rebellion, Monmouth said nothing but handed over a piece of paper on which he had written the only recantation he was prepared to make. It stated his regret at having been declared king, and his own reluctance in it, and confirmed that he knew his parents had never been married. He went no further. He made no statement of loyalty or penitence to James II, whom he called 'the King who is now', and asked only that he would not punish his children on his account.

The bishops tried again, but still Monmouth would not be drawn. He was sorry, he said, for everyone he had wronged: 'I forgive everybody, I have had many Enemies, I forgive them all.' He spoke of his gratitude to God 'that for these two years last past, I have led a Life unlike to my former Course and in which I have been happy'. Pressed hard to call his uprising a 'rebellion', Monmouth continued to resist. The most he would concede was his regret. 'I never was a man that delighted in Blood; I was very far from it,' he said. 'I am sorry for invading the Kingdom, and for the Blood that has been shed and,' – his voice dropping to a whisper – 'for the Souls which may have been lost by my means, I am sorry it ever happened.'

Around the scaffold stood an armed guard and beyond them the sheriffs and the crowd. When asked whether he would not say something to them to acknowledge his crimes, he stood quite still and was silent. The clerics could see they were going to extract no further confession, and so began the prayers. There on the wooden boards of the scaffold Monmouth knelt and bowed his head, and together with the kneeling clergymen intoned the Lord's Prayer and the words of love and reunion with which the soul of one about to die was commended to God. Still he remained calm, having made his own peace with God: 'I have now noe fear, as you may see by my Face, but there is something within me which does it, for I am sure I shall go to God.'

As he rose and the executioner stepped forward, the bishops tried one last time to extract words of obedience to James II. But when they said 'Lord Save the King', Monmouth did not repeat them. He might have done and said far more, but he knew that the lives of his wife and his imprisoned children depended on his behaviour. The bishops said the words again, and he answered only 'Amen'. Finally one of them asked him whether he would at least say something to the guards of the importance of remaining loyal to the king. Monmouth replied only: 'I will make no speeches, I come to die.' With the midday sun shining down, his servant came forward to help him undress. He removed his wig, refusing the cap and blindfold he was offered, and from his pocket he took a small silver object which he gave to his man along with six guineas. The money, he explained to the executioner, Jack Ketch, was for him if he performed his task well. He wanted a clean strike, and not the barbarous half-strikes he had wreaked on Lord Russell. Ketch replied, not without nervousness, 'I hope I shall'.

Monmouth then stretched out his long body and lowered his neck towards the block, which was just inches off the floor, but he then lifted himself up and asked to be allowed to feel the axe. Running his thumb along the blade's edge he told Ketch that it was not sharp enough. The executioner responded gruffly, but was already beginning to tremble at a task that daunted even him. Monmouth lay back down and placed his neck upon the block, doing so 'with all the calmnes off temper and composer of mind that ever hath bein observed in any that mounted that fatall scaffold before'. With the crowd motionless in awful anticipation, and the sonorous words of the clergymen chanting the 51st Psalm rising in the air, Ketch, legs apart, steadied himself. Reaching back he heaved the great axe through the air, but when it fell heavily it came down short, chopping deep into Monmouth's neck, causing his body to convulse and his head to turn, but without killing him. Now partially facing his victim, Ketch began to shake, and when he swung the axe again, he again failed to make a clear strike and took another bite from Monmouth's neck. The crowd groaned at each horrific hack. When his third swing also missed, Ketch's huge shoulders sagged, and he threw down his weapon down in despair, crying: 'God dame me I can doe noe more, my heart failles me.' The spectators roared with disbelief, as the butchered body of Monmouth lay, still alive, before them. Only the universal shouts and screams from the crowd and the furious order from the sheriffs caused him to pick up the axe and swing it twice more. Even then he had finally to take a knife to sever the remaining sinews of Monmouth's neck. When he held up the disembodied head, 'there was no shouting but many cried'. The emotion of the onlookers was overwhelming: 'if there had not been a guard before the souldiers to conduct the executioner away, the people would have torn him to pieces, soe great was their indignation at the barbarous usage of the late Duke of Monmouth'.[15]

Monmouth's head and body were placed in a velvet-lined coffin that stood by and taken into the Chapel of St Peter ad Vincula in the Tower of London and quietly buried. Anna's concern now was entirely for her children and, wiping away her tears, she decided against taking his body for burial at Moor Park in order to reinforce her absolute loyalty to James II. As one observer commented, Monmouth had already lost his life and now, going to his death without communion, he had sacrificed his soul to contest that Henrietta Wentworth was not a whore.

Henrietta herself heard the news of his execution in Holland, and shortly afterwards received the relics he had left her, including his watch and ring. Tragedy sapped her. She and her mother tried with little success to retrieve their possessions from the Dutch pawnbrokers. James II's ambassador to the Dutch Republic agreed to meet her, but was little help. She in turn treated him 'in a haughty kind of a way', determined to show Monmouth's own stoic indifference. But her face was already drawn with grief and illness. When she returned home that autumn an old friend found her 'in a most lamentable condition of health'. She was visited on her sickbed by Francis Turner, bishop of Ely, who confirmed that Monmouth's final hours had been calm and spent in communion with God and in defence of her honour. Just before he died, Turner explained, Monmouth had given him a note to give to her. On the king's instruction he was now delivering it. Henrietta unfolded the paper and read the words of a charm to keep her safe. She shook with sadness and murmured, 'Good God, had that poor man nothing to think of but me.' She lost consciousness and would last only a few months more. She died in the coming spring, aged just twenty-five.[16]

Many would reflect on the man who had fallen, both then and in the weeks and months that followed. Some of those who had supported him refused to believe he had died. It was rumoured that at the last moment his place on the scaffold had been taken by another, and that Monmouth would come again. John Bragg, a husbandman in Dorset, confided in his friend Soloman Andrew that 'Munmouth was noe more dead than he was and that wee should see other of his doinges here'. Princess Mary of Orange, for her part, commissioned the physician James Welwood to pen a history of recent events. Welwood, who had come to know Monmouth during his last years, wrote about him at length. He was careful to stress that he had read and partly transcribed Monmouth's diary and pocket book, and that, 'there is nothing deliver'd concerning this Unfortunate Gentleman, but what I have unquestionable Grounds for'. His words were an epitaph, for Mary, of the cousin and friend she remembered:

> Monmouth seem'd to be born for a better Fate; for the first part of his life was all Sunshine, though the rest was clouded. He was Brave, Generous, Affable, and extremely Handsome: Constant in his Friendships, just to his Word, and an utter enemy to all sorts of Cruelty. He was easy in his Nature, and fond of popular Applause which led him insensibly into all his Misfortunes; But wherever might be the hidden Designs of some working Heads he embark'd with, his own were noble, and chiefly aim'd at the Good of his Country.[17]

Epilogue

In the sweltering days after the battle of Sedgemoor hundreds of rebels had been taken prisoner on the Somerset Levels, tied roughly together and force-marched to temporary holding places. So strong was the stench of sweat and blood that the church wardens at Westonzoyland were still fumigating their church with incense weeks later. While the attainder against him had denied Monmouth any kind of legal hearing, the same was not true for those who had followed him, and in the months after his execution some 1,400 people were put on trial for their part in the rebellion. Responsibility for these hearings was given to Judge Jeffreys, whom James II had elevated to the House of Lords. He arrived in Dorchester in early September, by which time a number of prisoners had already died from the squalid and overcrowded conditions in the county gaols. The infamous trials that followed would be known, after the title of a pamphlet published four years later, as 'the Bloody Assizes'.

The scale of the mass justice of that autumn of 1685 was eye-watering. On a single day in September over 540 prisoners were tried and sentenced. Jeffreys told the incarcerated rebels that if they pleaded guilty the king would show mercy. He was expected to execute only the ringleaders, and this made sense. After all, the rank and file of the New Model Army had not been tried, let alone executed, in 1660. Instead it was the signatories of Charles I's death warrant who had been hunted down. Even in the rebellions of the sixteenth century the vast majority of grassroots recruits were pardoned.

After watching the first few who pleaded 'not guilty' being almost immediately condemned and executed, most of the remaining rebels did as Jeffreys advised and were accordingly convicted of 'levying war against the king' and other related crimes. But the horrifying realisation soon came that this time there would be almost no clemency. Over the weeks that followed 250 people would be hanged, drawn and quartered, while a further 850 were to be transported to the West Indies for ten years' labour. In all over 90 per cent were either executed or deported, and fewer than ten per cent pardoned.

The scale of the executions was such that the hangman Jack Ketch, who had so mutilated Monmouth on Tower Hill, complained that even with an assistant, one Pascha Rose, he could not hang, draw and quarter twenty-nine people in one day as he was being asked to. After the sentencing, the hangings themselves were systematically distributed across thirty-seven different locations in Dorset, Devon and Somerset to maximise their impact. The residents of modest market towns, Dunster and Dulverton, Wellington and Yeovil, looked on in horror as their friends and neighbours were hanged, disembowelled, decapitated, and hacked into quarters before their eyes. Their heads and limbs were then boiled in brine, tarred and put on public display. Jeffreys's lack of pity for the rebels was unsurprising, but it added to the profound sense of shock. One young woman of Lyme Regis pleaded on her knees before the judge to spare the life of her fiancé. The judge was reported to have looked down at her and to have remarked with a smirk that 'he could only spare her part of him; but as he knew what she wanted, it should be that part which she liked best, and he would give orders to the sheriff accordingly'. The sight and smell of the mutilated corpses, mounted as macabre trophies, was too much for many to bear. John Langford of Dorchester cut down the quarters of a friend, judging the consequent punishment worth enduring.

It was not just the rebels themselves who were given severe sentences. On his very first day in court Jeffreys tried the seventy-year-old Lady Alice Lisle, who though deaf and infirm was accused of allowing rebels to sleep in her stables. She maintained her innocence throughout and it was only through relentlessly hectoring and bullying the jury over many hours, and after rejecting a 'not guilty' verdict three times, that Jeffreys was able to force a conviction. When he did so, he remarked with satisfaction that 'if I had been among you and she had been my own mother, I should have found her guilty'. Despite a barrage of pleas for her life, Alice Lisle was hanged six days later. Another woman accused of aiding the rebels was Elizabeth Gaunt, a tallow chandler who had lodged with Mrs Smith in Amsterdam. The crime for which she was tried was that of helping to arrange a passage out of London for one James Burton, who was testifying against her to save his own skin. She was found guilty and on 23 October 1685 was burned alive at Tyburn. As the pyre was lit she held up a Bible and declared in a clear voice that she died to defend it. She would be the last woman in English history to be executed for treason.[1]

Others fared better. The ever-slippery Robert Ferguson eluded the search parties and made it to Amsterdam, where he resumed his career as a radical pamphleteer. William Williams, Monmouth's servant, would be pardoned and released the following spring, having stood as a witness for the king. Lord Grey made a full and detailed confession of the origins of the rebellion and of the 1683 Whig plot which, combined with his creditors' desire to keep him alive, spared him the scaffold. The value of his confession, which named every name, the hard cash produced by his family and his willingness to testify against his friends, brought him a pardon within a year and he was soon restored to his title and property. As he rode freely across his undulating Sussex lands, Grey must have pushed the memory of Monmouth, who had so often ridden with him, to the back of his mind. Meanwhile, to the hapless rebels themselves it seemed that the rich and well connected were pardoned while Monmouth and his impoverished supporters were condemned.[2]

In the end the defeat of Monmouth's uprising would mark the high point of a royal regime that was already plunging towards a precipice. James II's brief reign would be the shortest and most disastrous of any crowned monarch since the Middle Ages. Within a year he was confirming the fears that Monmouth's invasion literature had so luridly outlined, but which had then seemed to be scaremongering. His bloody-minded determination to bend Parliament to his will soon became apparent in his actions, as did his desire to make Catholicism once again the national religion – despite his solemn promises to protect the Anglican Church. After the Bloody Assizes, James II announced in the House of Lords that he was keeping the extra regiments that had been raised to fight Monmouth's rebels, so creating a permanent standing army of 20,000 to maintain national security. Furthermore, he explained, he had decided to dispense with the Test Act and had appointed a series of Catholics to senior military positions. He had no intention of seeking Parliament's views, let alone assent, for these decisions, but he expected it to grant the funds to pay for them. Outrage followed and Parliament was quickly prorogued.

Over the succeeding two years James II would alienate those who had been his greatest allies in the early 1680s – the Tories who had opposed both the Whigs and the Exclusion Bills tooth and nail. He gathered around him a tiny clique of advisers, many Catholic, including the Earl of Sunderland and Judge Jeffreys, who was now lord chancellor. Soon august establishment figures – among them the Archbishop of Canterbury and the fellows of Magdalen College, Oxford – were being expelled and incarcerated for daring to resist the king's authoritarian political and religious policies. When James saw that to achieve his goals he would have to call Parliament again, he and his ministers set about ensuring that only those loyal to him could be elected by initiating a programme of systematic electoral rigging the like of which England had never seen.

All the while, watching and waiting from the other side of the Channel, was William of Orange. The liberties and religious sensibilities of Britons did not much trouble him. Arguments about honour and obligation that had persuaded Monmouth to lead his doomed invasion left the unsentimental Dutchman cold. His primary concern had been, and remained, repelling Louis XIV. The difference that control of England, with its now enlarged army, could make to his efforts was obvious.

As James's catastrophic mismanagement of his kingdoms continued, William opened a quiet dialogue with the most disaffected English politicians. But with his wife, Princess Mary, still next in line to the throne it seemed that patience would be the best policy. Then, at Christmas 1687, it was announced that James II's queen, Mary Beatrice, was pregnant. Suddenly the opportunity to ascend the British throne, for which he had waited so long, seemed likely to elude William. By the time the queen gave birth to a healthy son William had already decided to invade.

The disaster of Monmouth's invasion provided his cousin with valuable lessons. William needed an invasion force strong enough to take the country without relying on English recruits. He also needed to secure concrete and conspicuous support from senior establishment figures at the very outset to give it the legitimacy Monmouth's insurgents had lacked. Over the late spring of 1688 William set about preparing an immense fleet in the docks at Hellevoetsluis. After the English politicians with whom he had been conferring had been told of his intentions, they put their names to what was couched as an 'invitation' to William to invade England for the protection of Protestantism and liberty. Of the seven signatories three had been closely connected to Monmouth and the Whigs of the early 1680s. Henry Sidney, the younger brother of Algernon, had fought in the St Denis campaign, had been visited by Monmouth on his sickbed afterwards, and had put the duke up in his house in The Hague in 1679. Edward Russell was Lord William Russell's first cousin and was devoted to the memory of his kinsman, 'a man I passionately love[d]'. William Cavendish, Earl of Devonshire, had sat with

Monmouth and Russell on the coalition Privy Council in 1679 and had been one of their colleagues in the attempts to pass the Exclusion Bills.[3]

William took almost exactly Monmouth's route when he sailed from the Dutch Republic to Lyme Bay in the autumn of 1688, arriving by chance on the auspicious Protestant date of 5 November. But the difference in scale was spectacular: from Monmouth's three vessels and eighty-three men, William's fleet comprised 500 ships and carried 21,000 professional soldiers. From Brixham in Devon where they landed they made for Exeter and then, in the weeks that followed, inched towards London. Recruits were at first slow to materialise, but James II started to dissolve both physically and mentally and the scales slowly tipped. Three weeks after the invasion John, now Lord Churchill, and second-in-command of the royal army, rode with the Duke of Grafton from their camp at Salisbury to join the Dutch. By Christmas Day, William had marched unopposed into London and James II had fled to France, never to return. The gentry had risen, officers of the royal army had defected, uprisings had broken out in other parts of the kingdom and there had been no fighting between the invaders and the royal army. Nearly everything that Monmouth had hoped for but had failed to achieve in 1685 fell in William's favour three years later.

After just two months, in February 1689, a newly elected 'convention' Parliament declared that King James II, having attempted to destroy Protestantism, law and liberty, had abdicated. It therefore offered the throne jointly to the Prince and Princess of Orange. The basis on which the offer was made was set out in an accompanying document, which would become statute that autumn as the Bill of Rights. This declared it illegal for sovereigns to suspend or override the law, to levy taxes or to create a standing army without Parliament's consent. It enshrined in law the requirement that Parliament should meet frequently, that there should be freedom of speech in its debates and that parliamentary elections should also be free. An additional clause preventing the throne from passing to a Catholic was added before it became law. The following spring, on William's initiative, a Toleration Bill was passed allowing Protestant non-conformists freedom of worship in houses licensed for the purpose and in 1694 he reluctantly ratified a Triennial Bill, requiring a new Parliament to meet every three years.

The Bill of Rights did not go as far as many of the Whigs had wanted – Monmouth's invasion declaration had called for annual Parliaments – but it gave written expression and statutory force to Parliament's place in the government of the kingdom and to the limits of royal authority. Henceforth no sovereign would try to rule England without Parliament and after 1707 no monarch would withhold royal assent from a bill passed by both houses. Power was shifting. As significant as the specific stipulations of what would be known as the 'Glorious Revolution' was the nature of the transaction itself. When William and Mary became joint monarchs by accepting an offer from Parliament, rather than by claiming sovereignty as a gift of God alone, the nature of monarchy in England changed. It would prove a turning point – arguably the greatest turning point in English constitutional history.[4]

Monmouth's friends would prosper under William III. James Vernon, his erstwhile secretary, became secretary of state, Lord Grey wormed his way into William's affections and was made Earl of Tankerville, and John Churchill became Duke of Marlborough, the champion of the endless wars with Louis XIV to which William now despatched the English army. Even the Earl of Sunderland, who had been James II's closest adviser, returned to England after the revolution to take a position in government once again. Judge Jeffreys, by contrast, was arrested for treason as James II fled and died in the Tower of London before he could be brought to trial. His body lay beside Monmouth's in the crypt of St Peter ad Vincula for a few years before it was reburied elsewhere with his first wife.

Monmouth's widow, Anna, had been allowed to keep the
Buccleuch titles and lands when the dukedom of Monmouth was
forfeit and in 1688 married Charles, Baron Cornwallis. She would
live into her eighties, outlasting her friend Mary II, her goddaughter,
Queen Anne, and the Hanoverian king, George I. The young
Princess of Wales, later Queen Caroline, adored her, and for the
delighted Georgian ladies Anna would recount colourful tales of
the court of King Charles with all the haughty humour of a dowager
duchess. But Monmouth's memory she cherished. When she rebuilt
her family's Scottish seat, modelling it on William III's residence,
Het Loo, she named it Dalkeith Palace. Here she kept the relics of
her first husband. A spectacular portrait of the duke on horseback
dominated the house, hanging prominently over the great stairs.
Half a dozen further paintings of him adorned the principal rooms,
while the panelling was designed to incorporate his eleven battle
paintings. Anna retrieved Monmouth's effects from the Rotterdam
pawn merchants and instead of having the gems of his Garter regalia
reset, she preserved the pieces intact. When she came to court after
George I had safely ascended the throne, she was known not as
Lady Cornwallis, nor even the Duchess of Buccleuch, but once
again as the Duchess of Monmouth.[5]

Those who succeed in taking the throne from another have their
names entered in the royal roll of history, while those who fail
tend to fade into obscurity or ignominy. Henry IV, Henry VII,
Mary I, William III and Mary II were among those who seized
English sovereignty from a relative and managed thereafter to
make it seem a foregone conclusion – it was in the interests of
no victor to do otherwise. Monmouth would be the last of a
sequence of brothers and sons, uncles and nephews, stretching
back centuries, to attempt and fail to wrest power from a
kinsman. While James II's descendants would try to raise rebellions in Scotland in the eighteenth century they were not royal
insiders, let alone part of its ruling establishment, and to them
Britain was a foreign country. William III may have been close

to Monmouth but he was not sentimental and had nothing to gain from perpetuating his cousin's memory, linked as it was to the uncomfortable truth that his own accession had not been inevitable and their two invasions not so dissimilar. Despite the Whigs' revival after 1688 there would be no rehabilitation for the Duke of Monmouth. His would be a forgotten sacrifice. His motives would be misrepresented and the satires against him taken as truths, until he became a historical caricature: arrogant, air-headed and absurd.[6]

That Monmouth had flaws is beyond question. He invariably acted from the heart rather than the head, often moved by an acute sense of fairness and justice rather than the cool political judgement that might have achieved much more. The political education and the experience that guided many around him were not his, and it told repeatedly. He was simply not capable of the strategies of shrewd self-interest which many politicians demonstrated to such effect. Instead Monmouth went on personal instinct, living almost entirely in the moment and thinking too little of the consequences of his actions. Crucially his devotion to honour and loyalty overwhelmed everything, causing him to make poor political judgements and to stay faithful to those who deserved it least. Perhaps it is not surprising that one who had been repeatedly abandoned by those he loved should have set such store by these virtues. His sudden and violent separation from his mother in 1657, his uncle's increasingly jealous antipathy in the 1670s and his banishment by his father in 1679 combined to make him determined not to visit such betrayals on others. It was his misery at forsaking Henrietta Wentworth rather than the prospect of his own execution that tortured him at the end. Concern for her was what drove him to his knees before his uncle on the day before his death, an act which must have been agony for him of all people, and which would cost him much in the eyes of posterity. He was not alone in such eleventh-hour pleading – Thomas Cranmer had repeatedly recanted his Protestantism in the days before his execution in Mary I's reign – but to Monmouth the mud would stick.

Against these shortcomings could be counted many qualities. Energy he had in abundance, not just for amusement but also for hard work, and as head of the army and Master of the Horse he showed intelligence, application and a commitment to reform. The charm for which he was famous across the courts of Europe was more than drawing-room finesse, but a genuine personal warmth and interest in others that was felt by numerous ordinary people from whom he had little or nothing to gain. He was humane and compassionate, abhorring gratuitous violence with all the feeling of one who knew what killing was, and concerned for the physical suffering of those in his charge. His innate empathy for the persecuted and the wronged, visible in his early career, was vividly revealed in his response to the government's treatment of the Lowland Scots. This was the incident that took him into politics. By the late 1670s he had made common cause with the Whigs in their mutual opposition to the Duke of York – his personal and theirs political. But it was not simply pique which joined Monmouth to them but a shared sense of grievance against an increasingly overbearing regime. Perhaps above all he had courage. He was prepared to stand and be counted, to act and not simply to observe. These qualities, so admirable and attractive in a man, were, however, his undoing as a politician. Had he only kept his pledge not to act in February 1685, his life, and perhaps British history, would have been quite different.

History would recall and embellish all Monmouth's vices and overlook his virtues. In his respected twentieth-century biography of James II, F. C. Turner remarked that: 'Of Monmouth it is safe to say that no man who appeared so attractive to his contemporaries, figures in history as so worthless and contemptible.' Here was a person 'so weak as to let himself be "made the cat's foot" by any politician who thought he could make use of him, and so vain that he thought that a brave carriage and popular manners could lead an aristocracy to overlook the defects of his birth.' This view has endured and the label to his portrait in the National Portrait Gallery in London, rehung in 2015, encapsulates him as 'charming, ambitious and unprincipled'.[7]

That one with such a keen sense of integrity and fairness should have been judged so harshly is only the last of the tragedies in which his short life concluded. But his political legacy is not to be found in such assessments. Posterity has tended to identify as the agents of history career politicians and administrators, lawyers and political thinkers, and not creatures of the court, bastard sons, dandies and leaders of uprisings that did not succeed. John Locke, who Monmouth last saw in Amsterdam only a few days before he sailed for Lyme Regis, made the intellectual case for government by consent of the governed. Thomas Jefferson would judge Locke one of 'the three greatest men that have ever lived, without any exception', and reproduce passages from his *Two Treatises of Government* almost verbatim in the American Declaration of Independence. But the great cause for which Locke had written would not have gathered such popular momentum had it not been for the Duke of Monmouth's participation and extraordinary personal appeal.

Monmouth helped make the Whigs and the Exclusion crisis not just a Westminster phenomenon but a genuinely national movement. It was he, not Shaftesbury or Sidney, Russell or Locke, who fired the crowds of common people and made the notion of intervening in the royal succession not only palatable but popular. While the Whigs' cause foundered in Monmouth's lifetime, the Exclusion crisis changed politics for ever. It gave voice to an argument that the Glorious Revolution would do much to settle, it gave ignited popular participation in parliamentary elections and brought political parties themselves into being. His paternity, his Protestantism and his Englishness taken together with his good looks, his personal magnetism and his public charisma, made Monmouth almost irresistible. He drew ordinary men and women to him, first to the streets and then to arms, to cheer and fight for one they wished could be their king. And while he, and they, would fail, in the end their cause did not.[8]

NOTES

Note on Sources

I have not, by and large, dwelt in the text on how my interpretation of Monmouth's life differs from other historians' (though it often does), on the basis that this is likely to be of limited interest to most readers. The footnotes contain the primary sources for Monmouth's life and actions and for my interpretation of events. They do not generally provide references for events that are well covered in scholarly secondary literature. Ronald Hutton's *Charles II* (1989), John Miller's *Charles II* (1991) and K. H. D. Haley's *The First Earl of Shaftesbury* (1968) all give excellent accounts of the period. The 2004 *Oxford Dictionary of National Biography* has been an indispensable source which I have not referenced specifically in the notes, but have used throughout. Robin Clifton's *The Last Popular Rebellion* (1984) is much the best book on Monmouth's rebellion and the character and experience of the rebels. Although it is not a biography it is also the best work on the duke himself since Elizabeth D'Oyley's *James, Duke of Monmouth* (1938). It should be acknowledged here that, while Monmouth's ancestry was Scottish, French and Welsh, this book considers him in an English context.

Abbreviations

Ailesbury Memoirs	*Memoirs of Thomas, Earl of Ailesbury written by himself*, 2 vols, the Roxburghe Club, London, 1890
BL	British Library, London
Bod. Lib.	Bodleian Library, Oxford
Bulstrode Papers	*The Collection of Autograph Letters and Historical Documents formed by Alfred Morrison. The Bulstrode Papers, Volume 1, 1667–1675*, London, 1897
Burnet, MJR	*Bishop Burnet's History of His Own Time*, M. J. Routh (ed.), 6 vols, Oxford, 1823
Burnet, OA	*Burnet's History of My Own Time*, Osmund Airy (ed.), 2 vols, Oxford, 1897

CCSP	*Calendar of the Clarendon State Papers Preserved in the Bodleian Library*, D. Dunn Macray and H. O. Coxe et al. (eds), 5 vols, Oxford, 1869–1932
Clarke, *Life of King James*	Clarke, J. S., *The Life of King James the Second King of England &c Collected out of the Memoirs Writ of his Own Hand Together with the King's Advice to his son and His Majesty's Will, published from the original Stuart manuscripts in Carlton House*, 2 vols, London, 1816
CSPD	*Calendar of State Papers, Domestic: Charles II*, Mary Anne Everett Green et al. (eds), 28 vols, London, 1860–1939
CSPVen	*Calendar of State Papers and Manuscripts Relating to English Affairs in the Archives and Collections of Venice*, Allen B. Hinds (ed.), 37 vols, 1916–35
D'Avaux	*Négociations de Monsieur le Comte d'Avaux en Hollande depuis 1679 jusqu'en 1684*, 3 vols, Paris, 1753
DRO	Dorset Record Office
EHR	*English Historical Review*
Entring Book	*The Entring Book of Roger Morrice, 1677–1691*, Mark Goldie et al. (eds), 7 vols, Woodbridge, 2007–9
Evelyn	*The Diary of John Evelyn*, E. S. De Beer (ed.), 6 vols, Oxford, 1955
Hatton	*Correspondence of the Family of Hatton: Being Chiefly Letters Addressed to Christopher First Viscount Hatton 1601–1704*, E. M. Thompson (ed.), 2 vols, Camden Society NS, 22, 23, London, 1878
Heroick Life	Anon., *An Historical Account of the Heroick Life and Magnanimous Actions of the Most Illustr. Protestant Prince James Duke of Monmouth, Containing an Account of His Birth, Education Places and Titles with His Martial Atchievements in Flanders and Scotland, His Disgrace and Departure from Court and Kingdom, &c*, London, 1683
HMC	Historical Manuscripts Commission
HMC Bath	*The Manuscripts of the Marquis of Bath*, 3 vols, London, 1904–8
HMC Buccleuch	*15th Report, Appendix, Part VIII: The Manuscripts of His Grace the Duke of Buccleuch and Queensberry, K.G., K.Y., preserved at Drumlanrig Castle*, 2 vols, London, 1897–1903
HMC Dartmouth	*11th Report, Appendix, Part V: The Manuscripts of the Earl of Dartmouth*, 3 vols, London, 1887
HMC Fitzherbert	*The Manuscripts of Sir William Fitzherbert, bart., and others*, London, 1893
HMC Foljambe	*15th Report, Appendix, Part V: The Manuscripts of F. J. Savile Foljambe of Osberton*, London, 1897

HMC Hamilton	*11th Report, Appendix, Part VI: The Manuscripts of the Duke of Hamilton*, London, 1887
HMC House of Lords	*11th Report, Appendix, Part II: The Manuscripts of the House of Lords 1678–1688*, London, 1887
HMC Le Fleming	*12th Report, Appendix, Part VII: The Manuscripts of S. H. Le Fleming, esq., of Rydall Hall*, London, 1890
HMC Ormonde	*The Manuscripts of the Marquis of Ormonde*, 8 vols, London, 1902–20
HMC Portland	*The Manuscripts of his Grace the Duke of Portland Preserved at Welbeck Abbey*, 10 vols, London, 1891–1931
HMC Rutland	*12th Report, Appendix, Part V: The Manuscripts of the Duke of Rutland at Belvoir Castle*, London, 1889
HMC Stopford-Sackville	*Report on the Manuscripts of Mrs Stopford-Sackville of Drayton House, Northamptonshire*, 2 vols, London, 1904
HMC 7th Report	*7th Report, Part II: Appendix (continued) and Index*, London, 1879
JHC	*Journal of the House of Commons*
JHL	*Journal of the House of Lords*
Luttrell, *State Affairs*	Luttrell, Narcissus, *A Brief Historical Relation of State Affairs from September 1678 to April 1714*, 6 vols, Oxford, 1857
Marvell	*Complete Works in Verse and Prose of Andrew Marvell*, A. B. Grosart (ed.), 4 vols, 1872–5
NAS	National Archives of Scotland, Edinburgh
ODNB	*Oxford Dictionary of National Biography*, H. C. G. Matthew and Brian Harrison (eds), 60 vols, Oxford, 2004
OPSH	*Original Papers containing the Secret History of Great Britain from the Restoration to the Accession of the House of Hannover to which are prefixed Extracts from the Memoirs of James II as written by Himself*, James MacPherson (ed.), 2 vols, London, 1775
Pepys	*The Diary of Samuel Pepys*, Robert Latham and William Matthews (eds), 11 vols, London, 1970–6
Reresby Memoirs	*The Memoirs of Sir John Reresby: The Complete Text and a Selection from his Letters*, Andrew Browning (ed.), second edition by Mary K. Geiter and W. A. Speck, London, 1991
Sidney–Savile	*Letters from the Honourable Algernon Sidney to the Honourable Henry Savile*, London, 1742

State Trials   *State Trials*, William Cobbett, T. B. Howell, T. J. Howell and David Jardine (eds), 33 vols, London, 1809–26

TNA   The National Archives, Kew, London

Welwood, *Memoirs*   *Memoirs of the Most Material Transactions in England for the Last Hundred Years Preceding the Revolution in 1688*, James Welwood (ed.), 6th edition, London, 1706

Chapter 1: Abduction

1 John Burke and John Bernard Burke (eds), *A Genealogical and Heraldic History of the Extinct and Dormant Baronetcies of England*, London, 1838, p. 490; *CCSP*, III, pp. 392–3, 394, 396; Timothy Crist (ed.), *Charles II to Lord Taaffe: Letters in Exile*, Cambridge, 1974, p. 217.

2 *CCSP*, III, p. 396.

3 David Laing (ed.), *The Letters and Journals of Robert Baillie*, 3 vols, Edinburgh, 1842, III, p. 88.

4 *CCSP*, I, p. 397.

5 N. A. M. Rodger, *The Safeguard of the Sea: a Naval History of Britain 660–1649*, London, 1997, pp. 420–5; *CCSP*, I, p. 426; S. R. Gardiner, *The History of the Great Civil War*, 4 vols, London, 1905, IV, pp. 166–74.

6 *CCSP*, I, pp. 426–30.

7 *The Perfect Weekly Account* (Thomason 72: E.453[19], 17), 12–19 Jul. 1658; M. Sainte-Beuve (ed.), *Mémoires de Madame de Motteville sur Anne d'Autriche et sa Cour*, 3 vols, Paris, 1855, I, p. 286.

8 *CCSP*, I, p. 431.

9 Edward Hyde, Earl of Clarendon, *The History of the Rebellion and Civil Wars in England Begun in the Year 1641*, edited by W. Dunn Macray, 6 vols, Oxford, 1888, IV, pp. 338, 360–1.

10 Mary Anne Everett Green, *Lives of the Princesses of England*, 6 vols, London, 1849–55, VI, p. 149; *The Parliament Kite, or the Tell-Tale Bird* (Thomason 72: E453[28], 9), 13–20 Jul. 1648; Hyde in his *History of the Rebellion*, IV, pp. 338, 349, implies that the Prince and Princess of Orange and the Prince of Wales remained in Hellevoetsluis for the week but Hyde was not in the country at the time.

11 TNA, E351/3265; E351/3267; LC5/134, p. 8, 260, SP16/375, no. 11, for their adjacent rooms at Richmond and St James's palaces.

12 *The Parliament Kite*, 13–20 Jul. 1648. The form of such dinners at the Binnenhof is indicated by the illustrations in Abraham van Wicquefort, *A Relation in Form of Journal*, trans. William Lower, The Hague, 1660; Pieter Geyl, *Orange and Stuart: 1641–1672*, London, 1939, 2001 edn, pp. 41–2.

13 Clarendon, *History of the Rebellion*, IV, pp. 338, 370–1.

14 George Scott, *Lucy Walter: Wife or Mistress?*, London, 1947, pp. 31–51.

15 'Cases brought before the committee: March 1647', Mary Anne Everett
   Green (ed.), *Calendar of the Proceedings of the Committee for Advance of
   Money 1642–1656*, London, 1888, II, pp. 780–99.

16 BL Add MS 28094, fos 71–2; *JHL*, 1629–42, pp. 283, 309, 454; *JHL*, 1645–7,
   pp. 470, 507, 696; *JHL*, 1647–8, pp. 16, 20, 25; *HMC: 6th Report, Part 1,
   Report and Appendix*, London, 1877, pp. 138–42, 156.

17 *JHL*, 1647–8, p. 25; BL Add MS 28094, fos 71–2.

18 *Evelyn*, II, pp. 561–2; Clarke, *Life of King James,* I, pp. 497–8; *OPSH*, I,
   pp. 76–7; *Memoirs of Sophia, Electress of Hanover 1630–1680*, trans. H.
   Forester, London, 1888, pp. 23–4.

19 Clarke, *Life of King James*, pp. 490–1; *OPSH*, I, pp. 76–9; Marika
   Keblusek, 'Een zwarte doos op een buiten bij Delft: Engelse Royalisten
   op "De Ruit" (1656–1660)', in E. den Hartog and R. M. Deuling (eds),
   *Kastelenstichting Holland en Zeeland: Buitenplaatsen in de omgeving
   van Delft*, Rotterdam, 2009; for Lucy's interest in gems: Thomas Birch
   (ed.), *A Collection of the State Papers of John Thurloe, Esq, Secretary
   first to the Council of State and Afterwards to the two Protectors, Oliver
   and Richard Cromwell*, 7 vols, London, 1742, V, pp. 161, 178.

20 BL Add MS 28094, fos 71–2; Arnold H. J. Baines, 'Monmouth, Kiffin
   and the Gosfrights', *Baptist Quarterly*, 20.3 (Jul. 1963), pp. 129–30; 'Mr
   Gospritt . . . blameing Mrs Barlows Mother for leaving her daughter
   abroad in an ill way of liveing', BL Add MS 28094, fos 71–2; Clarke, *Life
   of King James*, I, pp. 497–8.

21 James MacPherson (ed.), *The Life of Edward, Earl of Clarendon . . . in
   which is included a Continuation of his History of the Grand Rebellion*,
   3 vols, Oxford, 1827, II, pp. 252–6; *OPSH*, I, pp. 76–9; Clarke, *Life of
   King James*, I, pp. 490–1, 498. Charles's reticence and awkwardness was
   remarked on in France and Holland in the late 1640s: *The Letters and
   Journals of Robert Baillie, Principal of the University of Glasgow*, 3 vols,
   Edinburgh, 1842, III, p. 88; Sainte-Beuve (ed.), *Mémoires de Madame de
   Motteville*, I, p. 389.

22 *CCSP*, I, pp. 428–30; S. R. Gardiner (ed.), *The Hamilton Papers; being
   selections from original letters in the possession of His Grace the Duke of
   Hamilton and Brandon, relating to the years 1638–1650*, Camden Society,
   London, 1880, pp. 230–2.

23 *CSPVen*, 1647–52, pp. 80, 82.

24 BL Harl MS 6988, fos 222r–3v.

25 Roger Lockyer (ed.), *The Trial of Charles I: A Contemporary Account
   taken from the Memoirs of Sir Thomas Herbert and John Rushworth*,
   London, 1974, pp. 133–7.

Chapter 2: An Infamous Mother

1 *Evelyn*, II, pp. 561–2.

2 NAS, GD224/1059/10; Anna Keay, *The Magnificent Monarch: Charles II
   and the Ceremonies of Power*, London, 2008, p. 53.

3 NAS, GD224/1059/10.

4 *Heroick Life*, pp. 9–12; NAS, GD224/1059/10.

5 *CSPVen*, 1647–52, p. 204; *Memoirs of Mademoiselle de Montpensier Grand-daughter of Henri Quatre and niece of Queen Henrietta Maria Written by Herself*, 3 vols, London, 1848, I, pp. 169–71; Henri Courteault and Pierre de Vaissière (eds), *Journal de Jean Vallier, Maître d'Hôtel du Roi (1648–1657)*, 4 vols, Paris, 1902, III, pp. 42–3.

6 *Mercurius Politicus*, 8–15 Apr. 1652, p. 97; *Mercurius Politicus*, 15–22 Apr. 1652, p. 98; Keblusek, 'Een zwarte doos op een buiten bij Delft'.

7 Lambeth Palace Library, MS 645, no. 26.

8 *Historical Manuscripts Commission: The Laing Manuscripts at Edinburgh University*, 2 vols, London 1914–25, I, pp. 444–5; Lambeth Palace MS 646, no. 8 (fol. 15r, 16r); Birch (ed.), *State Papers of John Thurloe*, V, pp. 168–9; *OPSH*, I, pp. 76–9.

9 *Mercurius Politicus*, 10–17 Jul. 1656, 318, p. 21; Crist (ed.), *Charles II to Lord Taaffe*, p. 15.

10 Lambeth Palace Library, MS 646, no. 7 (fos 13r–14r), no. 8 (fos 15r, 16r).

11 Lambeth Palace Library, MS 645, no. 23.

12 Keblusek, 'Een zwarte doos op een buiten bij Delft'; G. E. Cockayne, *Complete Peerage*, revised edition, London, 1953, XII, p. 470.

13 TNA, PROB11/253, no. 407; 'Warrants of the Protector and Council', *CSPD*, 1655–56, p. 580; Birch (ed.), *State Papers of John Thurloe*, V, p. 161.

14 Birch (ed.), *State Papers of John Thurloe*, I, pp. 721–33; V, p. 161; *CCSP*, II, p. 110.

15 *Mercurius Politicus*, 10–17 Jul. 1656, pp. 318, 21; *Heroick Life*, pp. 9–12; BL Add MS 28094, fos 71–2.

16 Birch (ed.), *State Papers of John Thurloe*, V, pp. 161, 168–9, 178; *Heroick Life*, pp. 9–12; *Mercurius Politicus*, 10–17 Jul. 1656, pp. 318, 21.

17 *CCSP*, II, p. 211; Anna Keay, *The Magnificent Monarch*, pp. 51–3; *CSPVen*, 1657–59, pp. 1–11.

18 DRO, D/FSI, Box 268, General Household Accounts, 1658–59, *passim*; *CCSP*, III, p. 341.

19 Keblusek, 'Een zwarte doos op een buiten bij Delft'; Birch (ed.), *State Papers of John Thurloe*, V, pp. 161, 178.

20 This was a precursor to the 'black box' for which, two decades hence, all Europe would be searched, in the belief that it contained proof that Charles and Lucy Walter had been married, thus making their son James the legitimate heir to the throne of England.

21 Keblusek, 'Een zwarte doos op een buiten bij Delft'; Birch (ed.), *State Papers of John Thurloe*, VII, p. 347.

22 *CCSP*, III, 352; Birch (ed.), *State Papers of John Thurloe*, VI, pp. 458–69.

23 *CCSP*, III, p. 354.

24 Crist (ed.), *Charles II to Lord Taaffe*, p. 27; *CCSP*, III, pp. 392–4, 396, 401.

25 *CSPD*, 1657–58, p. 342; BL Add MS 28094, fos 71–2.

26 BL Add MS 28094, fos 71–2; Birch (ed.), *State Papers of John Thurloe*, VII, p. 337.

27 White Kennett, *A Complete History of England with the Lives of all the Kings and Queens*, 3 vols, London, 1719, III, p. 366; *OPSH*, I, pp. 76–9; Allan Fea, *King Monmouth: Being a History of the Career of James Scott, 'The Protestant Duke', 1649–1685*, London, 1902, p. 22; Clarke, *Life of King James*, I, pp. 490–2; MacPherson (ed.), *The Life of Edward, Earl of Clarendon*, II, pp. 252–6.

Chapter 3: A New Life

1 Birch (ed.), *State Papers of John Thurloe*, V, p. 178.

2 The painting, which belongs to the Duke of Buccleuch, hangs at Drumlanrig House in the dining room (2011); BL Add MS 15897, fol. 3r. Establishing the true date of Monmouth's birth was one of the questions behind the investigation of 1675, TNA, GD224/1059/10.

3 *CSPVen*, 1643–47, pp. 96–104; *CCSP*, II, pp. 124, 130, 139, 336; Clarendon, *History of the Rebellion*, V, pp. 343–4.

4 Birch (ed.), *State Papers of John Thurloe*, I, p. 260; *CCSP*, II, p. 139.

5 *CCSP*, II, pp. 337, 352.

6 Mary Anne Everett Green (ed.), *Letters of Queen Henrietta Maria including her Private Correspondence with Charles the First*, London, 1857, p. 260; Karen Britland, *Drama at the Courts of Queen Henrietta Maria*, Cambridge, 2006, pp. 122–3; Karen Britland, 'Exile or homecoming? Henrietta Maria in France 1644–69', in Torsten Riotte and Philip Mansel (eds), *Monarchy and Exile: The Politics of Legitimacy from Marie de Médicis to Wilhelm II*, London, 2011, p. 142; *Lettres de Henriette-Marie de France Reine d'Angleterre à sa Soeur Christine Duchesse de Savoie*, Rome, 1881, nos 9, 17, 55.

7 Britland, 'Exile or homecoming?', p. 138; Erin Griffey and Caroline Hibbard, 'Henrietta Maria's inventory at Colombes: courtly magnificence and hidden politics', *Journal of the History of Collections*, 24, 2 (2012), pp. 159–83; M. A. Chéruel (ed.), *Lettres du Cardinal Mazarin pendant son ministère*, 9 vols, Paris 1872–1906, IX, p. 187; *CCSP*, II, p. 434; III, p. 10.

8 *CCSP*, II, pp. 414, 430.

9 George F. Warner (ed.), *Nicholas Papers: Correspondence of Sir Edward Nicholas, Secretary of State*, Camden Society, 4 vols, London, 1886–1920, IV, p. 65; the queen may have met James as an infant when Lucy came to Paris in 1649, but this is not documented. The author of *Heroick Life* dates her involvement in James's education to 1650 when Charles II left the continent for Scotland. The date seems certain to be an error: James was still in Lucy's charge at this time, and Gough's responsibilities for his education clearly began soon after the summer of 1658.

10 *CSPVen*, 1661–64, pp. 168, 171; *Pepys*, III, p. 191.

11 *Heroick Life*, p. 12; *CSPVen*, 1661–64, p. 86; *OPSH*, I, p. 76; *Sidney–Savile*, London, 1742, p. 68.

12 MacPherson (ed.), *The Life of Edward, Earl of Clarendon*, II, pp. 252–6; *CSPVen*, 1661–64, p. 168; *Heroick Life*, p. 14; TNA, SP29/104, fol. 122 'my poor little Lord'.

13 *CSPD*, 1657–58, p. 342.

14 *Evelyn*, pp. 561–2; *CCSP*, II, p. 130.

15 Birch (ed.), *State Papers of John Thurloe*, VII, pp. 561–2 p. 370ff; F. Guizot, *Life of Oliver Cromwell*, London, 1887, p. 449.

16 *CCSP*, IV, pp. 239–40; F. J. Routledge, *England and the Treaty of the Pyrenees*, Liverpool, 1953, pp. 57–82.

17 *CCSP*, IV, p. 456.

18 C. H. Hartmann, *Charles II and Madame*, London, 1934, pp. 9–10.

19 William Fraser, *The Scotts of Buccleuch*, 2 vols, Edinburgh, 1878, I, p. 404.

20 This miniature (RC inventory no. 420645) is usually dated to *c.*1665 on the assumption that it was the miniature of Monmouth 'aged about 15 or 16' among Cooper's effects on his death. It is not clear, however, that the two are the same. Comparison with other images of Monmouth strongly suggests it shows the duke before his arrival at court in 1662. It may have been executed during 1658–60, when, in a period of political instability, Cooper's London commissions dropped away; Cooper was described as having 'lived long in France and Holland': George Vertue, *Anecdotes of Painting in England*, III, London, 1762.

21 On 1 May 1660 the Speaker of the House of Commons declared 'Parliament itself was violated before the horrid act against the late king, which we cannot think of without such a detestation and abhorrency as we want words to express it. But it was only the act of some few ambitious and bloody persons; true professors of religion, the nation itself, and Parliament were innocent of it,' *CSPD*, 1659–60, p. 429.

Chapter 4: Homecoming

1 *CSPVen*, 1661–64, p. 86.

2 Arthur Bryant (ed.), *The Letters, Speeches and Declarations of King Charles II*, London, 1935, p. 114; Maurice Lee, *The Heiress of Buccleuch: Marriage, Money and Politics in Seventeenth-Century Britain*, East Linton, 1996. Clarendon credited Lauderdale and Monck with proposing and brokering the marriage. They may have had a hand in it but the surviving letter from Lady Wemyss suggests she put the first suggestion to the king, and Clarendon admitted the whole affair was not discussed with the king's English ministers until the autumn of 1662; MacPherson (ed.), *The Life of Edward, Earl of Clarendon*, II, pp. 252–6.

3 Fraser, *Scotts of Buccleuch*, I, pp. 403–4.

4 Chéruel (ed.), *Lettres du Cardinal Mazarin*, IX, pp. 622, 632, 953; *CSPD*, 1660–61, p. 259; *CSPD*, 1661–62, p. 128; *CSPVen*, 32, pp. 150–63, 174; Bryant (ed.), *Letters*, p. 121; TNA, LC5/2, p. 38.

5 Bryant (ed.), *Letters*, p. 212.

6 *CSPVen*, 1661–64, p. 168; MacPherson (ed.), *The Life of Edward, Earl of Clarendon*, II, p. 252.

7 *Pepys*, III, p. 140.

8 Ibid., III, pp. 139–49; J. W. Willis Bund (ed.), *Diary of Henry Townshend of Elmley Lovett, 1640–1663*, 2 vols, London, 1915–20, I, pp. 92–3; *CSPVen*, 1661–64, pp. 168ff.

9 TNA, PRO31/3/110, fol. 206.

10 *Heroick Life*, p. 15; MacPherson (ed.), *The Life of Edward, Earl of Clarendon*, II, pp. 252–6; *CSPVen*, 1661–64, p. 171.

11 Maurice Exwood and H. L. Lehmann (eds), *The Journal of William Schellinks' Travels in England 1661–1663*, Camden Society, London, 1993, p. 53; *Pepys*, III, pp. 32, 138.

12 *Pepys*, III, *passim*; Exwood and Lehmann (eds), *Journal of William Schellinks' Travels passim.*

13 *Pepys*, III, pp. 190–1; John Bayley, *The History and Antiquities of the Tower of London*, London, 1830, p. 624; Simon Thurley, *Somerset House: The Palace of England's Queens 1551–1692*, London, 2009, p. 69; Exwood and Lehmann (eds), *Journal of William Schellinks' Travels*, p. 83.

14 'The Court is in confusion and grief unspeakable, the king is distressed and weeps bitterly, for he loved his brother tenderly, for he was amiable and most gracious . . . At present he has withdrawn himself and no one soever is allowed to approach him', *CSPVen*, 1659–61, p. 198.

15 'Mary, princess royal (1631–1660), princess of Orange, consort of William II', Marika Keblusek, *ODNB*; Everett Green, *Princesses*, VI, pp. 325–33.

16 *CSPVen*, 1661–64, p. 168; MacPherson (ed.), *The Life of Edward, Earl of Clarendon*, II, p. 253.

17 TNA, LC5/41, fos 12v–13r 74r; LC5/41; C. H. Hartmann, *The King My Brother*, London, 1954, p. 82; *Pepys*, III, p. 82, VII, pp. 371–3 *Evelyn*, III, pp. 347–8.

18 Fraser, *Scotts of Buccleuch*, II, p. 427; *OPSH*, I, p. 75; *CSPVen*, 1661–64, p. 215.

19 MacPherson (ed.), *The Life of Edward, Earl of Clarendon*, II, p. 252; *CSPVen*, 1661–64, p. 168; fol. TNA, SP29/140 fol. 64; 'he had a wonderful genius for every sort of exercise', Anthony Hamilton (ed.), *Memoirs of the Count of Grammont Containing the History of the English Court under Charles II*, London, 1890, p. 333; *Evelyn*, IV, p. 456.

20 Fraser, *Scotts of Buccleuch*, I, p. 417, for James's immaculate letter to the Earl of Wemyss, 11 Jun 1663.

21 *CSPVen*, 1661–64, pp. 168, 171, 204–16.

22 *Pepys*, VI, pp. 169–70.

23 TNA, WORK5/4, fos 102v, 111r; WORK5/5, fol. 75v; Simon Thurley, *The Whitehall Palace Plan of 1670*, London Topographical Society, 153, 1998; *Heroick Life*, p. 15; Fraser, *Scotts of Buccleuch*, I, p. 422.

24 *Pepys*, III, pp. 190–1.

25 Ibid., pp. 190–1, 300–1; Hamilton (ed.), *Memoirs of the Count of Grammont*, p. 333.

26 *Pepys*, III, pp. 190–1, 297, 299; *HMC Portland*, III, p. 294; *HMC Rutland*, II, p. 22.

27 MacPherson (ed.), *The Life of Edward, Earl of Clarendon*, II, pp. 252–6; *CSPD*, 1661–62, p. 552; Fraser, *Scotts of Buccleuch*, II, pp. 424–31.

28 TNA, SP29/62, fol. 159.

29 NAS, GD224/906/59/8; Fraser, *Scotts of Buccleuch*, I, p. 406.

30 NAS, GD122/3/11, 'Letters to Sir John Gilmour, President of the Court of Session, 1618–1663', no. 42.

31 *CSPD*, 1661–62, p. 579. The equivalence here is based on the Retail Price Index from 1660 to 2010.

32 NAS, GD122/3/11, 'Letters to Sir John Gilmour, President of the Court of Session, 1618–1663', no. 59.

33 Ibid., no. 51; Peter D. Anderson, *Robert Stewart, Earl of Orkney, Lord of Shetland*, Edinburgh, 1982, pp. 1–3.

34 NAS, GD157/3233; TNA, GD122/3/12, no. 48.

35 NAS, GD157/3233.

36 NAS, GD122/3/11, no. 58; 'by his Majties expres comand, red and approved by him', no. 59.

37 Ibid., nos 59, 61, 62, 64.

38 Ibid., 'Letters to Sir John Gilmour, President of the Court of Session, 1618–1663', no. 64. (Spelling modernised here for readability.)

39 *Pepys*, III, p. 238; IV, p. 376.

40 *Pepys*, III, p. 260, p. 297; *CSPVen*, pp. 204–16.

41 TNA, SP29/69, fol. 92.

42 NAS, GD224/906/59/7.

43 William Fraser (ed.), *Memorials of the Family of Wemyss of Wemyss*, 3 vols, Edinburgh, 1888, III, pp. 109, 126.

44 *Pepys*, V, p. 154; *HMC Le Fleming*, VII, pp. 29–30.

45 *Pepys*, IV, pp. 98–9, 108.

46 NAS, GD122/3/11, 'Letters to Sir John Gilmour, President of the Court of Session, 1618–1663', nos 75, 76; BL Add 23,210, fol. 35.

47 Hartmann, *The King My Brother*, p. 67; *Pepys*, IV, p. 107; *The Diary of John Lamont of Newton*, Maitland Club Publication, 7, Edinburgh, 1830, p. 161.

48 Hartmann, *The King My Brother*, p. 67; NAS, GD224/906/59/6.

49 *Pepys*, IV, pp. 113–14; C. H. Josten (ed.), *Elias Ashmole (1617–1692), His Autobiographical and Historical Notes, his Correspondence, and Other Contemporary Sources Relating to his Life and Work*, 5 vols, Oxford, 1966, III, pp. 914ff; TNA, SP44/9, pp. 361–2; TNA, LC5/107; TNA, SP 29/75 fol. 254; NAS, GD224/1059/10.

Chapter 5: Vicious and Idle

1 *CSPVen*, 1661–64, pp. 245–8.

2 Fraser, *Scotts of Buccleuch*, I, p. 422.

3 *CSPD*, 1663–64, pp. 264, 271, 275, 280–1; Andrew Clark (ed.), *Life and Times of Anthony Wood, antiquary, of Oxford, 1632–95*, 5 vols, Oxford, 1891, I, pp. 489–96.

4 Fraser, *Scotts of Buccleuch*, I, p. 420.

5 Clark (ed.), *Anthony Wood,* I, pp. 489–96.

6 Fraser, *Scotts of Buccleuch*, II, p. 391. In the end it was realised that the terms of the Buccleuch entail were such that Monmouth's children could be prevented from inheriting Anna's estates, were Anna to predecease him without bearing an heir, and an Act of Parliament was passed to overturn this on 1 Oct 1663: NAS, GD157/3238.

7 BL Add MS 51,326, fol. 8, in which Stephen Fox states that the couple lived separately 'till she cohabited with her husband at Oxford In the yeare 1665'.

8 *CSPD*, 1663–64, p. 539; BL Add MS 51,326, fos 8–9; DRO, FSI 275, Duchess of Monmouth's Accounts 1665–67, pp. 110, 130, 135, 137, fos 139–40; DRO, FSI 275, Duke and Duchess of Monmouth's Accounts 1667–68, pp. 11–12, 33–5; 'From Chisuik', Fraser (ed.), *Memorials of the Family of Wemyss of Wemyss*, III, p. 124; 'Chiswick: Other estates', *Victoria County History: A History of the County of Middlesex: Vol. 7: Acton, Chiswick, Ealing and Brentford, West Twyford, Willesden*, 1982, pp. 74–8.

9 *HMC Le Fleming*, VII, pp. 29–30l; TNA, WORK5/4, fol. 111.

10 *Pepys*, IV, p. 371.

11 TNA, WORK5/4, Extraordinary Account.

12 BL Add MS 15897; TNA WORK5/4, Extraordinary Account, fos 440–59.

13 Keay, *The Magnificent Monarch, passim.*

14 NAS, GD224/906/59, *passim.*

15 DRO, D/FSI, Box 275.

16 NAS, GD224/906/59, Miscellaneous Papers, Anna Buccleuch's Accounts Jul 1662–May 1663.

17 NAS, GC112/39/114/4.

18 'to gordon my old page goeing away', NAS, GD224/906/59/6.

19 DRO, D/FSI, Box 275, Monmouth's Accounts 1668–70; DRO, D/FSI, Box 274, Monmouth's debts before 1667.

20 TNA, SP29/105, f. 8; TNA, SP29/69, fol. 92.

21 DRO, D/FSI/274, Monmouth's debts before 1667, 26 May; D. R. Woolf, *Reading in Early Modern England*, Cambridge, 2000, p. 263.

22 Lambeth Palace Library, MS 931, no. 65; BL Royal MS 17 A XX, fos 1–26; Christopher Bond, 'The Phoenix and the Prince: the Poetry of Thomas Ross', *Review of English Studies*, 60, 246 (2009), pp. 588–604.

23 TNA, SP29/69, fol. 92; Fraser, *Scotts of Buccleuch*, II, pp. 391–2; *London Gazette*, 293, 3–7 Sep. 1668.

24 TNA, SP29/104, fol. 122.

25 BL Add MS 51,326, fos 8–9.

26 G. E. Aylmer, *The Crown's Servants: Government and Civil Service under Charles II, 1660–1685*, Oxford, 2002, p. 102; DRO, D/FSI, Box 275, Monmouth's Accounts 1667–68.

27 Fraser, *Scotts of Buccleuch*, II, pp. 485–7.

28 DRO, D/FSI/274, Monmouth's debts before 1667; DRO, FSI Box 275, 'Booke of . . . the Duke and Duchesse of Monmouth their Expence . . . 1667–1668', pp. 50, 56.

29 DRO, D/FSI, Box 275, Monmouth's Accounts 1667–68, p. 56.

30 DRO, D/FSI/274, Monmouth's debts before 1667, 'Claudius Sourceau for bill from Nov 1663 to Jan 1665', £833.

31 Fraser, *Scotts of Buccleuch*, II, pp. 485–7; DRO, D/FSI, Box 275, Monmouth's Accounts 1667–68, p. 56.

32 Fraser, *Scotts of Buccleuch*, II, pp. 485–7.

33 DRO, D/FSI/274, Monmouth's debts before 1667, Dec 1667: 'John Ball for interest on £2,000 borrowed from him by Mr Ross. £120'.

34 TNA, SP29/104, fol. 122; *CSPD*, 1663–64, p. 574; *CSPD*, 1664–65, pp. 230, 173.

35 *CSPD*, 1664–65, p. 256.

36 Clark (ed.), *Anthony Wood*, I, p. 58; J. N. P. Watson, *Captain, General and Rebel Chief: The Life of James, Duke of Monmouth*, London, 1979, p. 13; DRO, D/FSI, Box 275, Monmouth's Accounts 1667–68, p. 50.

37 *HMC Portland*, III, p. 294.

38 BL Add MS 51,326, fol. 18r.

39 Christopher Clay, *Public Finance and Private Wealth: the Career of Sir Stephen Fox 1627–1716*, Oxford, 1978; 'Chiswick: Manors', *A History of the County of Middlesex*, pp. 71–4; BL Add MS 51,326, fos 8–9.

40 DRO, FSI 275, Monmouth's Accounts 1670–72, p. 48.

41 Corpus Christi College, Oxford, Benefactor's Book, B/11/1/1, fol. 12r.

42 BL Add MS 51,326, fos 25–6, fol. 18r; *Calendar of Treasury Books*, 1667–68, pp. 153, 155, 404, 430, 527, 596, 610, 614; 1669–72, pp. 169, 417, 358, 532; *CSPD*, 1667–8, p. 290.

43 *Pepys*, VIII, pp. 184–5; Josten (ed.), *Elias Ashmole*, III, p. 1087.

44 *Memoirs of the Count Grammont*, p. 333; Bod. Lib., Carte MS 35, fos 285–6; *Pepys*, VI, pp. 167–8; VII, p. 411; VIII, p. 246. In November 1664 Ross complained: 'I shall hardly see him awake time enough tomorrow to make good his word' to write a letter, TNA SP29/104. fol. 122; 'Whoever wanted to recount all the dissipations of the Duke of Monmouth would have to make too long a search', *Lorenzo Magalotti at the Court of Charles II*, pp. 41–2, 79–81.

45 *CSPD*, 1664–65, pp. 392, 448; BL Royal MS 17 A XX, fos 1–25; Lambeth Palace Library, MS 931 Misc MSS, no. 65; N. A. M. Rodger, *The Command of the Ocean: A Naval History of Britain, 1649–1815*, London, 2005, pp. 63–9.

46 *Newes Published for the Satisfaction and Information of the People*, 52, 6 Jul. 1665; Clarke, *Life of King James*, I, p. 493.

47 MacPherson (ed.), *The Life of Edward, Earl of Clarendon*, II, pp. 389–90; 'Directions to a Painter', George de Forest Lord et al. (eds), *Poems on Affairs of State: Augustan Satirical Verse, 1660–1714*, New Haven and London, 1963–75, I, pp. 34–45.

48 Correlli Barnett, *Britain and her Army 1509–1970*, London, 1970; John Childs, *The Army of Charles II*, London, 1976, p. 1–21.

49 Charles Dalton, *English Army Lists and Commission Registers, 1661–1714*, London, 1904, I, p. 59; *CSPD*, 1665–6, p. 475.

50 *CSPD*, 1667, p. 177; 1666–67, pp. 108–33, 11 Sep 1666.

51 *HMC Le Fleming*, VII, p. 42; DRO, FSI 275, Duchess of Monmouth's Accounts 1665–67, p. 85; James Peller Malcolm, *Londinium Redivivum*, 4 vols, London, 1802–7, IV, p. 75.

52 *Pepys*, VIII, p. 255; DRO, D/FSI, Box 275, Duke and Duchess of Monmouth's Accounts 1667–68, p. 59; Duchess of Monmouth's Accounts 1665–67, pp. 129–30; *HMC Le Fleming*, VII, p. 49; TNA, SP29/204, fol. 58.

53 *CSPD*, 1667, p. 177; SP29/205, fol. 1.

54 TNA, SP29/204, fol. 59; SP29/205, fol. 1; *Pepys*, VIII, pp. 246, 282, 288.

Chapter 6: Coming of Age

1 *Pepys*, VIII, p. 524.

2 *Bulstrode Papers*, I, pp. 12, 15.

3 NAS, GD112/39/114/4; *Bulstrode Papers*, I, p. 19; *Lorenzo Magalotti at the Court of Charles II*, pp. 79–81.

4 A. P. Faugère, *Journal d'un voyage à Paris en 1657–1658*, Paris, 1862, pp. 427–9; A. and W. Galignani, *History of Paris from its Earliest Period to the Present Day*, London, 1825, 3 vols, II, pp. 533–4.

5 Hartmann, *Charles II and Madame*, pp. 197, 201.

6 Bryant (ed.), *Letters*, p. 214; Thomas-François Chabod, Marquis de Saint-Maurice, *Lettres sur la Cour le Louis XIV*, edited by C. Lévy, Paris, 1911–12, 2 vols, I, pp. 176–7.

7 Julia Cartwright, *Madame: A Life of Henriette Daughter of Charles I and Duchess of Orleans*, London, 1894.

8 *Memoirs of Mademoiselle de Montpensier*, III, pp. 2, 3–5; *London Gazette*, 30 Jan.–3 Feb. 1667/68; Hartmann, *Charles II and Madame*, p. 212; Marquis de Saint-Maurice, *Lettres sur la Cour de Louis XIV*, I, pp. 176–7; *Mémoires de Daniel de Cosnac*, 2 vols, Paris, 1852, II, p. 222; *Paris Gazette*, 4 Feb. 1668, N15, p. 124; 18 Feb. 1668, N21, p. 175.

9 *Memoirs of Mademoiselle de Montpensier*, III, pp. 3–5; *Mémoires de Daniel de Cosnac*, II, p. 222.

10 Hartmann, *Charles II and Madame*, p. 215.

11 Ibid., pp. 209, 212, 215; *HMC Le Fleming*, VII, p. 56; *Burnet*, OA, I, p. 435; *Bulstrode Papers*, I, pp. 44, 45.

12 *Calendar of Treasury Books*, 1667–68, pp. 382, 527; *CSPD*, 1667–68, p. 336; BL Add MS 5542, fol. 4v.

13 BL Add MS 5542, fol. 4v; Hartmann, *Charles II and Madame*, p. 212.

14 *Relation de la Feste de Versailles du Dix Huitième Juillet Mil Six Cens Soixante Huit*, Paris, 1668; *Louis XIV l'Homme et le Roi*, Nicolas Milovanovic and Alexandrew Maral (eds), Paris, 2009, pp. 150–3;

Paris Gazette, 21 Jul. 1668, N84, pp. 695–6; Hartmann, Charles *II and Madame*, p. 217.

15 *CSPD*, 1667–68, pp. 513, 534; *HMC Le Fleming*, VII, p. 59; Hartmann, *Charles II and Madame*, p. 364; TNA, SP 29/245 fos 10, 128; SP29/246, fol. 71; *Bulstrode Papers*, I, pp. 55, 58, 61.

16 *Pepys*, IX, p. 308; Christoffer Westergaard (ed.), *The First Triple Alliance: The Letters of Christopher Lindenov Danish Envoy to London*, New Haven, 1947, pp. 17–18; Lorenzo Magalotti, *The Travels of Cosmo the Third Duke of Tuscany through England*, London, 1821, p. 308.

17 Fraser, *Scotts of Buccleuch*, I, p. 429.

18 Eleonore Boswell, *The Restoration Court Stage* Cambridge, 1932, appendix C; *Pepys*, IX, p. 24; NAS, GD112/39/114/4.

19 Hartmann, *Charles II and Madame*, pp. 210–11; *Pepys*, IX, p. 191; *Bulstrode Papers*, I, p. 39.

20 BL Add MS 5542, Household Accounts 1669–71, fol. 25r; *Bulstrode Papers*, I, p. 51.

21 *CSPD*, 1667–68, p. 534; *Bulstrode Papers*, I, pp. 56, 60, 73.

22 DRO, FSI Box 275, Duke and Duchess of Monmouth's Accounts 1667–68, p. 48; BL Add MS 5542, Household Accounts 1669–71, fol. 25r [114]; *Bulstrode Papers*, I, p. 73.

23 *HMC Rutland*, II, p. 22.

24 Fraser, *Scotts of Buccleuch*, II, p. 396; DRO, F/FSI, Box 275, Monmouth's Accounts 1670–72, 'Pd Mr John Portman for a paire of Diamond Earreing set with 18 diamonds for her Grace. £1200'.

25 Westergaard (ed.), *The First Triple Alliance*, p. 17; *London Gazette*, 293, 3–7 Sep. 1668; *Heroick Life*, p. 19.

26 'Pd Mr Bootes for a Race Sute' £10 6s 6d, BL Add MS 5542, fol. 17r; *London Gazette*, 560, 27–30 Mar. 1671; *HMC Le Fleming*, pp. 62, 85.

27 Hartmann, *Charles II and Madame*, pp. 210, 241.

28 *Memoirs of the Count of Grammont*, p. 333.

29 F. C. Turner, *James II*, London, 1948, p. 61; *Burnet*, OA, I, p. 19.

30 *Lorenzo Magalotti at the court of Charles II: his* Relazione d'Inghilterra *of 1668*, edited and translated by W. E. Knowles Middleton, Waterloo, Ont., 1980, p. 77.

31 *HMC Rutland*, II, p. 27; Anne Somerset, *Ladies in Waiting: from the Tudors to the Present Day*, London, 1984, ch. 5; *Lorenzo Magalotti at the Court of Charles II*, pp. 41–2, 79–81.

32 Hartmann, *Charles II and Madame*, p. 209; *Pepys*, IV, p. 348; Agnes Strickland, *Lives of the Queens of England*, 11 vols, London, 1840–8, VIII, pp. 344–50.

33 TNA, SP 29/246 fol. 71.

34 *Lorenzo Magalotti at the Court of Charles II*, p. 34–7; John Miller, *James II*, New Haven, 1978 edition, p. 46; *Burnet*, OA, II, pp. 295–6.

35 *CSPVen*, 1669–70, pp. 71–81; Thomas-François Chabod, Marquis de Saint-Maurice, *Lettres sur la Cour de Louis XIV*, edited by C. Lévy, Paris, 1911–12, 2 vols, I, pp. 176–7; *Lorenzo Magalotti at the Court of Charles II*, p. 32.

36 C. Given Wilson and Alice Curteis, *Royal Bastards of Medieval England*, London, 1984, pp. 162–77; I am grateful to Ronald Hutton for his advice on the point of Henry VIII's marriages. Edward IV's illegitimate son, Arthur Plantagenet, and Henry VIII's son Henry Fitzroy had both been granted titles and offices, and had Henry Fitzroy survived into the turbulent years of the 1530s some sort of legitimation might well have been effected – but his ill health and early death prevented it.

37 *Pepys*, III, p. 303; IV, pp. 123, 376; V, p. 41; *CSPD*, 1663–64, p. 199; *JHL*, 1660–6, pp. 554–7.

38 *Pepys*, III, p. 238; TNA, SP29/232, fol. 134.

39 *Pepys*, V, pp. 56–8; VII, p. 411; *CSPVen*, 1669–70, pp. 79–80; *Lorenzo Magalotti at the Court of Charles II*, pp. 41–2.

40 *Pepys*, V, p. 58; DRO D/FSI, Box 275, *passim*.

41 DRO, D/FSI/274, Monmouth's debts before 1667; *CSPD*, 1678, p. 23.

42 TNA, SP29/62, fol. 159; Miller, *James II*, p. 56; *JHL*, 1666–75, pp. 351–3; John Ferne, *Blazon of Gentrie*, London, 1586, pp. 90, 150, refers to the 'son unnatural or illegitimate of a gentleman'; *CSPD*, 1673–75, pp. 327–8.

43 TNA, SP 29/93 fol. 66; SP 29/198 fol.13; AO3/290, p. 27; E351/2829, accounts of the office of the robes 1672–73, allowing embroidered leeks for Monmouth, his wife and child; *Pepys*, V, pp. 20–1.

44 Burnet, OA, I, pp. 469–70; SP29/232, fol. 134; *HMC: 10th Report, Appendix, Part IV: The Manuscripts of the Earl of Westmorland*, London, 1885, p. 114. See also K. H. D. Haley, *The First Earl of Shaftesbury*, Oxford, 1968, p. 277, for Lord Conway writing to Ormonde of the real expectation of the king's acknowledging he had married Monmouth's mother in November 1667.

45 *Pepys*, VII, p. 596.

46 Burnet, OA, I, pp. 469–70.

47 *CSPVen*, 1669–70, pp. 79–80; Saint-Maurice, *Lettres sur la Cour de Louis XIV*, I, pp. 176–7.

48 Miller, *James II*, p. 58; Clarke, *Life of King James*, I, pp. 400–1.

Chapter 7: The Soldier and the Sun King

1 Paul Sonnino, *Louis XIV and the Origins of the Dutch War*, Cambridge, 1988.

2 Carl J. Ekberg, *The Failure of Louis XIV's Dutch War*, Chapel Hill, 1979, ch. VII; Ronald Hutton, 'The religion of Charles II', in R. Malcolm Smuts (ed.), *The Stuart Courts and Europe*, Cambridge, 1996, pp. 228–47; Ronald Hutton, 'The making of the secret treaty of Dover', *The Historical Journal*, 29, 2, Jun. 1986, pp. 295–318.

3 Saint-Maurice, *Lettres sur la Cour de Louis XIV*, I, p. 417; Hartmann, *Charles II and Madame*, pp. 296–308.

4 Hartmann, *Charles II and Madame*, pp. 296–308; *London Gazette*, 469, 12 May 1670; *Memoirs of Mademoiselle de Montpensier*, III, pp. 54–60; PRO31/3/124, fol. 188v.

5 DRO, D/FSI, Box 275, Monmouth's Accounts 1668–70; BL Add MS 5542, Household Accounts of the Duke and Duchess of Monmouth, fol. 3r; Hartmann, *Charles II and Madame*, p. 308.

6 *CSPD*, 1670, pp. 222, 230, 234, 240; *Heroick Life*, pp. 22–3.

7 *Roscius Anglicanus: or an Historical Review of the Stage*, London, 1711, p. 29; BL Add MS 5542; Household Accounts of the Duke and Duchess of Monmouth, fol. 3r.

8 Hartmann, *Charles II and Madame*, pp. 329–37.

9 *CPSD*, 1670, p. 301.

10 Hartmann, *Charles II and Madame*, pp. 329–37; *Heroick Life*, pp. 24–5.

11 TNA, PC2/62, fol. 83v; *JHL*, 1666–75, pp. 351–3; BL Add MS 5542, Household Accounts of the Duke and Duchess of Monmouth, fol. 18v (99); *Bulstrode Papers*, I, pp. 155, 156.

12 *JHL*, 1666–75, *passim*.

13 *Burnet*, OA, I, pp. 488–9; *JHC* 1667–87, p. 188; *Marvell*, II, pp. 388–90; de Forest Lord et al. (eds), *Poems on Affairs of State*, I, pp. 169–71.

14 Westergaard (ed.), *The First Triple Alliance*, pp. 360, 365; *Reresby Memoirs* p. 81; *CSPVen*, 1671–72, pp. 1–14; *Marvell*, II, pp. 388–90.

15 *CSPD*, 1666–67, p. 263; *Marvell*, II, pp. 391–2; de Forest Lord et al. (eds), *Poems on Affairs of State*, I, pp. 172–6.

16 See, for example, National Maritime Museum, MEC0734.

17 Saint-Maurice, *Lettres sur la Cour de Louis XIV*, II, p. 77, 83–4; *Bulstrode Papers*, I, pp. 182, 184.

18 *CSPVen*, 1671–72, pp. 51–4; Sonnino, *Louis XIV and the Origins of the Dutch War*.

19 *CSPVen*, 1671–72, p. 51; *Bulstrode Papers*, I, p. 187.

20 *HMC Buccleuch*, I, p. 503; *Hatton*, I, pp. 77, 79; *CSPD*, 1671–72, p. 92.

21 *CSPVen*, 1671–72, pp. 172, 197.

22 Westergaard (ed.), *The First Triple Alliance*, pp. 503, 504; *CSPVen*, 1671–72, p. 170; *Bulstrode Papers*, I, p. 229.

23 TNA, LC5/139, 16 Mar 1672.

24 *HMC Buccleuch*, I, p. 514.

25 *CSPVen*, 1671–72, p. 197; Childs, *Army of Charles II*, pp. 245–6; Charles Dalton, *English Army Lists and Commissions, 1661–1714*, 6 vols, London, 1892–1904, I, p. xvi; M. Monmerque (ed.), *Lettres de Madame de Sévigné de sa Famille et de ses Amis*, Paris, 1862–6, 14 vols, III, pp. 57–9; *CSPVen*, 1671–72, pp. 197–200; M. Beryl Curran (ed.), *The Despatches of William Perwich, English Agent in Paris, 1669–1677*, London, 1903, pp. 214, 216; *CSPD*, 1671–72, p. 291; *Bulstrode Papers*, I, pp. 231, 236.

26 *HMC Le Fleming*, VII, p. 92; *London Gazette*, 682, 30 May–3 Jun. 1672; *Heroick Life*, pp. 31–7.

27 *London Gazette*, 686, 17–20 Jun 1672; *Memoirs of Mademoiselle de Montpensier*, III, p. 170; William Young, *International Politics and Warfare in the Age of Louis XIV and Peter the Great*, New York, 2004, pp. 129–31; Ekberg, *Failure of Louis XIV's Dutch War*, pp. 13–15.

28 Westergaard (ed.), *The First Triple Alliance*, pp. 326, 346–7, 356; *CSPVen*, 1671–72, pp. 249–50; *Memoirs of Mademoiselle de Montpensier*, III, p. 170; *Bulstrode Papers*, I, pp. 207, 240.

29 Saint-Maurice, *Lettres sur la Cour de Louis XIV*, II, p. 385; *CSPVen*, 1671–72, p. 269; BL Add 22,878, fos 129r–v, 131–5; *CSPD*, 1672–73, p. 529; *Bulstrode Papers*, I, p. 240.

30 TNA, SP29/311, fol. 250r; BL, Add 22,878, fos 131–5; Fraser, *Scotts of Buccleuch*, II, p. 397; *Bulstrode Papers*, I, p. 242.

31 BL Add 22,878, fos 131–5; TNA, SP105/101, *passim*.

32 D. J. H. Clifford (ed.), *The Diaries of Anne Clifford*, Stroud, 1990, p. 207.

33 'He talks of returning to the army immediately after the delivery of the duchess, his wife, which is expected at any moment', *CSPVen*, 1671–72, p. 271; *Bulstrode Papers*, I, p. 244; 'The Duke of Monmouth is also returned, and is friend now again with his wife', *CSPD*, 1672, p. 479.

34 Bod. Lib Carte MS 33, 421–2, James Buck, the Duke of Ormond's agent to Sir George Lane, on 7 Oct 1665 from Moor Park, 'my lady Monmouth is come to live in this Towne, and has greate inclination to be here . . .' For this reference and much other advice regarding Moor Park I am indebted to Dr Sally Jeffery.

35 TNA, LC5/201, p. 158 (for Monmouth's lodgings at Audley End in the autumn of 1668), p. 160 (for Monmouth's enormous lodgings at Newmarket in 1674).

36 *CSPD*, 1664–65, p. 582; 1665–66, pp. 35, 38; DRO, FSI 275, Duke and Duchess of Monmouth's Accounts 1667–68, pp. 58–9 includes £879 spent on building; TNA, WORK5/13, fol. 154; BL Add MS 5542, fol. 27r (118), for £1,536 spent on upholstery and furniture in 1669–70.

37 *HMC Ormonde*, III, p. 445; *Calendar of Treasury Books*, 1669–72, pp. 358, 417; BL Add MS 5542, Household Accounts of the Duke and Duchess of Monmouth, fol. 29v (125); DRO, FSI Box 275, Expenses 1668–70, pp. 134, 143; 'the purchase of Moor Parke was not approved of by Sr Stephen Fox till my Lord Duke was resolved upon it, and then twas best to get it paid for which he did and that with its furniture cost 13,200li', BL Add MS 51,326, fos 25v–26r, BL Add MS 5542.

38 DRO/FSI, Box 275, Monmouth's Accounts 1670–72, Jan.–Mar. 1672/73.

39 *CSPD*, 1673, p. 124; DRO, FSI 275, Monmouth's Accounts 1670–72, pp. 45–7.

40 DRO, FSI 275, Monmouth's Accounts 1670–72, pp. 53–8.

41 BL Add MS 51,326, fos 25v–26r; DRO, FSI 275, Monmouth's Accounts 1670–72, pp. 53–8; *Heroick Life*, pp. 37–9; TNA, LC5/107, 158v; *Bulstrode Papers*, I, p. 247.

42 *CSPVen*, 1671–72, p. 326; the household accounts make it clear that the Monmouths stayed at Moor Park on occasions through 1671 and 1672.

43 *CSPD*, 1672–73, pp. 286, 312–14; *Heroick Life*, pp. 40–1.

44 *CSPVen*, 1671–72, p. 321; *Hatton*, I, p. 98.

45   'Il a néanmoins offert au dit duc, afin qu'il eut quelque commandement considérable, de le faire brigadier et meme maréchal de camp. Il n'a voulu accepter que le premier de ces deux emplois disant qu'il n'en sait pas encore assez pour exercer celui de maréchal de camp, quoiqu'il ait servi la dernière campagne à la tête de son régiment, que ce soit un homme d'esprit et d'applicant et qui a eu une belle éducation. C'est un homme des mieux faits que j'aie vus et auquel le roi, son père, voudrait bien laisser sa couronne et il ne le fait servir dans les armées de terre et de mer que pour le mettre en estime dans l'esprit de ses peuples': Saint-Maurice, *Lettres sur la Cour de Louis XIV*, II, p. 476.

46   *Bulstrode Papers*, I, pp. 258, 261.

47   *London Gazette*, 778, 24–28 Apr. 1673; *CSPD*, 1673, p. 165; Guy Rowlands, *The Dynastic State and the Army under Louis XIV, 1661–1701*, Cambridge, 2010; *Heroick Life*, p. 44.

48   TNA, SP78/137, fos 116–117v.

49   James Falkner, *Marshal Vauban and the Defence of Louis XIV's France*, Barnsley, 2011, pp. 79–80.

50   Louis XIV, *Oeuvres de Louis XIV: Mémoires et Pièces Militaires*, Paris, 1806, III, pp. 333, 339–42; Curran (ed.), *Despatches of William Perwich*, p. 251; *London Gazette*, 792, 19–23 Jun. 1673; *Heroick Life*, pp. 46–53; TNA, SP78/137, fos 76r–v.

51   TNA, SP78/137, fos 87r–v.

52   Ibid., fos 112r–v.

53   Ibid., fos 112r–v, 114r, 116–117v, 130r–v; *London Gazette*, 790, Jun. 1673.

54   J. Balteau (ed.), *Dictionnaire de Biographie Française*, Paris, 1939.

55   '& did him that justice as to give him the honour of taking the Towne', TNA, SP 78/137, fos 141r, 143r–v, 144r, 165r, 166r–v, 169r, 190r; Louis XIV, *Oeuvres*, III, pp. 373–85; *London Gazette*, 790, 792, 19–23 Jun. 1673, 793, 23–26 Jun. 1673; Saint-Maurice, *Lettres sur la cour de Louis XIV*, II, pp. 563–6; *Hatton*, I, pp. 108–9; Gatien Courtilz de Sandras, *The History of the Life and Actions of . . . the Viscount de Turenne*, London, 1686, p. 369. For the certainty of Maastricht falling once the Half Moon had been secured, see Falkner, *Marshal Vauban*, pp. 33, 43–4.

56   Such was the celebrity that the siege of Maastricht brought that some then – and many historians since – sought to play down Monmouth's role. John Sheffield, Earl of Mulgrave, who loathed Monmouth, wrote in his memoirs that the whole thing was a sham, and that Louis had deliberately set up an easy victory which he kept ready 'on purpose 'till his [Monmouth's] day came of commanding': *The Works of John Sheffield, Earl of Mulgrave, Marquis of Normanby, and Duke of Buckingham*, 2 vols, London, 1729, II, p. 25.

57   TNA, SP 78/137, fos 143r, fos 144r.

58   Ibid., fol. 144r.

59   Curran (ed.), *Despatches of William Perwich*, pp. 252–3.

60   TNA, SP 78/137, fos 143r, 169r.

Chapter 8: A Rising Sun

1 Curran (ed.), *Despatches of William Perwich*, p. 253; W. D. Christie (ed.), *Letters Addressed from London to Sir Joseph Williamson while Plenipotentiary at the Congress of Cologne in the years 1673 and 1674*, 2 vols, Camden Society, New Series, VIII, I, pp. 62–4, 105; Louis XIV, *Oeuvres*, III, p. 412.

2 Christie (ed.), *Letters to Sir Joseph Williamson*, I, pp. 118–19.

3 Ibid., pp. 137, 140.

4 *Hatton*, I, p. 107; Christie (ed.), *Letters to Sir Joseph Williamson*, I, pp. 118–19.

5 DRO, D/FSI, Box 275.

6 *Pepys*, IV, pp. 98–9; London Metropolitan Archives, MR/R.S/001/2, nos 216, 218.

7 Christie (ed.), *Letters to Sir Joseph Williamson*, I, pp. 91–2, 105, 108, 118–19, 125; *Hatton*, I, pp. 109, 110; *CSPVen*, 1673–75, p. 78.

8 Donald Crawford (ed.), *Journals of Sir John Lauder Lord Fountainhill 1665–1676*, Edinburgh, 1900, p. 222; Charles R. Young, *The Royal Forests of Medieval England*, Leicester, 1979; *Manwood's Treatise of the Forest Laws*, London, 1717; *CSPD*, 1676–77, p. 415; *HMC: 10th Report, Appendix, Part IV: the Manuscripts of the Earl of Westmorland*, p. 166.

9 *CSPD*, 1673, p. 194; *Victoria County History: A History of the County of York East Riding, vol. 1: The City of Kingston upon Hull*, edited by K. J. Allison, London, 1969. I am grateful to Professor John Miller for his advice on the city of Hull.

10 *CSPD*, 1673, p. 480.

11 *Evelyn*, IV, p. 7.

12 Clarke, *Life of King James*, I, pp. 483–5.

13 *CSPD*, 1673, p. 377; Christie (ed.), *Letters to Sir Joseph Williamson*, I, p. 64.

14 Clarke, *Life of King James*, I, pp. 440–1; *A Church History of England*, London, 1742; *Burnet*, OA, I, pp. 295–8; Christie (ed.), *Letters to Sir Joseph Williamson*, I, p. 64.

15 *JHC*, 1667–87, pp. 281–2.

16 TNA, LC5/2, pp. 48–57.

17 *CSPD*, 1673, pp. 524–5; *HMC Le Fleming*, VII, p. 103; Christie (ed.), *Letters to Sir Joseph Williamson*, II, p. 13; *CSPVen*, 1673–75, pp. 105–6.

18 James Vernon to Secretary Williamson, 17 Nov. 1673 in Christie (ed.), *Letters to Sir Joseph Williamson*, I, p. 119; II, p. 73.

19 G. Wingrove Cooke (ed.), *The Life of the First Earl of Shaftesbury from Original Documents in the Possession of the Family*, 2 vols, London, 1836, II, p. 77; Tim Harris, 'Anthony Ashley Cooper, First Earl of Shaftesbury', *ODNB*; Haley, *Shaftesbury*, p. 343.

20 *Evelyn*, III, p. 620.

21 Fraser, *Scotts of Buccleuch*, II, p. 397.

22 TNA, SP29/140, fol. 64; *Pepys*, VII, pp. 371–3; *HMC Le Fleming*, VII, p. 62; *Works of John Sheffield*, II, p. 34.

23 TNA, PRO 30/24/42/57, 26 Feb 1673.

24 Christie (ed.), *Letters to Sir Joseph Williamson*, II, pp. 13, 20; *CSPVen*, 1673–75, p. 78; TNA, SP78/137, fol. 206r.

25 *CSPVen*, 1673–75, pp. 122, 129, 137–8.

26 Osmund Airy (ed.), *The Lauderdale Papers*, vol. III, 1673–1679, Camden Society, NS 38, London, 1895, III, p. 28; *CSPD*, 1673–75, p. 147; Christie (ed.), *Letters to Sir Joseph Williamson*, II, p. 152.

27 John Strype, *Survey of the Cities of London and Westminster*, London, 1720.

28 *Calendar of Treasury Books*, 1672–75, p. 514; *CSPD*, 1673–75, pp. 119, 224.

29 Edward Chamberlayne, *Angliae Notitia*, London, 1684, pp. 150–1.

30 H. M. Colvin (ed.), *The History of the King's Works*, 6 vols, London, 1963–82, IV (II), pp. 162–4; V, pp. 207–8.

31 Christie (ed.), *Letters to Sir Joseph Williamson*, I, pp. 99, 105, 106, 119; II, p. 90; Curran (ed.), *Despatches of William Perwich*, p. 256.

32 DRO, FSI 275, Duke and Duchess of Monmouth's Accounts, 1667–68, pp. 36, 45; *Calendar of Treasury Books*, 1669–72, pp. 169, 170; DRO, FSI 275, Duke and Duchess of Monmouth's Accounts 1667–68, p. 45.

33 DRO, FSI 275, Duke and Duchess of Monmouth's Accounts 1667–68, pp. 42–5.

34 Ibid., p. 50.

35 Ibid., pp. 33–5, 'And for Teaching ye Pages to write and Dance for 6 / mo ending 1669 At 20s each Master for each Page per month £24'.

36 Ibid., 'Rent for a House and Stables for 6 Months ending ye end of Septr 1670, £120'; TNA, SP 78/137, fol. 143r.

37 TNA, SP 29/69, fol. 92.

38 Westergaard (ed.), *The First Triple Alliance*, p. 491.

39 DRO, FSI 275, Duchess of Monmouth's Accounts 1665–67, p. 135; DRO, FSI 275, Monmouths' Accounts 1670–2, pp. 45, 46; Christie (ed.), *Letters to Sir Joseph Williamson*, II, p. 123; *CSPD*, 1673–75, p. 119.

40 *CSPD*, 1673, p. 124; *Calendar of Treasury Books*, 1672–75, p. 159; DRO, D/FSI/274, The Duke of Monmouths Accompt of old Debts contracted before Lady Day 1667, 'Remaines due to the workemen for building at the Mews, repaires and building at the Cockpitt} £657 5s 18d', undated, but mid-1670s; DRO, FSI 275, Duke and Duchess of Monmouth's Accounts 1667–8, pp. 58–9.

41 Hertfordshire Record Office, D/E Na O2, '1674 Duke of Monmouth Master of the Horse'.

42 Hertfordshire Record Office, D/E Na O2, unfoliated 31 Jul. 1674; Colvin (ed.), *History of the King's Works*, V, pp. 207–8.

43 *Survey of London: 16: St Martin-in-the-Fields I: Charing Cross*, London, 1935, pp. 5–16.

44 DRO DFSI/I, Box 269, James Duke of Monmouth, Master of the Horse Accounts.

45 DRO, FSI 275, Monmouths' Accounts 1670–2, pp. 55, 61; *CSPD*, 1672, p. 451; *Calendar of Treasury Books*, 1669–72, p. 1331.

46 *Evelyn*, IV, p. 6; Fraser, *Scotts of Buccleuch*, I, p. 432.

47 *Calendar of Treasury Books*, 1672–75, p. 149; *CSPD*, 1672, p. 479; Christie (ed.), *Letters to Sir Joseph Williamson*, I, p. 40.

48 *HMC Le Fleming*, VII, p. 111.

49 Marie Catherine Baronne d'Aulnoy, *Memoirs of the Court of England in 1675*, G. D. Gilbert (ed.), trans. Lucretia Arthur, London, 1927, pp. 3–9.

50 Paul Hammond (ed.), *Dryden: Selected Poems*, London, 2007, pp. 160–1: 'His motions all accompanied with grace / And paradise was opened in his face' (lines 29–30).

51 Fraser, *Scotts of Buccleuch*, II, pp. 427–8.

52 TNA, SP78/137, fos 116–117v.

53 *OPSH*, I, pp. 76–9; Hartmann, *Charles II and Madame*, pp. 201, 212.

Chapter 9: Care But Not Command

1 Keay, *The Magnificent Monarch*, p. 182; *Evelyn*, IV, p. 42; Anon., *A True Description of the New-Erected Fort at Windsor*, London, 1674; *HMC: Report on the Manuscripts of the Late Reginald Rawdon Hastings, Esq.*, 2 vols, London, 1930, II, p. 165; *CSPVen*, 1673–74, pp. 285–7.

2 TNA, SP78/137, fol. 206r.

3 Ibid., fos 118r, 143r.

4 *CSPD*, 1673–75, pp. 479–80, 547, 566–7; *CSPD*, 1675–76, p. 6.

5 *CSPD*, 1673–75, pp. 547, 575, 393–4; *CSPD*, 1675–76, pp. 6–7, 59; *CSPD*, 1676–77, pp. 410–12.

6 'Articles to be observed by the Duke of Monmouth's regiment of foot', *CSPD*, 1675–76, pp. 91–2, 101; *CSPD*, 1673–75, pp. 575, 603.

7 *CSPD*, 1675–76, p. 62.

8 TNA, SP 29/360 fos 179r–v.

9 *CSPD*, 1670, p. 27; Childs, *Army of Charles II*, pp. 91–3; Christie (ed.), *Letters to Sir Joseph Williamson*, I, pp. 94–108.

10 *Works of John Sheffield*, II, pp. 30–40. Arlington was thought to have been pleased with the arrangement which increased 'his own ease since it saved him the trouble of such affairs, without diminution either to his power or profit'.

11 *CSPD*, 1675–76, p. 303.

12 Ibid., pp. 200, 254–5; *CSPD*, 1673–75, pp. 327–8.

13 In November 1674 he told the Earl of Bath 'that every garrison should entertain one soldier of those that are superannuated and maimed and thereby disabled to do much duty', *CSPD*, 1673–75, pp. 76, 396, 595; *Survey of London*, 11, *Chelsea, Part IV: the Royal Hospital*, London, 1927.

14 *CSPD*, 1676–77, p. 316. See also pp. 41, 96, 346, 479.

15 Ibid., p. 316; *CSPD*, 1677–78, p. 6.

16 *HMC Bath*, II, p. 166; Bod. Lib. Carte MS 228, fol. 172r.

17 *OPSH*, I, pp. 73–4; Clarke, *Life of King James*, I, pp. 493–6; *Works of John Sheffield*, II, pp. 30–40; John Dalrymple, *Memoirs of Great Britain and Ireland*, 3 vols, London, 1790, I, p. 311.

18 *CSPD*, 1673–75, p. 305.

19 Lambeth Palace Library, MS 674, no. 5.

20 Ibid., no. 30; *CSPD*, 1673–75, p. 363; 1676–77, p. 413; 1677–78, pp. 309–10.

21 BL Sloane 1985, fol 95r. I am very grateful to Sandra Howat at Bowhill House for all her assistance with information on paintings, and to the Duke of Buccleuch for showing many to me; BL Add 15897, fol. 3–4; BL Add MS 5542, Household Accounts of the Duke and Duchess of Monmouth; DRO, FSI 275, Monmouths' Accounts 1670–72, pp. 53–8, 61.

22 Lambeth Palace Library, MS 674, no. 6 'My L[or]d D[uke] yesterday began to sitt to Mr Lilly (the best of Painters now) for his Picture in his St George's robes at length wch Lilly hath promised shall bee ready by that time the King comes to Newmarket'; C. H. Cooper, *Annals of Cambridge*, 5 vols, Cambridge, 1842–1908, III, p. 563; J. W. Goodison, *Catalogue of Cambridge Portraits*, Cambridge, 1955, p. xxvi.

23 BL Sloane MS 1985, fol. 95r; *HMC: Report on the Manuscripts of the Late Reginald Rawdon Hastings*, II, p. 165; *CSPD*, 1673–75, pp. 343–4; *HMC 7th Report*, I, p. 468.

24 Antony Griffiths, *The Print in Stuart Britain, 1603–1689*, London, 1998, pp. 225–7; F. W. H. Hollstein, *Dutch and Flemish Etchings, Engravings and Woodcuts, c.1450–1700*, 20 vols, 1929–78, II, pp. 224, 237, 244; *CSPD*, 1675–76, p. 194.

25 Clement Edwards Pike (ed.), *Selections from the Correspondence of Arthur Capel, Earl of Essex*, Camden Third Series, XXIV, London, 1913, pp. 59, 103, 140; Clement E. Pike, 'The Intrigue to Deprive the Earl of Essex of the Lord Lieutenancy of Ireland', *Transactions of the Royal Historical Society*, Third Series, vol. 5, 1911, pp. 89–103; *CSPD*, 1677–78, p. 202.

26 *CSPD*, 1673–75, p. 490; 1675–76, pp. 183–4, 194.

27 *Bulstrode Papers*, I, p. 311.

28 *HMC Rutland*, II, p. 34.

29 *London Gazette*, 955, 11–14 Jan. 1674; *London Gazette*, 1125, 28–31 Aug. 1676.

30 TNA SP29/437, fol. 121.

31 *OPSH*, I, pp. 76–9; *CSPD*, 1673–75, p. 366; 1675–76, pp. 153, 439, 497; 1680–81, pp. 687–8; 1675–76, pp. 63–7; Addenda 1660–85, pp. 346–7; 1678, pp. 499–500; Fea, *King Monmouth*, 'Appendix A: Mary Walter'; John Childs, *Nobles and Gentlemen and the Profession of Arms in Restoration Britain 1660–1688: A Biographical Dictionary of British Army Officers on Foreign Service*, London, 1987, p. 105; *Calendar of Treasury Papers*, vol. 1: 1556–1696 (1868), pp. 438–51; Pike (ed.), *Selections from the Correspondence of Arthur Capel*, p. 85; P. A. C. Wauchope, *Patrick Sarsfield and the Williamite War*, Dublin, 1992, chapter 1; H. C. Fanshawe, *The History of the Fanshawe Family*, Newcastle, 1927, pp. 256ff; Scott, *Lucy Walter, Wife or Mistress*, chapter 11; Anon., *A True and*

Wonderful Account of a Cure of the King's Evil by Mrs Fanshawe Sister to his Grace the Duke of Monmouth, London, 1681.

32 Peter Killigrew to his sister, 14 Mar 1675/76, sold at Sotheby's London, 27 May 2004, Sale L 04408, lot 224; George Etherege, *The Man of Mode*, John Barnard (ed.), London, 1979.

33 BL, Add MS 5542, Household Accounts 1669–71, fol. 30v; *HMC Rutland*, II, p. 27; *Bulstrode Papers*, I, pp. 304–5; Burke and Burke (eds), *Extinct and Dormant Baronetcies*, p. 546.

34 *HMC 7th Report*, I, p. 465; *Bulstrode Papers*, I, p. 311.

35 *HMC Rutland*, II, p. 27; d'Aulnoy, *Memoirs of the Court of England in 1675*, pp. 21–6; *Works of John Sheffield*, II, pp. 30–40; *HMC 7th Report*, I, p. 465; *CSPD*, 1683 (1), p. 372.

Chapter 10: The Ties Begin to Break

1 *JHC*, 1667–1687, pp. 314–16.

2 *JHL*, 1666–75, pp. 652–6; *History of the King's Works*, V, pp. 391–5; Philip Mansel, *Dressed to Rule: Royal and Court Costume from Louis XIV to Elizabeth II*, London, 2005, p. 15. Monmouth wore white shoes with red heels, which Louis XIV made fashionable in the early 1670s, in the full-length portrait in Garter robes by Peter Lely of the previous year and very likely wore them with his Parliament robes, as his father certainly did (see full-length portrait in Parliament robes by John Michael Wright in the Royal Collection).

3 Haley, *Shaftesbury*, p. 374.

4 *JHL*, 1666–75, pp. 652–6.

5 *JHC*, 1667–87, pp. 318–19.

6 *JHL*, 1695–81, pp. 3–35.

7 *JHL*, 1666–75, pp. 652–730; 1675–81, pp. 3–35.

8 *Letter from a Person of Quality to his Friend in the Country*, London, 1675.

9 *JHL*, 1675–81, pp. 41–2, 63–4; *HMC Portland*, III, p. 355; K. H. D. Haley, 'Shaftesbury's Lists of the Lay Peers and Members of the Commons, 1677–8', *Bulletin of the Institute of Historical Research*, 1940, 43, pp. 86–105.

10 BL Lansdowne 1236, fol. 128; *London Gazette*, 1284, 1–11 Mar. 1677.

11 *CSPD*, 1677–78, p. 278; *HMC 7th Report*, I, pp. 370, 469; Bod. Lib. Carte MS 39, fol. 58r.

12 *CSPD*, 1677–78, pp. 295, 312, 328, 347; Olaf van Nimwegen, *The Dutch Army and the Military Revolutions, 1588–1688*, Woodbridge, 2010, pp. 503–4.

13 *CSPD*, 1677–78, p. 347; *HMC Ormonde*, IV, p. 35.

14 *Reresby Memoirs*, p. 82.

15 *CSPD*, 1677–78, p. 431.

16 Ibid., p. 467.

17 George Percy Elliott (ed.), 'Diary of Dr Edward Lake, Chaplain and Tutor to the Princesses Mary and Anne, 1677–1678', *Camden Miscellany* I, 1847, pp. 5–10; *Evelyn*, IV, p. 122; *Hatton*, I, pp. 151–4; *HMC Ormonde*, IV, p. 54; *HMC Le Fleming*, VII, p. 141; *HMC 7th Report*, p. 494.

18 *CSPD*, 1677–78, p. 531.

19 *Reresby Memoirs*, pp. 133–4; *HMC Ormonde*, IV, p. 111.

20 *CSPD*, 1677–78, pp. 639, 641–2; 1678, p. 6.

21 *CSPD*, 1678, p. 6.

22 Ibid., pp. 8, 11, 15; TNA, SP44/52, p. 1.

23 Fraser, *Scotts of Buccleuch*, II, p. 400; BL Add MS 32,095, fos 81–2.

24 *CSPD* 1678, pp. 16–24.

25 TNA SP 44/52, p. 11; *HMC Rutland*, II, p. 48; *HMC Buccleuch*, I, 328; *CSPD*, 1678, pp. 23–4.

26 *JHL*, 1675–81, pp. 129–31.

27 *CSPD*, 1678, p. 110.

28 TNA, SP44/52, fol. 1.

29 *CSPD*, 1677–78, p. 582.

30 *HMC Ormonde*, IV, p. 108; *CPSD*, 1677–78, p. 582.

31 *CSPD*, 1672–73, p. 508; 1673–75, p. 250; 1676–77, p. 223.

32 *CSPD*, 1677–78, pp. 32–3.

33 Ibid., 1677–78, pp. 92–3.

34 Gillian H. MacIntosh, *The Scottish Parliament under Charles II 1660–1685*, Edinburgh, 2007.

35 Julia Buckroyd, *Church and State in Scotland*, Edinburgh, 1980, chapter 10; *Extracts from the Records of the Royal Burgh of Lanark*, Glasgow, 1893, p. 230.

36 *HMC Hamilton*, p. 164.

37 *HMC: 10th Report, Appendix, Part VI: The Manuscripts of the Marquess of Abergavenny, Lord Braye of c.*, pp. 183–5; Robert Wodrow, *The History of the Sufferings of the Church of Scotland*, 2 vols, London, 1721, II, pp. 434–44; *Register of the Privy Council of Scotland*, 3rd series, 16 vols, Edinburgh, 1908–70, V, pp. 420–1. It was not the first time an attempt had been made to lobby Monmouth on Scottish politics: 15 Mar. 1676, 'Some say Atholl's going up presently bott I don't beleiv't; he wes at the Wyms two days last week, and tho' his bussines be'nt certanly known, yett I believ its to mack that noble lady interpois with the Duke and Duchess of Monmuth to the Chancellor's prejudeice'; *HMC Hamilton*, p. 154.

38 TNA, GD112/39/124/16.

39 Airy (ed.), *Lauderdale Papers*, III, pp. 103–6.

40 Ibid., pp. 108, 241; Mark Goldie et al. (ed.), *Entring Book*, II, p. 56.

41 Airy (ed.), *Lauderdale Papers*, III, p. 115.

42 Ibid., p. 123.

43 Ibid., p. 116.

44 Ibid., pp. 121–2.

45 Ibid., pp. 125, 126–7, 145, 150.

46 *Burnet*, OA, II, p. 147.

47 Airy (ed.), *Lauderdale Papers*, III, pp. 152–3.

48 TNA, SP29/62, fol. 159; LC5/107, fol. 97r; *CSPD*, 1673–75, p. 305; Hertfordshire Record Office, D/E Na O2, unfoliated 31 Jul. 1674.

49 TNA, SP29/403, fol. 36; the warrant was reissued a week later with clarification on the geography of the command SP44/44, fol. 87.

50 TNA, SP29/403, fol. 124.

51 Clarke, *Life of King James*, I, pp. 496–7; TNA, SP30/G, fol. 729.

52 *HMC: The Laing Manuscripts at Edinburgh University*, I, London, 1914, p. 414.

Chapter 11: Finding New Friends

1 John A. Lynn, *The Wars of Louis XIV*, London, 1999, p. 154; John Childs, 'Monmouth and the army in Flanders', *Journal of the Society of Army Historical Research*, 52, 1974, pp. 3–12; Nimwegen, *The Dutch Army and the Military Revolutions*, p. 510; TNA, SP44/52, fos 63–75; *HMC 7th Report*, I, p. 494; *London Gazette*, 1328, 8–12 Aug 1678; *Heroick Life*, pp. 72–5; Aubrey du Maurier, *The Lives of All the Princes of Orange*, London, 1693, p. 299.

2 *CSPD*, 1678, pp. 355–56; TNA, SP44/52, fos 63–75.

3 *HMC Ormonde*, IV, p. 178; TNA, SP44/52, fos 63–75.

4 TNA, WORK5/1, fol. 190; WORK5/3, fol. 149v; WORK5/5, fol. 26; WORK5/11, fol. 83v; WORK5/21, fol. 79; TNA, PC2/66, p. 392; Simon Thurley, *Whitehall Palace: An Architectural History*, London and New Haven, 1999.

5 *Burnet*, OA, II, p. 157.

6 *CSPD*, 1678, p. 420.

7 Roger North, *Examen*, London, 1740, p. 225; *Burnet*, OA, II, p. 257.

8 TNA, PC2/66 fol. 396.

9 *CSPD*, 1674–79, p. 451; *Burnet*, OA, II, p. 161.

10 TNA, PC2/66, fol. 402.

11 *JHL*, 1675–81, pp. 198–9, 310–12.

12 *HMC House of Lords*, p. 17; *JHL*, 1675–81, pp. 331–4.

13 *JHL*, 1675–81, pp. 304–6; *HMC House of Lords*, p. 54.

14 *CSPD*, 1678, p. 542; *JHL*, 1675–81, pp. 350–5; *Heroick Life*, pp. 74–5.

15 John Kenyon, *The Popish Plot*, London, 1972, pp. 52–88.

16 TNA, PC2/66, fol. 397.

17 *JHL*, 1675–81, pp. 309–10.

18 North, *Examen*, p. 177.

19 *CSPD*, 1678, p. 453; *Reresby Memoirs*, p. 154.

20 George Treby, *A Collection of Letters and Other Writings Relating to the Horrid Popish Plot*, London, 1681.

21 *JHC*, 1667–87, pp. 536–7; *HMC Ormonde*, IV, pp. 467ff; *JHL*, 1675–81, pp. 345–6.

22 Tim Harris, *The London Crowds in the Reign of Charles II*, Cambridge, 1987, pp. 158–9; *HMC Ormonde*, IV, pp. 470, 473.

23 *HMC Ormonde*, IV, p. 207.

24 *JHC*, 1667–87, pp. 559–60.

25 *JHL*, 1675–81, pp. 409–10; *CSPD*, 1678, pp. 570, 584–5, 593, 1679–80.

26 *CSPD*, 1678, pp. 64, 528–9.

27 *CSPD*, 1679–80, pp. 104, 115, 116, 124–5, 127–9.

28 *HMC Ormonde*, IV, p. 493.

29 Haley, *Shaftesbury*, p. 449; TNA, PRO 31/3/139, 3/13 Jun. 1678.

30 *HMC Ormonde*, IV, p. 493.

31 Haley, *Shaftesbury*, p. 500.

32 Ibid., p. 512; *The Works of Sir William Temple Bart.*, 4 vols, London, 1814, II, pp. 491–2, 507; Clarke, *Life of King James*, I, p. 513.

33 *CSPD*, 1677–78, pp. 174, 590.

34 *HMC Ormonde*, V, p. 1; prints of Monmouth in the late 1670s include that engraved by Faithorne, sold by John Overton at Newgate, the Blooteling engraving of the Lely portrait in Garter robes, and an image of him on horseback entitled 'Princeps' sold on Bishopsgate Street.

35 Dalrymple, *Memoirs of Great Britain and Ireland*, I, p. 312.

36 *HMC 7th Report*, I, p. 465.

37 *CSPD*, 1673, p. 458; 1671–72, p. 291; 1673–75, p. 237; Christie (ed.), *Letters to Sir Joseph Williamson*, I, p. 137; *Calendar of Treasury Books*, 1672–75, p. 732; Pike (ed.), *Selections from the Correspondence of Arthur Capel*, p. 103.

38 *HMC 7th Report*, I, p. 472. See also the tortuous Chinese whispers of the rumour Monmouth was to be made Prince of Wales, in Danby's report of Nov. 1678, BL Add MS 28,043, fos 1r–v; Dalrymple, *Memoirs of Great Britain and Ireland*, I, pp. 258–9.

39 *JHC*, 1667–87, pp. 573–4; *Entring Book*, II, p. 115; *HMC Ormonde*, V, p. 8.

40 *Burnet*, OA, II, pp. 207–8; Haley, *Shaftesbury*, pp. 512–14; *CSPD*, 1679–80, p. 125; *HMC Foljambe*, p. 129; *Reresby Memoirs*, p. 176; *Works of Sir William Temple, Bart.*, II, pp. 510–12. For the debate about the genesis of the new Privy Council see E. R. Turner, 'The Privy Council of 1679', *EHR*, 30, 118 (Apr 1915), pp. 251–70.

41 TNA, PC2/68, fol. 3.

42 *JHC*, 1667–87, pp. 619–20; Haley, *Shaftesbury*, pp. 520–1.

43 *HMC Ormonde*, IV, p. 520.

44 *Ailesbury Memoirs*, I, p. 35.

Chapter 12: Icarus

1 David Symson, *A True and Impartial Account of the Life of the Most Reverend Father in God Dr James Sharp*, London, 1723, pp. 142–5; *Burnet*, OA, II, pp. 236–8; TNA, PC2/68, p. 104; *HMC Ormonde*, V, p. 127.

2 BL Add MS 23,244, fol. 5r; *CSPD*, 1679–80, pp. 163–4.

3 Henry Sidney, *Diary of the Times of Charles II,* edited by R. W. Blencowe, 2 vols, London, 1843, I, p. 9; C. Sanford Terry, 'The Duke of Monmouth's Instructions in 1679', *EHR*, 20 (77), Jan. 1905, pp. 127–9; *HMC 7th Report*, I, p. 472.

4 *HMC Ormonde*, IV, p. 524, V, p. 133; Sidney, *Diary*, I, p. 4.

5 Mark Napier (ed.), *Memorials and letters illustrative of the life and times of John Graham of Claverhouse, Viscount Dundee*, 3 vols, Edinburgh, 1859–62, I, pp. 386–7; *HMC Ormonde*, V, p. 135–6, Monmouth was given the right 'to pardon, treat and relax them of their burthens, as he shall see cause; else I hear he would not have gone on that errand . . .'; *Sidney–Savile*, London, 1742, p. 81.

6 BL Add MS 23,244, fos 8r–11; Sidney, *Diary*, I, p. 13; *Reresby Memoirs*, pp. 183–5; *Heroick Life*, p. 80.

7 *Sidney–Savile*, p. 72.

8 Airy (ed.), *Lauderdale Papers*, III, p. 261; BL Add MS 23,244, fol. 14; *HMC Hamilton*, p. 162.

9 BL, Add MS 23,244, fol. 12r; *Sidney–Savile*, pp. 114–16.

10 BL Add MS 23,244, fol. 16r ; *London Gazette*, 1419, 23–27 Jun 1679; Airy (ed.), *Lauderdale Papers*, III, p. 173; *HMC Ormonde*, IV, p. 527; Luttrell, *State Affairs*, I, p. 16; Anon., *A Further Account of the Proceedings against the Rebels in Scotland*, Edinburgh, 1679; Anon., *A True Account of the Great Victory Obtained over the Rebels in Scotland*, Edinburgh, 1679; *Heroick Life*, pp. 81–7.

11 *Burnet*, OA, II, p. 240; *HMC Foljambe*, p. 133; BL Add MS 23,244, fol. 45r; Clarke, *Life of King James*, I, p. 559; *Sidney–Savile*, p. 139; Alexander Shields, *A Hind Let Loose or an Historical Representation of the Testimonies of the Church of Scotland*, 1687, p. 128.

12 *HMC: Report on the Manuscripts of the Late Reginald Rawdon Hastings*, II, p. 388; Bod. Lib. Carte MS 39, fol. 68.

13 Andrew Browning, *Thomas Osborne, Earl of Danby and Duke of Leeds, 1632–1712*, 3 vols, Glasgow, 1944–51, I, pp. 298–9; Clarke, *Life of King James*, I, p. 525.

14 'Proceedings against Lord Danby, 1679', printed in Browning, *Danby*, III, p. 141.

15 'A list of the House of Lords', printed in Browning, *Danby*, III, p. 144.

16 'Lords names that votyed for and against the bill of attainder 79', printed in Browning, *Danby*, III, p. 149.

17 'Lords present, 10 May 1679, att the vote not to have a committee . . .', printed in Browning, *Danby*, III, p. 134.

18 *HMC Foljambe*, pp. 129–31; Clarke, *Life of King James*, I, pp. 552–3.

19 Clarke, *Life of King James*, I, p. 553.

20 TNA, PC2/67, fol. 62.

21 *CSPD*, 1679–80, p. 250.

22 Haley, *Shaftesbury*, p. 535; *Sidney–Savile*, p. 95; BL Add MS 32,682, fol. 5r.

23 'Lords present at the prorogation, 27 May 1679', printed in Browning, *Danby*, III, p. 137.

24 For an assessment of the options in May 1679, see *Sidney–Savile*, pp. 51–4.

25 *D'Avaux*, I, p. 61.

26 Monmouth was in touch with William III in Aug 1679, his continuing admiration expressed in the message of thanks he sent the stadtholder for 'the favours' William did Monmouth in relation to the army. BL Add MS 32,682, fos 10r–v.

27 NAS, GD224/882/7, no 4. The battle paintings are at Bowhill. I am grateful
    to Sandra Howarth and Crispin Powell for their assistance. One is now
    labelled 'Battle of Morville 1678', but perhaps shows the Battle of St Denis
    of that year in which Monmouth and William fought together.

28 *HMC Le Fleming*, p. 112; Colvin (ed.), *History of the King's Works*, V, p. 316.

29 TNA, LC5/193, pp. 54, 55, 58; *Calendar of Treasury Books, 1676–79*,
    pp. 1152–3.

30 BL Add MS 32,682, fol. 5r.

31 Temple, *Works*, II, p. 524; TNA, PC2/68, p. 161; *Sidney–Savile*, p. 124;
    Simon Thurley, *Hampton Court: A Social and Architectural History*,
    London and New Haven, 2003, p. 141.

32 Temple, *Works*, II, pp. 526–7; Airy (ed.), *Lauderdale Papers*, III, p. 173;
    Burnet, OA, II, p. 241; *CSPD, 1679–80*, p. 195; Clarke, *Life of King James*,
    I, p. 559; Anon., *News from Windsor*, London, 1679.

33 BL Add MS 32,682, fol. 9v.

34 *Entring Book*, II, p. 37.

35 Fraser, *Scotts of Buccleuch*, I, p. 437.

36 TNA, WORK5/23, fos 128v, 422–32; DRO, D/FSI/274, 'An Accompt of
    their Graces Debt', BL Sloane 1985, fol. 95r, suggesting that the building
    works were paid for by Monmouth but the fitting out by the Office of
    Works. DRO, D/FSI/274, Monmouths' debts before 1667, Mar–May 1667.

37 TNA, SP78/137, fol. 116v.

38 TNA, PROB11/349, fol. 195.

39 TNA, WORK5/23, fos 128v, 422–32; DRO, D/FSI/274, 'An Accompt of
    their Graces Debt'.

40 BL, Sloane MS 1985, fol. 95r.

41 *Memorials of the Family of Wemyss of Wemyss*, III, p. 123; Fraser, *Scotts of
    Buccleuch*, I, p. 434.

42 Sidney, *Diary*, I, p. 9; Clarke, *Life of King James*, I, pp. 566–7.

43 DRO, FSI, BOX 238 1661/2–1714; *CSPD, 1679–80*, p. 243; BL Add MS
    51,326, fol. 4–5; Howard Colvin and Alison Maguire, 'A collection of
    seventeenth-century architectural plans', *Architectural History*, 35, 1992,
    pp. 164–5.

44 *HMC Ormonde*, IV, p. 532; V, p. 178; *HMC Finch, Manuscripts of Allan
    George Finch*, 2 vols, London, 1913–22, II, p. 56; Haley, *Shaftesbury*, p. 547.

45 *Sidney–Savile*, pp. 131–3.

46 *HMC Foljambe*, p. 137; *CSPD, 1679–80*, pp. 226–8.

47 *CSPD, 1679–80*, p. 226.

48 Haley, *Shaftesbury*, p. 537; TNA, PC2/66, fol. 168; *Sidney–Savile*, p. 151.

49 William Temple, who counted Halifax and Essex as his friends and
    Monmouth as his enemy, ascribed their actions during the king's illness to
    self-interest: Temple, *Works*, II, pp. 531–4; Sidney, *Diary*, I, p. 176.

50 *HMC Foljambe*, p. 137; Temple, *Works*, II, pp. 531–4; Clarke, *Life of King
    James*, I, pp. 566–7. The Earl of Feversham also wrote to York along similar
    lines: *Ailesbury Memoirs*, I, p. 41; *Reresby Memoirs*, p. 187.

51 *CSPD*, 1679–80, pp. 226–70.

52 Clarke, *Life of King James*, I, pp. 566–7. For the king's shaving regime see Keay, *The Magnificent Monarch*, p. 48.

53 *Sidney–Savile*, p. 143.

54 *Hatton*, I, pp. 191–2; *HMC Foljambe*, p. 137; *HMC Fitzherbert*, p. 21; *Sidney–Savile*, p. 143.

55 Clarke, *Life of King James*, I, p. 567.

56 Temple, *Works*, II, pp. 531–4, *Sidney–Savile*, p. 143.

57 *Burnet*, OA, II, 243; *Hatton*, I, p. 194; *CSPD*, 1679–80, pp. 231, 240.

58 Keith Feiling and F. R. D. Needham (eds), 'The Journals of Edmund Warcup, 1676–84', *EHR* 40, 158, Apr. 1925, pp. 235–60, p. 243.

59 This had been Monmouth's own experience of the king, as he recalled to Sidney, *Diary*, I, p. 151.

60 TNA, PRO31/3/143, fos 63–8; *HMC Fitzherbert*, p. 21.

61 Feiling and Needham (eds), 'Journals of Edmund Warcup', p. 243; *HMC Foljambe*, pp. 137–8; *CSPD*, 1679–80, p. 240.

62 Clarke, *Life of King James*, I, pp. 571–4.

63 Bod. Lib. Carte MS 232, fol. 55; Clarke, *Life of King James*, I, pp. 570–2; *Burnet*, OA, II, 243; Sidney, *Diary*, I, pp. 127–8; *HMC Foljambe*, pp. 137–8.

64 *Hatton*, I, p. 194.

65 *HMC 7th Report*, I, p. 475.

66 *HMC Foljambe*, p. 138; *CSPD*, 1679–80, p. 244.

67 *CSPD*, 1679–80, pp. 245–6.

68 Ibid., pp. 243, 247, 250.

69 Ibid., p. 245.

70 Ibid., 1679–80, pp. 245–8.

71 TNA, SP44/164, fol. 25; PC2/68, fos 206, 209; *HMC Foljambe*, p. 138; *HMC 12th Report, Appendix, Part IX: The Manuscripts of the Duke of Beaufort, K.G., the Earl of Donoughmore, and others*, London, 1891, p. 85.

72 *Hatton*, I, p. 195.

73 *HMC Foljambe*, pp. 137–8.

74 TNA, PRO31/3/143, fos 69–70; *HMC 7th Report*, I, p. 495.

75 Sidney, *Diary*, I, p. 151; Bod. Lib. Carte MS 232, fol. 60.

76 *HMC 7th Report*, I, p. 475; Bod. Lib. Carte MS 232, fol. 60; *CSPD*, 1679–80, pp. 251–2; Luttrell, I, p. 21; TNA PROB31/3/143, fol. 77; *State Affairs Hatton*, I, pp. 206–7.

Chapter 13: Exclusion

1 BL Add MS 32,682, fol. 28v; *HMC Beaufort*, p. 85.

2 Bod. Lib. Carte MS 232, fol. 55.

3 Jonathan Israel, *The Dutch Republic*, Oxford, 1995.

4 Sidney, *Diary*, I, pp. 155–6.

5 Ibid., I, p. 130, *D'Avaux*, I, p. 59.

6   *D'Avaux*, I, pp. 58–62; BL Add MS 32,682, fol. 29r.

7   *D'Avaux*, I, pp. 58–9; BL Add MS 32,682, fol. 29r.

8   *D'Avaux*, I, pp. 60–1.

9   Sidney, *Diary*, I, pp. 154–6.

10 '. . . he said it would so vex the Duke', Sidney, *Diary*, I, pp. 154–6, 193.

11 Bod. Lib. Carte MS 232, fol. 60; Miller, *James II,* pp. 98–101; *Reresby Memoirs,* pp. 189–90.

12 *Reresby Memoirs*, pp. 189–90; Sidney, *Diary*, I, pp. 157, 161–2; *The London Gazette*, 1450, 9–13 Oct 1679; *HMC Ormonde*, V, p. 223; *Domestick Intelligence*, 28, 10 Oct 1679; Anon., *A True and Faithful Copy of a Real Letter written by a Friend in Utrecht*, Amsterdam, 1679; *Heroick Life*, p. 94.

13 BL Add MS 32,682, fol. 28v.

14 Sidney, *Diary*, I, pp. 166–8; *London Gazette*, 1452, 16–20 Oct. 1679; 1453, 20–23 Oct. 1679.

15 *CSPD*, 1679–80, p. 284; James Ferguson, *Robert Ferguson the Plotter*, Edinburgh, 1887, pp. 35–8.

16 *A True and Faithful Copy*, 1679.

17 *London Gazette*, 1462, 3–6 Nov. 1679; *Domestick Intelligence*, 20, 17 Oct. 1679.

18 Sidney, *Diary*, I, pp. 188, 190; TNA, PRO31/3/143, fos 106–10.

19 *London Gazette*, 1455, 27–30 Oct. 1679; 1462, 20–24 Nov. 1679; *Hatton*, I, p. 198; Feiling and Needham (eds), 'Journals of Edmund Warcup', p. 245.

20 *Hatton*, I, p. 200; *HMC Ormonde*, IV, pp. 553–7; Feiling and Needham (eds), 'Journals of Edmund Warcup', p. 246; *Heroick Life*, pp. 96–7.

21 *London Gazette*, 1457, 3–6 Nov. 1679; 1462, 20–24 Nov. 1679.

22 *Hatton*, I, p. 205.

23 *HMC Ormonde*, IV, p. 454; TNA PC2/68, p. 390; Sidney, *Diary,* I, p. 188; Haley, *Shaftesbury*, p. 210.

24 *D'Avaux*, I, p. 65.

25 Charles Blount, *An Appeal from the Country to the City*, London, 1679.

26 Sidney, *Diary*, I, p. 185.

27 *Hatton*, I, pp. 202, 205, 206–7; Clarke, *Life of King James,* I, pp. 579–80; *HMC Portland*, III, p. 364; *HMC Ormonde*, V, p. 244; Temple, *Works*, II, p. 546.

28 *Hatton*, I, p. 205; Harris, *London Crowds in the Reign of Charles II*, pp. 160–1; *Heroick Life*, p. 95.

29 *Hatton*, I, p. 206–7; *HMC Ormonde*, V, p. 244.

30 *HMC Ormonde*, V, pp. 244–5, 247; TNA, PRO31/3/143, fos 106–10; *HMC 7th Report*, I, p. 478.

31 *HMC 7th Report*, I, p. 477.

32 *Hatton*, I, p. 205; *HMC 7th Report*, p. 164.

33 *HMC Ormonde*, V, p. 244; Anon., *England's Happiness Restored*, London, 1679; Anon., *England's Overjoy at the Duke of Monmouth's Return*, London, 1679; *Hatton*, I, p. 206.

34 *CSPD*, 1679–80, pp. 292–6; *Entring Book*, II, pp. 208–9; *HMC Le Fleming* p. 164.

35 *HMC Ormonde*, V, p. 247.
36 *HMC 7th Report*, I, p. 478; TNA, PRO31/3/143, fol. 120; John Russell (ed.), *Letters of Rachel, Lady Russell,* 2 vols, London, 1853, I, p. 54.
37 *HMC Ormonde*, IV, p. 262; TNA, PRO31/3/143, fol. 122.
38 Sidney, *Diary*, I, pp. 240, 262–3.
39 *CSPD*, 1673–75, pp. 240–1.
40 Boswell, *The Restoration Court Stage*, p. 320.
41 Sidney, *Diary*, I, p. 262.
42 BL Egerton MS 1527, fol. 15r.
43 Bod. Lib. Carte MS 228, fol. 164r.
44 Bod. Lib. Carte MS 39, fol. 107.
45 Bod. Lib. Carte MS 243, fol. 444r.
46 *HMC 7th Report*, I, p. 472; *HMC Fitzherbert*, p. 21.
47 *Pepys*, III, p. 238; TNA SP29/232, fol. 134.
48 *HMC Ormonde*, V, p. 314; *CSPD*, 1679–80, pp. 449–50, 462–3, 466.
49 *CSPD* 1679–80, pp. 450, 462–3; BL Add MS 28,094, fos 71–2.
50 *HMC Le Fleming*, p. 167; G. Groen Van Prinsterer (ed.), *Archives ou Correspondance Inédite de la Maison d'Orange Nassau*, 15 vols, deuxième série, V, 1650–88, p. 393; TNA, PC2/68, p. 490; *Reresby Memoirs*, p. 182.
51 *CSPD*, 1679–80, p. 460; 'Some unpublished letters of Burnet, the Historian', *Camden Miscellany*, 1907, p. 19; de Forest Lord et al. (eds), *Poems on Affairs of State*, I, pp. 257–60.
52 TNA, PC2/68, p. 490; BL Add MS 32,095, fos 198, 200; *CSPD*, 1679–80, pp. 447–55; *Hatton*, I, p. 225; *HMC Ormonde*, V, p. 311; *Archives ou Correspondance Inédite de la Maison d'Orange Nassau*, p. 397.
53 'Some unpublished letters of Burnet, the Historian', p. 28; *Reresby Memoirs*, p. 194; *CSPD*, 1679–80, p. 497; Clarke, *Life of King James*, I, p. 590.
54 'Some unpublished letters of Burnet, the Historian', pp. 28, 35.
55 *CSPD*, 1679–80, p. 481; Luttrell, *State Affairs,* I, pp. 43, 50.
56 *CSPD*, 1679–80, p. 502; *London Gazette*, 1519, 7–10 June 1680; *HMC Ormonde*, V, p. 329.
57 BL Add MS 28,094, fos 71–2.
58 'Some unpublished letters of Burnet, the Historian', p. 31; Russell (ed.), *Letters of Rachel, Lady Russell*, I, p. 54; de Forest Lord et al. (eds), *Poems on Affairs of State*, I, p. 256: Rochester's poem 'Letter of the Duke of Monmouth to the King' has Charles II shouting to Monmouth: 'Oh! That my pr[ick] when I thy dam did f[uck] / Had in some turkey's a[rse], or a cow's been stuck / Then had I been, when the base deed was done / Sure to have got no rebel to my son' – a measure of the terms in which Lucy was spoken about.

Chapter 14: Opposition Leader

1   TNA, PRO31/3/146, fos 18–19; Bod. Lib., Carte MS 39, fol. 168r. For Monmouth's coaches and the liveries of his stables staff see DRO, D/FSI, Box 275. Monmouth's visit to Chichester with Lord Grey in February

1679/80 was an early instance of his combining hunting and/or horse racing with political canvassing: 'The Reception of the Duke of Monmouth at Chichester', *Sussex Archaeological Collections*, VII, 1854, pp. 169–72.

2   Bod. Lib. Carte MS 39, fol. 168r; *CSPD*, 1679–80, pp. 570, 600.

3   *CSPD*, 1679–80, p. 597; *Entring Book*, II, p. 234–5; *Heroick Life*, pp. 100–5.

4   *CSPD*, 1679–80, p. 604; *Entring Book*, II, p. 235; *HMC Le Fleming*, p. 170; Bod. Lib., Rawl. A 175, fols 174–6.

5   *Archives ou Correspondance Inédite de la Maison d'Orange Nassau*, p. 418; 'The Reception of the Duke of Monmouth at Chichester', pp. 169–72 (the date of the letter published here is Feb. 1679/80, so 1680 in New Series).

6   *Archives ou Correspondance Inédite de la Maison d'Orange Nassau*, p. 418; *Hatton*, I, p. 236.

7   Anon., *His Grace the Duke of Monmouth honoured in his Progress*, London, 1680; Anon., *A True Narrative of the Duke of Monmouth's late Journey into the West*, London, 1680. Real royal healing ceremonies were highly formalised events, and quite unlike this quick encounter in Crewkerne in almost every respect. In healing ceremonies proper (as Monmouth knew well) the king did not say 'God bless you' at any point, and the 'touching' was a very particular double-handed gesture of stroking the supplicant under the chin: see Keay, *Magnificent Monarch*, p. 117.

8   Haley, *Shaftesbury*, p. 584; TNA, PRO31/3/146, fol. 24r.

9   BL Add MS 34,692; *CSPD*, 1680–81, p. 31; *HMC Le Fleming*, pp. 171–2; *HMC Fitzherbert*, p. 23.

10   *HMC Ormonde*, V, p. 449.

11   Ibid., p. 454.

12   BL Add MS 28,938, fos 24r–v.

13   Bod. Lib. Carte MS 228, fol. 153r.

14   *HMC Ormonde*, V, pp. 445, 454, 458; *HMC Dartmouth*, I, p. 60; *Archives ou Correspondance Inédite de la Maison d'Orange-Nassau*, pp. 423–4; Burnet, OA, II, p. 268; *HMC Le Fleming*, p. 174; TNA, PRO31/3/146, fos 122–3; PRO 31/3/147, fol. 1v.

15   *Entring Book*, II, p. 240.

16   *JHC*, 1667–87, pp. 644–5; Lois G. Schwoerer, 'Russell, William, Lord Russell [called the Patriot, the Martyr] (1639–1683)', *ODNB*; 'The Hon. William Russell', *The House of Commons 1660–1690*, 3 vols, London, 1983, pp. 365–9.

17   H. C. Foxcroft (ed.), *The Life and Letters of Sir George Savile, Bart., first Marquis of Halifax*, 2 vols, London, 1898, II, p. 293; 'Debates in 1680: Nov 4th–8th', *Grey's Debates of the House of Commons*, vol. 7, 1769, pp. 415–33.

18   *HMC Ormonde*, V, p. 486.

19   Sidney, *Diary*, II, p. 118; *HMC 7th Report*, I, p. 479.

20   *CSPD*, 1680–81, p. 62; *HMC Le Fleming*, VII, p. 174; Christopher Phillison reported to his correspondent that Monmouth 'hath on his coach painted an heart wounded with two arrows, crosse, the plume of feathers, two Angells bearing up a scarf either side, which some say is P[rince] of

W[ales] Armes'. Some have concluded from this that Monmouth had had the arms of a Prince of Wales painted on his coach. In fact this is extremely unlikely. A heart wounded with arrows with a plume of feathers, with angel supporters, is nothing like the insignia of a Prince of Wales, and cannot in fact be identified as the arms of anyone of the period. If Monmouth really had had his coach painted with the insignia of a Prince of Wales it is unthinkable that it would not have caused more substantial comment than this single piece of hearsay. I am grateful to Patric Dickinson, Clarencieux King of Arms, for his advice on this point.

21 TNA, PRO31/3/147, fos 33r–34v; Bod. Lib. Carte MS 104, fol. 52r; *HMC Ormonde*, V, pp. 488–9.

22 Lambeth Palace Library, MS 674, no. 5; TNA, PRO31/3/147, fol. 34v; *HMC Ormonde*, V, p. 561–2; *Entring Book*, II, p. 419.

23 *JHL*, 1675–81, pp. 610–742.

24 *HMC Le Fleming*, p. 172.

25 *Entring Book*, II, pp. 263, 266; *JHC*, 1667–87, pp. 703–4.

26 TNA, PRO31/3/146, fos 122–3.

27 TNA, PRO31/3/147, fol. 34v; Haley, *Shaftesbury*, p. 603.

28 Haley, *Shaftesbury*, p. 604.

29 *CSPD*, 1680–81, p. 130.

30 Luttrell, *State Affairs*, I, p. 68; *CSPD*, 1680–81, pp. 159–60, 170; *Heroick Life*, pp. 106–8. For his visit the previous year see 'Reception of the Duke of Monmouth at Chichester', pp. 169–72.

31 *A True and Wonderful Account of a Cure of the King's Evil*; Luttrell, *State Affairs*, I, p. 64; Bod. Lib. Carte MS 104, fol. 57; *HMC Bath*, II, p. 169; 10 Feb. *CSPD*, 1680–81, p. 159.

32 *The Oxford Alderman's Speech to the D. of M.*, London, 1681; Anon., *An Answer to the Scoffying and Lying Libell*, London, 1681; Anon., *The Lady Gray Vindicated*, London, 1681; Bod. Lib. Carte MS 104, fol. 57.

33 Clark (ed.), *Anthony Wood*, II, pp. 514–34.

34 TNA, LC5/66, fos 7v–8r.

35 *History of Parliament: the House of Commons 1660–1690*, 'William Wright (1619–93)'; W. D. Christie, *A Life of Anthony Ashley Cooper, First Earl of Shaftesbury*, 2 vols, London, 1871, II, pp. 393–8; *CSPD*, 1680–81, p. 212; Clark (ed.), *Anthony Wood*, II, p. 522; Ford Grey, *The Secret History of the Rye House Plot*, London, 1754, pp. 11–13.

36 *Reresby Memoirs*, p. 219; *Burnet, OA*, II, p. 281.

37 Clark (ed.), *Anthony Wood*, II, p. 531; *CSPD*, 1680–81, p. 212; Bod. Lib. Carte MS 222, fol. 272r; *JHL*, 1675–81, pp. 745–57.

38 *HMC Ormonde*, VI, pp. 6–8; *HMC Beaufort*, pp. 83–4; Christie, *Shaftesbury*, II, Appendix VII, p. cxvi; *The Earl of Shaftesbury's Expedient to Settle the Nation Discoursed with His Majesty in the House of Peers at Oxford, 24 March, 1680/81*, London, 1681; Lionel K. Glassey, 'Shaftesbury and the Exclusion Crisis', in J. Spurr (ed.), *Antony Ashley Cooper, First Earl of Shaftesbury*, Swansea, 2011, pp. 207–31. The king told an agent of William of Orange a few months earlier that if he were able to

dispose of the crown himself he would give it to one of his own sons, but he knew too well that this was not in his power: *Archives ou Correspondance Inédite de la Maison d' Orange Nassau*, II, V, p. 452.

39 *JHL*, 13, 1675–81, pp. 754–6.

40 *Reresby Memoirs*, p. 222; *Burnet, OA*, II, pp. 280–6.

41 *HMC Ormonde*, VI, pp. 9–12, 20–1; *Ailesbury Memoirs,* I, pp. 56–8, 222; *JHL*, 13, 1675–81, pp. 756–7.

Chapter 15: Town and Country

1 Christie, *Shaftesbury*, II, pp. 391–401.

2 Mark Goldie (ed.), *John Locke: Selected Correspondence*, Oxford, 2002, pp. 84–6; Roger Woolhouse, *Locke: a Biography*, Cambridge, 2007. The date the two books of Locke's *Two Treatises of Government* were written remains the subject of debate, but recent work accepts it was in the period 1679–82. See Peter Laslett, *Locke, Two Treatises of Government*, Cambridge, 1988, and Richard Ashcraft, *Locke's Two Treatises of Government*, Cambridge, 1987.

3 BL Add MS 51,326, fos 8–9; *CSPD*, 1679–80, p. 570; Bod. Lib. Carte MS 228, fol. 164r; TNA WORK 5/35; Fraser, *Scotts of Buccleuch*, I, p. 450.

4 *CSPD*, 1679–80, p. 570; NAS, GD157/3278; Fraser, *Scotts of Buccleuch*, I, p. 440; DRO, FSI Box 274, 'Analysis of the financial affairs of the Duchess of Buccleuch'.

5 Bod. Lib. Carte MS 39, fol. 107; Luttrell, *State Affairs*, I, p. 53; BL Add MS 51,326, fos 4–5, 8–9; DRO, FSI Box 274, 'Analysis of the financial affairs of the Duchess of Buccleuch'.

6 BL Add MS 51,326, fos 25–6; 29 June 1681, *Calendar of Treasury Books*, 1681–85, pp. 185–203.

7 NAS, GD26/13/359, Letters from Anna Buccleuch and others, no. 4; *HMC Ormonde*, VI, p. 40. In 1680 the duke received two retrospective payments relating to his old office of Master of the Horse, one for over £4,000 and another for £1,000, *Calendar of Treasury Books*, 1679–80, pp. 627, 683, 739, all reimbursements of sums Monmouth had paid out personally when in office.

8 *CSPD*, 1680–81, p. 232; *HMC Ormonde*, VI, p. 40; *Protestant (Domestick) Intelligence or News Both from City and Country*, London, Friday 15 Apr. 1681, 114.

9 Feiling and Needham (eds), 'Journals of Edmund Warcup', p. 253; Haley, *Shaftesbury*, p. 642.

10 *Calendar of Treasury Books*, 1679–80, pp. 781, 783, 'Money warrant for 4,000 to the Duke of Monmouth for half a year to 1680, June 24, and for part of the succeeding quarter upon his annuity or yearly pension of 6,000l.', *Calendar of Treasury Books*, 1681–85, p. 84. Stephen Fox claimed later that the duke's allowance had been reduced to £4,000 per annum on his expulsion from court – representing the figure to which Anna was entitled in her own right; BL Add MS 51,326, fos 25–6; DRO, D/LRM/

T1, 6 Aug 1681. The contention that the allowance was for 'his son, Lord Doncaster' may have had some truth in it, *CSPD*, 1682, p. 396.

11 Feiling and Needham (eds), 'Journals of Edmund Warcup', pp. 256–7; *HMC Ormonde*, VI, p. 74. Monmouth was again conspicuously absent on 7 May 1681, when all the main Whig leaders attended the examination of Edward Fitzharris at the King's Bench: Haley, *Shaftesbury*, p. 646; *CSPD*, 1680–81, p. 270.

12 *HMC Ormonde*, VI, p. 91; Luttrell, *State Affairs*, I, p. 106; TNA, PC2/69, fol. 150.

13 *HMC Ormonde*, VI, p. 96.

14 Haley, *Shaftesbury*, p. 662.

15 *CSPD*, 1680–81, p. 572; Goldie et al. (ed.), *Entring Book*, II, p. 293; *Anon.*, *The Vindication of his Grace James Duke of Monmouth*, London, 1681.

16 *Hatton*, II. p. 10; *Dryden: Selected Poems*, pp. 150–228.

17 Gary S. De Krey, *London and the Restoration 1659–1686*, Cambridge, 2005, pp. 236–8; *Entring Book*, II, p. 294; *HMC Ormonde*, VI, p. 236–7.

18 *Entring Book*, II, p. 294; Luttrell, *State Affairs*, I, p. 148; *Reresby Memoirs*, p. 239.

19 *Reresby Memoirs*, pp. 239–40; *Entring Book*, II, p. 11; *HMC Ormonde*, VI, p. 252; Luttrell, *State Affairs*, I, p. 150.

20 *Hatton*, II, p. 11; *HMC Ormonde*, VI, p. 252.

21 *CSPD*, 1680–81, pp. 583–4.

22 *HMC Ormonde*, VI, pp. 236–7.

23 'Soho Square Area: Portland Estate, Monmouth House', *Survey of London*: vols 33 and 34, St Anne Soho, edited by F. H. W. Sheppard, London, 1966, pp. 107–13.

24 *HMC Westmorland*, p. 176; *CSPD*, 1682, p. 166; *Entring Book*, II, p. 315; *CSPD*, 1682, p. 147.

25 De Krey, *London and the Restoration*, p. 253; Newton E. Key, '"High feeding and smart Drinking", Associating Hedge-Lane Lords in Exclusion Crisis London', in Jason McElligott (ed.), *Fear, Exclusion and Revolution: Roger Morrice and Britain in the 1680s*, Aldershot, 2006, pp. 154–7; *CSPD*, 1682, p. 150.

26 The ceiling is still in situ at Moor Park, and a cartoon of the subject for a different room is in the Tate collection (T00916). I am grateful to Tabitha Barber of Tate for her information on the subject. DRO, FSI Box 274, 'Analysis of the financial affairs of the Duchess of Buccleuch', pp. 12–13.

27 Luttrell, *State Affairs*, I, p. 159; *HMC Ormonde*, VI, p. 298.

28 *HMC 7th Report*, I, p. 352; Bod. Lib. Carte MS 232, fol. 103; Carte MS 216, fos 47, 53r.

29 TNA, PC2/69, fol. 252v; Bod. Lib. Carte MS 216, fol. 55; BL Add MS 28,569, fol. 36r; Luttrell, *State Affairs*, I, p. 189; *State Affairs Reresby Memoirs*, pp. 265–6; *Letters to George, Earl of Aberdeen, Lord High Chancellor of Scotland 1681–1684*, Aberdeen, 1851, p. 21.

30　*CSPD*, 1682, p. 216; Halifax had talked earlier in 1682 about wanting to 'trample in pieces' the Duke of Monmouth: *Life and Letters of Halifax*, I, p. 31.

31　*HMC 7th Report, Graham manuscripts*, I, p. 264; *HMC Ormonde*, VI, p. 376; *Calendar of Treasury Books*, VII, 1681–85, 1, p. 494.

32　DRO, FSI Box 274, bound volume, 'Analysis of the financial affairs of the Duchess of Buccleuch', *passim*; *Calendar of Treasury Books*, VII, 1681–85, 1, p. 494.

33　Bod. Lib Carte MS 216, fos 55, 141r–v, 157r; *HMC Ormonde*, VI, p. 376; *Letters to George, Earl of Aberdeen*, p. 40.

34　*HMC Westmorland*, p. 176; *HMC Ormond*, VI, pp. 428, 430.

35　Clarke, *Life of King James*, I, p. 737; Bod. Lib. Carte MS 216, fol. 157r; *HMC Ormonde*, VI, p. 430; Haley, *Shaftesbury*, pp. 667, 701; John Bramhall (ed.), *The Rawdon Papers*, London, 1819, p. 276.

36　Philip Milton, 'Shaftesbury and the Rye House Plot', in Spurr (ed.), *Anthony Ashley Cooper*, pp. 233–68, p. 239; De Krey, *London and the Restoration*, pp. 262–4.

37　Luttrell, *State Affairs*, I, pp. 166, 179, 222; *Survey of London*, 33, pp. 42–51; *CSPD*, 1682, pp. 28, 396–7.

38　*HMC Ormonde*, VI, p. 430; Bod. Lib. Carte MS 216, fol. 159.

39　*CSPD*, 1682, pp. 380–410, 420–1, 427, 503–4, 510–11; *Hatton*, II, p. 20.

40　*CSPD*, 1682, pp. 380–410, 420–1; *HMC 7th Report*, I, p. 533; *HMC Ormonde*, VI, p. 445.

41　*CSPD*, 1682, pp. 396–7.

42　Ibid., pp. 342, 381, 388, 396–7, 406–7, 415–16, 423. For what happened at royal healing ceremonies see Keay, *Magnificent Monarch*, p. 117.

43　*CSPD*, 1682, pp. 313–14.

44　Ibid., pp. 398–9.

45　Ibid., pp. 408–9.

46　Ibid., pp. 391–2, 394.

47　Ibid., pp. 405ff.

48　*CSPD*, 1677–78, p. 33; *Heroick Life*, pp. 133–4.

49　*CSPD*, 1682, pp. 413, 415, 427.

50　*Hatton*, II, pp. 19–20; Bod. Lib. Carte MS 216, fol. 189; *CSPD*, 1682, p. 432.

51　*CSPD*, 1682, pp. 406–7.

52　Ibid., pp. 438–40.

Chapter 16: Desperate Measures

1　Haley, *Shaftesbury*, p. 662; Grey, *Secret History*, p. 26.

2　Milton, 'Shaftesbury and the Rye House Plot', pp. 238, 241; Grey, *Secret History*, pp. 3–5; BL Harl. MS 6845, fol. 266.

3　*Burnett, OA*, II, pp. 349–50; Milton, 'Shaftesbury and the Rye House Plot', p. 244; Grey, *Secret History*, pp. 25–7; *Ailesbury Memoirs*, I, pp. 66, 71.

4 *CSPD*, 1683, II, p. 80; *State Trials*, IX, pp. 432–3, 604; Luttrell, *State Affairs*, I, p. 227; *Burnett OA*, II, pp. 349–50; Milton, 'Shaftesbury and the Rye House Plot', pp. 248–9.

5 Milton, 'Shaftesbury and the Rye House Plot', p. 260; *State Trials*, IX, pp. 373, 432–3, 489, 605–6; *Burnet, OA*, II, pp. 349–51, 362–70; *Hatton*, II, p. 25; Grey, *Secret History*, pp. 26–36.

6 Milton, 'Shaftesbury and the Rye House Plot', p. 265; Haley, *Shaftesbury*, pp. 730–2; Grey, *Secret History*, pp. 35–40.

7 *CSPD*, 1682, pp. 528–30, 572; *Entring Book*, II, p. 330; *HMC 7th Report*, I, p. 481.

8 *State Trials*, IX, pp. 925, 963; *Burnet, OA*, p. 353–4; Jonathan Scott, *Algernon Sidney and the Restoration Crisis 1677–83*, Cambridge, 1991, pp. 276–7.

9 *State Trials*, IX, pp. 434, 817–18. Whether there was one meeting or two is unclear, as indeed is the concept of the group as a cabal at all: Scott, *Algernon Sidney*, pp. 282–5; Grey, *Secret History*, pp. 41, 45–58. Grey records Monmouth saying of Lord Howard that they 'had trusted him far too long to disoblige him now', p. 49. Lord Russell would claim shortly before his death that his involvement was largely to protect Monmouth: *State Trials*, IX, pp. 817–18.

10 *State Trials*, IX, pp. 432–7, 600–23, 925; Scott, *Algernon Sidney*, p. 275; *Burnet, OA*, pp. 354–5; Grey, *Secret History*, p. 42; *CSPD*, 1683, II, pp. 34–5; Bod. Lib. Carte MS 222, fol. 320r.

11 That Grey's account is unreliable is clear from many small points. For instance he claimed that Monmouth had been poised to raise a rebellion on the way back from Cheshire, and waited only for Lord Shaftesbury's approval to do so. Ferguson, by contrast, maintained that Monmouth had always been opposed to any such uprising, and that the duke had argued that those who cheered him on 'were wholly naked & destitute of Arms & come thither meerly out of curiosity to view, without the least thought of listing themselves soldiers', something Robert West, another of Shaftesbury's cronies, confirmed, Grey, *Secret History*, pp. 19–20, 46; Milton, 'Shaftesbury and the Rye House Plot', p. 241; *State Trials*, IX, p. 402.

12 Grey, *Secret History*, pp. 42–60, 52; *Burnet, OA*, pp. 353–5.

13 Grey, *Secret History*, p. 61.

14 *HMC 7th Report*, I, p. 359; *Entring Book*, II, p. 334.

15 *Hatton*, II, pp. 20, 25; Bod. Lib. Carte MS 222, fol. 327r; *Calendar of Treasury Books*, 1681–85, 1, p. 659; 2, pp. 736, 744, 784; TNA, LC5/107 fol. 102r.

16 Clarke, *Life of King James*, I, p. 739; PRO, PRO31/3/155, fol. 15r.

17 *State Trials*, IX, pp. 365–8; De Krey, *London and the Restoration*, pp. 359–70; *Burnet, OA*, pp. 360–3; Milne, 'The results of the Rye House plot and their influence on the revolution of 1688', *Transactions of the Royal Historical Society*, 1951, 5th series, I, pp. 91–108.

18 *State Trials*, IX, pp. 373, 402; *Burnet, OA*, pp. 364–8; *Ailesbury Memoirs*, pp. 75–7; TNA, PC2/70, pp. 6–18; Grey's account of Monmouth saying

'he would not consent to the muthering [murdering] the meanest creature (tho' the worst enemy he had in the world)' rings true: *Secret History*, p. 62.

19 *Letters to George, Earl of Aberdeen*, p. 135; TNA PC2/70, p. 14; *Burnet, OA*, p. 364; *State Trials*, IX, pp. 369–70; *Letters to George, Earl of Aberdeen*, p. 130; *CSPD*, 1683 (1), p. 347.

20 Scott, *Algernon Sidney*, pp. 291–3; *Burnet, OA*, II, p. 368; *State Trials*, IX, p. 489.

21 *Burnet, OA*, II, pp. 364, 368; Grey, *Secret History*, p. 63; Cobbett et al. (eds), *State Trials*, IX, pp. 600–1; TNA, PC2/70, p. 15; *London Gazette*, 28 Jun.–2 Jul. 1683; *Hatton*, II, p. 25; TNA, LC5/201, p. 317; George Roberts, *The Life, Progresses and Rebellion of James Duke of Monmouth*, 2 vols, London, 1844, I, p. 153; *Entring Book*, II, pp. 374, 397–8; *Ailesbury Memoirs*, I, pp. 74–5.

22 *CSPD*, 1683 (1), pp. 367–85; Graham MSS, *HMC 7th Report*, I, p. 363; *HMC Ormonde*, VII, p. 95.

23 J. W. Goodman, *Catalogue of Cambridge Portraits*, Cambridge, 1955, p. xxvi.

24 *CSPD*, 1683 (1), p. 372.

25 Ibid., pp. 358–9.

26 *Burnet, OA*, II, pp. 368–71.

27 *Hatton*, II, p. 29; *Burnet, OA*, II, pp. 371–3; *State Trials*, IX, pp. 600–23.

28 *Burnet, OA*, II, pp. 382–4.

29 Ibid., pp. 374–8; Lois G. Schwoerer, 'The trial of Lord William Russell, 1683: Judicial murder?', *The Journal of Legal History*, 1988, 9:2, pp. 142–68.

30 *Burnet, OA*, II, pp. 376–80.

31 *State Trials*, IX, pp. 377–8, 406; *CSPD*, 1683 (2), p. 80. Lord Howard claimed to have told Monmouth, before Shaftesbury's death, that the conspirators had designs upon the king's life, to which the duke reportedly replied: 'God-so, kill the King! I will never suffer that': *State Trials*, IX, p. 606; Grey, *Secret History*, p. 62.

32 *Ailesbury Memoirs*, I, p. 76.

33 Ibid., I, pp. 74–5.

34 *State Trials*, IX, pp. 817–18; Welwood, *Memoirs*, p. 143.

35 *Ailesbury Memoirs*, I, p. 77; *CSPD*, 1683 (1), p. 372.

36 *A History of the County of Bedford*, 3, Victoria County History, London, 1912, pp. 438–47; 'A Vanished Elizabethan Mansion: Toddington Manor House Bedfordshire', *Country Life*, 23 Mar. 1961.

37 *Ailesbury Memoirs*, I, pp. 77, 81, 120; Samuel and Daniel Lysons, *Magna Britannia*, 6 vols, London, 1806–22, I, pp. 143–4; BL Egerton MS 1527, fol. 56; Fraser, *Scotts of Buccleuch*, I, p. 449.

38 *CSPD*, 1683 (2), p. 309; *Ailesbury Memoirs*, I, p. 81.

39 Welwood, *Memoirs*, p. 319; *Reresby Memoirs*, p. 320.

40 TNA, SP29/433, fol. 247; *Burnet, OA*, II, pp. 405–6; Welwood, *Memoirs*, p. 319; *State Trials*, IX, p. 962.

41 NAS, GD224/903/27, no. 51; *Calendar of Treasury Books*, VII, part 2, pp. 910, 918; *CSPD*, 1683 (2), p. 35; Welwood, *Memoirs*, p. 320; PRO31/1/156, fos 63–7.

42 Welwood, *Memoirs*, p. 320; *Ailesbury Memoirs*, I, pp. 81–2. This may be the same Mrs Crofts Monmouth had visited in January 1682, *Hatton*, II, p. 12.

43 Burke and Burke (eds), *Extinct and Dormant Baronetcs*, p. 246; *Ailesbury Memoirs*, I, p. 82.

44 *Entring Book*, II, p. 399.

45 Welwood, *Memoirs*, p. 321.

46 Ibid.

47 TNA, SP29/434, fol. 141; Welwood, *Memoirs*, pp. 321–2. Unlike Monmouth's letter to the king of 15 October, which was written in his own hand, the letter done to placate York was in another hand, with just a stiff signature at the bottom.

Chapter 17: Love and Loss

1 *Reresby Memoirs*, pp. 319–22; Clarke, *Life of King James*, I, pp. 742–3; *Ailesbury Memoirs*, I, pp. 82–3; Dalrymple, *Memoirs of Great Britain and Ireland*, I, pp. 114–15; *HMC 7th Report*, I, p. 375.

2 TNA, PC2/70, p. 76; BL Add MS 4,159, Nov. 1683; TNA, PRO31/1/156, fos 63–7; *London Gazette*, 1880, 22–26 Nov. 1683; *Entring Book*, II, p. 410.

3 *Ailesbury Memoirs*, I, pp. 82–3; TNA, PRO31/1/156, fos 68–9; *HMC Dartmouth*, I, p. 101.

4 Welwood, *Memoirs*, p. 322; TNA, PRO31/1/156, fos 63–7; *Burnet, OA*, II, p. 406; Bod. Lib. Carte MS 228, fol. 77v.

5 Welwood, *Memoirs*, p. 322; TNA, SP29/433, fol. 247.

6 *Reresby Memoirs*, pp. 320–2; *HMC 7th Report*, I, pp. 368, 375; Burnet, OA, II, pp. 406–7; Welwood, *Memoirs*, p. 322; TNA, PRO31/1/156, fos 63–7; SP29/434, fol. 184.

7 *HMC Ormonde*, VII, p. 164.

8 Welwood, *Memoirs*, p. 322.

9 *London Gazette*, 1880, 22–26 Nov. 1683; TNA, PC2/70, p. 76; *State Trials*, IX, p. 973.

10 *Entring Book*, II, pp. 410, 414; *State Trials*, IX, p. 963.

11 *Journal of the Hon. John Erskine of Carnock 1683–1687*, Walter Macleod, ed., Edinburgh, 1893, p. 25; *CSPD*, 1683–84, p. 124; *HMC 7th Report*, I, p. 368.

12 *State Trials*, IX, pp. 899, 961.

13 *Ailesbury Memoirs*, pp. 83–4; Welwood, *Memoirs*, p. 322; TNA, PRO31/1/156, fos 73–5; *State Trials*, pp. 958, 961–73; *Entring Book*, II, p. 414.

14 *Entring Book*, II, pp. 417–20; TNA, PRO31/1/156, fos 76–8.

15 TNA, SP29/435, fol. 38; BL Add MS 27,402; Burnet, OA, II, p. 408; *State Trials*, IX, pp. 961–73.

16 *State Trials*, IX, pp. 961–73.

17 *State Trials*, IX, pp. 961–73; *Burnet, OA*, II, pp. 408–9; *Entring Book*, III, pp. 27–9.

18 *Entring Book*, II, pp. 418–21; Dalrymple, *Memoirs of Great Britain and Ireland*, I, p. 116; *HMC Ormonde*, VII, p. 165; Bod. Lib Carte MS 216, fol. 391; TNA, PC2/70, p. 89; Scott, *Algernon Sidney*, p. 347; TNA, PRO31/1/156, fos 79–82; *CSPD*, 1683–84, pp. 153–4; *CSPD*, 1683–84, pp. 153–4.

19 'A Discourse Concerning the Effects of the Great Frost, on Trees and Other Plants Anno 1683', *The Philosophical Transactions of the Royal Society*, 1753, 14, pp. 766–79; *Evelyn*, IV, pp. 350–60.

20 *Evelyn*, IV, p. 357.

21 Clarke, *Life of King James*, I, p. 744; *Hatton*, II, p. 42; Bod. Lib. Carte MS 216, fos 399, 401; Dalrymple, *Memoirs of Great Britain and Ireland*, I, p. 118; *HMC Hamilton*, p. 197.

22 *Life and Letters of Halifax*, I, p. 39; *Entring Book*, II, p. 446; *State Trials*, IX, pp. 1064–5.

23 *CSPD*, 1683–84, p. 281, 19 Feb. 1684; *HMC 7th Report*, I, p. 387.

24 TNA, PRO31/3/158, fos 3r, 29r; *D'Avaux*, III, pp. 104–5.

25 Bod. Lib. Carte MS 216, fol. 401r; Carte MS 232, fol. 141; Luttrell, *State Affairs*, I, pp. 303, 306; *HMC Portland*, III, p. 378; *CSPD*, 1684–85, p. 7i; *HMC 7th Report*, I, p. 499; TNA, PRO31/3/158, fol. 36v.

26 BL Add MS 41,832, fos 23r–v, 30v; Bod. Lib. Carte MS 216, fol. 488; *HMC 7th Report*, I, p. 499.

27 *HMC 7th Report*, I, p. 387; *CSPD* 1683–84, pp. 332–3; Grey, *The Secret History*, pp. 71–5.

28 BL Add MS 41,810, fol. 152, fol. 190, '. . . His Maty does constantly write to him every week'; TNA, PRO31/3/158, fos 15r, 36v. It is not surprising that Charles told the French ambassador he was angry with Monmouth, given that the duke was about to take up arms against Louis XIV.

29 *HMC Portland*, III, p. 378; *HMC 7th Report*, I, p. 499; *Calendar of Treasury Books*, VII, 1681–85, part 2, pp. 1114, 1116.

30 Dalrymple, *Memoirs of Great Britain and Ireland*, I, p. 118; *Archives ou Correspondance Inédite de la Maison d' Orange Nassau*, II, V, pp. 587–8; *D'Avaux*, IV, p. 16.

31 BL Add MS 41,832, fol. 31r; *D'Avaux*, III, pp. 104–5.

32 BL Add MS 41,810, fos 119r, 130; BL Egerton MS 1527, fos 72r–v.

33 BL Egerton MS 1527, fos 18–20.

34 *HMC Rutland*, II, p. 83; *AilesburyMemoirs*, I, p. 84.

35 BL Egerton MS 1527, fos 56r–v; *AilesburyMemoirs*, I, p. 77.

36 'endeavour'd to make up that Want, by applying himself to study, in which he made in short time no inconsiderable Progress', Welwood, *Memoirs*, pp. 149–50; BL Egerton MS 1527, fos 34v–42v; 43r; BL Add MS 41,818, 'Inventaire des Meubles arretes a Rotterdam Du Duc de Monmouth', fos 192r–193v.

37 BL Add MS 41,810, fos 128v, 135r; *D'Avaux*, IV, p. 16.

38 BL Add MS 41,810, fos 125r–28v; *D'Avaux*, IV, pp. 16, 24ff.

39 BL Add MS 41,812, fol. 2.

40 BL Add MS 41,410, fos 152, 157–8, 182–3; Dalrymple, *Memoirs of Great Britain and Ireland*, I, p. 124; Welwood, *Memoirs*, pp. 143–4; Burnet, OA, II, p. 410.

41 BL Add MS 41,810, fos 157–8, 182–3, 226, 240v, 302; Clarke, *Life of King James*, II, p. 13; *D'Avaux*, III, pp. 104–5, IV, pp. 211–12, 217, 225–7, 241–2.

42 BL Add MS 41,810, fos 188v–189r; BL, Add 41832, fos, 47–8, 55r; Grey, *The Secret History*, pp. 80–1; *D'Avaux*, IV, p. 87.

43 *D'Avaux*, IV, pp. 117–18, 'La Princesse d'Orange a fait des honneurs extraordinaires à une fille de qualité d'Angleterre, qui passe publiquement pour être la maitresse de M. de Montmouth'; Burnet, OA, II, pp. 453–5; BL Egerton 1527, fos 25r–v, 73r, 83v; BL Add MS 41,832, fol. 55r; *HMC 7th Report*, I, p. 378; Dalrymple, *Memoirs of Great Britain and Ireland*, I, p. 119.

44 BL Add MS 38,847, fos 84r, 123r.

45 Burnet, OA, II, pp. 453–5; Welwood, *Memoirs*, pp. 139, 144; *HMC Ormonde*, VII, p. 298; *Ailesbury Memoirs*, I, p. 103; *D'Avaux*, IV, p. 94.

46 BL Add MS 41,810, fol. 222; Welwood, *Memoirs*, pp. 322–3; John Willcock, 'The cipher in Monmouth's diary', *EHR*, 20, 80 (Oct. 1905), pp. 730–5; BL Egerton MS 1527, fos 74–5; Grey, *Secret History*, p. 82.

47 *CSPD*, 1684–85, pp. 273–4; BL Add MS 41,810, fos 182–3, 225, 240v; Bod. Lib. Carte MS 239, fol. 302; Luttrell, *State Affairs*, I, p. 318; *D'Avaux*, IV, pp. 87, 187–8.

48 Welwood, *Memoirs*, pp. 139, 144–5, 322–3; Burnet, OA, II, pp. 453–5; *Ailesbury Memoirs*, I, p. 113; *CSPD*, 1684–85, pp. 273–4; BL Add MS 41,810, fol. 226; *CSPD*, 1685, p. 1. Lord Grey gives a different account of Monmouth's intentions in the winter of 1684/85, but as he was well outside Monmouth's confidence at this point – Monmouth having in Grey's words 'laid [me] aside like other useless animals' – his information is far from reliable: Grey, *Secret History*, pp. 80–4.

Chapter 18: The Reluctant Rebel

1 *CSPD*, 1685, p. 1; 'Sir Patrick Hume's Narrative', in *Observations on the Historical Work of the Late Right Honourable Charles James Fox*, London, 1809, p. 5; *D'Avaux*, IV, p. 271.

2 'Sir Patrick Hume's Narrative', p. 8; Grey, *Secret History*, pp. 85–6.

3 BL Add MS 41,810, fol. 262r; C. E. Dobie (ed.), 'Correspondence of Henry Earl of Clarendon and James Earl of Abingdon', *Collectanea*, 3, Oxford Historical Society, 32, 1893, p. 255; Grey, *Secret History*, pp. 83–4.

4 *HMC Stopford-Sackville* I, p. 24; BL Harl MS 6845, fol. 269v.

5 Welwood, *Memoirs*, pp. 324–5; Luttrell, *State Affairs*, I, p. 365.

6 Welwood, *Memoirs*, pp. 324–5; BL Egerton MS 1527, fol. 176r; *Ailesbury Memoirs*, I, p. 113.

7 BL Add MS 41,812, fos 2, 7r, 20.

8 Grey, *Secret History*, p. 86; BL Add. MS 38,847, fol. 119; *State Trials*, IX, p. 409.

9 'Patrick Hume's Narrative', p. 12; BL Add MS 41,812, fos 9r, 15; *Journal of the Hon. John Erskine of Carnock*, p. 186; Welwood, *Memoirs*, p. 149; John Willcock, *A Scots Earl in Covenanting Times: being the Life and Times of Archibald, 9th Earl of Argyll*, Edinburgh, 1907.

10 'Sir Patrick Hume's Narrative', pp. 7–8, 17; Clarke, *Life of King James*, II, p. 32; *CSPD*, 1685, p. 8; Grey, *Secret History*, p. 94; *Journal of the Hon. John Erskine of Carnock*, p. 186; BL Add MS 41,812, Correspondence from English Envoys in Holland, fol. 15.

11 BL Harl MS 6845, fol. 270v; Grey, *Secret History*, p. 94; BL Add MS 41,818, fol. 181r; *State Trials*, XI, pp. 539–42.

12 Grey, *Secret History*, p. 93; *Burnet*, MJR, III, pp. 22–3.

13 *State Trials*, IX, pp. 377–8; *Burnet*, MJR, III, pp. 24–5.

14 *Burnet*, MJR, III, p. 25; Welwood, *Memoirs*, pp. 149, 325.

15 'Sir Patrick Hume's Narrative', pp. 12, 15; Grey, *Secret History*, p. 112; BL Harl MS 6845, fol. 270v; BL Add MS 41,812, fos 9r, 26v–27r; BL Lansdowne 1152, fos 303, 308; *Burnet*, MJR, III, pp. 22–5.

16 BL Harl MS 6845, fos 270–1; BL Lansdowne MS 1152, fos 301r, 310r–v; Grey, *Secret History*, p. 100–4.

17 BL Harl MS 6845, fos 270–1; Grey, *Secret History*, p. 112; *Burnet*, MJR, III, p. 26; *State Trials*, XI, p. 543.

18 John Miller, *James II*, New Haven and London, 1978.

19 BL Add MS 41,812, fos 2, 15; Dalrymple, *Memoirs of Great Britain and Ireland*, II, p. 13; *Burnet*, MJR, III, pp. 13–14; BL Add MS 16935, fos 18r–v.

20 Dalrymple, *Memoirs of Great Britain and Ireland*, II, pp. 16–17.

21 Ibid., pp. 19–20.

22 BL Add MS 41,812, fol. 65r; BL Harl MS 6845, fol. 271v.

23 BL Harl MS 6845, 271r–v; *HMC Stopford-Sackville*, I, p. 23.

24 BL Harl MS 6845, fol. 271r; BL Add MS 51,326, fos 6–7, 11–13.

25 BL Add MS 41,818, fos 192r–193v; Add MS 51,326, fos 6–7; Add MS 41,812, fos 156r–v; Grey, *Secret History*, pp. 99, 117–18.

26 BL Lansdowne MS 1152, fol. 237r; *HMC Stopford-Sackville*, I, p. 23; BL Harl MS 6845, fol. 272r; BL Add MS 41,812, fos 38v, 81r, 63–4, 85r, 112v; BL Add MS 41,818, fol. 11r; Grey, *Secret History*, p. 119.

27 Grey, *Secret History*, pp. 120–1; BL Harl MS 6845, fol. 272r; BL Lansdowne MS 1152, fol. 242r.

28 BL Harl MS 6845, fol. 272v; Grey, *Secret History*, pp. 118–22.

29 *Ailesbury Memoirs*, I, p. 117; *HMC Stopford-Sackville*, I, p. 22.

30 Clarke, *Life of King James*, II, p. 27; BL Add MS 41810, fol. 189r.

31 BL Add MS 41,812, fol. 65r.

32 BL Lansdowne MS 1152, fos 303, 310; BL Harl. MS 6845, fol. 271v; *Burnet, MJR*, III, p. 24.

33 Anon., *The Declaration of James Duke of Monmouth*, London, 1685; *Burnet, MJR*, III, p. 43; BL Lansdowne MS 1152, fos 242–3.

34 *Ailesbury Memoirs*, I, pp. 116–17; *HMC Stopford-Sackville*, I, p. 24.

35 BL Harl MS 6845, fos 273–74.

36 'Samuel Dassell's narrative', *Notes and Queries for Somerset and Dorset*, 27 (1955–60), Taunton, 1961, pp. 44–9.

37 'Samuel Dassell's narrative', pp. 44–9; BL Harl MS 6845, fos 273–4.

38 BL Harl MS 6845, fos 275–6.

39 'Samuel Dassell's narrative', pp. 44–9; BL Harl MS 6845, fos 273–4.

40 *JHC*, 1667–87, pp. 734–6; Luttrell, *State Affairs*, I, p. 346; *London Gazette*, 2042, 11–15 June 1685; Miller, *James II*, pp. 135–7; *Statutes of the Realm*, 6, 1685–94, ed. John Raithby, 1819, p. 2.

41 BL Lansdowne MS 1152, fol. 220; 'Samuel Dassell's narrative', p. 50; BL Harl 6845, fol. 278r.

42 Dalrymple, *Memoirs of Great Britain and Ireland*, II, p. 23; *HMC Stopford-Sackville*, pp. 7, 8.

43 BL Harl MS 6845, fol. 275; *Ailesbury Memoirs*, I, p. 118; DRO, DC/LR/A/3/1, p. 14.

44 BL Harl MS 6845, fol. 277r; Welwood, *Memoirs*, pp. 148–9; BL Lansdowne 1152, fol. 237v.

45 Welwood, *Memoirs*, pp. 148–9; *Ailesbury Memoirs*, I, pp. 115–16; *Hatton*, II, p. 57; *HMC Bath*, II, p. 171; BL Lansdowne MS 1152, fol. 310; BL Harl MS 6845, fol. 278r.

Chapter 19: The Last Battle

1 BL Harl MS 6845, fol. 278r; Daniel Defoe, *A tour thro' the whole island of Great Britain, divided into circuits or journies*, London, 1927, Letter 4, Part 2: Somerset and Wiltshire, Taunton.

2 BL Harl MS 6845, fol. 278r; John Whiting, *Persecution Exposed*, London, 1791, p. 297.

3 *HMC Bath*, II, pp. 170–1.

4 BL Harl MS 6845, fol. 278r; BL Lansdowne MS 1152, fos 242–3.

5 *CSPD*, James II, 1685, pp. 195, 201–2; Dalrymple, *Memoirs of Great Britain and Ireland*, II, p. 23.

6 BL Harl MS 6845, fol. 278r; *HMC Stopford-Sackville*, I, p. 12.

7 BL Harl MS 6845, fos 278r–v; *HMC Stopford-Sackville*, I, pp. 13–14; *London Gazette*, 2046, 28 June 1685; *HMC Rutland*, II, p. 89.

8 'Iter Bellicosum', *Camden Miscellany* XII, 3rd series, XVIII, 1910, p. 160; E. Black (ed.), *Kings in Conflict: Ireland in the 1690s*, Belfast, 1990, p. 41, no. 39, the Royal Armouries' straightened scythe blade associated with the

Monmouth rebellion. I am grateful to Dr Edward Impey, Master of the Armouries, for bringing this remarkable survival to my attention.

9 John Lauder, *Historical Observes of Memorable Occurents in Church and State 1680–1686*, Edinburgh, 1840, pp. 180–1; Willcock, *A Scots Earl in Covenanting Times*, p. 395.

10 BL Harl MS 6845, fos 274r–282r; *HMC Stopford-Sackville*, I, pp. 12–19; Lansdowne MS 1152, fos 237r–238, 240–1; DRO, DC/LR/A/3/1, p. 14; *London Gazette*, 2046, 28 Jun. 1685.

11 BL Harl MS 6845, fol. 279r. Local tradition that Monmouth and his officers held a meeting at the George seems likely to be true.

12 BL Harl MS 6845, fol. 279r; BL Lansdowne 1152, fos 237–8, 240–1, 242–3; *HMC Stopford-Sackville*, I, p. 23.

13 'Iter Bellicosum', p. 161; BL Harl MS 6845, fos 279, 280r; *HMC Stopford-Sackville*, I, p. 22; Whiting, *Persecution Exposed*, p. 29.

14 'Iter Bellicosum', p. 161.

15 BL Harl MS 6845, fol. 280r; BL Add MS 4162, fol. 125; G. Davies, 'Three letters on Monmouth's rebellion', *EHR*, 35, 137 (Jan. 1920), p. 115; *HMC Stopford-Sackville*, I, pp. 12, 15.

16 BL Harl MS 6845, fol. 280r; BL Add MS 4162, fol. 125; *HMC Stopford-Sackville*, I, p. 15; 'Edward Dummer: A Brief Journal', printed in David G. Chandler, *Sedgemoor, 1685 from Monmouth's Invasion to the Bloody Assizes*, Spellmount, 1995, pp. 128–9; *Entring Book*, III, pp. 27–9.

17 Edward Dummer described the night as 'a dark night and thick fogg covering the Moore'. 'Edward Dummer: A Brief Journal', p. 128. For a full account of the battle of Sedgemoor, see Robin Clifton, *The Last Popular Rebellion: the Western Rising of 1685*, Hounslow, 1984, chapter 7; BL Add MS 4162, fol 127r; BL Harl MS 6845 fol. 280v; Dalrymple, *Memoirs of Great Britain and Ireland*, II, p. 25.

18 BL Add MS 4162, fol. 125v; BL Harl MS 6845, fol. 280v.

19 Bernard Storer, *Sedgemoor: its History and Natural History*, Newton Abbot, 1972, chs 1, 2, 4 and 8.

20 BL Add MS 4162, fol. 126r; Bodleian Library, Ballard MS 48, fol. 74.

21 BL Harl MS 6845, fol. 281r; BL Add MS 4162, fol. 127v.

22 BL Add MS 4162, fol. 127v; 'Iter Bellicosum', p. 162; *HMC Stopford-Sackville*, I, pp. 16–19.

23 *HMC Ormonde*, V, p. 133; *Entring Book*, II, p. 160.

24 BL, Add MS 4162, fos 128r–v; BL Harl MS 6845, fos 276v, 281r, 295r; 'Edward Dummer: A Brief Journal', p. 128; *Entring Book*, III, pp. 27–9.

25 BL Harl MS 6845, fol. 281v.

26 *HMC Stopford-Sackville*, I, p. 19; Dalrymple, *Memoirs of Great Britain and Ireland*, II, p. 25.

27 BL Lansdowne MS 1152, fol. 237v; *HMC Stopford-Sackville*, I, pp. 16–19; BL Harl MS 6845, fol. 295r; Williams had been Monmouth's Groom of the Chamber since the mid-1660s, DRO D/FSI, Box 275.

28 *HMC Stopford-Sackville*, I, p. 20; BL Harl MS 6845, fos 281r–v, 295r; *Reresby Memoirs*, p. 385; *Burnet*, MJR, III, pp. 412–13.

Chapter 20: The End

1 *HMC Rutland*, II, pp. 90, 91–2, 93; *Reresby Memoirs*, p. 385; *The London Gazette*, 2049, 6 Jul.–9 Jul. 1685; Clarke, *Life of King James*, II, pp. 31–2; Anon., *An Account of the Defeat of the Rebels in England: As Also the Taking of the Duke of Monmouth, the late Lord Grey & c*, London, 1685; Tim Harris, *Revolution: The Great Crisis of the British Monarchy 1685–1720*, London, 2006, pp. 85–7.

2 *Burnet*, MJR, III, p. 412; G. Davies, 'Three letters on Monmouth's rebellion', *EHR*, 35, 137, Jan. 1920, pp. 115–16; *CSPD*, 1685, p. 260.

3 Clark (ed.), *Anthony Wood*, I, p. 58; TNA SP 44/22 fol. 137.

4 *Reresby Memoirs*, p. 385; Bod. Lib. Carte MS 117, fol. 473; *Burnet*, MJR, III, pp. 412–13; *Evelyn*, IV, p. 452; *Ailesbury Memoirs*, I, p. 119; *An Account of the Defeat of the Rebels in England*.

5 See *State Trials*, XI, p. 545, for Monmouth's sense of betrayal.

6 BL Add MS 38,847, fol. 123r; Anon., *An Account of what passed at the Execution of the late Duke of Monmouth*, London, 1685, p. 3.

7 BL Lansdowne 1236, fol. 229; Clarke, *Life of King James*, II, pp. 32–3; *An Account of what passed at the Execution of the Late Duke of Monmouth*, p. 4.

8 *Ailesbury Memoirs*, I, p. 119.

9 *Burnet*, MJR, p. 412; Fraser, *Scotts of Buccleuch*, I, pp. 447–8; *Ailesbury Memoirs*, I, pp. 118–21.

10 Dalrymple, *Memoirs of Great Britain and Ireland*, II, pp. 25–6; *CSPD*, 1685, p. 263; *State Trials*, XI, pp. 1075–6; Clarke, *Life of King James*, II, pp. 34–9; *Ailesbury Memoirs*, I, pp. 119–20; *Reresby Memoirs*, p. 385.

11 *CSPD*, 1685, p. 254; Luttrell, *State Affairs*, I, p. 352; *HMC Dartmouth*, I, p. 127; Fraser, *Scotts of Buccleuch*, I, pp. 447–9; *State Trials*, XI, pp. 1075–8; Dalrymple, *Memoirs of Great Britain and Ireland*, II, p. 26; *Burnet*, MJR, III, p. 413; Clarke, *Life of King James*, II, p. 39.

12 *CSPD*, 1685, p. 267.

13 *State Trials*, XI, pp. 1071–9; *Burnet*, MJR, III, pp. 413–14; *Evelyn*, IV, pp. 455–7; *Scotts of Buccleuch*, I, p. 450.

14 Luttrell, *State Affairs*, I, p. 354; *HMC Rutland*, II, pp. 93–4; *State Trials*, XI, p. 1081; *An Account of what passed at the Execution of the late Duke of Monmouth*, p. 1.

15 *An Account of what passed at the Execution of the late Duke of Monmouth*, p. 4; *HMC Rutland*, II, pp. 93–4; *Burnet*, MJR, p. 413; *HMC Stopford-Sackville*, I, p. 22; Luttrell, *State Affairs*, I, p. 354; *State Trials*, XI, pp. 1080–3; *Evelyn*, IV, pp. 455–7.

16 *Ailesbury Memoirs*, I, pp. 120–1; even her orange trees were impounded by those to whom Monmouth owed money, BL Add MS 38,847, fol. 133r; BL Add MS 41,812, fos 152v, 177v.

17 Welwood, *Memoirs*, p. 148.

Epilogue

1 Chandler, *Sedgemoor, 1685*, p. 105; *State Trials*, XI, pp. 371–4; Clifton, *Last Popular Rebellion*, chapter 8; 'The Gaol Book of the Western Circuit', printed in F. A. Inderwick, *Sidelights on the Stuarts*, London, 1888, pp. 398–427; Henry Pitman, *A Relation of the Great Suffering and Strange Adventures of Henry Pitman*, London, 1689, pp. 4–5; Richard Locke, *The Western Rebellion*, Taunton, 1782, p. 4; J. G. Muddiman, *The Bloody Assizes*, London, 1929, p. 78; Mary E. Lewis, 'A traitor's death? The identity of a drawn, hanged and quartered man from Hulton Abbey, Staffordshire', *Antiquity*, 82 (2008), pp. 113–24.

2 W. MacDonald Wigfield, *The Monmouth Rebels*, Gloucester and New York, 1985.

3 Russell (ed.), *Letters of Rachel, Lady Russell*, II, p. 183; Sidney, *Diary*, I, p. 163.

4 John Raithby (ed.), 'An Act declareing the Rights and Liberties of the Subject and Setleing the Succession of the Crowne', *Statutes of the Realm, 6, 1685–94*, London, 1819, pp. 142–5. For recent debates on the Glorious Revolution, see Jonathan Israel, *The Anglo-Dutch Moment: Essays on the Glorious Revolution and its World Impact*, Cambridge, 1991; Harris, *Revolution*.

5 *The Diary of Mary, Countess Cowper: Lady of the Bedchamber to the Princess of Wales*, London, 1864, p. 95; *HMC Portland*, VI, p. 187; *Gentleman's Magazine*, 1732, II, p. 630; NAS GD224/882/7, Inventories of Dalkeith Palace; I am indebted to the Duke of Buccleuch for showing me Monmouth's Garter regalia.

6 Gilbert Burnet, *The Ill Effects of Animosities among Protestants in England*, London, 1688, p. 5; Gilbert Burnet, *The Prince of Orange His Declaration shewing the Reasons why he Invades England with a short preface and some modest remarks*, London, 1688, p. 15.

7 Turner, *James II*, p. 161. See Robin Clifton, *Last Popular Rebellion*, and Tim Harris, 'Scott [Crofts], James, duke of Monmouth and first duke of Buccleuch (1649–1685)', *ODNB*, for much more nuanced modern assessments of Monmouth's character and career.

8 Merrill D. Peterson (ed.), *Jefferson: Writings*, New York, 1984, pp. 939–40; BL Add MS 41,812, Correspondence from English Envoys in Holland, fos 26–7, 44v–45r.

BIBLIOGRAPHY

Manuscript Collections

The Bodleian Library
The British Library
The Dorset Record Office
The Hertfordshire Record Office
Lambeth Palace Library
The London Metropolitan Archives
The National Archive of Scotland
The National Archives, Kew

Printed Primary Sources

Anon., *An Account of the Defeat of the Rebels in England: As Also the taking of the Duke of Monmouth, the late Lord Grey &c*, London, 1685

—, *An Account of what passed at the Execution of the late Duke of Monmouth*, London, 1685
—, *An Answer to the Scoffying and Lying Libell*, London, 1681
—, *An Appeal from the Country to the City*, 1679
—, *A Church History of England*, London, 1742
—, *The Declaration of James Duke of Monmouth*, London, 1685
—, *The Earl of Shaftesbury's Expedient to Settle the Nation Discoursed with His Majesty in the House of Peers at Oxford, 24 March 1681*, London, 1681
—, *England's Happiness Restored*, London, 1679
—, *England's Overjoy at the Duke of Monmouth's Return*, London, 1679
—, *A Further Account of the Proceedings against the Rebels in Scotland*, Edinburgh, 1679
—, *His Grace the Duke of Monmouth honoured in his Progress*, London, 1680
—, *An Historical Account of the Heroick Life and Magnanimous Actions of the Most Illustr. Protestant Prince James Duke of Monmouth, Containing an Account of His Birth, Education Places and Titles with His Martial Atchievements in Flanders and Scotland, His Disgrace and Departure from Court and Kingdom, &c*, London, 1683

—, *The Lady Gray Vindicated*, London, 1681

—, *News from Windsor*, London, 1679

—, *Poems on Affairs of State*, London, 1703

—, *Roscius Anglicanus: or an Historical Review of the Stage*, London, 1711

—, *A True Account of the Great Victory Obtained over the Rebels in Scotland*, Edinburgh, 1679

—, *A True and Faithful Copy of a Real Letter written by a Friend in Utrecht*, Amsterdam, 1679

—, *A True and Impartial Account of the Life of the Most Reverend Father in God Dr James Sharp*, London, 1723

—, *A True and Wonderful Account of a Cure of the King's Evil by Mrs Fanshawe Sister to his Grace the Duke of Monmouth*, London, 1681

—, *A True Description of the New-Erected Fort at Windsor*, London, 1674

—, *A True Narrative of the Duke of Monmouth's late Journey into the West*, London, 1680

—, *The Vindication of his Grace James Duke of Monmouth*, London, 1681

Archives ou Correspondance Inédite de la Maison d'Orange Nassau, G. Groen Van Prinsterer (ed.), 15 vols, deuxième série, V, 1650–1688

d'Aulnoy, Marie Catherine Baronne, *Memoirs of the Court of England in 1675*, trans. Lucretia Arthur, G. D. Gilbert (ed.),London, 1927

Bishop Burnet's History of His Own Time, M. J. Routh (ed.), 6 vols, Oxford, 1823

Burnet's History of My Own Time, Osmund Airy (ed.), 2 vols, Oxford, 1897

Burnet, Gilbert, *The Ill Effects of Animosities among Protestants in England*, London, 1688

—, *The Prince of Orange His Declaration shewing the Reasons why he Invades England with a short preface and some modest remarks*, London, 1688

Calendar of State Papers and Manuscripts Relating to English Affairs in the Archives and Collections of Venice, Allen B. Hinds (ed.), 37 vols, 1916–35

Calendar of State Papers, Domestic: Charles II, Mary Anne Everett Green et al. (eds), 28 vols, London, 1860–1939

Calendar of the Clarendon State Papers Preserved in the Bodleian Library, D. Dunn Macray and H. O. Coxe et al. (eds), 5 vols, Oxford, 1869–1932

Calendar of the Proceedings of the Committee for Advance of Money 1642–1656, Mary Anne Everett Green (ed.), London, 1888

Calendar of Treasury Books Preserved in the Public Record Office, 7 vols, William A. Shaw (ed.), London, 1904

Chamberlayne, Edward, *Angliae Notitia*, London, 1684

Charles II to Lord Taaffe: Letters in Exile, Timothy Crist (ed.), Cambridge, 1974

Clarke, J. S., *The Life of King James the Second King of England &c Collected out of the Memoirs Writ of his Own Hand Together with the King's Advice to his son and His Majesty's Will, published from the original Stuart manuscripts in Carlton House*, 2 vols, London, 1816

The Collection of Autograph Letters and Historical Documents formed by Alfred Morrison. The Bulstrode Papers, Volume 1, 1667–1675, London, 1897

A Collection of the State Papers of John Thurloe, Esq.: Secretary first to the Council of State and Afterwards to the two Protectors, Oliver and Richard Cromwell, Thomas Birch (ed.), 7 vols, London, 1742

Complete Works in Verse and Prose of Andrew Marvell, A. B. Grosart (ed.), 4 vols, 1872–5

Correspondence of the Family of Hatton: Being Chiefly Letters Addressed to Christopher First Viscount Hatton 1601–1704, E. M. Thompson (ed.), 2 vols, Camden Society NS, 22, 23, London, 1878

'Correspondence of Henry Earl of Clarendon and James Earl of Abingdon', C. E. Doble (ed.), *Collectanea*, 3, Oxford Historical Society, 32, Oxford, 1893

Davies, G., 'Three letters on Monmouth's rebellion', *English Historical Review*, 35, 137, Jan. 1920, pp. 113–16

Defoe, Daniel, *A tour thro' the whole island of Great Britain, divided into circuits or journies*, London, 1927

The Despatches of William Perwich, English Agent in Paris, 1669–1677, M. Beryl Curran (ed.), London, 1903

The Diaries of Anne Clifford, D. J. H. Clifford (ed.), Stroud, 1990

'Diary of Dr. Edward Lake, Chaplain and Tutor to the Princesses Mary and Anne, 1677–1678', George Percy Elliott (ed.), *Camden Miscellany*, I, 1847

Diary of Henry Townshend of Elmley Lovett, 1640–1663, J. W. Willis Bund (ed.), 2 vols, London, 1915–20

The Diary of John Evelyn, E. S. De Beer (ed.), 6 vols, Oxford, 1955

The Diary of John Lamont of Newton, Maitland Club Publication, 7, Edinburgh, 1830

The Diary of Mary, Countess Cowper: Lady of the Bedchamber to the Princess of Wales, London, 1864

The Diary of Samuel Pepys, Robert Latham and William Matthews (eds), 11 vols, London, 1970–6

Elias Ashmole, 1617–1692, His Autobiographical and Historical Notes, his Correspondence, and Other Contemporary Sources Relating to his Life and Work, C. H. Josten (ed.), 5 vols, Oxford, 1966

The Entring Book of Roger Morrice, 1677–1691, Mark Goldie et al. (eds), 7 vols, Woodbridge, 2007–9

Etherege, George, *The Man of Mode*, John Barnard (ed.), London, 1979

Extracts from the Records of the Royal Burgh of Lanark, Glasgow, 1893

Fanshawe, H. C., *The History of the Fanshawe Family*, Newcastle, 1927

Faugère, A. P., *Journal d'un voyage à Paris en 1657–1658*, Paris, 1862

The First Triple Alliance: The Letters of Christopher Lindenov, Danish Envoy to London, 1668–1672, Waldemar Westergaard (trans. and ed.), New Haven, 1947

Grey, Ford, Lord, *The Secret History of the Rye House Plot*, London, 1754

The Hamilton Papers; being selections from original letters in the possession of His Grace the Duke of Hamilton and Brandon, relating to the years 1638–1650, S. R. Gardiner (ed.), Camden Society, London, 1880

Historical Manuscripts Commission, 6th Report, Part 1: Report and Appendix, London, 1877

—, *7th Report, Part II: Appendix (continued) and Index*, London, 1879

—, *10th Report, Appendix, Part IV: The Manuscripts of the Earl of Westmorland*, London, 1885

—, *10th Report, Appendix, Part VI: The Manuscripts of the Marquess of Abergavenny, Lord Bray, G. F. Luttrell &c*, London, 1887

—, *11th Report, Appendix, Part II: The Manuscripts of the House of Lords 1678–1688*, London, 1887

—, *11th Report, Appendix, Part V: The Manuscripts of the Earl of Dartmouth*, 3 vols, London, 1887

—, *11th Report, Appendix, Part VI: The Manuscripts of the Duke of Hamilton*, London, 1887

—, *12th Report, Appendix, Part V: The Manuscripts of the Duke of Rutland at Belvoir Castle*, London, 1889

—, *12th Report, Appendix, Part VII: The Manuscripts of S. H. Le Fleming, esq., of Rydall Hall*, London, 1890

—, *12th Report, Appendix, Part IX: The Manuscripts of the Duke of Beaufort, K.G., the Earl of Donoughmore, and others*, London, 1891

—, *15th Report, Appendix, Part V: The Manuscripts of F. J. Savile Foljambe of Osberton*, London, 1897

—, *15th Report, Appendix, Part VIII: The Manuscripts of His Grace the Duke of Buccleuch and Queensberry, K.G., K.Y., preserved at Drumlanrig Castle*, 2 vols, London, 1897–1903

—, *The Laing Manuscripts at Edinburgh University*, I, London, 1914

—, *The Manuscripts of his Grace the Duke of Portland Preserved at Welbeck Abbey*, 10 vols, London, 1891–1931

—, *Report on the Manuscripts of the Late Reginald Rawdon Hastings, Esq.*, 2 vols, London, 1930

—, *The Manuscripts of Allan George Finch*, 2 vols, London, 1913–22

—, *The Manuscripts of Sir William Fitzherbert, bart., and others*, London, 1893

—, *The Manuscripts of the Marquis of Ormonde*, 8 vols, London, 1902–20

—, *Report on the Manuscripts of Mrs Stopford-Sackville of Drayton House, Northamptonshire*, 2 vols, London, 1904

History of Parliament: the House of Commons 1660–1690, Basil Duke Henning (ed.), 3 vols, London, 1983

Hyde, Edward, Earl of Clarendon, *The History of the Rebellion and Civil Wars in England Begun in the Year 1641*, W. Dunn Macray (ed.), 6 vols, Oxford, 1888

—, *The Life of Edward, Earl of Clarendon . . . in which is included a Continuation of his History of the Grand Rebellion*, 3 vols, Oxford, 1827

Inderwick, F. A., *Sidelights on the Stuarts*, London, 1888

'Iter Bellicosum', *Camden Miscellany* XII, 3rd series, XVIII, 1910

Jefferson: Writings, Merrill D. Peterson (ed.), New York, 1984

John Locke: Selected Correspondence, Mark Goldie (ed.), Oxford, 2002

Journal de Jean Vallier, Maître d'Hôtel du Roi, 1648–1657, Henri Courteault and Pierre de Vaissière (eds), 4 vols, Paris, 1902

Journal of the Hon. John Erskine of Carnock 1683–1687, Walter Macleod (ed.), Edinburgh, 1893

The Journal of William Schellinks' Travels in England 1661–1663, Maurice Exwood and H. L. Lehmann, eds, Camden Society, London, 1993

'The Journals of Edmund Warcup, 1676–84', Keith Feiling and F. R. D. Needham (eds), *English Historical Review*, 40, 158, April 1925, pp. 235–60

Journals of Sir John Lauder, Lord Fountainhall, 1665–1676, Donald Crawford (ed.), Edinburgh, 1900

The Lauderdale Papers, Osmund Airy (ed.), 3 vols, Camden Society, NS 38, London, 1884–5

Letter from a Person of Quality to his Friend in the Country, London, 1675

Letters Addressed from London to Sir Joseph Williamson while Plenipotentiary at the Congress of Cologne in the years 1673 and 1674, W. D. Christie (ed.), 2 vols, Camden Society, New Series, VIII, London, 1874

The Letters and Journals of Robert Baillie, David Laing (ed.), 3 vols, Edinburgh, 1842

Letters from the Honourable Algernon Sidney to the Honourable Henry Savile, London, 1742

Letters of Queen Henrietta Maria including her Private Correspondence with Charles the First, Mary Anne Everett Green (ed.), London, 1857

Letters of Rachel, Lady Russell, John Russell (ed.), 2 vols, London, 1853

The Letters, Speeches and Declarations of King Charles II, Arthur Bryant (ed.), London, 1935

Lettres de Henriette-Marie de France Reine d'Angleterre à sa Soeur Christine Duchesse de Savoie, Rome, 1881

Lettres de Madame de Sévigné de sa Famille et de ses Amis, M. Monmerque (ed.), 14 vols, Paris, 1862–6

Lettres du Cardinal Mazarin pendant son ministère, M. A. Chéruel (ed.), 9 vols, Paris, 1872–1906

The Life and Letters of Sir George Savile, Bart., first Marquis of Halifax, H. C. Foxcroft (ed.), 2 vols, London, 1898

The Life and Times of Anthony Wood, Antiquary, of Oxford, 1632–95, Andrew Clark (ed.), 5 vols, Oxford, 1891

Locke, John, *Two Treatises of Government*, Peter Laslett (ed.), Cambridge, 1988

Locke's Two Treatises of Government, Richard Ashcraft (ed.), Cambridge, 1987

Lorenzo Magalotti at the Court of Charles II: His Relazione d'Inghilterra *of 1668*, W. E. Knowles Middleton (ed.), Waterloo, Ont., 1980

Luttrell, Narcissus, *A Brief Historical Relation of State Affairs from September 1678 to April 1714*, 6 vols, Oxford, 1857

Magalotti, Lorenzo, *The Travels of Cosmo the Third Duke of Tuscany through England*, London, 1821

Manwood's Treatise of the Forest Laws, London, 1717

Mémoires de Daniel de Cosnac, 2 vols, Paris, 1852

Mémoires de Madame de Motteville sur Anne d'Autriche et sa Cour, M. Sainte-Beuve (ed.), 3 vols, Paris, 1855

Memoirs of Mademoiselle de Montpensier Grand-daughter of Henri Quatre and niece of Queen Henrietta Maria Written by Herself, 3 vols, London, 1848

The Memoirs of Sir John Reresby: The Complete Text and a Selection from his Letters, Andrew Browning (ed.), second edition by Mary K. Geiter and W. A. Speck, London, 1991

Memoirs of Sophia, Electress of Hanover 1630–1680, trans. H. Forester, London, 1888

Memoirs of the Count of Grammont Containing the History of the English Court under Charles II, Anthony Hamilton (ed.), London, 1890

Memoirs of the Most Material Transactions in England for the Last Hundred Years Preceding the Revolution in 1688, James Welwood (ed.), 6th edition, London, 1706

Memoirs of Thomas, Earl of Ailesbury written by himself, 2 vols, the Roxburghe Club, London, 1890

Memorials and letters illustrative of the life and times of John Graham of Claverhouse, Viscount Dundee, Mark Napier (ed.), 3 vols, Edinburgh, 1859–62

Memorials of the Family of Wemyss of Wemyss, William Fraser (ed.), 3 vols, Edinburgh, 1888

Négociations de Monsieur le Comte d'Avaux en Hollande depuis 1679 jusqu'en 1684, 3 vols, Paris, 1753

Nicholas Papers: Correspondence of Sir Edward Nicholas, Secretary of State, George F. Warner (ed.), Camden Society, 4 vols, London, 1886–1920

North, Roger, *Examen*, London, 1740

Oeuvres de Louis XIV: III Mémoires et Pièces Militaires, Paris, 1806

Original Papers containing the Secret History of Great Britain from the Restoration to the Accession of the House of Hannover to which are prefixed Extracts from the Memoirs of James II as written by Himself, James MacPherson (ed.), 2 vols, London, 1775

The Oxford Alderman's Speech to the D. of M., London, 1681

Pitman, Henry, *A Relation of the Great Suffering and Strange Adventures of Henry Pitman*, London, 1689

Poems on Affairs of State: Augustan satirical verse, 1660–1714, 7 vols, George de Forest Lord et al. (eds), New Haven and London, 1963–75

The Rawdon Papers, John Bramhall (ed.), London, 1819

'The Reception of the Duke of Monmouth at Chichester', *Sussex Archaeological Collections*, VII, 1854, pp. 169–72

Register of the Privy Council of Scotland, 3rd series, 16 vols, Edinburgh, 1908–70

Relation de la Feste de Versailles du Dix-Huitième Juillet Mil Six Cens Soixante-Huit, Paris, 1668

Saint-Maurice, Thomas-François Chabod, Marquis de, *Lettres sur la Cour de Louis XIV, 1667–1670*, C. Lévy (ed.), 2 vols, Paris, 1911–12

'Samuel Dassell's Narrative', *Notes and Queries for Somerset and Dorset*, 27, 1955–60, Taunton, 1961

Selections from the Correspondence of Arthur Capel, Earl of Essex, 1675–1677, Clement Edwards Pike (ed.), Camden Third Series, XXIV, London, 1913

Shields, Alexander, *A hind let loose or an Historical Representation of the Testimonies of the Church of Scotland*, 1687

Sidney, Henry, *Diary of the Times of Charles II*, R. W. Blencowe (ed.), 2 vols, London, 1843

'Sir Patrick Hume's Narrative', in *Observations on the Historical Work of the Late Right Honourable Charles James Fox*, London, 1809

'Some unpublished letters of Burnet, the Historian', *Camden Miscellany*, London, 1907

State Trials, William Cobbett, T. B. Howell, T. J. Howell and David Jardine (eds), 33 vols, London, 1809–26

Statutes of the Realm, 6, 1685–94, John Raithby (ed.), 1819

Strype, John, *Survey of the Cities of London and Westminster*, London, 1720

Terry, C. Sanford, 'The Duke of Monmouth's Instructions in June 1679', *The English Historical Review*, Vol. 20, No. 77, Jan. 1905, pp. 127–9

Treby, George, *A Collection of Letters and Other Writings Relating to the Horrid Popish Plot*, London, 1681

The Trial of Charles I: A Contemporary Account taken from the Memoirs of Sir Thomas Herbert and John Rushworth, Roger Lockyer (ed.), London, 1974

Wicquefort, Abraham van, *A Relation in form of Journal, of the Voiage and Residence which the most Excellent and most Mighty Prince Charles the II King of Great Britain, & c. hath made in Holland, from the 25 of May, to the 2 of June, 1660*, trans. William Lower, The Hague, 1660

The Works of John Sheffield, Earl of Mulgrave, Marquis of Normanby, and Duke of Buckingham, 2 vols, London, 1729

The Works of Sir William Temple Bart., 4 vols, London, 1814

Periodicals

Domestick Intelligence
The Gentleman's Magazine
Journal of the House of Commons
Journal of the House of Lords
The London Gazette
Mercurius Politicus
Newes Published for the Satisfaction and Information of the People
Paris Gazette
The Parliament Kite, or the Tell-Tale Bird
The Perfect Weekly Account
Protestant, Domestick Intelligence or News Both from City and Country

Secondary Sources

Anderson, Peter D., *Robert Stewart, Earl of Orkney, Lord of Shetland*, Edinburgh, 1982

Aylmer, G. E., *The Crown's Servants: Government and Civil Service under Charles II, 1660–1685*, Oxford, 2002

Baines, Arnold H. J., 'Monmouth, Kiffin and the Gosfrights', *Baptist Quarterly*, 20.3, Jul. 1963, pp. 129–30

Barnett, Correlli, *Britain and her Army 1509–1970*, London, 1970

Baxter, Stephen B., *William III*, London, 1966

Bayley, John, *The History and Antiquities of the Tower of London*, London, 1830

Black, E. (ed.), *Kings in Conflict: Ireland in the 1690s*, Belfast, 1990

Bond, Christopher, 'The Phoenix and the Prince: the Poetry of Thomas Ross', *Review of English Studies*, 60, 246, 2009

Boswell, Eleonore, *The Restoration Court Stage*, Cambridge, 1932.

Boutwood, James, 'A Vanished Elizabethan Mansion: Toddington Manor House Bedfordshire', *Country Life*, 23 Mar. 1961

Britland, Karen, *Drama at the Courts of Queen Henrietta Maria*, Cambridge, 2006

—, 'Exile or homecoming? Henrietta Maria in France 1644–69', in Torsten Riotte and Philip Mansel (eds), *Monarchy and Exile: The Politics of Legitimacy from Marie de Médicis to Wilhelm II*, London, 2011

Browning, Andrew, *Thomas Osborne, Earl of Danby and Duke of Leeds, 1632–1712*, 3 vols, Glasgow, 1944–51

Buckroyd, Julia, *Church and State in Scotland*, Edinburgh, 1980

Burke, John, and John Bernard Burke, *A Genealogical and Heraldic History of the Extinct and Dormant Baronetcies of England*, London, 1838

Cartwright, Julia, *Madame: A Life of Henriette Daughter of Charles I and Duchess of Orleans*, London, 1894

Chandler, David G., *Sedgemoor 1685: from Monmouth's Invasion to the Bloody Assizes*, Spellmount, 1995

Childs, John, 'Monmouth and the army in Flanders', *Journal of the Society of Army Historical Research*, 52, 1974

—, *The Army of Charles II*, London, 1976

—, *Nobles, Gentlemen and the Profession of Arms in Restoration Britain 1660–1688: A Biographical Dictionary of British Army Officers on Foreign Service*, London, 1987

Christie, W. D., *A Life of Anthony Ashley Cooper, First Earl of Shaftesbury*, 2 vols, London, 1871

Clay, Christopher, *Public Finance and Private Wealth: the Career of Sir Stephen Fox 1627–1716*, Oxford, 1978

Claydon, Tony, *William III and the Godly Revolution*, Cambridge, 2004

Clifton, Robin, *The Last Popular Rebellion: the Western Rising of 1685*, Hounslow, 1984

Colvin, H. M. (ed.), *The History of the King's Works*, 6 vols, London, 1963–82

Cooper, C. H., *Annals of Cambridge*, 5 vols, Cambridge, 1842–1908

Dalrymple, John, *Memoirs of Great Britain and Ireland*, 3 vols, London, 1790

Dalton, Charles, *English Army Lists and Commission Registers, 1661–1714*, London, 1904

De Krey, Gary S., *London and the Restoration, 1659–1683*, Cambridge, 2005

Dictionnaire de Biographie Française, J. Balteau (ed.), Paris, 1939

'A Discourse Concerning the Effects of the Great Frost, on Trees and Other Plants Anno 1683', *The Philosophical Transactions of the Royal Society*, 1753

D'Oyley, Elizabeth, *James, Duke of Monmouth*, London, 1938

Ekberg, Carl J., *The Failure of Louis XIV's Dutch War*, Chapel Hill, 1979

Falkner, James, *Marshal Vauban and the Defence of Louis XIV's France*, Barnsley, 2011

Fea, Allan, *King Monmouth: being a History of the Career of James Scott, 'The Protestant Duke' 1649–1685*, London, 1902

Ferguson, James, *Robert Ferguson the Plotter*, Edinburgh, 1887

Fraser, William, *The Scotts of Buccleuch*, 2 vols, Edinburgh, 1878

Galignani, A. and W., *A History of Paris from its Earliest Period to the Present Day*, 3 vols, London, 1825

Gardiner, S. R., *The History of the Great Civil War*, 4 vols, London, 1905, IV, pp. 166–74

Geyl, Pieter, *Orange and Stuart: 1641–1672*, London, 1939, 2001 edn.

Given Wilson, C., and Alice Curteis, *Royal Bastards of Medieval England*, London, 1984

Goodison, J. W., *Catalogue of Cambridge Portraits*, Cambridge, 1955

Green, Mary Anne Everett, *Lives of the Princesses of England*, 6 vols, London, 1849–55

Griffey, Erin, and Caroline Hibbard, 'Henrietta Maria's inventory at Colombes: courtly magnificence and hidden politics', *Journal of the History of Collections*, 24, 2, 2012

Griffiths, Antony, *The Print in Stuart Britain, 1603–1689*, London, 1998

Guizot, F., *Life of Oliver Cromwell*, London, 1887

Haley, K. H. D., 'Shaftesbury's Lists of the Lay Peers and Members of the Commons, 1677–8', *Bulletin of the Institute of Historical Research*, 1940, 43, pp. 86–105

—, *The First Earl of Shaftesbury*, Oxford, 1968

Harris, Tim, *The London Crowds in the Reign of Charles II*, Cambridge, 1987

—, *Revolution: the Great Crisis of the British Monarchy 1685–1720*, London, 2006

Hartmann, C. H., *Charles II and Madame*, London, 1934

—, *The King My Brother*, London, 1954

Hollstein, F. W. H., *Dutch and Flemish Etchings, Engravings and Woodcuts c.1450–1700*, 20 vols, 1929–78

Hutton, Ronald, 'The making of the secret treaty of Dover', *The Historical Journal*, 29, 2, June 1986, pp. 295–318

—, *Charles II: King of England, Scotland and Ireland*, Oxford, 1989

—, 'The religion of Charles II', in R. Malcolm Smuts (ed.), *The Stuart Courts and Europe*, Cambridge, 1996, pp. 228–47

Israel, Jonathan, *The Anglo-Dutch Moment: Essays on the Glorious Revolution and its World Impact*, Cambridge, 1991

—, *The Dutch Republic*, Oxford, 1995

Keay, Anna, *The Magnificent Monarch: Charles II and the Ceremonies of Power*, London, 2008

Keblusek, Marika, 'Een zwarte doos op een buiten bij Delft: Engelse royalisten op "De Ruit", 1656–1660', in E. den Hartog and R. M. Deuling (eds), *Kastelenstichting Holland en Zeeland: 'Buitenplaatsen in de omgeving van Delft'*, Rotterdam, 2008

Kennett, White, *A Complete History of England with the Lives of all the Kings and Queens*, 3 vols, London, 1719

Kenyon, John, *The Popish Plot*, London, 1972

Key, Newton E., '"High feeding and smart Drinking", Associating Hedge-Lane Lords in Exclusion Crisis London', ch. 9 of Jason McElligott (ed.), *Fear, Exclusion and Revolution: Roger Morrice and Britain in the 1680s*, Aldershot, 2006

Lauder, John, *Historical Observes of Memorable Occurrents in Church and State 1680–1686*, Edinburgh, 1840

Lee, Maurice, *The Heiresses of Buccleuch: Marriage, Money and Politics in Seventeenth-Century Britain*, East Linton, 1996

Lewis, Mary E., 'A traitor's death? The identity of a drawn, hanged and quartered man from Hulton Abbey, Staffordshire', *Antiquity*, 82, 2008, pp. 113–24

Locke, Richard, *The Western Rebellion*, Taunton, 1782

Lynn, John A., *The Wars of Louis XIV 1667–1714*, London, 1999

Lysons, Samuel and Daniel, *Magna Britannia*, 6 vols, London, 1806–22

MacIntosh, Gillian H., *The Scottish Parliament under Charles II 1660–1685*, Edinburgh, 2007

Maguire, Alison, 'A collection of seventeenth–century architectural plans', *Architectural History*, 35, 1992, pp. 164–5

Malcolm, James Peller, *Londinium Redivivum*, 4 vols, London, 1802–7

Mansel, Philip, *Dressed to Rule: Royal and Court Costume from Louis XIV to Elizabeth II*, London, 2005

Maurier, Aubrey du, *The Lives of all the Princes of Orange*, London, 1693

Miller, John, *James II*, New Haven and London, 1978

—, *Charles II*, London, 1991

Milne, Doreen J., 'The results of the Rye House Plot and their influence upon the Revolution of 1688', *Transactions of the Royal Historical Society*, 5th series, vol. I, 1951, pp. 91–108

Milovanovic, Nicolas, and Alexandre Maral (eds), *Louis XIV, l'Homme et le Roi*, Paris, 2009

Milton, Philip, 'Shaftesbury and the Rye House Plot', in John Spurr (ed.), *Anthony Ashley Cooper, First Earl of Shaftesbury 1621–1683*, Swansea, 2011, pp. 233–68

Muddiman, J. G., *The Bloody Assizes*, London, 1929

Nimwegen, Olaf van, *The Dutch Army and the Military Revolutions, 1588–1688*, Woodbridge, 2010

Pike, Clement E., 'The Intrigue to Deprive the Earl of Essex of the Lord Lieutenancy of Ireland', *Transactions of the Royal Historical Society*, 3rd Series, vol. 5, 1911, pp. 89–103

Roberts, George, *The Life, Progresses and Rebellion of James Duke of Monmouth*, 2 vols, London, 1844

Rodger, N. A. M., *The Safeguard of the Sea: a Naval History of Britain, 660–1649*, London, 1997

—, *The Command of the Ocean: A Naval History of Britain, 1649–1815*, London, 2005

Routledge, F. J., *England and the Treaty of the Pyrenees*, Liverpool, 1953

Rowlands, Guy, *The Dynastic State and the Army under Louis XIV, 1661–1701*, Cambridge, 2010

Schwoerer, Lois G., 'The trial of Lord William Russell, 1683: Judicial murder?', *The Journal of Legal History*, 1988, 9:2, pp. 142–68

Scott, George, *Lucy Walter: Wife or Mistress?*, London, 1947

Scott, Jonathan, *Algernon Sidney and the Restoration Crisis 1677–83*, Cambridge, 1991

Somerset, Anne, *Ladies in Waiting: from the Tudors to the Present Day*, London, 1984

Sonnino, Paul, *Louis XIV and the Origins of the Dutch War*, Cambridge, 1988

Spurr, John (ed.), *Antony Ashley Cooper, First Earl of Shaftesbury*, Swansea, 2011

Storer, Bernard, *Sedgemoor: its History and Natural History*, Newton Abbot, 1972

Strickland, Agnes, *Lives of the Queens of England*, 11 vols, London, 1840–8

Survey of London, 11, 'Chelsea, Part IV: the Royal Hospital', London, 1927

Survey of London, 16, 'St-Martin-in-the-Fields', I: Charing Cross, London, 1935

Survey of London, 33 and 34, 'St Anne Soho', ed. F. H. W. Sheppard, London, 1966

Tapsell, Grant, *The Personal Rule of Charles II: 1681–1685*, Woodbridge, 2007

Thurley, Simon, *The Whitehall Palace Plan of 1670*, London Topographical Society, 153, 1998

—, *Whitehall Palace: An Architectural History*, London and New Haven, 1999

—, *Hampton Court: A Social and Architectural History*, London and New Haven, 2003

—, *Somerset House: The Palace of England's Queens 1551–1692*, London, 2009

Turner, E. R., 'The Privy Council of 1679', *English Historical Review*, 30, 118, Apr. 1915, pp. 251–70

Turner, F. C., *James II*, London, 1948

Vertue, George, *Anecdotes of Painting in England*, III, London, 1762

Victoria County History: A History of the County of Bedford, 3 vols, London, 1904–12

Victoria County History: A History of the County of Middlesex: Volume 7: Acton, Chiswick, Ealing and Brentford, West Twyford, Willesden, 1982

Victoria County History: A History of the County of York East Riding: Volume 1: The City of Kingston upon Hull, K. J. Allison (ed.), London, 1969

Watson, J. N. P., *Captain, General and Rebel Chief: The Life of James, Duke of Monmouth*, London, 1979

Wauchope, P. A. C., *Patrick Sarsfield and the Williamite War*, Dublin, 1992

Whiting, John, *Persecution Exposed*, London, 1791

Wigfield, W. MacDonald, *The Monmouth Rebels*, Gloucester and New York, 1985

Willcock, John, *A Scots Earl in Covenanting Times: Being the Life and Times of Archibald 9th Earl of Argyll*, Edinburgh, 1907

Woolf, D. R., *Reading History in Early Modern England*, Cambridge, 2000

Woolhouse, Roger, *Locke: A Biography*, Cambridge, 2007

Wingrove Cooke, G. (ed.), *The Life of the First Earl of Shaftesbury from Original Documents in the Possession of the Family*, 2 vols, London, 1836

Young, Charles R., *The Royal Forests of Medieval England*, Leicester, 1979

Young, William, *International Politics and Warfare in the Age of Louis XIV and Peter the Great*, New York, 2004

ACKNOWLEDGEMENTS

While the Duke of Monmouth's English title died with him, his Scottish dukedom and his line did not. As a consequence many of his paintings and effects remain the property of his direct descendant Richard, 13th Duke of Queensberry and Buccleuch and I am immensely grateful to him for his assistance and encouragement. Charm and generosity are clearly in the family genes. Particular thanks are due to Sandra Howarth, the curator of the Buccleuch Heritage Trust and Dr Crispin Powell, the archivist, for their patient assistance on numerous questions. For advice or information I would like to thank Tabitha Barber, Andrew Barclay, Anthony Camp, Tony Claydon, Diana Dethloff, Anna Groundwater, Frances Harris, Tim Harris, Karen Hearn, Ronald Hutton, Edward Impey, Sally Jeffrey, Marika Keblusek, Catharine MacLeod, Philip Mansel, John Miller, the Hon. Mary Montague, Philip and Catherine Mould, James Peill. Particular thanks are due to Patric Dickinson, Clarencieux King of Arms; Peter Woodruff, formerly professor of psychiatry at the University of Sheffield; and Serve Minis for an expert tour of the remarkable surviving defences of the city of Maastricht. The Rev. Anne Crawford of St George's Church, Toddington, and the churchwardens of St Mary's, Bridgwater, St Mary the Virgin, Chedzoy and St Mary's, Westonzoyland each generously enabled me to visit their church.

Andrew Gordon of David Higham Associates overcame initial scepticism to be a wonderful supporter of this project. Michael Fishwick at Bloomsbury took the book on and has been both enthusiastic and unharrying – a perfect combination in an editor. His colleagues Anna Simpson, Kate Johnson, Marigold Atkey and Rachel Nicholson have each in their way helped turn a large email attachment into a real and respectable book. Professor Ronald Hutton generously read the manuscript in draft and saved me from many errors. Those that remain are, of course, entirely my own. Simon Thurley read the text and discussed scores of issues with me along the way; it has been his ceaseless encouragement that has, more than anything, made this book possible. My father, John Keay, read and helped refine the text. My mother, Julia Keay, would, I am sure, have felt about its subject as I do. I wish I could have shared it with her. As one who, unlike Monmouth, has had the best of parents, I dedicate this to mine with love and gratitude.

INDEX

'Abridgement of the English Military Discipline, An', 157
Act of Indemnity and Oblivion, 53
Acts of Succession, 101
Albemarle, Anne, Duchess of, 68
Albemarle, Christopher Monck, Duke of, 112, 237, 252
  commands Devon militia, 345, 350
Albemarle, George Monck, Duke of, 43–5, 57, 120, 142, 176, 214
  role as captain general, 156, 158
Alfonso VI, King of Portugal, 77
Alington, William, 129
American Declaration of Independence, 387
Amsterdam, exiled radicals in, 230–1
Anne, Princess (later Queen Anne), 100, 104, 162, 172, 210, 213, 215, 322, 383
  Protestant upbringing, 136, 151
  performs in *Calisto*, 240
Anne of Austria, Queen of France, 3
Apsley, Allan, 219
Argyll, Archibald Campbell, Earl of, 291, 330, 332–3, 335–7, 339–41, 343, 348
  defeated in Scotland, 352–3, 355
Arlington, Henry Bennet, Earl of, 107, 117–18, 129, 132, 138, 140–1, 147
  and exclusion crisis, 262–3
Armstrong, Sir Thomas, 211, 214, 250, 272, 348

military service, 115, 187, 200
returned as MP, 197
and marriage rumour, 241–2
secures writ of habeas corpus, 283
and opposition plotting, 287–8, 296–7
flees abroad, 304, 320
executed, 330
Arran, Richard Butler, Earl of, 251
Ashburnham, John, 66

Balliol College, Oxford, 260
Barillon d'Armoncourt, Ambassador Paul, 221, 246, 311
Barkstead, John, 27–8, 51–2
Bassett (or Bovett), Colonel Richard, 350
Batten, Sir William, 4
Battle of the Dunes, 40
bear gardens, closure of, 27
Bellasis, John, Baron, 134
Bentinck, Hans Willem, 228–9, 327
Berkenhead, Sir John, 111
Bettiscomb, John, 337
Bill of Rights, 382
Binnenhof Palace, 6, 12, 14, 20, 23
Birch, Sampson, 283
Blackburn, Robert, 61
Bloody Assizes, 377–9
Blooteling, Abraham, 160
Blount, Charles, 234
Bolton, Henrietta (née Crofts), Duchess of, 164

Bonfire Night, 289
Book of Common Prayer, 48
Boscobel Wood, 19
Bothwell Bridge, Battle of, 207,
    212–13, 363
Boughton, tailor drinks Monmouth's
    health, 281
Bowman, Francis, 70
Bragg, John, 376
Breda, 16, 239
Bridgwater, 350–1, 356–7, 359, 367
Bristol, George Digby, Earl of, 32, 100
Britannia, model for figure of, 71
Bruce, Thomas, Lord, 300–1, 303
Bryon (footman), 315
Bryte (footman), 74
Buccleuch, Anna, Countess
    of, see Monmouth, Anna,
    Duchess of
Buccleuch, Francis Scott, Earl of, 46
Buckingham, George Villiers, Duke
    of, 49, 57, 100, 104, 142, 169, 171,
    216
  and Dutch wars, 112–14, 117–18
  and the Cabal, 132, 138, 140
  replaced as chancellor of
    Cambridge, 158
Burford, Charles Beauclerk, Earl of
    (later Duke of St Albans), 160
Burnet, Bishop Gilbert, 181, 191, 204,
    245, 294, 299, 327
Bursfield, Charles, 31–2
Burton, James, 379
Busse, Thomas, 72
Buyse, Antony, 365–6

Cabal, the, 131–2, 138–40
Calvinism, 131, 176
Cambridge University, 62, 158–9, 255,
    297
Carbery, Richard Vaughan, Earl of, 7
Cardenas, Don Alonso de, 32–3
Carey, Robert, Earl of Monmouth, 58
Carisbrooke Castle, 4, 11
Carlingford, Theobald Taaffe, Earl
    of, 21, 23, 162
Caroline, Queen, 383
Carteret, Sir George, 77
Caryll, John, Sir Salomon
    Single, 109–10

Cassilis, John Kennedy, Earl
    of, 178–9, 205
Cassiobury House, 216, 298
Castlehaven, James Touchet, Earl
    of, 32
Castlemaine, Barbara (née Villiers),
    Countess of (later Duchess of
    Cleveland), 53, 56, 65, 71, 81, 83,
    97–8, 137, 148, 160
Catherine of Braganza, Queen, 49–50,
    56, 74, 76–7, 102, 137, 209, 307, 310
  infertility, 97–8, 100
  Monmouth appeals to, 367–8
Cavalier Parliament, 48, 196
Charleroi, 86, 89, 170, 172
Charles I, King, 2–5, 8, 210
  trial and execution, 11–12, 14–15,
    27, 43, 290
Charles II, King
  attempts abduction of
    Monmouth, 1–2, 17–19, 32–4
  campaigns as Prince of Wales, 2–7,
    10–11, 19–20
  relationship with Lucy Walter, 7,
    10, 17, 20, 22
  declared king of Scotland, 15, 19
  treaty with Spain, 22, 25, 28–9
  education, 38–9
  and his siblings, 41–2, 53–4
  relationship with Monmouth, 41–3,
    49–50, 52, 100–2, 148–50, 221–2,
    224, 324
  restoration, 43–5, 52–3
  and religious settlement, 47–8
  extramarital affairs, 53, 71, 96–8
  royal progress, 64–5
  and tennis, 67
  and Great Fire, 81–2
  and male pursuits, 95–6
  compared with Duke of York, 98–9
  and marriage rumour, 102–4, 234,
    241–5
  secret treaty and family
    reunion, 106–12
  receives news of Maastricht, 130
  clashes with Parliament, 165–70
  and Monmouth's
    commission, 183–4
  and Protestant succession, 194–5
  appoints coalition council, 201–2, 213

prorogues Parliament, 202–3
ill-health, 217–19, 243, 286
and Duke of York's return,
219–21
and Monmouth's banishment, 220–4
and Monmouth's return, 235–7
breach with Monmouth, 237–9, 241,
245, 269–70, 275–6
and exclusion crisis, 251–64
divorce proposal, 256
accepts French funds, 263
never recalls Parliament, 264
bans Whig dinner, 274
and Monmouth's reconciliation and
submission, 303–15
resumes correspondence with
Monmouth, 320–1
secret meeting with
Monmouth, 325–8
death and conversion, 328–9, 336, 343
Chatham, 82–3
Chester, welcomes Monmouth, 280–2,
284–5
Chesterfield, Philip Stanhope,
Lord, 81
Cheyne, Lord, 301
Chichester, welcomes
Monmouth, 248, 257–8
Chiffinch, William, 368
Chiswick House, 66, 75, 92, 144, 216
Christ Church College, Oxford, 65,
74, 259, 263
Christmas, suppression of, 27
Chudleigh, Thomas, 323–4, 327
Church of England, re-establishment
of, 45, 48
church bells, ringing of, 282, 284
Churchill, Arabella, 97–8
Churchill, John (later Duke of
Marlborough), 97, 128, 155, 353,
361–3, 382–3
City of London, as opposition
centre, 272–4
Clarendon, Edward Hyde, Earl of, 5,
7, 12, 17, 25, 32, 39, 45, 53, 65, 251
opposition to Monmouth's
dukedom, 57
and succession, 100–2
flees England, 104–5
Clarendon, Henry Hyde, Earl of, 369

Clerke, John, 143
Clifford of Chudleigh, Thomas,
Baron, 132, 135, 138, 140
Cliveden House, 216
coffee houses, 51, 59, 111, 198, 242
Colchester, Richard Savage,
Viscount, 275
Colman, Edward, 193–4
Colombes, 36–8, 41–2, 45, 47, 54, 58,
70, 133, 211, 258, 313
Condé, Prince de, 117
Conway, Edward, Viscount and Earl
of, 276
Cooke, Colonel, 264
Cooper, Samuel, 42
Corneille, Pierre, *Laodice*, 88
Cornwallis, Charles, Baron, 384
Corpus Christi College,
Oxford, 74–5, 259
Cosin, John, 34, 242
Cosnac, Daniel, 88
Coudenberg Palace, 1, 29–30, 32, 185,
319
Court of Justiciary, 332
Covenanters, 15–17, 176–7, 204, 239
Coventry, Sir John, 111–12
Coventry, welcomes Monmouth, 283
Cranbourne Lodge, 161
Cranmer, Thomas, 189, 385
Craven, William, Earl of, 18
Creede, Mr, 102
Crewkerne, 'healing' incident, 249,
257–8, 281
Crofts, Cecily, 37
Crofts, William, Baron, 36–9, 41–2,
47–9, 54–5, 68–70, 73, 211, 306
Crofts, Mrs, 306
Cromwell, Oliver, 1, 11, 13, 15, 21–2,
26–8, 40, 290
his head displayed in public, 52
his Council of State, 138
Cromwell, Richard, 40, 43
Crown Jewels, 25, 45
Crowne, John, *Calisto*, 239–40
Cumberland, Rupert, Duke
of, *see* Rupert, Prince

Dalkeith Palace, 383
Danby, Thomas Osborne, Earl
of, 138, 142, 166–7, 169, 172

and Scottish affairs, 177, 180–1
and Popish Plot, 189–90
fall of, 195–200, 208–10, 253
'Danby's Test', 167–8
Dangerfield, Thomas, 232, 235–6
D'Artagnan, Charles de Batz-
    Castelmore, Comte, 127–8
Dartmouth, George Legge, Baron, 293
Davenant, William, 109
de Haro, Don Luis, 40–1
De Ruit, 24, 30–1
De Ruyter, Admiral, 122
De Witt, Cornelius, 83, 119, 139
De Witt, Johan, 78, 107, 116, 119, 139
Dearlove, Thomas, 209
Declaration of Breda, 16
Declaration of Indulgence, 131–2
Delamere, George Booth, Baron, 280,
    337
Denham, John, 66
Derby, Ferdinando Stanley, Earl
    of, 279
Devonshire, William Cavendish, Earl
    of, 381
Dieren Palace, 321, 323–5
Disney, William, 336
divine right of kings, 265–6
Doncaster, Charles Scott, Earl of, 121,
    130, 141–2, 267
Doncaster, James Scott, Earl of, 147,
    214–15, 267
Dover Castle, 80, 109
Drumclog, Battle of, 205
Dryden, John
    The Indian Emperor, 93
    Absalom and Achitophel, 148, 271–2
Duke's Theatre, 163
Dunkirk
    sold to French, 100
    Monmouth visits, 113–14
Dutch East India Company, 13
Dutch Wars, 78–83
    French alliance, 106–7, 112–19,
        121–9
    flooding of Dutch republic, 116, 119
    disillusion and peace treaty, 139–41
    French continuation of, 154–5,
        169–71, 318–19
    Anglo-Dutch alliance, 172–5, 182–9
    'Treaty of Truce', 321

Earl of Strathmore's regiment, 178
Edinburgh Castle, 353
Edward III, King, 212, 221
Edward of the Palatinate, Prince, 49
Eliot, James, 18
Eliot, Thomas, 17–19
Elizabeth I, Queen, 80, 142, 189, 236,
    302, 323, 369
Elizabeth (née Stuart), Queen of
    Bohemia, 7, 231
Epsom racecourse, 279
Erskine, William, 34
Essex, Arthur Capel, Earl of, 198, 209,
    216, 218, 220, 233–4, 272, 289, 304
    dies mysteriously, 298–9
Essex, Robert Devereux, Earl of, 369
Etherege, George, The Man of
    Mode, 163–4, 239–40
Evelyn, John, 14, 17, 39, 91, 134, 139,
    147, 153
Exeter, welcomes Monmouth, 247–8

Falconbridge (or Fauconberg) Thomas
    Belasyse, Viscount, 222
Falmouth, Charles Berkeley, Earl
    of, 79
Fanshawe, Mary, 21, 162–3, 257, 362
Fanshawe, William, 163
Fariaux, General de, 128
Farrier, Thomas, 81
Ferguson, Robert, 231, 288–9, 320
    'Letter to a Person of Honour', 244
    and Rye House plot, 294, 296–7, 300
    and Monmouth's rebellion, 330–7,
        341–5, 347–8, 355, 366–8
    and invasion declaration, 342–5
    escapes to Amsterdam, 379
Feversham, Louis Duras, Earl of, 170,
    173, 353–4, 357, 359–60, 362–3
Ffloyd, Dr, 34
Filmer, Robert, Patriarcha, 265
Finch, Sir Heneage, 237, 264
Fonseca, Monsieur, 322
Ford, William, 72, 75, 215
Forrester, Andrew, 199
Foucault, Madame, 268
Four Days' Battle, 80
Fourille, Chevalier de, 125
Fox, Sir Stephen, 74–5, 90, 120, 147,
    157, 215, 223, 268, 372

Franche-Comté, 86–7, 89
Frederick, Elector Palatine, 231
Frederick Henry, Prince of Orange, 6, 23–4, 123

Gardiner, Bishop James, 133
Gaunt, Elizabeth, 379
general elections, 48, 166, 196–8, 217, 220, 233, 252, 257, 259–60
George I, King, 17, 383–4
Gerard of Brandon, Charles, Lord, 41, 92, 146, 224
Gerrard, Sir Gilbert, 242–3
Gettings, Mrs, 121
Ghysen, Claes, 17
Gilmour, Sir John, 59–61
Glorious Revolution, 382–3, 387
Godfrey, Colonel Charles, 143, 164, 224, 227, 233, 237, 284
Godfrey, Sir Edmund Bury, 190, 191–2, 237
Godolphin, Sidney, Baron, 115
Goodenough, Richard, 341
Gordon (page), 69
Gosfright, Margaret, 10, 24, 242
Gosfright, Peter, 10, 103, 174, 242
Gough, Fr Stephen, 38, 133, 210
Gracechurch Street pillory, 289
Grafton, Henry FitzRoy, Duke of, 65, 222, 238, 353–4, 363, 382
Grana, Otto del Caretto, Marquis of, 318–19, 321, 325, 331
Great Fire of London, 72, 81–2, 272
Great Plague, 74, 79, 258
Greenwich Palace, 49, 51
Grey, Lady Jane, 369
Grey, Ford, Baron Grey of Warke, 210, 239, 257–8
  and opposition plotting, 287–8, 291–2, 296
  flees abroad, 304, 320
  and Monmouth's rebellion, 330–2, 336, 341, 347–8, 355–6, 360–1, 364–7
  betrays Monmouth, 365–6
  pardoned under James II, 379
  prospers under William III, 383
Grey, Mary, Baroness Grey of Warke, 239, 257–8

Griffin, Edward, 306
Griffith, John, 18–19
Guildhall, 81, 172, 254
Guise, duc de, 114
Gwyn, Nell, 96, 148, 160, 238

habeas corpus, 283–4
Haberdashers' Hall dinner, 274–5
Halifax, George Savile, Earl and Marquis of, 190, 201, 209, 218, 220, 233–4, 254, 273, 276
  and Monmouth's reconciliation and submission, 303–8, 311–12, 314–15
  and Hampden's trial, 317
  and king's secret meeting with Monmouth, 326–8
Hamilton, William, 2nd Duke of, 4, 11, 13
Hamilton, William, 3rd Duke of, 177–81, 205–6
Hamilton, James, 89–90
Hamilton, Robert, 204, 206–7
Hampden, John, 290, 298, 308, 313, 315
  trial and sentence, 317–18
Hampton Court, Monmouth's public debut, 49–50
Harvey, John, 30
Harvey, Mrs, 17
Hatton, Charles, 232
Hedge Lane, 143, 238, 246, 254, 266, 274, 277
Helderenburg, 340
Hellevoetsluis, 5–6, 10–11, 381
Henri IV, King of France, 107, 211
Henrietta Maria, Queen, 26, 34, 47, 49, 87, 100, 242, 313
  exile in France, 3, 8, 14–15
  and Catholicism, 37–8, 175
  relationship with king, 41–2
  and Monmouth's title, 57
  opposition to Clarendon, 100
Henry IV, King, 384
Henry V, King, 58
Henry VII, King, 337, 384
Henry VIII, King, 55, 67, 101, 165, 211, 256
Henry, Prince, Duke of Gloucester, 37–8, 41, 53–4, 84

Herbert, Lord, 64, 284
Heron, John, 90
Highland Host, raising of, 177–82, 184
Hill, Anne, 27–8
HMS *Loyal London*, 83
HMS *Royal Charles*, 44, 70, 79, 83
HMS *Royal James*, 122, 161
HMS *Royal Oak*, 83
Holmes, Colonel Abraham, 362
Holmes, Sir Robert, Robert, 78, 276
Honourable Artillery Company, 232, 274
Hopkins, Richard, 283
Horton, and Monmouth's betrayal, 365–7
Howard, Mrs, 69
Howard, Thomas, 23–4, 26–8, 30–3
Howard of Escrick, William, Baron, 196, 269, 301, 312, 317
    and opposition plotting, 289–91, 298–9
Hucker, Captain John, 360
Huddleston, Fr John, 329
Hudson, Jeffrey, 37
Hyde, Sir Edward, *see* Clarendon, Lord

Ilchester, welcomes Monmouth, 248
Isabella, Archduchess, 1

Jacobite rebellions, 384
James, Duke of York (later King James II)
    and civil war, 4–5, 7
    criticisms of Lucy Walter, 34
    returns to England, 48–9
    and restoration, 53, 57, 66
    and Monmouth's 'legitimation', 60
    and Royal African Company, 77
    and Dutch wars, 78–9, 122
    and New York, 78
    contracts smallpox, 84
    and male pursuits, 95–6
    extramarital affairs, 96–8
    compared with Charles II, 98–9
    secret marriage, 99–100
    and kingly authority, 99, 137, 170
    and succession, 100–5
    converts to Catholicism, 106, 131–6, 138–40

and secret treaty, 107
    resigns offices, 135, 137, 151, 156, 194
    second marriage, 136–7, 139
    and Maastricht re-enactment, 152–3
    jealousy of Monmouth, 158, 161, 182–4, 209, 385
    portraits, 160–1
    and king's clash with Parliament, 165, 168–9
    stops attending Anglican services, 168
    and Scottish affairs, 180–2, 207
    and Monmouth's commission, 182–4
    and Popish Plot, 190, 193–5, 198
    goes into exile, 198, 209
    and Monmouth's changing allegiance, 208–9
    and exclusion, 209–12, 242, 247, 251–64
    returns from exile, 217–20, 230–2, 242
    and Monmouth's banishment, 220–4, 227–8
    arrives in The Hague, 229–30
    unpopularity, 234
    and marriage rumour, 242–4
    returns to London, 274, 277, 303–4
    meets Monmouth in Hyde Park, 277–8
    and Monmouth's reconciliation, 305–13
    and Monmouth's reception abroad, 320–1
    impending banishment, 328–9
    and Charles II's death, 329, 343
    proclaimed king, 331
    falling out with Argyll, 332
    accession, 337–8, 342–3, 346
    and Monmouth's landing, 346–7, 350, 353, 355
    and Monmouth's execution, 369
    political and religious policies, 379–80
    and William III's invasion, 381–2
James I and VI, King, 58, 142, 302
James V, King of Scotland, 59–60
Jefferson, Thomas, 386
Jeffreys, George, Baron, 285, 299, 317, 377–8, 380, 383

Jenkins, Sir Leoline, 253, 284, 293–4, 297, 307, 311, 314
Jennings, William, 248
Jones, Sir Henry, 131
Jones, Inigo, 49, 309
Jones, John, 361
Jones, William, 183–4
Juan José of Austria, Don (Governor-General of the Spanish Netherlands), 29–30, 33, 191, 211

Keeling, Josiah, 293–6
Kent, William, 146
Ketch, Jack, 374–5, 378
Keynsham Bridge, Battle of, 351–2, 354
Kid, John, 207
Killigrew, Peter, 163
King's Evil, touching for, 249, 257–8, 281
Kingdom, Lemuel, 197
Kirke, Diana (later Countess of Oxford), 97
Kirke, George, 164
Kirke, Mary (Moll), 97, 163–4, 353
Kirke, Percy, 164, 353–4, 363
Kneller, Godfrey, 36

la Chaise, François de, 193
Langford, John, 378
Langley, Robert, 224, 227
Lauderdale, John Maitland, Earl then Duke of, 60–1, 118, 132–3, 137–8, 140, 168, 189, 216, 251
    treatment of Scottish opposition, 177–81, 204–6, 210
    and raising of Highland Host, 177–81
le Blon, Daniel, 339–40
Le Nôtre, André, 91
Leicester, Robert Sidney, Earl of, 142
Lely, Peter, 97, 159–61
Les Invalides, 129, 157
Levellers, 269, 334
Leveson Gower, Sir William, 280
Life Guards, Royal, 92–3, 95–6, 131, 158, 222, 252
    attack Sir John Coventry, 111–12
    and Popish Plot, 191–2
    Albemarle appointed captain, 237, 252

Lindenov, Ambassador Christopher, 144
Lisle, Lady Alice, 378–9
Locke, John, 133, 139, 247, 260, 386–7
    Two Treatises of Government, 265–6, 387
Lockhart, Sir William, 125–6, 154
London
    and restoration, 50–2
    celebrates royal wedding, 171–2
    celebrates Protestant succession, 195
    popular support for Monmouth, 222–3, 235–7, 254, 289
    Whigs lose political control, 278, 289, 293, 334
    experiences extreme weather, 316–17
    and Monmouth's rebellion, 334, 341–2
    see also City of London; Great Fire of London; Great Plague
London Gazette, 244, 312
Longford, Francis Aungier, Earl of, 251
Loosduinen, 18
Lorges, Duc de, 124
Lorraine, Chevalier de, 88, 108
Louis XIII, King of France, 3
Louis XIV, King of France, 3–4, 14, 64, 136, 200, 231, 311, 380, 383
    and Treaty of Fuenterrabia, 40–1
    and Monmouth's French trips, 84–92
    annexations, 86–7
    Grand Divertissement, 90–1
    and wars of, 106–7, 112–19, 122–6, 128, 130, 140–1, 154–5, 169–71, 173, 185, 187–8, 318–19, 321, 324
    and secret treaty, 106–8
    honours Monmouth, 121–2
    and Popish Plot, 190, 193, 195
    and exclusion crisis, 246, 255, 263
Louvois, François Michel Le Tellier, Marquis de, 121, 154, 172
Lovelace, John, Baron, 250
Lowestoft, Battle of, 79, 104
Lumley, Richard, Baron, 365
Luxembourg, François Montmorency, Duc de, 186–8
Luxemburg, French attack, 319

Lyme Regis
  Monmouth's landing, 343–7
Lyttelton, Sir Charles, 272

Maastricht, 115, 122–30, 135, 141, 144,
    147, 149, 154, 200, 234,
    336
  re-enactment of campaign, 151–3,
    160
  French retain town, 169
Macclesfield, Charles Gerard, Earl
    of, 224, 269, 280–1, 337
Magdalen College, Oxford, 380
Magna Carta, 236
Malet, Miss, 76
Mandeville, Lord Robert, 81
Manley, John, 330
Marie-Thérèse, Queen of France, 41,
    86, 88, 115
maritime trade, 77–8
Mary Beatrice d'Este, Duchess of York
    (later Queen Mary 'of
    Modena'), 136–7, 161–2, 277–8,
    307, 310, 381
  her children, 162
Mary, Princess of Orange, 6–7, 20–2,
    78, 228
  death from smallpox, 53–4, 84
Mary (née Stuart), Princess of Orange
    (later Queen Mary II), 62, 100,
    162, 210, 227, 253
  Protestant upbringing, 136, 151
  marriage, 171–2
  and Duchess of Monmouth's
    visit, 215–16
  performs in Calisto, 240
  receives Monmouth, 321, 323–6,
    328
  commissions history of the
    period, 376
  and Glorious Revolution, 382–4
Mary I, Queen, 142, 151, 369, 384–5
Matthews, Edward, 337, 342
Maugridge, Mrs, 121
Maurice of the Palatinate, Prince, 7
May, Baptist, 327
May, Hugh, 212–13, 216
May, Mr (barber), 231
Mazarin, Cardinal Jules Raymond, 3,
    14, 36, 40–1, 46–7, 85–6

Meal Tub Plot, 232–3, 235
Medway Raid, 82–3, 106
Melville, George, Lord, 214
Mercurius Politicus, 28
Merton College, Oxford, 259, 263
Middlesex grand jury, 247
Minterne, Mary, 69, 215
Molière, Georges Dandin, 91
Monck, General
    George, see Albemarle, George
    Monck, Duke of
Monmouth and Buccleuch, Anna
    Scott, Duchess of
  engagement, 46–7, 49, 57–8, 61
  marriage, 62–3
  established at Chiswick
    House, 64–6
  education and accomplishments, 58,
    68–9
  and dancing, 69, 93–4
  her lady companions, 69
  income and extravagance, 71–5, 94,
    147, 176, 214, 267–8, 292, 305
  married life, 76, 119–20, 130, 141,
    147–8, 214–15, 277
  dislocates hip, 93–4
  and family reunion, 109
  her children, 119–21, 141–2, 147,
    214–15, 238, 241, 266–7, 293, 297
  friendship with York family, 161–2,
    215–16, 277–8, 322
  charged to look after Princess
    Anne, 172
  remodelled lodgings, 214–15
  imperiousness, 215–16
  relations with king, 238, 241, 266,
    269, 278, 295, 305
  travels to continent, 266–7
  returns to London, 277–8
  and Rye House plot, 295, 297
  and Monmouth's submission, 314
  marriage ends, 322
  and Monmouth's rebellion and
    execution, 369–73, 375
  and Monmouth's memory, 383–4
Monmouth and Buccleuch, James
    Scott, Duke of
  abduction attempts, 1–2, 17–19,
    32–4
  birth and childhood, 13–16

meets father near Antwerp, 25
attitude to his mother, 35–6
education, 38–40, 54–5, 69–71
relationship with king, 41–3, 49–50,
  52, 100–2, 148–50, 221–2, 224, 324
engagement, 46–7, 49, 57
comes to court, 49–56
good looks and energy, 54–5
assigned suite of rooms, 55–6
created Duke of Monmouth, 57–8
'legitimation', 59–61, 101
marriage, 62–3
and royal progress, 64–5
Whitehall apartments, 66–8
income and extravagance, 71–5,
  146–7, 176, 267–8, 292
extramarital affairs, 76–7, 96–7,
  163–4, 239–40
married life, 76, 119–20, 130, 141,
  147–8, 214–15, 277
first experience of war, 79–83
French trips, 84–92
embarks on military career, 92–3,
  117–19, 121–9
and male pursuits, 95–6
relationship with Duke of York, 98,
  104, 137, 160–2, 182–4
and succession, 100–5, 199–200,
  210–12, 227–9
takes seat in House of Lords, 103,
  111
coat of arms, 103
and family reunion, 109–11
comes of age, 111
joins Privy Council, 111
and attack on Sir John
  Coventry, 111–12
Dunkirk visit, 112–14
acquires Moor Park, 119–20
appointment in French army, 121–2,
  125
religious orthodoxy, 133, 135, 175
accumulates offices, 133–4, 153–4
and Duke of York's marriage, 136–7
declines political high office, 137,
  153
and his son's death, 141–2, 147
and Mastership of the Horse, 142–6,
  237, 273, 385
acts of kindness, 155

takes oversight of army, 156–8
appointed chancellor of
  Cambridge, 158–9
portraits, 159–61, 297
friendship with Nell Gwyn, 160
and his sister (Mary
  Fanshawe), 162–3
and Dutch alliance, 172–5, 182–9
appointed captain general, 175,
  182–4
and Scottish affairs, 175–82, 197,
  205–8
enters political arena, 181–3, 195–7
and Popish Plot, 189–97
disbands army, 196–7
growing reputation, 199–200
appointed to king's council, 201
change of political allegiance, 208–9
remodelled lodgings, 214–15
political naivety, 220, 292, 384–5
expulsion from court, 220–5,
  316–20
discharged from army
  responsibilities, 223
arrives in The Hague, 226–9
and Duke of York's recall, 230–1
and Meal Tub Plot, 232–3
returns to England, 235–7
relieved of royal appointments,
  237
breach with king, 237–9, 241, 245,
  269–70, 275–6, 385
sense of honour, 238–9
relationship with Henrietta
  Wentworth, 239–40, 301–3,
  322–3, 330–1, 370–2, 385
and horoscopes, 240, 369
western progress, 246–50, 282
and 'healing' incidents, 249, 257–8,
  281
speaks on Exclusion Bill, 254–5
ridiculed in print, 257–8
experiences financial
  pressures, 267–8
and his children, 267, 308, 326, 369,
  371, 373, 375
and Shaftesbury's arrest, 270–1, 273
meets Duke of York in Hyde
  Park, 277–8
Wallasey expedition, 279–82, 284

arrested, 283–5
and Whig plotting, 286–92, 317–18
appears before King's Bench, 292
seeks reconciliation, 292–3
and Rye House Plot, 295–301
reconciliation and submission,
    303–15
tries to save Hampden, 315
state of mind and spirituality, 321–2
marriage ends, 322
secret meeting with king, 325–8
learns of king's death, 328
drawn into rebellion, 329–40
pawns possessions, 339–40
lands in Dorset, 341–8
invasion declaration, 342–5, 382
proclaimed king, 347–50
defeated at Sedgemoor, 349–63
capture and execution, 364–76
appeals to James, 367–8
Montagu, Edward, see Sandwich,
    Edward Montagu, Earl of
Montagu, Ralph, 195, 199, 256
Montagu, Walter, 37
Montal, Comte, de, 124
Montburn, Marquis de, 95
Montpensier, Anne Marie Louise
    d'Orléans, Duchesse de, 88
Moor Park, 120–1, 130, 141, 144, 147,
    246, 277, 317, 375
rebuilding, 216–17, 223, 275
Moore, Sir Jonas, 271
Moorfields music hall, 50
Moray, Earl of, 180
Mulgrave, John Sheffield, Earl
    of, 163–4

Nantwich, welcomes Mon-
    mouth, 280–1
naval mutiny, 4–5
Needham, Eleanor, 163–4, 258, 297
New Model Army, 80, 377
New York (New Amsterdam), 78,
    122, 140
Newcastle, William Cavendish, Earl
    of, 39
Newmarket races, 61, 95, 292
Newport Pagnell, 196
Nieuwpoort, 173–4, 327
Nokes, David, 109–10

Norfolk, Henry Howard, Duke
    of, 57–8
North, Roger, 194
Northampton races, 268
Northumberland, George Fitzroy, Earl
    of, 160
Norton St Philip, 353–5, 361, 367
Nottingham Castle, 99

Oates, Titus, 190–5, 219, 232
Oglethorpe, Colonel, 364
O'Neill, Daniel, 22
Opdam, Jacob, 79
Order of the Garter, 16, 62–3, 76, 152,
    212, 311–12, 345, 366, 384
Orléans, Henriette Anne, Duchesse
    d', 42, 47, 53, 85, 87–9, 150
and family reunion, 108–11, 144
death in suspicious
    circumstances, 110–11
and Catholicism, 175
Orléans, Philippe, Duc d', 41, 47–8,
    85, 87–9, 108–10
and Dutch wars, 115, 122, 124–5,
    128
Ormonde, James Butler, Duke of, 15,
    76, 120, 175, 196, 258, 264, 279
Ossera, Marquis d', 174
Ossory, Thomas Butler, Earl of, 170,
    187, 199
Oxford, Aubrey de Vere, Earl of, 76,
    97, 200
Oxford, welcomes Monmouth, 250
Oxford Parliament, 257–64
Oxford University, 65, 258–9

Palmer, Roger, 53
Parcet, Elizabeth, 249, 257
peerages, Scottish and Irish, 58
Pegge, Catherine, 148
Pemberton, Justice, 298
Penn, William, 22
Pentland, Elizabeth, 24
Pepys, Samuel, 44, 55–6, 61, 63, 77, 79,
    82, 95, 101–2, 153
Philip IV, King of Spain, 2, 22, 25, 30,
    40, 86
Philip of the Palatinate, Prince, 7
Pinson, Monsieur, 143
playhouses, reopening of, 50

Plymouth, Don Carlos, Earl of, 148, 160, 170
'Popish massacre' pamphlet, 242
Popish Plot, 189–99, 208–9, 215
Port Meadow races, 250
Portman, Sir William, 247, 349
Portsmouth, Louise de Keroualle, Duchess of, 148, 160, 198, 213, 273, 310
  acts as go-between, 250–2, 270, 293
  and king's secret meeting with Monmouth, 326
Pregnani, Abbé, 95
Preston Moor, Battle of, 11, 13
Price, Goditha, 97
Pride's Purge, 11–12, 43
Progers, Edward, 33, 162

Quakers, 48, 248

Ramsay, Captain Robert, 155
Ramsey, John, 183–4
Ranelagh, Richard Jones, Earl of, 218
Raymond, Justice, 283
Reresby, John, 206
Richmond, Henry Fitzroy, Duke of, 57, 160, 211
  awarded Mastership of the Horse, 273, 276
Richmond and Lennox, Mary (née Villiers), Duchess of, 313
Rising Sun, 343, 345
Robartes, Lord John, 131
Robinson, William, 72
Roch Castle, 7, 9
Rochester, Laurence Hyde, Earl of, 303, 338, 350
Rocksavage House, 297
Rohanez, Duc de, 126
Rose, Pascha, 378
Ross, Thomas, 33, 39, 47, 54–5, 65, 69–72, 82, 103, 118, 162, 215
Rothes, John Leslie, Earl of, 45
Rowe, Anthony, 312
Roxalana (Hester Davenport), 76
Royal African Company, 77–8
Royal English regiment, 114–16, 121, 127, 140, 162–3
  uniforms, 114–15

in French service, 154–5, 168–70, 172
  winter pay, 154–5
Royal Exchange, 50, 81, 293
royal forests, 134, 140, 198, 223
Royal Hospital, Chelsea, 157
Royal Life Guards, *see* Life Guards
royal menagerie, 27, 51, 257
Royal Mews (stables), 142–6
royal tennis courts, 66–7
Rubens, Sir Peter Paul, 9
Rumbold, Richard, 294
Rump Parliament, 12
Rumsey, John, 288, 294–5, 300
Rupert, Prince, 5, 7, 49, 66, 77–8, 81, 103, 109, 135, 165, 171, 180, 189, 191, 252
  and Duke of York's marriage, 136–7
  and Monmouth's banishment, 226, 229–31
Russell, Edward, 381
Russell, Lord William, 85–6, 201, 205, 272, 304–6, 312–14, 387
  and exclusion crisis, 252–3
  and Monmouth's arrest, 284
  and opposition plotting, 287–8, 292, 294, 295–6, 298–9, 300–1
  execution, 299, 302, 313, 374
Rye House Plot, 293–301

St Albans, Henry Jermyn, Earl of, 41–2
St Augustine's Abbey, 109
St Bartholomew's fair, 51
St Clement Danes church, 133
St Denis, Battle of, 186–7, 197, 200, 212, 228, 381
St George's Chapel, Windsor, 62
St Germain-en-Laye, 3–4, 14–15, 17, 88
St James's Park, 146, 161, 190, 214, 241, 292
St-Martin-in-the-Fields, 175, 254, 276, 370
Saint-Maurice, Marquis de, 122, 128
St Paul's Cathedral, 25, 50, 81, 273
Sanbourne, Margaret, 102
Sandwich, Edward Montagu, Earl of, 44, 48–9, 101, 122, 139
Sarsfield, Charles and Charlotte, 162
Sarsfield, Mary, *see* Fanshawe, Mary
Sarsfield, Patrick, 162
Sarsfield, Captain William, 162–3, 362

Scone Palace, 19
Scott, Sir Gideon, 60
Scottish Parliament, and execution of
    Charles I, 15
Scottish Privy Council, 175–9, 206, 213
Scroggs, William, 219
Sedgemoor, Battle of, 350, 357–65,
    367, 377
Sévigné, Marie de Rabutin-Chantal,
    Marquise de, 115
Seymour, Francis, Baron, 64
Shadwell, Thomas, *The Sullen
    Lovers*, 109
Shaftesbury, Anthony Ashley Cooper,
    Earl of, 132–3, 138–40, 195
    clashes with king, 166–70
    imprisoned, 169–70
    alliance with Monmouth, 197–201,
        208–10
    and coalition council, 201, 205
    and succession, 211, 217–18
    and Meal Tub Plot, 232
    and Monmouth's return, 233–4
    and exclusion crisis, 247, 249–50,
        250, 254–6, 260–3, 268–9, 387
    his home at Wimborne St
        Giles, 247, 365
    tries to indict Duke of York, 247
    infirmity, 249, 260, 286
    and Locke's treatises, 265
    arrest and acquittal, 270–5
    secret approach to king, 278
    distanced from Monmouth, 279
    and Monmouth's arrest, 284
    and habeas corpus, 284
    and opposition plotting, 286–9, 294,
        304, 306
    death in Amsterdam, 289
    and Monmouth's rebellion, 332,
        335, 341, 348
Sharp, Archbishop James, 204–5
Sheldon, Archbishop Gilbert, 166
Shepherd (wine merchant), 288, 294, 296
Shute, Samuel, 274
Sidney, Algernon, 9–10, 218–19, 230,
    308, 387
    and opposition plotting, 289–91,
        295–6, 298
    execution, 313, 316
Sidney, Colonel Henry, 188, 210, 214,
    227–9, 233, 252, 381

Sidney, Colonel Robert, 10, 31
Simons, Fr, 105
Skelton, Bevil, 331, 338
Skinners' Company, 274
Slingsby, Sir Arthur, 1–2, 32, 35, 185
smallpox, 12, 20, 53–4, 84
Smith, Ann, 333, 337, 340, 379
'Smith, Mr', 334–6
Solebay, Battle of, 122, 139
Solemn League and Covenant, 15, 17,
    204
Somerset, Duke of, 57
Sourceau, Claude, 73, 240
Southhouse, Mrs, 121
Spanish Armada, 165
Spanish Netherlands, 1, 16, 25, 29, 31,
    116, 122, 311, 318, 327, 331, 338
    Louis XIV's designs on, 86–7, 106,
        169, 170
    England helps defend, 185–9
Speke, George, 248
Stafford, Monmouth's arrest in, 283–4
Staniers, Henry, 155
Stansfield, Sir James, 176
Strafford, Thomas Wentworth, Earl
    of, 253
Strasbourg, Battle of, 155
Stuart, Frances (later Duchess of
    Lennox and Richmond), 71, 96
Sully, Duke of, 38
Sun Tavern, 252, 293
Sunderland, Robert Spencer, Earl
    of, 154, 198–9, 201, 205, 209,
        218–20, 223, 227, 303
    and exclusion crisis, 250–1
    accompanies Monmouth, 269
    supports James II, 338, 380
    prospers under William III, 383
Sutton Street toll, 223

Taaffe, Theobald, *see* Carlingford,
    Theobald Taaffe, Earl of
Tarras, Walter Scott, Earl of, 46
Taunton, Monmouth proclaimed
    king, 349–50
Temple, Sir William, 201, 220, 233–4
Tenison, Thomas, 370–1
Test Act, 132–6, 138, 380
Texel, 340–2, 353
Thames, freezes over, 316–17
Thurland, Edward, 73

Thurlow, John, 26
Thynne, Sir James, 64
Thynne, Thomas, 247
Tilley, Joseph, 349
Tillotson, John, 301
Toddington manor house, 239, 297,
    300–3, 305, 311, 323, 326, 371
Toleration Bill, 382
Tonge, Israel, 190–1, 194
Tournai, 86, 89
Tower of London, 7, 25, 30, 50, 169,
    200, 236, 257, 311
  imprisonment of Monmouth, 26–8,
    368–72
  imprisonment of
    Shaftesbury, 270–1, 278, 286
  imprisonment of Rye House
    plotters, 296–8
  burial of Monmouth, 375
  burial of Jeffreys, 383
Townsend, Mary, 163
Trained Bands, 80
Treaty of Aix-la-Chapelle, 89–90, 106,
    115
Treaty of Fuenterrabia, 40–1
Treaty of Truce, 321
Treaty of Westminster, 140, 142, 154,
    169
Trenchard, John, 349
Triennial Bill, 382
Trinity College, Cambridge, 62
Triple Alliance, 87, 89
Turenne, Henri de La Tour
    d'Auvergne, Vicomte de, 113,
    117, 131
Turner, Bishop Francis, 375
Turner, F. C., 386
Tweeddale, John Hay, Marquess of, 46

United Provinces (the Dutch
    Republic), 16, 20, 106, 226, 227,
    230, 234, 318, 324–5, 331, 375, 381
  wars of, 78, 86–8, 106–8, 115–18, 122
  alliance with England, 171–5, 182–9
  and Dutch wars, 106, 115–16, 122,
    169–70, 185, 318
Upnor Castle, 83

van den Kerckhoven, Johann, 24
van Solms, Amalia, 6
Vanier, St Gill, 73, 188, 222, 240, 264

Vauban, Sébastien Le Prestre
    de, 123–4, 128
Vauxhall, New Spring Gardens, 50
Veldt, Gerrit, 30
Venner, Samuel, 341, 361
Vermeer, Johannes, 24
Vernatty, Diana, 69
Verneuil, Henri de Bourbon, Comte
    de, 211
Vernon, James, 137, 141, 154, 164, 183,
    187, 198
  elected MP, 197
  'authors' pamphlet, 258
  and Oxford Parliament, 259–60, 265
  urges rapprochement with king, 269
  prospers under William III, 383
Vernon, Sir Thomas, 164
Verrio, Antonio, 213, 218, 275
Versailles, Grand Divertissement, 90–1
Villa Hermosa, Carlos de Aragón de
    Gurrea, Duke of, 170, 174, 187

Wade, Nathaniel, 339, 341, 355
Wagstaffe, Moses, 330
Wallasey races, 279–81
Wallis, Dr, 260
Walter, Cornelia, 102
Walter, Elizabeth, 8–10
Walter, Justus, 24, 26, 30, 102
Walter, Lucy, 2, 7–10, 13–15, 20–8,
    30–4, 73, 99, 228, 290
  and abduction attempts, 1–2, 17–19,
    32–4
  relationship with king, 7, 10, 17, 20,
    22
  appearance, 9, 15
  promiscuity, 9–10, 21
  attempted poisoning, 20
  annual allowance, 22, 28
  attempts to murder maid, 23
  relationship with Thomas
    Howard, 23–4
  disinherited, 24
  imprisoned in the Tower, 26–8
  returns to Brussels, 30–1
  threatens to publish king's
    letters, 33
  death in Paris, 34, 242, 244
  and marriage rumour, 102–4, 234,
    241–5
  dying confession, 242

Walter, William, 8
Warcup, Edmund, 222, 232
Ward, Sir Patience, 273, 340
Wars of the Roses, 78
Watson, Francis, 215
Watts, Mr (tailor), 73
Watts, Paul, 18–19
Welwood, James, 376
Wemyss, David Wemyss, Earl
    of, 61–2, 65
Wemyss, Margaret Leslie, Countess
    of, 45–6, 57–62, 64–5
Wentworth, Henrietta Maria,
    Baroness, 163–4, 250, 267, 297,
    325–6, 336, 340, 365
    Monmouth's relationship with 239–
    40, 301–3, 322–3, 330–1, 370–2,
    385
    and Monmouth's death, 367, 370–2,
    375–6
Wentworth, Philadelphia,
    Baroness, 239–40, 301–3, 326
Wentworth, Thomas, Baron, 16, 164,
    239
West, Robert, 293, 295, 298, 300
Westminster Abbey, 50, 54, 142
Westonzoyland, 357–60, 377
Whig 'Anti-dinner', 274–5
Whigs and Tories, emergence
    of, 197–8
Whitehall Palace, 12, 16, 40, 50–1,
    54–6, 152, 193, 199, 206, 232, 237,
    252, 292, 294
    King's apartments, 62, 120, 180,
    224, 346
    Queen's apartments, 56, 71, 136
    Duke of York's apartments, 79, 84
    Secretary of State's office, 59, 141,
    181, 284, 309
    Great Hall theatre, 93, 239
    William of Orange's lodgings, 119,
    171
    Horse Guards, 146
    Council chamber, 56, 189–90, 295,
    309
    Banqueting House, 12, 68, 309
    Mr Chiffinch's room, 368
    see also Monmouth, Duke of and
    Monmouth, Duchess of for their
    lodgings

Whitelackington, welcomes
    Monmouth, 248
Whitley, Roger, 281
Wildman, Major, 334–5, 337, 339, 355
William the Conqueror, 27, 323
William II, Prince of Orange, 5–7, 20,
    78, 228
William III, Prince of Orange (later
    King William III), 6, 20, 54, 62,
    67, 78, 107
    and Dutch wars, 116–19, 139–40,
    170, 185–9, 318–19, 321
    relationship with Monmouth, 119,
    172, 187–9, 231
    marriage, 171–2
    Duke of York approaches, 200, 209,
    242
    and succession, 210–12, 227–9, 262
    and Monmouth's
    banishment, 227–9, 234
    and exclusion crisis, 248, 252, 262–3
    receives Monmouth, 318–19, 321,
    323–6, 328
    and dancing, 325–9
    and Charles II's death, 329
    and Monmouth's rebellion, 336,
    338–9, 367–8, 380–1
    and James II's accession, 338–9
    invasion of England, 380–3
    and Glorious Revolution, 382–4
Williams, William, 341, 362–3, 379
Williamson, Joseph, 118, 144, 183–4,
    190
Winchester, Charles Paulet, Marquis
    of, 261
Windsor Castle
    Maastricht re-enactment, 151–3
    remodelling of, 212–13, 216
Wolsey, Cardinal Thomas, 55
wool trade, 59
Worcester, Battle of, 19, 329, 365
Wren, Christopher, 192, 259
Wright, William, 260–1
Wyck, Jan, 212
Wyres, Thomas, 246

York, Anne Hyde, Duchess of,
    99–100, 103, 113
    converts to Catholicism, 135–6
Young, Drum Major William, 223

A NOTE ON THE AUTHOR

Born in the West Highlands of Scotland, Anna Keay read history at Magdalen College, Oxford, where she won two academic scholarships. She was awarded her PhD on the reign of Charles II by the University of London. She was formerly a curator for Historic Royal Palaces, Curatorial Director of English Heritage and is currently Director of the Landmark Trust. She is married with two children and divides her time between London and King's Lynn, Norfolk.

A NOTE ON THE TYPE

The text of this book is set in Linotype Stempel Garamond,
a version of Garamond adapted and first used by the Stempel
foundry in 1924. It is one of several versions of Garamond based
on the designs of Claude Garamond. It is thought that Garamond
based his font on Bembo, cut in 1495 by Francesco Griffo in
collaboration with the Italian printer Aldus Manutius. Garamond
types were first used in books printed in Paris around 1532. Many
of the present-day versions of this type are based on the *Typi
Academiae* of Jean Jannon cut in Sedan in 1615.

Claude Garamond was born in Paris in 1480. He learned how to
cut type from his father and by the age of fifteen he was able to
fashion steel punches the size of a pica with great precision. At the
age of sixty he was commissioned by King Francis I to design a
Greek alphabet, and for this he was given the honourable title of
royal type founder. He died in 1561.